West's®
Spanish-English /
English-Spanish
Law Dictionary

Translations of Terms, Phrases and
Definitions of Concepts of Modern Spanish
and English Legal Terminology

By

Gerardo Solís, LL.M.
Solís, Endara, Delgado y Guevara, Attorneys At Law

Contributing Authors

Eduardo Stagg
Attorney At Law

Rubén Levy
Kusnfecky Barsky & Levy Downie

Luis Chalhoub
Arellano, Chalhoub & Asociados
Law Professor Universidad Santa Maria la Antigua

Eva Solís de Castillo
The Chase Manhattan Bank, N.A.

Evangelina Díaz Lamoutte
Traducciones Profesionales

Efraín Padró, Editor
Attorney At Law, Denver, Colorado

and

Raúl A. Gasteazoro, Jr., Editor
Attorney At Law, St. Paul, Minn.

St. Paul, Minn.
West Publishing Co.
1992

COPYRIGHT © 1992 by West Publishing Company
610 Opperman Drive
P. O. Box 64526
St. Paul, MN 55164-0526
Printed in the United States of America
ISBN 0-314-00846-2
2nd Reprint-1997

Diccionario Legal Español-Inglés / Inglés-Español

Traducciones de Términos, Frases y
Definiciones de Conceptos de Terminología
Legal Moderna en Inglés y Español

Por

Gerardo Solís, LL.M.
Solis, Endara, Delgado y Guevara, Abogados

Co-Autores

Eduardo Stagg
Abogado

Rubén Levy
Kusnfecky Barsky & Levy Downie

Luis Chalhoub
Arellano, Chalhoub & Asocíados
Professor Universidad Santa Maria la Antigua

Eva Solís de Castillo
The Chase Manhattan Bank, N.A.

Evangelina Díaz Lamoutte
Traducciones Profesionales

Efraín Padró, Editor
Abogado, Denver, Colorado

y

Raúl A. Gasteazoro, Jr., Editor
Abogado, St. Paul, Minn.

St. Paul, Minn.
West Publishing Co.
1992

Prologue

This dictionary is meant to be a practical translation tool for anyone who requires a definition of a legal term in either Spanish or English. It also seeks to fill a void between two legal systems by providing an explanation of legal terms used in another legal system, be it the common law or the civil law. To accomplish this task, this work gathers commonly used legal words, and it explains their meaning in the second language.

This dictionary should be a valuable tool to numerous professionals who regularly utilize these terms in their daily affairs. Our goal has been to guarantee the accuracy and precision of the translated terms. It is not our aim to include useless terms or to give lengthy definitions which confuse rather than enlighten the reader. We have tried to strike a balance between simplicity and complexity in our definitions.

Over twelve thousand terms and words of frequent usage, together with their respective definitions, have been organized alphabetically. Terms of art have been translated to convey their meaning, both literally and conceptually. Where practical, ordinary language has been used in the definitions. Where there are several definitions for one term, these subdefinitions have been categorized.

When selecting words, we have omitted subsequent variants of the same term and we have suppressed obsolete terms. We have excluded those words not directly related to the law but have included those which have special significance in the economic, accounting and political arenas.

Also, we have translated and explained phrases, whose true context has no proper and literal translation in the second language, given the importance of understanding these in their true legal context. It has not been our objective to provide a mere dictionary of literally translated terms, but to explain the meaning of the consulted term. However, in some instances the terms are so distinctly expressed that an explanation is superfluous.

HOW TO USE THIS DICTIONARY

The dictionary is organized alphabetically. There are two sections: from Spanish to English and from English to Spanish. Please bear in mind that there are two letters in Spanish, the letters "Ch" and "Ll", which are not known in the English alphabet. In Spanish, the letter "Ch" and "Ll" follow the letters "C" and "L", respectively. No effort has been made to give a pronunciation guide for each of the translated terms. That will come in the future. Either a term or a phrase can be found using the traditional methods used to find words in a dictionary.

If a phrase contains two or more words, these can be used to find a translation of the phrase. If it is an important phrase, normally it is included as a definition or a subdefinition under one of the operative words used in the phrase. For example, the first phrase defined in the Spanish to English section is "Abogado Defensor". The operative word there is "Abogado" which is also defined in this section of the dictionary.

Should a phrase not be separately defined, the user should consult a translation of all terms used in the phrase to get a sense of the legal concepts surrounding its use. It was not the author's intention to include each and every phrase that can be used in Spanish since generally its meaning can be understood in the context of the operative words.

ACKNOWLEDGEMENT

The authors wish to thank all those who contributed to this dictionary, especially the following individuals: Lic. Luis García Campuzano, Leonor Urbain, Allison Gachne, Wendy E. Wenner, Jo Walsh and Barbara A. Kennedy. Also, the following institutions unselfishly contributed their assistance and support to this effort: the University of Minnesota Law School Library and Hamline University Law Library. If the authors have omitted anyone from this acknowledgement, we apologize and thank them.

Prólogo

Esta es una obra práctica que ofrece la traducción de más de doce mil (12,000) conceptos de uso frecuente en ambos idiomas, a la vez que se explican de manera clara y precisa las definiciones de los términos que pudiesen prestarse a interpretaciones ambiguas.

La necesidad que tienen los abogados y otros profesionales de intercambiar información en dos idiomas es cada día mayor. Con esta necesidad en mente, se ofrece esta obra.

Ha sido nuestra intención y así lo refleja esta obra, garantizar la exactitud y precisión en las explicaciones. No fue nuestra intención incluir términos inútiles, ni hacer explicaciones abundantes que en lugar de ilustrar, confunden. Tampoco tratamos de hacer simples definiciones, sino explicar adecuadamente en el idioma secundario lo que el término significa en el idioma primario.

Sin embargo, las diferencias lógicas entre dos idiomas, y en especial dos sistemas juridicos diferentes, imposibilita en ocasiones encontrar traducciones literales. De ser posible, se presentan las traducciones literales de los términos traducidos. Cabe precaver que hay veces que la traducción literal de un término no conlleva todos los matices que esa palabra tiene en el ámbito legal o para otras areas profesionales. De ser así, se ha explicado el término en forma simple para aclarar su significado. Hay palabras que captan conceptos legales que son complejos. Hemos tratado de explicar cada concepto complicado de forma tal que cualquiera persona pueda entender su significado.

Al seleccionar las palabras hemos considerado omitir variaciones subsecuentes de un mismo término y hemos suprimido términos que se encuentran en desuso; hemos excluido aquellos vocablos ajenos al derecho; sin enbargo, se han incluido aquellos que tienen especial importancia en la ciencia juridica. También incluye términos y frases, que si bien no tienen una correspondecia exacta con términos y frases en el segundo idioma, es necesario definirlos para abarcar conceptos legales de uso común en el primer idioma.

No ha sido nuestra intención únicamente ofrecer al lector un diccionario de términos traducidos literalmente, sino explicarle el significado del término consultado, mas en algunos casos hemos encontrado que la explicación sobra por lo explícito de la traducción.

La presentación de la obra es sumamente metódica, lo que facilita su uso. Su forma es simple y concisa y las explicaciones son amenas y sencillas. Esto facilita cualquiera consulta, tanto para aquellos que no están familiarizados con la hermenéutica jurídica como para aquellos familiarizados con los términos legales de un idioma que aspiran entender el sentido de una palabra juridica en el otro idioma.

COMO USAR ESTE DICCIONARIO

El diccionario esta organizado alfabéticamente. Hay dos secciones, del Inglés al Español y del Español al Inglés. No se ha intendado incluir para cada término la pronunciación correspondiente. Esta será una labor futura. Tanto una palabra como una frase se puede encontrar siguiendo normas tradicionales para el uso de un diccionario.

Si una frase tiene dos o más palabras, esta se puede encontrar bajo la definición de las palabras usadas en la frase. De ser una frase importante, normalmente se incluye una subdefinición de la frase, explicando su significaco, bajo las definiciones de una de las palabras usadas en la frase. Por ejemplo, la primera frase definida del Inglés al Español es "Abandonment of Lawsuit". Esta frase aparece bajo el término "Abandonment", no bajo el término "Lawsuit". El usuario debe consultar todas las definiciones para cada palabra usada en una frase. De esta manera, si la frase no aparece como una subdefinición en un termino independiente, el usuario tendrá una idea de los conceptos legales aplicables a cada palabra usada en la frase.

Esta obra no intenta definir cada frase existente dentro de la terminología jurídica. Por ejemplo, Black's Law Dictionary, en su quinta edición, contiene aproximadamente 35 frases cuando define la palabra "Contact". En esta obra, no se intenta abarcar cada frase incluida en Black's ya que se considera que el sentido de la mayoría de estas frases pueden obtenerse si el lector entiende la definición de cada palabra usada en la frase.

Abreviaciones de uso común se han incluido en el diccionario dentro del texto de cada letra del alfabeto. Por ejemplo, la primera abreviación usada del Inglés al Español es "A.G.". Bajo esta abreviación se han incluido los términos o definiciones de tal abreviación.

RECONOCIMIENTO

Los autores principales de esta obra están agradecidos a todos los que contribuyeron a ella, especialment las siguientes personas: Lic. Luis García Campuzano, Leonor Urbain, Allison Gachne, Wendy E. Wenner, Jo Walsh, y Barbara A. Kennedy. La Universidad de Minnesota y Hamline University contribuyeron libremente a este proyecto. Si hemos olvidado a alguien en nuestro reconocimiento, pedimos disculpas por ello.

TABLE OF CONTENTS / CONTENIDO

*

A

A BENEFICIO DE INVENTARIO. For the benefit of inventory. In civil law, testamentary heirs are liable for the charges and debts of the estate, but only to the extent of the value of the assets of the estate, by making an inventory of these assets and accepting or rejecting them within the time period and the manner prescribed by law.

A BUEN RECAUDO. Something kept under good custody.

A CONTRARIUS. (Lat.) To the contrary. An argument based on the juxtaposition of two opposing ideas.

A CONTRARIO SENSU. (Lat.) On the other hand; in the opposite sense.

A CUENTA DE. On behalf of. Phrase that describes that a person is acting on another's behalf. For the account of.

A FORTIORI. (Lat.) With stronger reason; much more. A term used in logic to denote an argument to the effect that because the ascertained fact exists, therefore another, which is included in it or is as probable, must also exist.

A LA ORDEN. To the order of. A direction to pay something to someone. These words are necessary to make a document a negotiable instrument. See "Efectos Negociables".

A LA VISTA O PRESENTACIÓN. At sight. With this phrase any negotiable instrument must be paid at the moment of its presentation.

A MANO ARMADA. Armed. A crime committed with firearms or where the use of firearms is threatened. They are classified as crimes "a mano armada" or armed crimes.

A POSTERIORI. (Lat.) From the effect to the cause; from what comes after. Means by which a concept or proposition is known or validated. A method of reasoning that starts with experiments or observations and attempts to discover general principles from them.

1

A PRIORI. (Lat.) From the cause to the effect; from what goes before. It also refers to the process of predicting facts without the benefit of historic experience, but from a general principle or admitted truth.

A QUO. (Lat.) From which. For example, a court "a quo" is a court from which a cause has been appealed to a superior court. It is also used in expressing the computation of time and the distance in space. In this sense it means the point or limit from which.

A RUEGO. At request. Expression before the signature of a person who signs for another one, who does not or cannot sign.

A TÍTULO GRATUITO. Title acquired gratuitously. What has been granted without consideration.

A TÍTULO ONEROSO. Title acquired by purchase or any other way than gratuitously. Acquired upon exchange of valuable consideration.

A TÍTULO PRECARIO. The use of property which is granted as a courtesy or with permission but without the conveyance of any rights.

AB INITIO. (Lat.) From the beginning; from the first act. It is commonly used to indicate that the validity of certain acts relates back to their inception or creation.

AB INTESTATO. (Lat.) In civil law, without a will, an intestate deceased. It is also used to refer to the judicial procedure that follows the death of a person without a will.

ABANDERAR. To register a vessel. The act by which a vessel acquires its nationality by enrollment in the register of ships of a country after fulfilling all the necessary requirements.

ABANDONAR. To abandon. To relinquish or give up with intent of never again resuming one's right or interest.

ABANDONO. Abandonment. Effect of being abandoned, to give up without intent of reassuming one's right.

ABASTECER. To supply. To provide with food and other things essential to life.

ABASTECIMIENTO. Supplying. The act of providing food and other things essential to life.

ABASTO. Supply. Provisions of food.

ABDICACIÓN. Abdication. The act of a sovereign in renouncing and relinquishing his or her government or throne, so that either the throne is left entirely vacant, or it is filled by a successor appointed or elected.

ABDUCCIÓN. Abduction. Kidnapping. The criminal offense of taking away a person who is in the care of another.

ABERRACIÓN. Aberration. A deviation from what is normal, typical, correct or right. Conceptual misunderstanding, mistake or false concept of something. May also refer to mental derangement.

ABIGEATO. Abigeus. (Lat.) In civil law, the stealing or driving away of cattle or other animals.

ABIGEO. One who steals or drives away cattle or other animals.

ABINTESTATO. Intestate proceedings. Judicial proceedings to distribute the estate of a person who died without a will among his or her heirs according to the law. If no heirs exist, the state inherits.

ABJURAR. To abjure. To renounce a belief under oath, before an authority. To retract.

ABOGACÍA. Legal profession. The profession of those licensed to practice law.

ABOGADO. Lawyer; attorney at law. A person learned in the law and licensed to practice law. A person admitted to practice law in his or her respective state and authorized to perform both civil and criminal legal functions for clients, including drafting of legal documents, giving legal advice, and representing such clients before courts, administrative agencies, boards, etc.

ABOGADO ACUSADOR. Prosecuting attorney. The attorney who on behalf of the plaintiff lodges a complaint or suit against the defendant, who is suspected of the commission of the crime.

3

ABOGADO DEFENSOR. Defense attorney. The attorney who acts on behalf of the defendant in a civil or criminal case.

ABOGADO DE OFICIO. Court appointed attorney. The attorney who is selected by the court to represent a defendant when he or she does not have the means to hire the services of an attorney.

ABOGAR. To advocate. To act as an attorney. To defend or plea for another.

ABOLENGO. Lineage. Line of descent from an ancestor.

ABOLICIÓN. Abolition; abrogation. The act of revoking a law, decree, use or custom.

ABOLIR. To repeal, revoke or abolish something.

ABONAR. To credit, satisfy or pay on an obligation. (1) Normally used to denote an installment payment. To partially pay an account. (2) To inscribe someone, normally by a payment, so that he or she may enjoy some service or benefit on a periodic basis.

ABONO. Installment. A partial payment of a debt. A voucher or guarantee. To discharge part of a debt.

ABORDAJE. Collision or fouling of two vessels. (1) In criminal law, the offense of one vessel approaching another with the purpose of taking whatever goods are inside. (2) In maritime and air law, an impact or sudden contact between two moving vessels. It could be due to negligence, recklessness, an unavoidable collision, or the negligence of both vessels.

ABORTAR. To abort. (1) When the fetus is naturally expelled from the womb before it is viable. (2) Legally, the willful expulsion or extraction of a fetus from the womb other than to produce a live child or remove a dead fetus.

ABORTO. Abortion. When the fetus is expelled from the womb before the moment determined by nature. See "Abortar".

ABREVADERO. Drinking trough. Place conditioned so that cattle can drink water.

ABREVIACIÓN. Abridgment. Condensation of a larger work. Abbreviation.

ABRIGO TRIBUTARIO. Tax shelter. Any device used to reduce the payment of taxes.

ABROGACIÓN. Abrogation. The annulment of a previous law, rule or regulation by the authorities or by usage. To repeal.

ABROGAR. To abrogate, to repeal. To annul or repeal a law, by an act of the legislative power, by constitutional authority, or by usage.

ABSENTISMO. Absenteeism. Whenever a person is not in his or her place of usual residence for a certain act, for example, to cast a vote while away (absentee ballot).

ABSOLUCIÓN. Absolution. The sentence or verdict by a judge, whereby the proceedings are concluded, the defendant is declared free, and the charges formulated against him or her are dismissed.

ABSOLUTO. Absolute. Without restrictions. Full or unlimited. Complete. Perfect.

ABSOLUTORIO. Absolutory. That which implies release or discharge from a debt, obligation or duty. See "Absolución".

ABSOLVER. Absolve; release. To set free or release from a debt or other responsibility.

ABSTEMIO. The one who practices abstention. The person who deprives him- or herself of something.

ABSTENCIÓN. Abstention. To deprive oneself voluntarily of something. To forgo an activity.

ABSTINENCIA. Abstinence. The act of giving up certain pleasures or activities. Normally refers to sexual abstinence.

ABSUELTO. Acquitted. Whenever a person accused of a crime is absolved or released from all charges.

ABSURDO. Absurd. What is contrary to reason or impossible.

ABUELASTRO(TRA). The step-mother or step-father of a parent. The second spouse of a grandparent.

ABUSO. Abuse; misuse. To make excessive or improper use of a right, a person or a thing, or to employ it in a manner contrary to the natural or legal rules for its use.

ABUSO DE AUTORIDAD. Abuse of authority. The improper use or the misuse by a public officer of the authority conferred upon him or her by law.

ABUSO DE CONFIANZA. Breach of trust. An act of the trustee in excess of his or her authority to the detriment of the trust.

ABUSO DE DERECHO. Conduct by an official which abuses his or her authority and which results in prejudice to someone.

ACAPARAMIENTO. To monopolize. The acquisition and retention of large quantities of a product to dominate or affect the marketplace.

ACÁPITE. Paragraph. Any part or subdivision of a writing. Subhead.

ACARREAR. To carry. To transport goods or people from one place to another. To convey.

ACATAMIENTO. Obedience; to comply with. To respect an authority or the order of an authority.

ACCEDENTE. Person who accedes or agrees.

ACCEDER. To accede. To agree to what has been requested or contracted.

ACCESIÓN. Accession. The right to own things that become, either naturally or artificially, a part of something already owned.

ACCESO. Access. To approach. To arrive. Entrance.

ACCESO CARNAL. Sexual intercourse. Sexual penetration between a male person and another of either sex, by normal or abnormal means.

ACCESORIO. Accessory (e.g., to a crime); appendant; additional. Anything which is joined to another thing as an incident or as subordinate to it or which belongs to or with it.

ACCIDENTAL. Accidental. (1) What is casual and happens by chance. What is caused by accident. See "Accidente". (2) What is not essential.

ACCIDENTE. Accident, casualty. A fortuitous circumstance, event or happening. An occurrence by chance and not by design.

ACCIDENTE DE TRÁNSITO. Traffic accident. An accident involving at least one person and one automobile.

ACCIÓN. Action; lawsuit; share of stock; stock certificate. (1) In procedural law, it is the right of one party to prosecute another to enforce or protect a right, to redress or prevent a wrong, or to punish a public offense. (2) In commercial law, a written instrument evidencing a share in the ownership of a corporation.

ACCIÓN ADMINISTRATIVA. Administrative action. Proceedings before administrative agencies to reclaim whatever right a person thinks he or she has, because of wrongful administrative act.

ACCIÓN CAMBIARIA. An executory action derived from a negotiable instrument known as the "letra de cambio."

ACCIÓN CAUSAL. A lawsuit demanding compliance with the undertaking which caused the issuance of a "letra de cambio."

ACCIÓN DECLARATIVA. Declaratory action. A lawsuit to determine a justifiable issue where the plaintiff is in doubt as to his or her legal rights or obligations.

ACCIÓN DIRECTA. Direct action. (1) The action taken by a person, in his or her own name against an assign of the person with whom he or she contracted but excluding said person. (2) Action against an insurer under the indemnity policy rather than against the insured tortfeasor.

ACCIÓN EJECUTIVA. Enforced collection action. To compel a debtor, by means of judicial proceedings, to settle or make partial payment on a debt.

7

ACCIÓN ESTIMATORIA. Quanti minoris (Lat.). The name of an action in civil law, brought by one who purchased an article, for a reduction of the agreed price because defects in the thing diminish its value.

ACCIÓN EXHIBITORIA. Discovery action. When a person interested in a thing asks a judge to order the person that holds it to exhibit it for the purpose of clarifying the lawsuit or obtaining the necessary evidence.

ACCIÓN NEGATORIA. Action that re-establishes, in favor of the owner of real estate, the free exercise of his or her right over the land that had been appropriated or possessed by third persons.

ACCIÓN OBLICUA. Action that authorizes creditors to exercise all the rights of the debtor, except personal rights, for the purpose of protecting their interests.

ACCIÓN PENAL. A penal action; a criminal prosecution seeking to impose a penalty.

ACCIÓN PERSONAL. In Personam Action (Lat.). (1) In civil law, an action seeking to enforce an obligation against a person, as opposed to one brought to enforce rights in a thing against the whole world (in rem). (2) In common law, an action brought for the recovery of some debt or for damages for some personal injury.

ACCIÓN PETITORIA. Petitory action. One in which the plaintiff seeks to establish and enforce, by an appropriate legal proceeding, his or her right, or his or her title to the property or domain in dispute.

ACCIÓN PIGNORATICIA o PRENDARIA. Pignoratitia   actio (Lat.). An action against pledged property, or founded on a pledge, that permits the creditor to claim the payment from the debtor with the pledge as guaranty. It also authorizes the debtor to retrieve the pledged property after full payment to the creditor.

ACCIÓN POSESORIA. Possessory action. Action brought to obtain or recover the possession of the thing lost or to protect its actual possession.

ACCIÓN REAL. In rem action. Action instituted against the thing. One which is taken directly against property or one which is brought to enforce a right in the thing itself.

ACCIÓN REDHIBITORIA. Redhibitory action. An action to avoid or rescind a sale on account of some vice or defect in the thing sold, which renders its use impossible or so inconvenient and imperfect that the buyer would not have purchased it had he or she known of the vice.

ACCIÓN REIVINDICATORIA. Recovery action; actio realis (Lat.) Action to obtain by formal judgment or decree from a competent court the restoration or vindication of a person's property rights which were taken or withheld.

ACCIÓN REVOCATORIA o PAULIANA. Action brought by a creditor that annuls every fraudulent act by the debtor to the detriment of the creditor.

ACCIONANTE. Plaintiff. The person who brings an action against another.

ACCIONES. Shares of stock. Certificates which represent the rights of the stockholder to a proportional interest in a corporation.

ACCIONISTA. Stockholder; shareholder. A person who owns shares of stock in a corporation.

ACEFALÍA. Quality of being acephalous, lacking a head. This term is usually applied to a public office without an incumbent officer.

ACEPTACIÓN. Acceptance. Act by means of which a person admits or acknowledges what another has offered or affirmed.

ACEPTACIÓN DE LA HERENCIA. Acceptance of the inheritance. Declaration of the heir in which he or she agrees to receive the patrimony of the deceased.

ACEPTACIÓN DE LETRA. Acceptance of a bill of exchange. Engagement to pay the bill of exchange in money once it is due.

ACEPTACIÓN DE MANDATO. Acceptance of the mandate. Said of the acceptance by the mandatary of the mandate issued by the mandator. See "Mandato".

ACEPTACIÓN DE PODER. Acceptance of power. The acceptance by the proxy holder of the power granted by the constituent.

ACEPTACIÓN EXPRESA. Express acceptance. The unequivocal agreement by word of mouth or in writing to what has been contracted.

ACEPTACIÓN TÁCITA. Implied acceptance. Whenever the acts of the acceptor indicate that he or she has agreed to what has been contracted.

ACEPTANTE. Acceptor. The person who agrees with a proposition.

ACEPTAR. To accept or admit something as true.

ACERVO. Assets. The aggregate of undivided common property, money or other, belonging to a person or a group of persons.

ACLAMACIÓN. Acclamation. To praise, applaud or honor someone. To adopt an agreement by a majority vote.

ACLARACIÓN DE SENTENCIA. Clarification of the judge's decision or sentence.

ACOGER. To receive. To accept or recognize, for example: plaintiff's demands.

ACOMETER. To attack. To intentionally assault or threaten to assault another to cause injury. Also to undertake a task.

ACOMETIDA. Attack. Assault.

ACOMETIMIENTO. Assault. An intentional show of force or movement that could reasonably make the person approached feel threatened or in danger of harmful physical contact.

ACOMODACIÓN. Accommodation. An arrangement made without consideration. Adjustment. A favor.

ACORDADO. Stipulated. Agreed-upon. When two parties to a lawsuit agree as to the existence of a fact or on a point of procedure.

ACORDAR. To agree or resolve. To pass a resolution, by the courts or judges, which will be communicated to the parties. To resolve by common agreement or majority of votes.

ACOSAMIENTO. Pursuit. (1) Action and effect of pursuing. (2) To badger a witness.

ACOTACIÓN. Annotation. A written commentary of something intended to explain or illustrate its meaning.

ACOTAMIENTO. Annotation. To make remarks or annotations. See "Acotación".

ACOTAR. To annotate. To survey, map and mark boundaries. To select a property for a specific use. To set aside land.

ACRECENTAR. To increase. To enrich, foster or promote.

ACRECER. To increase. Also the right to accretion. The right of heirs to aggregate to their share of the estate any portion that another heir cannot or will not accept.

ACREDITAR. To assure; to prove; to credit. (1) To establish a fact or hypothesis as true by satisfactory and sufficient evidence. (2) To grant to a debtor the right to defer payment of a debt.

ACREEDOR. Creditor. A person to whom a debt is owing by another person who is the "debtor."

ACREEDOR COMÚN o SIMPLE. General creditor; creditor at large. One who has no security for the payment of his or her claim.

ACREEDOR HIPOTECARIO. Mortgagee. One who has his or her credit guaranteed by a mortgage.

ACREEDOR PIGNORATICIO O PRENDARIO. Pledgee. One who has secured another's debt by a pledge.

ACREEDOR PRIVILEGIADO. Preferred creditor. Creditor with preferential right to payment over all other creditors.

ACREEDOR QUIROGRAFARIO. One who can prove his or her credit by a written document.

ACREEDOR SOLIDARIO. Joint and several creditor. Said of the creditor which can compel any debtor to discharge the whole debt. Once this has been done, he or she has the duty to give to each creditor his or her portion.

ACRIMINAR. To accuse, incriminate. To accuse of a crime or felony.

ACTA. Minutes. Written record of meetings, proceedings, acts and deeds.

ACTA JUDICIAL. A court record. A memorandum written by the court's secretary attesting facts, declarations, or agreements.

ACTA NOTARIAL. Notarial certificate. A document written by a notary public to attest that a fact occurred in his or her presence or under his or her authorization.

ACTAS. Minutes of a meeting or proceedings.

ACTIO. Actio (Lat.). An action or cause of action.

ACTIVO. Assets. All money, property, and money-related rights owned by a person or an organization.

ACTIVO CAPITAL. Capital assets. All capital invested plus surplus or undivided profits.

ACTIVO FIJO. Fixed capital. Cost of all property, equipment and investments acquired to carry a business.

ACTO. Act. External manifestation of actor's will. Something done voluntarily by a person.

ACTO ADMINISTRATIVO. Administrative act. Act by an administrative body which is necessary to carry out the legislative policy and purpose already declared by the legislative body.

ACTOR. Plaintiff. Person who brings an action, who complains or sues.

ACTOS DE ADMINISTRACION. Administrative acts for the preservation or benefit of an estate.

ACTOS DE COMERCIO. Commercial transactions. Those transactions between merchants regulated by commercial codes and complementary legislation.

ACTOS ENTRE VIVOS. Inter vivos acts. Acts done between the living. In contrast to those acts done in contemplation of death (mortis causa) or which take place as the result of succession.

ACTOS JURÍDICOS. Juridical acts. Those designed to have legal effects before the courts.

ACTOS MORTIS CAUSA. Mortis causa acts. Those in which the transmission of rights does not have effect until the death of the person transmitting the rights.

ACTOS PROCESALES. All acts effected within the context of a judicial process.

ACTOS SOLEMNES. Solemn acts. Those which require the accomplishment of certain indispensable formal prerequisites in order to be legally valid and effective.

ACTUACIÓN. Proceeding. The conduct of juridical business before a competent judicial body or officer. Performance.

ACTUACIONES JUDICIALES. Judicial acts. The acts of a judicial body following established procedures.

ACTUAR. To act. To perform or take action. To discharge a duty. To litigate or otherwise enter into judicial proceedings.

ACTUALIDAD. Present time. What takes place currently.

ACTUARIO. (Lat.) Actuarius; clerk of the court, secretary of the court. Generally, the officer of the court who files pleadings, motions, judgments, etc., issues process, and keeps records of court proceedings.

ACUERDO. Agreement. The coming together of two minds on a given proposition.

ACUMULACIÓN DE ACCIONES. Joinder of actions or claims. Joining several causes of action or claims in a single lawsuit.

ACUMULACIÓN DE PENAS. Cumulative sentences. Whenever a defendant is convicted as a result of an indictment of several counts each for a different crime.

ACUSACIÓN. Accusation. A formal criminal charge against a person filed before a court or magistrate having jurisdiction to inquire into the alleged crime.

ACUSADO. Defendant, accused. Person against whom relief or recovery is sought in a suit, or the accused in a criminal case.

ACUSADOR. Complainant, accuser. Party who accuses or files a complaint. The accuser may be a private prosecutor (acusador particular o privado) or a public prosecutor (acusador público).

ACUSE. Acknowledgment. To admit verbally or in writing to have received something.

AD HOC. (Lat.) For this special purpose. Said of an interim appointment of a tutor, prosecutor or other officer appointed for a special purpose or a specific case.

AD HONOREM. (Lat.) What is done gratuitously; just for the honor of doing it.

AD LITEM. (Lat.) For the purposes of the suit.

AD QUEM. (Lat.) To which. Term used in the computation of time or distance, meaning the end of the period or point of arrival.

AD VALOREM. (Lat.) According to the value.

ADEUDAR. To owe. Obligation to pay for goods or services acquired. To debit.

ADEUDO. Indebtedness. Debt or obligation to pay a sum of money.

ADHESIÓN. Adhesion. Consent one party gives to the proposition of another. See "Contrato de Adhesion".

ADICIONAR. To add. To aggregate, unite or attach.

ADJUDICACIÓN. Adjudication. A judicial act that determines the legal rights or duties of the parties.

14

ADJUDICADO. Said of the thing that is allocated by the judge. See "Adjudicación".

ADJUDICADOR. Adjudger. Judge or person that declares that something belongs to another by good title to it or for the settlement of a debt. See "Adjudicación".

ADJUDICATORIO. Awardee. The person who receives the thing by the order of the court. See "Adjudicación".

ADJUNTO. Attached. Bound, fastened, joined or connected. Enclosed herewith.

ADMINISTRACIÓN. Administration; management. (1) The persons and political party currently running the government. (2) Managing or running a business, organization, or branch of government. (3) Supervision and management of the estate of a dead person.

ADMINISTRACIÓN DE PEQUEÑA EMPRESA. Small Business Administration.

ADMINISTRACIÓN DE VETERANOS. Veterans Administration.

ADMINISTRACIÓN PÚBLICA. Public Administration. All entities responsible for the governance of a political body.

ADMINISTRADOR. Administrator; manager. A person appointed by the court to supervise the management of an estate.

ADMISIBLE. Qualified. Admissible. Term used to denote that the arguments or the evidence presented is worthy of admission and consideration.

ADMISIBILIDAD. Admissibility. Said of what is admissible. See "Admisible".

ADMISIÓN. Admission; confession. A voluntary statement that a fact or a state of events is true.

ADMITIDO. Admitted. Said of a fact stipulated or recognized by all parties. Something accepted. This expression is also utilized to describe a lawyer admitted to the bar.

ADMITIR. To admit. To confess, to recognize one's acts and assume the responsibility thereof. To receive, to accept.

ADMONICIÓN. Admonition. Warning or reprimand. Common when an accused is discharged; if he or she is found punished more severely.

ADOLESCENCIA. Adolescence. That age which follows puberty and precedes the age of majority.

ADOLESCENTE. Adolescent. Person who is in the state of adolescence. See "Adolescencia".

ADOPCIÓN. Adoption. To take into one's family a child, who is not a natural heir, and give him or her the rights, privileges, and duties of a natural one.

ADOPTADO. Adopted. Person who is taken into a family as if he or she were its natural born child. See "Adopción".

ADOPTANTE. Adopter. Person who adopts a child. See "Adopción".

ADOPTAR. To adopt. To take into one's family a child, who is not a natural heir, and give him or her the rights, privileges and duties of a natural one.

ADOPTIVO. Adoptive. Refers to adoption or to the parties involved.

ADQUIRIENTE. Purchaser. One who buys, purchases or acquires.

ADQUIRIR. To legally increase one's rights or assets in property.

ADQUISICIÓN. Acquisition. To acquire property. To increase patrimony.

ADQUISITIVO. Acquisitive. Said of the person with the faculty to acquire.

ADSCRITO. Person enrolled in an organization.

ADUANA. Customs. A public office established for the inspection and assessment of duties on imported goods.

ADUCIR PRUEBAS. To adduce evidence. To produce proof in a court of law.

ADULTERAR. To adulterate. (1) To commit adultery. (2) To falsify. To mix and taint something of quality with something of lesser quality. To alter scales and balances.

ADULTERINO. Adulterine. Proceeding from adultery. Usually refers to the bastard child, the product of adulterous relations.

ADULTERIO. Adultery. Voluntary sexual intercourse of a married person with a person other than the offender's spouse.

ADÚLTERO. Adulterous. Person who commits adultery. See "Adulterio".

ADULTO. Adult. One who has attained the legal age of majority; generally 18 years.

ADVERADO. Attested. Whenever an act or document is witnessed.

ADVERTIR. To warn. To point out danger. To give notice. To observe.

ADVERTENCIA. Warning. To indicate or recommend an action be taken or not. Usually it means the admonishment by the judge to comply with a law or regulations.

AFECTACIÓN. Charge. Wherever a claim is made against property. Encumbrance. Also appropriation.

AFECTAR. To affect. To charge, mortgage, pledge or otherwise encumber property to assure the payment of money or performance or non-performance of a certain act.

AFIANZAR. To bail. To bond. To guarantee the fulfillment of an obligation, by means of bailment. See "Fianza".

AFIDAVIT. (Lat.) Affidavit. A written or printed statement of facts, made voluntarily and confirmed by the oath or affirmation of the party making it, taken before a person having authority to administer such oath or affirmation, usually a notary public.

AFILIACIÓN. Affiliation. To form part of a group or organization as a member.

AFILIADO. Member of a group or organization.

AFÍN. Similar. Related. Related by marriage.

AFINIDAD. Affinity. The connection existing, as a consequence of marriage, between each of the married persons and the kindred of the other.

AFIRMACIÓN. Affirmation. To affirm, to confirm or ratify something as true.

AFIRMAR. To affirm. To state something as the truth. To confirm or ratify. To establish.

AFORO. Appraisal. To gauge the value of property by persons qualified to do so.

AFRENTA. Affront. An insult. Shame and dishonor caused by something said or done.

AGENCIA. Agency. Relation in which one person acts for or represents another by the latter's authority.

AGENTE. Agent. A person authorized by another person to act for him or her; a person entrusted with another's business.

AGENTE DE POLICÍA. Policeman. Person whose duty is to enforce the law and to preserve order and peace.

AGENTE DE SEGUROS. Insurance broker or agent. The persons who act as middlemen between the insurance company and the insured.

AGIOTAJE. Agiotage. A speculation on the rise and fall of the public debt or public funds or securities.

AGNACIÓN. Agnation. Kinship by the father's side.

AGNADO. Agnate. Person whose relationship is traced exclusively through males. See "Agnación".

AGRARIO. Agrarian. That which refers to the field. Relating to land and crops.

AGRAVANTE. Aggravating circumstances. Whenever a crime is committed in such a way that the circumstances augment the responsibility of the author.

AGRAVIADA, PARTE. Aggrieved party. Person or persons who are wronged, offended or injured.

AGRAVIADOR. Offender. Person who commits an offense. Violator of the law. Tortfeasor.

AGRAVIAR. To injure, to cause harm, damage or to offend.

AGRAVIO. Injury, damage; tort. A legal wrong done to another person.

AGREDIDO. Person against whom an aggression is committed.

AGREDIR. To assault. To physically attack another with intent to harm.

AGREGAR. To add. To join, annex or attach.

AGRESIÓN. Aggression. Assault. Any willful attempt or threat to inflict injury upon another person.

AGRESOR. Aggressor. The person who attacks or assaults another with intention to cause harm.

AGRICULTOR. Farmer.

AGUAS FLUVIALES. (Lat.) Fluvius. Water from rivers, that can be utilized for watering crops, drinking and navigation.

AGUAS SUBTERRÁNEAS. Subterranean waters. Said of all water that is underground.

AGUINALDO. Gift. Voluntary reward in the form of money that employers give to employees, sometimes by reason of special festivities such as Christmas.

AHIJADO. Godchild. One person in respect of his or her Godfather.

AHOGAR. To drown. To kill by suffocation, by immersion into water or by choking.

AHOGADO. Person who has drowned. See "Ahogar".

AHORCADO. Hanged. Person hung by the neck. Suspended.

AHORCAR. To hang. To suspend a person by the neck until death.

AHORRAR. To save. Not to consume everything and set aside something, usually money.

AHORROS. Savings. What has been spared and not consumed.

AISLAR. To isolate. To separate a thing or persons from others. To detach.

AJENO. (1) What belongs to another. (2) Foreign or strange.

AJUAR. The goods, furnishings and items in a household.

AJUSTAR. To adjust. (1) To conform one thing to another. (2) To agree to a price for services rendered.

AJUSTES. Adjustments. Whenever differences or discrepancies are settled or arranged.

AJUSTICIADO. Executed criminal. Person convicted of a crime who has been put to death by the state.

AJUSTICIADOR. Executioner. Person who carries out the death penalty.

AJUSTICIAR. To execute. To punish with death.

AL CONTADO. Cash. A cash sale. When payment is tendered as soon as the goods are delivered; as distinguished from a sale on credit.

ALARDE. (1) To review. Monthly revision of cases by the courts. Also regular visits by court appointed officers to the jails to establish how the prisoners are being treated. (2) To boast.

ALBACEA. Executor, executrix. A person appointed by a testator, a judge, or by law to carry out the directions and requests of the deceased and to dispose of his or her property.

ALBEDRÍO. Free choice. The power to act by one's own decision.

ALCABALA. Tax or duty paid to a fiscal entity by the seller of a good, normally a percentage of the sale price.

ALCAHUETE. Procurer. Person who procures for another the gratification of his lust. Pimp. Panderer.

ALCALDE. Mayor. A governmental figure who is generally the principal administrative officer of a city or other municipal entity.

ALCANCE. Scope. Extent. Comprehension. Balance due.

ALCOHÓLICO. Alcoholic. Containing or relating to alcohol.

ALDEA. Village. Small town without its own jurisdiction.

ALEATORIO. Aleatory. Uncertain or insecure. This word is utilized to describe contracts where the parties stipulate certain clauses which depend on the occurrence of some future uncertain act, i.e., insurance contract, lottery, etc.

ALEGAR. To plead. To assert, claim, declare or state, by a party to an action, in order to set forth what he or she expects to prove.

ALEGATO. Allegation. The written document in which the lawyer details the reasons why his or her client's petitions should be granted.

ALEVOSÍA. Perfidy, treachery. The act of one who has pledged to act, but willfully betrays his word by failing to act.

ALGUACIL. Bailiff; constable; court officer.

ALIADO. Allied. United with another for defense and attack.

ALIANZA. Agreement or pact. Alliance. The union of two or more persons or states for mutual purposes.

ALIAS. Alias. Short for "alias dictus" or "otherwise called." A fictitious name used in place of a person's real name.

ALIENACIÓN. Alienation. To transmit property to another.

ALIMENTANTE. Person who pays alimony or allowance to another.

21

ALIMENTISTA. Person who receives alimony or allowance from another.

ALIMENTOS. Support, maintenance. The furnishing by one person to another, for his or her support, of the means of sustenance such as food, clothing, shelter, etc., particularly where the legal relation of the parties is such that one is bound to support the other, as between father and child, or husband and wife.

ALMIRANTAZGO. Admiralty. Maritime court with jurisdiction in controversies arising out of maritime contracts, torts, injuries or offenses.

ALMONEDA. Auction.

ALOJAMIENTO. Lodging. Housing. Quartering.

ALOJAR. To lodge. To house or quarter.

ALQUILAR. To rent. See "Alquiler".

ALQUILER. To lease, rent. A contract by which a person owning a property (real or personal) grants to another the right to possess, use and enjoy it for a specified period of time in exchange for periodic payment of a stipulated price, referred to as rent, while the owner retains ultimate legal ownership. See "Arrendamiento".

ALTA CORTE DE JUSTICIA. High Court of Justice. A court of high powers and extensive jurisdiction.

ALTA MAR. High seas. Portion of the ocean considered as international waters.

ALTA TRAICIÓN. High treason. The crime of having contact with the enemy in war times to betray one's country. Rendering aid and comfort to the enemy.

ALTERACIÓN. Alteration. Change or modification of a thing or an instrument into a different one.

ALTERADO. Altered. Person who is disturbed, upset or angered.

ALTERAR. To alter. (1) To disturb, upset or irritate. (2) To falsify.

ALTERNATIVO. Alternative. The right to choose between two or more options.

ALUCINACIÓN. Hallucination. A trick of the senses.

ALUCINAR. To hallucinate. To be deluded or dazzled.

ALUMBRAMIENTO. (1) Childbirth. (2) To discover subterranean water, and to bring it to the surface.

ALUVIÓN. Alluvion. The increase or accession of land on a shore by the force of the water which is so gradual that no one can judge how much is added at each moment of time.

ALZADA. Appeal. To resort to a superior court for it to review the decision of an inferior one.

ALZAMIENTO. (1) Uprising. Insurrection. (2) Raising, lifting.

ALLANAMIENTO. The act of accepting a claim or a decision.

ALLANAMIENTO DE MORADA. Trespass, unlawful entry. Breaking into a house, with or without any right, without the owner's permission.

ALLANAR. To break into. To enter a place, with or without the right to do so, without the owner's or occupant's consent. To raid or trespass.

A.M. ANTE MERIDIANO. A.M. The first twelve hours of the day.

AMA DE CASA. Housewife.

AMANCEBAMIENTO. Concubinage.

AMANTE. Lover. (1) A person who loves. (2) Adulterer.

AMBIGÜEDAD. Ambiguity. State of the word or text that is not clear and which requires further interpretation.

AMBIGUO. Ambiguous. Word or text that is not clear and which requires further interpretation.

AMENAZA. Threat. Menace. A declaration of intention to harm, punish or otherwise cause damage to another.

AMISTOSO. Amicable. Person favorably disposed. Friendly.

AMICUS CURIAE. (Lat.) Friend of the court. A party voluntarily appearing to aid the court in deciding an important case.

AMNISTÍA. Amnesty. Pardon granted by a government to a group of persons who have been guilty of a crime, generally political in nature.

AMOJONAMIENTO. Marking with landmarks the boundaries of a property.

AMONESTACIÓN. Admonition. Warning from a judge to the person discharged informing him or her that if he or she is convicted of the same crime or offense, he or she will be punished with severity.

AMORTIZACIÓN. Amortization. The payment of a debt by installments.

AMOTINAR. To mutiny. To rise against lawful or constituted authority, particularly a mutiny by the naval or military services.

AMPARO. Constitutional remedy to guarantee the inviolability of the rights and guaranties set forth in the Constitution.

AMPLIACIÓN. Enlargement. Augmentation. Extension.

ANALOGÍA. Analogy. Reasoning or arguing by similarities. Way of interpretation of the law consisting in the application of cases on a different subject matter, to cases where there is no precedent in point, but are governed by the same general principle.

ANARQUÍA. Anarchy. The absence of government.

ANATOCISMO. Anatocism. (1) Agreement whereby the debtor agrees to pay interest on interest which is due and unpaid. (2) Repeated or doubled interest; compound interest, usury.

ANCIANO. Elder. Person who is aged or old.

ANCLAR. To anchor. To keep a vessel stationary by dropping the anchor.

ANCLAJE. Anchorage. To station a vessel at a berth.

ANFICTIÓN. In Roman law, representative to the Roman cities' confederacy.

ÁNIMO. Animus (Lat.). State of mind or intention.

ÁNIMO DE LUCRO. Animus lucrae (Lat.). The intention to gain or profit.

ANÓNIMO. Anonymous. Nameless, unsigned.

ANOTACIÓN. Entry.

ANTECEDENTES. Precedent. (1) A court decision on a question of law that gives authority or direction on how to decide a similar question of law in a later case with similar facts. (2) Something that must happen before something else may happen.

ANTECEDENTES PENALES. Criminal records of a particular person. A document stating the crimes and misdemeanors of a person evidencing his or her past conduct.

ANTECESOR. Predecessor. Person who precedes another in time. Ancestor.

ANTEDICHO. Aforesaid. What has been said before. Above-mentioned.

ANTEPASADO. Before last. Ancestor. Grandfather or other remote predecessor.

ANTEPROYECTO. Preliminary sketch, first draft. Generally, the first draft written by specialists on a subject matter that will be used as the basis for the elaboration of a law.

ANTE. Before. In the presence. Before someone.

ANTES. Before. What comes prior to something. Preceding.

ANTICIPADO. (1) Advance on funds. (2) Treacherous attack.

ANTICIPACIÓN. Anticipation. Advancement. Payment or collection before it is due. Doing something before the due date.

ANTICIPO. Anticipation. See "Anticipación".

ANTICONSTITUCIONAL. That which is contrary to or in conflict with a constitution.

ANTICRESIS. An agreement by which the debtor, or a third person on behalf of the debtor, gives to the creditor the income from the property he or she has pledged, in lieu of the interest on his or her debt.

ANTIGÜEDAD. Seniority. (1) Time a person has labored in his or her job. (2) Special bonus for years labored.

ANTIGUO. Ancient. Antique. Veteran. Senior.

ANTIJURÍDICO. Unlawful. That which is contrary to, prohibited by, or unauthorized by law.

ANTIMONOPOLIO. Antitrust. Against monopolies.

ANTINOMIA. A contradiction between two or more judicial norms.

ANTISEMITA. Antisemitic. Person or group of persons who dislike and often advocate the persecution of the Jews.

ANTISOCIAL. Antisocial. A person who rebels against the existence of any social order. Said of the person whose conduct reflects a lack of respect for the law. A criminal.

ANUALIDAD. Annuity. A fixed sum of money, usually paid to a person periodically during a fixed period of time or for life.

ANUENCIA. Consent. Whenever one agrees with the proposition of another and demonstrates this agreement actively.

ANULABLE. Voidable. That which may be declared with no legal force or binding effect.

ANULACIÓN. Annulment. The act of making null and void. Cancellation. Defeasance. Vacation.

ANULAR. To annul, void, cancel or dismiss. To set aside, invalidate, reverse or vacate. To defeat, quash, abate. To write off or disaffirm.

ANUNCIO. Advertisement. Statement, report, omen.

ANVERSO. Obverse. The face of a document or coin.

AÑO. Year. Twelve months. The period from January 1st through December 31st.

APARCERÍA. Sharecropping. Type of agricultural arrangement in which the landowner leases land and equipment to a tenant or sharecropper who, in turn, gives to the landlord a percentage of the crops as rent.

APARCERO. Partner; each one of the parties to a partnership.

APAREJOS. Rigging. Tools, instruments, and accessories of a vessel indispensable for navigation.

APARENTE. Apparent. (1) That which is evident. (2) Not real. (3) Convenient.

APARIENCIA. Appearance. Resemblance. Conjecture. Coming to court.

APARTAMENTO. Apartment. To abandon a claim, right or action.

APÁTRIDA. Stateless. One without a nationality, without a country.

APELABLE. Appealable. That which can be appealed. See "Apelación".

APELACIÓN. Appeal. Resort to an appellate court requesting that it review the decision of an inferior court.

APELADO. That which has been appealed. See "Apelación". Person favored with an appeal.

APELANDO. State of a person who is requesting an appeal.

APELAR. To appeal.

APELLIDO. Surname; last name; family name.

27

APERCIBIMIENTO. Warning or notice. Generally, a warning to a public officer by a higher authority to cease and desist from improper conduct.

APERSONAMIENTO. Appearance. Whenever a person comes into court as a party to a suit, either as plaintiff or defendant.

APERSONARSE. To appear. Whenever a person comes into court.

APERTURA DE CRÉDITO. Contract where a fixed limit of credit is granted by a creditor to a customer (debtor) for the latter's use but which should not be exceeded. Opening of a credit line.

APERTURA DE LA SUCESIÓN. Opening of the inheritance. Whenever a person dies, his or her inheritance is "opened" so that the property can be transmitted to the heirs.

APERTURA DEL TESTAMENTO. Opening of a will at the time of death or presumption thereof; the act of opening and reading the deceased's last will and testament.

APLAZAR. To postpone. To adjourn or extend; to put off, defer or delay, to summon.

APLICACIÓN. Enforcement to make effective; to put into execution.

APLICACIÓN DE DERECHO. Those executory actions intended to enforce a judicial decision through legal channels.

APLICAR. To adjudicate, to award; to allocate, to appropriate or apply.

APÓCRIFO. Apocryphal. False, imitated. That whose authenticity is questioned.

APODERADO. Attorney, agent. One who is appointed and authorized to act in the place or stead of another.

APODERAR. To empower. To grant a power of attorney.

APODO. Nickname. A short name applied to some persons generally because of some personal characteristics.

APOLOGÍA DEL DELITO. Defense of the crime. To excuse or to advocate the commission of a crime.

APORTE. Contribution. To furnish goods, money, time, work, or other things of value for a common enterprise.

APOSTAR. To bet. To place a bet or wager. To gamble.

APOSTADO. (1) What has been wagered. (2) A soldier stationed at his or her post.

APREHENDER. To seize; arrest. See "Arrestar".

APREMIO. Writ. An order issued from a court compelling payment or fulfillment of a specified act. Enforced collection action.

APRENDIZ. Apprentice. Person who is not learned in a particular discipline and is being trained by a skilled tutor.

APRESAMIENTO. Capture. To seize a vessel or aircraft by the use of force.

APRESAR. To capture. To seize.

APRISIONAR. To imprison. To confine or restrain a person's liberty in any way.

APROBACIÓN. Approval; to consent to another's act; to confirm, ratify, acquiesce or sanction.

APROBADO. Approved. That which has been confirmed, ratified, acquiesced or sanctioned. See "Aprobación".

APROPIACIÓN. Appropriation. The act of appropriating a thing; to make a thing the subject of property.

APROPIACIÓN INDEBIDA. Misappropriation. (1) A crime consisting in the malicious retention of another's goods or assets received temporarily for deposit in violation of a duty to hold and return the property. (2) The crime of utilizing the goods entrusted for a different purpose than that ordered.

APROVECHAMIENTO. Advantage. To obtain profit or gain. To exploit to full potential. To utilize.

29

APTITUD. Aptitude. Fitness or capacity for employment or other acts. Competence.

APTO. Apt. Person with aptitude. See "Aptitud".

APUESTA. Bet. Wager between two or more persons where the happening of an event or the proof of a solution or fact in favor of one of the parties results in winning money or other valuable property.

AQUIESCENCIA. Acquiescence. Agreement or consent by a person to a transaction, event or fact.

ARANCEL. Tariff. The list or schedule of articles on which a duty is imposed upon their importation into a foreign country, with the rates at which they are taxed.

ARBITRAJE. Arbitration. An agreement to abide by the judgment of selected persons (arbitrators) in some disputed matter, instead of litigating before a court with the purpose of avoiding the formalities, delay, expense and vexation of ordinary litigation.

ARBITRADOR. Arbitrator. A private, disinterested person, chosen by the parties to a disputed question, for the purpose of hearing facts and arguments and rendering a judgment, at his or her own discretion, on the disputed question.

ARBITRARIEDAD. Arbitrariness. Conduct that is contrary to the law, justice or reason. Arbitrary and capricious conduct which is an abuse of power.

ARBITRARIO. Arbitrary. That which depends on the will or whim of someone.

ARBITRIO. Arbitrament. Decision or award of an arbitrator to settle a dispute in arbitration.

ÁRBITRO. Arbiter. A person chosen to decide a controversy according to the rules of law and equity.

ARCAS. Vaults. Place where money and valuables are kept.

ARCHIVOS. Archives. Place destined for the filing and conservation of documents in an orderly fashion so that they can be consulted.

ARGUMENTO. Argument. The effort to establish a belief by reasoning and logic.

ARISTOCRACIA. Aristocracy. Government by which a class of people rule.

ARMA. Weapon. Any instrument destined to attack or defend.

ARMADOR. Shipowner. The person who equips a ship, supplying all the necessary equipment to navigate, and who uses it commercially.

ARMISTICIO. Armistice. The end of hostilities between belligerent nations.

ARQUEO. Audit. (1) Amounts contained in "arcas" or vaults. (2) The measure of the cubic capacity of cargo of any vessel.

ARRAIGO. Bailment. Whenever the court protects one of the parties by seeking real estate, a surety, or money to secure the payment of a judgment.

ARRAIGADO. Subject to bail. See "Arraigo".

ARRAS. Earnest money, down payment. A sum of money paid by the buyer at the time of entering a contract to indicate the intention and ability of the buyer to carry out the contract. Normally it is applied to the purchase price and it is forfeited if the buyer defaults.

ARREGLADOR. Adjuster. A person who either determines or settles the amount of a claim or debt.

ARREGLO. Settlement, agreement, understanding, arrangement, compromise, composition or accommodation.

ARRENDADOR. Landlord. The owner of a land or a building that is rented or leased to one or more tenants.

ARRENDAMIENTO. To lease, rent. A contract by which a person owning a property (real or personal) grants to another the right to possess, use and enjoy it for a specified period of time in exchange for periodic payment of a stipulated price, referred to as rent, while the owner retains ultimate legal ownership. See "Alquiler".

ARRENDATARIO. Tenant. Person who rents or leases real property. Lessee. One who occupies another's property for a price during a fixed period of time. See "Alquiler".

ARREPENTIRSE. To repent; to reconsider, to withdraw or revoke.

ARRESTADO. Person who has been arrested.

ARRESTAR. To arrest. To deprive a person of his or her liberty by legal authority.

ARRESTO. Arrest. To deprive a person of his or her liberty by legal authority.

ARRIENDO. Rental. A contract by which a person owning real or personal property grants to another the right to possess, use and enjoy it for a specific period of time in exchange for periodic payment of a stipulated rent, while the owner retains ultimate legal ownership.

ARROGACIÓN. Arrogation. (1) To assume or acquire immaterial things like jurisdiction. (2) To adopt an orphan as one's child.

ARSENAL. Arsenal. (1) Place where weapons are kept. (2) Place where ships are built or repaired.

ARTICULADO. Series of articles or paragraphs of a statute or law.

ARTÍCULO. Article. Every one of the numbered propositions of a treaty, code, book, etc.

ASALARIADO. Wage earner. Person who collects his or her pay for services rendered to an employer on a regular basis.

ASALTANTE. Assailant. Person who commits an assault. See "Asalto" and "Asaltar".

ASALTAR. To rob. To overcome someone suddenly and unexpectedly with the intention of taking money, personal property or any other valuable articles against his or her will, and accomplished by means of force or by inflicting fear.

ASALTO. Assault. An armed robbery.

ASAMBLEA. A convention to address matters of common concern.

ASAMBLEA CONSTITUYENTE. Constitutional convention. A duly constituted assembly of delegates or representatives of the people of a state or nation for the purpose of revising or amending its constitution.

ASAMBLEA DE ACCIONISTAS. A shareholder's or stockholder's meeting.

ASAMBLEA LEGISLATIVA. Legislature. Body of persons that enacts statutory laws for a state or nation.

ASCENDIENTE. Ascendant. Person with whom one is related in the ascending line (e.g., parents, grandparents, etc.).

ASCENSO. Promotion. To be promoted to a higher position with more authority and/or wages.

ASEGURADO. The insured. The person who is covered by insurance.

ASEGURADOR. Insurer; the underwriter or insurance company with whom a contract of insurance is made.

ASEGURAR. To assure; to give security about what has been said; to insure; to keep persons or things from harm; to guarantee the performance of an obligation.

ASENTAR. To seat. To place. To establish. To award. To settle. To inscribe. See "Asiento".

ASENTIMIENTO. Assent. Compliance; approval of something done or to be done.

ASESINAR. To assassinate, to murder. The unlawful killing of a human being by another with malice aforethought, either express or implied.

ASESINATO. Assassination. The unlawful killing of a human being by another with malice aforethought, either express or implied.

ASESINO. Murderer. Person who kills another. See "Asesinato".

33

ASESOR. Assessor; a person learned in a particular science who gives advice; consultant; adviser.

ASIENTO. Inscription. Registration of a civil or commercial act in general, in an official ledger kept in a public record office.

ASIGNACIÓN. Allotment; a share or portion granted; allowance, quota.

ASIGNACIÓN TESTAMENTARIA. Bequest. To give a gift of personal property as stated in one's will. A legacy.

ASILO. Asylum. In public international law, the protection or refuge given to political criminals of a state by diplomatic representatives of another in their buildings, preventing the taking of said political criminals without the consent of the diplomatic representative. Refuge granted to political persecutees obtained by entry into a country which grants asylum.

ASISTENCIA. Attendance; action of being present. Also assistance, to help or aid.

ASISTENTE. Assistant. One who is present. One who helps or aids.

ASOCIACIÓN. Association. Body of persons who have joined together for some special purpose. Company, partnership, union.

ASOCIACIÓN EN PARTICIPACION. A joint venture contract where one party gives money, goods or services in exchange for a share in the profits in the venture.

ASOCIADO. Associate. Member of an association. A member of a syndicate.

ASTUCIA. Cunning. Trick or artifice to deceive another.

ASUETO. Day off; short time off.

ASUMIR. To assume. To take possession of a duty or post.

ASUNCIÓN DEL RIESGO. Assumption of risk. Whenever the plaintiff assumes consequences of the injuries of the defendant, even though no fault lies with the plaintiff; for example, in an insurance contract.

ASUNTO. Matter. Subject, issue, or affair.

ATACADO. Attacked. (1) Person who has been assaulted. (2) Affirmation that has been contested.

ATACANTE. Assailant. Person who commits an assault.

ATACAR. To attack or assault. To oppose, contest, rebut or challenge.

ATENTADO. Attempt. The attempt or assault of a person, his or her rights or goods.

ATENTAR. To attempt. To attempt or commit a crime.

ATENUANTE. Extenuating circumstance. Circumstance which renders a crime less evil or blameworthy than it would otherwise be.

ATESTADO. Attestation. (1) Official document in which certain facts are stated. (2) Deposition.

ATESTAR. To attest. To bear witness to, to depose or certify.

ATESTIGUAR. To declare or testify as a witness.

ATRACADO. Moored. (1) Situation of a vessel at berth. (2) Person who has been assaulted.

ATRACAR. To assault; to attack; to moor, to make shore.

ATRACO. Holdup. To assault. See "Asaltar".

ATRASADO. Delinquent, not paid at the time required. In arrears, late.

ATROCIDAD. Atrocity. Extreme and perverse cruelty.

ATROPELLAR. To violate; to run over; to treat arbitrarily.

ATROZ. Atrocious. What is committed with atrocity. See "Atrocidad".

AUDIENCIA. Hearing. Proceeding wherein evidence is taken for the purpose of determining an issue or fact and reaching a decision on the basis of that evidence.

AUDITOR. Auditor. Person who verifies the accuracy of financial statements or accounts.

AUDITORÍA. (1) An account statement. Counting the assets and liabilities. (2) Judge or legal advisor.

AUSENCIA. Absence. The condition of the person whose whereabouts are unknown.

AUSENTE. Absent. The person who is not present in the place he or she should be.

AUTÉNTICA. Attestation; the act of witnessing an instrument in writing and subscribing to it as a witness.

AUTENTICIDAD. Authenticity. That which is authentic or true.

AUTENTICACIÓN. To authenticate. The act of giving authority or legal authenticity to a statute, record or other written instrument or a certified copy thereof.

AUTENTIFICAR. To authenticate; to give full value to a document or a certified copy thereof, for it to be legally admissible.

AUTO. Interlocutory order; decree; writ; warrant.

AUTOCRACIA. Autocracy. A government at the will of one person, unchecked by constitutional restrictions or limitations.

AUTONOMÍA. Autonomy. The right and power of self-government. Rights which are independent.

AUTOPSIA. Autopsy; the examination of a dead body to establish the cause of its death.

AUTOR. Author; a creator or originator of something. Principal; perpetrator of a crime.

AUTORIDAD. Authority. The right to exercise powers, to enforce and implement laws and control.

AUTORIZACIÓN. Authorization; a permission or power given for a certain act. To authorize an act.

AUTORIZADO. Authorized. The person or act authorized to do something.

AUTOS. Record of the case. The official collection of all the trial pleadings, exhibits, orders and testimony that took place during the trial.

AVAL. Aval. To guarantee a negotiable instrument by placing one's signature at the bottom of a promissory note or of a bill of exchange.

AVALADO. The guarantee. The secured party to a guaranty.

AVALAR. To vouch for; to back, support, or otherwise guarantee something; to endorse.

AVALISTA. The guarantor. One who makes a guaranty.

AVALORAR. To appraise. To value or price a thing.

AVALUADOR. Appraiser. Person appointed by competent authority to establish the true value of property.

AVALUAR. To appraise; to assess; to ascertain or fix the value of something.

AVALÚO. Appraisement. A just valuation of property; appraisal.

AVENIMIENTO. Agreement. A mutual assent to do or not to do something. A compromise intended to end a civil action or trial.

AVENIRSE. To agree; to settle or compromise.

AVERÍA. Average. In maritime law, loss or damage accidentally suffered by a vessel or to its cargo during a voyage.

AVISO. Notice; announcement. Knowledge of certain facts.

AVOCACIÓN. See "Avocamento".

AVOCAMENTO. Evocation. In French law, the withdrawal of a cause from the cognizance of an inferior court, and bringing it before another court or judge.

AVOCAMIENTO. See "Avocamento".

AVULSIÓN. Avulsion. A sudden and perceptible loss or addition to land by the action of water, or a sudden change in the bed or course of a stream.

AYUDA. Assistance. Help or aid.

AYUDANTE. Assistant. Subordinate that helps or aids.

AYUNTAMIENTO. Municipal council which governs the municipality.

AZAR. Chance. Casualty. Fate. Misfortune.

B

BACHILLER. Bachelor. (1) One who has finished high school. (2) One who has taken the first degree in a college or university. (3) **Bachiller en Leyes.** Bachelor of Laws.

BAJO PALABRA, LIBERTAD. On parole. A conditional release of a person from imprisonment.

BAJO PROTESTA. Under protest. To act under a formal declaration of dissent or disapproval, in order to preserve some right or to be exonerated from responsibility.

BALANCE. Balance. An amount left over. The difference between assets and liabilities.

BALANZA DE PAGOS. Balance of payments. The net difference resulting from the commercial trade between one nation and its trade partners.

BALANCE GENERAL. Balance sheet. A statement that shows the assets and liabilities of a business.

BALDÍO. Uncultivated or undeveloped piece of land either private or public.

BALÍSTICA. Ballistics. The science that studies the movement of projectiles, bullets.

BANCA. Banking. The business of issuing notes payable on demand intended to circulate in lieu of money; receiving money in deposit; discounting commercial papers; making loans; and in general being involved in the business of handling money.

BANCA o BANCO CENTRAL. Central Banking or Bank. A country's bank which administers its monetary policy.

BANCARROTA. Bankruptcy. Legal status of one who cannot meet his or her monetary obligations and is insolvent.

BANCO. Bank. An institution whose business is the banking business. See "Banca".

BANDA. Gang. A group of criminals or terrorists associated to commit crimes.

BANDERA. Flag. (1) A national standard which displays certain emblems; an ensign; a banner. (2) In maritime law it refers to the nationality or country under which a vessel has been registered, making it subject to the laws of that country.

BANDIDO. Bandit; an outlaw; a gunman or robber. A racketeer, thief.

BANDO. Side. Usually refers to the political inclination or party of a person.

BANDOLERO. Thief; bandit.

BANQUILLO DE ACUSADOS. Defendant's seat in court.

BARATERÍA. Fraud, barratry. Commercial Law: Committing fraud in a business transaction. Maritime Law: A fraud committed by the Captain or the crew of a vessel against the shipowner, the cargo owner or the insurer.

BASE. Base; basis. Group of ideas or material support on which one sometimes relies or leans on. What is fundamental.

BARCO. Vessel. See "Buque".

BASE IMPONIBLE. Tax base. The total assessed value of all the property in a given area which determines the rate at which an individual property is taxed.

BASTANTEAR. To recognize as valid; to declare valid and to admit the legality of a power given to an attorney.

BASTANTEO. The act of admitting the legality of a power given to an attorney. See "Bastantear".

BASTARDO. Bastard; a child born out of wedlock.

BAUTISMO. Baptism. Act of becoming a Christian and being entitled to rights and obligations according to the Catholic Church.

BAUTIZO. Baptism. See "Bautismo".

BEBIDAS ALCOHÓLICAS. Alcoholic beverages. Beverages containing alcohol which are considered intoxicating.

BELIGERANTE. Belligerent. A state engaged in war. Also a state not directly at war which assists (openly or covertly) another state at war.

BENEFICIARIO. Beneficiary. One for whose benefit a trust is created or insurance is acquired. One receiving benefits.

BENEFICIENCIA SOCIAL. Welfare. Public financial assistance to certain categories of poor or dispossessed persons.

BENEFICIO. Benefit. Advantage, gain, profit.

BENEFICIO DE EXCUSIÓN. Benefit of exclusion. Right of a guarantor to compel a creditor to exhaust his or her remedies against the debtor before having recourse against the guarantor.

BENEFICIO DE INVENTARIO. See "A Beneficio de Inventario".

BENEFICIOS MARGINALES. Fringe benefits. Those fringe benefits received by an employee as consequence of his or her work.

BESTIALIDAD. Bestiality, sodomy. Crime consisting of unnatural sexual intercourse between human and animals.

BICAMERAL. Bicameral. Legislative system in which the legislature or parliament is formed by two chambers, the Senate or upper one and the House of Representatives or lower one.

BIEN. Good, singular of "Bienes." See "Bienes".

BIEN RAÍZ. Real estate. Land and the property affixed to it.

BIEN RELICTO. Estate left by a decedent.

BIENES. Assets, goods, possessions; property of all kinds, real and personal, tangible and intangible, belonging to a person, association, corporation, or estate.

BIENES ACCESORIOS. Accessions. Property which has become permanently affixed to land, such as land building up on a river bank. The owner of the land will also own the new land.

BIENES COMUNES. Common property. Those goods that can be used by everyone and are private property. In real estate refers to the common part of the property that belongs communally to every one of the unit owners in a building complex.

BIENES DE CONSUMO. Consumer goods. Goods which are purchased primarily for personal, family or household purposes.

BIENES CORPORALES E INCORPORABLES. Tangible and intangible goods.

BIENES DE DOMINIO PRIVADO. Private property. Property that belongs absolutely to an individual, and over which he or she has the exclusive right of disposition.

BIENES DE DOMINIO PÚBLICO. Public property. Those things considered as being owned by "the public" (the entire state or community), and not restricted to the dominion of a private person.

BIENES DEL ESTADO. State property. Property that belongs to the State.

BIENES DEL QUEBRADO. Bankrupt's property. Property that belongs to a person who has been declared in bankruptcy.

BIENES FUNGIBLES. Fungible goods. Movable goods. Things that are easily replaced one for another. For example, a pound of sugar is fungible because it may be substituted for its equivalent.

BIENES FUTUROS. Future goods. Goods which are neither existing nor identified.

BIENES GANANCIALES. Property acquired during married life which is held jointly.

BIENES INCORPORALES. Intangible property.

BIENES INDIVISIBLES. Property that cannot be divided without altering its essence.

BIENES INEMBARGABLES. Properties that by virtue of law cannot be subject to sequestration.

BIENES INMUEBLES. Real estate. Land and anything permanently affixed to the land.

BIENES LITIGIOSOS. All goods or property involved in a lawsuit.

BIENES MOSTRENCOS. Unclaimed property. Property whose owner is unknown and therefore passes to the state.

BIENES MUEBLES. Movable property. All goods that are subject to property excluding real estate.

BIENES MUEBLES TANGIBLES (o CORPORALES). Tangible personal property.

BIENES NO FUNGIBLES. Specific goods. Goods that have been already ascertained and cannot be replaced.

BIENES PARAFERNALES. Paraphernal property. Separate property of a married woman, other than that which is included in her dowry.

BIENES PRIVATIVOS. Separate property. In a community property state. This is the property not included in the marital estate because it was acquired before marriage or, if acquired during marriage, is considered to belong exclusively to one of the spouses.

BIENES RAICES. Real estate. Plural of "Bien Raíz". See "Bien Raíz."

BIENESTAR. Well-being; welfare.

BIENES SEMOVIENTES. Livestock. Property that can move itself. The term is used to refer to animals.

BIGAMIA. Bigamy. The state of a man who has two wives, or of a woman who has two husbands, at the same time.

BILATERAL. Bilateral. On both sides. For example, a deal that involves promises, rights, and duties on both sides is said to be bilateral in nature.

BILLETE. Note or currency, can be the equivalent of money.

BILLETE DE LOTERÍA. Lottery ticket.

43

BINUBA, BINUBO. Person married for the second time.

BISABUELO, BISABUELA. Great-grandparent. See "Ascendiente".

BISNIETO, BISNIETA. Great-grandchild. See "Descendiente".

BLASFEMIA. Blasphemy. Something said or done to injure God or something sacred.

BLOQUEO. Blockage. See "Boicot". Sanctions.

BODA. Wedding, marriage.

BOICOT O BOICOTEO. Boycott or sanctions. Concerted refusal to do business with a particular person, business or country in order to obtain concessions or to express displeasure with certain acts or practices of the latter.

BOLETA. Ticket slip, certificate. Citation or summons issued to a violator of a law. Also a slip or certificate that evidences some property right.

BOLETÍN JUDICIAL. Judicial bulletin. Periodical publication in which judicial notice of a document or act is inserted for publication.

BOLETÍN OFICIAL O GACETA OFICIAL. Official gazette. Daily publication in which the laws, decrees, municipal or state resolutions, and any judicial document that requires notice by publication are inserted.

BOLETO. Ticket. A certificate that shows that a fare or fee has been paid and which contains the rights or privileges for whom it was issued.

BOLSA DE VALORES. Stock exchange. An organized market or exchange where shares (stocks), commercial papers, and bonds are traded.

BONA FIDE. (Lat.) Good faith. See "Buena Fe".

BONA IMMOBILIA. (Lat.) Fixed good.

BONIFICACIÓN. Bonus, allowance. An extra or irregular payment given as a gratuity.

BONO. Bond. A certificate or evidence of a debt where the issuing company or governmental body promises to pay the bondholder a specified amount of interest for a specified length of time, and to repay the principal on the expiration date.

BORRACHO. Alcoholic, drunk. Person intoxicated by the use of alcohol and under its influence and thus impaired in his or her reasoning and senses.

BORRADOR. Rough draft. A provisional writing of a document used to make corrections and amendments before it is prepared in final form.

BORRAR. To erase, delete.

BUEN COMPORTAMIENTO. Good behavior. Circumstance in which a convict can be released from jail on parole.

BUEN NOMBRE. Good reputation.

BUEN PADRE DE FAMILIA. Literally, a good family father. Said of the standard of behavior required from the moderate or average person (father) to exercise reasonable care in his or her acts.

BUEN RECAUDO. Secure. Something kept in good hands or under good custody.

BUENA CONDUCTA. Good behavior. Law-abiding conduct.

BUENA FE. Good faith. State of mind denoting honesty of purpose, free from intention to defraud.

BUENAS COSTUMBRES. Good manners. To behave in accordance with accepted moral principles.

BUENOS OFICIOS. Mediation. (1) In public international law the offering, by a third state, to mediate between two belligerent states, with the purpose of resolving the conflict through negotiation instead of war. (2) The acting of a person to facilitate or accomplish something for another.

BUFETE. Law office. Private office where lawyers carry on their legal business.

45

BUQUE. Ship, vessel. Any craft used, or capable of being used, to navigate in water.

BURDEL. A brothel; a house of prostitution. Said of the place where sexual pleasures are offered for sale.

BURGUESÍA. Bourgeoisie, middle class. This was the intellectual and artistic class that originated during the French Revolution in 1789. Nowadays refers to the social class formed by professionals.

BUROCRACIA. Bureaucracy. An organization, such as an administrative agency, with the following general traits: a chain of command with fewer people at the top than at the bottom; well-defined positions and responsibilities; fairly inflexible rules and procedures; "red tape" (many forms to be filled out and difficult procedures to go through); and delegation of authority downward from level to level.

BURÓCRATA. Bureaucrat. One who is part of a bureaucracy.

BURLAR. To deceive. To make fun of.

BURSÁTIL. Having to do with the stock market or exchange.

C

CABAL. Right, exact, accurate, perfect. (1) **Un Hombre Cabal.** A perfect man. (2) **De Juicio Cabal.** To be of sound mind.

CABAL JUICIO. Sound mind. The mental condition in which a person is fully capable of acting and not impaired.

CABECEADOR. Name formerly given to an executioner.

CABECILLA. (1) Person who commands a group of people who often pledge a fanatic compliance to his or her instructions. (2) Leader of a group of rebels. (3) In civil war, the person who commands the forces opposing the established government. (4) The head of a gang of criminals.

CABEZA. Head. One who governs or leads any body, community, town.

CABEZA DE FAMILIA. Head of family or household. The person who maintains, supports and takes care of the affairs of other persons, usually living in the same house. Head of a family.

CABEZA DE PROCESO. Said of the court order which initiates a criminal procedure. Said order may be the result of an accusation made by the victim or another person.

CABEZA DE SENTENCIA. Preamble to court's judgment. Caption. This is the heading of the judgment in which the names of the plaintiffs and the defendants (in a civil suit) or the parties (if it involves a criminal case) and the object or controversy is mentioned, to identify the proceeding and the persons bound by the judgments.

CABEZADERO. Name given in ancient Spanish law to the executioner.

CABILDEAR. To lobby. To attempt to persuade a legislator to vote a certain way on a bill or to introduce a bill. To have a bill approved by using pressure. To press upon.

CABILDEO. In old Spanish law, lobbying. Speculation.

CABILDERO. Meeting of a town's council; the place where said meeting is held. Lobbyist. One who pressures to have a bill passed. One who schemes, speculates.

CABILDO. A municipal council. Meeting of a town's council.

CABOTAJE. Coastal traffic. (1) Dues paid by coasting vessel. (2) **Barco De Cabotaje.** Landing vessel.

CADÁVER. Corpse, dead body. Body of a dead person.

CADENA. Chain. Term of a sentence or of prison.

CADENA PERPETUA. Life imprisonment. A criminal punishment consisting in the loss of personal liberty for the rest of the prisoner's life.

CADUCABLE. Forfeitable. Having an end.

CADUCAR. To forfeit, expire; become invalid; lapse.

CADUCIDAD. Lapsing; expiration. Termination of a right or privilege by virtue of law or by the passing of time.

CADUCIDAD DE LA INSTANCIA. Lapsing of a legal right or privilege. Termination of a privilege or right to do something during a trial by failing to do it within a certain time.

CADUCO. Lapsed, expired. Void. Without legal validity. A contract that is not valid any more. Also, termination of an insurance policy because of failure to pay the premium.

CAER. (1) To disappear or diminish, as a ministry or monarchy. (2) To lose fame, fortune or a job. (3) to fall into a category or denomination. (4) To incur in error, ignorance, harm or danger.

CAÍDO. Due, matured. Fallen.

CAÍDOS. Arrears.

CAJA. Cash box. Cashier's office. Used to keep money or valuables in a bank or commercial establishment.

CAJA DE SEGURIDAD. Safe deposit box. A service offered by many banks consisting of the rent of a metallic box installed in a special section of the bank for the purpose of keeping things of value.

CAJERO. Teller. Cashier. Bank's employee responsible for receiving and/or paying money. Anyone who receives payment at a commercial establishment.

CALABOZO. Cell; jail. A place used to confine prisoners.

CALAMIDAD. Misfortune. Unfortunate event or occurrence that harms many persons. It is considered an aggravating circumstance if a crime is committed to a person already in dire need because of such occurrence or event.

CÁLCULO DEL IMPUESTO. Tax computation. Process of appraising the value of something and ascertaining the amount of tax imposed.

CALENDARIO. Calendar. Almanac. A table with the year divided into months, weeks and days.

CALIBRE. Calibre. (1) Diameter of projectile or missile. (2) Gauge. (3) Importance or capacity. (4) Diameter of the cannons of firearms and their projectiles.

CALIDAD. Quality. Capacity. Condition or requisite to a deal. Class, nobility. Personal data and qualifications needed for a determined position. Junction. Post.

CALIFICACIÓN. Qualification, judgment. Evaluation, assessment. Mark of a test.

CALIFICACIÓN DE LA QUIEBRA. Bankruptcy qualification. Judicial resolution establishing the nature of the bankruptcy, which can be by accident, fault or fraud. The determination, by the judge, of the nature of the bankruptcy, i.e., whether it was fraudulent, involuntary, fortuitous or due to bad management.

CALIFICACIÓN DE UN DELITO. Determination of the nature of the crime, identification of a criminal and the penalty related to the crime.

CALIFICACIÓN REGISTRAL. An official review to determine whether or not documents submitted to a public registry are eligible for registration.

CALIFICADO. Qualified, skilled. Evaluated. Conditioned.

CALIFICAR. To weigh the merit of a witness' testimony or the value of evidence in general. Also, to ascertain the eligibility for registration of written documents.

CALÍGRAFO. Handwriting expert. Person versed in calligraphy who can give expert testimony on civil or criminal cases.

CALUMNIA. Calumny; defamation. Crime consisting of falsely accusing someone of a crime or offense.

CÁMARA. Chamber; room.

CÁMARA DE COMPENSACIONES. Clearing house. An organization created by banks for the purpose of settling their daily balances by the exchange of checks and drafts drawn on each other.

CÁMARA DE DIPUTADOS. Legislative chamber. Parliament. Congress. The branch of government entrusted with the enactment of laws.

CAMBALACHE. Swap, exchange. To barter for cheap things or items. Second hand shop.

CAMBIAR. To exchange, to change. To exchange one item for another. To exchange currency of one country for that of another.

CAMBIARIO. Related to a bill of exchange.

CAMBIO. Exchange; commission. Exchange rate. Barter. To trade equivalent things without setting a price. Also to compare the value of one currency to another country's currency.

CAMBIO MERCANTIL. Mercantile exchange. Said of those commercial exchanges between merchants and not between original manufacturers and consumers.

CAMBISTA. Cambist, trader in international bills or exchange. One who deals in the exchange of currency from different countries.

CAMPAÑA. Campaign. (1) Period when the army is in a military operation or at war. (2) Electoral campaign.

CAMPO. Field. A large area of land in the countryside. Jurisdiction, order of ideas or matters. In political campaigns or civil war, the army or party to which a person belongs.

CANAL. (1) Canal. Artificial waterway which links two seas or rivers used for navigation. (2) Channel, means of expression or communication.

CANCELACIÓN. Cancellation. To destroy the force, effectiveness, or validity of something. To annul.

CANCELACIÓN DE HIPOTECA. Discharge of mortgage. Whenever a mortgage loses its enforceability by (a) consent of the parties, (b) judicial order or judgment, or (c) payment of the loan.

CANCELAR. To cancel, to discharge. To settle, to pay a debt. To honor a draft, to pay a bill.

CANCILLER. Minister of foreign affairs. Cabinet level officer in charge of the foreign policy of a country.

CANCILLERÍA. Ministry of foreign affairs, chancellery. Office in charge of writing diplomatic documents.

CANJE. Exchange, clearing of checks.

CANJEABLE. Exchangeable, convertible.

CANJEAR. To exchange, to clear (checks). To convert (one currency into another).

CANJES INVOLUNTARIOS. Involuntary conversions. The loss of property by destruction, seizure, theft, casualty or condemnation.

CANON. (1) Rent. Compensation or fee paid, usually periodically, for the use of any property, land, building, etc. (2) Canon, precept, or rule.

CANÓNICO, DERECHO. Canon law. System of judicial norms that regulates the internal and external relationship of the church.

CANTIDAD. Quantity. All that can be counted, measured or weighed.

CANTIDAD NETA RECIBIDA. Amount realized. Amount received by a taxpayer upon the sale or exchange of property. It is the starting point for arriving at realized gain or loss for tax purposes.

CANTÓN. Canton. Territorial division typical of small federal republics such as in Switzerland.

CAPACIDAD. Capacity, competency. Legal competency of a party or person in a determined judicial setting to become active or passive subjects.

CAPACIDAD CIVIL. Legal capacity. Ability to understand the nature and effects of one's acts, and being bound by them. Capability to enter into contractual relations and enforce them. Commonly refers to a state required to grant or receive certain rights in family law, real estate, inheritance, etc.

CAPACIDAD DE PRODUCIR INGRESO. Earning capacity. Capability of a person to earn income based on a set of factors such as any impairment from an accident or disability, occupation, nature of injury, age at time of injury, wages prior to and after the injury.

CAPACIDAD JURÍDICA. Legal capacity. Ability of a person to enjoy rights, be bound and liable by certain obligations. Also, capacity set by law to exercise civil, political and social right. See "Capacidad Civil".

CAPITAL. Capital. (1) The accumulated goods, possessions and assets used for the production of profits and wealth. (2) The principal political city of a state from where the national or state governments exercise power.

CAPITALIZAR. To capitalize, convert, compound (as in interest). (1) To convert a periodic payment into an equivalent capital sum. To compute the present value of an income extended over a period of time. (2) To raise money for an investment by issuing securities.

CAPITAL SOCIAL. Capital stock. All stock issued in exchange for money by a corporation which represents the ownership interest of the stockholders and its capital funds.

CAPITALISMO. Capitalism. Economic doctrine by which the economy is divided in two forces, labor and capital, each theoretically acting freely according to the law of supply and demand.

CAPITALIZACIÓN. Capitalization. To compute the value of an asset in relation to the income it produces.

CAPITÁN DE BUQUE. Captain of a vessel. The person in charge of the government and direction of a vessel. He or she is entrusted with many duties including the registration of births and deaths aboard his or her ship, the celebration of wills and marriages and the punishment of any insubordinate crew member.

CAPITULACIONES MATRIMONIALES. Marriage articles, antenuptial agreement. Contract or agreement between a man and woman before marriage, but in contemplation and generally in consideration of marriage, whereby the property rights and interests of either the prospective husband or wife, or both of them, are determined.

CAPÍTULO. Chapter. (1) Leading title, military order or congregation. (2) Collegiate body which acts as senate or council to the bishop. (3) Important subdivision of extensive codes or laws.

CAPTURA. (1) The seizure of an enemy ship or of a neutral ship that assists the enemy, by contraband, circumventing blockades or transmitting information or news. (2) The apprehension of a person by virtue of a judicial order.

CARÁCTER. Character. Nature of a person. Attribute of a person due to his or her state, nature or rank.

CÁRCEL. Jail. A building or group of buildings utilized for the confinement of those persons awaiting trial or who are serving a sentence for crimes or misdemeanors.

CAREAR. To confront. In criminal law, the act of setting a witness face to face with the accused, in order that the latter may make any objection he or she has to the witness, or so that the witness may identify the accused.

CAREO. Confrontation. The act of setting opposing parties face to face to extract the truth.

CARGA. Cargo. The load of a vessel, train, truck, airplane or other carrier.

CARGA PROCESAL. Within a judicial process the obligations of each party involved, mainly those related to the plaintiff who has to prove a fact or a right.

CARGAMENTO. Load. The cargo transported by ships. Shipment.

CARGO. (1) Position, duty. Responsibility given to someone. (2) Count, charge. The underlying substantive offense contained in an accusation or indictment. A claim. A declaration of facts constituting the plaintiff's cause of action. (3) Load.

CARNAL. Carnal. Related by blood.

CARRERA. Career. Profession which requires a higher level of studies (university). Profession, course.

CARTA. Letter, chart.

CARTA CREDENCIAL. Credentials. Documentary evidence given by the government of a country to its ambassadors or diplomatic ministers to accredit their position before other countries' governments.

CARTA DE CIUDADANÍA o DE NATURALIZACIÓN. Naturalization papers. Document verifying that a person has acquired the nationality of a country different from his or her native one.

CARTA DE CRÉDITO o CARTA DE ORDEN DE CRÉDITO. Letter of credit. A letter authorizing one person to pay money or extend credit to another on the credit of the issuer. A negotiable instrument.

CARTA MAGNA. The Great Charter. (1) A document, signed by the English King in 1215, that first defined and gave many basic rights in England. These included personal and property rights, limits on taxation and religious interference, etc. (2) Generally speaking, the Constitution of a nation.

CARTA ROGATORIA. Letters rogatory. The medium whereby one country, through one of its courts, requests another country, acting through its own courts and by methods of court procedure peculiar thereto and entirely within the latter's control, to assist the administration of justice in the former country.

CARTEL. Cartel. A close (often formal) association of countries or companies formed to control the production, sale, and price of a determined product, to their mutual benefit. It has the same effect as a trust.

CARTERA. (1) Portfolio. Collective term for all the securities held by one person or institution. (2) Office of a Minister. Any department entrusted to a cabinet minister.

CASA. House. Firm. Concern.

CASA DE EMPEÑOS. Pawnshop. A place in which money is lent, usually in small sums, on security of personal property deposited or left in pledge.

CASA DE EXPÓSITOS. Foundling house or hospital. Charitable institutions that take care of infants forsaken by their parents.

CASA MATRIZ. Main office. The principal place of business of an organization that has a subsidiary or branch.

CASACIÓN. Cassation (French), annulment. To quash, to render void. To resort to the highest court or to the court of cassation to review the ultimate decision of an inferior court in order to annul it. Generally the revision by the highest court is limited to issues of law and is not allowed to review the facts.

CASADO(A). A married man or woman. One who was married even if later was divorced or widowed.

CASAMIENTO. Marriage. The contract and the act of joining a man and a woman to live together as husband and wife.

CASAR. (1) To marry. To join legally one man and one woman as husband and wife. (2) To annul a judgment. To quash or declare a court decision void.

CASARSE. To marry. To get married.

CASERO. Landlord. Caretaker. One who has property for rent. One who administers the estate of another. One who takes care of the house of another while away.

CASICONTRATO. Quasi-contract. An obligation similar to a contract that does not arise from an agreement but rather a unilateral act.

CASO. Case. (1) Lawsuit; a dispute that goes to court. (2) The judge's opinion deciding a legal dispute. (3) A judicial proceeding.

CASO FORTUITO. Act of God. An act, event, happening, or occurrence due to natural causes that is in no sense attributable to human agency. The inevitable accident that one could not have prevented.

CASTIGABLE. Punishable. Capable of being punished.

CASTIGAR. To punish; to penalize. See "Castigo".

CASTIGO. Punishment. Pain, penalty, confinement or other measure inflicted on a person by lawful authority for the commission of an offense or crime.

CASUAL. Casual. By chance, accidental. Unpremeditated, occasional. Fortuitous.

CATASTRAL. Cadastral. Relating to cadastre. See "Catastro".

CATASTRO. Cadastre. (1) Tax inventory and assessment of real property. (2) The government office entrusted with the inventory and valuation of real property.

CÁTEDRA. Chair. (1) Senior teaching post. (2) Podium or place where lectures are given.

CATEO. Warrant. Prospecting. To search for minerals with the authorization of the government. Court order to search for another's property.

CAUCIÓN. Bail. (1) The surety or sureties that procure the release of a person under arrest, by becoming responsible for his or her appearance at the time and place designated. (2) Guaranty. Security that assures the fulfillment of a contract or obligation. It can be decreed by the court or agreed upon by the parties to the contract.

CAUCIONAR. To pledge, to guarantee, to stand bail for someone.

CAUDAL. Wealth. Possessions, assets, patrimony of a person. All kinds of goods.

CAUDAL HEREDITARIO, PATRIMONIO. Estate. The whole property, rights, interest belonging to a dead person before it has been taxed or distributed according to the law or as a result of a will.

CAUDILLO. Leader. One who leads a people to war. Name also given to the one who leads or manages a community, society or union.

CAUSA. (1) Cause. Something that precedes and brings about an effect or a result. (2) Suit, trial. Any question, civil or criminal, litigated or contested before a court of justice. (3) Consideration.

The motive or reason to enter into a contract. This is one of the essential elements needed to have an enforceable contract. Without consideration there can be no contract. The consideration needs also to be a legal one in order to have a valid contract.

CAUSA RAZONABLE. Reasonable cause. (1) The state of facts which causes a reasonable person to act. (2) Justified cause. The argument or motive set by law as fair. Justification to fire an employee.

CAUSAHABIENTE. Assignee, subrogee. Successor to the property or estate; rights and obligations of a decedent.

CAUSAL. Cause. Reason or motive. Grounds.

CAUSANTE. Originator. Constituent. Principal. The one who does something and brings about an effect. Steps to avoid.

CAUSAR. To cause. To start a lawsuit. To make happen.

CAUTELAR. Precautionary, preventive. (1) To take precautions. (2) **Medidas Cautelares.** Preventive measures.

CEDENTE. Assignor, transferor. Grantor. The person who assigns, transfers or grants property or rights to another. The person who receives is known as assignee or grantee.

CEDER. To yield, to assign, to transfer, to submit to, to cede a territory.

CEDIBLE. Transferable. A right which can be transferred to another party.

CEDIDO. Transferred, assigned, assignee.

CÉDULA. Document. Identity card. Official document which is utilized to identify a person.

CÉDULA DE IDENTIDAD PERSONAL. Identification card, issued by the government as proof of identity.

CÉDULA HIPOTECARIA. Mortgage bond. Bond against which real estate or personal property is pledged as security to assure the bond will be paid as stated in its terms.

CELDA. Cell. The rooms where prisoners are locked in a jail.

CELEBRACIÓN. Celebration, formalization. (1) Formalization of an act or contract in compliance with the established requisites. (2) The execution of an act or contract with the fulfillment of all legal requirements.

CELEBRAR. To formalize. To execute or carry out an act or contract.

CENSO. Census. The official counting or enumeration of people of a state, nation, district, or other political subdivision.

CENSO ENFITÉUTICO. Emphyteusis. The real right by which a person is entitled to enjoy another's estate as if it were his or her own, and to dispose of its substance, as far as can be done without deteriorating it.

CERTIFICACIÓN. Certification. The formal assertion in writing of some fact.

CERTIFICADO. Certificate. A written assurance, or official representation, that some act has or has not been done, or has been complied with. A declaration in writing containing a statement signed by the party certifying.

CERTIFICADO DE ORIGEN. Certificate of origin. A written and official assurance that a product comes from a determined country or place.

CERTIFICADO DE DEFUNCIÓN. Death certificate. Certificate in which the death of a person is established.

CERTIFICADO DE NACIMIENTO. Birth certificate. Certificate issued by competent authority attesting to the date, place, parents, gender, name and other information on a person's birth.

CERTIFICADO DE PAZ Y SALVO. Tax cleared certificate. Certificate which proves a person has paid a certain tax for a particular period.

CERTIFICAR. To certify. To guarantee. To register, to attest.

CESACIÓN. Cessation. Suspension, final, discontinuation. To terminate one's function.

CESANTÍA. Unemployment. State of the person not working or not employed; also severance pay.

CESE. Cessation. (1) Discontinuation, order for the suspension of payment. (2) **Cese De Fuego.** Cease fire.

CESIBLE. Transferable, assignable. What can be transferred.

CESIÓN. Cession, assignment. The act of ceding, giving up property rights, or credits.

CESIÓN DE BIENES. Assignment of goods. General assignment in favor of creditors. The surrender of property that a debtor makes of all his or her property to his or her creditors, when the debtor finds himself or herself unable to pay his or her debts.

CESIONARIO. Assignee, transferee, cessionary, grantee. The person who receives property from other.

CESIONISTA. Assignor. Transferor, grantor; one who transfers property.

CIRCUITO. Circuit, track, course. Section of a territory specially defined. Jurisdiction in which a judge is empowered to act.

CIRCUNSCRIPCIÓN. Circumscription. Subdivision of an administrative, military, electoral or ecclesiastical territory.

CIRCUNSTANCIAS. Circumstances. The surrounding at the commission of an act.

CIRCUNSTANCIAS AGRAVANTES. Aggravating circumstances. Any circumstance that adds to the punishment, to the crime or fault committed.

CICUNSTANCIAS ATENUANTES. Extenuating circumstances. Any circumstance that lessens the crime or fault committed and consequently mitigates its punishment.

CIRCUNSTANCIAS EXIMENTES. Exculpatory circumstances; any circumstance that justified the action taken.

CIRCUNSTANCIAL. Circumstantial. Subordinate or indirect. Something not relevant. Accompanying events or conditions. Those facts that indicate the probability or improbability of something. Circumstances from which a fact can be inferred; that proves something indirectly.

CITA. Appointment, meeting, to arrange to meet someone. Date.

CITACIÓN. Citation, summons. (1) An order of a court of competent jurisdiction requiring a person therein named to appear on a given day and do something therein mentioned, or show cause excusing compliance. (2) Writing or oral reference to something already said or written.

CITAR. To make an appointment with. To quote. To summon. To call to witness, to sue or prosecute, to indict.

CIUDAD. City, town.

CIUDADANÍA. Citizenship. The status of being a citizen of a country and therefore entitled to the enjoyment of full civil rights established by the Constitution of that country.

CIUDADANO. Citizen. A person who is a member of a political community such as a country and entitled to rights and obligations established by it for their mutual interest and protection.

CÍVICO. Civic. Relating to citizenship or citizens.

CIVIL. Civil. (1) Refers to private relations, rights, obligations, remedies. (2) Private law as opposed to public law. (3) Not military. (4) The law containing statutes and regulations referring to private citizens and their property, and private, family relations. (5) Generally what is in the civil code and not in the criminal one. (6) The legal system evolved from the Roman empire, different from the common law system.

CIVILISTA. Person specialized in civil law. Lawyer versed in civil law.

CLASIFICACIÓN. Classification, sort, classing.

CLASIFICAR. To classify. To sort. To grade according to class.

CLÁUSULA. Clause. Any subdivision of a legal document, such as contract, deed, or statute.

CLÁUSULA CIF. CIF clause. Clause sometimes inserted in commercial sales contracts, whereby the established sale price includes the cost, the insurance and the freight.

CLÁUSULA COMPROMISORIA. Arbitration clause. A clause inserted in a contract providing for compulsory arbitration in case of dispute as to rights or liabilities under such contract.

CLÁUSULA DE CADUCIDAD. Caducity clause. See "Caducidad".

CLÁUSULA F.A.S. Free along side clause. A clause used in sales price quotations, indicating that the price includes all costs of transportation and delivery of goods alongside the ship.

CLÁUSULA F.O.B. Free on board clause. A clause in which the seller is committed to transport and deliver, at his or her risk and expense, the goods to a certain location, after which goods pass from seller to buyer.

CLÁUSULA PENAL. Penalty clause. (1) Any provision in a contract which calls for the exacting of a penalty instead of actual money damages. (2) Clause whereby a party agrees to pay to the other a fine of money if the first one does not do what was agreed or if it is not done on time.

CLÁUSULA REBUS SIC STANTIBUS. (Lat.) "Rebus sic stantibus" clause. A tacit condition in some contracts and generally in treaties by which it (the contract or treaty) will cease to be obligatory if the facts and conditions upon which it was founded have changed substantially.

CLAUSURA. Closing. (1) In religion, term used to describe the place (monastery or nunnery) where persons of the opposite sex are not permitted. (2) Term also used to describe the end of sessions of an assembly.

CLEMENCIA. Clemency; mercy. Whenever mercy is requested and/or granted.

CLEPTOMANÍA. Kleptomania. An irresistible impulse to steal objects regardless of their value for the sake of taking possession and not for economic need.

CLEPTÓMANO. Kleptomaniac. See "Cleptomanía".

CLIENTE. Client. A person who seeks the professional services of another. Customer.

61

COACCIÓN. Compulsion, duress. Force or violence against a person to oblige him or her to say something or execute an act.

COACCIONAR. To coerce. To force. See "Coacción".

COACREEDOR. Joint creditor. One of many to whom another owes.

COACTIVO. Coactive. Compulsory. Coercive. Compelling. Coercing.

COALICIÓN. Coalition. Confederation. Union. Association.

COARTADA. Alibi. A defense argued by the defendant of having been elsewhere when the alleged act was committed.

COASEGURADOR. Co-insurer. Special type of insurance agent, where the insurance is composed of several partial contracts, and each one covers a portion of the risk. The insurer of an insurer.

COAUTOR. Co-author. One who does something with another.

COBRADOR. Collector. Payee. One who asks for payment.

COBRANZA. Collection. To hand in for payment. Recovery. In process of collection.

COBRAR. To collect; recover; demand payment.

CODEMANDADO. Co-defendant. When another person is charged in the same indictment with others.

CODEUDOR. Co-debtor. Any person who, as or with the principal debtor, could be compelled to pay a claim.

CODIFICACIÓN. Codification. Tendency to compile in codes the legislation of different branches of the law.

CODIFICADOR. Classifier, codifier. The author of a code.

CODIFICAR. To codify, to classify. See "Codificación".

CÓDIGO. Code. A systematic collection, compendium or revision of laws, rules or regulations.

COERCIÓN. Coercion. (1) Compulsion or force; making a person act against his or her free will. (2) To force or restrain a person from doing or saying something by the use or threat of violence.

COERCITIVO. Coercive, restraining, restrictive. See "Coerción".

COGNACIÓN. Descendants related by blood through the maternal line. Kindred by maternal consanguinity.

COGNADO. Cognate. Blood relative by the mother.

COGNICIÓN. Cognition, knowledge. Process of cognition refers to the phase of the proceeding in which a decision is made, by a judge or jury, in favor or against the parties involved.

COHECHO. Bribe, bribery. The offering of a gift or consideration in money with the object of corrupting or unduly influencing the judgment or conduct of the recipient; generally, a public officer or governmental employee.

COHEREDERO. Co-heir. One of several to inherit by will or law.

COIMA. Bribe. Graft. Illegal payment made to someone, usually a public employee, to have him or her do or not do something.

COITO. Sexual contact with penetration.

COLABORACIÓN. Collaboration, contribution. Work done between two or more authors.

COLACIÓN. Comparison, collation, hodgepodge (inheritance), to mention. To produce as proof. Bestowal of clerical benefit, granting of a degree.

COLATERAL. Collateral. (1) Relative by consanguinity, not of direct descent. Not lineal, i.e., brothers, cousins, uncles. (2) Guaranty. Surety. That which secures payment of a debt.

COLECTA. Collection, receipts. Collection for charity. Gathering of people in church, money collected in church. General collection of money goods, food for charity.

COLECTIVIDAD. Collectivity, community. Group of people joined together by similar interests or goals, with a common plan of action.

COLECTIVO. Joint, collective, communal, common. Commonly owned by a group of people. Collection or gathering for a common purpose.

COLEGA. Colleague, counterpart, fellow member, associate.

COLEGIACIÓN. Association. To join or form an association of members from the same profession, such as lawyers, doctors, teachers.

COLEGIADO. Collegiate. Member of a professional association.

COLEGIO. College, professional association. High school.

COLIGACIÓN. Association. The act of joining the members of any profession.

COLINDANTE. Abutting owner or property. (1) One who owns property which adjoins other property. (2) Property contiguous to another.

COLISIÓN. Collision. Striking together of two objects, one of which may be stationary.

COLONO. Colonist, colonial, tenant farmer.

COLUSIÓN. Collusion. An agreement between two or more persons to defraud or cheat another person.

COMANDITA. Commandite (Fr.). Limited partnership where one group is responsible for all the acts of the company while another group provides funds for the company and is only responsible up to the amount of funds provided.

COMARCA. Region, area. Territory divided by common history, geography, and economics which encompasses several towns.

COMERCIANTE. Merchant. A person who deals in goods or otherwise by his or her occupation holds himself out as having knowledge or skill peculiar to the sale or purchase of the goods involved.

COMERCIANTE AL DETAL. Retailer. See "Comerciante Al Por Menor".

COMERCIANTE AL POR MAYOR. Wholesaler. A merchant who sells goods and buys in large quantities.

COMERCIANTE AL POR MENOR. Retailer. Person engaged in the sale and purchase of goods in small quantities.

COMERCIO. Commerce. Lucrative activity which consists of acting as middleman between producers and consumers. Trade. Buying and selling of goods.

COMETER. To commit, to entrust, to perpetrate, to charge, to commission.

COMETIDO. Duty, assignment, charge, task, moral obligation.

COMICIO. Election Board. Assembly or reunion of those duly appointed to elect persons to particular posts.

COMICIOS. Electoral meetings. Elections. Voting poll.

COMISAR. To forfeit. To confiscate. To seize.

COMISARÍA. Commissariat. Police station. Place and office where the commissary performs his or her functions. Headquarters of a commissioner.

COMISARIO. Deputy. Delegate. Commissioner. (1) A person who executes a task as the representative of his or her superior. (2) Rank in the police or guard service, sheriff, chief of police.

COMISIÓN. Commission. (1) The authority or instruction under which one person conducts business or negotiates for another. (2) Fee. Amount of money paid to the person acting on behalf of another. (3) Group of people meeting to do something, usually appointed by someone.

COMISIONADO. Commissioner. Person in charge of performing a duty entrusted by another.

COMISIONAR. To commission, to empower, to entrust, to appoint. To entrust one's duty to another person. To delegate.

COMISIONISTA. Agent. Person who works on commission, regularly and professionally. Representative.

COMITÉ. Committee, commission. Group of people charged to perform a task or duty, by a corporation or government. In politics, refers to the different structures political parties have within.

COMITENTE. Constituent, principal. One who entrusts another (agent) with a commission or charge, by order and in name of the principal. Commissioning.

COMODANTE. Lender. Person who gives a good on a loan. Free loan. The item in reference is borrowed free of charge. Bailor.

COMODATARIO. Borrower, person who receives an item as a loan without any charge. Bailee.

COMODATO. Commodatum. In civil law, when one person lends gratuitously to another some object not consumable to be restored to him or her in kind at a given period.

COMPAÑÍA. Company, corporation, society. See "Sociedad". (1) Generally refers to a contract whereby two or more persons agree to create a juridical person in order to conduct some business. (2) Legal entity created by statute after certain formalities are observed that is different from its incorporating members, and capable of having its own rights and obligations without any liability to its shareholders.

COMPARECENCIA. Appearance (in court). Coming to court either as plaintiff or defendant.

COMPARECER. To appear in court.

COMPARECIENTE. Appearing. One who appears either orally, in writing, in person, or by a representative before a judicial authority.

COMPENSACIÓN. Compensation. (1) Payment for loss, injury, or damages. (2) Payment of any sort for work or services performed. (3) One of the legal forms to terminate obligations. It occurs when two persons owing to each other agree to set off both obligations or at least to the extent of the lesser one.

COMPETENCIA. Competency. As applied to courts and public officers, it is the jurisdictional and legal authority to deal with the particular matter in question. Also the capacity of a public authority to hear a particular case or carry on a trial and judge it. The legal capacity of a court or judge to hold a trial in a particular jurisdiction.

COMPENTENCIA DESLEAL. Unfair competition. Any dishonest or fraudulent actions in trade or commerce, with the intent to deceive the customer in the marketplace for the benefit of the actor. It is a crime.

COMPETENTE. Competent. Capable. Able. The quality of having the required ability or qualification to do something.

CÓMPLICE. Abettor, accomplice. One who knowingly and voluntarily aids in the commission of a crime or protects a criminal or assists him or her to escape from justice.

COMPOSICIÓN. Settlement. Agreement or adjustment, payment or satisfaction.

COMPRA. Purchase, buy. To acquire personal (bona mobilia) or real (bona immobilia) property upon payment of the purchase price.

COMPRADOR. Buyer; purchaser. The person acquiring a thing by paying the purchase price to the seller.

COMPRAVENTA. Buying and selling. Sale. A contract by which one of the parties called the seller (vendor), in consideration of the payment or promise of payment of a certain sum of money, transfers to the other party, called the buyer, good title and possession of property.

COMPROBANTE. Voucher. Proof, invoice.

COMPROBAR. To check. To audit, verify, prove, or to establish something. To ascertain.

COMPROMETER. To compromise. To arbitrate. (1) Mutual agreement to have a dispute settled by persons different from the parties in conflict. (2) To have a commitment. To undertake.

COMPROMISO. Obligation; commitment; undertaking. Engagement, appointment, compromise.

COMPULSA. Attested copy of a document, deed, instrument, verified against the original.

COMPULSIÓN. Compulsion. Force or intimidation used on a person, by order of an authority, to compel him or her to do something.

COMPULSIVO. Compulsive. An order by competent authority that forces the person to act in a specific way, i.e., to undergo examination in court.

COMÚN. Common. (1) What does not belong privately to someone, but belongs to many, and everyone has the right to its use. (2) What is ordinary and accepted by everyone.

COMUNICADO. Official announcement. Public letter or statement.

COMUNICAR. To announce, to inform, to transmit. To pass on, to make known.

COMUNIDAD DE BIENES MATRIMONIALES, BIENES GANAN-CIALES. Community property. The property acquired during the marriage either by the husband or wife and which is considered to belong to both equally.

COMUNÍQUESE. Let it be known. Phrase used in certain written documents and also in orders from the authorities so that the contents of the document or order are published and known to the public.

COMUNISMO. Communism. Marxism. Political and ideological doctrine in which the state, being more important than individuals, controls all the means of production that should belong to the community. It proclaims a society without classes.

CONATO. Attempted crime. Whenever a crime is attempted but not actually committed.

CONCEDENTE. Grantor, licensor. The person who grants, consents, accepts.

CONCEDER. To grant, to allow, to concede. To give or grant a right or a thing. To allocate the execution of a work or public service through direct assignment or bid.

CONCEPCIÓN. Conception. Action and effect of conceiving. To become pregnant.

CONCERTAR. To arrange, to adjust, to agree. To arrange a business to agree upon, to coordinate. To come to. To conclude. To arrive at an agreement.

CONCESIÓN. Concession. A grant of specific privileges by a government to someone, for a specific purpose. Franchise.

CONCESIONARIO. Concessionaire. Holder of a concession, license.

CONCIENCIA. Equity. To judge in fairness. Conscience.

CONCILIACIÓN. Conciliation. The adjustment and settlement of a dispute in a friendly manner. Used in courts before trial with a view towards avoiding trial. Also used in labor disputes.

CONCLUSIÓN. Conclusion. The end, close or termination of something. Final plea or address to the jury.

CONCLUYENTE. Conclusive. Determining. Conclusive evidence, convincing argument.

CONCORDANCIA. Conformity. Agreement or harmony in form. Concordance.

CONCORDAR. To agree. To be in accord. To be in agreement, to reconcile.

CONCORDATO. Concordat. (1) In French law, a compromise effected by a bankrupt party with his or her creditors, by virtue of which he or she engages to pay within a certain time a certain proportion of his or her debts, and by which the creditors agree to discharge the whole of their claims in consideration of the same. (2) Treaty with the Vatican or between two countries regarding the Catholic Church or ecclesiastical matters.

CONCUBINA. Concubine. Woman who lives with a man as a wife but who is not married to him.

CONCUBINATO. Concubinage. The act of living together, man and woman, without being legally married.

CONCURRENTE. Concurrent. Having the same rank or authority. Acting or agreeing together.

CONCURRIR. To concur. To agree, also to meet or attend.

CONCURSADO. Bankrupt. A trader who is ruined financially; who cannot meet his or her monetary obligations.

CONCURSANTE. Bidder. One who takes part in a meeting. Participant. Contestant. A competitor in a contract.

CONCURSAR. (1) To declare bankruptcy. When a debtor is declared insolvent, whether permanently or temporarily, by his or her creditors. (2) To compete. To compete in a contest.

CONCURSO. Meeting; conference; assembly. Contest. (1) Bid made by those who want to acquire a concession to do something. (2) Pageant.

CONCURSO CIVIL DE ACREEDORES. Insolvency proceedings. Suit to enable creditors to enforce their claims against an insolvent debtor.

CONCUSIÓN. Graft. When a public officer fraudulently obtains public money because of position, rank, or superior influence, without rendering services, or to render a service he or she is already required to do. It is a crime.

CONDENA. Penalty. Sentence. Jail term. (1) Juridical decision in which a party to a lawsuit is compelled to satisfy the other's demand. (2) Judgment whereby a person is convicted and sentenced to jail or punished.

CONDENAR. To condemn, to sentence, to find guilty, to fine.

CONDENADO. Convicted, sentenced. Condemned, prisoner, criminal.

CONDENATORIO. Condemnatory, pronouncing.

CONDICIÓN. Condition. A future and uncertain event upon the happening of which the existence or the termination of an obligation depends.

CONDICIONAL. Conditional, requirement, subject to a condition.

CONDICIÓN RESOLUTORIA. Resolutory or dissolving condition. That condition which obliges the creditor of an obligation to restore what he or she has received in case the event provided for in the condition takes place.

CONDICIÓN SUSPENSIVA. Suspensive condition. A condition which prevents a contract from going into operation until the event has been fulfilled.

CONDOMINIO. Condominium. An estate in real property consisting of an individual unit interest in a multi-unit complex, with some private and common areas of ownership. Real estate rights to a single apartment in a building or townhouse which gives owners a separate right to their own units and a common right to the common areas of the building or complex. (1) Joint ownership. Right over real estate that several people have, which cannot be divided. When a person buys a floor or apartment, one has sole ownership. However, one shares in a condominium the ownership of the land, roof, stairway, elevator, and other common areas.

CONDONACIÓN. Condonation; to forgive or forget a debt, penalty, or fine.

CONDONAR. To condone, to forgive. The forgiveness of a debt, totally or partially. This is a unilateral act by the creditor to terminate an obligation without payment.

CONDUCENTE. Pertinent, relevant, conducive, leading.

CONDUCTA. Behavior, conduct, way a person behaves. Behavior or conduct of a person in relation to his or her social status, environment, local ordinance, and current general customs.

CONFABULACIÓN. Conspiracy, plotting. Action and effect of conspiring. To be in accord with two or more persons over a business in which they are not the only parties interested.

CONFABULARSE. To conspire, to plot, to scheme.

CONFERENCIA. Conference, interview, congress, assembly. Conversation between two or more persons to discuss a point of view or business. Meeting among state representatives to address international affairs.

CONFERIR. To confer, to consult. To award. To deal or study something among several, to be assigned an award, a job, faculty or rights.

CONFESAR. To confess, To admit. See "Confesion".

CONFESIÓN. Confession. To admit or acknowledge guilt of the crime for which one is charged.

CONFESIÓN JUDICIAL. Judicial confession. Confession made before court in the due course of legal proceedings.

CONFESIÓN EXTRAJUDICIAL. Extrajudicial confession. Confession made out of court.

CONFESO. A person who confesses or admits. Convict who admits and describes his or her crime. Defendant who admits to the other party something which might compromise or harm it.

CONFIABLE. Trustworthy, reliable, dependable.

CONFIAR. To trust, to rely, to depend. To entrust, to confide, to count on someone.

CONFIDENCIAL. Confidential; entrusted with confidence by another to keep certain affairs secret.

CONFINAMIENTO. Confinement. A penalty consisting in the imprisonment of a person.

CONFIRMACIÓN. Confirmation, acknowledgment. Corroboration of a testimony, affirmation. To acknowledge the truth.

CONFIRMADA. Confirmed. Something that has been corroborated. It refers to the judgment that after being appealed has not been declared void.

CONFIRMAR. To confirm. To ratify what was originally done without authority. To verify or approve something, leaving it without doubt.

CONFISCACIÓN. Confiscation. The seizure of private property by the government without compensation to the owner, often as a consequence of conviction for a crime, or because possession or use of the property was contrary to law.

CONFISCAR. To confiscate. Expropriate. Condemn. Generally to confiscate something after conviction of a crime and without indemnization.

CONFLICTO. Conflict. Clash.

CONFLICTO DE INTERESES. Conflict of interest. Term used to describe the ethical dilemma present when a public officer or fiduciary may be impaired in the performance of his or her duty due to matters of private interest or gain.

CONFLICTO DE LEYES. Conflict of laws. (1) Inconsistency or difference between the laws of different states or countries. (2) That part of the law of a state that determines what effect is to be given to the fact that the case may have a significant relationship to more than one state. It happens when two or more statutes can be applied to one situation but there would be an incompatibility in the application of either law. (3) In criminal law, the more favorable law is to be applied to the defendant. (4) In labor law, the more favorable law to the worker is to be chosen.

CONFORME. Consistent, correct, congruent, alike, agreeable.

CONFUSIÓN DE DERECHOS. Confusion of rights. A union of the qualities of creditor and debtor in the same person. The effect of such a union is, generally, to extinguish such a debt.

CONGRESO. Congress. A formal meeting of delegates or representatives that integrate the legislative power of a nation or a group.

CONGRUENCIA. Congruity. The suitability of the remedy and scope of the judgment rendered in relation to what was petitioned and litigated by the parties.

CONJETURA. Conjecture. A probable fact based on weak evidence. Circumstantial evidence.

CONMINACIÓN. Admonition, judgment, threat. Action and effect of a threat, warning or intimidation.

CONMINAR. To threaten with punishment by an authority or judge.

CONMOCIÓN. Commotion, shock, political upheaval, disturbance. Unrest. Concussion of the brain.

CONMUTACIÓN. Commutation. Consists of reducing the sentence of a prisoner or changing same for a lesser one. Usually to commute the death sentence to life imprisonment.

CONMUTACIÓN DE LA PENA. Commutation. In criminal law, changing a punishment to one which is less severe. This is within the authority of the President or governor but not of the judiciary.

CONMUTAR. To commute, to barter, to exchange.

CONOCER. To know, to take cognizance of, to observe, to consider, to recognize. To inform someone of something.

CONOCIMIENTO. Knowledge, cognizance, notice. (1) Document or signature required of the person who seeks to collect a bill of exchange, check or promissory note. (2) Acknowledgment a witness makes before a notary.

CONOCIMIENTO DE EMBARQUE. Bill of lading. Document evidencing receipt of goods for shipment, contract for their carriage, and title to those goods, issued by a person engaged in the business of transporting or forwarding goods.

CONSANGUÍNEO. Consanguineous. A person related by blood.

CONSANGUINIDAD. Consanguinity. Relationship between people who have a common ancestry. Related by blood.

CONSECUENCIA. Consequence. Effect or result derived from another. Caused.

CONSECUENCIAL. Consequential, as a result of, as a consequence of. To have or bring consequences.

CONSECUENTE. Consequential, consistent, consecutive. According to the effect.

CONSEJO. Council. An assembly of persons created to give advice on a given subject.

CONSEJO DE GABINETE. Council of ministers. An advisory body selected to aid the executive.

CONSENSO. Agreement. Consensus, general or majority approval.

CONSENSUAL. Consensual. Contract where the concurrence of wills is present.

CONSENTIMIENTO. Consent. To accede. To yield to.

CONSIDERANDO. Whereas. Every reason or conclusion of law upon which a judicial resolution is founded.

CONSIGNACIÓN. Consignment. (1) Judicial deposit of any quantity or any value, made by a debtor when the creditor cannot or does not want to receive them. (2) In commercial law, the delivery of goods in trust.

CONSIGNADOR. Consignor. The person who consigns. The one who sends merchandise consigned to another called consignee.

CONSIGNAR. To allocate, to assign, to consign. To put in storage. To transfer income from an estate as settlement of a debt. Contract whereby one gives merchandise to another for sale without receiving payment until the goods are sold. To send something through an intermediary to another.

CONSIGNATARIO. Consignee, trustee. Person in whose name the allocation or consignment is made. In transportation refers to the person in whose name the merchandise is shipped to and thus receives the merchandise sent on consignment for another person.

CONSOLIDACIÓN. Consolidation, merger, conversion of a debt. Action and effect of consolidation.

CONSOLIDAR. To consolidate, to merge. To fuse, to fund, to combine. To fund or fuse the usufruct with the real estate. To reinforce a regime or government.

CONSORCIO. Consortium, cartel, syndicate. Association of corporations or private persons who have their own funds, established to achieve common aims with a single administrative entity.

CONSPIRACIÓN. Conspiracy. When two or more persons join together for an unlawful purpose.

CONSPIRADOR. Conspirator, plotter. See "Conspiración".

CONSPIRAR. To conspire, to plot, to combine forces against the authorities. To agree to act against someone or something.

CONSTANCIA. Record, evidence, constancy, perseverance, to put on record. Certainty.

CONSTAR. To be evident, to be recorded, to be clear, to be registered.

CONSTITUCIÓN. Constitution. The organic and fundamental law of a nation or state, stating the basic principles to which its internal life is to be conformed. Magna Carta.

CONSTITUCIONAL. Constitutional. Consistent with the constitution. To abide by the constitution not against the constitution.

CONSTITUCIONALIDAD. Constitutionality. Nature of constitutional. Principles that mediate between laws, decrees, ordinances or resolutions prescribed by administrative agencies in relation to the norms contained in the constitution.

CONSTITUIR. To organize; to incorporate. To become.

CONSTITUTIVO. Constitutive, essential, component, constituent.

CONSTITUYENTE. (1) Constituent. One who gives authority to another to act for him or her. (2) A voting member of a particular electoral district, who is represented by a legislator in public affairs.

CONSUETUDINARIO. Customary. According to custom or usage. What has been generally done. It can be considered to be legally binding if not prohibited by law. Also refers to the doctrines of common law used in many countries.

CÓNSUL. Consul. A country's foreign representative, below the rank of ambassador, who usually handles the country's and its citizens' business and private matters, but not political matters.

CONSULADO. Consulate. The residence and/or offices of a consul.

CONSULTA. Consultation. Opinion given by a lawyer about a legal question. To request an opinion.

CONSULTAR. To consult, to consider, to review, to discuss. To deliberate about.

CONSULTOR. Consultant. A person (e.g., lawyer) who gives advice.

CONSUMACIÓN. Consummation; act of completing what was intended. Completion.

CONSUMIBLE. Consumable. What can be consumed.

CONTABILIDAD. Accounting. System to set accounts and to register income and expenses.

CONTABLE. Accountant. See "Contador".

CONTADOR. Accountant. Person skilled in keeping books or accounts.

CONTADOR PÚBLICO AUTORIZADO. Certified public accountant. Said of the accountant that has passed the special requirements to be licensed as a public accountant.

CONTENCIOSO. Contentious, contested, in litigation, litigious. Concerning legal actions. What is subject to controversy.

CONTENCIOSO–ADMINISTRATIVO. Administrative law matters. The jurisdictional act which resolves conflicts that arise from the public administration.

CONTENDOR. Opponent, competitor, rival, antagonist, disputant, litigant.

CONTESTACIÓN. Answer, reply, dispute, argument, defendant's plea. Allegation.

CONTESTACIÓN A LA DEMANDA. Plea. The answer which the defendant in an action at law makes to the plaintiff's complaint.

CONTESTAR. To answer, reply.

CONTINGENCIA. Contingency; a fortuitous event. An event which may occur without design or expectations. A casualty.

CONTRABANDO. Smuggling. The offense of secretly importing or exporting prohibited or taxable articles.

CONTRADEMANDA. Counterclaim, cross demand. A claim presented by a defendant in opposition to or deduction from the claim of the plaintiff.

CONTRAINTERROGAR. Cross-examine. The questioning of an opposing witness during a trial or hearing.

CONTRALOR GENERAL. Comptroller general. Public officer of a state charged with the duty of examining and auditing national accounts and reporting on financial matters from time to time.

CONTRAPARTE. Counterpart. The opposing part to a contract or lawsuit.

CONTRAPRESTACIÓN. Consideration. Something of value (e.g., money) which one ordinarily accepts voluntarily in exchange for something else.

CONTRAPROPOSICIÓN. Counter-offer. a rejection of an offer and a new offer made.

CONTRAPRUEBA. Rebutting evidence, counterproof. Evidence to disprove previous evidence.

CONTRARIAR. To contradict, to oppose, to annoy, to interfere. To obstruct.

CONTRARIO. Adversary, opponent of the other party to a suit. One who is in opposition to the ideas or interest of another.

CONTRARRECLAMACIÓN. Counter-claim. See "Contra-demanda".

CONTRASENTIDO. Opposite meaning, mistranslation, misinterpretation, nonsense. Contradiction.

CONTRATANTE. Contracting party. Part of a contract. The contracting parties, contractor.

CONTRATAR. To make a contract, to trade, to hire, to sign a contract.

CONTRATO. Contract. An agreement between two or more persons which creates an obligation to give, to do or not to do a particular thing.

CONTRATO A TÍTULO GRATUITO. Gratuitous contract. A contract which benefits one of the parties to it, without any profit or advantage or consideration to the other party.

CONTRATO DE TÍTULO ONEROSO. Onerous contract. Contract where the obligations attached to it come from the advantage to be derived from it. The contract in which the benefits to each part originate in the obligation of the other.

CONTRATO ALEATORIO. Aleatory contract. A mutual agreement where performance and the contract's effects depend on an uncertain event.

CONTRATO CONMUTATIVO. Commutative contract. (1) Contract where each of the contracting parties gives and receives consideration which is considered equivalent. (2) Contract where the parties know the extent of their obligations.

CONTRATO DE ADHESIÓN. Adhesion contract. Standard contract form offered by one party to another on an essentially "take it or leave it" basis without affording opportunity to bargain.

CONTRATO DE ARRENDAMIENTO. Lease contract. See "Arrendamiento".

CONTRATO DE FLETAMENTO. Charter party contract. See "Fletamento".

CONTRATO INNOMINADO o ATÍPICO. Innominate contract. Special contract or one not specifically provided for by law.

CONTRATISTA. Contractor. The entrepreneur who with his or her own resources performs work entrusted by third parties.

CONTRAVENCIÓN. Infraction, misdemeanor. A violation of a municipal statute for which the only sentence authorized is a fine or imprisonment for a short period of time.

CONTRAVENIR. To violate, to infringe, to transgress. To contravene.

CONTRAYENTE. Contracting party. Person who enters into a contract. Also, each of the persons marrying each other.

CONTRIBUCIONES. Assessments. (1) Deciding on the amount to be paid by each of several persons of a common fund. (2) A payment beyond what is normally required of members of a group. (3) Contribution, tax, quota. Obligatory contribution that is impersonal and established by law which is required to be paid periodically, in order to distribute among the taxpayers the burden of public expenses.

CONTRIBUYENTE. Taxpaying. Contributor, taxpayer. One who is required to pay contributions, taxes.

CONTROVERSIA. Controversy. A dispute. A litigated question.

CONTUBERNIO. Cohabit. Whenever a man and a woman live together as husband and wife without being married. Sexual intercourse.

CONTUMACIA. Contumacy. Nonappearance, default, contempt of court. The refusal or intentional omission of a person who has been duly cited before a court to appear and defend the charges against him or her.

79

CONTUMAZ. Contumacious; guilty of contempt of court.

CONVALECER. To recover legal efficacy. To convalesce. To recover.

CONVALIDACIÓN. To validate, confirm. To make legally valid what was imperfect or uncertain.

CONVALIDAR. To ratify, to validate, to confirm. To make valid and with legal efficacy an action previously voidable.

CONVENCIÓN. (1) Convention, assembly. (2) Contract, agreement. Generally between countries or international organizations.

CONVENCIÓN COLECTIVA DE TRABAJO. Collective bargaining agreement. An agreement between an employer and a labor union which regulates the terms and conditions of employment.

CONVENCIÓN CONSTITUYENTE. Constitutional convention. See "Constituyente".

CONVENIO. Agreement. Accord. See "Contrato".

CONVENCIONAL. Conventional, customary, contractual, by agreement; member of an assembly, delegate.

CONVENIR. To convene, to agree, to assemble, to concur, to come to an agreement. To be convenient for. To be of interest to someone.

CONVICCIÓN. Conviction. When the person brought to trial is found guilty of the crime he or she is accused of. Certainty.

CONVICTO. Convict. (1) A person in prison. (2) To find a person guilty of a criminal charge.

CONVIVENCIA. Convivence. To voluntarily fail to see or to tolerate the transgressions of subordinates. To live with others.

CONVOCACIÓN. Meeting, convocation, summoning, convening, convoking.

CONVOCAR. To summon, to convene, to call a person.

CONVOCATORIA. Notice of meeting. (1) Decree that calls for elections on certain elected posts mentioned therein. (2) Notice of the day, month, place and purpose of a meeting; summons.

CONYUGAL. Conjugal. Married.

CÓNYUGE. Spouse. Husband or wife.

COOPERATIVA. Cooperative. A corporation or association organized for the purpose of rendering economic services, without gain to itself, to shareholders or members who own and control it.

COPIA. Copy; faithful reproduction of an original.

COPIADOR. Copying, letter book, copybook.

COPROPIEDAD. Joint ownership, joint estate. Property held in common.

COPROPIETARIO. Co-owner, joint owner, co-proprietor.

CÓPULA. Carnal knowledge. Sexual intercourse between a man and a woman. Coitus, copulation.

CORPORACIÓN. Corporation, company. An organization that is formed under state or federal law and exists, for legal purposes, as a separate being or an artificial person.

CORPORAL. Corporeal. Corporal. Material.

CORRECCIONAL. Correctional, corrective. Penitentiary established for the serving of prison time on medium term sentences.

CORREDOR. Broker. A person who is employed by different persons to buy, sell, make deals, or enter into contracts.

CORREGIDOR. Magistrate. In Spanish law, a magistrate has jurisdiction over various misdemeanors and of certain civil matters.

CORRESPONDENCIA. Mail, correspondence. Letters and other postal documents.

CORRETAJE. Brokerage. Go-between who puts buyers and sellers together in order to have a deal or transaction concluded.

CORROBORAR. To corroborate, to confirm, to support, to back up.

CORROMPER. To corrupt, to seduce, to bribe, to pervert, to turn bad.

CORRUPCIÓN. Corruption. Bribery, seduction. Corruption of minors. Perversion.

CORTE. Court. An organ of the government belonging to the judicial branch whose function is the application of the laws to controversies brought before it and the public administration of justice.

CORTE DE APELACIÓN. Court of appeals. Superior court which reviews the decisions made by the lower courts.

CORTE DE CASACIÓN. Court of cassation. An appellate court. See "Casación" and "Recurso de Casación".

CORTE SUPREMA DE JUSTICIA. Supreme Court. Court of last resort.

CORTESÍA. Courtesy. Grace period. Extension of time for payment. Formal ending of a letter.

COSA. Thing. Every material object that may have a value. Affair. Something.

COSA JUZGADA. (Lat.) Res judicata: Rule that a final judgment rendered by a court of competent jurisdiction on the merits is conclusive as to the rights of the parties and their privies, and, as to them, constitutes an absolute bar to a subsequent action involving the same claim, demand or cause of action.

COSTAS. Court costs. A pecuniary allowance, made to the successful party (and recoverable from the losing party), for his or her expenses in prosecuting or defending an action or a distinct proceeding within an action.

COSTEAR. To finance, to pay for, to defray the expenses of, to pay for itself.

COSTO. Cost, expense. The price in money of a thing or service.

COSTUMBRE. Custom. A usage resulting from a long series of actions, constantly repeated, which have, by such repetition and by uninterrupted acquiescence, acquired the force of a law with respect to the place or subject-matter to which it relates.

COTEJO. Comparison. Action of comparing. To collate. (1) To confront or compare something with another thing or things. (2) This expression is commonly used to compare the handwriting of a person, when his or her signature or handwriting is neither confirmed nor denied.

CREDENCIALES. Credentials. In international public law refers to the document which evidences and proves to the government of a state that the person bearing the documents is the authorized diplomatic representative of another state. The official document which serves for an employee to take possession of a post without prejudice to his or her later obtaining the corresponding title.

CREDIBILIDAD. Credibility. What is credible.

CRÉDITO QUIROGRAFARIO. Unsecured credit. A loan that is not guaranteed. Whenever there is no collateral mortgaged or pledged on a debt to assure payment.

CRIMEN. Crime. An act in violation of a penal law.

CRIMINAL. Criminal. Person charged with committing a crime.

CRIMINALIDAD. Criminality. Quality or circumstance which makes an action criminal. Number of crimes committed in a determined territory and time.

CRIMINOLOGÍA. Criminology. Complementary science of criminal law which studies criminality and criminal behavior in order to obtain a better understanding of criminal activities and thus formulate adequate criminal policies and penalties.

CRUELDAD. Cruelty. What is cruel.

CUANTÍA. Quantity. Sum of money claimed or asked for in a suit.

CUASICONTRATO. Quasi contract. An obligation created by law or equity in the absence of an agreement.

CUASIDELITO. Quasi crime. Refers to the damage, injury, loss, or prejudice caused to another without intention or malice due to a criminal cause. Unconscious and illegal will in carrying out an act.

CUATRERO. Cattle thief or horse thief.

CUENTA. Account; bill; statement.

CUENTA CONJUNTA o MANCOMUNADA. Joint account. A bank account in two or more names, e.g., with equal rights and obligations to all owners.

CUENTA CORRIENTE. Current account. Checking account. A contract with a bank by which a person deposits a sum of money and can make payments based on that sum of money, through checks.

CUERPO. Body. (1) Organic substance which composes the human body. (2) Any real estate or personal property. (3) Dead body. (4) Group of public officials or civil servants of a determined branch of service.

CUERPO DEL DELITO. (Lat.) Corpus delicti. Body of a crime. The material substance upon which a crime has been committed.

CUESTIÓN. Question. Matter, affair, issue, subject. Question made in order to find out the truth of a controversial thing. Exposition of reasons or arguments over a thing.

CUESTIONAR. To question, to debate, to issue, to argue.

CUESTIONARIO. Questionnaire, survey. Group of questions to be answered.

CUIDADO. Care, caution, charge, attention, worry.

CULPA. Guilt. That quality which imparts criminality to a motive or act, and renders the person amenable to punishment by law.

CULPABLE. Culpable. Guilty; to blame a person responsible for a crime or fault.

CULPA GRAVE o LATA. Gross negligence. The absence of even the slightest diligence, by action or omission; to act recklessly.

CULPA LEVE. Ordinary negligence. The omission of that care which a person of common prudence would usually undertake.

CULPABILIDAD. Guilt, culpability. Possibility of charging a person with a crime. To have committed a fault or crime.

CULPOSO. Culpable; guilty. Said of the person responsible for doing something without the intention.

CUMPLIMIENTO. Performance, fulfillment, completion, execution. To reach a determined age counted by computation of a time period. To reach the expiration date or the date of performance.

CUMPLIMIENTO VOLUNTARIO. Voluntary compliance.

CUMPLIR. To perform, to fulfill, to complete, to execute, to do, to carry out, to honor.

CUMULATIVO. Cumulative; forming an aggregate.

CUÑADO. Brother-in-law. The brother of a spouse.

CUÑADA. Sister-in-law. The sister of a spouse.

CUOTA. Quota; a proportional part, a share.

CURADOR. Guardian. (1) A person lawfully vested with the power, and charged with the duty, of taking care of a person and managing the property and rights of that person, who, for defect of age, understanding, or self-control, is considered incapable of administering his or her own affairs. (2) Curator, administrator, tutor. Person named to take care of another and administer the goods, assets, property of another person who, due to age or instability or sickness, is incapable of handling his or her affairs.

CURATELA. Guardianship; curatorship. See "Curador".

CURSO. Course, direction of things. School year. Academic year. Treatise on a branch of law. The course of things, history.

CUSTODIA. Custody, safekeeping, care, deposit. Condition of a person who is under police surveillance.

CUSTODIAR. To have custody of, to watch over, to take care of.

CUSTODIO. Custodian, guardian. The one in charge of the custody.

CH

CHALANERÍA. To handle business with knowledge. To take care of matters with dexterity and craftiness.

CHALECO SALVAVIDAS. Life vest.

CHAMBÓN. Unhandy. The person who does something without skill.

CHANCHULLO. Unlawful act to achieve something, usually to make profit.

CHANTAJE. Blackmail. Extortion. Crime committed by unlawfully demanding something from a person who is threatened with disclosures of a secret that could be harmful.

CHANTAJEAR. To blackmail. See "Chantaje".

CHANTAJISTA. Blackmailer. The person who commits the crime of blackmail.

CHARADA. Charade. Enigma.

CHAUVINISMO. Chauvinism. Theory that preaches the superiority of the man and the inferiority of the woman.

CHAUVINISTA. Chauvinist. The person who acts in a chauvinistic way.

CHEQUE. Check. A draft drawn upon a bank and payable on demand signed by the drawer, containing an unconditional promise to pay a certain sum in money to the order of the payee.

CHEQUE CERTIFICADO. Certified check. A check drawn by a depositor and that the bank has marked as accepted or certified. This check becomes an obligation of the bank. The bank assures that sufficient funds have been set aside and that it is holding that money to pay the certified check when presented to the bank.

CHEQUE DE GERENCIA. Cashiers check. A check drawn by a bank upon itself, signed by an authorized official of the bank. This check can be cashed by the payee immediately after presentation to the bank. The bank has the obligation to pay it upon demand.

CHEQUE DE VIAJERO. Travelers check. A monetary instrument purchased from a bank, money exchange company, or the like, in various denominations which can be used as cash upon the counter-signature by purchaser.

CHEQUE EN BLANCO. Blank check. A check signed by the drawer but where the amount, date, and/or payee has been left blank.

CHEQUE PERSONAL. Personal check. One drawn on an individual's own account.

CHEQUE POST-FECHADO. Post-dated check. A check dated after the date on which it was actually drawn. It is drawn one day with the intention that it be payable on the stated date. Its negotiability is not affected by being post-dated. Nevertheless, some jurisdictions consider it payable on demand regardless of the date specified.

CHICANERÍA. Trickery. Sharp practice. The practice of delaying legal proceedings.

CHICANERO. Shyster lawyer. The lawyer who uses artifices to delay legal proceedings.

CHIFLADO. Crazy. Not sound of mind.

CHISME. Gossip. A tale or story told with malice with intent to create discord.

CHOCAR. To clash. To collide.

CHOQUE. Collision, conflict. Violent clash between two things. Generally refers to a car accident.

CHOQUE NERVIOSO. Nervous breakdown.

CHOZNO(NA). The son or daughter of the great-great-grandchild.

CHUSMA. Rabble. People with no education, civility or manners.

D

DACIÓN EN PAGO. Payment; payment in kind. A giving by the debtor and receiving by the creditor of something other than money in payment of a debt.

DACTILAR. Digital. Pertaining to the fingers.

DACTILOSCOPÍA. Dactyloscopy. Auxiliary science to criminology which studies the identity of persons by their fingerprints.

DÁDIVA. Gift, donation, grant, bribe. (1) Something given voluntarily and without asking for any consideration. (2) Any money or good given by a person to induce an action of a person in public office.

DADOR. (1) Drawer, issuer. (2) **De Préstamo.** Lender. (3) Giver.

DAMA. Lady. Any adult female person. Could also mean a concubine or mistress.

DAMNIFICADO. Injured. Any victim of an unlawful civil or criminal act or deed, of a public disaster or natural catastrophe.

DAMNIFICAR. To injure, damage. To do harm or hurt someone's person, rights, reputation or property.

DAÑADO. Spoiled, aggrieved, damaged. Something that becomes useless.

DAÑAR. To damage. See "Daño".

DAÑINO. Harmful. Capable of producing damage, injury or destruction.

DAÑO. Damage. Loss, injury, or deterioration, caused to another's person or property by the negligence, design or accident of one person.

DAÑO EMERGENTE. Consequential damages. Injury derived, not directly, from the act of the party but from the results of such act.

DAÑO IRREPARABLE. Undue hardship.

DAÑOS Y PERJUICIOS. Said of damages and their consequences such as loss of income or profit.

DAR. To give. To confer, to deliver.

DAR FE. To attest. To give faith to the veracity of a fact or act.

DATA. Date. Data. Items of an account.

DATO. Fact. A piece of information. (Pl.) **Data.** Details, items of an account.

DEBATE. Debate. Discussion among two or more persons.

DEBE. Debit. Account of the sums owed by one person to another.

DEBENTURE. Debenture stock. A promissory note or bond backed by the general credit of a corporation and usually not secured by a mortgage or lien on any specific property.

DEBER. Duty. Legal or moral obligation.

DÉBIL. Weak, impaired, or ailing. Lack of strength or energy.

DEBILIDAD MENTAL. Feeble mind. Intellectual deficiencies which denote different degrees of mental illness from the psychological point of view and which negate the feebleminded person's legal responsibility or capacity.

DÉBITO CONYUGAL. The mutual obligation of the spouses to live together as husband and wife for the reproduction of humankind.

DÉCADA. Decade. Passing of ten days or ten years.

DECÁLOGO. Decalogue. The Ten Commandments.

DECALVAR. To shave. Kind of punishment consisting in the shaving of a person's hair.

DECANO. Dean. Administrative or academic head of school, college or university.

DECAPITAR. To decapitate. The act of beheading.

DECAPITACIÓN. Decapitation. The action of killing a person by slashing off the head.

DECENCIA. Decency. Value influencing judicial decisions. Dignity of acts and words pursuant to the condition or quality of the persons.

DECENTE. Decent. An honest, respectable person.

DECESO. Death, natural or civil.

DECIDIR. To decide. To make up a definitive judgment or discernment.

DECIR. To say. To express one's mind with words.

DECISIÓN. Decision; verdict; judgment. Any formal deciding of a dispute, such as a judge's resolution of a lawsuit.

DECISORIO. Decisive. That which decides, defines or determines a subject matter.

DECLARACIÓN. Declaration; statement; report. An unsworn statement made out of court.

DECLARACIÓN CONJUNTA. (1) Joint return. (2) Joint declaration, written or verbal statement by two or more persons. Usually refers to the joint tax return made by spouses.

DECLARACIÓN DE AUSENCIA. Declaration made by a judge under which a person, who has been lost for a considerable period of time, is considered absent and therefore his or her goods are ordered to be administered by a guardian.

DECLARACIÓN DE BIENES. Declaration of wealth. A statement reporting all the assets and valuables of a person.

DECLARACIÓN DE IMPUESTOS. Tax return. Forms required by a taxing authority to be completed by every taxpayer, disclosing all the necessary information to compute the taxes due as well as the computation itself.

DECLARACIÓN DE INCONSTITUCIONALIDAD. Declaration of unconstitutionality. Declaration by which the conflict of a statute with some provisions of a constitution is stated. When a statute is found to be unconstitutional it is considered void, therefore all rights and duties or obligations that derive from it are also void.

DECLARACIÓN DE QUIEBRA. Declaration of bankruptcy. See "Quiebra". Declaration made by a merchant, a judge or a creditor of a person's state of bankruptcy.

DECLARACIÓN DE REBELDÍA. Declaration of contempt of court, contumacy. See "Rebeldía".

DECLARACIÓN EXTRAJUDICIAL. Extrajudicial statement. Out of court statement. Any declaration, written or oral, made out of court.

DECLARACIÓN INDAGATORIA. Unsworn statement made by someone accused of committing a crime before a court officer or a judge.

DECLARACIÓN JUDICIAL. Court order. A decree of the court pronounced on hearing and understanding all the points at issue. It is a declaration of the court announcing the legal consequences of the facts it has found. Statement or declaration made before a court officer or a judge.

DECLARACIÓN JURADA. Sworn declaration; affidavit. A written or printed declaration or statement of facts, made voluntarily, and confirmed by an oath or affirmation of the party making it, taken before a person having the authority to administer such oath or affirmation.

DECLARANTE. Deponent. One who testifies regarding certain facts while under oath.

DECLARAR. To declare. To make a statement, to testify, to pronounce clearly some opinion or resolution.

DECLARATIVO. Declaratory. To decide what was uncertain or doubtful.

DECLINAR. To decline. To refuse an appointment or jurisdiction.

91

DECORO. Propriety. Honor, honesty and prudence in a person's behavior.

DECOMISAR. To confiscate, seize.

DECOMISO. Forfeit, seizure. The act of taking possession of private property, without compensation to the owner, often as a consequence of the owner's being convicted of a crime, or because the owner's original possession or use of the property was contrary to law.

DECRÉPITO. Decrepit. Someone who is disabled and worn down due to old age or other causes, rendering the individual comparatively helpless in contrast with someone healthy and strong.

DECRETAR. To decree, decide, resolve.

DECRETAR UN PARO. To call a strike.

DECRETAR UNA LEY. To enact a law. Judgment. Order.

DECRETO. Decree.

DECRETO DE GABINETE. Cabinet decree. A decree pronounced by the executive council comprised by all the ministers of the executive branch.

DECRETO LEY. Decree law. An executive decree having the force of law pronounced by the executive power holding all the powers of the state or by delegation of these powers by Congress.

DE CUJUS. (Lat.) From whom. Term used to designate the person by, through, from or under whom another claims. Usually refers to a deceased person.

DE DERECHO. By law, legitimate, lawful. In accordance to law. See "De Jure".

DEDUCIBLE. Deductible. Any item which may be subtracted from income for tax purposes.

DEDUCIR. To deduct. To subtract, to take a part away.

DEDUCCIÓN. Deduction. The part which is taken away. The income subtracted from gross income resulting in net income for tax purposes. In civil law the right of an heir to take a portion from the total succession before partition takes place.

DE FACTO. (Lat.) In fact, actually. (1) Act or situation that must be accepted for all practical purposes but that is illegitimate. (2) Said of a government that takes power illegitimately. (3) Said of a new government of a nation that seized power by force to replace the legitimate authorities.

DEFECTO. Defect, flaw, fault. The absence of some legal requirement that makes a thing legally insufficient or non-binding.

DEFECTOS DE FORMA. Defects of form. (1) Imperfection in the style, manner, or non-essential parts of a legal document. (2) Lack or insufficiency of all the necessary formal elements required for the validity of any judicial act.

DEFECTO LEGAL. Legal defect. The omission of something legally required.

DEFECTUOSO. Defective, faulty. That which needs to be corrected.

DEFENDER. To defend. To protect. To represent a defendant in administrative, civil or criminal proceedings.

DEFENSA. Defense. (1) That which is put forward to diminish plaintiff's cause of action or defeat recovery altogether. (2) A response to the claims of the plaintiff, setting forth reasons why the claims should not be granted.

DEFENSA DE OFICIO. Defense at the court's initiative. A lawyer appointed by the government to defend indigents and any accused who refuses to defend himself or herself. Defense provided by the court.

DEFENSOR. Counsel for the defense. (1) Attorney who gives legal advice and assistance to a person sued or accused of a crime. (2) Defense attorney. Lawyer who files appearance on behalf of the defendant and represents him or her in a civil or criminal case.

DEFERIR. To yield. To relinquish or surrender. In civil procedure law it is to submit to the other party's declaration under oath.

DEFERIDO. In civil prodecural law, when a party is not able to independently prove his or her case and in order to prevail must rely on the adversary's sworn testimony.

DEFICIENTE. Handicapped. Deficient. Lacking in something necessary.

DÉFICIT. Deficit, shortage. A deficiency of revenues compared with expenditures.

DEFINICIÓN. Definition. A brief description or explanation of the meaning of a word or term.

DEFINIR. To define. The action of deciding or determining something. To explain the meaning of words. In relation to space, to set or determine boundaries with precision.

DEFINITIVO. Definite. Something final, determined, bound.

DEFRAUDACIÓN. Defraud. A mispresentation of an existing material fact, deliberately.

DEFRAUDACIÓN FISCAL. Tax evasion. Knowingly avoiding the payment of taxes.

DEFRAUDAR. To defraud; to cheat.

DEFRAUDADOR. Defrauder. A person who misrepresents an existing material fact, knowing it to be false for the purpose of deceiving.

DEFUNCIÓN. Death, demise. Permanent and irreversible cessation of all vital functions and signs.

DEGENERACIÓN. Degeneration. A process involving deterioration of a substance which may arise from decay or corrosion. A decline from a higher physical or moral condition.

DEGENERADO. Degenerate. A person who has fallen from his or her former higher moral or physical values.

DEGRADAR. To degrade. To deprive one of honor, titles, and privileges due to dishonorable conduct.

DEJAR. To leave. To bequeath. The action of the testator in favor of the heirs.

DE JURE. (Lat.) By law. Rightful, legitimate. Said of the way the persons and intitutions of a nation abide by the law and the constitution.

DELATAR. To accuse, denounce. To inform against someone.

DELATOR. Accuser, informer.

DELEGACIÓN. (1) Delegation, committee. An entire group of delegates or representatives. (2) Delegation of power. The giving of authority by one person to another.

DELEGADO. Delegate, deputy, representative. A person chosen to represent another person or group of persons.

DELEGAR. To delegate. To commission or entrust a person with the power to act in the name or on behalf of the one who deputized him or her.

DELIBERACIÓN. Deliberation. To consider the reasons for and against a contemplated act or course of conduct.

DELIBERAR. To deliberate, ponder. To carefully consider, discuss, and work towards forming an opinion or making a decision.

DELICTIVO. Criminal. That which in any manner violates or infringes the criminal law.

DELINCUENCIA. Delinquency. Human behavior punished by criminal law because of its injurious consequences to the peace or security of the community.

DELINCUENTE. Delinquent. One who has committed a crime or offense.

DELINCUENTE HABITUAL. Habitual offender. Those offenders that either by organic or physical problems or other factors violate or break the law repeatedly.

DELINQUIR. To commit a crime.

DELITO. Crime, criminal offense. A positive or negative act in violation of criminal law.

DELITO CIVIL. Tort. A private or civil wrong, other than breach of contract.

DELITO CONSUMADO. Said of a crime that has been committed fully. Completed crime.

DELITO CONTINUADO. Continuing offense. A single crime, such as a conspiracy, that can contain many individual acts over time.

DELITO CULPOSO. Crime committed without the intention to produce the effect caused. It is committed by negligence.

DELITO DOLOSO. Deceitful crime. Crime for which deceitfulness is required.

DELITO FRUSTRADO. Frustrated crime. When a person undertakes all necessary acts to commit a crime but is frustrated in the commission of the crime.

DEMAGOGO. Demagogue. A person who uses public emotions and prejudices for personal or political power.

DEMANDA. Lawsuit. Petition. A formal written application to a court requesting judicial action on a certain matter.

DEMANDADO. Defendant. The party against which relief or recovery is sought in a legal action or suit.

DEMANDANTE. Plaintiff. A person who brings an action to a court seeking relief for an injury to his or her rights.

DEMANDAR. To demand, to claim; to file a lawsuit; to sue.

DEMASÍA. Excess. An extreme or excessive amount that goes beyond that which is usual, proper or necessary.

DEMENCIA. Insanity. Disorder of the mind or intellect to the degree that it negates the individual's legal responsibility or capacity.

DEMENTE. Demented, insane. A person not in control of all his or her mental faculties.

DEMOCRACIA. Democracy. (1) The form of government in which the sovereign powers reside in and are exercised by the people through a system of representation. (2) The form of government in which the whole of the people of a nation intervene or have their opinion voiced with regard to the persons who govern said nation.

DEMORA. Delay. Retardation.

DENEGACIÓN. Denial, refusal. Decline to accept a demand or request.

DENUNCIA. Denunciation. In criminal law, the act by which an individual informs a public officer, whose duty is to prosecute offenders, that a crime has been committed.

DENUNCIAR. To denounce; to report, accuse, arraign.

DENUNCIO. Denouncement. A formal accusation.

DE OFICIO. (Lat.) By virtue of an office. Those acts performed by judges by their own initiative and without request of the parties to a lawsuit.

DEPENDENCIA. Dependency. To be under or subordinated to an authority. Generally, it is the acknowledgment of a greater power and subjection to it.

DEPENDIENTE. Dependent. One deriving support from another in whole or in part. (1) For tax purposes any individual supported by the taxpayer and bearing a specific relationship with the latter. (2) Person who is subordinated to another. (3) One who is supported by another.

97

DEPONENTE. Deponent. Person who gives testimony or makes statements under oath.

DEPONER. To depose, attest. To give sworn testimony out of court.

DEPORTACIÓN. Deportation. (1) A punishment by which a condemned person is sent away to a foreign country. (2) The sending back of an alien to his or her native country.

DEPOSICIÓN. Deposition. The testimony of a witness that is reduced to writing and duly authenticated.

DEPOSITANTE. Depositor. One who commits money or anything else to the care of a bank or another.

DEPOSITARIO. Depositary. The person or institution taking responsibility for the money or goods placed on deposit.

DEPÓSITO. (1) Deposit. An act by which a person receives the property of another, binding himself or herself to preserve and return it. (2) Warehouse. Structure used for the reception and storage of goods and merchandise.

DEPÓSITO ADUANERO. Customs deposit. Amount put down as a guarantee or pledge for the payment of custom duties. Bonded warehouse.

DEPÓSITO DE CADÁVERES. Morgue. A place where the bodies of dead people are kept until identified or buried.

DEPÓSITO IRREGULAR. Irregular deposit. A deposit where the receiver does not have to give back the same item deposited, but something equivalent in quantity and quality.

DEPÓSITO JUDICIAL. Judicial deposit. A deposit made by order of a court in the course of some proceeding.

DEPRECIACIÓN. Depreciation. A decline in value of property due to age or use.

DEPRECIAR. To depreciate. To lower the value of something.

DEPURACIÓN. Depuration. The act of purifying.

DEPURAR. To depurate. To free from impurities.

DERECHO. (1) Law. Prescribed rules of action or conduct commanding what is right and prohibiting what is wrong. (2) Right. Power, privilege or faculty inherent in one person.

DERECHO ADMINISTRATIVO. Administrative law. The group of rules and principles of public internal law which regulates the public administration (power and duties of administrative agencies).

DERECHO AERONÁUTICO. Air law. The branch of the law that deals with air traffic and all matters related to it.

DERECHO BANCARIO. Banking law. Group of rules which refers to the persons, the operations and the business and laws of banking.

DERECHO CIVIL. Civil law. The part of the law that establishes the general requirements of private acts, family and private property.

DERECHO CONSUETUDINARIO (NO ESCRITO, DE COSTUMBRE). Common law. The law that becomes such and persists by custom.

DERECHO COMPARADO. Comparative law. The science that compares the differences and similarities in the law of two or more countries or legal systems.

DERECHO CONSTITUCIONAL. Constitutional law. Branch of law which deals with the organization of the state, its powers and the individual rights and duties.

DERECHO DEL TRABAJO. Labor law. The branch of law which deals with the legal rights and duties in the relationship between employers and employees.

DERECHO DE REPRESENTACIÓN. Right of representation. In the law of distribution and descent, the principle upon which the issue of a deceased person takes or inherits the share of an estate which its immediate ancestor would have taken or inherited, if living.

DERECHO DE RETENCIÓN. Lien. Right to retain possession of property of another until payment or satisfaction of a debt or claim.

DERECHO FISCAL. Tax law. Laws about the relationship of the public treasure, the taxpayers and the collection of taxes.

DERECHO INTERNACIONAL PRIVADO. Private international law. Rules by which the law to be applied to any civil, commercial, criminal or labor relation among persons of different nationalities are determined.

DERECHO INTERNACIONAL PÚBLICO. Public International Law. Group of laws that regulate the relationship among different states and between them and international entities.

DERECHO LITIGIOSO. Litigious right. In civil law, a right which cannot be exercised without undergoing a lawsuit.

DERECHO MARÍTIMO. Maritime law. Branch of law that deals with business transacted at sea or which deals with maritime commerce and navigation generally.

DERECHO MERCANTIL o COMERCIAL. Commercial law. The branch of the law which rules commercial acts and relations of persons engaged in trade or commercial pursuits.

DERECHO PENAL. Criminal law. Branch of the law which establishes crimes and their punishments. Set of laws enacted to preserve public order by defining offenses and imposing corresponding fines and penalties for their violation.

DERECHO PROCESAL. Procedural law. Adjective law or law of procedure. Rules by which rights are enforced and redress is obtained.

DERECHO REAL. Real right, right in rem. Right of a person over one or more things subject of property.

DERECHOS INDIVIDUALES. Individual rights. Those belonging to every citizen of a state and which are established by the Constitution.

DEROGACIÓN. Derogation. The partial repeal or abolishment of a law, as by a subsequent act which limits its scope or impairs its utility and force.

100

DEROGAR. To annul, repeal, revoke.

DEROGATORIO. Derogatory. Having a repealing or retracting effect.

DERRELICTO. Derelict. The abandonment of a vessel or a person.

DERRIBAR. To overthrow. To cast down as from a position of power.

DERROCAR. To overthrow. To bring down a government through force and violence.

DERROCHE. Waste. Squandering of one's wealth or resources.

DERROTA. Defeat. To lose, be overcome in any contest.

DESACATO. Contempt. A willful disregard or disobedience of public authority.

DESACUERDO. Disagreement. Difference of opinion.

DESAFÍO. Defiance. Provoking to combat. A challenge objecting or excepting, to call or put in question.

DESAFORAR. To deprive someone of a privilege or immunity; to disbar.

DESAFUERO. Lawlessness. Any violent act against the law, customs or reason. In procedural law, the denial or loss of a right or privilege.

DESAGRAVIO. Indemnity, redress, relief. Compensation given to a person from a loss already sustained.

DESAHUCIAR. To give notice to quit. To dispossess, evict. When a landlord notifies a tenant of an intention to repossess the property.

DESAHUCIO. Dispossession. Notice to quit. A written notice given by a landlord to a tenant, stating that the former desires to repossess the premises, and that the latter is required to quit and move from the same by a designated time.

DESALOJO. Eviction. Dispossession by process of law.

DESALQUILAR. To vacate. To leave the premises.

DESAMPARAR. To abandon, forsake. To leave a person or thing without protection or help.

DESAPARECER. To disappear. To vanish from sight or cease to be or exist.

DESAPARICIÓN. Disappearance. The act of vanishing.

DESAPROBAR. Disapprove. To refuse consent to.

DESAPROPIAR. To transfer property.

DESARMADO. Without guns or weapons.

DESARMAR. To disarm. To divest oneself of weapons.

DESARROLLAR. To develop. To evolve to a higher, more useful stage, to bring about growth or cause to become active.

DESARROLLO. Development. The act or process of advancement to a higher, more progressive stage through changes.

DESASTRE. Disaster. Any unfortunate event or catastrophe causing widespread damages and suffering.

DESAUTORIZAR. To deprive of authority.

DESAVENENCIA. Disagreement, discord. Hostility, antagonism.

DESCANSO. Repose. Cessation or break from activity. Ease or inactivity after exertion or labor.

DESCANSAR. To rest. To recover from motion or activity.

DESCARGA. Unloading. To remove the burden, such as a load or cargo, or to get rid or dispose of anything burdensome.

DESCARGO. Release. Discharge from an obligation or debt. Acquittal, as from a charge.

DESCENDENCIA. Descent. The order or series of persons who have descended one from the other or all from a common ancestor.

DESCENDIENTE. Descendent. Those persons who are in the bloodline of the ancestor. Those descended from another.

DESCENTRALIZAR. To decentralize. To remove from direct connection with a central power or authority. To disperse industries and commerce from cities to outlying areas.

DESCONOCER. To disavow. In procedural law, to contest any judicial situation. To repudiate the acts of an agent.

DESCONTAR. To discount, deduct. (1) An allowance from an original price or debt, given as an incentive for prompt payment. (2) To discount. A deduction from an original price or debt. In banking terms, a deduction made upon its loans of money or upon a negotiable instrument payable at a future date transferred to the bank. It means subtracting from a note the interests which will accrue during the term of the debt at the time of disbursement.

DESCRIPCIÓN. Description. A delineation or enumeration of the characteristics and qualities of a person or object.

DESCUBRIMIENTO. Discovery. A disclosing or bringing to light of that which was hidden or concealed. The finding of land previously unknown to civilized people and which is claimed by a sovereign nation.

DESCUBRIR. To discover. The action of uncovering what was hidden or unknown.

DESCUENTO. Discount. A deduction from an original price or debt, allowed for paying promptly or in cash. Markdown.

DESCUIDO. Carelessness. Negligence. Failure to do or perform some work or duty that can be done or that is required to be done. Lack of attention or care in the doing or omission of a given act.

DESEMBARGAR. To lift an embargo.

DESEMBARGO. Lifting an embargo.

DESEMPEÑAR. To redeem. To free from debt or from a pawn shop. To accomplish.

DESERCIÓN. Desertion. A willful abandonment of a job or duty in violation of a legal or moral obligation.

DESERTOR. Deserter. A person who renounces his or her responsibilities and evades his or her duties in violation of a legal or moral obligation.

DESESTIMAR. To dismiss. To reject or overrule an action or suit without any further consideration.

DESFALCAR. To embezzle, defalcate. To fraudulently and secretly take money or property by one who has been entrusted with it.

DESFALCO. Defalcation. Misappropriation of funds or money entrusted and which were held in a fiduciary capacity.

DESFALCADOR. Defaulter. One who misappropriates money held by him or her in a fiduciary character.

DESFLORACIÓN. Defloration. The act by which a woman is deprived of her virginity.

DESGLOSAR. To detach. To remove a document from a court record, leaving a copy of it in its place. To break down or separate.

DESGLOSE. Removal of footnotes or marginal comments or pages from a legal file of papers or duly paged instrument, leaving a copy of its contents and the name of the one by whom the removal was made. Breakdown or separation.

DESGRAVAR. To lower duties; to remove a lien. Disencumber.

DESHABITADO. Uninhabited. Unoccupied by people.

DESHACER. To undo, cancel, dissolve, destroy, annul (as in a contract).

DESHEREDADO. Disinherited. The person deprived of the right to inherit, who would otherwise be an heir, by the acts of the owner of the estate.

DESHEREDAR. To disinherit, abdicate.

DESHIPOTECAR. To release, discharge or cancel a mortgage.

DESHONESTIDAD. Dishonesty. Lack of integrity.

DESIERTO. Forfeited, lapsed. The expiration of rights or privileges because of the failure to exercise these within some limit of time.

DESIGNAR. To designate. (1) To appoint, nominate for a special purpose or assign to a particular function. (2) To appoint a person to perform a task or duty or to hold a specific post.

DESINCORPORAR. To dissolve a corporation. To separate what was incorporated before.

DESISTIMIENTO. Waiving a right; abandonment. To give up, renounce or abandon voluntarily a right or a claim.

DESLEAL. Disloyal. Not faithful to.

DESLIGAR. Unbind. To untie a bond, to excuse from an obligation.

DESLINDE Y AMOJONAMIENTO. To bound and demarcate. To establish the boundaries between two parcels of land and to mark them by physical means.

DESMEDRO. Deterioration. The act of growing worse or inferior in quality.

DESOBEDECER. To disobey. To neglect or refuse to obey.

DESOCUPAR. To empty, vacate. To cease from occupancy.

DESOLLAR. To skin. To strip or deprive of a skin.

DESORDEN. Disorder. Lack of order; tumult; disruption; disturbances.

DESPACHAR. (1) To dispatch: a sending off. (2) To dismiss: from employment.

DESPACHO. (1) Mandamus. A writ issuing from a court of competent jurisdiction, commanding an inferior tribunal, board, corporation, or person to perform a purely ministerial duty imposed by law. (2) Office.

DESPEDIR. To fire. To dismiss or discharge an employee.

DESPIDO. Layoff. A termination of employment by a decision of the employer.

DESPOBLADO. Uninhabited place, to become depopulated.

DESPOJAR. To dispossess. To deprive someone of property.

DESPOJO. Dispossession. Violent dispossession of real estate. An act whereby the wrongdoer gets the actual occupation of land or hereditament.

DESPOJOS. Corpse. Remains of a dead body.

DESPOSAR. To wed. To get married.

DESPOSEER. To dispossess, divest.

DÉSPOTA. Despot. A ruler with absolute power who exercises it with oppression and autocracy as in a tyranny.

DESTIERRO. Exile. Expelling and sending a person from one country to another.

DESUSO. Disuse, obsolete. No longer in use.

DESTINATARIO. Addressee. Person to whom an object is sent.

DESTINO. Destination. The final place where an object should be transported.

DESTITUCIÓN. Destitution. Deprivation of something.

DESTRUCCIÓN. Destruction. The act of ruining something completely, which may include a taking of rights or property.

DESVALIJAR. To rob. To steal the contents of a bag or container.

DETECTOR DE MENTIRAS. Lie detector. A machine that reads blood pressure, perspiration rate, and other body signs, and gives a rough indication of whether a person is giving truthful answers to questions asked. Also called a "polygraph."

DETENCIÓN. Detention. (1) The restraint of a person's personal liberty against his or her will because he or she is suspected of having committed a crime. (2) The privation of liberty. The act of holding a person or thing.

DETENER. To detain, delay; to arrest.

DETENTACIÓN. In the legislation of some countries it is just a tenure, for others it is the act of keeping a tenure unlawfully and in bad faith.

DETENTADOR. Deforciant. One who wrongfully keeps lands and tenements from possession of the owner.

DETENTAR. To detain. To withhold someone's property.

DETERIORO. Deterioration. Material damage suffered by any good or real estate.

DETRIMENTO. Detriment, damage. That which injures or causes damage.

DEUDA. Debt. What is owed to someone.

DEUDA HEREDITARIA. Debt of the decedent payable from the assets of the estate.

DEUDA INCOBRABLE. Bad debt. Debt that cannot be collected.

DEUDOR. Debtor. A person who owes money.

DEUDOR HIPOTECARIO. Mortgagor. Person who mortgages his or her property as a guarantee for payment of a loan.

DEUDOR MANCOMUNADO. Joint debtor. A debtor liable for his or her separate portion of the debt.

DEUDOR SOLIDARIO. Joint and several debtor. One of several debtors, each of whom is liable for the whole debt.

DEVALUACIÓN. Devaluation. Reduction in value of a currency.

DEVENGADO. Accrued. Amount of monies or interests earned or due; funds that are entitled to be received.

DEVENGAR. To earn, to draw interest, to gain a benefit as recompense for a service or labor.

DEVOLUCIÓN. Refund. To refund money in restitution or repayment.

DEVOLUTIVO. Returnable. In civil procedure law, one of the effects given to an appeal by which the inferior court is separated from the deliberations of the case.

DÍA FERIADO. Holiday. A day of exemption from labor.

DÍA HÁBIL. Working day. Day on which courts are in session.

DIARIO. (1) Daily. (2) Ledger, journal. (3) Log book. (4) Newspaper. (5) Diary.

DICCIONARIO. Dictionary. A book containing words listed in alphabetical order, with their meanings, pronunciations and other information or which conveys information under alphabetically arranged subjects or entries.

DICTADOR. Dictator. A person who exercises absolute political power and authority oppressively, violating all constitutional strictures and individual liberties.

DICTADURA. Dictatorship. Government in which absolute power is concentrated in one individual.

DICTAMEN. (1) Judgment. The official decision of a court about the rights and claims of each side in a lawsuit. (2) Opinion, report.

DICTAMINAR. To pass judgment on. To decide about a controversial point submitted to one's consideration.

DIETA. Special remuneration for personal services like the daily expense allowance to public officials for services outside of their normal duties or of their domicile.

DIFAMACIÓN. Defamation. See "Difamar".

DIFAMAR. To libel, defame. To injure, diminish or destroy the reputation, respect or goodwill of someone.

DIFUNTO. Deceased. A dead person.

DIGESTO. Digest. A compendium or collection of many books, subjects, articles, and topics arranged in alphabetical order. An index to reported cases arranged by subjects and subdivided by jurisdiction and courts.

DIGITALES. Digits, fingerprints. Pertaining to a finger.

DIGNIDAD. Dignity. (1) Decency. (2) An honor rank or office.

DILACIÓN. Delay. Retardation.

DILATORIO. Dilatory. Causing delay.

DILIGENCIA. (1) Affair, business. (2) Diligence, care, service.

DILIGENCIA JUDICIAL. Judicial proceeding. Any proceeding in which judicial action is invoked.

DILIGENCIAS PRELIMINARES O PREPARATORIAS DEL JUICIO. Pre-trial discovery. Procedural devices used by the parties to an action prior to trial to obtain information and preliminary evidence for use at trial.

DILIGENTE. Diligent. A person who carries out his or her work or duties with painstaking care and perseverance; industrious.

DIMITIR. To resign. To leave one's employment.

DINERO. Money. Currency.

DIPLOMA. Diploma. Instrument conferring some honor, privilege or authority.

DIPLOMACIA. Diplomacy. The art and practice of carrying out negotiations between countries through their representatives for the accomplishment of mutually satisfactory political and economic relations.

DIPLOMÁTICO. Diplomat. The person representing his or her government in negotiations with other governments or international organizations.

DIPUTADO. (1) Deputy. (2) Congressman. (3) A person appointed to act on behalf of another. (4) The term usually refers to those persons who represent the people of a nation in the legislative branch.

DIRECCIÓN. Address, direction, administration, management.

DIRECTIVA. Management, board of directors. A group of persons who form the governing body of an association.

DIRECTOR. Director. In commercial law, any person appointed or elected according to law, authorized to manage and direct the affairs of a corporation or company.

DIRIMENTE. Annulling. Impediment that absolutely bars or makes null a marriage.

DIRIMIR. To solve, to settle, to adjust differences. To determine.

DISCERNIMIENTO. Discernment. Acuteness in judgment. The ability to perceive or recognize clearly.

DISCERNIR. To discern. To see or understand differences, to judge.

DISCONFORME. Disagreeing, dissenting. Not in agreement.

DISCONFORMIDAD. Nonconformity, dissent, objection. Disapproval.

DISCORDANCIA. Discordance, difference, dissent.

DISCONTÍNUO. Discontinuous. Something intermittent, changing or irregular. Not produced any more.

DISCRECIONAL. Discretionary. What is done in free will and in good judgment.

DISCRIMINACIÓN. Discrimination. Unfair treatment of persons because of their race, age, nationality, religion or other factor.

DISCULPAR. To excuse. To pardon. To free from any obligation or duty.

DISCURSO. Discourse, speech. Dissertation. Oral communication of ideas.

DISENSO. Lack of conformity. Not agreeing with.

DISENTIR. To dissent, differ, disagree. To differ in opinion.

DISFRAZ. Disguise. To conceal or hide by false representation.

DISFRUTE. Enjoyment. The exercise of a right, satisfaction or pleasure in the possession of a material object or property right or privilege.

DISIDENCIA. Dissent. See "Disentir".

DISIDENTE. Dissident. One who does not agree with the opinion of the majority.

DISIMULAR. To pretend. To allege falsely. Untruthful appearance or representation.

DISIMULO. Pretense. The act of make-believe.

DISOLUCIÓN. Dissolution. Termination, act of dissolving.

DISOLVER. To dissolve. To break up, terminate.

DISPARO. Shot. A discharge from a firearm or other weapon.

DISPENSA. Dispensation. An allowance to do something forbidden or to omit something required. To exempt.

DISPONIBILIDAD. Availability. That which is attainable or accessible.

111

DISPONIBLE. Available. That which may be used.

DISPOSICIÓN. Disposition. Order. Provision. Regulation.

DISPUTA. Dispute, contest, argument. A disagreement between persons about their rights and their legal obligations to one another.

DISTINGUIR. To distinguish. To differentiate or set apart.

DISTRITO. District. One of the territorial areas into which an entire state or country, municipality or other political subdivision is divided, for judicial, political, electoral, or administrative purposes.

DITA. Bondsman. Person who guarantees payment.

DIVIDENDO. Dividend. Earnings and profits designated by the board of directors of a corporation to be paid pro-rata among the outstanding shares.

DIVISA. Currency. Coined money and such banknotes or other paper money as are authorized by law and do in fact circulate from hand to hand as the medium of exchange and legal tender.

DIVISIÓN. Division. (1) Administrative unit of an organization. (2) The act of separating or distributing.

DIVORCIO. Divorce. The legal separation of spouses, effected by the judgment or decree of a court, either totally dissolving the marriage relation or suspending its effects so far as concerns the cohabitation of the parties.

DIVULGACIÓN. To make public.

DOBLE NACIONALIDAD. Dual citizenship. A person who enjoys the nationality of two countries at the same time.

DOCENTE. Educational. Pertaining to teaching and education.

DOCTRINA. Doctrine. A legal principle or rule.

DOCUMENTACIÓN. Documentation. All the papers, instruments, citations, references, etc., which may be used in support of an argument or case. The use of documentary evidence.

DOCUMENTADOR PÚBLICO. Notary public. A semi-public officer who can administer oaths, certify the validity of documents, and perform other testimonial duties needed for business and legal matters.

DOCUMENTAL. Documentary. A dramatic or instructive film representation.

DOCUMENTO NEGOCIABLE. Negotiable. Negotiable instrument. See "Efectos Negociables".

DOCUMENTO PRIVADO. Private document. A document written by the parties without the intervention of a notary public or any other authority with competence to legalize documents.

DOCUMENTO PÚBLICO. Public document. A document authorized or legalized by a notary public or any other public officer.

DOLO. Dolus (Lat.). Fraud, deceit. In civil law, a fraudulent action, artifice or trick used to deceive someone.

DOLOSO. Guiltful. Deceitful. What is made fraudulently to trick another who is ignorant of the truth, to prejudice or damage him or her.

DOMICILIO. Domicile. That place where a person has his or her true, fixed, and permanent home or principal establishment, and to which whenever he or she is absent, he or she has the intention of returning.

DOMINANTE. Dominant. The one who controls or rules.

DOMINIO. Domain. The complete and absolute ownership of land.

DOMINIO ÚTIL. Beneficial ownership. Ownership by a person who does not have title to the property but has the same rights of enjoyment or usufruct.

DONACIÓN. Donation. Gift. A voluntary transfer of property to another person, made gratuitously and without any consideration.

DONANTE. Donor. The party conferring a gift or power.

113

DONATARIO. Donee. The recipient of a gift.

DORSO. Back. Rear part of something, as opposed to the front.

DOTE. Dowry. The property which a woman brings to her husband in marriage.

DOTAL. Dotal. Pertaining to or related to a dowry.

DOTANTE. Endower. The person giving a dower.

DUDA RAZONABLE. Reasonable doubt. Standard of proof used in criminal cases and defined as the type of doubt that would cause prudent persons to hesitate before acting in matters important to themselves.

DUDOSO. Doubtful, dubious. What is uncertain, questionable.

DUELO. (1) Duel. A prearranged combat between two persons according to a code of honor. (2) Mourning. The time during which one grieves.

DUEÑO. Owner. The person vested with the title of property.

DUPLICA. Rejoinder. The answer to the plaintiff's pleadings.

DUPLICADO. Duplicate. A copy of an original.

DURACIÓN. Duration. The period in which anything exists.

E

EBRIEDAD. Drunkenness. Under the influence of intoxicating beverages. The condition a person is in after consuming alcoholic beverages. The characteristic of this condition is the impairment of the mental functions.

EBRIO. Drunk. Person under the influence of intoxicating beverages. The person whose mental abilities are impaired because of ingestion of alcoholic beverages.

ECHAZÓN. Jettison. (1) The act of throwing overboard from a vessel part of the cargo, in case of extreme danger, to lighten the ship's load. (2) The things thrown overboard from a vessel to lighten the ship's cargo.

ECLECTICISMO. Eclecticism. Manner of thought or action that is intermediate and not extreme. Philosophical principle that believes in the use of any doctrine or method or system when its arguments are reasonable.

ECLESIÁSTICO. Ecclesiastical. Pertaining to the church. Priest or minister.

ECONOMÍA. Economy. (1) Prudent administration of goods and services. (2) Frugality.

ECONOMÍA POLÍTICA. Political economy. The science that studies the process of production, distribution and consumption of wealth.

ECUÁNIME. Equable, calm, stable. Marked by a lack of extreme variation or inequality.

EDAD. Age. (1) The time a person has lived since birth. (2) The time something has been in existence.

EDICIÓN OFICIAL. Official edition. Written material published and sanctioned by a government.

EDICTO. Edict. (1) A written form used to make public a court resolution. (2) A proclamation or notice. The written publication of news or facts which an authority wants to make public.

EDICTO JUDICIAL. The means by which the court notifies the defaulting party of a lawsuit of the proceedings. It is also used to make some information about the case public when it is required to be published.

EDICTO MATRIMONIAL. Publication by which the general public is placed on notice of a future wedding with the purpose of letting anyone express to the court any reason why the marriage should not occur.

EDICTO EVOLUTIVO. Consequence produced by an appealed court order, when it is sent to a superior court to decide whether it is valid or not, without suspending the effects of the appealed order. The effect of the appealed order will be revoked if declared void by the superior court; if not, its effects were never suspended.

EDIL. Roman magistrate in charge of the care of public buildings and temples.

EE. UU. Common abbreviation of "Estados Unidos" or United States of America.

EFECTIVO. (1) Effective, efficient. (2) Cash, ready money. (3) Current, actual.

EFECTO. Effect. (1) To do, produce, accomplish, or force. (2) Value, consequence. (3) Actual, current.

EFECTO RETROACTIVO. Retroactive effect. Whenever the law creates a new obligation on transactions or considerations already past, or destroys or impairs vested rights.

EFECTOS. Goods, effects, chattel. Merchandise.

EFECTOS AL PORTADOR. Bearer paper. A check or other financial document that is made out "payable to bearer," endorsed in blank, or made out to "cash" or other indication that no one specific person is meant to cash it.

EFECTOS NEGOCIABLES. Negotiable instruments. A signed document that contains an unconditional promise to pay an exact amount of money, either when demanded or at an exact future date.

EFECTOS PERSONALES. Personal property; personal effects.

EFECTUAR. To effect, carry out.

116

EFICAZ. Effective, efficacious. Something that produces the intended effects.

EFÍMERO. Ephemeral. Lasting a very short time. With little value or consequence.

EGOLATRÍA. Self-idolatry. The flattery of oneself.

EJECUCIÓN. Execution; fulfillment; enforcement. (1) The last phase of the legal proceeding consisting of the enforcement and application of the judgment to make it effective. (2) The performing of the necessary acts to carry out the intended purpose. The completion of something by fulfilling the formalities required to the perfecting of it.

EJECUCIÓN DE LA LEY. Enforcement of the law.

EJECUCIÓN DE SENTENCIA. Enforcement of judgment. The carrying out of the mandate contained in a court resolution. The act of enforcing the court's judgment by requiring compliance with its decision.

EJECUTABLE. Executory. Capable of being enforced. Not yet executed, that which can be completed and taken into performance.

EJECUTADO. One whose property is attached because of a debt. (1) It is the judgment debtor whose property has been seized and sold according to the law to meet his or her debt. (2) The person killed by death penalty or assassination.

EJECUTANTE. Executant. One who forecloses or executes. The plaintiff creditor who sues to foreclose on the goods or property of the debtor in order to satisfy the debt in arrears.

EJECUTAR. To perform, execute, to complete, carry out. To make an execution. To fulfill the formalities in order to make something valid and enforceable.

EJECUTIVO. Executive. One of the powers of the nation. The one in charge of executing the law. Usually vested in the President or Prime Minister.

EJECUTOR. Executor. Executioner. (1) The person in charge of the execution. (2) The person who carries out the death penalty. (3) The one appointed by the deceased to carry out the last will by distributing the estate according to the will.

EJECUTORÍA. A judgment which is considered to have the effect of "res judicata." It is the condition of a judgment that has already decided something and can be enforced anytime because the opportunity to challenge it has passed.

EJEMPLO. Example. (1) Manner or conduct of one which can influence others to imitate said conduct. (2) Used to demonstrate or show something.

EJERCER. To practice. (1) The exercise of any profession. (2) To use, to carry on.

ELECCIÓN. Election. The act of choosing one or more from a number of persons. The choice left to someone between alternatives.

ELECTO. Elected. The person who has been chosen.

ELECTOR. Voter. The person who chooses between alternatives.

ELECTORADO. Voting population. Those who have the right to vote in an election.

ELEGIBLE. Eligible. With the capacity to be chosen, particularly for public office. Qualified.

ELEGIR EL JURADO. To draw or select a jury. The act of choosing the group of people who are called to serve as jury in a case. The jury is the body who determines the guilt or innocence of the defendant.

ELEMENTO. Element; material or substance; ingredient; constituent. One component of a thing.

ELEVAR. To raise. Elevate, increase.

ELEVAR A ESCRITURA PÚBLICA. To convert a private document into a public one by satisfying the formalities required.

ELOCUCIÓN. Elocution. Way of choosing words to express thoughts.

ELOCUENCIA. Eloquence. The art of speaking or writing with facility and the ability to persuade.

ELOCUENTE. Eloquent. Expressing one's thoughts with eloquence.

ELUSIÓN. Avoidance. To escape or evade.

EMANCIPACIÓN. Emancipation. (1) The act by which a minor child who was under the guardianship of his or her parents is rendered free from parental supervision. (2) The act by which one who was unfree, or under the power and control of another, is rendered free, or set at liberty and made his or her own master.

EMANCIPAR. To emancipate. To render free one who was under the control of another. The term is generally used to refer to the emancipation of a minor child by his or her parents.

EMBAJADA. Embassy. Body of diplomatic representatives of a country headed by an ambassador.

EMBAJADOR. Ambassador. A public officer vested with high diplomatic powers, commissioned by a government to transact the international business of his or her government with a foreign government.

EMBALAJE. Packing of goods for transport.

EMBALSAMAR. To embalm. To perfume and/or preserve dead bodies from decay.

EMBARAZO. Pregnancy. The existence of the condition beginning at the moment of conception and terminating with delivery of a child.

EMBARGABLE. Attachable, garnishable. Suitable to be garnished. (1) The person whose property can be seized or subjected to garnishment. (2) The property that can be garnished or seized.

EMBARGADO. Garnishee. Person affected by a process of garnishment. (1) The defendant in a garnishment proceeding. (2) The garnished goods. Garnishment.

EMBARGADOR. Garnishor. Lienor. (1) The creditor or plaintiff who establishes a lien or initiates garnishment proceedings. (2) The court ordering the garnishment or lien against a defendant or debtor.

EMBARGO. Garnishment. An accessory action to a judgment rendered in a principal action, which is resorted to as a means of obtaining satisfaction of the judgment by attaching goods, money or property of the judgment debtor.

EMBARGO EJECUTIVO. The kind of lien or garnishment established to obtain satisfaction of a judgment. According to this process of garnishment, the property affected by it is attached to be sold in order to satisfy the judgment already rendered.

EMBARGO PREVENTIVO. The detention or attachment of property during the main action or proceeding in order to ensure that the property is available to satisfy a possible judgment.

EMBAUCADOR. Deceptive, tricky. One who deceives. The person who cheats with malice to take advantage of another.

EMBLEMA. Emblem. The symbol used to represent something.

EMBRIAGUEZ. Drunkenness. State of being under the influence of intoxicating beverages.

EMERGENTE. Emergent. That which results or comes from another.

EMIGRACIÓN. Emigration. To move from one country or state to another. The movement of people or animals from one place to another.

EMIGRANTE. Emigrant. Person who abandons his or her country to live and reside elsewhere.

EMIGRAR. To emigrate or to migrate. To move from one place to another. To leave one's country in order to find a new life or work in another.

EMITENTE. Drawer of a check or bill. The one who signs a check or negotiable note and delivers it to another.

EMITIR. To issue. To deliver a commercial paper or document to a holder or a remitter.

EMISIÓN. Emission, issuance. To put into circulation.

EMISOR. Issuer. The person who issues a check or bill, or puts these into circulation.

EMOLUMENTO. Emolument. That which is received as compensation for services.

EMPADRONAMIENTO. Census, voting list. Act of recording, in a special registry, various characteristics of the population for the purpose of statistical, taxing or electoral count.

EMPEÑAR. To pledge, pawn. (1) Handing over physical possession of a piece of personal property to another person, who holds it until payment of a debt is effected to that person. (2) To undertake. To promise.

EMPEÑO. Purpose. Pawn. Pledge. (1) Desire or purpose. (2) The contract by which one person turns property over to another to assure to the latter that a debt secured with that property will be paid.

EMPLAZADO. The person whose presence is requested by a judge or court. The person against whom the summons or subpoena is directed in order to have him or her appear before the court.

EMPLAZADOR. Summoner. (1) The judge or court which issues the subpoena. (2) The court officer who serves the subpoena. The one who delivers the summons.

EMPLAZAMIENTO. Summons, citation. A mandate or writ requiring the appearance of a defendant in an action under penalty of having judgment entered against him or her for failure to do so.

EMPLAZAR. To summon or subpoena. The act of requiring the presence of a person before the judge or court.

EMPLEADO. Employee. A person in the service of another pursuant to a contract, where the employer has the power or right to control and direct the employee in the material details of how the work is to be performed.

EMPLEADO A MEDIO TIEMPO. Part-time employee. One hired to perform a job for another on a part-time basis; one employed at uncertain or irregular times.

EMPLEADO A TIEMPO COMPLETO. Full-time employee. The person who has been hired to work for another during all of his or her hours of labor. The employee must be present at work during that time.

EMPLEADO PÚBLICO. Public employee. Public officer. A person hired to perform a job or to work for the city or state. The employee hired by the government, whether local or national.

EMPLEADOR. Employer. One who employs the services of others in exchange for wages or salaries. The person who pays another who has performed the required services.

EMPLEO. Employment. Occupation. The activity in which one person is engaged as a means of earning his or her salary or wages for a living.

EMPRESA. Enterprise. A venture or undertaking, especially one involving financial commitment. A business.

EMPRESARIO. Businessman. The person who puts money into a business. Also the one who manages the business itself.

EMPRÉSTITO. Loan. A sum of money lent for a period of time and repayable with interest.

EN CINTA. Pregnant. The condition of a woman who is expecting a baby.

EN COMANDITA. Limited Partnership. The partnership in which two partners join together for a common business. One partner, called General Partner, is responsible for the management of the business and whose liabilities extend beyond his or her capital contribution to the partnership; the other partner, called Limited Partner, has liabilities that are limited to his or her capital distribution. See "Sociedad en Comandita".

EN COMANDITA SIMPLE. The limited partnership in which the capital contribution of the limited partner is not represented by shares. See "En Comandita".

EN COMANDITA POR ACCIONES. The limited partnership in which the capital contribution of the limited partner is represented by shares.

ENAJENACIÓN. Alienation, transfer. Voluntary and absolute transfer of title and possession of real property from one person to another. The act by means of which property is transferred to another person.

ENAJENACIÓN (DE BIENES). Disposition (of property).

ENAJENACIÓN MENTAL. Insanity. Not of sound mind. The condition of a person after suffering a psychic disorder.

ENAJENADOR. The person who transfers his or her properties by any means.

ENAJENANTE. See "Enajenador".

ENAJENAR. To alienate, transfer, sell, or otherwise dispose of.

ENCABEZAMIENTO. Beginning. The words used to begin a document.

ENCAJE. Cash reserve. The funds kept by banks and insurance companies in a reserve account as required by law to protect the banks or insurance companies from losses.

ENCARCELACIÓN. Imprisonment. Act of confining to prison. To put a person in prison. The confinement of a person in a specific place.

ENCARCELAR. To imprison. To place a person in confinement.

ENCARECIDO. Gone up in value. Dearest. (1) Having suffered an increase in its value. (2) Showing a lot of consideration and friendship.

ENCAUSADO. Defendant. Person against whom a legal action is brought. This action may be civil or criminal. Generally the term is used to refer to the defendant in a criminal action.

ENCAUSAR. To prosecute. To carry on a judicial proceeding against a person.

ENCOMENDADO. Commissioned. Subject to commission being entrusted.

ENCOMIENDA. Commission. (1) Mandate given to a person to do a specific commission. (2) The thing given according to the mandate.

ENCOMIENDA POSTAL. Parcel post. Package shipped by mail.

ENCUBRIDOR. Accessory after the fact, one who conceals a crime. A person who, knowing a felony has been committed by another, receives, shelters, shields, comforts or assists the felon, in order to enable him or her to escape from punishment.

ENCUBRIMIENTO. Concealment. (1) Criminal conduct by one who aids a person who has committed a crime in order to help that person avoid being caught. (2) The act of hiding the instruments used to perpetrate a crime or the stolen goods.

ENCUESTA. Survey, inquiry, investigation. Study conducted to obtain information in order to analyze it.

ENDEUDADO. Indebted. Person being in debt. The person who is indebted to another called a creditor. One who has the obligation to pay a debt.

ENDORSAR. To endorse. See "Endosar".

ENDORSO. Endorsement. See "Endoso".

ENDOSABLE. Endorsable. Capable of being endorsed. The negotiable instrument, note, bill or check which can be endorsed.

ENDOSADO. Endorsee. Endorsed. (1) The new beneficiary of a negotiable note or check to whom it was being transferred by endorsement. (2) The negotiable document that has been transferred upon an endorsement.

ENDOSANTE. Endorser. The beneficiary of a negotiable note who endorses it to have it transferred to another.

ENDOSAR. To endorse. To make an endorsement. To transfer the rights and obligation of a negotiable note to another by signing on the back of the note. The act of signing a check or negotiable instrument on the back transferring it to another. This is done by the beneficiary of the negotiable note with the intent to transfer it.

ENDOSATARIO. Endorsee. The person to whom a negotiable instrument is assigned by endorsement.

ENDOSO. Endorsement. The act of a payee, drawee, accommodation endorser, or holder of a bill, note, check, or other negotiable instrument, in writing his or her name upon the back of the same, with or without further or qualifying words, whereby the property in the same is assigned and transferred to another.

ENEMIGO. Enemy, adversary. The person or state which is at war with another.

ENEMIGO PÚBLICO. Public enemy. (1) A person is deemed to be a public enemy when he or she commits frequent crimes. A notorious felon. (2) A problem which affects the social and economic condition or welfare of the population.

ENFERMEDAD PROFESIONAL. Occupational disease. A disease resulting from exposure during employment to conditions or substances detrimental to one's health. The impairment of the health of workers caused by exposure to harmful conditions during the course of employment. See "Riesgos Profesionales".

ENFERMEDAD VENÉREA. Venereal disease. A sexually transmitted disease.

ENFITEUSIS. Emphyteusis. The real right by which a person is entitled to enjoy another's estate as if it were his or her own, and to dispose of its substance, as far as can be done without deteriorating it, for perpetuity or for a long time.

ENFITEUTA. The person entitled to enjoy the right of emphyteusis.

ENGANCHE. Down payment. Money given to the seller of something with the purpose of having it reserved for a period of time until the balance of the price is cancelled.

ENGAÑAR. To cheat, defraud, deceive. The act intended to misrepresent something for the purpose of defrauding another.

ENGAÑO. Cheat. To misrepresent something to make it look or appear to others different from what it is.

ENGENDRAR. To create. To cause. The act of giving life to a creature.

ENGENDRO. (1) An unborn creature. (2) A creature born with substantial defects.

ENJUICIADO. Defendant. (1) The person against whom the plaintiff is seeking relief. The one subject to an indictment. (2) The cause that already has been on trial.

ENJUICIAMIENTO. Trial. The judicial proceedings carried out before a court to settle a conflict. Generally refers to criminal proceedings.

ENJUICIAR. To prosecute. To carry on a legal action or judicial proceeding, by due course of law and before a competent tribunal, for the purpose of determining the validity of a charge.

ENMENDAR. To amend. To change, correct or revise. The act of making a modification or change in something to make it different from what it was.

125

ENMIENDA. Amendment. Modification, deletion or addition proposed or made to a bill, law, constitution, etc. A change made to alter something.

ENLACE. Union. (1) The connection of two things. (2) The relation between different things. (3) Wedding. The act of getting married.

ENRIQUECIMIENTO SIN CAUSA. Unjust enrichment. The legal principle that when a person obtains money or property unfairly at another's expense, it should be returned. According to this principle, nobody can get richer at another's expense without a valid cause.

ENSAÑAR. To irritate, gloat. Aggravating circumstances in the commission of a crime which increase the penalty for the crime. Consisting in causing unnecessary pain and damage while committing a crime.

ENSERES. Implements. The equipment needed to perform a job. Personal goods.

ENSERES DOMÉSTICOS. Household appliances. Those kinds of appliances which belong to a family household. Implements of a house.

ENTABLAR. To bring. To procure. Generally used to refer to bringing an action or suit. Initiation of legal proceedings.

ENTABLAR JUICIO. Bring an action. The presentation of a pleading to begin a lawsuit. The presentation of charges against one person to initiate the case.

ENTERRAR. To bury. To place underground.

ENTIDAD. Entity; bureau, department, agency. An organization created to perform a duty or carry on a business.

ENTIERRO. Funeral. The act of burial.

ENTRADA BRUTA. Gross receipts. The complete and total amount of money or value or other consideration received from a transaction.

ENTRADAS. (1) Income, revenue, receipts. (2) Money gained from business, work or investment. (3) All financial gains. (4) Doors used to enter a place. (5) Tickets.

ENTRE LÍNEAS. Between lines. What is written between the lines of a document. Interlineation.

126

ENTREGADOR DE LA CITACIÓN. Summoner. Process server. A person with legal authority to formally deliver court papers such as writs and summonses to defendants.

ENTREGA. Delivery. The act of giving something or handing it over to someone else's authority or possession.

ENTREGAR. To deliver. The act by which an object or substance of something is placed within the actual, constructive possession or control of another. To place something under the authority or control of someone.

ENTREGARSE. To surrender. The act of giving oneself. To have sexual intercourse.

ENUNCIAR. To announce. To declare. The act of stating something.

ENVENENAR. To poison. To administer a substance capable of destroying life.

ENVIADO. Envoy.

ENVIADO DIPLOMÁTICO. Diplomatic official of one country who has been sent to serve in another.

ENVIAR. To remit or send.

ENVICIAR. To vitiate. The act of corrupting or creating addiction.

ENVIUDAR. To became a widow(er). To survive the spouse.

EPÍGRAFO. (1) Epigraph, heading, title. (2) Inscription on a building. (3) Annotation prefixed to a literary work.

EQUIDAD. Equity. Spirit and habit of fairness, justice, and right, which regulates the dealings between individuals. The principle of law which permits a flexible application of the law in light of the circumstances to reach a just and equitable result. A complement to the strict letter of the law by the use of equity.

EQUIPAJE. Luggage. The property carried by a passenger during his or her travels.

EQUITATIVO. Equitable. Consistent with the principles of justice and right.

ERARIO. State or public treasury. Place where public revenues are deposited and kept.

ERGA OMNES. (Lat.) In front of everybody; with respect to all. It is used to refer to rights which affect everybody and not just one person or a particular group of persons.

ERROR. Error. A mistaken judgment or incorrect belief as to the existence or effect of matters of fact, or a false or mistaken application of the law.

ERROR DE DERECHO. Error of law. The mistake committed when determining the meaning of a statue or law. The false knowledge of the law.

ERROR DE HECHO. Error of fact. The mistake committed upon the knowledge of an event, person or thing.

ERROR JUDICIAL. Judicial error. Any mistake committed while trying a case. Any error in the proceedings.

ESCALA. Stopover. The place or one of the places where a vessel, aircraft or traveler stops during a trip.

ESCALAFÓN. Military listing in order of importance. The rank and name of all the members of the organization.

ESCALAMIENTO. Burglary, housebreaking. Breaking and entering into a place without permission with the purpose of committing a crime therein.

ESCÁNDALO PÚBLICO. Public scandal. A misdemeanor consisting of the disorderly alteration of the normal behavior of the society. Especially the violation of the moral conduct.

ESCAPADO. Having escaped. See "Escapar".

ESCAPAR. To escape. To avoid. The action of leaving the custody of the authority under which one is confined, before the sentence is over or without any justification.

ESCLAVITUD. Slavery. Civil relation in which one has absolute power over the life, fortune, and liberty of another.

ESCRIBANO. Court clerk; notary public. The person authorized to attest the authenticity of documents and acts taking place before his or her presence.

ESCRIBIENTE. Clerk. Person responsible for keeping records, especially in public offices.

ESCRITO. Brief; a document in writing. Generally consisting of a statement prepared by the parties in which they present their arguments, facts and the law to support their positions in the case.

ESCRITURA. Contract; deed; legal instrument; handwriting. A written document.

ESCRITURA PRIVADA. Private document. Any written instrument neither certified nor recorded by a notary public. The authenticity of a signature may be attested by the notary public without making it a public document.

ESCRITURA PÚBLICA. Public document. A written document that has been recorded by a notary public. Generally it has to be written in a special paper furnished by the notary. The notary not only attests to the authenticity of the signature, but also keeps a record of it.

ESCRUTINIO. Canvass, scrutiny. The act of examining and counting the votes cast in a public election to determine the authenticity of the results.

ESCUELA. School. (1) An institution in charge of teaching. (2) Group of philosophers who think in the same way and agree on basic principles.

ESCUELA DE DERECHO. Law school. The faculty and student body in a university where law is taught.

ESCUELA PRIMARIA. Elementary school. The institution in charge of giving the basic education for up to six years to children.

ESCUELA SECUNDARIA. High school. The institution which continues the education of a child who already has an elementary education. The child with a high school education is ready to enter college or university.

ESPECIE. Kind, sort. Class; generic class. A group of things classified for their common characteristics.

ESPECIFICACIÓN. Specification. (1) Means to acquire title to a thing by working it into new forms or species from the raw material. (2) Description of the elements or quality of something.

ESPÍA. Spy.

ESPIONAJE. Espionage. (1) The federal crime of "gathering, transmitting or losing" classified information regarding the national defense so that the information will be used to the advantage or detriment of another nation. (2) This word is also applicable to the gathering or disclosure of secrets.

ESPONSALES. Betrothal, engagement to marry. Mutual promise between a man and woman to marry.

ESPOSA. Wife. Woman united to a man by marriage.

ESPOSO. Husband. A married man.

ESTABILIDAD. Stability, permanence. In Roman law it is a right of the employee to continue indefinitely in his or her employment unless the employee becomes involved in acts legally determined to give rise to a justified cause for dismissal.

ESTABLECIMIENTO. Establishment. In commercial law, a place of business.

ESTADÍA. Stay. In maritime law, the time during which a vessel is allowed to stay in port beyond the time allowed for loading and unloading.

ESTADIDAD. Statehood. The condition of a state.

ESTADO. State. A body of people occupying a definite territory and politically organized under one government.

ESTADO CIVIL. Status; marital status. Legal condition or civil status of an individual concerning his or her rights, duties, capacities and incapacities with respect to the rest of the community.

ESTADO DE GANANCIAS Y PÉRDIDAS. Profit and loss statement. The statement evidencing the commercial activity of a business during an established time. It lists income and expenses over a specific period of time.

ESTADOS UNIDOS. United States. A union of states.

ESTAFA. Fraud. An intentional perversion of truth for the purpose of inducing another, in reliance upon it, to part with some valuable thing belonging to him or her.

ESTAFADO. Defrauded. The person against whom a fraud has been committed. The victim of fraud.

ESTAFADOR. Swindler. A person who commits fraud.

ESTAFAR. To defraud. To commit a crime consisting of cheating. To induce another to do something that otherwise he or she would not do.

ESTAMPILLA. Stamp. Small label printed and sold by the government, and required to be attached to all mail or for certain tax matters or documents.

ESTATAL. Related to the state.

ESTATUTO. (1) Statute. Law enacted and established by the legislature. (2) Bylaws. Regulations adopted by an association or corporation.

ESTIGMA. Stigma. Mark which affects adversely the reputation of a person.

ESTIMAR. To estimate, appraise. Estimating the value of something by an impartial expert.

ESTIPENDIO. Fee, stipend. Compensation for a particular act or service. Payment given to a person for the performance of a service.

ESTIPULACIÓN. Stipulation. (1) An agreement between lawyers on opposite sides of a lawsuit. (2) One point in a written agreement.

ESTIPULAR. To stipulate, specify, agree, covenant.

ESTIRPE. (Lat.) Lineage; stirps. Person from whom a family is descended. "Per stirpes" is the method of dividing a deceased's estate by giving out shares equally "by representation" or by family groups (as opposed to "per capita," or each individual taking in his or her own right).

ESTORBO PÚBLICO. Common nuisance. The unpleasant activity which annoys and causes an unreasonable disturbance to the public in general and not to one particular person.

ESTRADO. Important part of the courtroom in which legal actions take place. Board in which notes are affixed to give public notice of some of the court orders.

ESTUDIANTE A TIEMPO COMPLETO. Full-time student. The one registered and attending all the courses required by the faculty during the semester.

ESTUDIANTE A TIEMPO PARCIAL. Part-time student. The student registered and attending some of the courses required by the faculty during the semester.

ESTUPEFACIENTE. Narcotic substance. Any drug which deprives its user of mental sharpness or induces sleep.

ESTUPRADOR. Rapist. The person who commits the crime of having sexual intercourse with a woman without her consent or against her will.

ESTUPRO. Stuprum. In Roman and civil law, unlawful sexual intercourse between a man and an unmarried woman. Some laws require her to be a minor.

ÉTICA. Ethics. (1) Professional standards of conduct for lawyers and judges. (2) Standards of fair and honest conduct in general. Most of the time it is used to refer to morals.

EUTANASIA. Euthanasia. The act of painlessly putting to death a person suffering from an incurable disease as an act of mercy.

EVACUAR. To evacuate. To vacate. (1) The act of leaving empty. (2) To carry on an action.

EVADIR. To evade. (1) To escape in any way the punishment of the law. (2) Illegal nonpayment of taxes due.

EVALUADOR. Appraiser. The person who is entrusted with the duty of determining the correct value of something.

EVASIÓN. Evasion. (1) To avoid or escape from imprisonment. (2) The act of evading due payment of taxes.

EVENTO. Event. Something that happens.

EVICCIÓN. Eviction. The act of depriving a person of the possession of land or rental property which he or she has held or leased.

Dispossession of property against the holder by someone with superior legal title to recover it.

EVIDENCIA. Evidence, proof. Any means by which the truth alleged by any party at trial is ascertained.

EVITABLE. Avoidable. Preventable. That which can be avoided.

EVITAR. To avoid. The act which prevents something from happening. To prevent from occurrence.

EX LEGE. (Lat.) By force of law; as a matter of law. According to the law.

EX NUNC. (Lat.) From now; from this moment.

EX TUNC. (Lat.) Since then.

EXACCIÓN. To request payment. The act intended to collect money owed.

EXAMEN. Test. Analysis. Inspection.

EXAMINAR. To examine. To inquire into; to test someone's knowledge.

EXCARCELACIÓN. The act of setting free a convict with the consent of the judge. To avoid imprisonment by paying bail.

EXCARCELAR. To release a prisoner from jail with the authorization of the court.

EXCEDENTE. Excess, surplus. That which goes beyond the ordinary limit.

EXCEPCIÓN. Exception. A plea by which the defendant when answering the plaintiff's complaint alleges facts that constitute a defense against the cause of action. In the exception the defendant does not deny the plaintiff's cause of action. The defendant alleges a fact which prevents the plaintiff from obtaining what he or she seeks.

EXCEPCIÓN DILATORIA. Dilatory defense. Dilatory plea. The exception intended to retard the progress of the trial. An allegation by the defendant intended to obstruct the plaintiff's complaint until the impediment is removed. It does not challenge the merits of the case. Lack of jurisdiction is one kind of dilatory defense.

EXCEPCIÓN PERENTORIA. Peremptory exception. Peremptory plea. The defense alleged by the defendant with the intent to destroy the plaintiff's complaint. The defendant alleges facts which oppose and deny the merits of the cause of action. One example of this peremptory exception is "Res Judicata."

EXCLUSIÓN. Exclusion. To segregate, to separate. That which is not admitted. The act of excluding something.

EXCLUSIVO. Exclusive. Restrictive to. Solely. Appertaining to the subject alone, not including any other.

EXCUSA. Excuse. A reason given to justify the action or omission of the person charged or accused.

EXCUSIÓN. Right given to the guarantor of an obligation which allows him or her to request the creditor of the obligation to go against the debtor of the obligation and use all the remedies available to the creditor before recourse is allowed against the guarantor.

EXENCIÓN. Exemption, immunity. Being free from an obligation. To be exempt, privileged.

EXENCIÓN DE IMPUESTO. Tax exemption. That property or part of the income which is not subject to taxation and should be subtracted from the taxable one.

EXENCIONES PERSONALES. Personal exemptions. Those personal expenses which are allowed by law to be deducted by the taxpayer. These expenses are to be subtracted from the gross income.

EXENTO. Exempt. Free. Quality of the thing which has been set free from a duty. Exempt is what is relieved from liability, taxation, attachment. The class of property not subject to a levy.

EXEQUÁTUR. Exequatur. (1) A written official recognition and authorization of consular officer, issued by the government to which he or she is accredited. (2) In another sense, it is the authorization given by the judicial authority of a country to execute within its jurisdiction a judgment given in a foreign country.

EXHEREDAR. Disinherit.

EXHIBICIONISTA. Exhibitionist. A person who exposes his or her private body parts in public places. Exposure of sexual organs at an improper place and time and in an indecent manner.

EXHORTAR. To issue letters rogatory or requisitorial.

EXHORTO. Letters rogatory. Request sent by one court to another one of like hierarchy in a different jurisdiction to execute an action required in proceedings taking place before the court that has issued the letter rogatory.

EXHUMACIÓN. The act of unburying a dead person.

EXHUMAR. To unbury. To take away the rest of the deceased from where it has been buried.

EXILADO. A person who has been banished. A person punished by compelling him or her to leave his or her country.

EXILIO. Exile. Banishment from a country. Punishment inflicted upon a person by compelling him or her to leave his or her country.

EXIMENTE. Exempting. (1) Excuse for acting or failing to act. (2) Clearing the defendant from alleged fault or guilt. It is an affirmative defense alleged to present new circumstances which constitute a defense to the charge against the defendant. It does not tend to disprove the charge but to show that there is a reasonable justification to dismiss the case.

EXISTENCIAS. Inventory. A detailed list of the existing goods in stock.

EXONERACIÓN. Exoneration. Removal of a burden, responsibility, or duty.

EXPEDIDO. Issued. Sent.

EXPEDIENTE. File, record, proceedings. Group of papers, from the original complaint to the final judgment, including all pleadings of a case, arranged in order and kept for preservation and reference purposes. The file of the documents containing the acts and proceedings of a case.

EXPEDIR. (1) To ship, send, forward. (2) Forward. (3) To issue.

135

EXPEDIR UN CHEQUE. Issue a check. The act of writing and signing a check to make it payable.

EXPEDITO. Expeditious, quality of being prompt. Performed with haste and speed.

EXPENDER. Expend. To sell. To give something in exchange for money.

EXPENDIO. Store. Place in which goods are for sale.

EXPERTO. Expert. (1) A person possessing special knowledge or experience who is allowed to testify at trial not only about facts, but also about the professional conclusions he or she draws from these facts. (2) The person who has particular knowledge of a matter or subject.

EXPIACIÓN. Atonement. See "Expiar".

EXPIAR. To atone. To purify oneself by suffering the punishment, to serve the time of the sentence.

EXPIRAR. To expire, lapse. Loss of a right or privilege caused by lapse of time. Termination caused by lapse of time.

EXPONER. To expose. To show to others. The act of making a public display of something; to risk. To place anything in a risky position.

EXPOSICIÓN. Exposition. Act of exposing. Action intended to show something to others.

EXPOSICIÓN DE MOTIVOS. Preamble delineating the reasons or motives for enacting a new law or agreeing upon something. They are not binding but are given to explain the meaning and intent of the document.

EXPRESO. Express. Speedy. (1) With rapidity; expeditious. (2) Clear; done with the intent; specifically with that purpose.

EXPROPIACIÓN. Expropriation. The taking of property in exchange for compensation or indemnization. A seizure of property by the government under eminent domain.

EXPROPRIAR. Expropriate, condemn. To take private property for public use. The act of seizing another's property under eminent domain. It is done by the government with a superior public interest.

EXPULSAR. To expel.

EXPULSIÓN. Expulsion. Ejection. Expelling. The act of throwing something out. The banishment of someone from an activity or body.

EXTENDER. To extend. To prolong further than the original limit.

EXTENDER UN CHEQUE. To issue a check. The signing of a check.

EXTINCIÓN. To extinguish. Termination or cancellation of the effects and consequences of a right or obligation. No longer in existence. The end of something.

EXTINGUIR. To put an end to something. To terminate, extinguish.

EXTINTO. Extinct. That which is already extinguished and lacks existence. Without life.

EXTORSIÓN. Extortion, blackmail. The obtaining of property from another induced by wrongful use of actual or threatened force, violence, or fear.

EXTORSIONADO. Blackmailed. The person who is suffering from an extortion. The victim forced to act against his or her will under threat.

EXTORSIONAR. To extort. The act by means of which one person is forced to do or give something under fear of violence or intimidation.

EXTORSIONISTA. Extortioner. Blackmailer. The criminal who demands something from another by inflicting fear or threatening to cause injury or harm.

EXTRACONTRACTUAL. Not in the contract. That which is effected outside the terms of the contract.

EXTRADICIÓN. Extradition. The surrender by one state or country to another of an individual accused or convicted of an offense outside its own territory and within the territorial jurisdiction of the other.

EXTRAJUDICIAL. Extrajudicial, out of court. That act done or performed outside the judicial proceedings and beyond the scope of the court. Not within the judge's authority.

EXTRALIMITACIÓN. Overstepping. To go beyond the limits of. To carry on an act without the power to do it. To do something without authorization.

EXTRAMATRIMONIAL. Out of wedlock. A relation taking place between a married person and another one not married to the first one.

EXTRANJERO. Alien. Person born outside a country and who is not considered a citizen of it. A foreign person.

EXTRAOFICIAL. Unofficial. Not formal. Not sanctioned by an authorized person or entity. Given outside the scope of the official course of dealing.

EXTRATERRITORIAL. Extraterritorial. Occurrence beyond the limits of a specific territory. Having effects beyond the judicial boundaries of a state.

EXTRATERRITORIALIDAD. Extraterritoriality. Principle which grants validity to some acts in one state when they have occurred outside the limits of its territory. That which extends beyond the boundaries of one state and has effects in another country.

EXTREMISTA. Extremist. The person whose ideas and acts go beyond reasonable limits. Quality of being at one extreme of a continuum. Beyond the average and normal conduct.

F

FABRICADO. Fabricated (evidence). Something that has been done for the purpose of demonstrating or proving something else.

FACIO UT DES. (Lat.) "I do if you give." This is a Latin expression used in a contract to show the kind of consideration involved.

FACIO UT FACIAS. (Lat.) "I do if you do." Expression from Latin by which the parties state the reason to enter into a contract.

FACCIÓN. Faction. (1) Group or band of rebels. (2) Features of a human face.

FACSÍMIL. Facsimile. An exact copy of the original.

FACTO. In fact. Something done. It refers to things or events taking place by themselves or without considering the law, but not necessarily against the law. In a political sense it means the kind of government installed with violence after overthrowing another one.

FACTOR. Factor. An agent employed by a businessman to buy, sell and in general administer a particular business or businesses.

FACTUM. Fact. The facts involved in the lawsuit as opposed to those pertaining to the law itself, known as questions of law.

FACTURA. Invoice, bill. A written itemized statement detailing the quantity, value or prices of merchandise shipped or sent to a purchaser.

FACULTAD. Faculty. Power. Authority. Capability. (1) The power to do something, especially those things permitted or not prohibited by law. (2) The teaching body of a university or school.

FACULTAR. To empower. To give someone else the power to do something.

FACULTATIVO. Pertaining to faculty. (1) Relative to empower. (2) Those things that may or may not be done at one's will.

FALACIA. Deceit, fallacy, lie.

FALENCIA. Deceit, bankruptcy. (1) Said or done with the intent to lie. (2) Unable to pay its debts.

FALIBILIDAD. Fallibility. Liable or likely to err.

FALSA PRUEBA. False evidence. Fabricated evidence presented to a court with the intent to deceive said court.

FALSARIO. Falsifier. Forger. The person telling a lie or forging.

FALSAS APARIENCIAS. False pretenses. A lie told to deceive another person out of his or her money or property.

FALSEDAD. Falsehood. Lack of truth or authenticity. Not real or untrue. Fabricated act or statement known to be untrue and told or done to deceive.

FALSIFICACIÓN. Falsification. Forgery. To alter something or give it a false appearance by imitation, alteration or addition. It is considered a crime.

FALSIFICADOR. Counterfeiter, forger.

FALSIFICAR. To falsify. Counterfeit, forge.

FALSO. Fake. Forged. False. Untrue.

FALSO TESTIMONIO. Perjury. Crime committed when a witness, a translator or another deliberately distorts, denies or refrains from stating the whole or part of the truth while under oath.

FALSOS PRETEXTOS. False pretenses. See "Falsas Apariencias".

FALTA. Fault. Defect. Flaw. Misdemeanor. Minor violation or infraction of the law.

FALLAR. To rule, to pass judgment. To err or miss. To decide or resolve a dispute arising from a trial, determining the rights and obligations of the parties.

FALLECIMIENTO. Decease, death. Permanent cessation of all vital biological functions and signs.

FALLIDO. Bankrupt. When a person is unable to pay his or her debts because his or her liabilities are larger than his or her assets.

FALLO. Verdict. Judgment. Action and effect of passing judgment in a controversy. It can refer to the award given by an arbitrator in a dispute submitted to his or her knowledge.

FAMA PÚBLICA. Reputation. What people in a community think about a person.

FAMILIA. Family. Group of two persons or more living together under one head or management. A group of blood-relatives.

F.A.S. Free along side. Clause or article in a contract for the delivery of goods at the port next to the vessel or carrier.

FASCISMO. Fascism. A centralized system of government which promotes the supremacy of the State over individuals through a strong national policy.

FATAL. Fatal. Final.

FE. Testimony; credence. (1) **Dar fe.** To attest. (2) **De buena fe.** In good faith. Done with good intention and thinking it was right. (3) **De mala fe.** In bad faith. Done with intent to harm.

FE PÚBLICA. Authority to attest documents. Authority given to some public officers to attest the authenticity of documents.

FECHA. Date. The time (day, month, year) in which something happened.

FECHA CIERTA. Fixed date. Time from which private documents have full value to the parties and to third persons affected by it.

FECHORÍA. Malfeasance, misdeed.

FEDATARIO. One who attests or certifies. Notary Public.

FEDERACIÓN. Federation. Association or group of persons who have a common interest, purpose or goal.

FEDERAL. (1) A federal union comprises two or more states into one strong central government with many powers left to the states. (2) The United States federal government is the national, as opposed to state, government.

FEHACIENTE. Authentic. Certifying with full credibility.

FELÓN. Felon. Criminal. A person who commits a major crime (a felony) and is still serving time for it.

FELONÍA. Felony. (1) A serious crime. (2) Generally a crime with a sentence of one year or more.

FERIADO. Holiday. Days in which the public offices are closed. These days do not count during the computation of time in a court proceeding.

FESTIVO. Holiday. See "Feriado".

FETICIDA. One guilty of killing a fetus.

FETICIDIO. Feticide. The act by which someone kills a fetus. It is in essence an abortion punishable by law.

FETICHISMO. Fetishism. It is a psychological diversion in which the sexual instinct is aroused by touching, looking at, or smelling objects.

FETO. Fetus. An unborn child. The unborn offspring of a viviparous animal.

FEUDAL. Feudal. Relative to feudalism. Usually the lord who charged the vassal for the use of his land during the 9th through 15th century in Europe.

FEUDALISMO. Feudalism. Social and political system in which the vassal paid the lord for protection and for the use of his land in Europe during the 9th through 15th century.

FIADOR. Surety. One who undertakes to pay money or to do any other act in the event that his or her principal fails to do so.

FIADOR JUDICIAL. Bailor. The person who becomes surety for the appearance of a defendant in court.

FIANZA. Bond (surety); bail. An obligation of a person (the guarantor) to pay a second party upon default by a third party to the second party.

FIANZA DE CUMPLIMIENTO. Performance Bond. Guaranty protecting against loss due to non-performance of the obligation contracted.

FIAR. To give credit. To assure. To bail. To trust someone or something. To have confidence in someone.

FIAT. (Lat.) "Let it be done;" a command.

FICCIÓN LEGAL. Legal fiction. Assumption of law that something which is or may be false is true. It is a supposition of a fact upon a rule of law which allows something to be established as true.

FIDEDIGNO. Reliable. Something that can be trusted because it emanates from a source worthy of credit.

FIDEICOMISARIO. Trustee. Fiduciary. "Cestui que" trust. (1) The "cestui que" trust or person in favor of whom a trust was created. The beneficiary of a trust. (2) The term is also used to describe the trustee itself. See "Fiduciario". The person to whom confidence is given to act or manage in benefit of another. (3) Recently this word is used as "fiduciario" to call the person in charge of the management of debentures for another. It is the person empowered to act as the legal representative of the debenture holder.

FIDEICOMISO. Trust. A right of property, real or personal, held by one party for the benefit of another. The arrangement by which property is transferred to a trustee to manage it for the benefit of another called "cestui que" trust.

FIDEICOMITENTE. Settlor. One who creates a trust. The person who gives property to another called trustee for the benefit of a third one called cestui que trust.

FIDELIDAD. Fidelity. Faithfulness. Honor. Loyalty.

FIDUCIARIO. Trustee. Person who holds property in trust for another. The person empowered to administer property in trust for the benefit of another called cestui que trust.

FIJACIÓN o FIJAR EN LISTA. To fix or place in a board. The act of posting documents at the court's board for a period of time during the proceedings for the parties to be informed of them.

FILIACIÓN. Filiation. (1) Relation of children with parents. (2) Dependence or relation of some things upon others. (3) The act of taking notice or writing down the personal data.

143

FILIACIÓN PARTIDISTA o POLÍTICA. To enroll or register oneself in a political party.

FILIAL. Filial. A branch. An establishment depending on another one called headquarters or main office.

FILICIDA. Filicide. One who kills his or her child.

FILICIDIO. Filicide. The act of murdering one's own child.

FILIGRANA. Filigree. Filigrane. Transparent line or mark made in the paper during its elaboration. It is important to determine its authenticity.

FILOSOFÍA DEL DERECHO. (1) Jurisprudence. The science which has for its function to ascertain the principles on which legal rules are based. (2) The interpretation of the law by the courts.

FIN. End. Termination. Purpose. Goal.

FINADO. Deceased. Dead person.

FINANZA. Finance. The administration of money.

FINANZAS PÚBLICAS. Administration of public and government funds. It refers to the collecting and managing of money and properties belonging to one state.

FINCA. Property. Real estate. Farm.

FINIQUITO. Release. Written evidence in which the discharge of an obligation is expressed.

FIRMA. Signature. Office. Law office. (1) A written representation of a person's name to attest the validity of an instrument. (2) Place where business is conducted, especially the office where lawyers work.

FIRMA COMERCIAL. Firm name. The name or title under which a company transacts its business.

FISCAL. (1) The district attorney. Prosecutor. A public official who represents the state in the case against a person accused of a crime. (2) Anything pertaining to the treasury.

FISCALÍA. District attorney's office.

FISCO. State or national treasury.

FLAGRANTE. Flagrant. Crime detected while being perpetrated.

FLETADOR. Freighter. The charterer of a vessel that transports persons or cargo. The tenant of a ship.

FLETAMENTO. Charter. A contract by which one person (the charterer) takes over the use of the whole or part of a ship belonging to another (the owner) for the conveyance of goods or persons to one or more places.

FLETANTE. Shipowner. One who owns any means of transport for hire. The shipowner whose vessel has been rented to transport persons or goods.

FLETAR. To charter, to hire. The renting of a ship to transport persons or goods.

FLETE. Freight. The price or compensation paid for the transportation of goods by a carrier.

FLOTA. Fleet. (1) The group of vessels of one nation or company. (2) Ships sailing together.

FLUJO DE FONDOS. Cash flow. Amount of cash left from cash receipts after payments are made.

FLUVIAL. Pertaining to river.

F.O.B. F.O.B. "Free on Board." The selling price of goods includes transportation costs to the F.O.B. point, which is a specific place named in the contract.

FOJA. Page.

FOLIAR. To foliate. To number pages of a book or file.

FOLIO. Folio. Page of a book, notebook or file.

FONDO. Bottom. Essence. Base.

FONDO MONETARIO INTERNACIONAL. International Monetary Fund. Agency of the United Nations established to stabilize international exchange and promote balanced international trade.

FONDOS. Funds. A sum of money or other liquid asset set aside for a specific purpose, or available for the payment of debts or claims.

FONDOS PÚBLICOS. Public funds. Money or liquid assets available to be used by the government.

FORENSE. Forensic. Legal. Belonging to or connected with law. (1) **Médico forense.** Forensic doctor. The doctor who applies his or her medical knowledge for the benefit of the law.

FORMA. Form. Legal or technical manner or order to be observed in legal instruments or judicial proceedings, or in the construction of legal documents or processes.

FORMAL. Formal. Pertaining to form as opposed to substance.

FORMAS DE GOBIERNO. Kinds of government. Different ways in which the nation can organize its political structure.

FORMALIDAD. Formality. The conditions required by law in the making of contracts or in conducting legal proceedings, to insure their validity and consistency.

FORMULARIO. Formulary. Printed blank form.

FORNICACIÓN. Fornication. Unlawful sexual intercourse between two unmarried persons.

FORNICAR. To fornicate. Having sex outside marriage.

FORO. (1) Forum. A place of litigation. (2) Bar. The whole body of the members of the legal profession.

FORTUITO. Fortuitous, casual. Occurring by chance or accident. (1) **Caso Fortuito.** Act of God. Fortuitous event. That unavoidable and unforseen event which occurs either by an act of the nature or by the hand of the man. It is just cause for the breach of a contract. See "Fuerza Mayor".

FORTUNA. Luck. Fate. Fortune. Wealth.

FORZADO. Forced. (1) Person convicted to hard labor. (2) Something that has been forced.

FORZAMIENTO. Done with violence. Breaking into. Forcing.

146

FORZAR. To force. To break. To rape. To do something by strength.

FORZOSO. Unavoidable, compulsory. Obligatory.

FRACTURA. To break.

FRAGRANTE. Flagrant. See "Flagrante".

FRANCO. Duty free. Honest.

FRANCO A BORDO. Free on board. F.O.B. The selling price already includes the cost of transportation of goods and delivery at seller's expense to the specified destination.

FRANQUEAR. To exempt, to pre-pay. To set free from a duty or from taxation. To pay proper postage.

FRANQUICIA. Franchise. (1) The license given by the owner of a trademark or trade name permitting another to sell a product or service under that name or mark. (2) Exempt from taxes. (3) Unit used to establish the amount of coverage in an insurance.

FRATERNIDAD. Fraternity. Brotherhood.

FRATICIDA. Fratricide. A person who murders his or her brother or sister.

FRATICIDIO. Fratricide. The killing of a brother or sister.

FRAUDE. Fraud. Deceit, trick.

FRAUDE DE ACREEDORES. Fraud committed against creditors. It refers to all those acts of the debtor done with the intent to deceive his or her creditors.

FRAUDE ELECTORAL. Political crime committed to prevent or obstruct voting or the proper counting of votes in an election.

FRENTE. Front. It also refers to political coalitions.

FRONTERA. Frontier, border. Boundary line between two countries.

FRUSTRADO. Thwarted. Frustrated. It refers to the punishable conduct of doing all the acts required to commit a crime that nevertheless is defeated by causes outside the criminal's control.

147

FRUTOS. Fruit. Benefit. Profit. Rent.

FRUTOS CIVILES. Rent, income, interest.

FRUTOS INDUSTRIALES. Goods or profits produced by cultivation or work.

FRUTOS NATURALES. Products from nature. Spontaneous production from nature like animals and fruits.

FUENTES DE DERECHO. Sources of the law. The origin from which particular laws derive their authority and force.

FUENTES DE LAS OBLIGACIONES. Sources of obligation. The acts and facts from which obligations and liabilities are originated. They are "contratos", "cuasi contratos", "delitos", "cuasi delitos" and the law. See these terms.

FUERO. Privilege. (1) Benefit enjoyed by a person, company or class, beyond the common advantage of other citizens. (2) Name given to some laws or compilation of laws. (3) Territorial jurisdiction in which a court has authority to act.

FUERO SINDICAL. Legal rights of organized labor. Privilege given to some union, activist and leaders by means of which their labor conditions may not be diminished.

FUERZA. Violence. Strength. Force.

FUERZA FÍSICA. Violence. Unjust use of physical force. The exercise of actual force against a person to have him or her do, not do or give something. It is an unlawful abuse of force. Its use is cause to render void the act performed.

FUERZA MAYOR. Force majeure, acts of God. Fortuitous event. Cause outside the control of the parties in a contract, that cannot be avoided by exercise of due care. An event caused entirely by nature alone. It is a fortuitous event. Formerly there was a distinction between "Fuerza Mayor" and "Caso Fortuito". The first was used to refer to unforseen acts caused by man and the second one to unforseen acts caused by nature. Nowadays these two terms refer to the same unforseen and unavoidable act and both are just cause for non-compliance or performance of an obligation.

FUERZA MORAL. Intimidation. Unlawful use of coercion. The exercise of duress against a person's will in order to have him or her do, not do or give something. Its use is cause for the annulment of the act.

FUERZA PÚBLICA. Public force. The body of agents in charge of keeping the order in a country.

FUGA. To escape. To elope. Leak.

FUGITIVO. Fugitive. A person who commits a crime and either leaves the area or hides to avoid prosecution.

FUNCIONARIO PÚBLICO. Public official. The holder of a public office, and who exercises a portion of the sovereign power.

FUNDACIÓN. Foundation. Permanent fund established and maintained by contributions for charitable, educational, religious or other benevolent purpose.

FUNDAMENTO JURÍDICO. Legal base or legal ground. The main reason on which a legal argument is based.

FUNDO. Rural property. Country property. Land.

FUNDO DOMINANTE. Dominant tenement. That particular parcel of land that is benefited as a result of an easement on a servient estate.

FUNDO SIRVIENTE. Servient tenement. The estate upon which an easement is placed for the benefit of another.

FUNGIBLE. Fungible, consumable. Movable goods which may be easily replaced one for another.

FUSIL. Rifle. Arm used to kill.

FUSILAMIENTO. To shoot and kill a person with a firing squad. This was one way of executing the death penalty.

FUSIÓN (DE EMPRESAS). Merger. The fusion or absorption of one thing into another. The term is generally used in commercial law to refer to the absorption of one company by another, the absorbing company retaining its own name, identity and assets, and the absorbed company ceasing to exist as a separate business entity.

G

GABARRO. (1) Flaw or defect in goods. (2) Error or mistake. (3) Burdensome obligation.

GABELA. In a general sense any (1) tax, duty or contribution which is paid to a government; (2) advantage or edge given to someone in a game.

GABINETE. Cabinet. The body of ministers which counsels the leader of a nation.

GACETA. Gazette. Official publication of laws, regulations and affairs of state. A newspaper which publishes the laws and contracts in which the nation is involved. The official newspaper in which the nation makes public the executive regulations, laws and judiciary orders.

GAJE. Wage. Salary. Payment received for the performance of a service or job.

GAJES DEL OFICIO. Expression used in a figurative sense to represent those inconveniences which one has to suffer while performing a service or job.

GALAFATE. Artful thief. Cunning rogue.

GALLARDETE. Pennant, flag.

GANADO. Livestock, cattle, herd, flock. Also means earned.

GANANCIA. Gain. The profit obtained by means of work or lucrative activity. Difference between cost and sale price. Benefit received. The benefit received from a transaction minus the cost of said transaction.

GANANCIA REALIZADA. Gain or profit realized.

GANANCIA RECONOCIDA. Recognized gain or profit.

GANANCIAS DE CAPITAL. Capital gains. Profit made in a capital asset transaction. The surplus over the basis or cost resulting from the sale of a capital asset.

150

GANANCIAS Y PÉRDIDAS. Profit and loss. The gain or benefit arising from a transaction and the expenses or loss from the transaction. The accounting of what is owed or lost and what is earned or gained in a transaction.

GANANCIALES. Property held jointly by husband and wife. It is a contract by means of which husband and wife agree to hold in common the property acquired by either one during marriage. Some jurisdictions consider community property rights to be in effect upon marriage if not otherwise specified. Other states do not consider it an implied contract and require that the spouses expressly agree to it.

GANAR. Gain. (1) To earn money or acquire goods. (2) To win.

GANCHO. (1) Hook. (2) Crook. Enticing through cunning and deceit.

GANGA. Anything acquired for less than its real value.

GARANTE. Guarantor. Person who gives a guaranty. One who becomes secondarily liable for another's debt.

GARANTÍA. Guaranty. (1) Contract whereby security for a debt or performance is given. (2) Warranty. An expressed statement that some situation or thing is as it appears to be. (3) **Bono de garantía.** Surety bond.

GARANTÍAS CONSTITUCIONALES o INDIVIDUALES. Constitutional rights. Rights guaranteed to the citizens by the constitution.

GARANTIZADO. Guaranteed, warranted.

GARANTIZAR. To guarantee, warrant.

GASTOS. Costs. Expenses incurred to acquire goods or services. Money paid for the procurement of something.

GASTOS DE REPRESENTACIÓN. Business expenses. Those expenses incurred during business and directly related to the business. Money allowed to be expended by a high level employee for the purpose of conducting business or maintaining a status.

GASTOS JUDICIALES. Costs. Fee, expenses and cost established by law payable by the losing party in a lawsuit to the winning party for expenses incurred during the legal proceedings. This money is awarded by the court.

GENERALES DE LA LEY. Personal data. Personal circumstances as to which one person must be questioned to identify oneself. The information which describes a person. It refers to the name, occupation, age, civil status, residency, etc.

GÉNERO. Gender. A general class of the same kind or kin.

GENOCIDIO. Genocide. To systematically kill a specific racial, political, or cultural group.

GENTE. People. Folk. Crowd. Nation.

GENTIL. Gentile. Pagan, worshiper of idols.

GENTILICIO. Relative to a nation.

GERENTE. Manager. Person in charge of the administration of a corporation or mercantile enterprise.

GESTIÓN. Effort. Action taken for the accomplishment of a goal.

GESTIÓN DE NEGOCIO AJENO. A quasi contract in which one party acts for the benefit of another without having been authorized to do so by the other party. Nevertheless, expenses incurred are recoverable.

GESTOR. Agent. Person who promotes functions or events for the benefit of third parties.

GIRADO. Drawee. The person requested to pay or honor a draft. In a check the drawee is the bank that issues the check book from which the check was drawn. The drawee is the one accepting to pay the money to the payee specified in the draft by the drawer who has drawn the negotiable note.

GIRADOR. Drawer, maker. Person who draws a bill or draft. In a check, the drawer is the one who signs it.

GIRAR. To draw. To draw and sign a negotiable instrument. To write a negotiable instrument and sign it. To draw a draft.

GIRO. Draft. The issuance through a bank of a payment order. Money order. It is a negotiable instrument by which one party, called the drawer, gives an instruction to another, called the drawee, to pay the amount of money therein specified to the beneficiary called payee. It is a written instruction drawn by the drawer directed to the drawee to pay the sum of money therein established at the given date to the payee or to his or her order.

GLOSA. Gloss. Explanation, commentary or interpretation of a text.

GOBERNADOR. Governor. (1) The chief executive officer of a state in the United States. (2) The highest public official from the executive branch in a specific geographic section of one country.

GOBERNAR. To govern; to manage, direct.

GOBIERNO. Government. The whole class or body of officeholders or functionaries considered in the aggregate, that handle the executive, judicial, legislative and administrative business of the state.

GOCE. Enjoyment. Possession and use of a right with satisfaction.

GOLPE DE ESTADO. Coup d'état. Political move to overthrow the existing government by force.

GRABADO. Engraved. Carved. Etching. Illustration.

GRACIA. Pardon. (1) Amnesty or commutation of sentence granted by the executive power. (2) **Período de Gracia.** Period of time in which an obligation will not be enforced or will not have to be performed. Compliance with an obligation is exempt during this time.

GRADO. Grade. Degree. (1) Class of value or quality. (2) Legal extent of guilt or negligence in a crime. (3) Measure of the distance in the relationship of two persons whether by blood or affinity.

GRADO DE AFINIDAD. Degree of affinity. The distance which separates two persons who are related by affinity.

GRADO DE CONSANGUINIDAD. Degree of consanguinity. Kindred degree. The measure of the distance in the relationship by blood between two persons.

GRADUACIÓN. Grading. (1) The act of receiving or giving an academic degree. (2) Measuring something by degree or grade.

153

GRADUACIÓN DE ACREEDORES. Rating or classification given to creditors in order to establish the respective place or preference between them and with regard to the debtor.

GRADUACIÓN DE LA PENA. The judge's determination of the time of imprisonment established according to the limits set by law.

GRAN JURADO. Grand jury. Group of persons which receives complaints and accusations of crime, hears preliminary evidence on the complaining side, and makes formal accusations or indictments.

GRANJA PRISIÓN. Prison ranch. Farm where prisoners work the land and do other chores for the benefit of the state.

GRATIFICACIÓN. Gratification. Monetary reward for merit or services rendered.

GRATUITO. Gratuitous. (1) Free, given for nothing. (2) **Contrato Gratuito.** Contract in which there is no consideration. It is a valid contract in which something is given without receiving any consideration in exchange or something is received without giving any consideration in exchange.

GRAVADO. Affected with an encumbrance. Taxed. (1) Property upon which an encumbrance, lien or mortgage is placed. (2) Good or property that has been taxed.

GRAVAMEN. Encumbrance. A claim placed on a property. Lien.

GRAVAR. To tax.

GRAVE. Grave. Of importance, weighty. Something important and of great consequence.

GRAVIDEZ. Pregnant.

GREMIO. Guild, labor union. Organized group of persons who share the same profession.

GUARDIA. Guard. Person entrusted to keep or protect something or someone.

GUERRA. War. Armed conflict between two or more nations.

GUERRILLA. Guerrilla. Independent army organized to fight for a cause.

GUÍA. Bill of lading. Guide.

GUÍA AÉREA. Air bill of lading. A document evidencing receipt of goods, contract for their carriage, and title of goods which are transported by air.

GUÍA DE EMBARQUE. Bill of lading. See "Conocimiento de Embarque".

H

HABEAS CORPUS. (Lat.) Literally, "you have the body." Written petition commanding that a person detained be brought before competent authority. The purpose of this writ is to have an accused person released from unlawful imprisonment, regardless of guilt or innocence. A person has a constitutional right to be free unless he or she was lawfully imprisoned.

HABER. To have. Property.

HABER HEREDITARIO. Estate. The property left by a deceased to be inherited.

HABERES. Properties.

HÁBIL. Skillful, capable, able to understand; apt, qualified, of great ability or proficiency; expert. **Día Hábil.** Working day. Not a holiday.

HABILITACIÓN. Authorization; qualification. (1) Action whereby competency is granted to an incompetent party. (2) To adhere the necessary stamp duty to a petition or document for it to acquire full force and effect.

HABILITACIÓN DE BANDERA. Concession to a foreign vessel to engage in coastal trade.

HABILITAR. To authorize. To enable. To validate. To make something capable of being properly used.

HABITACIÓN. House. Building or place where people live. Also a room in a house, generally the bedroom.

HABITANTE. Inhabitant. Person who dwells on a permanent basis in a particular place.

HABITAR. To inhabit. To reside.

HABITUAL. Habitual. Usual or customary. Something happening with frequency or that which is common.

HACER. To make. The act of doing something.

HACER CONSTAR. To put on record. To take note for further reference.

HACER CUMPLIR. To enforce.

HACER RESPONSABLE. To find responsible or guilty.

HACER SABER. To let know. Expression used when something needs to be notified.

HACIENDA PÚBLICA. Public treasury. Aggregate of goods, real property and money which the government manages on behalf of a nation.

HALLAZGO. Find. Act of finding or recovering something lost.

HAMPÓN. Bold, valiant, licentious; daring, fearless, very free in behavior or manner; taking liberties, shameless; gangster. In its frequent sense means thief.

HECHO. Act, fact. A thing that took place, an event. It is the occurrence whether actual or past which creates, modifies or extinguishes rights and obligations.

HECHO FORTUITO. Casualty. It is the event that cannot be foreseen or prevented. These happenings are circumstances which justify the breach of a contract.

HECHURA. (1) Workmanship; to make something. (2) What's paid to a worker for completing a job.

HEREDAD. Parcel of land. Any property that is inheritable. An estate.

HEREDAD DOMINANTE. Dominant estate or tenement. It is the real estate in favor of which an encumbrance is created.

HEREDAD SIRVIENTE. Servient tenement. The real estate upon which an encumbrance is created for the benefit of another.

HEREDAR. To inherit.

HEREDERO. Heir, legatee, inheritor. Person who by virtue of law or by testament has a right to inherit property.

157

HEREDERO A INTESTATO. Intestate heir. One called to inherit when there is no will.

HEREDERO ABSOLUTO. Unconditional heir. One who inherits without reservations or conditions.

HEREDERO BENEFICIARIO. Beneficiary heir. One who inherits under the benefit of inventory. This heir will be responsible for the debts of the deceased only to the extent of the succession.

HEREDERO FORZOSO. Forced heir. Heir who cannot be disinherited. This heir is protected by law and cannot be excluded from a part of the estate unless there is just cause for disinheritance. A fixed portion is set by law to be inherited by this forced heir.

HEREDERO LEGAL. Legal heir. Heir who has a right, by virtue of law, to receive a fixed portion of the estate.

HEREDERO PURO Y SIMPLE. Unconditional heir. The one who inherits without reservation and thereby becomes responsible for all the debts of the deceased, even if these debts exceed the estate of the deceased. The one who inherits without benefit of inventory.

HEREDERO TESTAMENTARIO. Testamentary heir. One who is appointed as such in the testament of the decedent.

HEREDERO UNIVERSAL. Unconditional heir. The one who takes the whole or part of the estate and inherits all the corresponding rights and obligations of the deceased.

HERENCIA. Inheritance, legacy. Property received from a dead person, either by the effect of laws, or through a will. it is also known as the estate. It is the property left by a deceased.

HERENCIA VACANTE. Vacant estate. Estate without known or existing heirs, or with heirs that are incompetent or who have waived their right to inherit. The estate is then transferred to the state or city.

HERENCIA YACENTE. Undecided estate. Whenever an heir has not yet received his or her portion of the estate. This is the name given to the estate left by the decedent during the period of time between the opening of the succession and the acceptance of the estate by the heir.

HERIDA. Injury. Wound to break the continuity in the body tissue. Mental or physical damage.

HERMAFRODITA. Hermaphrodite. Having both female and male organs. Being both man and woman or not being either one.

HERMANOS. Brothers. Males who share the same parents, or the same father or mother. (Feminine would be "hermanas.")

HERMANO BASTARDO. Bastard brother. An illegitimate child who shares a parent with a legitimate child.

HERMENÉUTICA. The science which interprets books and establishes their meaning.

HERMENÉUTICA JURÍDICA. Jurisprudence. The art of interpreting the law and legal texts.

HIC ET NUNC. Here and now. Latin expression of importance for its reference to place and time of rights and obligations.

HIDALGO. Noble. Person entitled to certain rights by virtue of being of noble descent.

HIJA. Daughter. The immediate female descendant of a person.

HIJASTRA. Stepdaughter.

HIJASTRO. Stepson.

HIJO. Son. The immediate male descendant of a person.

HIMEN. Hymen. The vaginal membrane through which the menstruation flows. It is torn when virginity is lost.

HIPOTECA. Mortgage. The putting up of real property in exchange for a loan. An "in rem" right created upon real property to guarantee the performance of a certain act. It is a lien or pledge of real estate to secure the performance of an obligation. This conveyance secures with property the performance of an obligation or debt. Conveyance of title does not occur unless the debt is not satisfied. The property securing the debt needs to be real property. Vessels and aircrafts can be mortgaged to secure a debt.

HIPOTECA NAVAL. Naval mortgage. Mortgage where the object which guarantees the performance of an obligation is a vessel.

HIPOTECANTE. Mortgagor. One who pledges his or her property as security for a debt. The owner of real estate that secures the payment of debt.

HIPOTECAR. To hypothecate, to pledge, to mortgage. The pledging of property to a creditor as security for the payment of a loan.

HIPOTECARIO. Mortgagee. One who takes or receives a mortgage. The creditor to whom the payment of a debt is guaranteed with real estate or other property.

HIPOTÉTICO. Hypothetical. The process of setting up a series of facts, assuming that they are true, and asking for an answer to a question based on those facts.

HISPANO. Spanish.

HISPANOAMERICANO. Spanish-American.

HISTERIA. Hysteria. Affliction of the nervous system which causes substantial changes in one's behavior.

HISTORIAL. Record, history, antecedents.

HISTORIAL PENAL Y POLICIVO. Criminal record. A written account of a person's crimes or misdemeanors. A document submitted by an authorized officer containing the history in successive order of the crimes, misdemeanors or violations committed by one person, used as evidence of that person's past conduct.

HITO. Landmark. Milestone. A sign placed to establish a limit or to mark a boundary.

HOGAR. Homestead. Home. A place occupied by the owner and his or her family and exempted from seizure or forced sale to meet general debts.

HOJA. Page. Leaf. Sheet.

HOJA DE SERVICIOS. Document in which the working history of one person is recorded.

HOJA DE VIDA. Curriculum vitae, résumé. A written account of one person's life. A history of the important events in one's existence.

HOLÓGRAFO. Holograph. The testament written entirely by the decedent. Handwritten and signed by the deceased.

HOMENAJE. Homage. Allegiance. Respect. Faculty.

HOMICIDA. Murderer. (1) The author of a homicide. The person who kills another. The criminal who takes another life. (2) Anything used to cause death.

HOMICIDIO. Homicide. Death caused to a person by another. The killing of a person. It does not necessarily constitute a crime. It is punishable only when knowingly intended to cause death.

HOMICIDIO CULPOSO. Excusable homicide. homicide by misadventure or necessity. Negligence homicide. It is a kind of homicide in which there is a total lack of the intent to kill. It could occur when doing something permitted by law which then results in a death or when acting in self-defense or while trying to arrest an escaping criminal or when committed with negligence.

HOMICIDIO DOLOSO. Murder. The willful and intended killing of a human being.

HOMICIDIO PRETERINTENCIONAL. Manslaughter. The killing of a human being, without premeditation, in the act of committing another crime. The death caused to a person by one who intended a harm or injury but not the killing itself.

HOMOLOGACIÓN. Homologation. (1) Confirmation by a court of justice of certain acts and agreements of the parties. (2) The implicit confirmation or acceptance of the parties to the arbitrator's award because it has not been appealed on time.

HOMOSEXUAL. Homosexual.

HOMOSEXUALIDAD. Homosexuality. The manifestation of erotic attraction of an individual to others of the same sex.

HONESTIDAD. Honesty. Refraining from lying, cheating, or stealing; being truthful, trustworthy or upright.

HONESTO. Honest. Decent. The quality of a person who acts honestly.

HONOR. Honor. Quality of the person who is respected because of compliance with established moral principles.

HONORABLE. Reputable, honorable, reliable. Of good reputation.

HONORARIO. (1) Honorary. An office or position held as an honor only, without service or pay. (2) Fee, honorarium. A voluntary donation.

HONORARIOS. Fees. Stipend paid for services rendered.

HONORARIOS DE ABOGADOS. Attorney's fees.

HONRADEZ. Honesty, integrity. The quality or state of being of sound moral principle; upright, honest, and frank.

HONRAR. (1) To honor. High regard or great respect given, received, or enjoyed. (2) To accept and pay when due; to meet an obligation.

HONRA. Honor. Respect and esteem of own dignity.

HONRAS FÚNEBRES. Funeral honors. Last respects showed at the funeral.

HORARIO DE TRABAJO. Working schedule. Specific hours of labor for each day of the week.

HORAS EXTRAORDINARIAS. Overtime. Work performed beyond the regular working schedule. Work performed during this time should be paid at an additional rate.

HORAS LABORABLES. Working hours. Time of the day in which an employee is regularly scheduled to work.

HOSTILIDAD. Hostility. Acts of war. Armed conflict.

HUELGA. Strike. A willful withholding or slowing-down by employees to extract concessions from an employer. A cessation of work by employees to demand better working conditions or higher wages or to enforce compliance with a collective bargaining agreement.

HUELLAS DIGITALES. Fingerprints. Impressions left by the fleshy tips of the fingers.

HÚERFANO. Orphan. Person (particularly a minor or infant) who has lost a father or mother or both.

HUMANIDAD. Humanity. Science which studies the nature, philosophy and culture of mankind.

HUMANISTA. Humanist. Said of the person who preaches the principles of mankind.

HURTAR. To rob, steal. See "Hurto".

HURTO. Theft. Act of taking property of another without violence or consent for the purpose of gain.

I

ID EST. (Lat.) That is.

IDEM. (Lat.) The same; the same as that previously mentioned.

IDENTIDAD. (1) Identity. The condition or fact of being some specific person or thing; individuality. (2) Sameness. When the persons or things before the judge are identical to what they have claimed to be.

IDENTIFICACIÓN. Identification. The act of proving that a person, subject, or article before the court is the very same that he, she or it is alleged, charged, or reputed to be.

IDENTIFICAR. To identify. To establish the identity or nature of something.

IDEOLOGÍA. Ideology. Branch of the philosophical sciences that deals with the origin and classification of ideas.

IDEOGRAMA. Symbol which conveys a message or an idea.

IDIOTA. Idiot. In civil law, any individual mentally inferior to a two-year-old child. The term is relevant to determine what legal consequences an act by an idiot may produce.

IDIOTEZ. Idiocy. An idiotic act. A degree of mental inferiority (usually equivalent to a two-year-old child) which negates an individual legal responsibility or capacity.

IDONEIDAD. Competence. Fitness to carry out a post. Legally speaking an expert is considered competent when he or she is able to issue an informed opinion regarding the specific matters or problems brought to his or her attention.

IDÓNEO. Competent. Fit to perform a task or duty. Capable.

IGNORADO. Ignored. Not noted, acknowledged or paid attention to.

IGNORANCIA. Ignorance. The condition or quality of being ignorant; lack of knowledge, facts, education, etc.

IGNORANTIA NON EXCUSAT LEGEM. (Lat.) Ignorance of the law is no excuse. In most jurisdictions, ignorance of the law is not a valid excuse for non-compliance.

IGUALA. Agreement. Convention or stipulation whereby parties reach an accord.

IGUALDAD. Equality. Possessing the same qualities, quantities or nature as another thing or person.

IGUALDAD ANTE LA LEY. Equal protection under the law. Constitutional principle that no person or class of persons shall be denied the same protection of the laws which is enjoyed by other persons or other classes in similar circumstances.

IGUALITARIO. Equitable. Just; conforming to the principles of justice and right.

ILEGAL. Illegal, unlawful, prohibited by law. Against the law. Generally all unlawful acts are null and void.

ILEGALIDAD. Illegality. All which is contrary to the law.

ILEGISLABLE. That which cannot be legislated.

ILEGITIMIDAD. Illegitimacy. The fact, condition, or quality of being illegitimate, specifically, bastardy.

ILEGÍTIMO. Illegitimate. (1) Children born out of lawful wedlock. (2) Illegal. That which is contrary to law.

ILESO. Unharmed. Unhurt. Unscathed. Sound.

ILÍCITO. Illicit, unlawful, prohibited, unauthorized, improper. Not allowed by law, custom, etc.

ILICITUD. Illicitness. What is not permitted morally nor legally.

ILÍQUIDO. Unliquidated, unpaid. Not determined, assessed or ascertained in amounts.

ILUSIÓN. Illusion. A mental impression or image which does not correspond with reality.

IMBÉCIL. Imbecile. Any individual mentally inferior to a child between two and seven years old. It is less serious in degree than an idiot. See "Idiota".

IMBECILIDAD. Imbecility. A degree of mental inferiority (usually equivalent to a child between two and seven years old) which negates legal responsibility or capacity.

IMITACIÓN. Imitation. The result or product of imitating. Artificial likeness, copy; a counterfeit. Made to resemble something else.

IMITADO. Imitated, copied. Something which has been reproduced or mimicked.

INMOBILIA. Real estate. "Bona Immobilia." In rem property. See "Inmuebles".

IMPAGABLE. Unpayable. Obligation which cannot be satisfied by the debtor.

IMPARCIAL. Impartial, fair. Favoring no side or party more than another; without prejudice or bias.

IMPARCIALIDAD. Impartiality. The act of being impartial.

IMPARTIR. To impart. To give, convey, or grant something.

IMPAVIDEZ. Intrepidity. Without fear.

IMPEDIDO. (1) Disabled, disqualified. Unable or unfit. Crippled, incapacitated. (2) Legally incapable.

IMPEDIMENTO. (1) Hindrance. Obstacle to the fulfillment of a contract, or to the holding of a public post. (2) Estoppel. When a party is prevented by his or her own acts from claiming a right to the detriment of the other party who was entitled to rely on such conduct and has acted accordingly.

IMPEDIR. To hinder. To bar or prevent an action. To stop.

IMPEDITIVO. Preventive. What stops or deters from doing something. It impedes the happening of an event.

IMPENSAS. Expense. Any cost or charge incurred in doing something.

IMPERATIVO. Imperative. Mandatory. Domineering.

IMPERATIVO LEGAL. Requirement of law. A mandatory provision which must be complied with.

IMPERDONABLE. Unpardonable. A fault so serious that the aggravated party or the judge cannot forgive it.

IMPERFECTO. Imperfect. Not of the best possible quality. Not complete. Containing defects.

IMPERIALISMO. Imperialism. Political system advocating the expansion of a nation at the expense of another until universal domination is achieved.

IMPERICIA. Incapacity; ineptitude. Lack of skill.

IMPERIO. Judicial authority. Jurisdiction. Imperium. The right to command, which includes the right to employ force to uphold the law.

IMPERMUTABLE. Unchangeable. That which cannot be changed.

IMPERTINENCIA. Impertinent. Not connected with the matter at hand.

IMPERTINENTE. Impertinent, irrelevant. Not relating or applicable to the matter at issue.

IMPLANTAR. To implant. To introduce and execute new practices. To set firmly in position.

IMPLICAR. Imply. To intend or infer, as opposed to actually expressing a thing in words.

IMPLÍCITO. Implicit, constructive, tacit. Capable of being understood without being said.

IMPLORAR. Implore. To call upon in supplication; beseech. To beg.

IMPONEDOR. Assessor. An officer chosen or appointed to appraise, value, or assess property.

IMPONENTE. Imposing. (1) Something that causes a strong impression because of its characteristics (i.e., size). (2) That which imposes something.

IMPONER. To assess, impose. To levy or exact by authority; to lay, as a burden, tax, duty or charge.

IMPONIBLE. Taxable. That which may be levied for purposes of taxation. See "Impuesto".

167

IMPORTACIÓN. Importation. The act of bringing goods and merchandise into a country from a foreign country.

IMPORTANTE. Important. Meaning a great deal; having much significance, consequence, or worth.

IMPORTE. Amount. Value or price of a thing.

IMPOSIBLE. Impossible. Not capable of being done or attained.

IMPOSIBILIDAD. Impossibility. That which may not be or not exist.

IMPOSIBILITAR. To prevent, to make impossible, to stop from doing or to impede an event.

IMPOSICIÓN. Imposition, an assessment, contribution or tax.

IMPOSITIVO. Burdensome, relating to taxation.

IMPOSTERGABLE. Undeferrable. That which may not be postponed or delayed.

IMPOSTOR(A). Impostor, impostress. One who pretends to be what he or she is not in order to cheat somebody.

IMPOTENCIA. Impotence. (1) The quality or state of being impotent. Lacking in power, strength, or vigor. (2) The inability to copulate.

IMPREMEDITADO. Unpremeditated. What was not planned beforehand.

IMPRESCINDIBLE. Essential. What is absolutely necessary.

IMPRESCRIBILIDAD. Non-prescriptible. Said of the actions and rights which are not extinguished due to the passage of time even if they are not enforced.

IMPRESCRIPTIBLE. Imprescriptible. That which may not be lost or barred because of inactivity by an interested party during a determined period of time. The term is usually used to refer to actions and rights and the possibility of exercising them after a long period of inactivity.

IMPRESIÓN DIGITAL. Fingerprints. The impression of a fingertip on any surface.

IMPREVISIBLE. Unforeseen. That which may not be known before-hand. That which may not be expected.

IMPREVISTO. Unforeseen, unexpected. What cannot be expected. Important in contract law since this lack of vision can affect the binding nature of a given contract. See "Clausula Rebus Sic Stanti-bus". Something that has not been foreseen.

IMPRECAR. Imprecate, invoke injury. To verbally express a wish that someone be harmed. To utter a curse.

IMPROCEDENTE. What cannot proceed. That which would not be admitted for lack of importance or relation to the current proceed-ings.

IMPRORROGABLE. Not extendible, not postponable.

IMPRUDENCIA. Imprudence. Lacking prudence or discretion.

IMPRUDENCIA CONCURRENTE. Contributory negligence. The omission or wrongful act by a person legally responsible for the care of the plaintiff which results in contributing negligence.

IMPRUDENCIA TEMERARIA. Gross negligence. The intentional act or failure to act without giving importance to the life or property of another. Reckless disregard.

IMPÚBER. Below the age of puberty.

IMPUESTO. Tax. Assessment. A monetary burden placed on indi-viduals, business entities, or property to support and carry on the legitimate functions of the government.

IMPUESTO DE SEGURO SOCIAL. Social security tax. Taxes paid by employers and employees. All resources collected from all work-ers and employers are then pooled and utilized for retirement or disability in the workforce.

IMPUESTO ESTIMADO. Estimated tax. Tax paid on a preliminary basis, taking into consideration the previous year's declaration. It is adjusted yearly when a final tax return is rendered.

IMPUESTO HEREDITARIO. Inheritance tax. Tax paid to receive the property from a decedent at death.

IMPUESTO INMOBILIARIO. Real estate tax. Tax levied for the ownership of real property.

IMPUESTO SOBRE BIENES INMUEBLES. Real estate tax. Taxes levied on the value of real properties.

IMPUESTO SOBRE LA RENTA. Income tax. See "Impuesto sobre Ingresos".

IMPUESTO SOBRE INGRESOS. Income tax. Tax levied on a person's income, including commission, wages and all other earnings.

IMPUESTO SOBRE VENTAS. Sales tax. Tax imposed on the sale of goods. The tax is paid by the buyer, but the seller is the person responsible to remit the tax to the state.

IMPUESTOS. Taxes. Sum of money collected from individuals, business entities, or property owners for the operation of the government.

IMPUGNABLE. Impeachable. Open to objection, legally vulnerable.

IMPUGNACIÓN. Impugnation. Objection, exception, refutation, legal attack. To contest the validity of an act.

IMPUGNANTE O IMPUGNADOR. Opposer, challenger. One who requests annulment or opposes any resolution or action.

IMPUGNAR. Impugn. To oppose, object, dispute, take exception. To request an annulment.

IMPULSO PROCESAL. The actions and steps performed during the course of a legal proceeding in order to move it forward.

IMPUNIDAD. Impunity. Exemption or protection from penalty or punishment.

IMPUTABLE. Imputable, chargeable. Being liable or responsible for conduct or omission.

IMPUTADO. Imputed. Attributed vicariously. Something is imputed to a person if, even though that person is not responsible for it, he or she is ultimately liable since the duty falls upon someone under his or her care or control.

IN ABSENTIA. (Lat.) In absence.

IN ARTICULO MORTIS. (Lat.) At the time or point of death.

IN DUBIIS ABSTINE. (Lat.) When in doubt, abstain.

IN DUBIO PRO OPERARIO. (Lat.) When there is doubt, favor the worker.

IN DUBIO PRO REO. (Lat.) When there is doubt, favor the defendant.

IN EXTREMIS. (Lat.) In the last illness.

IN FRAGANTI. (Lat.) In the act.

IN FRAUDEM LEGIS. (Lat.) In fraud of the law. With the intent or purpose of evading the law.

IN MEMORIAM. (Lat.) In memory.

IN PERSONAM. (Lat.) With reference to a person.

IN REM. (Lat.) With reference to property.

INABROGABLE. Indefeasible. That which may not be cancelled or repealed. Usually used to refer to laws or rights.

INACTUABLE. Not actionable. That for which an action will not lie.

INACEPTABLE. Unacceptable. That which may not be received or approved.

INADMISIBLE. Inadmissible. That which, under the established rules of law, cannot be admitted or received into evidence; for example, evidence obtained during an illegal search, or certain types of hearsay testimony.

INALIENABLE. Inalienable. That which cannot be bought or sold, or given away; for example, certain personal rights such as the right to be free.

INAMOVIBLE. Not removable from office. Right of certain public officers not to be removed from their posts until their office is terminated or only if proceedings prove their misconduct during their tenure.

INAPELABLE. Unappealable. Which cannot be appealed.

INAPLAZABLE. Undeferrable. That which may not be postponed or delayed.

INAPLICABLE. Inapplicable, irrelevant. That which lacks importance or significance. That which will not be applied.

INCAPACIDAD. Incapacity, incompetence. (1) Lack of legal capacity or ability to act. (2) An injury which prevents working.

INCADUCABLE. Not voidable. That which may not be lost or barred by the lapse of time. That which will not expire.

INCAPACITADO. Incapacitated, disabled; legally incompetent.

INCAPAZ. Incapable. Not qualified, incompetent. Said of the person who lacks the aptitude to exercise rights and contract obligations.

INCAUTACIÓN. Attachment of property, seizure, levy. The act or process of taking or seizing persons or property, by virtue of a judicial order, and bringing the same into the custody of the court for the purpose of securing satisfaction of the judgment ultimately to be entered in the action.

INCAUTAR. To impound, attach. To seize property pursuant to a writ of attachment.

INCENDIAR. Arson. To set on fire. The act of setting aflame.

INCENDIARIO. Arsonist. Person who sets property on fire willfully, with intent to cause harm.

INCENDIO. Fire, blaze. A crime against property by burning it.

INCESTO. Incest. Sexual intercourse between persons too closely related by blood to legally marry.

INCIERTO. Uncertain. Doubtful. Untrue. Unknown.

INCIDENCIA. Incidence. Something that happens in the course of an act and which is related to it.

INCIDENTAL. Incidental. Depending upon something else which is primary.

INCIDENTE. Incident. Occurrence. That which depends upon, pertains to, or follows another matter that is more worthy.

INCIPIENTE. Incipient. That which begins to exist.

INCISO. Division, section. Any distinct part into which a text is divided.

INCITADOR. Agitator. Instigator. One who urges or stimulates another to do something or take some action.

INCITAR. To incite. Instigate. Urge, provoke, strongly encourage, or stir up.

INCLUSIÓN. Inclusion, incorporation. The adding of something. Annexing.

INCOADO. Started, initiated. Something that has commenced or begun.

INCOAR. To initiate. To put into motion; to begin to do.

INCOBRABLE. Uncollectible. What cannot be recovered or collected.

INCOMPATIBILIDAD. Incompatibility, inconsistency. (1) Incapability of existing or being united together. (2) As grounds for divorce, it refers to such deep and irreconcilable conflict in personalities or temperaments between spouses that a normal marital relationship is impossible.

INCOMPATIBLE. Incompatible. That which may not be joined or coexist at the same time and place.

INCOMPETENCIA. Incompetency, incompetence. Lack of physical or legal ability or fitness to discharge the required duty.

INCOMPETENTE. Incompetent. (1) Lacking the qualities needed for effective action. (2) Not legally qualified.

INCOMUNICADO. Incommunicado. Status of a detained person who is denied permission to speak to anyone other than those in charge of his or her custody.

INCONCLUSO. Inconclusive. That which may be disproved or rebutted. That which is not completed.

INCONDICIONAL. Unconditional, absolute. Not limited by any conditions.

INCONFORME. In disagreement. One who is not in harmony or in accordance with someone or something.

INCONFORMIDAD. Unconformity. Not in accordance with someone or something.

INCONMUTABLE. Unexchangeable. That which may not be interchanged. That which may not be given in exchange for another.

INCONSECUENTE. Inconsequent. That which does not produce any effect. That which does not follow an order.

INCONSTITUCIONAL. Unconstitutional. Contrary to the constitution.

INCONSTITUCIONALIDAD. Unconstitutionality. Not in accordance with what the constitution prescribes.

INCORPORAR. Incorporate. To create a corporation; to grant a corporate franchise to certain persons engaged in a common enterprise.

INCORPÓREO. Incorporeal, intangible. That which does not have matter or substance or body.

INCOSTEABLE. Too expensive. That which may not be affordable or paid.

INCRIMINAR. Incriminate. To charge with a crime, to expose to an accusation or charge of crime.

INCULPADO. Accused, defendant. Person against whom a legal action is brought. One charged with committing a crime.

INCULPAR. To inculpate, accuse, incriminate. To charge someone with a crime.

INCUMPLIMIENTO. Noncompliance, default, failure of performance, breach of duty.

INCURRIR. To incur. To commit.

INDAGACIÓN. Investigation, examination. A careful inquiry seeking data or information.

INDAGADO. Inquired. A person who is under investigation.

INDAGADOR. Investigator. The person who conducts an inquiry.

INDAGAR. To investigate, to examine, to inquire into.

INDAGATORIA. Inquiry, investigation. The process of observing or studying by close examination and systematic inquiry.

INDAGATORIO. Inquiry. Investigation. Interrogatory. Process in search of the truth.

INDEBIDO. Unlawful, improper. What is not correct.

INDECENCIA. Indecency. What is morally incorrect.

INDECENTE. Indecent. One who acts improperly. Morally incorrect.

INDECISO. Undecided. One who has not made up his or her mind.

INDECLINABLE. Undeniable. That which may not be refused or denied or declined.

INDEFENDIBLE. Indefensible, vulnerable. That which may not be protected from an attack.

INDEFENSO. Without defense. That has means to defend itself.

INDELEBLE. Indelible. That which cannot be removed, washed away, or erased.

INDEMNIDAD. Indemnity. (1) Legal exemption from penalties or liabilities. (2) A contract to compensate or reimburse a person for possible losses of a particular type.

INDEMNIZACIÓN. Indemnity, indemnification. Compensation given to a person who has suffered a loss or damages.

INDEMNIZACIÓN POR DESPIDO. Severance pay. Payment to an employee upon termination of his or her employment.

INDEMNIZADO. Indemnified. One who has received an indemnity or a repayment of what was lost.

INDEPENDIENTE. Independent. Free from influence or control of others. Self supported.

INDEROGABLE. That which may not be revoked or annulled.

INDETERMINADO. Indeterminate. That which is uncertain, or not particularly designated.

175

INDICIO. Indication. Sign. Circumstantial evidence. A clue to what is unknown or unresolved. A fact which implies the existence of another.

INDICIOS. Indicia. Signs. Indications. Circumstances which point to the existence of a given fact as probable, but not certain.

INDILIGENCIA. Carelessness, negligence. The failure to exercise a reasonable amount of care in a situation that causes harm to someone or something.

INDIRECTO. Indirect. That which does not go straight to the point.

INDISOLUBLE. Undissoluble. Incapable of being dissolved, annulled, or undone.

INDISPENSABLE. Necessary, essential. What cannot be dispensed with. What is required.

INDISPUTABLE. Indisputable. Unquestionable, incontestable. That which is not disputable.

INDIVIDUAL. (1) A single person, as distinguished from a group or class. (2) A private or natural person, as distinguished from a partnership or corporation.

INDIVISIBLE. Indivisible. Not susceptible of division or apportionment; inseparable; entire.

INDIVISO. Undivided. That which has not been yet divided into parts.

INDOCUMENTADO. (1) Said of the person lacking documents required by law. (2) Not documented.

INDUBITABLE. Doubtless, or unquestionable. What is sure, certain. That which does not admit doubts.

INDULGENCIA. Forbearance, leniency, clemency.

INDULTAR. To pardon. To forgive, to exempt from punishment.

INDULTO. Amnesty. Total or partial pardon, by the governing power, of the sanctions imposed by a court of law.

INDUSTRIA. Industry. (1) Skill or ability to make something. (2) The manufacturing process or business.

176

INDUSTRIAL. Industrial, industrialist. Related to industry. One engaged in the business of production.

INEFICACIA. Inefficiency. (1) Quality of not being efficient. (2) Lacking legal effect.

INEFICAZ. ineffective. That which does not produce the expected effects.

INEFICIENTE. Inefficient, incompetent. Not capable of producing the desired results.

INEMBARGABLE. That which by virtue of law cannot be attached.

INEPTITUD. Ineptitude. Lack of competency, skill or ability to perform.

INEPTO. Inept. Not capable or competent for the desired purposes. A person lacking knowledge. Ignorant.

INEQUÍVOCO. Unequivocal. What is clear; that which does not admit more than one meaning. Certain.

INEVITABLE. Inevitable. Incapable of being avoided. That which will occur.

INEXIGIBLE. Not requireable. That which cannot be demanded.

INFALIBILIDAD. Infallibility. Quality of a person who is incapable of error, and who is not liable to mislead, deceive, or disappoint.

INFAMACIÓN. Defamation, slander. To purposely offend another's reputation.

INFAMIA. Infamy. The loss of a good reputation by conviction of a major crime, and the loss of certain legal rights that accompanies this conviction.

INFANCIA. Infancy. A general state of childhood. When something is new. In some states, however, it means the same as "minority."

INFANTICIDA. Infanticide. One who kills a child or a baby.

INFANTICIDIO. Infanticide. The murder of an infant soon after its birth.

INFERENCIA. Inference. A truth or proposition drawn from a fact which is assumed or admitted to be true.

INFERIOR. Inferior. (1) What is situated lower than another thing. (2) What is of less quantity, quality, authority, etc.

INFIDELIDAD. Infidelity. Unfaithfulness. Usually referring to commission of adultery by one spouse.

INFIEL. Unfaithful. Someone who cannot be trusted. Not loyal.

INFLUENCIA. Influence. Authority, power to cause the desired effects because of position or wealth.

INFLUENCIAR. To influence. To exercise the necessary power or authority upon another to produce a desired effect.

INFLUYENTE. Influential. One who has the required power to obtain the results he or she wants.

INFORMACIÓN. Information; report; brief.

INFORMADOR. Informer, informant. An undisclosed person who confidentially volunteers material information on crimes to law enforcement officers.

INFORMAL. Informal. That which does not require protocol or observance of fixed rules or customs.

INFORMANTE. Informer. See "Informador".

INFORME. Report. Verbal or written exposition regarding a particular matter.

INFRACTOR. Transgressor. One who breaks the law.

INFRACCIÓN. Infraction. Breach or infringement of a law, treaty, covenant, or agreement.

INFRA PETITA. (Lat.) Below what was claimed or requested. Whenever the court concedes less than was originally claimed.

INFRASCRITO. (Lat.) Undersigned, subscriber.

INFRINGIR. To infringe, breach, fail to observe the terms. Violation of a law or regulation.

178

INGERENCIA. Interference. To intervene in another's affairs.

INGRATITUD. Ingratitude. When a person does not appreciate the benefits or kindness received.

INGRESO o RENTA. Income. All earnings, salaries, rents or other income received by a person; income received on a monthly or annual basis or some other regular and periodic basis.

INGRESO BRUTO. Gross income. All income before any tax or deductions have been substracted.

INGRESO NETO. Net income. Income after all deductions allowed by law are subtracted from the gross income.

INGRESO TRIBUTABLE. Taxable income as computed on a tax return. Income upon which tax is to be paid.

INGRESOS. Earnings, receipts, income. The return in money from one's business, labor, or capital invested.

INHÁBIL. Unqualified, incompetent. Not having the required qualifications.

INHABILIDAD. Incompetence. Disability. Lack of ability, competency or skill. That which does not have the requirements to perform a duty or job.

INHABILITACIÓN. Disqualification. Disability. (1) The lack of legal capacity to perform an act. (2) Penalty that prohibits the exercise of certain rights or the eligibility for specific posts.

INHABILITADO. Unable. One who according to law is not capable of releasing an act with legal effects.

INHERENTE. Inherent. What exists in and is inseparable from something else.

INHIBICIÓN. Inhibition. To hold, to restrain.

INHIBIRSE. When a judge disqualifies himself or herself from presiding over a case because of a conflict of interest regarding one of the parties.

INHIBITORIO. Inhibitory. What restrains or prevents the happening of an event.

INHUMANIDAD. Inhumanity. A cruel action. Not having the sensibility that characterizes a human being.

INHUMAR. Inhume, inter. To bury a lifeless body.

INICIAR. To initiate. To start. To put in practice or use.

INICIATIVA. Initiative. The power or ability of introducing new ideas. The power of proposing laws to a legislative assembly for discussion and approval or consideration.

INÍCUO. Iniquitous. What is not in accordance with principles of justice and right.

INIQUIDAD. Iniquity. Gross injustice, action contrary to equity.

ININTELIGIBLE. Unintelligible. That which cannot be understood.

INJUSTIFICABLE. Unjustifiable. What may not prove that which is just or right. That which cannot be justified.

INJUSTIFICADO. Unjustified. What is not just, fair. Something that has not yet been justified.

INJURIA. Injury. To damage another's reputation. Oral defamation. Wrongdoing.

INJURIAR. To willfully insult, defame or damage another's reputation. To injure.

INJUSTICIA. Injustice. The denial of justice by an act, fault or omission of a court of law.

INJUSTO. Unjust, contrary to justice, unfair.

INMATERIAL. Immaterial. Not material, essential, or necessary; not important or pertinent.

INMEMORIAL. Immemorial. What is so old that it cannot be remembered. What is not kept by memory.

INMIGRACIÓN. Immigration. The coming into a country from another, for purposes of permanent residence.

INMOBILIARIO. Real estate. Land and anything permanently affixed to the land. The term is generally synonymous with real property.

INMORAL. Immoral. Contrary to good morals; detrimental to the public welfare. Not according to the standards of a given community, as expressed by law or otherwise.

INMORALIDAD. Immorality. The state of immorality. See "Immoral".

INMUEBLES. Immovables. Property which cannot be moved from one place to another, either by its nature or its attachment to an immovable object. Real or fixed property. See "Inmobiliario".

INMUNE. Immune; exempt. Not capable of being affected by sickness or by restrictions. See "Inmunidad".

INMUNIDAD. Immunity. (1) Exemption, as from serving in an office, or performing duties which the law generally requires other citizens to perform, e.g., exemption from paying taxes. (2) Freedom from duty or penalty. (3) Special privilege.

INNAVEGABLE. (1) Unseaworthy. A vessel which is unable to withstand the perils of an ordinary voyage at sea. (2) As applied to streams, not capable of or suitable for navigation; impassable by ships or vessels.

INNEGOCIABLE. Not negotiable, not transferable. Not subject to negotiation.

INNOVACIÓN. Innovation. (1) The introduction of something new. (2) A new idea, method, or device.

INOCENCIA. Innocence. The absence of guilt or wrongdoing.

INOCENTE. Innocent. Free from guilt.

INOFICIOSO. Inofficious. The term is used to refer to a will which is not in accordance with the moral duties of the testator to the heirs.

INQUILINO. Tenant, lessee. Person who rents in whole or in part a particular place for residential or commercial purposes.

INQUISICIÓN. Inquisition. Canonical institution or tribunal created for investigating and prosecuting crimes of heresy.

INSANIA. Insanity. A condition which renders the affected person unfit to enjoy liberty of action because of the unreliability of his or her behavior with accompanying danger to himself and others.

INSANO. Insane. See "Insania".

181

INSATISFECHO. Unsatisfied. One whose desires or requirements have not been satisfied.

INSCRIBIBLE. Recordable. That which may be registered in a public record or registry.

INSCRIBIR. To register, list, book; to record. To get registered.

INSCRIPCIÓN. Inscription. Registration, record.

INSCRITO. Recorded. A document which has been presented and recorded in a public registry.

INSECUESTRABLE. Not attachable. What may not be taken in order to guarantee satisfaction of a judgment or to secure the payment of a debt.

INSOLVENCIA. Insolvency. The inability to pay one's debts.

INSOLVENTE. Insolvent, bankrupt. When a person or organization either cannot pay its debts as they become due or whose assets are less than their liabilities.

INSPECCIÓN. Inspection. To examine; scrutinize; investigate; look into.

INSPECTOR. Inspector. Examiner. The person who investigates.

INSTANCIA. Instance. Petition. The processing, filing and prosecuting of a lawsuit. Stage of the proceeding in a judicial process.

INSTAR. To urge. To press, to incite.

INSTIGACIÓN. Instigation, abetment. Act of encouraging, inciting or aiding another.

INSTIGADOR. Instigator. One who incites another to do something (i.e., to commit a crime).

INSTIGAR. Instigate. To stimulate or encourage another to perform an action.

INSTITUCIÓN. Institution. (1) Establishment. An established or organized society or corporation. (2) Any custom, system, organization, etc., firmly established.

INSTITUCIONAL. Institutional. Related to an institution or an organization.

INSTITUIR. To found, to establish. To initiate something (i.e., an organization).

INSTITUTO. An established organization founded for promoting the arts, science or education.

INSTRUCCIÓN. Education. Proceeding. To teach something. The word is also used to refer to the formal organization and development of a trial. Order.

INSTRUCCIÓN DEL SUMARIO. To draw up or prepare an indictment. To carry on the necessary acts to find the truth in a criminal investigation.

INSTRUIR CARGOS. Arraign. To bring a defendant before a judge to hear the charges against him or her and to enter a plea of guilty or not guilty.

INSTRUMENTO. Instrument. A written document which states, proves or justifies something.

INSTRUMENTOS DE TRABAJO. Tools. Equipment needed to do a task or a job.

INSTRUMENTO PRIVADO. Private document. A particular document done without the participation of a notary public so that it is not public.

INSTRUMENTO PÚBLICO. Public document. The document prepared or signed before a notary public.

INSUBSANABLE. Irreparable. That which may not be corrected.

INSUBSISTENTE. Groundless. Lack of substance or foundation. Said of the office that has been eliminated.

INSUFICIENCIA. Insufficiency. That which does not satisfy the needs of someone. Lacking something that is required.

INSUFICIENTE. Insufficient. Not adequate.

INSURRECTO. Insurgent, rebel. Person who opposes by force the execution of the law or a regime.

INTANGIBLE. Intangible. What cannot be touched. Incorporeal.

INTEGRACIÓN. Integration. To remove barriers in order to join as a whole.

INTEGRANTES. Members, participants. Any person who is part of a group.

INTEGRAR. To integrate. To put together.

INTENCIÓN. Intention. Determination to act in a certain way or to do a certain thing.

INTENCIONAL. Intentional. Done with intention or design.

INTENCIONALIDAD. Premeditation. To deliberate on a contemplated act; prior thought; plotting or planning; a design formed to do something before it is done.

INTENCIONALMENTE. Intentionally. To do something on purpose. To do something with the determination of producing a specific effect.

INTENDENCIA. Intendancy. Mayoralty. Department of the executive power in a municipality, or district.

INTENDENTE. Intendant. Chief administrative officer of an intendancy. See "Intendencia".

INTENTAR. To attempt; intend. Trying to do something.

INTENTO. Attempt, design, try. Try to do something (i.e., to commit a crime).

INTERDICCIÓN. Interdiction. Prohibition. Restraint. Status of a person who on account of insanity or disability is incapable of administering his or her own affairs.

INTERDICTO. (1) Interdict. A decree which prohibits something. (2) Interdiction. A judicial decree, by which a person is deprived of the exercise of his or her civil rights.

INTERÉS. Interest. (1) Monetary compensation given for the use of money. (2) A right, claim, title or legal share in something.

INTIMACIÓN DE PAGO. Demand for payment. Request to have a debt paid.

INTERESADO. Interested party. Party in interest. Also a person who does something to obtain a benefit.

INTERINIDAD. Temporariness. Condition of that which is not permanent.

INTERINO. Provisional, temporary, acting, for the time being.

INTERIOR. Interior. Internal or domestic. Within a country.

INTERLOCUTORIA. Interlocutory decree. A provisional or preliminary decree, which is not final and does not determine the suit, but directs some further proceedings in preparation for the final decree.

INTERLOCUTORIO. Interlocutory. Provisional; interim; temporary; not final.

INTERMEDIARIO. Intermediary. Mediator. One who intervenes into a dispute in order to settle differences. An arbitrator or mediator. One who is employed to negotiate a matter between two or more parties, and who for that purpose may be an agent for all of the parties.

INTERPELACIÓN. Interpellation. Summons, citation. Writ issued by the court or other body (i.e., legislature) requesting the presence of a person.

INTERPELAR. Interpellate. To ask for aid or for an explanation.

INTERPONER. To present, to file. To present a document (i.e., a plea) to a public office (i.e., the court).

INTERPRETACIÓN. Interpretation. The act or process of discovering and ascertaining the meaning of a statute, will, contract, or other written document.

INTÉRPRETE. Interpreter. (1) A person sworn at a trial or other court proceeding to interpret the evidence of a foreigner or deaf person to the court, as well as interpret the proceedings to the foreigner or deaf person. (2) Translator.

INTERROGAR. To interrogate, question, examine.

INTERROGATORIO. Interrogatory. Series of questions made to the parties and witnesses to establish the facts.

185

INTERROGATORIO CRUZADO. Cross examination. The questioning of an opposing witness during a trial or hearing.

INTERROGATORIO DIRECTO. Direct examination. The first questioning in a trial or proceeding of a witness by the side that called that witness.

INTERRUPCIÓN. Interruption. A break in the continuity of something.

INTERRUPCIÓN DEL PROCESO. Stay of court proceedings. Any break or delay in the judicial process.

INTERVENCIÓN. Intervention. The procedure by which a third person, not originally a party to the suit, but claiming an interest in the subject matter, comes into the case to protect his or her right or interpose his or her claim.

INTERVENIR. (1) To intervene. The act of interposing a claim in an action or other proceeding with the leave of the court. (2) To introduce oneself into another's affairs. (3) To transfer the management of a business or other entity to a third party under judicial authority to satisfy the entity's debts.

INTER VIVOS. (Lat.) Between the living; from one living person to another.

INTESTADO(A). Intestate. Person who dies without making a will.

INTIMACIÓN. Intimation. In civil law, notification to a party that some step in a legal proceeding is asked or will be taken.

INTIMIDACIÓN. Intimidation. Unlawful coercion; duress; putting in fear.

INTOXICACIÓN. Intoxication. When, by reason of taking intoxicants, an individual does not have the normal use of his or her physical or mental faculties.

INTRANSFERIBLE. Not transferable. What cannot be assigned or negotiated.

INTRASPASABLE. Untransferable. That which may not be turned over to another person.

INTRUSIÓN. Intrusion, encroachment. Act of wrongfully entering upon or taking possession or property of another.

INTRUSO. Intruder. One who has not been welcomed. One who forces himself or herself or enters without authorization or any color of right, into an office or place.

INTUITO PECUNIAE. (Lat.) Whenever a contract is formalized, taking into account the capital or monetary contribution and not the parties involved, since the latter would be "Intuito Personae".

INTUITO PERSONAE. (Lat.) Whenever a contract is formalized, taking into account the person involved and not the funds involved.

INVALIDACIÓN. Invalidation, to make void an act.

INVALIDAR. To invalidate, to nullify so that the act loses legal force.

INVASIÓN. Invasion. Penetration by the armed forces of a country into the territory of another, to conquer or plunder it.

INVASIÓN DE DERECHOS. Invasion of rights. An encroachment upon the rights of another.

INVENCIÓN. Invention. A creation. What was created or designed by someone. Something that has been made up.

INVENTARIO. Stock. Inventory. An itemized list of the various articles constituting a collection, estate, stock in trade, etc., with their estimated or actual value.

INVENTO. Invention. See "Invención".

INVENTOR. Inventor. One who devises or designs something.

INVERSIÓN. Investment. An expenditure to acquire property or other assets in order to produce revenue.

INVERSIONISTA. Investor. One who commits assets, usually money, to earn a financial return.

INVERTIR. To invest. To put money into any kind of business (i.e., property, securities, etc.) in order to get profits.

INVESTIGACIÓN. Investigation. To examine carefully. To research something in order to find out the facts.

INVESTIR. To invest. To provide authority.

INVIOLABILIDAD. Inviolability. The state or quality of being secured against violation. Safe from trespass or assault. That which cannot be opened without the consent of the owner.

INVOCAR. To invoke. To cite a law in defense of oneself.

INVOLUNTARIO. Involuntary. That which happens without one's control. Not intentional.

IPSO FACTO. (Lat.) By the fact itself; by the mere fact.

IPSO JURE. (Lat.) By the law itself, by the mere effect of the law.

IRRAZONABLE. Unreasonable. What is immoderate or excessive under the circumstances. Contrary to reason.

IRRECUPERABLE. Irrecoverable. Which cannot be rectified or retrieved. That which cannot be obtained again.

IRRECURRIBLE. Not appealable. That which does not admit an appeal. Usually refers to a final decision. Without further appeal.

IRRECUSABLE. (1) Unimpeachable, unchallengeable. (2) A certain class of contractual obligations recognized by the law imposed on a person without his or her consent and without regard to an act of his or her own. (3) That which may not be denied. That which has to be accepted (i.e., competency of a court, judge, etc.).

IRREDIMIBLE. Irredeemable. Not recoverable.

IRREFUTABLE. Irrefutable. That which may not be disproved. What is firm. What cannot be contested or challenged.

IRREGULAR. Irregular. Contrary to the rule or norm. Not in accordance with what is usual. Not ordinary.

IRRELEVANTE. Irrelevant. Not related to the matter or issue at hand. For example, irrelevant evidence is evidence that will not help to either prove or disprove any point in a lawsuit.

IRRENUNCIABLE. Unrenounceable. What may not be surrendered or abandoned. What may not be waived.

IRREPARABLE. Irreparable. That which may not be repaired or fixed or corrected. A harm that cannot be corrected or remedied.

188

IRRESPONSABILIDAD. Irresponsibility. The quality or state of lacking a sense of responsibility.

IRRESPONSABLE. Irresponsible. Unreliable person. Not capable of assuming responsibilities.

IRRETROACTIVO. Not retroactive. That which cannot affect situations or conditions previously existing. Not intended to act on things that are established.

IRREVERSIBLE. Irreversible. That which cannot be annulled. What is final, especially matters concerning legal decisions.

IRREVISABLE. Not revisable, not reviewable. That which cannot be reexamined.

IRREVOCABLE. Irrevocable. That which cannot be revoked or recalled; indefeasible.

IRREVOCABILIDAD. Irrevocability. The quality of being irrevocable. That which cannot be overturned, undone, or declared void.

J

JACTANCIA. Brag. Boasting about something to the detriment of another's right. (1) The act of claiming rights upon the property of another without any justification. (2) Also boasting about having done an act which constitutes a crime. This is a crime in some jurisdictions.

JEFATURA. Headquarters, department, division.

JEFE. Chief, head, boss.

JEFE DE ESTADO. Chief of state. Prime Minister, President. The maximum leader of a nation.

JERARQUÍA. Hierarchy. List detailing the name and rank in order of importance. It shows the different levels of an organization.

JERGA. Jargon, slang. Type of language used by people engaged in the same activity consisting of words proper to their practice.

JERIGONZA. Jargon, slang. Kind of language used by people engaged in the same activity. It is language formed by terms hard to understand.

JORNADA. Working day. Time during which an employee is available to work and perform the services he or she has been hired to do.

JORNAL. Daily wages. Salary paid to an employee for the work performed during each working day.

JUBILACIÓN. (1) Retirement. Withdrawal from one's position or occupation. (2) Right to withdraw oneself from work and yet receive money in consideration for one's years of employment.

JUBILADO. (1) One retired from one's position or occupation. (2) The person who is enjoying the right to receive money without working in consideration of his or her age and years of employment.

JUBILAR. (1) To retire. (2) To pension. To withdraw oneself from work and keep receiving money. To receive a pension.

190

JUDICATURA. Judicature. The judicial branch of a government. (1) The body of magistrates and judges of a given jurisdiction. (2) The act of giving a judgment.

JUDICIAL. Judicial. Having to do with a court or a judge. Referent to the lawsuit, trial, judges, justice.

JUEZ. Judge. The person given the authority to judge in a court of law. The judge is in charge of the proceedings, the rendering of the judgment and the ordering of its execution. The judge and the magistrate are both in charge of the administration of justice. Generally, in civil law, the magistrate is invested with a higher rank or authority than the judge.

JUEZ A QUO. Judge from whom. The judge who has issued a judgment or order, which has been appealed. It is the lower court judge when referring to a case which is being revised by an appellate court.

JUEZ AD QUEM. The judge to whom an appeal is submitted.

JUEZ CIVIL. The judge with the jurisdictional authority to try civil cases of any kind except criminal and military ones.

JUEZ CONTENCIOSO ADMINISTRATIVO. The judge with the aptitude to handle matters in which one of the parties to the case is the government and the other a private citizen.

JUEZ DE CIRCUITO. Circuit judge. The judge who has the power to hear cases within a specific territory called a circuit. Generally the circuits form a district. The circuit judge is inferior in rank and authority to the district judge.

JUEZ DE DISTRITO. District judge. The judge who is vested with the power to handle cases within a specific territory called district. The district is formed by various circuits, therefore the circuit judge is in a lower position and the district judge is superior.

JUEZ DE LA APELACIÓN. The superior judge to whom an appeal has been presented in order to have a judgment revoked.

JUEZ DE LA CAUSA. The judge of the case. The one in charge of trying that particular matter. The judge before whom a trial is taking place.

JUEZ DE LO CIVIL. A Civil judge. See "Juez Civil".

JUEZ DE LO CONTENCIOSO ADMINISTRATIVO. See "Juez Contencioso Administrativo".

JUEZ DE LO PENAL. See "Juez Penal".

JUEZ DE PRIMERA INSTANCIA. The first judge to try a case. The trial judge to whom a case is first presented for adjudication in a judicial process.

JUEZ DE SEGUNDA INSTANCIA. The judge to whom an appeal is presented or who is hearing a case that has been appealed.

JUEZ DE TRABAJO. The judge who has been empowered to try labor law cases. The one in charge of deciding the conflicts arising out of labor relations.

JUEZ DE TURNO. Whenever there are various judges with the same rank and ability, the law establishes that only one is in charge of receiving the lawsuits which are presented for the first time. This duty is given to one judge at a time and it rotates from one judge to another by turn.

JUEZ DEL CONOCIMIENTO. See "Juez de la Causa".

JUEZ PENAL. The judge that has the power to try criminal cases. Generally this judge specializes in criminal law and does not try any other matters.

JUICIO. Trial. Judgment. (1) The proceeding and the official decision of a court of law upon the dispute litigated before it. It is the proper examination of a conflict presented in a lawsuit to a court, for final adjudication of the rights and obligations therein invoked. (2) The capacity or wisdom to distinguish between good and evil, truth and falsehood.

JUICIO ARBITRAL. Arbitration hearing. Arbitrage. The case voluntarily submitted by the parties for arbitration by the decision of a knowledgeable person called arbitrator. The final decision given according to the proceedings established is called an award.

JUICIO CIVIL. Any kind of trial which involves civil matters as opposed to criminal and military ones. The proceeding established to decide a conflict regulated by the Civil Code.

192

JUICIO CONTENCIOSO. Trial in which there is a conflict to be resolved. It presents the position of one party against the other. It opposes the trial in which the parties are only asking for a declaratory judgment.

JUICIO CONTENCIOSO ADMINISTRATIVO. The trial in which there is a conflict to be resolved between the parties when one of them is the government and the other a private citizen.

JUICIO DE DIVORCIO. Divorce proceedings. Trial in which the parties being married request the termination of their relationship. There could be a conflict if one spouse opposes the complaint.

JUICIO DECLARATIVO. Declaratory judgment. Proceedings established by a plaintiff when in doubt as to his or her rights and seeking a determination by the judge. It is a binding adjudication of the rights and status of the parties, even though no consequential relief is awarded.

JUICIO EJECUTIVO. Executory process. An expedited process, short and quick, by which a plaintiff holding a specific privilege seeks to garnish the defendant's property and put it up for sale in order to satisfy the defendant's debt.

JUICIO EN REBELDÍA. The trial carried out without the appearance of the defendant. Proceeding taking place when the defendant is in contempt of court.

JUICIO ORDINARIO. Plenary action. The trial in which the merits of the case are decided according to a complete and entire proceeding.

JUICIO ORDINARIO DE MAYOR CUANTÍA. A court with jurisdiction to hear a plenary action where the amount in the controversy is superior to the specific amount established for small claims court.

JUICIO ORDINARIO DE MENOR CUANTÍA. A court with limited jurisdiction to hear actions where the amount in the controversy is for small claims resulting in an expedited handling of the case.

JUICIO PENAL. Criminal action. Trial or proceeding in which the cases involved are those dealing with criminal law. Its purpose is to establish if a crime has been committed, find the person responsible for it, convict the guilty party and sentence him or her to the punishment established by law.

JUICIO SUCESORIO. Inheritance proceeding. The process established to obtain acquisition of property left by a decedent. It can be testate when the distribution of the estate is done according to a will or intestate when there is no testament.

JUICIO SUMARIO. Summary proceeding. A short and quick judicial proceeding by means of which a judgment can be obtained rapidly. It is different from a plenary action which involves the regular procedures of a case.

JUNTA. Board. A representative group created to carry on a specific purpose assigned to them. Meeting.

JUNTA DE ACCIONISTAS. Stockholders or shareholders meeting. A meeting of stockholders is the supreme body in the organization of a corporation which decides relevant matters of concern to the corporation.

JUNTA DE ACREEDORES. Meeting of creditors. The meeting of the creditors of the bankrupt party to decide the course of action to be taken against the bankrupt party's estate.

JUNTA DE CONCILIACIÓN Y DECISIÓN. Conciliation and Decision Board. The Board in charge of hearing a labor dispute and reaching a settlement in a friendly manner to avoid a trial or arbitration.

JUNTA DIRECTIVA. Board of Directors. The body in charge of governing a corporation. Its members are appointed by the stockholders. This Board is empowered to oversee the management of the business and select the officers of the corporation.

JUNTA EXTRAORDINARA. Special meeting. A meeting called outside the ordinary schedule of meetings for the special purpose of deciding a particular matter.

JUNTA ORDINARIA. Regular meeting. Those meetings taking place during the time and place indicated in the by-laws or statutes of the corporation.

JURA NOVIT CURIA. (Lat.) The court knows the law; the court recognizes rights. Expression which informs the parties to state the facts only, since the judge knows the laws. Nevertheless the parties are required to express the law which supports their petition.

JURADO. Jury. A group of persons selected by law and sworn in to look at certain facts and determine the truth.

JURADO DE CONCIENCIA. Jury. A group of citizens called to hear a trial and decide according to their judgment the guilt or innocence of the defendant.

JURAMENTO. Oath, swearing. A formal swearing that a person will tell the truth in a particular matter (an "assertory oath") or will act in a particular way (a "promissory oath").

JURAR. To swear; to give or take an oath.

JURICIDAD. Quality of being done or decided according to the law.

JURÍDICO. Juridical. Relating to the administration of justice, or office of a judge. According to the law. An act done within the scope of the law.

JURISCONSULTO. Jurist, jurisconsult, lawyer. A person who studies the law and can give legal advice.

JURISDICCIÓN. Jurisdiction. The authority by means of which a court can hear and decide a particular matter within a specific territory. It gives the court the ability to try a case. It makes special reference to the type of cases which can be tried depending on the subject matter involved and the territory in which a case can be decided.

JURISDICCIÓN CIVIL. Authority empowering a court to decide cases which involve matters regulated by the Civil Code as opposed to those of a criminal or military nature.

JURISDICCIÓN CONTENCIOSO ADMINISTRATIVA. The authority given to a court to hear lawsuits in which one of the parties to a conflict is the government and the other is a private citizen.

JURISDICCIÓN LABORAL. The jurisdiction which allows a court to handle a labor dispute between employers and employees.

JURISDICCIÓN MARÍTIMA. The power which a court has to decide cases involving maritime law.

JURISDICCIÓN MILITAR. Jurisdiction entrusted to a special court to decide military cases or cases in which the military is involved or involving a civilian during the course of a military action.

JURISDICCIÓN PENAL. Authority given to a court empowering it to hear cases in which there is a violation of criminal law.

JURISPRUDENCIA. Jurisprudence. (1) The study of the law and legal philosophy. (2) The interpretation of the law by the courts. It embodies the precedents and group of cases already decided in the same manner.

JURISTA. Jurist. (1) A judge. (2) A legal scholar.

JURIS TANTUM. (Lat.) A presumption which is good until proof to the contrary is produced.

JURO. (1) Right of perpetual ownership of a thing. (2) Pension.

JUS. Law. Judge.

JUS AD REM. (Lat.) A right to a thing. A right exercised by one person over a particular article of property by virtue of a contract or obligation incurred by another person in respect to it, and which is enforceable only against or through such other person. For example, the right of the mortgagee in case of default.

JUS IN RE. (Lat.) A right in a thing. A right of a person regarding an article of his or her property, and implying complete ownership with possession, and defensible against the whole world.

JUS SANGUINIS. (Lat.) The right of blood. The principle that a person's citizenship is determined by the citizenship of his or her parents.

JUS SOLI. (Lat.) The law of the place of one's birth. The principle that a person's citizenship is determined by the place of birth rather than by the citizenship of one's parents.

JUSTA CAUSA. Just cause; a lawful ground. (1) A legal transaction of some kind. (2) Proper consideration.

JUSTICIA. Justice. Fairness in treatment by the law. According to the law.

JUSTIFICACIÓN. Justification. Legal excuse or reason for an intentional action that would otherwise be unlawful. A just cause.

JUSTIPRECIO. Appraisal. To determine the exact valuation of something by an expert called an appraiser.

JUSTO. Just, fair. (1) Legal or lawful. (2) Morally right; fair.

JUSTO PRECIO. Fair price.

JUSTO TÍTULO. Just or fee title. Title received from the real owner, provided the title were such as to transfer rightful ownership of the property. The act by means of which property is acquired by one person and becomes protected by law.

JUZGADO. Court of law. Courtroom. Courthouse. The place where the judge hears and tries a case. The conflict decided. Generally the court in which there is only one judge.

JUZGADO CIVIL. Those courts in which the judge tries cases involving civil matters not regulated by criminal or military law.

JUZGADO DE CIRCUITO. Circuit court. The courtroom with jurisdiction to try cases within a specific territory called a circuit. It is inferior to the district court.

JUZGADO DE PRIMERA INSTANCIA. Courtroom in which a lawsuit has been tried for the first time.

JUZGADO DE SEGUNDA INSTANCIA. The courtroom with jurisdiction to decide whether a judgment or order is to be revoked or not as a result of the appeal.

JUZGADO DE TRABAJO. The court with the authority to hear cases involving a labor dispute between employee and employer.

JUZGADO DE TURNO. The court whose turn it is to receive the complaint presented for the first time by the plaintiff when there are various courts with jurisdiction over the same cases. See "Juez de Turno".

197

JUZGADO DE LO CIVIL. A court having jurisdiction to handle cases pertaining to matters regulated by the Civil Code.

JUZGADO DE LO PENAL. The court having the authority to try a case in which there is a criminal count.

JUZGADO PENAL. The court with the authority and power to hear the cases against the person accused of committing a crime.

JUZGAR. To judge; to decide a case.

K

KAISER. Kaiser. Emperor, ruler of an empire.

KARTELL (CARTEL). Cartel. A combination or agreement between political parties, unions, independent business enterprises or other kinds of organizations, executed to share power (economic or political) to limit competition or form a joint venture.

KIBUTZ. Kibutz. Collective group of people who jointly own and harvest land. The base of its economy is the community of property.

KILO. Kilo. Kilogram. A measure of weight that represents one thousand grams.

KILOMÉTRICO. Kilometric. Distance in which there are many kilometers. Said of something long. Long duration.

KILÓMETRO. Kilometer. A unit used to measure distance. It is used to establish the measure of a territory. This unit represents one thousand meters.

KIOSKO. A small house or store used to dwell or sell goods.

KREMLIN. Kremlin. (1) Citadel of a Russian city. (2) Name given to identify the Russian government.

LL

LLAMADO(DA). Call, summons, invitation. To announce authoritatively. A request or command to come or assemble.

LLAMAMIENTO. (1) Call. (2) Summons, citation. A document notifying a person that an action has been commenced against him or her in the court from where the process issues, and that he or she is required to appear, on a day named, and answer the complaint in such action.

LLAMAR. To call, summon. The act of making a call; see "Llamada".

LLAVE. Key, goodwill. (1) Instrument used to open a lock. (2) The value of a company as an operating business for its good name, namely customers and other such factors that have built up over a considerable time.

LLAVE FALSA. Said of the instrument other than a key used to open a lock with criminal intentions.

LLEGAR. To arrive, reach. To get to some place.

LLENAR. To fill. To fill an empty space.

LLEVAR. To carry; to transport; to bear, to wear; to induce; to bring. (1) To take something from one place to another. (2) To carry with or in oneself. (3) To carry in accounts.

LLEVAR REGISTROS. Keep records.

L

L.A.B. (Libre a bordo). F.O.B. (Free on board.) Means generally that the seller assumes all responsibilities and costs up to the point of delivery, including insurance, transportation, etc.

LABOR. Labor. Work or task.

LABORABLE. Working day as opposed to a holiday.

LABORAL. Labor, with reference to work or employment matters. The term is used to refer to the body of law which deals with the rights and obligations arising between master and servant.

LABORALISTA. Scholarly writer who specializes in the doctrines and principles of labor law.

LABORIOSIDAD. Quality of being productive and efficiently performing a task.

LACERAR. Lacerate. To mangle, damage, or tear in pieces. To cause harm or injuries.

LACTANCIA. Lactation. Period of time during which babies are fed with the mother's milk or its substitute.

LACTANTE. The baby who is fed with the mother's milk or its substitute.

LADRÓN. Thief. One who steals; one who commits a theft or larceny. The person who commits the crime of stealing.

LAGUNA LEGAL. Legal gap. Questions or issues not covered by statutory law. The unforeseen event not regulated by the law. Any circumstance, fact or occurrence not subject to the law.

LAICO. Laity; the person who is not a priest. Also one who does not admit any religion.

LAISSEZ FAIRE, LAISSEZ PASSER. (French) Let it be, let it pass. Eighteenth century doctrine advocating free enterprise and commerce without any involvement or interference by the state.

201

LANZAMIENTO. Eviction, ouster. Dispossession by process of law; the act of depriving a person of the possession of land or rental property which he or she has held or leased. The execution of the judgment in which the dispossession has been ordered.

LANZAR. To dispossess, evict, oust. To oust a person from land by legal process; to eject; to exclude from realty.

LAPIDACIÓN. Lapidation. Stoning to death. The act of killing a person sentenced to death by stoning.

LAPSO. Lapse. Period of time.

LARGO PLAZO. Long-term. An extensive period of time. Said of the contract in which the obligation is to be performed during more than seven years.

LASCIVIA. Lewdness, lasciviousness. Gross and wanton indecency in sexual relations.

LASCIVO. Lewd. The behavior carried out with excess of lust.

LASTIMADO. Injured. One who has been hurt or damaged in any way.

LASTO. Voucher. A document that authorizes the giving out of something, usually cash. Extension of territory belonging to one person.

LATIFUNDIO. Latifundium. Large landed estate.

LATO. Wide, extensive.

LATO SENSU. In a broad sense. To interpret the law in a broad sense as opposed to literally.

LATROCINIO. Theft, robbery, larceny. The practice or custom of defrauding another.

LAUDO. Award, finding. (1) To give or grant by formal process. (2) The decision of an arbitrator or other non-judge in a dispute submitted to him or her.

LECTIVO. Pertaining to the education. Time during which the schools are opened for teaching.

LECTURA DE ACUSACIÓN. Arraignment. The bringing of a defendant before a judge to hear the charges against him or her and to enter a plea.

LEGACIÓN. Legation. Embassy. Diplomatic commission given to a person to act as a foreign representative in another state.

LEGADO. Legacy, bequest. (1) A disposition of property by will. A clause in a will intended to give property, whether real or personal, to a person other than an heir. (2) The highest official of an embassy.

LEGADO ALTERNATIVO. Alternate legacy. A legacy by which the testator gives one of two or more things without designating which; therefore, the legatee is given a choice.

LEGADO CONDICIONAL. Conditional legacy. A legacy which is liable to take effect or to be defeated according to the occurrence or non-occurrence of some uncertain event.

LEGAJO. Bundle of papers, file. Instrument which keeps documents together.

LEGAL. Legal. Conforming or pertaining to the law; required or permitted by law; not forbidden by law.

LEGALIDAD. Legality. Coming from the law. Lawfulness. The quality of being done according to the law.

LEGALIZACIÓN. Legalization. The act of legalizing or making legal or lawful. A statement by which an authorized officer declares or certifies the authenticity of a document by recognizing the signature.

LEGALIZAR. To legalize. To make legal or lawful. (1) To confirm or validate what was before void or unlawful. (2) Declaration that the signature of a document is true.

LEGALMENTE. Legally; lawfully; according to law.

LEGAR. To bequeath, to devise. To give real or personal property by will to another.

LEGATARIO. Legatee. Person who receives a legacy. The person to whom property, whether real or personal, is transferred by bequest in a will upon the death of another.

LEGISLACIÓN. Legislation. (1) The act of giving or enacting laws; the power to make laws; the act of legislating. (2) Body of laws by which a state or a particular subject is governed.

LEGISLADOR. Legislator. A member of a city, state or federal legislative body, entrusted with making laws.

LEGISLAR. To legislate. To enact laws or pass resolutions via legislation, as opposed to court-made law.

LEGISLATIVO. Legislative. Pertaining to the function of law-making or to the process for the enactment of laws.

LEGISLATURA. Legislature. (1) The department, assembly, or body of persons that makes statutory laws for a state or nation. (2) The period of time during which the legislators meet to carry on their duties.

LEGÍTIMA DEFENSA. Self-defense. The protection of one's person or property against some injury attempted by another.

LEGITIMACIÓN. Making legal or legitimate; giving legal standing or competency.

LEGITIMAR. To legalize, to legitimate. To make legal or lawful. The act of giving a valid reason to justify an action otherwise illegal.

LEGITIMIDAD. Genuineness, legitimacy. (1) Legality or conformity with the law. (2) Lawful birth; the condition of being born in wedlock; the opposite of illegitimacy or bastardy.

LEGÍTIMO. Legitimate. (1) (verb) To make lawful; to confer legitimacy. (2) (adj.) That which is lawful, legal, or according to law.

LEGO. Layperson. One of the laity, and not one of the clergy; one who is not of a particular profession.

LEGULEYO. Shyster. (1) One who carries on any business or profession in a deceitful, tricky or dishonest way. (2) One who without knowing the law in depth, delays proceedings with unscrupulous practices. Being, among jurists, what a quack is to physicians.

LENOCINIO. Pandering. To pimp; to cater to the gratification or the lust of another. The contract in which one party receives unfair and unreasonable benefits to the detriment of the other.

LEONINO. One-sided, unfair. Advantage favoring a party to the detriment of the other.

LESA PATRIA. Expression applied to crimes against the security of a nation, especially high treason.

LESBIANA. Lesbian. A woman who has sexual relations with another woman.

LESBIANISMO. Lesbianism. Female homosexuality.

LESIÓN. Lesion. Damage; injury; detriment; wound. (1) Any change in the structure of an organ due to injury or disease. (2) Detriment which a party to a contract suffers due to a specific performance clause or because no provision for changes of circumstances due to the passage of time was included therein.

LESIONADA. Injured person. Person who has suffered an injury.

LESIONAR. To injure. To violate the legal right of another or inflict an actionable wrong. To do harm to, damage, or impair.

LESIVO. Injurious, damaging, prejudicial. That which violates the legal rights of another or inflicts an actionable wrong.

LETAL. Lethal. Deadly, fatal, mortal.

LETRA. (1) Handwriting. The peculiar and unique style each person has of writing, distinguishing the style from that of any other person. (2) Letter. A commission, patent, or written instrument containing or attesting the granting of some power, authority or right.

LETRA DE CAMBIO. Bill of exchange. Contract whereby a person orders another to pay a certain sum of money on his or her behalf to a third party therein named at a definite future time.

LETRA MUERTA. Dead letter. (1) A term sometimes applied to a law that has become obsolete by long disuse. (2) A letter that is undeliverable by the postal service because of insufficient address or postage and absence of return address.

205

LETRADO. (1) Learned, erudite. (2) Lawyer, advocate, counselor.

LEVANTAR. To raise, lift. To build. (1) To start a revolution or rebellion. (2) To terminate a garnishment. (3) To write something down, to keep a record.

LEX. (Lat.) A system or body of laws, written or unwritten. The law.

LEX FORI. (Lat.) The law of the forum or court; that is, the law of the state, country, or jurisdiction wherein the court is located.

LEX LOCI. (Lat.) The law of the place. The substantive rights of the parties to an action are governed by the law of the place where the rights were acquired or liabilities incurred.

LEX LOCI CONTRACTUS. (Lat.) The law of the place where the contract was made, or the place of its performance.

LEX REI SITAE. (Lat.) The law of the place where the thing is situated.

LEY. Law. Statutory act. That which is laid down, ordained or established. Any juridical rule governing the acts, rights and liabilities arising out of the relations between persons. Those rules of conduct that must be obeyed by every person living in a given society. Solemn expression of the will of the legislative body of the state or nation. A body of rules of action or conduct prescribed by controlling authority, and having binding legal force.

LEY ADJETIVA. Adjective law, procedural law. The rules of how to carry on a lawsuit; detailing the procedural aspects of a civil or criminal action. Procedural law. Those laws containing the methods and ways by which another law, regulating rights and obligations, is to be applied.

LEY CIVIL. Civil law. (1) The body of law which every nation, state, or city has established for itself, as opposed to natural law or international law. (2) Laws concerned with civil or private rights and remedies, as contrasted with criminal laws.

LEY DE LA OFERTA Y DEMANDA. Law of supply and demand. Economic principle dealing with the relationship between supply and demand.

LEY DEL FORO. "Lex forum." Law of the forum. Expression used to refer to the law of the territory in which the court has jurisdiction to try cases.

LEY DEL LUGAR. "Lex loci." Law of the place. This expression makes reference to the law of the place in which the event pertaining to the case took place or occurred.

LEY MARCIAL. Martial law. Legal regime found during times of war or when the civilian government is ineffective.

LEY PENAL. Penal law, criminal law. That law enacted for the purpose of preventing harm to society, which (a) declares what conduct is criminal, and (b) prescribes the punishment to be imposed for engaging in such conduct.

LEY SUBSTANTIVA. Substantive law. The part of law which creates, defines, and regulates rights and obligations, as opposed to procedural law, which establishes the procedures for their enforcement.

LIAR. To tie. To bind.

LIBELO. Libel. (1) A type of defamation expressed by print, writing, pictures or signs. (2) Any written petition or complaint. (3) A written document.

LIBERACIÓN. Liberation. Cancellation. Release. The act of setting free. To liberate. To terminate an obligation by any means.

LIBERAL. Liberal. Free in giving; generous. Not strict or narrow-minded.

LIBERALIDAD. Generosity. Transfer of property or rights made without receiving any consideration or benefit in exchange for the thing given.

LIBERALISMO. Liberalism. Political philosophy which advocates the principle of total freedom for human beings.

LIBERAR. To free. (1) To release, discharge or exempt of obligation, encumbrance or duty. (2) To free a prisoner.

LIBERTAD. Freedom. Liberty. Quality of being able to decide for oneself what to do or not do.

LIBERTAD BAJO FIANZA. Free on bail. To be free from imprisonment by posting bail to assure that the prisoner will appear before a judge when summoned.

LIBERTAD BAJO PALABRA. Free on parole. A release from imprisonment done upon the condition that the prisoner will be under supervision for a specified period of time.

LIBERTAD CONDICIONAL. Free on parole. The conditional release from prison of a person who has served part of the jail sentence and is still subject to penal supervision.

LIBERTAD DE ASOCIACIÓN. Freedom of association. The constitutionally protected right allows any person to associate freely and hold meetings.

LIBERTAD DE CONCIENCIA. Liberty of conscience. Liberty for each individual to decide for himself or herself what to do.

LIBERTAD DE CULTO. Freedom of religion. Constitutional right which protects the freedom to adopt, practice and exercise any kind of religion or belief the person wishes.

LIBERTAD DE EXPRESIÓN. (1) Freedom to express oneself, whether orally or in writing, without previous censorship. (2) Freedom of expression. Freedom granted by the First Amendment of the U.S. Constitution, which includes freedom of religion, speech, and press. (3) The constitutional right which allows every person to express oneself freely without disturbing public order. It includes the right to publish and speak one's views and thoughts.

LIBERTAD DE RELIGIÓN. Freedom of religion. Right protected by the constitution that allows anyone to express his or her religious preference in any way.

LIBERTAD DE TRABAJO. Freedom of work. Constitutional right which protects every person's right to work in any job and earn a decent wage.

LIBERTAD DE TRÁNSITO. Freedom of movement. The constitutional right by which every person in society has the ability to move freely from place to place.

LIBERTAD PROVISIONAL. Free on parole. The act of allowing a prisoner to leave the prison before serving the complete sentence based on good behavior during the time served.

LIBRADO. Drawee. Person to whom a bill of exchange is addressed, and who is requested to pay the amount of money therein mentioned. The person who has to pay the beneficiary the amount established in the note.

LIBRADOR. Drawer. Person who issues or draws a bill of exchange. The person who signs a check is the drawer of it.

LIBRAMIENTO. Draft. Warrant. Order of payment.

LIBRANZA. Draft. Bill of exchange. A check. A written order by the first party (drawer), instructing the second party (drawee, usually a bank), to pay a certain amount of money to a third party (payee).

LIBRAR. To issue. To draw a bill of exchange or other negotiable instrument. To free, release, discharge.

LIBRE. Free. Not subject to legal constraint. Exempt from obligations. Unmarried. Without encumbrances.

LIBRE ALBEDRÍO. Free will. The power of choosing a course of action without restraint or interference from an outside source. Freedom to act according to one's ideas.

LIBRE ARBITRIO. Free will. The ability to govern one's conduct according to one's free will.

LIBRE DE GRAVAMEN. Free from encumbrance. Said of the property which is not affected by any encumbrance, lien or mortgage.

LIBRE DE IMPUESTO. Duty free. The property or goods that have been exempt from taxes. That which is not subject to the obligation to pay taxes.

LIBRO. Book. One of the sections in which a code of law is divided. The code is divided in books, the book in titles, the title in chapters, the chapters in sections, the section in articles, the articles in paragraphs, literals or numerals.

LIBRO DE ACCIONES. Stock record. The book required to be kept by corporations when issuing or selling stocks to record the stockholders, amount of stocks, dates, etc.

LIBRO DE ACTAS. Minutes record. Book in which the corporation records the resolutions and minutes adopted by the board of directors or stockholders.

LIBRO DE INVENTARIOS Y BALANCES. Inventory and balance record. Book required by law to be filled by merchants to keep an adequate record of their inventory and balance sheet. It should have the inventory of all the assets and the balance sheets of their commercial activities.

LIBRO DIARIO. Journal. The book in which the merchant is required to keep record of each and every one of his or her day-by-day transactions in progressive order.

LIBRO MAESTRO. Ledger. The book of accounting in which the merchant should keep a record of his or her business transactions in two columns, one for credits and the other for debits. This is the principal accounting book of the business in which, at a glance, the debits and credits of each account can be found.

LIBRO MAYOR. Ledger. See "Libro Maestro".

LIBROS DE COMERCIO. Book of accounts. Those containing a detailed statement of the business transactions in the form of credits and debits. These books are required by law to be filled by merchants. They are: Ledger, Journal and Inventory and Balance record. See "Libro Mayor", "Libro Diario" and "Libro de Inventarios y Balances".

LICENCIA. License, permit. Authorization or permission. (1) The permission by competent authority to do an act which, without such permission, would be illegal, a trespass, or a tort. (2) A permit granted by the government to perform a business.

LICENCIA DE ALIJO. Unloading permit. Permit granted to unload merchandise from a ship or any other kind of vessel.

LICENCIA DE CAMBIO. Exchange permit. Generally, permit granted to buy foreign currency or exchange one's currency for another at market or established rates.

LICENCIA DE CONDUCIR o DE GUIAR. Driver's license. Permit issued by pertinent authorities to allow driving within a given state's jurisdiction.

LICENCIA DE CONSTRUCCIÓN o PARA EDIFICAR. Building permit. Authorization required by local governmental bodies for new buildings, or major alterations or expansions of existing structures.

LICENCIA DE FABRICACIÓN. Manufacturing rights. Permit or patent given to an inventor, producer or manufacturer for the exclusive production or manufacturing of a product, idea or good.

LICENCIA DE GUIAR. Driver's license. Same as "Licencia de Conductor."

LICENCIA DE IMPORTACIÓN. Import permit. License or permit which allows the introduction of goods or merchandise into a country from a foreign country.

LICENCIA DE PATENTE. Patent license. License which gives a producer the right to the exclusive manufacture and sale of an invention or patented article.

LICENCIA MARITAL. License or permission which a married woman is required to obtain from her husband before taking independent legal action.

LICENCIA MATRIMONIAL o PARA CASARSE. Marriage license. A license or permission granted by a public authority to persons who intend to marry, usually addressed to the minister or magistrate who is to perform the ceremony.

LICENCIADO. Professional person, such as lawyer. Generally, a title given to the student who has successfully completed the undergraduate studies at the university.

LICITACIÓN. Licitation. (1) The act of bidding or making an offer by a buyer to pay a designated price for property which is about to be sold at auction. (2) Process through which bids are submitted to the government as a result of public notice for an intended purchase, and a public contract is awarded to the lowest bidder.

LÍCITO. Lawful, legal, legitimate.

LICITUD. Quality of being legal. What is legal and moral.

LID. Legal dispute.

LÍDER. Leader. Principal, director or conductor of a group.

LIDERAZGO. Leadership. Quality of being a leader.

LIDIAR. To fight, contend or struggle.

LIGA. League. Alliance.

LIGAMENTO. Legal impediment to marriage caused by a prior marriage which has not been legally dissolved.

LIMITACIÓN. Limitation. Whenever there is a restriction. That which cannot be done without some restriction.

LÍMITE. Limit. Boundary. That used to define the beginning and end of something.

LIMÍTROFE. Bordering. Landmark used to establish the boundaries of a territory.

LINAJE. Lineage. Line of descent from an ancestor; family, race, stock.

LINDERO. Boundary; property line.

LÍNEA COLATERAL. See "Colateral".

LÍNEA RECTA. The lineage line, descending or ascending, which unites persons to a common ancestor.

LIQUIDACIÓN. Liquidation. (1) Process of reducing assets to cash, discharging liabilities, leaving a surplus or a deficit. (2) To sell merchandise at a big discount. (3) To kill. To end another's life.

LIQUIDADOR. Liquidator. (1) Person who carries out the liquidation or winding up of a company. (2) Trustee in bankruptcy. The person who has the duty to execute a liquidation.

LIQUIDEZ. Liquidity. Quality of having enough cash to pay one's debts.

LISIADO. Cripple. Person who is lame or physically disabled, be it partially or totally.

212

LISTA. List.

LITERAL. Literal. (1) Strict compliance with or interpretation of the letter of a text. (2) The letter used to identify one of the sections of the article which is one of the segments in which a case is divided.

LITIGANTE. Litigant. A party to a lawsuit; one engaged in litigation. The plaintiff or defendant to a case in conflict.

LITIGAR. To litigate. To dispute or contest in a court of law; to carry on a suit.

LITIGIO. Lawsuit, litigation. Legal action, including all proceedings therein. A judicial contest, a judicial controversy, a suit at law.

LITIGIOSO. Litigious. (1) That which is the subject of a lawsuit or action. (2) Fond of litigation; prone to engage in suits.

LITIS. (Lat.) Process, lawsuit.

LITIS CONTESTATIO. (Lat.) The contestation of a suit; the process of contesting a suit by the opposing statements of the respective parties.

LITIS CONSORTE. (Lat.) Associate in a lawsuit. Each party on the same side of a lawsuit whenever there are several parties on each side.

LITIS PENDENCIA. "Lis pendens." A pending suit. A case that is being tried. It is a dilatory action to extend the time of the trial.

LITORAL. Littoral. Belonging to shore, as in the coasts of seas and great lakes.

LOCACIÓN. Lease. Contract where a party grants another the use of his or her property for a price.

LOCADOR. Landlord. The owner of property rented. The one who gets paid for the use of his or her property.

LOCAL. (1) Place of business. (2) Local. Belonging or confined to a particular place.

LOCATARIO. Tenant. The one who pays money to the landlord for the use of leased property.

LOCO. Mad, lunatic, insane.

LOCURA. Insanity. A mental disorder or condition which renders the affected person unfit to enjoy liberty of action due to unreliable behavior with concomitant danger to himself or herself and others. In law, the term is used to denote that degree of mental illness which negates the individual's legal responsibility or capacity.

LOCUS REGIT ACTUM. (Lat.) The laws of the place where the acts were celebrated should apply.

LOGRERO. Usurer. Profiteer. Money lender.

LONJA. Public building used as a market, business center, or stock exchange.

LOTE. Lot. Piece of land. A part of something that has been divided. Real estate consisting of a piece of land.

LOTERÍA. Lottery. A chance to win a prize for a price. Raffle. Game.

LUCIDEZ. Of sound mind. Ability to understand the consequences of one's acts.

LUCRO. Profit or gain. Benefit received from an investment.

LUCRO CESANTE. Loss of profits; business interruptions. The loss suffered by one party because of the other's breach of a contract.

LUGAR. (1) Space, site, room. (2) Reason.

LUGAR DE PAGO. Refers to the place where the obligation should be performed or the place of payment for a debt. Generally it is the debtor's office or residency.

LUGAR Y FECHA. Place and date. Refers to the place and time in which an obligation begins, should be performed or carried out and terminated.

LUJURIA. Lust. Lewdness. Indecent behavior connected with sexual relations. Something performed with obscenity and in an immoral manner. Sexually related conduct intended to offend another's sense of morality.

LUTO. Mourning, sorrow, grief for the death of a loved one.

214

M

MACANA. Stick. A weapon made of wood used by some Indians in Central and South America.

MACERO. Sergeant at arms.

MÁCULA. Stain, spot or blemish. That which is done with the intent to cause dishonor.

MACUQUERO. Unlawful worker of an abandoned mine.

MACHO. Male. A man or a male animal.

MACHETAZO. Blow inflicted with a machete.

MACHISMO. Said of the theory or belief which supposes the superiority of men over women.

MACHUCAR. To pound or bruise. To cause any injury.

MADRASTRA. Stepmother. The wife of one's father by virtue of a subsequent marriage.

MADRE. Mother. A woman who has borne a child.

MADRE PATRIA. Motherland. The country, nation or place where a person is born.

MADRE POLÍTICA. Mother-in-law. The mother of one's spouse.

MADRINA. Godmother. (1) A woman who sponsors a person at baptism. (2) Protectress.

MAESTRE. Master of a merchant ship. Second in command after the captain of a ship.

MAESTRO. Teacher. Person who imparts knowledge to others by means of lessons.

MAFIA. Mafia. A secret organization of criminals.

MAGISTRADO. Magistrate. Justice. Any public officer vested with legislative, executive or judicial power. Generally the highest level justice who decides with others any legal conflicts presented in a judicial proceeding.

MAGISTRATURA. Magistracy. Those invested with the duty, honor and post of a magistrate. See "Magistrado".

MAGNA CARTA. The great charter. The name of the charter granted by King John of England in 1215, and regarded as the foundation of English constitutional laws and liberties.

MAGNO. Great; grand. Having importance.

MAL. Evil. Harm. Injury. Malady. Fault.

MALA CONDUCTA. Misconduct. A transgression or violation of some established and definite rule of action.

MALA FE. Mala fides; bad faith. The conscious and willful doing of a wrong for a dishonest or fraudulent purpose.

MALBARATAR. To squander. To sell something below its real value.

MALCORTE. The cutting of trees in violation of the law.

MALCRIADO. Spoiled. A stubborn or insolent child.

MALCRIAR. To spoil. To raise and educate one's children poorly.

MALDISPUESTO. Indisposed. Unwilling or unable to do something.

MALEANTE. Perverse person; a crook, rogue, rascal.

MALÉFICO. Malicious. Involving malice; having, or done with, wicked or mischievious intentions or motives.

MALHECHOR. Malefactor. Criminal who has been convicted of a crime or offense. A person who does not do any good.

MALICIA. Malice. The intentional doing of a wrongful act without just cause or excuse, with an intent to inflict an injury or under circumstances where the law will imply such evil intent.

MALOS TRATOS. Bad or poor treatment of a person with whom the offender has a close and continuous relationship. This term is most commonly used in family and labor law.

MALUM IN SE. (Lat.) A wrong in itself.

MALUM PROHIBITUM. (Lat.) Wrong prohibited.

MALVERSACIÓN. Misappropriation. The act of turning something to a wrong purpose; wrongful appropriation.

MALVERSAR. To misappropriate. To turn something to a wrong purpose.

MAMOTRETO. Bulky book. Large bundle of papers.

MANCEBA. Concubine. A woman who cohabits with a man to whom she is not married. A mistress.

MANCIPACIÓN. In Roman law "Mancipatio." In a broad sense, any transmission of rights or goods.

MANCIPATIO. Mancipatio (Lat.). In Roman law, a ceremony required to perfect the sale of certain types of property called "res mancipi" (slaves, cattle, land or houses).

MANCIPAR. To mancipate. To subject or to enslave. Also to dispose of "res mancipi" in accordance with the Roman requirement of "mancipatio."

MANCOMUNADA Y SOLIDARIAMENTE. Jointly and severally. When the existing liability for a single obligation is both individual for a proportional part and jointly for the whole.

MANCOMUNAR. (1) To associate. To unite forces, resources or persons for a common purpose. (2) To oblige two or more persons in a single obligation, either for the whole or for a proportional part of the liability.

MANCOMUNIDAD. Joint or concurrent liability. Where two or more joint obligors are equally liable for the same obligation.

MANDAMIENTO. Mandate. A command or direction authoritatively given; rule or regulation. Any legitimate order given by a superior.

MANDAMIENTO JUDICIAL. Writ, mandamus. An order issued by a court commanding the performance of a specified act.

MANDANTE. Mandator. Person who orders another to perform an act on his or her behalf. While the person who gives the order is called

217

a principal ("Mandante") or constituent ("constituyente"), the person who complies is the mandatory ("mandatario") or agent ("agente").

MANDAR. To send; to order. The act of governing.

MANDATARIO. Mandatary. Attorney; representative; agent or proxy. The person entrusted with the representation of another. One to whom a power of attorney has been given to perform an act on behalf of the principal.

MANDATO. Mandate, power of attorney. An instrument authorizing another to act as one's agent or attorney. The mandate can be gratuitous or onerous.

MANDO. Command. Power to give orders to subordinates. Authority extended over citizens or subjects.

MANDO Y JURISDICCIÓN. Authority and jurisdiction. This expression is used to describe the scope of the authority or immunity held by a public officer in space. For example, the President has both authority and jurisdiction throughout a nation, the same as a Supreme Court judge. However, circuit courts only have these powers within their respective circuit.

MANÍA. Mania. Mental disorder which manifests itself from inordinate desires to frenzy and madness. Its relevance hinges on its degree, since in its extreme form a person cannot be considered legally responsible for his or her acts.

MANICOMIO. Insane asylum. A hospital or asylum where the insane are cared for.

MANIFESTACIÓN. Manifestation. A statement or declaration; a public demonstration. That which is intended to show or express something.

MANIFESTACIÓN DE IMPUESTO. Tax return. Forms for reporting income, deductions and exemptions which are forwarded with the tax payment to the taxing authorities.

MANIFESTANTE. Deponent. Person who testifies to the truth of certain facts. A person who makes a written statement under oath.

MANIFESTAR. To manifest; to show. A public declaration. To express something.

MANIFIESTO DE EMBARQUE. Ship's manifest. Shipping document containing a list of the contents, value, origin, carrier and destination of the goods shipped.

MANO DE OBRA. Labor. (1) The work required to do something. (2) The number of workers existing at a given time in the labor market. (3) The services performed by workers for wages as distinguished from those rendered by entrepreneurs for profits.

MANTENIDO. Dependent. One who derives his or her main support from another. One who does not work and receives money or support from another to satisfy his or her basic needs.

MANTENIMIENTO. Maintenance. The act of maintaining, keeping up, supporting; livelihood; means of sustenance.

MANUFACTURA. Manufacture. The process of making products by hand or machinery.

MANUSCRITO. Manuscript. Literally, written by hand. A writing; a paper written with the hand; a writing that has not been printed.

MANUTENCIÓN. Maintenance, support. (1) (verb) Furnishing funds or means for maintenance; to maintain; to provide for; to carry on. (2) (noun) All such means of living as would enable one to live in the degree of comfort suitable and becoming to his or her station in life.

MAÑA. Faculty and ability of being handy, skilled or clever.

MAQUETA. Mock-up. Model. Scale model of a construction, monument or building.

MAQUINACIÓN. Machination, scheme. The act of planning or contriving a scheme for executing some purpose, particularly an evil purpose; an artful design formed with deliberation.

MARBETE. Label, tag adhered to boxes, bottles, baggage, bags, etc., containing the brand name, the address of the addressee, and other instructions.

MARCA DE FÁBRICA. Manufacturer's trademark. A distinctive mark of authenticity through which the products of particular manufacturers may be distinguished from those of others.

MARCA REGISTRADA. Registered trademark. A trademark filed at the relevant trademark and patent office.

MARIDO. Husband. A married man. A woman's spouse or companion.

MARINA MERCANTE. Merchant marine. Ships of a country designated for maritime commerce.

MARITAL. Marital. Related to, or connected with, the status of marriage.

MARTILLAR. (1) To sell at auction. (2) To hammer or knock down.

MARXISMO. Marxism. Doctrine elaborated by Marx and Engels. Politically, it pretends to have a state without classes.

MÁS ADELANTE. Hereinafter or hereafter. Futurity. Always used in statutes and legal documents as indicative of future time, excluding the present and the past.

MASA. Mass, volume. Group of goods or things or people. Assets, wealth, estate.

MASA DE ACREEDORES. Group of creditors of a bankrupt debtor.

MASA DE LA QUIEBRA. Assets of a bankruptcy. The group of assets of a bankrupt debtor which are subject to the claims of the recognized creditors, and that will bear the expenses of the insolvency and the bankruptcy proceeding.

MASA HEREDITARIA. Assets of the estate of a decedent. The property object of the succession left by the deceased. The property and goods which are going to be transferred upon the death of the owner. That which is going to be inherited by the heirs.

MASCULINO. Masculine. Male. Virile.

MASOQUISMO. Masochism. Perversion in which sexual pleasure is augmented when one is dominated and maltreated by the other party.

MATANZA. Slaughtering. (1) To slaughter. (2) To butcher (animals) for food. (3) Heavy casualties in war.

MATAR. To kill. To deprive of life.

MATERIA. Matter. (1) Subject-matter of a controversy. (2) Transaction, event, occurrence. (3) Substance as distinguished from form.

MATERIAL. Material. Important; more or less necessary; having influence or effect; going to the substance, as opposed to the form.

MATERNIDAD. Maternity. The character, relation, state or condition of a mother.

MATERNO. Maternal. Related to or belonging to a mother. Motherly.

MATRICIDIO. Matricide. The murder of a mother by her son or daughter.

MATRÍCULA. Register, list. (1) Inscription of persons, things, acts or circumstances in a central registry for the purpose of public record-keeping. (2) Tuition. The fee to be paid to enter a school or university.

MATRIMONIO. Matrimony. Marriage in the sense of the relation or status, not of the ceremony.

MATRIMONIO NATURAL. Common-law marriage. One not solemnized in the ordinary way (that is, non-ceremonial), but created by an agreement to marry, followed by cohabitation.

MATRIMONIO POR PODER. Marriage by proxy. Marriage contracted by one or more agents rather than by the parties themselves.

MATRIMONIO PUTATIVO. Putative marriage. One contracted in good faith but in ignorance of some existing impediment on the part of at least one of the contracting parties.

MÁXIMA. Maxim. A principle of law universally admitted as being a correct statement of the law, or as agreeable to reason.

MAYOR CUANTÍA. Involving more than a certain sum. It refers to judicial proceedings involving more than a specified sum established by law.

MAYORÍA. Majority. (1) Age at which a person is entitled to the management of his or her own affairs and to the enjoyment of civic rights. (2) Any number of votes greater than half the total cast.

221

MAYORÍA ABSOLUTA. Absolute majority. A number greater than half of any aggregate total.

MAYORÍA RELATIVA. Relative majority. Plurality. The largest number of votes cast in an election involving more than two contestants, but which does not amount to more than half of the votes.

MAYORISTA. Wholesaler. One who buys in comparatively large quantities, and then resells, usually in smaller quantities, to a retailer, who in turn sells to the consumer.

MAYORITARIO. That which has the character of being approved or rejected by the majority.

MEDIACIÓN. Mediation. (1) The act of a third person in intermediating between two contending parties with a view to persuading them to adjust or settle their dispute. (2) The friendly interference of a neutral nation in the controversies of others, for the purpose of keeping the peace in the family of nations.

MEDIADOR. Mediator. Disinterested person who intervenes between parties to reconcile them.

MEDIANERO. Mediatory. Each of the owners of abutting property.

MEDIAR. To mediate. To intervene as a broker or middleman.

MEDICINA. Medicine. The science and art of preventing and curing diseases of the human body.

MEDICINA FORENSE. Forensic medicine. Branch of medicine which permits the application of specific medical knowledge to the purposes of the law.

MÉDICO FORENSE. Coroner. Public official, charged with the duty of inquiring into the causes or circumstances of any death which occurs through violence or suddenly and with marks of suspicion.

MEDIDAS CAUTELARES. Precautionary measures. Measures previously taken to prevent mischief or to secure a good result.

MEDIDAS PREVENTIVAS. Precatory measures. Action taken to prevent failure of the proposed end.

MEDIOS FRAUDULENTOS. False pretenses. Offense consisting of representing a fact or circumstance which is not true in a way calculated to mislead.

MEDIOS Y ARBITRIOS. Ways and means. In a legislative body, the "committee on ways and means" is a committee appointed to inquire into and consider the methods and sources for raising revenue, and to propose means for providing the funds needed by the government.

MEGALOMANÍA. Megalomania. Insanity. (1) That degree of mental illness which negates the individual's legal responsibility or capacity. (2) Delusion of grandeur.

MEJOR POSTOR. Highest bidder. The person who offers the highest sum of money in an auction.

MEJORAS. Improvements. Enhancement or valuable additions made to real property.

MELLIZO. Twin. Either of two offspring produced at birth.

MEMBRESÍA. Membership. To belong to or be a member of a group, association or other organization.

MEMBRETE. Letterhead; heading; memorandum. A sheet or paper bearing a special seal or symbol used to identify the writer. The seal itself.

MEMORÁNDUM. Memorandum. An informal note utilized to keep something that must be remembered in writing. A brief written outline of an agreement or transaction.

MEMORIAL. Memorial. A formal written petition in a court or administrative body or other entity, requesting action on a certain matter before it.

MENDICIDAD. Mendicancy. State and life of a person who lives on charity obtained through begging.

MENGUA. (1) Diminution, decrease. (2) Waning. (3) Poverty, want.

MENOR. Minor. Person under the age of legal competence.

MENOR CUANTÍA. Involving less than a certain sum. The judicial proceeding which involves a case where the sum in conflict is less than a specific sum established by law to make a difference between cases.

MENOR EMANCIPADO. Emancipated minor. A person under 18 years of age who is totally self-supporting. The minor who has received authorization to act on his or her own behalf and be fully responsible for the act done.

MENOS. Less. That which is lower or fewer than another.

MENOSCABO. Detriment. A loss, damage or miscredit suffered by a person.

MENOSPRECIAR. To underestimate. To undervalue something. To despise.

MENSAJERO. Messenger. Person who bears news or messages.

MENS REA. (Lat.) Guilty mind; a guilty or wrongful purpose; a criminal intent.

MENSUAL. Monthly. That which occurs every month, whether a payment of rent, the accruing of interest or other.

MENSURA. Measurement. Any actions in which measures are taken, particularly applied to real estate.

MENTIRA. To lie, deceive. To willfully be false or deceptive or not tell the complete truth.

MENTIROSO. Liar. The person who lies. See "Mentira".

MERCADERÍA. Merchandise. Said of all salable goods. Any object capable of being sold.

MERCADER. Merchant. One who is engaged in the purchase and sale of goods.

MERCADO. Market. Place of commercial activity where articles are bought and sold. It usually refers to the place where food is bought.

MERCADO DE VALORES. Securities or stock market. An organized market or exchange where securities are traded.

MERCANCÍA. Merchandise. All goods which merchants buy and sell.

MERCANTE. Merchant. The person who sells. One who is in the sales business. See "Mercader".

MERCANTIL. Mercantile, commercial. All that refers to commerce or trade or the business of buying and selling merchandise.

MERCENARIO. Mercenary. (1) In general, all persons who receive a salary. (2) Voluntary soldier who receives payment for services rendered.

MERITORIO. Meritorious. Possessing or characterized by "merit" in the legal sense of the word.

MESA ELECTORAL. Board of elections. Board which receives and counts electoral votes, and oversees the electoral process to ensure it is conducted fairly.

MESADA. Monthly pay, wages or allowance. Money given to another.

MESOCRACIA. Government by the middle class.

METEDOR. Smuggler. Person who imports or exports prohibited articles without paying the duties chargeable to them.

MÉTODO. Method. The mode or way of operating, or the means of attaining an object.

METRÓPOLI. Metropolis. (1) Principal city or capital of a nation, state or region. (2) A large important city.

MIEDO. Fear. Apprehension of harm; dread; consciousness of approaching danger.

MIEMBRO. Member. One of the persons constituting a group (for example, a family, partnership, etc.).

MIGRACIÓN. Migration. (1) Movement of people from one country or region to another. (2) The department or agency of the government in charge of the registration and status of foreigners within a country.

MILICIA. Militia. (1) The science of waging war. (2) The body of citizens in a state, enrolled for discipline in a military force, but not engaged in actual service except in emergencies, as distinguished from regular troops or a standing army.

MINISTERIO. Ministry, governmental department.

MINISTERIO PÚBLICO. Attorney general's office. It is the institution formed by all public prosecutors and the attorney general entrusted to defend the rights of the state and society.

MINISTRO. Minister. Person acting as agent for another in the performance of specified duties or orders.

MINORÍA. Minority. (1) The smaller number of votes of an assembly. (2) The state or condition of a minor.

MINORISTA. Retailer. Merchant who sells goods to the public in small quantities.

MINORITARIO. Pertaining to the minority, i.e., a minority vote.

MINUTA. (1) Rough draft of a contract or public deed. (2) Draft, extract or notes from a contract, transaction or proceeding.

MISHNA. (Heb.) Oral Jewish law. The collection of Jewish traditions compiled about 200 A.D. and made the basic part of the Talmud.

MISIÓN. Mission. A specific task or duty undertaken by a person or a group of persons.

MITIGACIÓN. Mitigation. Alleviation, reduction, abatement or diminution of a penalty or punishment imposed by law.

MITIGAR. To mitigate. To reduce or alleviate a penalty or punishment.

MITIN. Meeting. Assembling of people to discuss and act upon a matter in which they have a common interest.

MOBILIARIO. Movables, chattel. (1) Things which may be carried from one place to another, whether they move by themselves or whether they are inanimate objects capable of being moved by extraneous power. (2) Household furnishings.

MOCIÓN. Motion. (1) The proposition by a member of a deliberative body submitting a certain measure for consideration by the assembly. (2) An application made to a court or judge to obtain a rule or order directing some act to be done in favor of the applicant.

MOCIONANTE. One who makes a motion. The person who submits to the court or others a proposal.

MOCIONAR. To make a motion. The act of expressing one's opinion or proposal.

MODELO. Model. Example worthy of imitation. A pattern.

MODIFICACIÓN. Modification. An alternation which changes certain aspects but leaves the nature and use of the thing unchanged.

MODIFICAR. Modify. To alter; to change in incidental or subordinate features; to amend.

MODO. Mode. System or manner to do things.

MODUS VIVENDI. Method or way of living. A rule of conduct.

MOJÓN. Landmark, milestone. Demarcations made of stones, trees, or other objects, marking the boundaries of an estate or a public road.

MONEDA. Currency. Coined money, bank notes or paper money which are the medium of exchange.

MONEDA DE CURSO LEGAL. Legal tender. Coin and paper money which by law is good to satisfy public and private obligations.

MONEDA FALSA. Counterfeit money. Money copied or imitated, without authority or right, with a view to defraud, by passing the copied money as genuine.

MONEDERO FALSO. Counterfeiter. One who unlawfully makes base coin in imitation of the true metal, or forges false currency, with the intention of deceiving another.

MONETARIA. Monetary. What refers to money, whether paper or coins.

MONOGAMIA. Monogamy. The marriage to one spouse only.

MONOPOLIO. Monopoly. A form of market structure in which one or only a few entities or corporations dominate the total sales of a product or service.

MONUMENTO. Monument. Anything by which the memory of a person, thing, science, art, idea or event is preserved or perpetuated.

MORA. Delay, default. Tardiness in the compliance of an obligation. Arrears. Delay in performing an obligation.

MORADA. Abode. The place of residence. Home.

MORAL PÚBLICA. Said of the moral principles and values adopted by the majority regarding behavior, honesty, etc.

MOROSIDAD. Delinquency. Being tardy or untimely in meeting one's obligations.

MORATORIA. Moratorium. Delay or postponement of an action or proceeding. Extra time allowed to meet or perform an obligation or debt that has matured and should have been performed.

MORFINA. Morphine. The principal alkaloid extracted from opium which is used in the form of a soluble salt as an analgesic and sedative. A highly addictive narcotic.

MORGUE. Morgue. Repositary where cadavers are kept until identified and claimed by relatives or their release for burial.

MOROSO. Delinquent, slow pay. Person who does not pay a debt at the time appointed. The person who is in arrears. Also the obligation itself that has not been fulfilled in due time.

MORTALIDAD. Mortality. The relative incidence of death.

MORTIS CAUSA. By reason of death; in contemplation of death.

MOSTRAR CAUSA. To show cause. To present to the court such reasons and considerations as one has to offer why a particular order, decree, injunction, etc., should not be confirmed, take effect, be executed, etc.

MOSTRENCO. (1) Having no known owner. (2) Stray. Having no house or home. Any kind of property which can be owned by anyone because it has been abandoned.

MOTE. Motto; nickname; slogan.

MOTÍN. Mutiny. An insurrection of soldiers or sailors against the authority of their commanders; a sedition or revolt in the army or navy.

MOTIVO. Motive. Cause, reason or basis which induces an action.

MOTU PROPIO. (Lat.) Of his or her own initiative. When a person acts voluntarily.

MÓVIL. Motive. Intent. The purpose which encourages one person to do something. See "Motivo".

MUDO. Mute, speechless. One who cannot or will not speak.

MUEBLE. (1) Movable thing which may be carried from one place to another. (2) Furniture.

MUERTE. Death. The cessation of life.

MUERTE ACCIDENTAL. Accidental death. Death caused by sickness or casual violence.

MUERTE NATURAL. Natural death. Death from causes other than an accident or violence.

MUERTE PRESUNTA. Presumptive death. Death which is presumed after a certain period of unexplained absence, although no body has been found.

MUERTE VIOLENTA. Violent death. Death caused by violent external means.

MUJER. Woman. A person of the female sex.

MULTA. Fine. (1) (noun) Monetary punishment imposed by a lawful tribunal on a person convicted of a crime or misdemeanor. (2) (verb) To impose a monetary punishment or verdict.

MULTAR. To fine, impose a penalty. Obligation to pay a certain sum of money.

MUNDANO. Mundane. Characterized by the practical, transitory, and ordinary.

MUNICIPIO. Municipality. A legally incorporated association by the inhabitants of a limited area for local government or other public purposes.

MURMURACIÓN. Gossip; slander. A rumor or report of an intimate nature.

MUTATIS MUTANDIS. (Lat.) With the necessary changes of details. This phrase is utilized to indicate that the contract or matter is the same as another but should be changed where necessary.

MUTILACIÓN. Mutilation. (1) As applied to written documents, rendering the document imperfect by recoving from it some essential part (by cutting, tearing, burning, or erasure) but without totally destroying it. (2) In criminal law, depriving a person of the use of any of those limbs which may be useful in a fight. (3) To mutilate a body.

MUTUALIDAD. (1) Mutuality. Reciprocation; interchange. An act by each of two parties. (2) Mutual association. One based on reciprocal contracts and which requires that each member receive benefits as a matter of right. Commonly a fraternal or social organization which provides insurance for its members on an assessment basis.

MUTUANTE. Lender. Said of the person that gives to the borrower a loan for consumption. See "Mutuo".

MUTUARIO. Borrower. Said of the person who receives a loan of chattels for consumption and agrees to return an equivalent in kind and quantity. See "Mutuo".

MUTUO. (1) In Roman law, "mutuum." Loan for consumption; a loan of chattels, upon an agreement that the borrower may consume them, returning to the lender an equivalent in kind and quantity. (2) Mutual. Common to both parties.

MUTUO CONSENTIMIENTO. Mutual consent. An agreement by all parties on a specific subject.

N

NACIMIENTO. Birth. The emergence of a new individual from the body of its mother.

NACIÓN. Nation. (1) The inhabitants of a country ruled by the same government. (2) The territory of the same country. (3) A group of persons with the same ethnic origin and having the same language.

NACIONAL. National. Pertaining to a nation. Person who has acquired nationality either by birth or nationalization.

NACIONALIDAD. Nationality. The quality or character which arises from a person's belonging to a nation or state. It can arise by either birth or naturalization.

NACIONALIZACIÓN. Nationalization, naturalization. (1) The granting of the quality or status of a "national" to a foreigner. (2) The acquisition of private property or business by the government.

NACIONALIZAR. To nationalize, naturalize. To acquire nationality. See "Nacionalización".

NACIONES UNIDAS. United Nations. An international organization created to prevent war, provide justice and promote human rights.

NARCÓTICO. Narcotic. Generic term for any drug which dulls the senses or induces sleep and which commonly becomes addictive after prolonged use. In law these substances are important in relation to the influence they have upon the will of an individual.

NASCITURUS. (Lat.) That shall hereafter be born. A term used in marriage settlements to designate the future issue of the marriage, as opposed to a child already born.

NATALIDAD. Natality. Birth rate. Number of births during a given period of time.

NATIVO. Native. A citizen by birth, as distinguished from a citizen by naturalization.

NATO. Ex officio. By virtue of the office. Inherent or implied in an office or position.

NATURAL. Natural. That which has to do with nature. What is customary or normal. When this word is applied to a son or daughter it signifies that the person was born out of wedlock; however, at the time of conception his or her parents could marry since no legal impediment existed.

NATURALEZA. Nature. (1) Naturalization. The process by which a person acquires nationality after birth. See "Naturalización". (2) The essence and characteristics of each being.

NATURALIZACIÓN. Naturalization. The process by which a person acquires nationality after birth and becomes entitled to the privileges of citizenship.

NAUFRAGIO. Shipwreck. The loss of a vessel, caused by grounding or by the violence of winds and waves in a tempest.

NAVE. Ship, vessel, boat. Any craft used, or capable of being used, for navigation.

NAVEGABILIDAD. Navigability. Determination by competent authority that a vessel is capable of safe navigation.

NAVEGACIÓN. Navigation. The art and science of conducting and handling vessels.

NAVIERO. (1) Shipowner. Owner of a shipping company. (2) Related to ships or shipping.

NECESIDAD. Necessity. (1) An irresistible impulse or force which compels one to act. (2) The lack of food or things indispensable to live.

NECROLOGÍA. Necrology. (1) A list of the recently dead. (2) Obituary.

NECROPSIA. Autopsy. Post-mortem examination of a human body to establish the cause of death.

NEGABLE. Deniable. What can be denied or refused. Whenever the defendant can deny the allegations of the plaintiff. Traverse.

NEGACIÓN. Traverse. Whenever the defendant denies the allegations of the plaintiff.

NEGAR. To deny. To reject or refuse a fact or allegation.

NEGATIVA. Negative. Refusal of what has been requested. This word may be construed as contempt of court.

NEGLIGENCIA. Negligence. An omission which a reasonable person, guided by ordinary prudence and care, should do to protect others, or the doing of something which a reasonable and prudent person would not do and which harms the interests of others.

NEGLIGENCIA COMPARATIVA. Comparative or ordinary negligence. When negligence is measured in terms of a percentage, and any damages allowed are diminished in proportion to the amount of negligence attributable to the person injured, damaged, or which seeks recovery.

NEGLIGENCIA CONCURRENTE. Concurrent negligence. Arises where the injury is proximately caused by the concurrent wrongful acts or omissions of two or more persons acting independently.

NEGLIGENCIA CONTRIBUYENTE. Contributory negligence. Conduct by a plaintiff which is below the standard to which he or she is legally required to conform for his or her own protection and which is a contributing cause which cooperates with the defendant's negligence in causing the plaintiff's harm.

NEGLIGENCIA CRASA. Gross negligence. The intentional failure to perform a manifest duty in reckless disregard of the consequences that affect the life, safety, or property of another.

NEGLIGENCIA CRIMINAL. Criminal negligence. Such a flagrant and reckless disregard of the safety of others, or willful indifference to the injury to follow, as to convert an act otherwise lawful into a crime because it results in personal injury or death.

NEGLIGENCIA DERIVADA. Imputed negligence. Doctrine that places on one person responsibility for the negligence of another. Such responsibility of liability is imputed by reason of some special relationship of the parties, such as parent and child, husband and wife, driver and passenger, etc.

NEGLIGENCIA GRAVE. Gross negligence. See "Negligencia Crasa".

NEGLIGENTE. Negligent. Person who is careless, by omission or commission, of the interest of others. See "Negligencia".

233

NEGOCIABILIDAD. Negotiability. Said of all documents that are negotiable, which may be transferred by endorsement or delivery.

NEGOCIABLE. Negotiable, assignable. Legally capable of being transferred by endorsement or delivery.

NEGOCIACIÓN. Negotiation. (1) The conversation and exchange which passes between parties or their agents in the course of or incident to the making of a contract. (2) The act by which a check, promissory note, or negotiable instrument is put into circulation by transfer from one person to another person.

NEGOCIACIONES COLECTIVAS. Collective bargaining. A procedure for making collective agreements between employer and accredited employee representatives, concerning wages, hours, and other employment conditions, which requires that each party deal with the other in good faith and with an open mind.

NEGOCIADOR. Negotiator. Person who acts between parties in a negotiation. See "Negociación".

NEGOCIO. Business. (1) Employment, occupation, profession or commercial activity engaged in for gain or livelihood. (2) Commercial establishment. Activity in which a merchant is involved. The course of dealings of a commercial establishment.

NEPOTISMO. Nepotism. When those in power appoint their own relatives to hold public offices.

NETO. Net. That which remains after all allowable deductions, such as charges, expenses, discounts, commissions, taxes, etc., are made.

NEUTRAL. Neutral. Impartial in a discussion or lawsuit. Not taking sides between two parties in conflict.

NEUTRALIDAD. Neutrality. State of being neutral. Quality of being neutral.

NEXO. Bond, tie, union or relations between persons and/or things.

NIETO, NIETA. Grandchild. A child of one's child.

NIÑO ILEGÍTIMO. Illegitimate child. Child who is born at a time when his or her parents, though alive, are not married to each other.

NOCHE. Night. Lapse during which there is no sunlight.

NOCIVO. Noxious. Harmful; offensive; offensive to the smell. That which causes or tends to cause injury, especially to health or morals.

NOCTURNIDAD. What has to do with the night. Aggravation of an offense because it was committed at night.

NO ES CULPABLE. Not guilty. Verdict in criminal cases where the defendant is acquitted of the charge.

NO HA LUGAR. Expression utilized by the judge to reject a petition, claim or objection presented by one of the parties to a lawsuit.

NOMBRADO. Appointed. A person who has been chosen to perform a specific task, duty or to fill a post.

NOMBRAMIENTO. Appointment. The designation of a person, by the person or persons having the authority therefor, to discharge the duties of some office or trust.

NOMBRAR. To name. To appoint, or designate someone to fill a post.

NOMBRE. Name. Word or words given to identify objects. The first name of a person to distinguish him or her from others.

NOMBRE COMERCIAL. Commercial name. Trade name; firm name. The name under which a commercial establishment carries on its business.

NOMINACIÓN. Nomination. An appointment or designation of a person to fill an office or discharge a duty.

NOMINADO. Said of the contract that is established and regulated by law.

NOMINAL. Nominal. Titular; existing in name only; not real or substantial; connected with the transaction or proceeding in name only, not in real interest.

NOMINAR. Nominate. To name, designate, appoint, or propose for election or appointment.

NOMINATIVO. Nominative. In the name of a determined person. In stocks, the opposite of bearer shares.

NORMA. Norm. Rule of conduct, law, standard, criterion.

NORMATIVO. Normative. (1) Said of the contract in which two or more persons agree and establish future rules for future contracts among themselves and are bound by those rules as if they were imposed by law. (2) Said of something imposing rules.

NOTARÍA. Notary's office. The place in which a notary public performs his or her duties. See "Notario".

NOTARIADO. What has been approved by a notary public. The notary gives faith of the acts or signatures brought before him or her.

NOTARIAL. Notarial. Taken by a notary public; performed by a notary in his or her official capacity; belonging to a notary and evidencing his or her official character, as a notarial seal.

NOTARIO. Notary public. A public officer who is authorized by the state or federal government to administer oaths, and to attest to the authenticity of signatures and acts.

NOTICIA. Notice. News. See "Notificación".

NOTIFICACIÓN. Notification. Information, an advice, or written notice or warning intended to apprise a person of some proceeding in which his or her interests are involved, or informing him or her of some fact which it is his or her right to know and the duty of the notifying party to communicate.

NOTIFICADOR. Process server. Person authorized by law (e.g., a sheriff) to serve process papers on defendants.

NOTIFICAR. To notify. See "Notificación".

NOTORIO. Notorious. What is known to all as a fact.

NOVACIÓN. Novation, substitution. Substitution of an existing contract, debt, or obligation for a new one, between the same or different parties.

NOVAR. To substitute. The substitution of the object or one of the subjects in an obligation, therefore the original obligation is terminated and a new or substitute obligation is created.

NOVATORIO. Novatory. The state of being or having to do with a novation. See "Novar".

NOVIA. Fiancée. A woman engaged to be married.

NOVIO. Fiancé. A man engaged to be married.

NOVICIO. Novice; new. Inexperienced. Freshman; apprentice.

NUERA. Daughter-in-law. With respect to a person, the wife of his or her son.

NUEVO(VA). New. Previously unknown. Fresh.

NUEVO JUICIO. New trial. A re-examination of an issue of fact, or some part or positions thereof, after the verdict by a jury, report of a referee, or a decision by the court.

NULIDAD. Nullity, invalidity. An act or proceeding in a cause which the opposite party may treat as though it had not taken place, or which has absolutely no legal force or effect.

NULIFICAR. To annul, nullify. To reduce to nothing; to make void or of no effect; to abolish; to do away with.

NULO. Null, void, invalid, of no legal force. That which cannot be enforced because it lacks an essential element for its validity.

NUNCIATURA. Nunciature. Office of a nuncio, the official representative of the Pope in a foreign nation.

NUNCIO. Nuncio. (1) Person who transmits news. (2) Papal diplomatic representative before a government.

NUNC PRO TUNC. (Lat.) Now for then. Phrase applied to acts allowed to be done after the time when they should be done, with a retroactive effect, that is, with the same effect as if regularly done.

NUNCUPATIVO. Nuncupative. Said of an oral will declared or dictated by the testator before witnesses, and afterwards reduced to writing.

NUPCIAS. Matrimony. The ceremony and not the contract of marriage. The wedding.

O

OBEDIENCIA. Obedience. Compliance with a command, prohibition, known law or rule or duty.

OBCECACIÓN. Obfuscation, obsession. A violent emotional state that affects the will and conscience of a person. It can be a mitigating circumstance if a crime is committed in this state of mind.

OBCECADO. Person who is in a state of obfuscation. See "Obcecación".

ÓBITO. Decease. To depart from life. To die. Death.

OBITUARIO. Obituary. Ledger in which deaths and funerals are registered in one's parish. Also the name of the newspaper section advising a person's demise.

OBJECIÓN. Objection. Act of objecting; that which is, or may be, presented in opposition; an adverse reason or argument.

OBJETIVO. Impartial. Fair and not biased.

OBJETO. (1) (verb) To interpose a declaration, during a legal proceeding, to the effect that the particular matter or thing under consideration is not done or admitted with the consent of the party objecting, but is considered improper or illegal, and referring the question of its propriety or legality to the court. (2) (noun) End aimed at; the thing sought to be accomplished or attained; the aim or purpose; the objective.

OBJETO DE LA ACCIÓN. Object of the action. The thing sought to be obtained by the action; the remedy demanded or the relief or recovery sought or prayed for.

OBJETIVIDAD. Objectivity. Said of an open and unbiased mind, that can judge impartially based on the facts without preconceived notions.

OBJETIVO. Objective. (1) That which refers to an object. (2) Impartial. Without bias.

OBLACIÓN. Oblation. (1) Offering or gift made to the church. (2) Payment.

OBLIGACIÓN. A generic word having many, wide and varied meanings, according to the context in which it is used. That which a person is bound to do or forbear; any duty imposed by law, promise, contract, relations of society, courtesy, kindness, etc.

OBLIGACIÓN ACCESORIA. Accessory obligation. One which depends upon or is collateral to the principal obligations. Whenever the principal obligation is extinguished, the accessory obligation is also extinguished.

OBLIGACIÓN ALTERNATIVA. Alternative obligation. Said of the obligations that encompass two or more duties or undertakings; once one of these is accomplished or delivered, the obligation is discharged.

OBLICACIÓN A PLAZO. Conditional obligation. Said of the obligation that must be complied with by a certain date.

OBLIGACIÓN BILATERAL. Bilateral obligation. Said of the obligations in which all parties exchange mutual undertakings.

OBLIGACIÓN COLECTIVA. Joint or several obligations. A "joint obligation" is one in which two or more obligors bind themselves to the performance of the obligations. A "several obligation" is one where the obligors bind themselves each to independently fulfill the engagement.

OBLIGACIÓN CONVENCIONAL. Contractual obligations. The one which arises from a contract or agreement.

OBLIGACIÓN DE DAR. Obligation to give. Said of the obligation to deliver a thing or transfer a right to another.

OBLIGACIÓN DE HACER. Obligation to do. Said of the obligation that requires that an action be taken.

OBLIGACIÓN DE NO DAR. Obligation not to give. This is the obligation not to act or perform, since what is required is a negative action. See "Obligación de No Hacer".

OBLIGACIÓN DE NO HACER. Obligation not to do. Said of the obligation in which a particular action is prohibited.

OBLIGACIÓN DE PROBAR. Burden of proof. See "Onus Probandi".

OBLIGACIÓN DE TRACTO SUCESIVO. Successive performance obligation. Said of the obligation that requires successive compliance in time, i.e., the payment of rent for an apartment, the payment of wages to an employee, etc.

OBLIGACIÓN DE TRACTO ÚNICO. Said of an obligation that requires a one-time or immediate compliance, i.e., the delivery of goods to the purchaser, etc. It is the opposite of the successive performance obligation. See "Obligación de Tracto Sucesivo".

OBLIGACIÓN DIVISIBLE. Divisible obligations. One which, being a unit, may nevertheless be lawfully divided, with or without the consent of the parties.

OBLIGACIÓN ÉTICA. Moral obligation. One which rests upon ethical obligations alone, and is not imposed or enforced by law, since no contract or law has been breached.

OBLIGACIÓN EXPRESA. Express obligation. One by which the obligor binds him or herself in express terms to perform his or her obligations.

OBLIGACIÓN IMPLÍCITA. Implied obligation. One that is raised by the implication or inference of the law from the nature of the transaction.

OBLIGACIÓN INCONDICIONAL. Absolute obligation. One which gives no alternative to the obligor, but requires fulfillment according to the engagement.

OBLIGACIÓN INDIVISIBLE. Indivisible obligation. One which is not susceptible of division.

OBLIGACIÓN LÍCITA. Lawful obligation. Said of the obligation which complies with the law.

OBLIGACIÓN MANCOMUNADA. Concurrent obligation. Said of the obligation in which there are a number of debtors or creditors. However, each creditor can only claim his or her share and each debtor is only responsible for his or her share of the debt.

240

OBLIGACIÓN NATURAL. Natural obligation. One which cannot be forced by action, but which is binding on the party in good conscience and fairness.

OBLIGACIÓN PERSONAL. Personal or heritable obligation. One where the heirs and assigns of one party may enforce the performance against the heirs of the other party.

OBLIGACIÓN PRINCIPAL. Principal obligation. One which arises from the principal object of the engagement between the contracting parties.

OBLIGACIÓN PURA. Pure obligation. One which is not suspended by any condition.

OBLIGACIÓN SIMPLE. Simple obligation. One which is not dependent for its execution on any event provided for by the parties, and which will not become void on the happening of any such event.

OBLIGACIÓN SINALAGMÁTICA. Synallagmatic obligation. Said of the obligation that is unilateral in principle but that can be converted to bilateral.

OBLIGACIÓN SOLIDARIA. Solidary obligation. One which binds each of the obligors for the whole debt. Joint and several obligations in which each debtor is responsible and can be requested to discharge the whole debt and not just his or her share.

OBLIGACIÓN TRIBUTARIA. Tax liability. The obligation to pay taxes to the government.

OBLIGACIÓN UNILATERAL. Unilateral obligation. Said of the obligations in which only one party is bound to the other, without mutual engagements.

OBLIGADO. Debtor. Person who contracts to do, not to do or give something.

OBLIGATORIEDAD. Obligatory. The need to act due to an obligation.

OBLIGATORIO. Compulsory. What has to be done due to legal, moral or contractual obligation.

OBRA. Work; act; labor. A thing produced by an artist (work of art), a builder (building), a writer (book), etc.

OBREPCIÓN. Obreption. To obtain something by fraud, surprise or false representations.

OBSCENIDAD. Obscenity. The character or quality of being obscene; conduct tending to corrupt the public morals by its indecency and lewdness.

OBSCENO. Obscene. Objectionable or offensive to accepted standards of decency.

OBSEQUIO. Gift. A transfer of property without consideration. Donation.

OBSERVANCIA. Observance. The proper execution of the command of one's superior. Compliance with the law.

OBSERVAR. To observe. (1) To perform that which has been prescribed by some law or usage. To adhere to or abide by. (2) To watch or look out.

OBSERVACIÓN. Observation; remark.

OBSOLESCENCIA. Obsolescent. Condition of that which is obsolete and no longer in use.

OBTENCIÓN. Obtainment. Action and effect of obtaining. To get possession of, procure, preserve or maintain.

OBSTRUCCIÓN. Obstruction. What hinders or prevents an action.

OBVENCIÓN. Perquisite. Fringe benefit or other incidental profit or benefit attaching to an office or position.

OBVIAR. To obviate. To make unnecessary; to see beforehand and dispose of.

OCASIÓN. Occasion. Opportunity or chance in time or place to do, obtain or procure something. Opportunity favorable to act.

OCASIONAL. Occasional. The product of the opportunity favorable to act.

OCCISIÓN. Violent death.

OCCISO. Person who has died violently.

OCIO. Idleness, leisure; recreation, pastime.

OCIOSIDAD. Idleness. Said of the situation of the person who cannot or will not work.

OCIOSO. Idler. Person who cannot or will not work.

OCULTACIÓN. Concealment. A withholding of something which one knows and which one, in duty, is bound to reveal.

OCULTAR. To conceal. To hide or withhold from view or knowledge of others.

OCUPACIÓN o NEGOCIO. Trade or business.

OCUPADOR. Occupier. Person who is in possession of a thing.

OCUPANTE. Occupant. Person who occupies. One who takes possession of a thing no one owns.

OCUPAR. To occupy. To take possession of something.

OCURRENCIA. Occurrence. An event or happening. Any incident or event, especially one that happens without being designed or expected.

ODIO. Hatred. Aversion of one person to another person or thing.

OFENDEDOR. Offender. See "Ofensor".

OFENDER. To offend. To infringe, violate. To transgress the moral or civil rights of another.

OFENDIDO. Victim of an offense.

OFENSA. Offense, crime. A felony or misdemeanor; a breach of the criminal laws.

OFENSOR. Offender. Commonly used in statutes to indicate a person implicated in the commission of a crime and includes a person guilty of a misdemeanor or traffic offense.

OFERENTE. Offeror. Natural or juridical person who makes an offer.

243

OFERTA. Offer. A proposal to do a thing or pay an amount, usually accompanied by an expected acceptance or counter-offer, in return for a promise or an act.

OFICIAL. Official. (1) (noun) Officer, functionary; a person invested with the authority of an office. (2) (adj.) Pertaining to an office; invested with the character of an officer; proceeding from, sanctioned by, or done by, an officer.

OFICIALIZAR. To make official.

OFICIAR. To officiate; to give official notice.

OFICINISTA. Clerk. Office worker, person employed in a public or private office.

OFICIO. Occupation, work. One's regular business or employment.

OFICIOSO. Officious. (1) Active. (2) That is not official. (3) A diplomatic gesture of mediation in good faith.

OFRECEDOR. Offeror. In contracts, the party who makes the offer and looks for an acceptance from the offeree.

OFRECER. To offer, bid, quote. To bring to or before; to present for acceptance or rejection; to exhibit something that may be taken, accepted or rejected.

OFRECIDO. Offeree. In contracts, the person to whom an offer is made by the offeror.

OFRECIMIENTO DE PAGO. Offer of payment. When a debtor recognizes his or her debt and informs the creditor of his or her willingness to pay.

OFUSCACIÓN. Obfuscation. Mental confusion. See "Obcecación".

OLIGOPOLIO. Oligopoly. A market in which each of a few producers affects but does not control the market.

OLÓGRAFO. (1) Holographic. That which is written in the proper hand of the author. (2) Holograph. A will or deed written entirely by the testator or grantor with his or her own hand and not witnessed.

OLVIDO. Forgetfulness. Lack of memory or the ability to remember. Negligence of a duty.

OMISIÓN. Omission. Neglecting to perform what the law requires.

ONEROSO. Onerous. (1) When the obligations attaching to a contract, lease, or other right are unreasonably burdensome or exceed the advantage to be derived from it. (2) Any obligation which is not gratuitous.

ONUS PROBANDI. (Lat.) Burden of proof. The necessity or duty of affirmatively proving a fact or facts in dispute on an issue raised between the parties in a cause.

OPCIÓN. Option. (1) The act of choosing. (2) An agreement which gives the optionee the power to accept an offer for a limited time.

OPCIÓN DE COMPRA. Option to purchase. Clause commonly agreed upon where the lessor and lessee agree to give to the latter the option to buy the property leased.

OPERACIÓN. Operation. (1) Any action in general. (2) To enter in a business transaction. (3) Banking or trading transaction. (4) Medical intervention.

OPERAR. To operate. To realize an operation.

OPERARIO. Operator, workman, worker.

OPONIBILIDAD. Opposition. The right a person has to defend his or her rights against any third parties.

OPINIÓN. Opinion. (1) A document prepared by an attorney for a client, setting forth the attorney's understanding of the law as applicable to the state of facts submitted to him or her for that purpose. (2) The statement by a judge of the decision reached in regard to a cause tried or argued before him or her, expounding the law as applied to the case, and detailing the reasons upon which the judgment is based.

OPONER. To oppose. To present a contrary opinion.

OPONERSE. To oppose. To be against. See "Oponer".

OPONIBLE. Opposable. Being likely to cause objection; objectionable.

OPOSICIÓN. Opposition. (1) Act of opposing or resisting; antagonism; state of being opposite or opposed; antithesis. (2) Political party opposed to a government.

OPOSITOR. Opposer. One who opposes; objector.

OPRESIÓN. Oppression. An act of cruelty, severity, unlawful exaction, or excessive use of authority.

OPROBIO. Opprobrium. Affront. Offense or dishonor.

OPTATIVO. Optional. That which involves an option or alternative; not compulsory.

OPUGNACIÓN. To contradict or oppose by force of reason.

OPULENCIA. Opulence. Abundance, wealth, excess of money.

ORADOR. Orator. Speaker. Person who addresses a group of persons.

ORATORIA. Oratory. The art of speaking in public eloquently or effectively.

ORATORIA FORENSE. Oral participation by the parties' attorneys in a judicial proceeding.

ORDEN. Order. (1) A mandate; precept; command or direction authoritatively given; rule or regulation. (2) Sequence, succession.

ORDEN JUDICIAL. Court order.

ORDEN MORAL. Moral order. The whole group of opinions, institutions, traditions and mores which constitute the moral and ethical structure of a country, society or community.

ORDENAMIENTO. Ordinance, law. A rule established by authority; a permanent rule of action.

ORDENANZA. Ordinance. See "Ordenamiento".

ORDENAR. To order, command.

ORDINARIO. Ordinary. (1) Normal, common or habitual. (2) Of little value.

ORFANDAD. Orphanhood. Person who has lost one or both parents.

ORGÁNICO. Organic. (1) That which relates to an organ or organism. (2) The fundamental law of a state or institution.

ORGANISMO. Organism. (1) Entity composed of different branches that work together to achieve a goal. (2) The total sum of all the organs a human body is made of.

ORGANIZACIÓN. Organization. (1) To organize; to put into working order. (2) A corporation; government or governmental subdivision or agency; business trust; estate; trust; two or more persons having a joint or common interest; or any other legal or commercial entity.

ORGANIZADOR. Organizer, incorporator. Something used to organize. The person in charge of the organization.

ORIGEN. Origin. Beginning. Place where one or one's parents are born.

ORIUNDO. Originating. That which is native or originates from somewhere or something.

ORTODOXO. Orthodox. Person who accepts a dogma without question.

OTORGADOR. Grantor. The person who gives or grants something to another. See "Otorgante".

OTORGAMIENTO. Granting. To issue, grant or execute a document.

OTORGANTE. Grantor, maker. (1) The person who makes a grant. (2) A transferor of property. (3) The creator of a trust.

OTROSÍ. Moreover. An expression utilized to add something omitted.

OYENTE. Hearer. Person who hears.

P

PABELLÓN. Pavilion. (1) A large and often sumptuous tent. (2) National flag. (3) Flag utilized by ships to indicate their port of registry.

PACTA SUNT SERVANTA. (Lat.) The agreements of the parties in a contract must be complied with.

PACTANTE. (1) Contracting party. Party with whom a contract is made. (2) Covenantee; party with whom a covenant is made.

PACTAR. To agree. To enter into an agreement, to convene. To concur; come into harmony; give mutual assent.

PACTO. Agreement between two or more persons to do, to give or not to do something. A contract or covenant.

PACTO ACCESORIO. Accessory covenant. Said of the contract to assure performance of a principal contract. Whenever the principal contract is extinguished, the accessory contract is extinguished as well.

PACTO ANTICRÉTICO. Antichretic covenant. Said of the contract in which the debtor and creditor agree that the latter is entitled to receive the income from the property pledged, in lieu of interest as security on the debt.

PACTO COMISORIO. The covenant in which the parties can rescind the contract if one of the parties has defaulted.

PACTO DE CABALLEROS. Gentlemen's agreement. An unsigned and unenforceable agreement made between parties who expect its performance because of good faith.

PACTO DE CUOTA LITIS. Agreement between a lawyer and his or her client in which in addition to fees, said lawyer will receive a portion of the damages recovered in the lawsuit.

PACTO DE NO HACER ALGO. Negative covenant. A provision in an employment agreement or a contract for sale of a business which prohibits the employee or seller from competing in the same area or market. Such restriction must be reasonable in scope and duration.

PACTO DE TRABAJO. Employment contract. An agreement between employer and employee in which the terms and conditions of one's employment are provided.

PACTO RESTRICTIVO. Restrictive covenant. Provision in a deed limiting the use of the property and prohibiting certain uses. See also "Pacto de No Hacer Algo".

PACTO SOCIAL. (1) Partnership agreement. The document embodying the terms and conditions of a partnership and sometimes referred to as the articles of partnership. (2) Articles of incorporation. Terms and conditions by which a corporation is organized.

PADECER. To suffer. To have the feeling or sensation that arises from the action of something painful, distressing, or the like.

PADRE. Father. A male parent.

PADRE DE FAMILIA. Head of household. Said of a man with children.

PADRE PUTATIVO. Putative father. The alleged or reputed father of an illegitimate child.

PADRINO. Godfather. Patron; protector; best man (in a wedding).

PADRÓN. Census. A periodic population list of the residents of a town. It is usually effected for tax reasons or prior to elections.

PAGA. Payment. Fee, wages, salary or satisfaction of a debt or obligation.

PAGADERO. Payable. Capable of being paid; suitable to be paid; admitting or demanding payment; justly due; legally enforceable.

PAGADO. Paid. To be charged a debt. To settle an obligation in the manner and time frame contracted.

249

PAGADOR. Payer; disburser. One who pays, or who is to make a payment.

PAGADOR DE IMPUESTOS. Taxpayer. Person who pays taxes; one whose income is subject to taxation.

PAGADURÍA. Public office where payments are made.

PAGA MÍNIMA. Minimum wage. The least wage on which an ordinary individual can be self-sustaining and obtain the ordinary requirements of life. Such minimum wages are set and required by federal statutes of employers engaged in businesses which affect interstate commerce.

PAGAR. To pay. To discharge a debt with money or goods.

PAGARÉ. Promissory note. A document which recognizes the existence of a "sum certain" debt and contains the promise to pay a specific sum at a certain time or on demand to the person named therein or to his or her order.

PAGARÉ A LA ORDEN. Negotiable note. Note legally capable of being transferred by endorsement or delivery.

PAGARÉ A LA VISTA. Demand note. A note which expressly states that it is payable on demand, on presentation or at sight.

PAGARÉ AL PORTADOR. Bearer note. Bonds payable to the person having possession of them. Such bonds do not require endorsement to transfer ownership but only the transfer of possession.

PAGARÉ CON GARANTÍA PRENDARIA. Collateral note. Loan secured by a pledge of specific property.

PAGARÉ FISCAL. Treasury bill. Short-term obligations of a governmental entity.

PAGARÉ HIPOTECARIO. Mortgage note or bond. Note for which real estate or personal property is pledged as security that the note will be paid as stated in its terms.

PAGO. Payment. (1) The fulfillment of a promise, or the performance of an agreement. (2) **Dación en pago.** Payment in kind. Payment not made in money, but of something different with a corresponding value in money equivalent to the debt.

PAGO BAJO PROTESTA. Payment under protest. A payment made under compulsion while the payor asserts that he or she waives no rights by making the payment.

PAGO DIFERIDO. Deferred payment. Payment of principal or interest postponed to a future date.

PAGO EN EXCESO. Overpayment. Payment in excess of what is really owed.

PAGO INCOMPLETO o INSUFICIENTE. Underpayment. Payment of less than what was due.

PAGO JUDICIAL. Payment forced by legal means. Payment ordered by a court.

PAGO PARCIAL. Partial payment. Whenever the debt is not settled in full by the payment.

PAGO POR CONSIGNACIÓN. Consignment. The judicial deposit of any quantity or any value, made by the debtor when the creditor cannot or refuses to receive payment. By delivering payment to the court the debtor cannot be sued for nonpayment.

PAGO SUSPENDIDO. Stop payment order. An order by the drawer of a draft (check) ordering the drawee not to make payment on such.

PAGO TOTAL. Payment in full.

PAÍS. State. Fixed territory with inhabitants sharing a common government, language, culture, history and customs.

PALABRAS COMPROMETEDORAS. Compromising words. Words or expressions that jeopardize or compromise a party's case.

PALACIO DE JUSTICIA. Courthouse. The building occupied for the public sessions of a court, with its various offices.

251

PALPABLE. Palpable. Easily perceptible, plain, obvious, readily visible, noticeable, patent, distinct, manifest.

PANCARTA. Poster, sign, notice.

PANDILLA. Gang of criminals.

PANDILLERO. Gangster, racketeer. A member of a gang of criminals, thieves, or the like.

PAPEL. Paper. Document. Role.

PAPEL BANCABLE. Bankable paper. Notes, checks, bank bills, drafts and other securities for money, received as cash by banks.

PAPEL COMERCIAL o DE COMERCIO. Commercial paper. Bills of exchange (drafts), promissory notes, bank checks, and other negotiable instruments for the payment of money, which, by their form and on their face, purport to be such instruments.

PAPEL DE SEGURIDAD. Safety paper. A special paper utilized for printing of negotiable documents which prevents alterations to said documents as they would become easily perceptible.

PAPEL MONEDA. Paper money. Bill issued by a government against its own credit with a promise to pay the amount specified therein in money.

PAPEL SELLADO o TIMBRADO. A stamped or taxed paper. The paper stamped with a special national emblem or seal which is utilized in the execution of public documents.

PAPELES. Papers. All documents: securities, obligations, pledges, mortgages, deposits, liens, etc., given by a debtor in order to assure the payment or performance of his or her debt, by furnishing the creditor with a resource to be used if the debtor defaults in his or her principal obligation.

PAR. Par. In commercial law, equal; equality. An equality between the nominal or face value of a bill of exchange, share of stock, etc., and its actual selling value.

PARADERO. Whereabouts. Place or general locality where a person or thing is.

PARÁSITO SOCIAL. Social parasite. Person who lives on welfare even though he or she is fit and able to work.

PARCELA. Parcel. (1) A small package or bundle. (2) A part or portion of land. A contiguous quantity of land in the possession of an owner; a lot.

PARCELACIÓN. The act of dividing an estate in lots.

PARCELERO. Sharecropper. Type of tenant farmer who lives on and works the land of another, his or her compensation being a portion of the crops minus any advances for seed, food, tools, etc.

PARCIAL. Partial. Relating to or constituting a part; not complete; not entire or universal; not general or total.

PARCIALIDAD. Partiality. Bias, prejudice. A predisposition to decide a cause or an issue in a certain way, which does not leave the mind open to conviction.

PARCIONERO. Partner. A member of a partnership or firm; one who has united with others to form a partnership in business.

PARENTELA. Kin. Relation or relationship by blood or consanguinity. Relatives by blood; by birth.

PARENTESCO. Kinship, relationship. The state of being kin. See "Parentela".

PARENTESCO COLATERAL. The relationship established by consanguinity rather than direct descent. For example, brothers between themselves, cousins, uncles, etc.

PARENTESCO CONSANGUÍNEO. The relationship established by blood, in which all persons descend from a common ancestor.

PARENTESCO DE DOBLE VÍNCULO. Kinship by sharing two common ancestors (mother and father), such as brothers, as opposed to half brothers, who share only one common ancestor.

PARENTESCO DE SIMPLE VÍNCULO. Kinship of sharing a single ancestor (mother or father) i.e., half brothers. See "Parentesco de Doble Vínculo".

PARIDAD CAMBIARIA. Par of exchange. The precise equality or equivalency of any given sum or quantity of money of one country, and the like sum or quantity of money of any other sovereign country into which it is to be exchanged.

PARIENTES. Relatives. Kinsmen; persons connected with one another by blood or affinity.

PARIENTES MÁS PRÓXIMOS. Next of kin. (1) A person's nearest blood relations according to the law of consanguinity, or (2) those entitled to take under statutory distribution of an intestate's estate.

PARIENTES POR AFINIDAD. In-laws. Persons related by marriage rather than blood.

PARIFICAR. Prove through an example or comparison what is being affirmed.

PARLAMENTARIO. A member of parliament or congress.

PARLAMENTO. Parliament. (1) The supreme legislative assembly of Great Britain and Ireland, consisting of the king and queen and the three estates of the realm: The lords spiritual, the lords temporal, and the commons. (2) Name given to the legislative body of a state.

PARO. Stoppage. Strike. Suspension of work.

PARO OBRERO. Worker's strike. The act of quitting work by a body of workers for the purpose of coercing their employer to accede to some demand they have made upon him or her, and which he or she has refused.

PARO FORZOSO. Lockout. Cessation of furnishing of work to employees or withholding work from them in an effort to get from the employees more desirable terms.

PARO PATRONAL. Lockout. See "Paro Forzoso".

PARRICIDA. Parricide. A person guilty of killing his or her father.

PARRICIDIO. Parricide. The crime of killing one's father.

PARTE. (1) Report, communication, dispatch. (2) A person involved in a lawsuit as a defendant or plaintiff. (3) A share, interest or part of something. (4) One of the persons bound by a contract, agreement, matter or transaction.

PARTE ACTORA. Plaintiff. A person who brings an action; the party who complains or sues in a civil action and is so named on the record.

PARTE CONTENDIENTE. Adverse party in a suit. A party to an action whose interests are opposed to or opposite the interests of another party to the action.

PARTE DE INTERÉS ADVERSO. Adverse party. See "Parte Contendiente".

PARTE DEMANDADA. Defendant. The person defending or denying a claim; the party against whom relief or recovery is sought in an action or suit, or the accused in a criminal case.

PARTE DEMANDANTE. Plaintiff. See "Parte Actora".

PARTE INCULPABLE. Innocent party. Person who did not consciously or intentionally participate in the crime, event, transaction, etc., claimed by the opposing party.

PARTE PERJUDICADA. Aggrieved party. One whose legal right is invaded by an act complained of, or whose pecuniary interest is directly affected by a decree or judgment.

PARTE QUERELLADA. Defendant. See "Parte Demandada".

PARTE REBELDE. Party in contempt of court. Said of the party that does not show up in court when summoned or does not send a person to represent it.

PARTICIÓN. Partition. Distribution. The giving out or division among a number; sharing or parcelling out; allotting; dispensing; apportioning.

PARTICIPACIÓN. Participation. To have a share of something. To have a share of the profits.

PARTICIPACIÓN DE UTILIDADES o EN LOS BENEFICIOS. Profit-sharing. When an employer establishes a plan under which his or her employees or their beneficiaries participate in the employer's profits.

PARTIDA. Partition. Division, portion, certificate. (1) Certificate issued by a competent authority. (2) Departure. (3) Allowance. Money allocated for a specific purpose.

PARTIDA DE DEFUNCIÓN. Death certificate. A certificate detailing the date, age, cause of death and the information of a deceased.

PARTIDA DE NACIMIENTO. Birth certificate. A certificate detailing the date of birth, sex, parents, name and other information of an individual's birth.

PARTIDO. (1) Political party. (2) District or territory.

PASADOR. Smuggler. One who imports or exports prohibited goods or articles without paying the duties chargeable on them.

PASAPORTE. Passport. A document identifying a citizen, in effect requesting foreign powers to allow the bearer to enter and to pass freely and safely, recognizing the right of the bearer to the protection and good offices of his or her country's diplomatic and consular offices.

PASIVO. (1) Passive. Inactive, permissive; consisting of endurance or submission, rather than action. (2) Liabilities; all character of debts and obligations.

PASIVO CONSOLIDADO. Funded debt. Debt represented by bonds or other securities.

PASIVO CORRIENTE o EXIGIBLE. Current liabilities. A liability that is presently enforceable, and that will be paid in the normal operation of a business at an early date, usually within one year.

PASIVO EVENTUAL. Contingent liability. A liability not yet fixed but dependent on events to occur in the future.

PATENTABLE. Patentable. Suitable to be patented; entitled by law to be protected by the issuance of a patent.

PATENTADO. (1) Patented. That which has been protected by the issuance of a patent. (2) Patentee. Person to whom a patent has been granted.

PATENTAR. To patent. To register one's creation in order to have the protection of the law.

PATENTE. Patent; permit. Grant of some privilege, property, or authority, made by the government or sovereign of a country to one or more individuals.

PATENTE DE INVENCIÓN. Letters patent. An instrument issued by the government to the patentee, granting or confirming a right to the exclusive possession and enjoyment of land, or of a new invention or discovery.

PATENTE DE NAVEGACIÓN. Navigation patent. Maritime certificate issued by the country of registry which should be kept aboard, which describes the vessel's owner, call sign letters, type of vessel, tonnages, dimensions and engine specifications among other data.

PATENTE PENDIENTE. Patent pending or applied for. Designation describing the legal status of a patent application while a search is conducted by the patent office as to the patentability of the invention.

PATERNIDAD. Paternity. The state or condition of being a father.

PATERNO. Paternal. Related to the father.

PATÍBULO. Gallows, platform. Scaffold or other public platform where the death penalty is executed.

PATRIA. Motherland; native country to which a person belongs.

PATRIA POTESTAD. Patria Potestas (Lat.). The group of rights and obligations conferred by law to parents for the care, education and guardianship of their children until their legal age.

PATRIMONIO. Proprietorship. (1) All the things that belong to a person. (2) That which is inherited from one's father or mother.

PATRÓN o PATRONO. (1) Employer. One who employs the services of others. (2) Landlord.

PATRULLA. Patrol. Squad. A detachment of persons employed for reconaissance, security or combat.

PEAJE. Toll. Fee paid for the right to use something, generally a road, bridge, or the like, of a public nature.

PEATÓN. Pedestrian. A person traveling on foot.

PECULADO. Peculation. Graft, embezzlement. The unlawful appropriation of public funds by a public officer for his or her own benefit or the benefit of others. See "Malversación".

PECULIO. Peculium. (1) Private resources. Money that a particular person has. (2) Estate or wealth of little value or importance.

PECUNIARIO. Monetary. That which relates to money.

PECHAR. To pay taxes or a tribute.

PEDIDO. Petition. Request; order. See "Petición".

PEDIMIENTO. Petition. See "Petición".

PEDIMIENTO DE AVOCACIÓN. Bill or writ of certiorari. An order by the appellate court indicating whether or not it will hear an appeal.

PEDIR. To request; to demand.

PELIGRO. Danger. Jeopardy; exposure to loss or injury; peril.

PELOTERA. Riot. When three or more persons commit or threaten to commit an act of violence, commit a crime, prevent or coerce official action.

PENA. Penalty. A punishment or sanction imposed by law. It can be civil or criminal in nature.

PENA CAPITAL. Capital punishment. Death penalty. Supreme penalty as punishment for murder or other capital crimes.

PENA CONVENCIONAL. Contract penalty. Penalty pursuant to a default of a contract or agreement.

PENA CORPORAL. Corporal punishment. Physical punishment as distinguished from pecuniary punishment or a fine; any kind of punishment inflicted on the body.

PENA CRUEL Y DESUSADA. Cruel and unusual punishment. Such punishment as would amount to torture or barbarity, and any cruel or degrading punishment not known to the common law; any punishment so disproportionate to the offense as to shock the moral sense of the community.

PENA DE MUERTE. Death penalty. See "Pena Capital".

PENA PECUNIARIA. Fine. A pecuniary punishment imposed by a lawful tribunal upon a person convicted of a crime or misdemeanor.

PENADO. Convict. Prisoner. One who has been adjudged guilty of a crime and is serving a sentence as a result of the conviction.

PENAL. Penal. (1) Related to criminal (penal) law or criminal matters. (2) Concerning to a penalty. (3) **Cláusula penal.** Penalty clause. Agreement to pay money when non-performance of a contract occurs.

PENALIDAD. Penalty. A punishment imposed by law or contract.

PENALIZAR. To penalize, to impose a penalty.

PENDENTE LITE. (Lat.) Pending the outcome of the suit; during the actual progress of a suit; during litigation.

259

PENDIENTE. Pending. Begun, but not yet completed; unsettled; undetermined; in abeyance.

PENITENCIARÍA. Penitentiary. A prison or place of confinement where convicted felons serve their prison terms.

PENSADO. Premeditated, deliberate. Having thought of committing an act beforehand; having planned the execution of an act.

PENSIÓN. Pension, annuity, benefit.

PENSIÓN ALIMENTICIA. Alimony. Allowance which one spouse pays to the other pursuant to a court order for maintenance while they are separated, or while divorce proceedings are pending, or after they are divorced.

PENSIÓN DE ARRENDAMIENTO. Rent. Consideration paid for use or possession of property.

PENSIÓN DE INVALIDEZ. Disability benefit. Benefit received by an employee pursuant to the workers' compensation laws after he or she has been injured while on the job.

PENSIÓN DE JUBILACIÓN. Retirement pension. Benefits received pursuant to a plan established and maintained by an employer to provide such benefits to his or her employees, or their beneficiaries, over a period of years (usually for life) after retirement.

PENSIÓN DE RETIRO. See "Pensión de Jubilación".

PENSIÓN PARA HIJOS MENORES. Child support. In a marriage dissolution or child custody action, money paid by one parent to another toward the expenses of the children of the marriage.

PEQUEÑO JURADO. Petty or petit jury. The ordinary jury for the trial of a civil or criminal action; so called to distinguish it from the grand jury.

PER CÁPITA. Per capita (Lat.). By the head or polls, according to the number of individuals.

PÉRDIDA. Loss. The act of losing or the thing lost; that which is gone and cannot be recovered.

PÉRDIDA CONSIGUIENTE. Consequential loss. Loss not directly caused by damage, but rather arising from results of such damage.

PÉRDIDA CONSTRUCTIVA. Loss resulting from such injuries to the property, without its destruction, rendering it valueless to the owner or preventing its restoration to its original condition except at a cost exceeding its value.

PÉRDIDA DE NEGOCIO. Business loss. Loss from the sale, exchange or other disposition of property used in the trade or business.

PÉRDIDA EFECTIVA. Direct or actual loss. One resulting immediately and proximately from the occurrence and not remotely from some of the consequences or effects thereof.

PÉRDIDA FORTUITA. Casualty loss. As defined for tax purposes it is the complete or partial destruction of property resulting from an identifiable event of a sudden, unexpected or unusual nature.

PÉRDIDA PARCIAL. Partial loss. A loss of a part of a thing or of its value, or any damage not amounting, actually or constructively, to its entire destruction.

PERDÓN. (1) Pardon. An executive action authorized by the law which mitigates or sets aside for the offender the punishment the law inflicts for a crime. (2) Remission or forgiveness of a debt.

PERDONAR. To pardon. To exempt; to forgive.

PERENTORIO. Peremptory. Imperative; final; absolute; not admitting of question, delay, reconsideration or any alternative.

PERFECCIÓN. Perfection. Legal validity. State of being complete, finished, having taken all the steps required by law.

PERFECTO. Perfect. Legally correct; binding; valid; without defect.

PERÍODO. Period, term. Determined space of time.

PERÍODO CONTABLE. Fiscal period. In accounting the period of time usually covered by financial statements. (Could be a year, month, quarter, etc.)

PERÍODO DE GRACIA. Grace period. Days of grace. An extra specified time (usually measured by days) granted to a debtor (bound either to perform an act or make a payment) after the date of performance on an obligation. Certain time after the official deadline during which a taxpayer can pay his or her taxes without incurring a penalty.

PERÍODO DE PRUEBA. Test period. Probation. (1) In procedural law time allowed to parties in litigation to produce evidence on which the case rests. (2) In labor law, the initial period of employment in which the worker must prove capable in order to be considered permanently in such a position.

PERÍODO ELECTORAL. Electoral period. A space of time between the starting and ending of the electoral process.

PERÍODO FISCAL o PERÍODO IMPOSITIVO. Accounting period. In tax law the period of time over which a taxpayer must determine his or her tax liabilities.

PERÍODO PRESIDENCIAL. The president's term of office. Period during which an elected president is entitled to hold office.

PERITAJE. Expert testimony, appraisal. Opinion rendered by some person who possesses special skills or knowledge in the arts, sciences, professions or business and for the purpose of clarifying evidence or the facts in issue. Valuation or estimation of value of goods or real estate.

PERITO. Expert. Appraiser. One skilled. One who by reason of education or specialized experience possesses knowledge superior to the average person's regarding an art, science, profession or business.

PERITO CALÍGRAFO. Handwriting expert. An expert specially skilled to distinguish the peculiarities of one's handwriting who may render an opinion about its genuineness.

PERITO CATASTRAL. Appraiser. An expert specially skilled in estimating the value of real estate.

PERITO TÉCNICO. Expert witness. A witness who has been qualified as an expert and who thereby will be allowed, through answers to questions posed, to assist the jury in understanding complicated

262

and technical subjects not within the understanding of the average lay person.

PERJUDICADO. Injured. Damaged, aggrieved party. One who has suffered loss or injury.

PERJUDICAR. To damage, harm, injure. To cause loss or detriment of any kind to a person.

PERJUDICIAL. Prejudicial, injurious. That which causes injury or impairs.

PERJUICIO. Injury. Damage, detriment, harm, loss; prejudice; tort. Loss or detriment suffered by one to his or her person or property as a result of another's action or omission.

PERJURAR. To commit perjury. Lie under oath.

PERJURIO. Perjury. The crime of lying while under oath. False swearing. Act by which a person under oath in a judicial proceeding willfully makes a false statement or lies.

PERJURO. Perjurer. One who commits perjury. See "Perjurio".

PERMISIVO. Permissive. (1) Allowed, allowable; that which may be done. (2) Lenient; tolerant.

PERMISO. Permit. License; leave of absence. Any document which grants the person the right to do some act not forbidden by law but not allowable without it. Temporary absence from employment or duty with intention to return.

PERMISO DE CIRCULACIÓN o DE CONDUCIÓN. Driver's license. Authorization given by competent authority to operate any vehicle on public roads.

PERMISO DE CONSTRUCCIÓN o EDIFICACIÓN. Building permit. Authorization given by local governmental bodies to build or expand existing structures.

PERMISO DE EXPORTACIÓN. Export permit. Authorization required to export goods.

PERMUTAR. To barter. The exchange between parties of one thing or right for another without using money.

PERPETRADOR. Perpetrator. The person who actually commits a crime, or by whose immediate agency it occurs.

PERPETUIDAD. Perpetuity. Continuing forever. Without limit on time.

PER SE. (Lat.) By itself; in itself; taken alone; inherently; unconnected with other matters.

PERSONA. Person. Any being entitled to rights and charged with duties.

PERSONA FICTICIA. A legal entity, created by or under authority of the laws of a nation, which has similar rights and duties to a natural person.

PERSONA JURÍDICA. Artificial person, legal person. See "Persona Ficticia".

PERSONA MORAL. Legal entity. See "Persona Ficticia".

PERSONA NATURAL. Human being; natural person. Any human.

PERSONA PRIVADA. Private person. Not occupying a public office.

PERSONALIDAD. Personality. Capacity. Required attitude to be legally qualified to be the subject of the law.

PERSONERÍA. Legal capacity. Position or authority of an official representative or attorney in fact. Required ability to be used or to be brought into courts.

PERSONERÍA GREMIAL O PERSONERÍA JURÍDICA. Capacity of a legal entity. Ability required from legal entities (i.e., unions, associations) to be subjects of law.

PERSONERO. Delegate. Attorney, proxy. Solicitor. (1) A person who has been entrusted by another to represent him or her or act for him or her. (2) The attorney for the government in a small territorial division in charge of the prosecution of crimes.

PERTENENCIAS. Belongings. Property of a person. Possessions.

PERTINENTE. Pertinent, relevant, material. When evidence is directed to the issue or matters in dispute, and legitimately tends to prove the allegations of the party offering it.

PERTRECHOS. Equipment, supplies. Needed materials or provisions specially for navigation.

PERTURBACIÓN DEL ORDEN PÚBLICO. Breach of the peace. Disturbance of peace. Riot. A violation or disturbance of the public tranquility and order.

PERTURBACIÓN MENTAL. Mental disorder. Mental illness. Insanity.

PERTUBADOR. Agitator. One who stirs up, excites, perturbs people to produce changes. One who incessantly advocates a social change.

PESAS Y MEDIDAS. Weights and measures. System used by a country to weigh and measure things and persons.

PESO DE LA PRUEBA. Burden of proof. In the law of evidence, the necessity or duty of affirmatively proving a fact or facts in dispute on an issue raised between the parties in a lawsuit.

PESQUISA. Investigation, inquiry. A careful search in order to discover all circumstances under which a crime was committed.

PETICIÓN. Petition. Motion. A formal, written application to a court or other entity requesting action on a certain matter.

PETICIONANTE. Petitioner. Applicant, movant. One who presents a petition to a court, officer, or legislative body.

PETICIONAR. To petition, solicit. To ask a court or other entity to do something. To act.

PICAPLEITOS. Quarrelsome person (one who likes to pick a fight); shyster lawyer, ambulance chaser. Lawyer who performs in a dishonest way.

PIGNORACIÓN. Pignoration. Pledge. The delivery of property to a creditor as security or collateral for a debt. To pawn.

PIGNORAR. To pawn, to pledge. See "Pignoración".

PILLAJE. Pillage. Loot. Plunder; the forcible taking of private property by an invading or conquering army from the enemy's subjects. The act of taking goods, money, etc., by force.

PIRATA. Pirate. One who attacks and robs property and persons within a ship or an airplane.

PIRATERÍA. Piracy. Those acts of robbery and depredation upon the high seas and against a ship or property or persons within. To commit those acts within an airplane.

PIROMANÍA. Pyromania. Compulsion to start fires.

PISO. Floor, apartment. Any horizontal level of a building. Usually refers to an apartment in a building.

PISTA. Clue. Suggestion or piece of evidence which may or may not lead to the solution of a crime or puzzle.

PISTA DE ATERRIZAJE. Runway, landing strip or landing field.

PISTOLA. Handgun. Pistol. Any firearm which could be used with one hand.

PLACA DE AUTOMÓVIL. License plate. An identifying plaque given by governmental entities to be carried by vehicles driven on public roads.

PLAGIO. Plagiarism. The act of appropriating the literary composition of another, or parts or passages of another's writings, or the ideas or language of the same, and passing them off as the product of one's own mind.

PLANES DE PENSIÓN. Pension plans. A plan established by an employer or by a governmental entity to provide benefits to the employees or their beneficiaries such as payment of an amount of money, normally monthly.

PLANTEAR. To establish, to state.

PLANTEAR UNA APELACIÓN. To file an appeal. See "Appeal".

PLAZA. Square. Position. Employment. The word "plaza" may be used in different senses. (1) As square: an open area in a city used as park and limited by street or buildings; (2) as market: a place were goods are bought and sold; (3) as position: offer of employment.

PLAZO. Time, duration. Extent or time during which an obligation or any act may be fulfilled.

PLAZO CONMINATORIO. Time allowed to do something followed by the threat of a punishment.

PLAZO CONVENCIONAL. Conventional time. Time fixed by interested parties to do something.

PLAZO DE GRACIA. Grace period. See "Término de Gracia".

PLAZO DE PRESCRIPCIÓN. Limitation. Time allowed to a person to take action (i.e., sue, to claim), after which, if he or she remains silent, he or she will lose the right to act.

PLAZO DEL CONTRATO. Contract time limit. Time period during which the contract may be executed.

PLAZO JUDICIAL. Judicial term. Time allowed by court according to law.

PLAZO LEGAL. Legal turn or legal term. Time prescribed by law to do something, as accomplished.

PLAZO PROBATORIO. Test or trial period. See "Término de Pruebas".

PLENARIA. Plenary. Full, entire, complete, absolute, perfect, unqualified. Part of the proceedings in which the investigation is completed and a decision is to be rendered.

PLESBICITO. Plebiscite. A vote of the people expressing their choice for or against a proposed form of government, submitted to them.

267

PLEITO. Any conflict or quarrel. Lawsuit, litigation. A process in law instituted by one party to compel another to do that person justice.

PLENO. Full. Complete. Having no open space. (1) **Tribunal en pleno.** Full court. A complete court with all the judges present. (2) **De pleno derecho.** By full right.

PLENOS PODERES. Full powers. The empowering of an agent by a nation. To conduct special business with a foreign government.

PLICA. Escrow. A sealed envelope which contains documents. A will or an order that is to be open after the happening of a certain condition.

PLIEGO. Sealed letter or document. Document containing the specifications requested in a public bid. Document containing a request.

PLURALIDAD. Plurality. Meaning more than one, the state of being plural.

PLUS PETITIO. (Lat.) In Roman law, a phrase used to denote the claiming of more than what is owed by a debtor. It is also used to refer to a judgment which grants the plaintiff more than what was asked for.

PLUSVALÍA. Unearned increment value.

PLUTOCRACIA. Plutocracy. A state whose government is run by wealthy people.

POBLACIÓN. People, population. All the individuals of a state.

POBRE. Poor. A pauper. A person who has no means of support.

POBREZA. Poverty. The state of being poor.

PODER. Power. Authority, power of attorney, proxy. Authority given to a person to do any act on behalf of another.

PODER EJECUTIVO. Executive power. One of the three branches into which a government of a state is divided, charged with the duty of executing the laws and securing their due observance.

PODER ESPECIAL. Special power of attorney. Authorization given to someone to perform specified acts.

PODER GENERAL. General power of attorney. Authorization given to a person to perform any act within the normal authority of the grantor or principal.

PODER HABIENTE. Proxy holder. Person who substitutes another or represents him or her and acts on his or her behalf.

PODER JUDICIAL. Judicial power. One of the three branches of government which is charged with the duty of deciding controversies between people according to what the law says, interpreting the law and exercising judicial authority.

PODER PÚBLICO. Sovereign power. Superior power within a state which authorizes it to rule in order to accomplish the legitimate ends of government.

PODERDANTE. Constituent. Person who grants to another the power to represent him or her.

POLICÍA. Police, officer. (1) Governmental department charged with the duty of preservation of public order and the prevention and detection of crimes. (2) One of the members of the police.

POLICÍA JUDICIAL. Judiciary police. Department under judicial power or authority whose function is to investigate crimes and capture criminals.

POLICÍA MARÍTIMA. Maritime police. A state force whose duty consists of the enforcement of navigation rules within territorial waters.

POLIGAMIA. Polygamy. The offense of having more than one spouse at the same time.

POLÍGAMO. Polygamist. Person who has more than one spouse at a time.

POLÍGRAFO. Polygraph. Lie detector. A device which measures some psychophysics changes such as respiration, pulse, etc.

POLÍTICA. (1) Politics. The science of government; the art or practice of administering public affairs. (2) Policy. The general principles by which a government is guided in its management of public affairs, or the legislature in its measures.

POLÍTICA ECONÓMICA. Economic policy. General principles by which government is guided in its management of its taxing and expenditure policies.

POLÍTICA EXTERIOR. Foreign policy. General principles by which a government is guided in its relations with other nations in the international community.

POLÍTICO. Political. Politician. (1) Pertaining or relating to the policy or the administration of a government, state or nation. (2) Person actively engaged in party politics as a profession; one engaged in conducting the business of government.

PÓLIZA. Policy, contract. Check, draft. Usually used to refer to the document which contains all the terms and conditions agreed upon by the parties to a contract. It is also used as a draft. Insurance agreement.

PÓLIZA DE FLETAMENTO. Charter-party contract. The document which contains all the contractual conditions by which the owner of a ship authorizes another person (a charterer) to use it for the conveyance of goods or persons to one or more places.

PÓLIZA DE SEGURO. Insurance policy. Policy of insurance. A written insurance contract. The document which establishes the contractual conditions agreed upon by the parties in an insurance contract.

POLIZÓN. Stowaway. One who hides aboard a vessel or an aircraft in order to get free passage.

PONENTE. Presiding judge. Proponent. (1) The judge who directs proceedings as chief officer and prepares the opinion of the court. (2) One who offers or makes a motion. (3) Chairman of a committee.

PONERSE DE ACUERDO. To come to an agreement. To agree.

POR MAYOR. Wholesale. Refers to sales in large quantities.

270

POR MENOR. Retail sale. The sale of goods in small quantities.

POR ESTIRPE. Per stirpes (Lat.). Term used in inheritance law and distribution to denote a system of dividing an intestate estate by class or group of distribution instead of per capita.

PORCENTAGE. Percentage. A given part in every hundred.

PORCIÓN. Portion, party; share, allotment. Any part into which something is divided.

POSTDATAR. To post-date. To assign a later date than the actual one to a document.

PORNOGRAFÍA. Pornography. The depiction of obscene sexual behavior, as in pictures or writing, intended to cause sexual excitement.

PORTADOR. Bearer. The person in possession of an instrument, document of title, or security payable to bearer or endorsed in blank.

PORTAR ARMAS. Bear arms. To carry arms.

PORTE. Portage, carrying charge; freight; postage. Carriage of something from one place to another. What is charged for carrying freight, merchandise or cargo.

PORTEADOR. Carrier. A person or an organization engaged in the business of transporting goods or passengers for a pecuniary compensation.

PORTEAR. To carry. To transport goods or persons from one point to another.

PORTE DEBIDO. Freight to be paid. See "Porte".

PORTE PAGADO. Freight prepaid. See "Porte".

POSEEDOR. Possessor. One who possesses; holds property, for his or her use and enjoyment. The word is also used to refer to an owner or a holder.

POSEEDOR DE BUENA FE. Possessor bona fide (Lat.). Good faith holder or owner. One who possesses anything as owner without knowing of any defect in the title of ownership.

POSEEDOR DE MALA FE. Possessor mala fide (Lat.). Bad faith holder or owner. One who assumes the condition of owner of something knowing the title is defective.

POSEER. To possess. To hold something as property.

POSESIÓN. Possession. (1) The detention and control, or the manual or ideal custody, of anything which may be the subject of property, for one's use and enjoyment, either as owner or as the proprietor of a qualified right in it, and either held personally or by another who exercises it in one's place and name.

POSESIÓN ACTUAL. Actual possession. When a person is under real control and enjoyment of a thing.

POSESIÓN ARTIFICIAL. Constructive possession. When possession is assumed to exist.

POSESIONARIO. To take possession. To take office.

POSESOR. Possessor, holder. One who has possession.

POSESORIO. Possessory. Relating to possession; founded on possession.

POSFECHADO. Post dated. An instrument dated at a later time than when it is really made.

POSICIONES. Written interrogatories; questions and answers; depositions. Interrogatory made by one party to another in a litigation.

POSTERIDAD. Posterity. All the descendants of a person in a direct line to the remotest generation. Future generations.

POSTULAR. Postulate. Demand, request, petition; to nominate for office or for employment.

PÓSTUMO. Posthumous. After death. (1) **Hijo póstumo.** Posthumous child. A child born after the death of his or her father.

POSTOR. Bidder. The person making an offer at an auction.

POSTURA. Bid. Amount of money offered in an auction.

POTESTAD. Power. Authority, jurisdiction. The right to do something.

POTESTATIVO. Optional, facultative. That which may be legally done or not done.

PRÁCTICA FORENSE. Clerkship. Period during which a law student or lawyer works in order to learn how to practice law.

PREÁMBULO. Preamble. Clause at the beginning of the constitution or document explaining the reason for its enactment and the objects sought to be accomplished.

PREAVISO. Notice. In labor law, the notification that either the employer or employee is obliged to give on whether they will end the labor contract.

PRECARIO. Precarious. That which has to be returned to at the request of another. Uncertain right.

PRECARISTA. One who has an uncertain right on something.

PRECEDENTE. Precedent. (1) An adjudged case or decision of a court, considered as furnishing an example or authority for an identical or similar case arising afterwards. (2) Prior in time or order.

PRECEPTIVO. Preceptive. Containing a command; obligatory.

PRECEPTO. Precept. An order, writ or warrant. Rule imposing standard of conduct or action.

PRECIADOR. Appraiser. A person who ascertains and states the true value of goods or real estate.

PRECIAR. To appraise, value. To estimate the value of something.

PRECIO. Price. Charge, worth. Estimated monetary value of a thing. Monetary value asked or paid for something.

273

PRECIO AFECTIVO. Sentimental price or value. Estimated worth of something taking into consideration the sentiments, memories and other intangibles.

PRECIO ALZADO o GLOBAL. Lump sum, fixed price. Settled amount of money paid in exchange for goods or services.

PRECIO CORRIENTE o DE MERCADO. Market price, going price. The current market value of an article at a determined time and place.

PRECIO NOMINAL. Par value. The monetary value assigned to a security (i.e., stocks) by the issuer.

PRECIO REAL. Real price, market price, true value. The current market value of a security at a determined time and place.

PRECIO IRRISORIO o VIL. Ridiculously small price. Notoriously inferior price compared with the true price of a thing.

PRECLUSIÓN. Preclusion, estoppel. Prohibition to do something by virtue of law or because the time for doing it has elapsed.

PREDECESOR. Predecessor. One who goes before.

PREDIO. Real estate. Real property. Any portion of land.

PREDIO DOMINANTE. Dominant estate. Land whose owner enjoys an easement over an adjoining estate.

PREDIO RÚSTICO. Farm. Tract of land devoted to agriculture, pasturage or similar uses.

PREDIO SIRVIENTE. Servient estate. An estate subject to a servitude for the benefit of another.

PREDIO URBANO. Town property. Tract of land which will be used to build dwellings.

PREDISPONER. To predispose, to prejudice.

PREDISPOSICIÓN. Predisposition. Bias, prejudice. A predisposition to decide a cause or an issue in a certain way, which does not leave the mind open to conviction or a change.

PREFECTO. Prefect. Chairman. The presiding officer of an assembly, public meeting, convention, legislative body, etc.

PREFECTURA. Prefecture. Superintendency.

PREFECTURA DE POLICÍA. Police headquarters.

PREGONERO. Auctioneer. Announcer. A person authorized or licensed by law to sell lands or goods at public auction.

PREGUNTA. Question.

PREGUNTA CAPCIOSA. Deceptive question. A misleading question. One which intends to get a specific answer by making the witness believe what is not true.

PREGUNTA HIPOTÉTICA. Hypothetical question. A process of setting up a series of facts, assuming that they are true, and asking for an answer to a question based on those facts.

PREGUNTA SUGERENTE. Leading question. Question which instructs the witness how to answer or puts into his or her mouth words to be echoed back. One which suggests to the witness the answer desired.

PREJUICIO. Prejudice, bias, preconceived opinion, prejudgment. A leaning towards one side of a cause for some reason other than a conviction of its justice.

PREJUZGAR. To prejudge. To judge or decide something beforehand.

PRELACIÓN. Priority. Preference. A legal preference between two persons having similar rights with respect to the same subject matter, but where one is entitled to exercise his or her right to the exclusion of the other due to a priority.

PREMEDITACIÓN. Premeditation. Malice aforethought. Decision or plan to commit a crime before committing it.

PREMEDITADO. Premeditated. The mental purpose, the formed intent to commit an act.

PREMIO o RECOMPENSA. Prize (award). A reward or recompense for some act done; a valuable thing offered by a person for something done by others.

PREMORIENCIA. Predecease. To die before another person.

PREMORIR. See "Premoriencia".

PRENDA. Pledge. Security. A bailment or pawn of goods to a creditor as security for some debt or engagement.

PRESCRIBIR. Limitation. To acquire or lose a thing or a right by action or inaction over a period of time as required by law.

PRESCRIPCIÓN. Prescription, extinguishment limitation. Securing an absolute and perpetual right of ownership to property, or the discharge of a debt or obligation by the effects of time, and under conditions regulated by law.

PRESCRIPCIÓN ADQUISITIVA. Adverse possession. Method of acquiring title to real property by possession for the statutory period under certain conditions.

PRESCRIPCIÓN EXTINTIVA O LIBERATORIA. Limitation. Prescription. Peremptory and perpetual bar to a cause of action caused by the inactivity of an injured party during a period of time.

PRESENTAR. To present. To introduce. The act of showing something. To submit before someone.

PRESENTE. Present. Being in the place or within sight. The fact of having existence in the actual time. A gift.

PRESIDENCIA. Presidency. The act and action of presiding. The place where the act of presiding is occurring. The house and office of the president.

PRESIDENCIABLE. Having the ability to become a president.

PRESIDENTE. President. Chairman. The person who occupies the maximum position in the executive branch. The one who has the supreme authority to control.

PRESIDENTE DE LA CORTE SUPREMA. Chief Justice of the Supreme Court. The supreme judge who has been selected to preside over the court.

PRESIDENTE DE LA JUNTA. Chairman of the board. The person appointed to direct or moderate the meeting. This is the presiding officer of the assembly.

PRESIDENTE DEL JURADO. Foreman of the jury. The presiding member of a grand or petit jury, who speaks or answers for the jury to the court.

PRESIDENTE ELECTO. President-elect. The person who, having been elected to be president, has not yet occupied the presidency.

PRESIDIARIO. Convicted. The person who, having been found guilty of a crime, is serving the term of imprisonment. See "Preso".

PRESIDIO. Prison. Jail. The place in which a convict is confined to serve the term of imprisonment established in the sentence.

PRESO. Prisoner. A person who is detained under suspicion of having committed a crime. Also a convict who is serving the term of a sentence in prison. An inmate in a jail or penitentiary, as a result of a conviction of a crime.

PRESTACIÓN. Obligation. One of the essential elements of a contract without which there can be no binding contract. This specific word means the content, kind or type of obligation. It is the object or performance of the contract. The doing, not doing or giving something.

PRESTACIÓN DE DAR. Obligation undertaken in a contract by one party consisting of the giving of something to the other party. The giving of something.

PRESTACIÓN DE HACER. Obligation contracted by which one party has the duty to do something according to the contract. Rendering of service.

PRESTACIÓN DE NO HACER. Obligation undertaken by one party consisting of not doing something pursuant to the contract. The not doing of something.

PRESTACIONES LABORALES. Fringe benefits. Non-wage benefits which accompany or are in addition to a person's employment, such as paid insurance, recreational facilities, sick-leave, etc.

PRESTACIONES SUPLEMENTARIAS. See "Prestaciones Laborales".

PRESTADOR. Lender. A person who lends money to another. The one who lends.

PRESTAMISTA. Lender. The person who, in a loan, lends money to another and then receives the principal and interest on the loan.

PRÉSTAMO. Loan. Contract whereby one person agrees to lend money to another who agrees to repay the money to the first one. The delivery by one party, to and received by another party, of a sum of money upon agreement, express or implied, to repay it with or without interest.

PRÉSTAMO DE CONSUMO. Contract by which one party agrees to give certain kind and amount of goods to be consumed by another who agrees to give back the same amount and kind of goods. See "Mutuo".

PRÉSTAMO DE USO. Commodate. Contract by which one party gratuitously agrees to give something to another for the latter's use and the lender expects it back after a certain time. See "Comodato".

PRÉSTAMO HIPOTECARIO. Mortgage loan. A loan secured by a mortgage on real estate in which the borrower is the mortgagor and the lender the mortgagee.

PRÉSTAMO SIMPLE. The loan in which one party gives a certain amount and kind of goods to another who has the right to consume the goods and the obligation to return an equal amount of the same kind of goods. This type of loan is also known as "mutuum" (Lat.). See "Préstamo de Consumo".

PRESTATARIO. Borrower. The person to whom money is lent. The one who receives something with the obligation to pay it back or return it.

PRESTAR. To lend. The act of lending money to another for a period of time, usually with an interest charge to be incurred by the borrower.

PRESUMIR. Presume. To assume beforehand. To believe or accept upon probable evidence.

PRESUMIBLE. Supposable. A presumption. That which can be presumed.

PRESUNCIÓN. Presumption. A rule of law, statutory or judicial, by which the finding of a basic fact gives rise to the existence of a presumed fact, until the presumption is rebutted.

PRESUNCIÓN ABSOLUTA. Absolute presumption. The one in which the presumed fact is established without rebuttal.

PRESUNCIÓN CONCLUYENTE. Conclusive presumption. One in which proof of a basic fact renders the existence of the presumed fact conclusive and irrefutable.

PRESUNCIÓN DE DERECHO. The one which does not permit evidence to the contrary. The presumption is not refutable.

PRESUNCIÓN DE HECHO. Presumption of fact. Presumption which (1) does not compel a finding of the presumed fact but which warrants one when the basic fact has been proven; (2) does not admit proof to the contrary.

PRESUNCIÓN DE INOCENCIA. Presumption of innocence. A criminal law principle where the defendant is presumed innocent and where the government has the burden of proving every element of a crime beyond a reasonable doubt and the defendant has no burden to prove his or her innocence.

PRESUNCIÓN DE LEY. Presumption of law. One which, once the basic fact is proved and no evidence to the contrary has been introduced, compels a finding of the existence of the presumed fact.

The presumption can be rejected once evidence to the contrary has been presented.

PRESUNCIÓN DE MUERTE. Presumption of death. A presumption which arises upon the disappearance and continued absence of a person from his or her customary location or home for an extended period of time without any apparent reason for such absence.

PRESUNCIÓN JURIS ET DE JURE. Irrefutable presumption. The conclusive presumption requiring a finding of the presumed fact once the underlying evidence is presented. It does not admit evidence to the contrary.

PRESUNCIÓN JURIS TANTUM. Rebuttable presumption. A presumption that can be overturned if evidence to the contrary is presented.

PRESUNCIÓN REFUTABLE. Rebuttable presumption. A presumption that can be overturned upon the showing of sufficient proof.

PRESUNTO. Presumed. Probably. Likely.

PRESUPUESTO. (1) Presupposition. Something supposed beforehand. (2) Budget. A plan for the coordination of resources and expenditures. The amount of money that is available for, required for, or assigned to a particular purpose.

PRESUPUESTOS PROCESALES. Circumstances about the proceeding which need to be satisfied in order to begin the trial.

PRETENDIENTE. Petitioner. The person requesting.

PRETENSIÓN. Pretension. (1) An allegation of a right. (2) A claim or an effort to establish a claim.

PRETERINTENCIÓN. Beyond the intent. Quality of the act the effect of which is criminal but was not intended with the resulting purpose.

PRETERINTENCIONALIDAD. Consequence beyond the intent. See "Preterintención".

PREVARICACIÓN. Prevarication. Crime committed by a public officer who fails in the performance of the duty entrusted. It refers specially to the administration of justice.

PREVARICADOR. Prevaricator. The public officer who fails in the performance of the duty entrusted. Specially the judge who renders a judgment against the law, regardless of the intent.

PREVARICAR. To commit the crime of prevarication. See "Prevaricación".

PREVARICATO. Prevarication. The acting with unfaithfulness and lack of honesty; deceitful, crafty, or unfaithful conduct, particularly as is manifested in the concealing of a crime.

PREVENCIÓN. Prevent. The act of preparing beforehand to obtain a goal to foresee. Something done to avoid.

PREVENIR. Prevent; to avoid; to stop; to warn.

PREVENTIVA. Name given to a special kind of detention where a detainee is held until formal charges are made.

PREVENTIVO. Preventive. Able to prevent. Cautionary.

PREVIO. Before. Subject to be anticipated.

PREVIO ACUERDO. Subject to agreement. Expression meaning that before something is done, an agreement has to be reached.

PREVIO PAGO. Against payment. Expression meaning that before performance, an obligation must be met or paid.

PREVISIBILIDAD. Foreseeability. The ability to be foreseen or known in advance.

PREVISIBLE. Foreseeable. That which can be foreseen.

PREVISIÓN. Foresight. Heedful thought for the future.

PRIMA. Premium. (1) In insurance law, the amount paid to the insurer to cover the risk involved. (2) In labor law, a bonus given to the worker for increased or better quality production.

PRIMERA INSTANCIA. Proceeding by which a case is first tried. When a case is at the trial level, not on appeal.

PRIMO. Cousin. The child of one's uncle or aunt.

PRIMOGÉNITO. First-born son.

PRIMOGENITURA. Primogeniture. The state of being the first-born among several children of the same parents; seniority by birth in the same family.

PRINCIPAL. Principal. (1) Chief. Most important; primary; head of a business; employer. (2) The capital sum of a debt or obligation, as distinguished from interest or additions to it. (3) In criminal law, a chief actor or perpetrator, or an aider or abettor actually or constructively present at the commission of a crime, as distinguished from an "accessory." (4) In agency law, one who has permitted or directed another (an agent or servant) to act for his or her benefit and subject to his or her direction and control.

PRINCIPIO. Beginning. Principle. A fundamental truth or doctrine of law; a comprehensive rule or doctrine which furnishes a basis for others. That which constitutes the essence of a body. Origin.

PRIORIDAD. Priority. That which has occurred before in time with respect to another.

PRISIÓN. Prison. (1) A place for the long-term custody of persons convicted of a crime. (2) Punishment consisting in the confinement or imprisonment of a convict.

PRISIONERO. Prisoner. A person convicted to serve time in a prison as a result of a sentence.

PRIVACIÓN. To deprive someone from something.

PRIVADO. Private. Opposed to public. That which is of personal concern.

PRIVAR. To deprive. To take away.

PRIVATIVO. Exclusively. That which pertains solely to one person or small group. A privilege granted to few.

PRIVILEGIADO. Privileged. One who has been granted a privilege or immunity.

PRIVILEGIO. Privilege. A particular and peculiar benefit enjoyed by a person, company, or class, beyond the common advantages of other citizens.

PRIVILEGIO PERSONAL. Personal privilege. The benefit granted to one person without the possibility of transferring it.

PROBABLE. Probable. Having more evidence for than against; supported by evidence which inclines the mind to believe, but leaves some room for doubt; likely.

PROBADO. Proved. What has been demonstrated with evidence.

PROBAR. Prove. To establish or make certain; to establish a fact or hypothesis as true by satisfactory and sufficient evidence.

PROBATORIO. Probationary. Suitable to prove. Capable of proving.

PROCEDENCIA. Origin. The place where something comes from.

PROCEDER. To conduct. To act. To proceed.

PROCEDIMIENTO. Proceeding. The mode of proceeding to enforce a legal right, including all possible steps in an action from its commencement to the execution of judgment within a judicial action or lawsuit.

PROCEDIMIENTO CIVIL. Civil procedure. Body of law concerned with methods, procedures and practices in civil litigation.

PROCEDIMIENTO CRIMINAL. Criminal procedure. Body of law concerned with the procedural steps through which a criminal case passes, starting with the initial investigation of a crime and concluding with the conviction of the offender.

PROCEDIMIENTO EJECUTIVO. Executive proceeding. A short proceeding established to obtain a quick and expeditious judgment against the debtor.

PROCEDIMIENTO JUDICIAL. Judicial proceeding. The rules governing the ways and manners in which a case should be tried in the court. The principles by which a judicial proceeding is to be conducted by the judge and carried out by the parties to a lawsuit.

PROCEDIMIENTO PENAL. Criminal procedure or proceeding. Rules which regulate the procedure of a trial in criminal cases. See "Procedimiento Criminal".

PROCEDIMIENTO SUMARIO. Summary procedure or proceeding. Any proceeding by which a controversy is settled, a case disposed of, or trial conducted, in a prompt and simple manner, without the aid of a jury, without extensive proof, or in other respects out of the regular course of the procedures established for deciding judicial disputes.

PROCESADO. Defendant. The party against which a criminal case is tried.

PROCESAL. Procedural, pertaining to legal process.

PROCESALISTA. An attorney expert in procedural law. Attorney who specializes in the steps and procedures that are common to a trial.

PROCESAR. To process. To sue; prosecute; to arraign; to indict.

PROCESO. Process. A mode, method or operation whereby a result is produced. Proceeding, trial, action.

PROCESO ACUMULATIVO. Joinder. Joining or coupling together; uniting two or more constituents or elements in one; uniting with another person in some legal step or proceeding.

PROCESO ANORMAL. Irregular process. Process not followed in strict conformity with the law, whether the defect appears on the fact of the process, or by reference to extrinsic facts, and whether such defects render the process void or only voidable.

PROCURADOR. Procurator. Attorney, counselor, proctor, solicitor.

PROCURADOR GENERAL. Attorney general. The chief law officer of a state or country in charge of prosecuting the criminals by investigating the cases where a crime is suspected or committed.

PROCURADURÍA. The attorney general's office.

PRODUCIR. To produce. (1) To yield, return; to bring forward; to bring into view or notice. (2) The process of transforming raw materials into a final and useful product.

PRODUCTO. Product. Income. What has been transformed from raw material to a useful good. The rent. Benefit.

PRODUCTOS BÁSICOS. Commodities. Those things which are useful or serviceable, particularly articles for merchandise movable in trade.

PROFANACIÓN. Profanation. Inappropriate use of something sacred. Also the crime committed by one who opens a grave without being duly authorized.

PROFANO. Profane. The person who shows no respect for the principles of morality. The one who violates a grave. Indecency.

PROFECTICIO. The property which comes from the father.

PROFESAR. To profess. To exercise. The act of performing the services of a profession. To practice a religion.

PROFESIÓN. Profession. The ability. Job or work carried out by a person. Principal occupation.

PROFESIONAL. Professional. Pertaining to a profession. The person who practices a profession.

PROFESIONALISMO. Quality of something done in the form of a profession.

PROFESIONALIDAD DELICTIVA. (1) A criminal whose profession consists of committing crimes for a living. (2) The illegal exercise of a profession.

PRÓFUGO. Fugitive from justice. A person who, having committed a crime, flees from the jurisdiction of the court where the crime was committed or departs from his or her usual place of abode and conceals himself or herself.

PROGENITOR. Progenitor. The person who has issued children.

PROHIBICIÓN. Prohibition. Inhibition; interdiction. Act or law prohibiting something.

PROHIBICIÓN JUDICIAL. Injunction. A judicial process or order addressed to a person who is directed to do or refrain from doing a particular thing.

PROHIBIR. To prohibit. To enjoin; to forbid by law; to prevent. A command restraining from doing something.

PROHIJAR. Adopt. To take into one's family through legal means another's child as if he or she were one's own.

PRO INDIVISO. A real estate right belonging to many persons in an undivided portion of a whole. The common ownership of an undivided thing or good.

PROLE. Issue. The people descending from one. Descendant.

PROLETARIO. Proletarian. The very poor people who do not own private property and work to earn money to support themselves.

PROMEDIABLE. Averageable.

PROMESA. Promise. Pledge. A statement of the intent to act or refrain from acting in a specific way. A declaration which binds the person who makes it to do or forbear a certain act, and which gives the person to whom made a right to expect or claim the performance of some particular thing.

PROMESA COLATERAL. Collateral promise. Promise to answer for the debt or default of another.

PROMESA DE COMPRA-VENTA. A contract by which the person promises to buy and the other promises to sell a certain good at a given price on a specified date.

PROMESA DE PAGO. Promise to pay. I.O.U. A memorandum of debt containing the debtor's signature. A promissory note executed by the debtor.

PROMESA IMPLÍCITA. Implied promise. Fiction which the law creates to render one liable on a contract theory so as to avoid fraud or unjust enrichment.

PROMESA SIN CAUSA. Naked promise. One given without any consideration, equivalent, or reciprocal obligation, and for that reason not enforceable by law.

PROMETEDOR. Promisor. One who makes a promise. The person who expresses his or her intention to do or not to do something.

PROMETER. To promise. (1) The act of declaring the intent to do or not to do something. (2) To state a truth.

PROMITENTE. Promisor. The person who has made a promise or declaration of intent to act or not act in a certain way.

PROMITENTE COMPRADOR. Promisor to buy. The one who commits to buy according to a buy-sell contract.

PROMITENTE VENDEDOR. Promisor to sell. The party who has committed to sell in a buy-sell contract.

PROMISCUIDAD. Quality of promiscuity. (1) Circumstance in which father, mother and children live in a house without privacy. (2) The practice of sexual libertinage.

PROMISCUO. Promiscuous. The person who practices sexual libertinage. Licentious.

PROMOCIÓN. Promotion. Promotion of grade. Class. (1) The act of promoting something to make it famous. (2) The act of advancing a person to a higher position. (3) A group of people who have finished studies and advanced academically.

PROMOTOR. Promotor. The person who promotes.

PROMULGACIÓN. To promulgate, enact or publish some act or foster or sponsor an event.

PROMULGAR. Promulgate; enact. (1) Publish, proclaim, to announce officially. (2) The formal act of announcing a statute or rule of court.

PRONTUARIO. Record. A history of the past conduct or acts performed. Criminal record of a person that evidences his or her past conduct.

PRONUNCIAMIENTO. (1) Coup d'état. Rebellion carried out by the military to overthrow the government. (2) Declaration. Expression of one's ideas.

PROPAGANDA. Advertisement. Ad.

PROPENSIÓN DELICTUAL. Tendency in a person to commit crimes. The psychological condition of the person who has an inclination for crime.

PROPIEDAD. Property. That which belongs to someone. Rights recognized and protected by law. Everything subject to ownership. The right of possession, using, enjoying, and disposing of something. Things with value. The ability to use and transfer something without the interference of anyone else. Belongings.

PROPIEDAD ABSOLUTA. Fee simple absolute. An estate limited absolutely to a person and his or her heirs and assigns forever without limitation or conditions.

ROPIEDAD APARENTE. Apparent owner. The person who is reputed by all appearances to have the title to possession of property.

PROPIEDAD ARTÍSTICA. Literary property. Right which entitles an author and his or her assigns to all the use and profit of his or her work. The absolute right to dispose of an artistic creation.

PROPIEDAD HORIZONTAL. Legal status of a building in which there are more than one right to ownership of individual units. It is also the single real property parcel with unit owners having a right to use and share common sections of a whole, keeping separate ownership to the individual units.

PROPIEDAD INDUSTRIAL. The right to patents, trademark, words or symbols which are distinctive of a registered product.

288

PROPIEDAD INTELECTUAL. Literary property. The right recognized to authors to the use of their intellectual work. The exclusive right to the corporeal body in which the intellectual creation is made.

PROPIEDAD LITERARIA. Literary property. The rights to use, possess and transfer the benefits of a literary work. See "Propiedad Intelectual".

PROPIEDAD PRIVADA. Private property. The property held by a private citizen. It can be held separate or undivided by one or more persons. That which is not belongs to the general public.

PROPIEDAD PRO INDIVISO. Condominium. Common ownership of an undivided thing.

PROPIETARIO. Owner. Proprietor. The person who is entitled to or has legal right. The one who has the exclusive title to anything. The one in whom ownership is vested. He or she who has possession and ownership.

PROPIETARIO CONJUNTO. Joint owner. One of many persons who jointly holds property. All owners having a common title of ownership to the same property.

PROPIETARIO INSCRITO. Record owner. The owner of property according to the office where deeds and titles are required to be registered to be valid.

PROPIO. One's own. Suitable. Private. Adequate.

PROPONENTE. Proponent. One who proposes or argues in favor of something; one who makes a proposal.

PROPONER. To propose, to make an offer.

PROPOSICIÓN. Proposition, proposal. An offer; something proffered. The initial overture or preliminary statement for consideration by the other party to a proposed agreement.

PROPÓSITO. Purpose. Intent. The objective for which something is done.

289

PROPUESTA. Proposal. See "Proposición".

PRORRATA. Pro rata. Proportionately; according to a certain rate, percentage, or proportion. Part corresponding to one person after a proportional distribution has been made.

PRORRATEAR. Allocate. The distribution of something in proportional parts.

PRÓRROGA. Extension, postponement. An increase in the length of time to accomplish something. The extension of the duration.

PROSCRIBIR. To proscribe. To censure something. The act of prohibiting. To outlaw.

PROSCRITO. Outlaw. Proscribed. (1) The person who has committed a crime and is at large. (2) Something that has been banned or prohibited.

PROSECUCIÓN. Prosecution. A criminal action; a proceeding instituted and carried on by due course of law, before a competent tribunal, for the purpose of determining the guilt or innocence of a person charged with a crime.

PROSELITISMO. Proselytism. The act of recruiting people who agree to one's ideas.

PROSÉLITO. Proselyte. The person who has been called to join or agree to another's idea.

PROSPERAR. To prosper. To be successful, to gain.

PROSTÍBULO. Place of prostitution. The place in which women carry on the business of having sex in exchange for money.

PROSTITUCIÓN. Prostitution. Performing or offering to perform for hire an act of sexual intercourse or any unlawful sexual act.

PROSTITUTA. Prostitute. A woman who indiscriminately provides sexual acts for hire. The woman who has sex with anyone who agrees to pay for it.

PROTESTA. Protest. A formal declaration made by a person interested or concerned in some act about to be done, or already performed, whereby he or she expresses his or her dissent or disapproval, or affirms the act against his or her will.

PROTESTAR. To protest. The act of making a statement of disagreement.

PROTESTO. Protest. A formal declaration made by the person compelled to honor a negotiable note or to satisfy payment of a debt in which he or she denies the duty to pay with the intent to recover the amount he or she is being forced to pay.

PROTOCOLIZACIÓN. To protocolize. The act of turning a private document into a notarized document.

PROTOCOLO. Protocol. (1) A brief summary of the text of a document. (2) The minutes of a meeting which are generally initiated by the parties. (3) The etiquette of diplomacy and the ranking of officials.

PROVECHO. Benefit. Profit. What is earned as income, profit.

PROVEEDOR. Furnisher. The person in charge of providing something. The act of giving or supplying something. The act of rendering a judgment.

PROVEER. (1) To provide, supply, furnish. (2) To decide. The act of giving or supplying something. The act of rendering a judgment.

PROVEÍDO. Judgment, decision. (1) That which has been already decided. (2) An interlocutory order requiring some act during the proceeding.

PROVIDENCIA. Order. Writ. Interlocutory judgment. Any decision of a court in which a mere procedural question is handled. An order given by a court demanding the performance of a specified act.

PROVINCIA. Province. One of the divisions of a territory. An extension of land into which a government has divided its jurisdiction.

291

PROVISION DE FONDOS. Funds in deposit. Amount of money deposited with the drawee to guarantee that the amount specified in the negotiable note will be honored.

PROVISIONAL. Provisional. Temporary. Not permanent.

PROVOCACIÓN. Provocation. The act of inciting another to do a particular thing. The provoking of a person to act in a desired way. To instigate.

PROXENETA. Pimp. Panderer. The one who procures a person to have sex with another in exchange of money. One who obtains customers for a whore or prostitute.

PROXENITISMO. Panderism. To pander. The act and action of inducing a person to consort with another for prostitution. To use people to satisfy the lust of another for profit.

PROYECTO. Project. Plan. A draft. Intention.

PROYECTO DE LEY. Proposed bill. The draft of a bill or law that is in discussion and has not been approved yet.

PRUDENCIA RAZONABLE. Reasonable care. That degree of care which a person of ordinary prudence would exercise in the same or similar circumstances.

PRUEBA. Evidence. That used to prove. The probative evidence used to present a fact to the court in order to have something established as true or in existence. The means to prove something like testimony or documents.

PRUEBA ABSOLUTA. Full proof. Evidence which tends to prove to the jury in absolute terms the truth of the fact in dispute, to the entire exclusion of every reasonable doubt.

PRUEBA ADMISIBLE. Admissible or competent evidence. When the evidence introduced is of such a character that the court or judge is bound to receive it; that is, allow it to be introduced at trial.

PRUEBA CIRCUNSTANCIAL. Circumstantial evidence. Evidence of facts or circumstances from which the existence or non-existence of a fact at issue may be inferred.

PRUEBA CONCLUYENTE. Conclusive evidence. Evidence which is incontrovertible, either because the law does not permit it to be contradicted, or because it is so strong and convincing as to overbear all proof to the contrary and establish the proposition in question beyond a reasonable doubt.

PRUEBA CORROBORATIVA. Corroborating or corroborative evidence. Evidence supplementary to that already given and tending to strengthen or confirm it.

PRUEBA CUMULATIVA. Cumulative evidence. Additional or corroborative evidence on the same point. That which goes to prove what has already been established by other evidence. See also "Prueba Corroborativa".

PRUEBA DECISIVA. Conclusive evidence. Evidence which is incontrovertible, either because the law does not permit it to be contradicted, or because it is so strong and convincing as to overbear all proof to the contrary and establish the proposition in question beyond a reasonable doubt.

PRUEBA DEMOSTRATIVA. Demonstrative evidence. Evidence which is addressed directly to the senses without intervention of testimony. Such evidence may include maps, diagrams, photographs, etc. See also "Prueba Material".

PRUEBA DE PERITOS. Expert testimony. Opinion of a person who possesses special skill or knowledge in some science, profession or business which is not common to the average person and which is possessed by the expert by reason of his or her special study or experience.

PRUEBA DE REFERENCIA. Hearsay evidence. Testimony in court of a statement made out of court, the statement being offered as an assertion to show the truth of matters asserted therein, and thus resting for its value on the credibility of the out-of-court asserter.

PRUEBA DIRECTA. Direct evidence. Evidence in the form of testimony from a witness who actually saw, heard or touched the subject of interrogation.

PRUEBA DOCUMENTAL. Documentary evidence. Evidence derived from written instruments, inscriptions, documents of all kinds, and any inanimate objects admissible for the purpose, as distinguished from oral evidence or that delivered by human beings by speaking.

PRUEBA ESCRITA. Documentary evidence. Written evidence. See "Prueba Documental".

PRUEBA IMPERTINENTE. Irrelevant evidence. Evidence which has no tendency to prove or disprove any issue or fact involved. Evidence having no relation to the fact intended to be proven.

PRUEBA INDIRECTA. Indirect evidence. Evidence which only tends to establish the issue by proof of various facts which agree with a given hypothesis. It consists of both inferences and presumptions.

PRUEBA INEFICAZ. Inconclusive evidence. Evidence which may be disproved or rebutted; not preventing further proof or consideration. Instrumental. Documentary evidence. The evidence obtained from writing. See "Prueba Documental".

PRUEBA MATERIAL. Real evidence. Evidence furnished by things themselves, on view or inspection, as distinguished from a description of them by the mouth of a witness. See also "Prueba Demostrativa".

PRUEBA ORAL. Parol evidence. Oral or verbal evidence; evidence which is given by live testimony; the ordinary kind of evidence given by witnesses in court.

PRUEBA ORIGINAL. Original evidence. An original document, writing, or other material object introduced in evidence, as distinguished from a copy of it or from extraneous evidence of its content.

PRUEBA PERICIAL. Expert testimony. Opinion of a person who possesses special skill or knowledge in some science, profession or business which is not common to the average person and which is possessed by the expert by reason of his or her special study or experience. Same as "Prueba de Peritos".

PRUEBA PERTINENTE. Relevant evidence. That evidence which tends to prove the alleged fact regardless of its effectiveness. It has to be taken into consideration by the trier of fact.

PRUEBA PLENA. Full proof. That evidence which by itself demonstrates a fact. The proof sufficient to consider a fact as true.

PRUEBA POR INDICIOS. Circumstantial evidence. Evidence of facts or circumstances from which the existence or non-existence of a fact in issue may be inferred.

PRUEBA PRIMA FACIE. (Lat.) Prima facie evidence. Evidence good and sufficient on its face. Evidence which, if unexplained or uncontradicted, is sufficient to sustain a judgment in favor of the issue which it supports, but which may be contradicted by other evidence.

PRUEBA PRIMARIA. Primary evidence. Original or firsthand evidence; the best evidence that the nature of the case admits of; the evidence which is required in the first instance, and which must fail before secondary evidence can be admitted.

PRUEBA TASADA. The evidence already valuated by the law. Evidence that if presented in a case and accepted by the judge has to be given the value already established by law.

PRUEBA TESTIMONIAL. Oral or testimonial evidence. Oral or verbal evidence; evidence which is given by word of mouth; the ordinary kind of evidence given by witnesses in court.

PÚBER. Pubescent. The child who has reached puberty. The earliest date in which a young person acquires the ability to have children. Usually 12-16 years old.

PUBERTAD. Puberty. The earliest age at which persons are capable of begetting or bearing children.

PÚBLICO. Public. Not private. That which pertains to the general population. Not subject to private property.

PUDOR. Bashfulness, shy, timid, self-conscious. Modest behavior with regard to sexual matters.

PUEBLO. Town. Population. The poorest people in a city.

PUERTO. Port. The place where vessels arrive to load and unload persons or cargo.

PUGNA. Conflict.

PUJA. Outbid. The act of countering with a higher bid over another's bid.

PUNIBILIDAD. Punishable. That which is subject to punishment. The condition of being able to be punished.

PUNIBLE. Punishable. That which can be punished.

PUNITIVO. Punitive. Relating to punishment; having the character of punishment or penalty; inflicting punishment or a penalty.

PUPILO. Pupil. (1) A ward or infant under the age of puberty. (2) A person under the authority of a tutor. (3) A student.

PURGAR. To clear of a criminal charge.

PUTATIVO. Putative. The condition in which something is by appearing to be something else. That which is reputed to be another thing.

Q

QUASI CASI. (Lat.) As if. Almost.

QUEBRADO. Bankrupt. The state or condition of an entity (natural person, corporation, etc.) that is unable to pay its debts when due.

QUEBRANTADOR. Lawbreaker. One who violates or infringes the law.

QUEBRANTAMIENTO. Violation, infringement, breach. The breaking or violation of a law, right, contract, obligation, or duty, either by commission or omission.

QUEBRANTAR. To violate, break, breach.

QUEBRAR. To go into bankruptcy; to break; crush.

QUEDA, TOQUE DE. Curfew. A signal that warns citizens not to exit, transit or travel during certain hours.

QUEJA. Complaint, charge. The initial pleading by which an action is commenced and which sets forth a claim for relief. It can be informal, to a private person, officer, administrative agency, or before a judge.

QUEJARSE. To complain. (1) To express grief, pain or discontent. (2) To make a formal accusation or charge.

QUEMARROPA. Very close. To shoot very near the target.

QUERELLA. Complaint, accusation. See "Queja".

QUERELLADO. Defendant, accused. The person defending or denying in a lawsuit, or the accused in a criminal case.

QUERELLANTE. Plaintiff, complainant. One who approaches the courts for legal redress by filing a complaint.

QUERIDA. (1) Dear. Someone loved. (2) Mistress. A woman having a love affair with another woman's husband.

QUID. (Lat.) The main reason.

QUID PRO QUO. (Lat.) Literally, "something for the equivalent." The mutual consideration which passes between the parties to a contract, and which renders it valid and binding.

QUIEBRA. Bankruptcy. State of being bankrupt. See "Quebrado".

QUIEBRA CASUAL o FORTUITA. Fortuitous bankruptcy. The bankruptcy which results from circumstances not connected with the ability of the bankrupt one, who has acted with prudence.

QUIEBRA CULPABLE. Bankruptcy due to mismanagement. It occurs as a result of the errors or omissions of the bankrupt person; disproportionate expenses, negligence or other.

QUIEBRA FRAUDULENTA. Fraudulent bankruptcy. Whenever the bankrupt person has acted to defraud his or her creditors, by simulating debts, losses or expenses. Also, if fraudulent preferences are granted to one creditor to the detriment of others, or if certain goods are hidden or substracted from the assets of the bankrupt estate.

QUIEN CALLA, OTORGA. Silence shows consent.

QUIEN CONCIERNE, A. To whom it may concern.

QUINCENA. (1) A period of time consisting of fifteen days. (2) Payment (to workers) issued every fifteen days.

QUINQUENIO. Period of five years.

QUIROGRAFARIO. (1) An unsecured debt. (2) A general creditor, not given any preference or privileges in a bankruptcy action. (3) Handwritten.

QUIRÓGRAFO. (1) (masc.) Promissory note, I.O.U. A promise in writing to pay a specified sum at a certain time, or on demand, or at sight, to a specified person, or to his order, or to bearer. (2) (adj.) Unsecured. (3) Handwritten.

QUITACIÓN. Release, discharge, waiver.

QUITANZA. Receipt of payment in full accord and satisfaction.

QUORUM. Quorum. The number of members who must be present in a deliberative body before business can be transacted.

QUO WARRANTO. (Lat.) Literally, "by what authority." An extraordinary proceeding, prerogative in nature and belonging to the state, addressed to prevent the continued exercise of unlawfully asserted authority.

QUOTA LITIS, PACTO DE. (Lat.) Agreement between a lawyer and his or her client in which in addition to fees, said lawyer will receive a portion of the benefit obtained after the lawsuit.

R

RÁBULA. Shyster lawyer. Lawyer who carries on his or her profession in a deceitful, tricky or dishonest way.

RACIAL. Racial. Having to do with race or an ethnic group, or characterized by it.

RACISMO. Racism. A belief that race is the primary determination of human traits and capacities and that racial differences produce an inherent superiority of a particular race.

RADICAR. To file, establish.

RADICARSE. To locate. The act of establishing an office or house in a specific place.

RAMA. Branch. (1) An offshoot, lateral extension, or subdivision. (2) A branch of a family stock is a group of persons related by descent from a common ancestor, and related to the main stock by a common ancestor descending from the original founder or progenitor.

RAMO. Branch or a special part of a profession, art or science.

RAMERA. Prostitute. A woman who offers her body for sexual purposes in exchange for money. See "Prostituta".

RANGO HIPOTECARIO. Mortgage rank. Position occupied by a mortgage in relation to other mortgages on a property. It is established by the order of registration.

RAPIÑA. Rapine. Violent and open theft of another's property.

RAPTADA. A female victim of a rape or kidnapping.

RAPTAR. To rape, to kidnap; abduct. To rob. (1) The act of sexual intercourse by force or seduction without legally valid consent. (2) In a less common usage, it also means to rob.

RAPTO. Abduction. The offense of taking away a wife, child, or other, by fraud and persuasion or open violence.

RAPTOR. (1) Kidnapper, abductor. (2) The one who commits the crime of rape. Thief.

RAQUETERO. Racketeer. A person who makes money through extortion and coercion. Wrecker.

RASTRA. The act of dragging along. (1) The consequences of a crime or an act which results in liability. (2) A track or mark left on the ground.

RASTREAR. To trace. To follow a clue, to investigate.

RASTRO. Trace, vestige. A sign or indication that something has happened or has been somewhere.

RATA PARTE. See "Prorrata".

RATEAR. (1) Pilfer. To steal petty things or to pick one's pocket. (2) To divide something proportionally.

RATERÍA. Larceny. A crime consisting of stealing things of small value.

RATERO. Pick pocket. Thief who takes money and other objects from the pockets of unaware victims.

RATIFICACIÓN. Ratification. The confirmation of a previous act. The means by which something is validated. The acceptance of.

RATIFICAR. Ratify. To approve and sanction; to make valid; to confirm; to give sanction to.

RATIHABICIÓN. Ratification. The act of approving what has been previously done. The affirmance of an act that was reported to be done on his or her behalf. The validation of an act done either by oneself or by another claiming to be representing oneself.

RATIO DECIDENDI. (Lat.) The rationale or reason for a decision. The point which determines a judgment in a case.

RAZA. Race. A group of humans with the same ethnic characteristics.

RAZÓN. Reason. (1) The mental capacity to distinguish truth from falsehood, good from evil, and which enables the possessor to deduce inferences from facts or from positions. (2) An inducement, motive, or ground for action. (3) Ratio, rate. (4) Explanation.

RAZÓN SOCIAL. A corporation's name, its trade name.

RAZONABLE. Reasonable. Fair, proper, just, moderate, suitable under the circumstances. That conduct which would be the expected of a common or ordinary person.

RAZONAMIENTO. Reasoning. The act of exercising mental capacity by analyzing facts and ideas in order to reach a proper conclusion from the propositions at hand.

REA. Woman defendant in a criminal case.

REABRIR. Reopen. The act of allowing access or entrance to something that was previously opened and is already closed. To investigate or try again a case already closed.

READMISIÓN. Readmission. (1) To re-admit a document that was withdrawn and that is presented again. (2) The act by which someone or something is admitted for a second time.

READMITIR. To readmit. To accept once more what has been accepted before.

REAFIRMAR. Reaffirm. The ratification of a former affirmation. To declare with the intent to confirm something already said or written.

REAJUSTAR. To readjust. To change the form or substance of something in order to accommodate it once again. The act of changing the terms and conditions of a contract or covenant.

REAJUSTE. Readjust. To alter or modify something in order to settle a difference. A change in a contract.

REAL. Real. (1) That which exists and is concrete. (2) That which has to do with a monarchy. (3) Opposed to personal, as between personal property and real property. (4) Royal coin.

REALIZAR. To realize. To make real or bring into action.

REANUDAR. To begin again. To continue something that once was moving.

REARGÜIR. To reargue.

REASEGURO. Reinsurance. Secondary contract by which an insurer procures a third person to insure him or her and share the risk and liability created by reason of an original insurance contract.

REAVALUAR. Revaluation. The act of reasserting the already estimated value of property. To make a new appraisal.

REAVALÚO. Reappraisement. The new estimated value of property calculated by an independent expert.

REBAJA. Discount. A deduction from an original price or debt.

REBAJA DEL IMPUESTO. Abatement of tax.

REBATIR. (1) To refute, rebut. To take away the effect of something. (2) To deduct, to take away, abate.

REBELARSE. To rebel. To oppose or disobey one in authority or control.

REBELDE. Rebel. Defaulter, person in contempt of court. Said of the defendant who does not appear before court when requested by the judge.

REBELDÍA. Non-appearance, default. When a person duly summoned to court does not appear before it, or if the person appears but later leaves the courtroom. Contempt of court.

REBELIÓN. Rebellion. Deliberate, organized resistance, by force and arms, to the laws or operations of the government, committed by a subject or citizen.

REBUS SIC STANTIBUS. (Lat.) Literally, In these circumstances. A tacit condition in all treaties under which a treaty will cease to be obligatory if the original facts and conditions that it was based on change substantially.

RECABAR. To ask, to solicit. To gather something; i.e., evidences, documents, facts, information, etc.

RECADO. (1) Message transmitted verbally and in person. (2) Document which justifies the items in a bill.

RECAPACITAR. To recapacitate. See "Rehabilitar". To think it over.

RECARGAR. To charge again. Also to load in excess of its capacity.

RECARGO. Surcharge. (1) (noun) An overcharge; an exaction, impost, or encumbrance beyond what is just and right, or beyond one's authority or power. (2) (verb) The imposition of personal liability on a fiduciary for willful or negligent misconduct in the administration of his or her fiduciary duties.

RECAUDABLE. Collectible. Debts, obligations, demands and liabilities that one may be compelled to pay by means of legal process.

RECAUDACIÓN. The act of collecting money. It can be either (a) to raise funds for a cause, or (b) to collect payment of taxes or a debt.

RECAUDACIONES. Collections, revenue. The act of collecting money.

RECAUDACIONES FISCALES. Tax collections. Collecting tax payments.

RECAUDADOR. Collector. One authorized or appointed to collect debts for another.

RECAUDADOR DE IMPUESTOS. Tax collector.

RECAUDAR. (1) To collect. (2) To gather and put something under custody.

RECAUDAR IMPUESTOS. To collect taxes.

RECAUDO. Collection; bond, surety. Custody. (1) Money collected for taxes or the payment of debts. (2) The keeping of something in a secure place.

RECEPTAR. To abet or conceal a crime.

RECEPTOR. Receiver. The one who receives something, someone who is appointed to receive debts, documents, taxes, etc.

RECEPTORÍA. Office of the tax collector or other collector.

RECESO. Adjournment. A putting off or postponing of business or of a session until another time.

RECIBIDO. Received. That which has been delivered and is under the possession of another. Goods or property that have entered the custody of another.

RECIBIR. To receive, accept. To admit.

RECIBO. Receipt. Written acknowledgment of payment. A declaration stating that something has been received.

RECIPIENTE. Recipient. That used to receive other things. The person who receives something. The beneficiary or victim. The one to whom something is given.

RECIPROCIDAD. Reciprocity. Mutuality. In international law, the relationship existing between two states when each of them gives the subjects of the other certain privileges, on condition that its own subjects enjoy similar privileges in the latter state.

RECÍPROCO. Reciprocal, bilateral. Something that is mutual between two persons such as a right, an obligation, etc. Behavior or act that pertains to both parties. What is owed or given from one person to another and from the latter to the former.

RECLAMACIÓN. Claim. To demand as one's own or as one's right; to assert; to urge; to insist.

RECLAMANTE. Claimant. One who demands or asserts a right or claim.

RECLAMAR. (1) To claim. To demand that some right be respected. (2) To complain. To oppose something considered unjust; to show disapproval.

RECLAMO. Claim. Complaint. The manifestation by which someone expresses disconformity with something and requires compensation. The act by which an explanation or remedy is demanded.

RECLUSIÓN. Imprisonment. The act of confining a person in prison.

RECLUIR. To imprison. To put in reclusion. To isolate.

RECLUSO. Prisoner; imprisoned. One who is convicted of a crime and sentenced to a prison, penitentiary or jail.

RECLUTAMIENTO. Recruitment. To enroll people for a purpose, i.e., military reasons.

RECOBRABLE. Recoverable. Quality of what can be obtained again. Anything suitable of being collected after having paid it. What has been lost and can be recovered.

305

RECOBRAR. To recover. To get or obtain again, to collect, to get renewed possession of; to win back.

RECOBRO. Recovery, repossession. The obtainment of a thing by the judgment of a court, as the result of an action brought for that purpose.

RECOGEDOR. Collector. See "Recaudador".

RECOMENDACIÓN. Recommendation. (1) To give advice or suggestions. (2) To vouch for someone.

RECOMENDAR. Recommend. To propose one's ideas in order to have others accept and act according to them. To speak well of a person.

RECOMPENSA. Reward. A recompense offered or given for some service or attainment. Award.

RECOMPENSAR. Reward. A sum of money given as recompense for performing a special service.

RECONCILIACIÓN. Reconciliation. The renewal of amicable relations between two adversaries.

RECONDUCCIÓN. The act of renewal of a lease. See "Reconducir".

RECONDUCIR. To renew a leasing contract expressly or tacitly.

RECONOCER. To recognize, examine, acknowledge. (1) One nation's recognition of a new nation or a new established government in another. (2) Carefully examining a person or thing to establish the identity. (3) To acknowledge something has been said, done, signed, etc.

RECONOCIMIENTO. Recognizance; canvass; survey; examination, exploration; admission, acknowledgment.

RECONSIDERACIÓN. Reconsideration. (1) A proceeding that asks the judge to leave without effect an interlocutory judgment. (2) To ask someone to reconsider something.

RECONSIDERAR. To reconsider. The act of considering again. To study or analyze what has been previously decided. Remedy available to the party against whom a decision has been rendered, in order to have the issuing officer consider it again.

RECONSTITUIR. Reconstitute. To make again. To do something for the second time.

RECONVENCIÓN. A claim presented by a defendant in opposition to the claim of the plaintiff.

RECONVENIR. To counterclaim; to countercharge. Also see "Reconvención". The act by means of which the defendant presents a claim against the plaintiff.

RECOPILADOR. Compiler. The person who gathers or collects something.

RECOPILACIÓN. Compilation. A bringing together of laws and rules in an arrangement designed to facilitate their use.

RECRIMINACIÓN. Recrimination. Charge made by the accused against the accuser. Countercharge.

RECRIMINAR. Recriminate, countercharge. Also see "Reconvención".

RECTIFICACIÓN. Rectification. The correction of an error.

RECTITUD. Rectitude. What is straight. Those qualities of honesty and integrity attributed to a person.

RECTO. Straight. Correct. Said of an honest and just person.

RECTOR. Dean. The person who is in charge of directing an organization, especially a school.

RECUPERABLE. Recoverable. What can be collected back. To get back what has been paid.

RECUPERACIÓN. Recovery, recapture, salvage. The obtainment of a thing by the judgment of a court, as the result of an action brought for that purpose.

RECUPERAR. To recover, recapture; to repossess. (1) To regain possession of something. (2) To regain one's health or state.

RECURRENTE. Petitioner, appellant. The party who takes an appeal from one court or jurisdiction to another.

307

RECURRIBLE. Recoursable. That which allows the possibility to demand a remedy. The judicial or administrative order or act that can be considered again.

RECURRIDO. The act or decision against which a recourse has been presented.

RECURRIR. To resort to, have recourse to, appeal to.

RECURSO. Remedy. An extraordinary proceeding to dispute a sentence or resolution; extraordinary remedy; motion, appeal, petition, a resort.

RECURSO CONTENCIOSO ADMINISTRATIVO. A claim or an appeal filed against resolutions dictated by a public administrator or the executive branch of the government contesting those resolutions on the grounds that they diminish a person's rights or affect matters of public interest.

RECURSO DE ACLARACIÓN (DE ACLARATORIA). A petition presented to the same court that has dictated a sentence or resolution, to clarify certain aspects of it or to correct a mathematical error but not to change the sentence or resolution itself.

RECURSO DE APELACIÓN. Appeal. Resort to a superior court to review the decision of an inferior court.

RECURSO DE CASACIÓN. An extraordinary appeal filed to a supreme court challenging a sentence of a superior court as contrary to the law or the doctrine created by the jurisprudence on the subject, or not complying with the proceedings stated by law; this appeal serves to annul the sentence and correct the error of law, sometimes by reconciling, contending or divergent positions in the law.

RECURSO DE HECHO. An appeal filed at the superior court alleging that a lower court has rejected or neglected to admit a motion or certain facts in its deliberation.

RECURSO DE INCONSTITUCIONALIDAD. Resort to a competent court to review a law, decree, resolution or an act by an authority that goes against the supreme law of a nation as stated in its constitution.

RECUSABLE. Exceptionable. Subject to disqualification for being biased or having a conflict of interests in the case. Action intended to have another judge or justice hear the dispute because the first one may have a personal or conflicting interest that would affect the decision.

RECUSACIÓN. Recusation; challenge, objection, exception. Act of disqualifying a judge, or judge disqualifying himself or herself, from a case because of bias or personal interest.

RECUSADO. The one who has been disqualified from a case. See "Recusación".

RECUSANTE. The one who objects to or challenges a judge.

RECHAZAR. To reject, refuse, decline.

REDACCIÓN. Writing. The place where publications are made. Also the people who work there.

REDACTAR. To compose, draft, edit. To put something in writing.

REDADA. Raid. Police action intended to search for criminals.

REDENCIÓN. Redemption. Release of an obligation, encumbrance, charge or mortgage.

REDHIBICIÓN. Redhibition. The nullification of a sale due to hidden defects unknown to the buyer at the time of purchase.

REDIMIBLE. Redeemable. Subject to redemption; admitting redemption or repurchase.

REDIMIR. To redeem, call in, pay off. (1) To free someone (a slave) or something (a property or article) by paying a price or debt. (2) To buy back or repurchase something.

RÉDITO. Revenue, profits, return. Interests or income from a sum of money.

REDUCCIÓN. Reduction. Any discount or subtraction. Diminution.

REELECCIÓN. Re-election. The act of presenting as a candidate to a new election a person already elected.

309

REEMBOLSAR. To reimburse, refund. To pay back, in return or requital. The act of refunding.

REEMBOLSO. Reimbursement, repayment, refund. That which is refunded.

REEMBOLSO DE IMPUESTO. Tax refund. An amount returned to the taxpayer after he or she has made full payment of the tax.

REEMPLAZAR. To replace. To put something or someone in the place of another thing or person.

REEMPLAZO. Replacement, substitution. One who replaces another. See "Reemplazar".

REENVÍO. Remand. To send back. (1) The remand by the appellate court of the case to the lower court from which it came, for the purpose of having some further action taken on it. (2) In private international law, **Teoría del Reenvío.** Doctrine that establishes the principle to be applied in a conflict of law. Whenever a judge is to apply a foreign law, he or she has to take into consideration the references that the foreign law makes to the law of the court which is handling the case.

REFERENCIA. Reference. (1) To allude to something. (2) A person who will provide information for another about the other's character, credit, etc.

REFERENDUM. Referendum. The process of ratification by the electorate of a proposed or new state constitution or amendment (constitutional referendum) or a law passed by the legislature (statutory referendum).

REFORMA. Reform. Reformation, amendment. (1) New form. (2) A modification or change.

REFORMAR. To reform. (1) To correct, rectify, amend or remodel. (2) Removal of moral or other faults.

REFORMATORIO. Reformatory. A correctional institution for youthful offenders where the emphasis is on reformation of the juvenile's behavior.

REFRENDACIÓN. Legalization. Action and effect of making legal or lawful. Authentication.

REFUGIADO. Refugee. Person who, as a consequence of war, revolution or political persecution, takes refuge in a foreign country.

REFUTACIÓN. Refutation. To disprove or rebut something.

REGALÍA. Right, privilege; bonus; commission; royalty. (1) Compensation paid for the use of one's property (tangible or intangible) by another. (2) Remuneration.

REGALO. Gift. A transfer of property without consideration. A voluntary transfer from one person to another without receiving anything in exchange for the given property.

REGATEAR. To bargain over the price of something. To request a discount from the stated price. To offer less money than the price already set.

REGENCIA. Regency. The act of governing. Authority to rule.

REGENTE. Magistrate. Person empowered as a public civil officer, or a public civil officer vested with executive or judicial powers.

REGIDOR. Justice of the peace. The person vested with the power to hear and decide cases involving small claims or short punishments in a small jurisdiction.

RÉGIMEN. Regime. A system of rules and regulations.

REGIÓN. Region. A portion of a territory. A section of land or water.

REGIONALISMO. Regionalism. A practice proper of a region. Something common of a specific section.

REGIR. To govern; to be in force. The quality of the law which is enforceable.

REGISTRADOR. Registrar. Filing officer. The person in charge of the public filing office, where documents need to be recorded or registered for their validity or publicity.

REGISTRAR. To register, to record, file, enter; inspect.

REGISTRO. Record, file, docket; search or inspection; booking or registration; office for official registration, registry.

REGLA. Rule. An established regulation or standard.

REGLAMENTAR. To regulate. To establish the rule. To discuss, approve and issue regulations or by-laws.

REGLAMENTARIO. Regulatory, that which refers to regulations.

REGLAMENTO. By-law; regulation, rule. Set of rules that regulate something.

REGULACIÓN. Regulation. The act in which the rules are contained. The rule itself.

REGULAR. Ordinary. (1) To regulate, the act of making rules. (2) Something common.

REHABILITACIÓN. Rehabilitation. To reinstate or restore a person with some right, authority, or dignity formerly held.

REHABILITAR. To rehabilitate. To give another person his or her suspended rights. The act of reforming a criminal to make him or her a good citizen. To give back one's rights and privileges.

REHÉN. Hostage. An innocent person held captive by one who threatens to kill or harm him or her if specific demands are not met.

REINA. Queen. (1) Monarch of a kingdom. (2) The wife of a king. (3) A sweet manner in which to address a woman.

REINADO. Reign. Period during which a sovereign governs.

REINCIDENCIA. Recurrence; second offense. Characteristic of a person who commits a crime or offense a second time or, after being previously convicted for other crimes, commits new crimes.

REINCIDENTE. Relapsing person. One who has committed a crime or misdemeanor and does it again. To repeat the same error once more. The quality of the person who makes mistakes.

REINCIDIR. To relapse. To commit crimes. The condition of the one who commits the same type of crime many times. Also the condition of habitually committing crimes.

REINICIAR. To reopen (a case).

REINTEGRO. Re-integration. Restitution. To replace in the same position.

312

RELACIÓN LABORAL, DE TRABAJO. Work relationship.

REINTEGRACIÓN. Restoration, restitution, reimbursement. To recover something lost.

REINTEGRAR. To refund (bonds); to repay, reimburse; to restore, rehabilitate.

REINVERSIÓN. Rollover.

REITERANTE. Habitual criminal offender.

REITERAR. Reiterate. The act of repeating what has been previously said or done.

REIVINDICACIÓN. Replevy, recovery. To recover one's property wrongfully held by someone who has no right to it.

REIVINDICAR. To recover, regain possession of; to replevy. To restore goods (which had been wrongfully obtained) to the original owner. The vindication or recovery by authorities of property or rights that had been taken from the owner. To recover what belongs to one.

RELACIÓN. Relation, report, account. (1) A brief report made by the court clerk to the judge about the state of a case or issue. (2) Personal relations.

RELACIONES DIPLOMÁTICAS. Diplomatic relation. Bilateral relationships between two states with special delegates appointed to each other.

RELATAR. To narrate, report.

RELEVANTE. Relevant. Applying to the matter in question; affording something to the issue.

RELEVAR. To release; to relieve; to acquit. Giving up or abandoning a claim or right to a person against whom a claim exists or against whom a right is to be exercised.

REMANENTE. Remnant. The part which is left from something. The residue. What is left over.

REMATAR. To auction; to finish. (1) To buy or sell at auction. (2) To give a final and deadly stroke.

313

REMATE. An auction sale; end, finish. (1) A public sale of property to the highest bidder. (2) To give a final deadly blow.

REMATE JUDICIAL. Judicial auction or sale. A sale made under the authority of a court with competent authority to order it.

REMEDIO. Remedy, recourse, appeal. The means by which a right is enforced or the violation of a right is prevented, redressed, or compensated.

REMESA. Shipment, remittance, payment. Said of each shipment of something.

REMISIÓN. Remission; waiver; remittance. A release or extinguishment of a debt.

REMISIÓN DE LA DEUDA. Cancellation of a debt. A creditor's voluntary waiver of an obligation or part of it.

REMITENTE. Sender, shipper; remitter. The name and address of the one who sends something.

REMITIR. To remit, to dispatch, transmit or forward. Something sent to a third person.

REMUNERACIÓN. Remuneration. The compensation, salary or recompense. Payment to employees. Payment that a person earns for doing a job or service.

REMUNERAR. To remunerate. To compensate or pay, for something given or for a service received.

REMUNERATORIO. Remunerative, profitable. Onerous. When the obligations attaching to a contract unreasonably counterbalance or exceed the advantage to be derived from it.

RENDICIÓN. To render, surrender. Yield, profit. (1) The act of surrending to the enemy in a conflict. (2) The financial gain that results from selling products or services.

RENDICIÓN DE CUENTAS. To submit a report explaining what has been done on a given business or matter.

RENDIMIENTO. Surrendering. Productivity. (1) The act by which one gives up control to another. (2) The production of something.

The profit derived from an activity. The revenue derived from an act or process.

RENDIR. To render, yield, produce, submit.

RENEGOCIAR. To renegotiate. To negotiate new terms for a previous agreement.

RENOVACIÓN. Renovation, renewal. (1) To keep an agreement alive by rehabilitating it. (2) A change of something old to something new.

RENTA. Rent, income, revenue. (1) The compensation or fee paid, usually periodically, for the use of any property, land, buildings, etc. (2) The return in money from one's business, labor, or capital investment.

RENTA GRAVABLE. Taxable income.

RENTABLE. Profitable. Said of a business that at least pays its bills and produces some profits. With profit.

RENTAR. (1) To rent. To lease. (2) To yield, produce an income.

RENUNCIA. Resignation; waiver. Formal renouncement or relinquishment of an office, right, or possession of something.

RENUNCIABLE. Subject to renouncement. What can be given up or abjured.

RENUNCIANTE. Renouncer. The person who renounces his or her rights or property. The one who abjures, who gives up something.

RENUNCIAR. To resign, waiver, renounce. To voluntarily relinquish some possession, right, job, etc.

REO. (1) Convict. One who has been found guilty of a crime and is serving a sentence as a result. (2) Defendant. A person accused of a crime, who is under custody.

REPARACIÓN. Repair; indemnify; redress. Satisfaction for an injury or damages sustained.

REPARAR. To restore. The act or action of repairing what is broken. To put attention to. To fix.

315

REPARO. Objection. Repair. That which is remarked or criticized.

REPARTICIÓN. Distribution. To divide and distribute by parts.

REPATRIACIÓN. Repatriation. To send or return to one's country.

REPERTORIO. Repertory. Index or abridged edition which refers to subjects covered in detail in other books. Plays to be presented in a theater.

REPETIR. To repeat. Also, to claim restitution from a third party.

RÉPLICA. Reply. To answer another's complaint.

REPLICANTE. Respondent. In appellate practice, the party who responds to the applicant's request for review.

REPLICAR. To reply, respond, repeat. To make, return to, an answer.

REPONER. To replace. To reinstate. To reply, to recover lost health.

REPOSESIÓN. Repossession. To recover goods sold on credit or in installments when the buyer fails to pay for them.

REPOSICIÓN. (1) Reinstatement. In insurance law, a restoration of the insured's rights under a policy which has lapsed or been cancelled. (2) Reversal. The annulling or setting aside by an appellate court of a decision by a lower court.

REPREGUNTA. Cross-examination. The examination of a witness by a party other than the direct examiner upon a matter that is within the scope of the direct examination of the witness.

REPREGUNTAR. To cross-examine. The procedural way of asking questions to the witness called by the opposing party in a trial.

REPRENDER. To reprimand. To reprove severely; to censure formally, especially with authority.

REPRESALIA. Reprisal. Any action taken by one person either in spite of or as a retaliation for an assumed or real wrong by another.

REPRESENTACIÓN. Representation. (1) To represent someone. (2) Any conduct capable of being turned into a statement of fact. (3) A group of people that represents an institution, government or corporation.

REPRESENTANTE. Representative. One who stands in the place of another. Attorney-in-fact. Agent.

REPRESENTANTE LEGAL. Legal representative. The person who is empowered to act on behalf of someone and acquires duties and obligations which bind the person represented.

REPRESENTAR. To represent. To act on behalf of another. To appear in the place of someone and act in his or her name.

REPRESIÓN. Repression, restraint. To use force to control dissent or maintain the public order.

REPRESIÓN DEL COMERCIO. Restraint of trade. Contracts or combinations which tend or are designed to eliminate or stifle competition, effect a monopoly, artificially maintain prices, or otherwise hamper or obstruct the course of trade and commerce. Actions which impede the natural economic development of trade and commerce.

REPRIMIR. To repress. To exercise control and quell an action, using force.

REPROBACIÓN. Reprobation. Act intended to express one's rejection to an idea or act. To condemn something not acceptable.

REPRODUCCIÓN. Reproduction. To submit again. To present once more something already produced. To procreate and extend the species. To copy.

REPRODUCIR. To reproduce. To produce or do something again.

REPÚBLICA. Republic. That form of government in which the administration of affairs is open to all its people.

REPUDIACIÓN. Repudiation. Rejection; disclaimer; renunciation. The rejection or refusal of an offered or available right or privilege, or of a duty or relation.

REPUDIAR. To repudiate; to disaffirm; to renounce, relinquish.

REPUESTO. Recovered. Accessory. (1) One who has recovered good condition or health. (2) The spare part of a machine.

317

REQUERIMIENTO. Requirement. Demand; injunction; summons. (1) To demand a person do or not do something. (2) **Requerimiento de pago.** To demand a person pay something.

REQUERIR. To require, need; to summon; to investigate. (1) To request with authority. (2) To examine the condition of something. (3) To court a woman.

REQUIRENTE. Requirer. The person who requests.

REQUISA. Inspection. The act of reviewing with the intent to inspect it.

REQUISICIÓN. Requisition. (1) A demand in writing, or formal request or requirement. (2) The taking or seizure of property by government.

REQUISITO. Requisite. Requirement. (1) Necessary condition. (2) Something wanted or needed.

RES. (Lat.) A thing, an object.

RES GESTAE. (Lat.) Things done. The "res gestae" rule is that where a remark is made spontaneously and concurrently with an affray, collision or the like, it carries with it inherently a degree of credibility and will be admissible because of its spontaneous nature.

RES IPSA LOQUITUR. (Lat.) The thing speaks for itself. Rebuttable presumption or inference that defendant was negligent which arises upon proof that the instrumentality causing the injury was in defendant's exclusive control, and that the accident was one which ordinarily does not happen in the absence of negligence.

RES JUDICATA. (Lat.) A thing or matter settled by another judgment. Rule that a final judgment rendered by a court of competent jurisdiction on the merits is conclusive as to the rights of the parties and their privies, and, as to them, constitutes an absolute bar to a subsequent action involving the same claim, demand or cause of action.

RESARCIMIENTO. Compensation, indemnity. Reparation of damage.

RESARCIR. To compensate. To repair a damage.

RESCATAR. To rescue. Action performed to save from danger.

RESCATE. Rescue. The act of saving from danger.

RESCINDIR. To rescind. To abrogate, annul, avoid, or cancel a contract. Particularly, nullifying a contract by the act of a party.

RESCISIÓN. Rescission. Annulment, cancellation. The act of leaving without effect something such as a contract or an obligation.

RESEÑA. Mark. (1) A symbol or signal that allows to recognize or distinguish something. (2) An abridged version or brief description of a work, play, book, etc.

RESERVA. Reserve, exception, reservation. (1) To hold back a thing or right. (2) A sum of money set aside to meet future needs, losses or claims.

RESERVAMOS TODOS LOS DERECHOS, SE RESERVAN TODOS LOS DERECHOS. All rights reserved.

RESERVARSE. Reserved. To be reserved. That which has been set aside with a specific purpose.

RESERVAS BANCARIAS. Bank reserves. Deposits established by law that commercial banks must maintain in governmental banks or institutions to comply with government rules and regulations. A means to control the monetary supply of a country.

RESGUARDO. Security, collateral, receipt. (1) Property which is pledged as security for the satisfaction of a debt. (2) Border personnel for customs purposes. (3) A written acknowledgment by some institution or business of a deposit or payment.

RESIDENCIA. Residence. A place where a person lives all or part of the time. Sometimes this is the same as "domicile".

RESIDENTE. Resident. Any person who occupies a dwelling within the state, and has a present intent to remain there for a period of time.

RESIDUAL. Residual. Being a residual or remainder. That which is left over.

RESIDUO. Residue, remainder. That which is left over.

RESIGNACIÓN. (1) Resignation, from a job or position. (2) Not to fight against what is opposed and accept its consequences passively.

RESISTENCIA A LA AUTORIDAD. Resisting an officer. The criminal act of attempting to stop or hinder a police officer from performing a duty such as making an arrest, serving a writ, or keeping the peace. This may be a crime whether or not force is used.

RESISTIR. To resist. To oppose and not give up against what is not accepted.

RESOLUCIÓN. Resolution. (1) Solution of a problem or conflict. (2) A formal expression of the opinion or decision of an organized group. (3) Annulment.

RESOLVER. To resolve, decide, solve. To end a conflict with a decision.

RESOLUTORIO. Resolutory. (1) Referring to a resolution. That which is used to resolve a dispute. (2) Used to analyze. (3) Causing the termination. Bringing to an end.

RESPALDO. Backing; security, guaranty. Something that is backing another thing.

RESPETO. Respect. Honor and distinction given to honest and important people. That which is admired. To abide by.

RESPONSABILIDAD. Responsibility, accountability; liability.

RESPONSABILIDAD CIVIL. Civil liability. Liability for a civil act as opposed to responsibility for the consequences of a criminal act.

RESPONSABILIDAD PENAL. Criminal liability. Responsibility for the commission of a criminal act.

RESPONSABLE. Responsible. (1) Liable to be called upon to answer for one's acts or decisions. (2) One who is responsible; responsible party. (3) Reliable. Able to fulfill an obligation.

RESPUESTA. Answer, response, reply. (1) The satisfaction or solution to a question. (2) The reaction to an action.

RESTITUCIÓN. Restitution. Restoration of anything to its rightful owner; the act of making good or giving the equivalent for any loss, damage, or injury; indemnification. The giving back to the owner what has been taken. The restoration of rights or property.

RESTITUIR. To restore, return; to refund, pay back; to reinstate. (1) To give back the possession of something to its previous holder or owner. (2) To put back into a previous state.

RESTRICCIÓN. Restriction; limitation; restraint. A limitation imposed to restrain and prohibit.

RESTRICCIÓN DEL DOMINIO. A limitation placed on the use of a property.

RESUMEN. Summary, digest, abstract. A concise statement of the history of something; a concise highlight of the main points.

RESULTADO. Results, consequences, effects. The product of.

RETENCIÓN. Retention; withholding; detention. Something or an amount that is held back.

RETENER. To retain. (1) The act of withholding from someone. Keeping something back from the person entitled to it. (2) To detain a person.

RETIRAR. Retire, to call in; to withdraw, to revoke. (1) To withdraw something from where it was deposited. To take funds from an account. (2) To withdraw from an activity.

RETIRO. Retirement, withdrawal, retreat. (1) Pension of a retired employee. (2) To take back something; in most cases, money, from where it was deposited. (3) A place of privacy or safety. (4) Withdrawal. The act of drawing money from an account. (5) To retire from work.

RETO. Dare. To challenge.

RETRACTACIÓN. Retraction, redemption. The act of withdrawing or taking back something.

RETRACTO. Retract. (1) The act of not affirming what has been declared. To go back on one's testimony. (2) The right reserved to the seller to buy back from buyer at a specified price what has been sold.

RETRASADO. Delayed. Not on time. (1) An occurrence which is overdue or that which is late in occurring. A payment which is not on time. (2) Retarded, mentally deficient.

RETRASO. Delay. To be late or to delay. What is not on time.

RETRIBUCIÓN. Retribution. Fee, compensation; remuneration. Something given or demanded in payment. Payment for services rendered; salary; recompense.

RETROACTIVIDAD. Retroactivity. The quality of that law which has effects upon events that have occurred before the law is enacted.

RETROACTIVO. Retroactive. Made effective on a date prior to enactment, promulgation, or imposition.

RETROTRAER. To date back. To date an instrument to a time before it was written. To bring back to a prior date.

RETROVENTA. The sales contract in which seller reserves the right to buy back from buyer what is being sold.

REUNIÓN. Reunion, meeting; assembly; pool or syndicate. A group of people gathering together for a purpose.

REUNIR LOS REQUISITOS. To qualify. To meet all the conditions required for something.

REVÁLIDA. (1) Revalidation. (2) Bar examination.

REVALIDACIÓN. Revalidation. Confirmation or ratification of a previous act.

REVALORIZACIÓN. To re-evaluate, to give a new value.

REVELACIÓN o DIVULGACIÓN. Disclosure. Revelation; saying what is secret or not fully understood.

REVENDEDOR. Re-seller. (1) The one who sells merchandise occasionally for profit. Retailer. (2) All merchants.

REVENTA. Resale. When the purchaser resells his or her property.

REVERSIÓN. Reversion. Any future interest retained by a person who transfers away property.

REVERSO. The back of a document.

REVISAR. Review. The act of inspecting with the intent to correct possible mistakes.

REVISIÓN. Revision, review, inspection. Audit.

REVISOR. Inspector; auditor. The person charged with reviewing things, such as documents presented to him or her.

REVISTA. (1) Rehearing, new trial. A second consideration of a case or issue for the purpose of calling to the court's or administrative board's attention any error, omission, or oversight in the first consideration. (2) Magazine.

REVISTA JURÍDICA. Law journal. A periodic and specialized publication on law issues. Legal magazine. Publication containing relevant articles about the law.

REVOCABLE. Revocable. Susceptible to being revoked, withdrawn, or cancelled.

REVOCACIÓN. Revocation. The recall of some power, authority, or thing granted, or a destroying or making void of some deed that had existence until the act of revocation made it void.

REVOCAR. To revoke. To avoid or make void by recalling or taking back; to cancel, rescind, repeal, or reverse.

REVOLUCIÓN. Revolution. Complete overthrow of an established government by means of force by those who were previously subject to it. A revolt.

REVOLUCIONARIO. Revolutionary. Relative to revolution. Person who favors changing the order and authority of a nation through revolution.

REVUELTA. Revolt, altercation, sedition, upheaval. An attempt to overthrow the government. Politically, a large-scale revolt is called a rebellion, and if it is successful it becomes a revolution.

REY. King. (1) Monarch of a kingdom. (2) Husband of a queen.

RIBEREÑO. Pertaining to, being, or living on the bank of a river.

RIESGO. Risk. The element of uncertainty in an undertaking.

RIESGOS PROFESIONALES. Those risks which impair the health of a worker caused by accident or exposure to conditions arising during the course of employment.

RIÑA. Quarrel. Dispute. A fight between two or more people.

RIQUEZA. Wealth. Quality of being rich.

RITUALIDAD. Ritualism. Relative to a ritual.

RIVAL. Rival. The person against whom one has to compete. A competitor.

RIVALIDAD. Rivalry. Quality of being a competitor. Condition existing between two persons who oppose each other.

ROBAR. To rob, steal, plunder. The crime of stealing, using violence in the process.

ROBO. Robbery. Felonious taking of another's property by force or violence.

ROGATORIO. Rogatory. The document which one court sends to another court in a different jurisdiction for the purpose of requesting the execution of a judicial request, order or judgment.

ROL. Role. The function or action to be performed.

ROLLO. Roll (noun). Record of the proceedings of a court or public office.

ROMPER. To break, shatter, destroy.

RÓTULO. Label. Used to describe a product or store. Add. Title.

RÚBRICA. Mark. Seal. Symbol used to identify something.

RUBRO. Seal. Item. (1) A portion into which something is divided, such as titles or headings. (2) Also a symbol used to identify something.

RUEDA. Session. A meeting.

RUEGO. Request. Plea. Verbal or written petition.

RUFIÁN. Ruffian. A person whose conduct is against the law. One who behaves in a disorderly way, violating regulations. A destructive person.

RUMOR. Rumor; hearsay. (1) A story circulating from one person to another without any known source or authority for the truth of it. (2) A statement, other than one made by a witness while testifying at trial, offered in evidence to show the truth of the matter assented.

RUPTURA. Rupture. Break, breach. The breaking or interruption of what is established, such as relations, law, obligations, etc.

RURAL. Rural. Not pertaining to the city. Relative to the countryside.

RUTINA. Routine, habitual. A habitual way of acting. An act being practiced regularly and customarily.

S

SABIENDAS, A. Knowingly. With knowledge; consciously; intelligently; willfully.

SABOTAJE. Sabotage. (1) The willful destruction or injury of, or defective production of, war material or national defense material, or harm to war premises or utilities. (2) Also the willful destruction of property with the intention of interfering with its normal operation.

SABOTEADOR. The person who carries out the sabotage.

SABOTEAR. To sabotage.

SÁDICO. Sadistic. The person who enjoys acting with cruelty to another. Acting with sadism.

SADISMO. Sadism. A sexual perversion where one provokes his or her own arousal by committing cruel acts upon another person. On the other hand, in masochism, the sexual perversion consists in achieving excitement by submitting oneself to the cruelty of another person.

SALA. Courtroom. Name given to the different branches of the court. Group of judges forming one of the branches of the court.

SALA CIVIL. Civil court. The section of the court which handles any kind of civil lawsuit including family matters, except criminal matters.

SALA PENAL. The court which handles the violations to criminal laws.

SALARIADO. Salaried. Remuneration given to the work performed by labor through wages. A person who receives a salary.

SALARIO. Salary, wage. A fixed periodic compensation paid for services rendered. Every kind of compensation paid to a person for services rendered during a period of time, including money, salary bonus, tips, payment of any kind, etc. The term includes any remuneration received in connection with the work rendered.

SALARIO MÍNIMO. Minimum wage. The lowest wage by which an individual can meet the ordinary requirements of life. It is set by law taking into consideration the cost of living such as housing, health, recreation, food, inflation, the Gross National Product (GNP).

SALDAR. To balance.

SALDO. Balance. Amount owed by one party to another after the bill or account between them has been closed. Also, a credit which has been partially paid. (1) An equality between the sum total of the two sides of an account. (2) The excess or amount left over on either side of an account.

SALDO PENDIENTE. Balance due. See "Saldo".

SALTEAR. To hold up, rob.

SALUD PÚBLICA. Public health. (1) The general health of the population. (2) The department of the government in charge of the general health of the people. See "Sanidad Pública".

SALVAMENTO. Rescue, refuge. (1) Port or place where people or ships shelter against danger. (2) The rescue of shipwrecked persons or the salvage of ships in case of wreck.

SALVEDAD. Condition. Qualification. Note inserted at the end of a document in order to correct an error or to express an amendment to the text. Qualification, exception, reservation.

SALVOCONDUCTO. Safe-conduct. Document issued by an authority which empowers the holder to go through a prohibited area without risk.

SANA CRÍTICA. Rule of evidence which lets the juror, judge or arbitrator use his or her best judgment when deciding which evidence is more important or conclusive to prove or show something.

SANCIÓN. Sanction. Penalty. To make valid. (1) The unfavorable juridical consequence that the nonfulfillment of a duty produces. Part of a law designed to secure its enforcement by imposing a penalty for its violation or offering a reward for its observance. (2) To approve a law or regulation which has legal effect.

SANCIÓN PROCESAL. Penalty for breach of rules of procedure.

SANCIÓN PUNITIVA o PENAL. Penalty. See "Sanción".

SANCIONAR. To authorize. Approve. To penalize. (1) To impose a penalty. (2) To sign a law or statute, thus making it valid and enforceable.

SANEADO. Free of encumbrance. Without defect.

SANEAMIENTO. Indemnification. Reparation. To restore the victim of a loss, in whole or in part, by payment, repair, or replacement. It is a legal warranty, whether or not established by contract where the seller is forced to indemnify the buyer of a good, generally real estate, if there is any defect in the title transferred.

SANIDAD PÚBLICA. Public health. The part of the government in charge of taking care of the population's health. See "Salud Pública".

SANO JUICIO DE. Of sound mind. Mental state where a person's faculties of perception and judgment are ordinarily well developed, and not impaired by mania, insanity, or other mental disorder.

SAQUEAR. To plunder. To seize with violence. To sack, plunder, pillage. To take property from persons or places by open force, in the course of war or by unlawful hostility, as in the case of pirates or robbers. To obtain property through violence and vandalism.

SATÉLITE. Satellite. Refers to heavenly bodies lacking their own light that rotate around a planet.

SATÉLITE ARTIFICAL. Artificial satellite. Objects launched from earth that upon reaching a desired altitude start rotating around a planet.

SATISFACCIÓN. Satisfaction. (1) The discharge of an obligation by paying a party what is due to it, or what is awarded to it, by the judgment of a court or otherwise. (2) Clause in a contract by which one party undertakes to perform an obligation to the satisfaction of the other.

SATISFECHO. Satisfied. An obligation already discharged. What has been done in accord and satisfaction. A debt that has been paid.

SECECIÓN. Secession. Means by which a particular territory obtains its independence from another.

SECRETA. Secret. That which cannot be revealed. Information that must be kept from public knowledge.

SECRETARÍA. (1) Executive department of government. A branch of the executive government in charge of one specific public function. (2) The office of a secretary or clerk.

SECRETARIO(A). Secretary. Clerk. The officer in charge of filing, and keeping record of the activity in his or her office. The court employee whose job is to keep record of the court proceedings. ·

SECRETARIO DE ESTADO. Secretary of state, minister. The maximum public officer in charge of a particular branch of the executive government, at the cabinet level.

SECRETO PROFESIONAL. (1) Professional secret. The duty of members of certain professions such as doctors, lawyers, notarys, etc., to not reveal to a third party the facts known through the practice of their profession, unless specially permitted by law. The duty imposed upon the members of some professions to withhold and retain information obtained during the course of their professional activity. Privilege which prevents one from being compelled to testify on what has been learned during the performance of professional duty. (2) Trade secret. A formula, pattern, device or compilation of information used in one's business and which gives one opportunity to obtain advantage over competitors who do not know or use it.

SECUESTRAR. To confiscate. To appropriate an object and deposit it into the hands of a third party until its ownership is resolved. Also to kidnap a person. (1) To sequester, seize, attach. (2) To kidnap, abduct. (3) The preventive action taken to assure that property is going to be available for sale to satisfy a debt. (4) The criminal conduct of illegally restraining another's freedom of movement.

SECUESTRO. Seizure. Kidnapping. (1) Preventory action consisting of legally holding someone else's property before establishing a lawsuit in order to assure that the property seized will be available to satisfy the complaint if judgment is rendered for the plaintiff. (2) Crime committed by one who detains or holds another person against his or her will.

SECUESTRO JUDICIAL. Judicial seizure. To deposit into the hands of a third party an object under lawsuit, until its ownership is decided.

SECULARIZACIÓN. Secularization. The transfer of a property owned by the church or a religious community to state-owned property.

SEDE. Main office. Headquarters. The principal place of business. The place where the government has its principal offices.

SEDICIÓN. Sedition. Efforts to arouse a popular, collective and violent uprising against the authorities, public order or military discipline that fails as a rebellion. Communication or agreement which has as its objective the stirring up of treason or certain lesser commotion, or the defamation of the government. Insurrectionary movement, smaller than a rebellion, tending to overthrow a government.

SEDUCCIÓN. Seduction. Misleading a minor into engaging in a sexual act. Act of a man enticing a woman to have unlawful intercourse with him by means of persuasion, solicitation, promises, bribes, or other means without the use of force. Generally against a minor.

SEDUCTOR. Seducer. A person who seduces a minor to have sexual relations with him or her.

SEGÚN. Pursuant to. Happening in relation to.

SEGÚN LO CONVENIDO. As agreed. Done according to what has been stipulated. According to the intent of the parties.

SEGÚN LO PACTADO. As agreed. See "Según lo Convenido".

SEGÚN MI LEAL SABER Y ENTENDER. "To the best of my knowledge and belief." Expression used when making a statement with the intent to say the truth as it is honestly understood.

SEGUNDA HIPOTECA. Second mortgage. Second levy constituted upon goods or property already mortgaged in favor of another creditor and for a different obligation. A mortgage of property which ranks in priority below a first mortgage. An encumbrance which guarantees a different credit upon a property already bearing another encumbrance.

SEGUNDA INSTANCIA. Appeal, suit. First appeal. The proceedings established to review a case which has been appealed. During the appeal.

SEGUNDAS NUPCIAS. Second marriage. A new matrimony engaged in after dissolution of the first one. A new marriage after the termination of the first one.

SEGURIDAD. Security. Safety. Exempt from risk. Certainty. Having accuracy. A guaranty that something will occur as stated. Bail, protection.

SEGURIDAD SOCIAL. Social Security. System of social benefits created to protect people upon the occurrence of certain acts.

SEGURO. Insurance. Contract known as policy whereby a person, the insurer or underwriter, for an agreed consideration, called premium, undertakes to compensate or indemnify the insured from loss in the event a stipulated risk occurs.

SEGURO CONTRA ACCIDENTES. Accident insurance. Policy which protects the insured by means of compensation or indemnity in case of the occurrence of an accident.

SEGURO CONTRA INCENDIO. Fire insurance. Contract to protect the insured in case of a fire.

SEGURO CONTRA ROBO. Type of insurance in which the policy-holder is to be indemnified if the interest protected is stolen.

SEGURO DE HOSPITALIZACIÓN o MÉDICO. Health insurance. Policy whereby the insured is compensated for medical expenses in case of a disease, sickness, disability or occurrence of a particular risk.

SEGURO DE VIDA. Life insurance. Contract by which the insurer agrees to pay a stipulated amount of money to a beneficiary upon the death of the insured.

SEGURO SOCIAL. Social security. National program of contributory social insurance whereby employees, employers and the self-employed pay contributions which are pooled in special trust funds. When earnings stop or are reduced because the worker retires, dies, or becomes disabled, monthly cash benefits are paid to replace part of the earnings the person or family lost.

SELLAR. To seal; to close; to stamp.

SELLO. Seal; stamp.

SEMOVIENTE. Livestock. Judicial qualification given to animals. This terminology is used for large animals domesticated by man. Capable of movement. Any kind of animal, especially those used by man for certain tasks.

SENADO. Senate. Name of the upper chamber, or less numerous branch, of the Congress.

SENADOR. Senator. Legislator. Member of the legislative body of a nation in charge of enacting the law.

SENECTUD. Senility. Of old age. The person who has lived a long time. Quality of being an old person.

SENIL. Senile. Old.

SENILIDAD. Senility. Of old age.

SENTENCIA. Judgment. Award, verdict, finding, decision, sentence. The final, official and authentic decision of a court of justice resolving the rights or claims presented during a trial or judicial proceeding. Generally it establishes the obligations or rights of the parties. The sentence is the last word of the court ending a civil or criminal matter.

SENTENCIA ABSOLUTORIA. Acquit. The court's decision finding a person, who has been accused of a crime, not guilty.

SENTENCIA ACUMULATIVA. Cumulative sentence. That sentence which imposes a conviction on a person who has been found guilty of other charges and which is to begin at the end of the sentence served in prison for the prior conviction.

SENTENCIA CONCURRENTE. Concurrent sentence. That sentence imposed upon a convicted person which is served at the same time as another sentence.

SENTENCIA CONSECUTIVA. Cumulative sentence. See "Sentencia Acumulativa".

SENTENCIA CONDENATORIA. Conviction. Judgment finding the accused guilty as charged.

SENTENCIA DECLARATIVA. Declaratory judgment. The decision rendered in a declaratory action, establishing the parties' rights.

SENTENCIA DEFINITIVA o FINAL. Final judgment. The judgment that terminates the controversy as to all the claims of the litigation. It is distinguished from the "Sentencia Interlocutoria".

SENTENCIA EN CONTUMACIA o EN REBELDÍA. Default judgment. Sentence given in a proceeding where there is a non-appearance by a defendant.

SENTENCIA EJECUTORIADA o FIRME. A judgment which has "res judicata" consequences. It is the final judgment that has been agreed upon by the parties or that has not been appealed.

SENTENCIA EXTRANJERA. Foreign judgment. Sentence given by the courts of another country. To make it enforceable in the country where its effects are sought, it has to comply with the requirements set forth by that jurisdiction.

SENTENCIA INTERLOCUTORIA. Interlocutory judgment. The judgment which only decides one subordinate claim of the cause. It does not determine the whole dispute but terminates some particular question(s).

SENTENCIA NULA. Void judgment. The judgment with no legal validity because it was rendered against the law or in violation of some essential element.

SENTENCIAR. To sentence; to pass judgment. The act of rendering a judgment in any kind of legal dispute that has been tried.

SEÑALAMIENTO. Designation. (1) Designating a day (date) for an oral or sight judgment. Matter that will be treated on the day designated. (2) Designation, act of designating a date for a hearing or trial. (3) The pointing out and identification of someone as responsible.

333

SEÑALAR. To designate a date for a hearing. To mark or establish signals. To point out, identify.

SEÑAS PARTICULARES o PERSONALES. Personal description. Physical details that permit the identification of a person. Physical characteristics of a person distinguishing him or her from another person.

SEÑORÍA. Your honor. Expression used to show respect to a judge.

SEPARACIÓN. Separation. Act done with the intent to separate. That which is not part of a whole. Removal. The act of dismissing someone from his or her job.

SEPARACIÓN CONYUGAL. Legal separation. Situation in which married couples find themselves when they stop living together. Interruption of the married life by agreement of the spouses or by judicial decision, without extinguishing the marriage itself.

SEPARACIÓN DEL CARGO. The act by which a person is removed from the duties entrusted. To dismiss from a job, commission or assignment. The expression implies that the person has been fired but is not necessarily true.

SEPARACIÓN DE HECHOS. Situation that occurs when married couples agree to separate permanently without previous juridical decision.

SÉPASE. Be it known. Word used to mean that the information should be disclosed or made public.

SEPULTURA. Grave. The place where the body has been buried.

SERVICIO. Service. (1) An act of serving. The act and action of using. (2) Toilet. The water closet of a building. (3) Performing a service.

SERVICIO ACTIVO. On duty.

SERVICIO DOMÉSTICO. Servant. Household employee. The person hired to carry out the household duties. The gardener, maid, chauffeur.

SERVICIO PÚBLICO. Public service. The service rendered to the general population to satisfy a public need.

SERVICIOS PROFESIONALES. Professional services. Those rendered by any professional in the course of his or her profession. The legal services of an attorney. The services of a doctor.

SERVIDUMBRE. Easement, servitude, servitus. Burden placed on one site, called servient, for the benefit of another, called dominant tenement. It is a right of use over another property.

SERVIDUMBRE ACCESORIA. Appurtenant easement. Incorporeal right attached to a superior right and inherent in land to which it is attached and is in the nature of a covenant running with the land.

SERVIDUMBRE ACTIVA, AFIRMATIVA o POSITIVA. Positive or affirmative easement. One where the servient tenement must permit something to be done thereon.

SERVIDUMBRE APARENTE. Apparent easement. Right which exists upon the construction or condition of one of the tenements.

SERVIDUMBRE CONTINUA. Continuing easement. The enjoyment of which can be had without interruption.

SERVIDUMBRE DE ACCESO. Easement of access. The right of an abutting owner to ingress and to egress from his premises.

SERVIDUMBRE DE AGUAS. Water rights. The servient tenement must permit the course of water coming from another estate. It's also the right to use water from a natural stream.

SERVIDUMBRE DE CAMINO. Right of way. Right to pass over another's land.

SERVIDUMBRE DE DESAGÜE. Drainage rights. A right to have the water course or drainage of the dominant tenement passing over the servient one, without any destruction or diversion that may cause damage to the dominant tenement.

SERVIDUMBRE DE LUCES Y VISTAS. Light and view easement. The right obtained from an adjoining landowner to protect against the obstruction of light and air.

SERVIDUMBRE DE PASO. Right of way. See "Servidumbre de Camino".

SERVIDUMBRE DE UTILIDAD PÚBLICA. Public easement. Right established by statute for the enjoyment of the general public.

SERVIDUMBRE DE VÍA. Right of way. See "Servidumbre de Camino".

SERVIDUMBRE DISCONTINUA. An easement that can only be enjoyed through the action of a person (i.e., hunting on the land).

SERVIDUMBRE INTERMITENTE. Intermittent easement. Usable or used only at times, and not continuously.

SERVIDUMBRE NEGATIVA. Negative easement. The owner of the servient estate is prohibited from doing something otherwise lawful.

SERVIDUMBRE PERSONAL. Easement in gross. It is an easement consisting of a personal right or interest to use land of another and it is not appurtenant to any estate. It usually ends with the death of the grantee.

SERVIDUMBRE POR PRESCRIPCIÓN. Easement by prescription. Mode of acquiring title to property by immemorial or long continued use.

SERVIDUMBRE POSITIVA. Affirmative easement. See "Servidumbre Activa".

SERVIDUMBRE PREDIAL. Appurtenant easement. See "Servidumbre Accesoria".

SERVIDUMBRE REAL. Appurtenant easement. See "Servidumbre Accesoria".

SERVIDUMBRE TÁCITA. Implied easement. Easement which the law imposes upon the parties, although it was not expressly bargained for by the parties.

SERVIDUMBRE VISIBLE. Apparent easement. See "Apparent".

SERVIDUMBRE VOLUNTARIA. Easement created by contract.

SESIÓN. Session. Meeting. Gathering of people to exchange ideas or impressions.

SESIÓN EXTRAORDINARIA. Extraordinary meeting. A reunion held outside the regular schedule of meetings to discuss a particular matter.

SESIÓN ORDINARIA. Regular meeting. Any meeting held according to the normal and ordinary schedule.

SESIONAR. To meet. To hold a meeting.

SEUDÓNIMO. Pseudonym, pen name. Name chosen by a person to conceal his or her real identity, in any activity undertaken. A fictitious name.

SEVICIA. Cruelty. Brutality, constitutes a cause for divorce. Extreme cruelty. (1) It is a cause of action for a divorce decree. (2) Circumstances which allow sentencing with a maximum term.

SEXO. Sex. Organic characteristic that distinguishes male from female in animals and plants.

SICARIO. A person hired to kill another. A hired murderer.

SIGLO. Century. A period of one hundred years in progressive order one after the other.

SILENCIO ADMINISTRATIVO. The attitude assumed by the government when receiving a petition which consists of not doing anything and implying a negative answer.

SIMULACIÓN. Simulation. The act by means of which something is altered to seem like another thing.

SINALAGMÁTICO. Bilateral. To give obligatory character to the different parts of a judicial act. Imposing reciprocal obligations. The kind of contract in which both parties have agreed to take on obligations.

SINDICADO. Accused. The person against whom a criminal charge has been made. The defendant in a criminal case.

SINDICAR. To accuse. (1) To charge someone with a criminal violation. (2) To form a union or association.

SINDICATO. Union. Grouping formed to defend the common economic interests of the members. Syndical union. An association of individuals, formed for the purpose of conducting and carrying out some particular business transaction, ordinarily of a financial character, in which the members are mutually interested.

SÍNDICO. Trustee. The person entrusted with the power to supervise the management of an organization and safeguard the business. The accountant or attorney in charge of the liquidation of a bankrupt estate and the settlement of the debtor's obligations.

SINE QUA NON. (Lat.) Indispensable condition. Without which it would not be.

SINGULAR. Singular. Individual.

SINIESTRO. Disaster. (1) Act of fate that produces great damage or loss. Disaster, damage, loss. (2) Left. (3) Important or great loss. Generally consisting of death, fire, shipwreck, accident.

SIN PERJUICIO DE TERCEROS. Expression used to protect the interests of third parties who have not participated in a transaction. It means that whatever has been agreed will not harm the right of a third person.

SIRVIENTE. Servient. Quality of performing a service.

SITIAL. Chair of presiding officer; bench in courtroom.

SITIO. Place.

SOBERANÍA. Sovereignty. The supreme, absolute, and uncontrollable power by which any independent state is governed.

SOBORNADO. Bribed. The public official who has solicited or received money or any value to act under influence.

SOBORNADOR. Briber. The person who offers or gives money or any other value to a public officer to influence his or her action.

SOBORNAR. To bribe. To corrupt with gifts in order to carry out or permit wrong, immoral or illicit doings. To offer, give, receive or solicit anything of value to influence a public official.

SOBORNO. Bribery, subornation. Crime consisting in the corrupt tendering or receiving of a price for official action.

SOBREASEGURADO. Overinsured. Insured for an amount greater than what can be lost.

SOBRECARGO. Commissioner. Represents the interests of the load.

SOBREGIRADO. Overdrawn. Having paid or ordered in excess of the budgeted amount.

SOBREGIRAR. To overdraw. To draw upon a person in excess of the funds remaining to the drawer's credit with the drawee, or to an amount greater than what is due. To issue a draft for an amount superior to the funds from which the draft is to be paid.

SOBREGIRO. Overdraft. (1) Draft, note or check drawn against the unavailable funds. A check written on a checking account containing less funds than the amount of the check. (2) Credit given to the drawer by the drawee when paying an overdraft.

SOBRENOMBRE. Nickname. Appellative that a person may add to his or her real name. Also known as.

SOBRESEER. To stay a cause; to abandon a purpose; to desist. To stop the proceedings by means of a court order.

SOBRESEIMIENTO. Stay of proceedings; dismissal; nonsuit.

SOBRESEIMIENTO DEFINITIVO. Dismissal. It puts an end to the proceedings without possibility of reopening the case. The finding of no evidence or lack of sufficient evidence to convict a defendant.

SOBRESEIMIENTO PROVISIONAL o TEMPORAL. Temporary stay. A stop to the proceedings because of lack of evidence to incriminate the defendant. It is not definitive; therefore, the case can be reopened.

SOBRETASA. Surtax, surcharge. A tax on a tax.

SOBREVENCIDO. Overdue. Delayed or unpaid. In arrears. An obligation that is past due.

SOBREVENDIDO. Sold in excess of its capacity.

SOBREVIVENCIA. Survival. Act of surviving. Staying alive.

SOBREVIVIENTE. Surviving. The person who lives after another has died. To live after a disaster.

SOBREVIVIR. To survive. To live after another. To stay alive.

SOBRINO(A). Nephew or niece. The son or daughter of a brother or sister.

SOCIALISMO. Socialism. Social organizational system that affirms the superiority of collective interests over those of individuals.

SOCIALISTA. Socialist. Supporter of socialism.

SOCIEDAD. Corporation, partnership, association, society.

SOCIEDAD ACCIDENTAL o EN PARTICIPACIÓN. An association without a partnership agreement or formal incorporation, temporarily created to accomplish a specific purpose. The rights or obligations fall on the acting partner, whose liability goes beyond his or her capital contribution.

SOCIEDAD ANÓNIMA. Corporation. An artificial person or legal entity created under the authority of the law and capable of rights and obligations. In some states it can be organized by one person. It has a capital stock divided into shares and the stockholders are liable only to the extent of their contributions.

SOCIEDAD COLECTIVA. General partnership. One in which all the partners are jointly and severally responsible for the partnership, sharing the profits and losses without limitation beyond their capital contribution.

SOCIEDAD COMANDITARIA o EN COMANDITA. Limited partnership. A partnership formed by at least one general partner responsible beyond his or her contribution and by whom the business is conducted and by at least one limited partner whose liability is limited to the partnership agreement or to his or her capital contribution. When the limited partner's contribution is not divided in stocks it is called "Sociedad Comanditaria o En Comandita Simple" and when the capital contribution of the limited partner is divided in stocks it is called "Sociedad Comanditaria o En Comandita por Acciones".

SOCIEDAD CONYUGAL. Joint ownership of property by husband and wife. Combination of property affected by the common interests of marriage.

SOCIEDAD EN COMANDITA POR ACCIONES. Limited partnership. An unincorporated business enterprise with ownership interests represented by shares of stock. See "Sociedad Comanditaria".

SOCIEDAD DE BENEFICENCIA. Eleemosynary or alms-giving corporation. A non-profit organization created for charitable purposes.

SOCIEDAD DE GANANCIALES. Community property. Community of property between husband and wife acquired during marriage. It is the property owned in common by the spouses each having one half interest in the marital patrimony. The partnership formed by husband and wife over property acquired during marriage.

SOCIO. Partner. Member of a group or association. One involved in a business with others as a partnership. A member of a firm.

SOCIO ADMINISTRADOR. Managing partner. The partner in charge of the management. It is the partner fully and personally liable and responsible for the debts of the partnership because of his or her involvement in the management.

SOCIO APARENTE. Ostensible partner. The person whose name is shown to cause the impression that he or she is a member of the firm as a partner, regardless of whether the person has a real interest or participation in the business.

SOCIO CAPITALISTA. Limited or special partner. A partner who is responsible or liable for the debts of the partnership only to the extent of his or her contribution. Whether or not the name appears to the world as partner.

SOCIO COMANDITADO. General partner. The partner who participates in the management of a limited partnership and who is presumably liable and responsible for the debts of the partnership beyond the amount of his or her contribution to the business.

SOCIO COMANDITARIO. Limited or special partner. A partner of a limited partnership whose liability is limited and restricted only to the amount of his or her contribution to the partnership and who is not involved in the management of the business.

SOCIO OSTENCIBLE. Ostensible partner. See "Socio Aparente".

SOCIO OCULTO o SECRETO. Dormant partner. The partner whose name does not appear as partner. Nevertheless a contribution has been made to the firm and he or she has a real interest in the profit and losses. The name of the dormant partner is not known to others as partner and he or she is simply passive in the management because no active part is taken in the business.

SODOMIA. Sodomy. Carnal copulation by human beings with each other against nature, or with a beast. Anal penetration.

SOLARIEGO. Held in fee simple. Real estate completely owned by one person. The owner is entitled to the whole property without limitations.

SOLEMNE. Solemn. Regarding legal acts and contracts, refers to their authenticity and effectiveness when they have followed all the forms required by law for their validity. Legal, complete. Quality of a document which means it is perfect, valid, enforceable because all the formal requirements have been completed or fulfilled.

SOLEMNIDAD. Solemnity. Quality of being solemn.

SOLICITANTE. Petitioner. One who presents a petition to a court, officer or legislative body.

SOLICITUD. Demand; petition.

SOLIDARIDAD. Solidarity. Participating in the same amount. Circumstance which allows the same condition to the parties. That which gives everyone having this condition the ability to act independently.

SOLIDARIDAD ACTIVA. Active solidarity. The power given to each creditor which makes him or her able to enforce the whole right against the debtor.

SOLIDARIDAD PASIVA. Passive solidarity. Quality of each debtor which makes him or her liable and responsible for the full amount of the obligation.

SOLIDARIO. Solidary. Individually and collectively liable. Any solidary debtor can be held responsible for the whole debt. Any solidary creditor can enforce the totality of his or her right against any debtor.

SOLTERO. Unmarried, single. The one who has not been married or whose marriage has been annulled. The legal status of a person who is not married.

SOLTURA. Release from jail or imprisonment. Free. Not in captivity.

SOLVENCIA. Solvency. Excess of assets over liabilities. Ability to meet one's obligation.

SOLVENTAR. To settle, satisfy.

SOLVENTE. Solvent. Debtor who can meet his or her obligations at maturity or when due. Responsible, sound. Able to pay debts as they become due.

SOMETER. To submit. (1) **Someter al arbitraje.** To submit to arbitration. (2) **Someter a votación.** To put to a vote.

SO PENA DE. Under penalty of. Warnings that a penalty will be imposed.

SOPLÓN. Informer, squealer.

SORTEO DE JURADOS. To choose a jury by drawing lots.

SOSPECHOSO. Suspect. A person reputed or thought to be involved in a crime.

STATUS QUO. (Lat.) Existing state of things.

STRICTO SENSU. Strictly speaking, as it arises from literal interpretation.

SUBALQUILER. Sublease. Transaction where tenant grants an interest in leased premises less than his own, or reserves to him or herself a reversionary interest in the property. See "Subarrendador, Subarrendatario, Subarrendar".

SUBARRENDADOR. A tenant who subleases to another tenant. When a tenant rents property to another, either for the rest of the tenant's own lease or for a portion of it.

SUBARRENDATARIO. A tenant who subleases from another tenant.

SUBARRENDAR. To sublease. To lease what has been already leased.

SUBASTA. Auction. The public sale of goods to the highest bidder by one licensed and authorized for that purpose.

SUBCONTRATISTA. Subcontractor. One who takes a portion of a contract from a principal contractor or another subcontractor.

SUBCONTRATO. Subcontract. A contract subordinate to another contract and with the object of performing the main contract.

SUBDIRECTOR. Assistant manager. Deputy manager, personal replacement of a director.

SÚBDITO. Subject of a country. One who owes allegiance to a sovereign and is governed by his or her laws.

SUB JUDICE. (Lat.) Under judicial consideration. Undermined. Said of the case which is undergoing judicial proceedings.

SUBPOENA DUCES TECUM. (Lat.) Order to appear and produce documents.

SUBREPTICIO. Surreptitious. Stealthily or fraudulently done, taken away, or introduced.

SUBROGACIÓN. Subrogation. Substitution of a person or object in place of another. The lawful substitution of a third party in place of a party having a claim against another party. The rights to recover from another debtor what has been paid to the creditor.

SUBSANABLE. Reparable. That which can be amended, ratified or corrected. That which may be corrected or overcome.

SUBSANACIÓN. Amendment of an error. Rectification of a mistake, correction of a defect.

SUBSECRETARIO. Undersecretary. The second after a minister. The one in charge of one of the main branches of a ministry.

SUBSIDIO. Subsidy. A grant of money made by the government in aid of an enterprise which is considered a proper subject for government aid, because it is of benefit to the public.

SUBSTANCIACIÓN. Substantiation. To conduct a matter or judgment through the correct legal proceeding until a sentence is pronounced.

SUBSTANCIADOR. The judge who is in charge of a case that is being tried.

SUBSTANCIACIÓN. The act of trying a case. Actions by the person in charge of the proceedings.

SUBSTITUCIÓN. Substitution, subrogation. To put a person in the place, right or interest of another.

SUBSTITUCIÓN DE HEREDERO. Second heir. The designation of a second heir by a testator in case the main heir does not wish or is unable to accept the inheritance. Act by which one heir is replaced according to the will in case he or she does not want to inherit. The transfer of property to a second heir named in the testament if the first one repudiates the estate.

SUBSTITUCIÓN DEL MANDATO. Power of attorney substitution. The agent or attorney may delegate to another the execution of what has been commended to him. Provision made in a contract where a power of attorney is granted by which the agent or attorney can be replaced by another attorney or agent.

SUBSTITUTO. Substitute. The one called to replace another. The second heir called to accept the estate in case the first one refuses to inherit.

SUBSTRAER. To steal, to withdraw, to misappropriate.

SUBTERFUGIO. Subterfuge. That to which one resorts for escape or concealment.

SUBVENCIÓN. Assistance, aid. Grant given to help someone else achieve the goal set. Generally involving a public benefit.

345

SUBVERSIÓN. Subversion. Revolution. Destruction of moral values. The act or process of overthrowing, destroying, or corrupting. Generally to overthrow a government.

SUBVERSIVO. Subversive. The person or act intending to overthrow, destroy or corrupt.

SUCEDER. To inherit. To follow.

SUCESIÓN. Succession. (1) The placing or continuance of one person or thing in the place of another. (2) It also means the descendants. (3) The acquisition of rights or property upon the death of another according to the civil law, whether or not there has been a will.

SUCESIÓN AB INTESTATO. Intestate succession. See "Sucesión Intestada".

SUCESIÓN HEREDITARIA. Hereditary succession. It is the inheritance by law whether or not there is a testament. Means of acquiring rights or property upon the death of another.

SUCESIÓN INTESTADA. Intestate succession. The acquisition of property by an heir when the decedent dies without a will or when the testament made is declared null.

SUCESIÓN LEGÍTIMA. Legal succession. The succession set by law to benefit the heir in the nearest relation, to a deceased person.

SUCESIÓN LEGAL. See "Sucesión Legitima".

SUCESIÓN TESTADA. Testate succession. See "Sucesión Testamentaria".

SUCESIÓN TESTAMENTARIA. Testamentary succession. It is the succession in which the estate is acquired by the heir designated in a will, given according to the formalities of the law.

SUCESIÓN UNIVERSAL. Universal succession. The one by which an heir, called universal successor, inherits the whole estate with its rights and obligations.

SUCESO. Occurrence. Any event.

346

SUCESOR. Successor. One who succeeds or follows. One who takes the place that another has left, and sustains the like part or character; one who takes the place of another by succession.

SUCESORIO. Successory. Relative or pertaining to a succession.

SUCURSAL. Branch. Commercial or industrial establishment located in a different location from the headquarters or main office. An offshoot, lateral extension, or subdivision of a commercial establishment.

SUEGRA. Mother-in-law. To each spouse, the mother of the other. The mother of one's spouse.

SUEGRO. Father-in-law. To each spouse, the father of the other. The father of one's spouse.

SUELDO. Pay, monthly salary. Payment for the work, services or labor performed for another.

SUELTO. Free. That which has been set free.

SUFRAGIO. Suffrage. Electoral system through which the designation of people to occupy certain positions is determined by votes. A vote; the act of voting; the right or privilege of casting a vote at public elections.

SUGESTIÓN. Suggestion. Act of suggesting or presenting one idea indirectly. Hint or insinuation. The act of inducing one person to act according to another's will.

SUICIDA. Suicide. The person who commits suicide or attempts to suicide. The one who kills him or herself.

SUICIDIO. Suicide. To end one's own life.

SUI GENERIS. (Lat.) Unique, peculiar, in a class by itself.

SUI JURIS. (Lat.) Of his or her own right.

SUJETO. Subject to. A person.

SUMARIAS. Proceedings. The file containing the acts done towards the investigation of the facts and truth in a criminal case.

SUMARIO. Summary, proceeding. The process by which all the necessary elements, to decide whether or not a person(s) may be accused of committing a crime during a plenary proceeding, are gathered. (1) A short proceeding toward an expedited judgment. (2) In criminal law the judicial proceeding and action tending to gather the evidence prior to the hearings.

SUMINISTRO. Supply. Contract by which one party undertakes the obligation to furnish or give something to another generally in a periodic way.

SUMISIÓN. Submission. (1) Submit one's will to the will of another. (2) To submit a legal proceeding to a judge with jurisdiction over the case.

SUPERAVIT. Surplus, excess. Refers to excess of income over expenses. Positive balance. That which results when income exceeds expenses. When referring to the national budget it means that there is a positive balance because the expenditure was less than the general income.

SUPERSTICIÓN. Superstition. Fear of the unknown which makes a person believe in irrational occurrences.

SUPÉRSTITE. Surviving. The one who survives over another. The spouse who becomes a widow(er).

SUPERVIVENCIA. Survivorship. To live longer than another or after his or her death. Survival. The act of living through a disaster. See "Sobrevivencia".

SUPERVIVIENTE. Survivor. The person whose life continues after the death of another. The one who lives after a disaster.

SUPERVIVIR. To survive. The act of staying alive.

SUPLETORIO. Additional. Supplementary. What complements or replaces. That which is added to a thing to complete it.

SÚPLICA. Petition, request, prayer for relief.

SUPRA. (Lat.) Above, preceding.

SUPREMA CORTE DE JUSTICIA. Supreme court of justice. The ultimate or highest court.

SUPRIMIR. Suppress. To put an end to a thing actually existing; to prevent, subdue, or end by force.

SUPOSICIÓN. Supposition. Assumption.

SUSCRIBIR. To underwrite. To sign at the end of a document as an author or giving concurrence. To subscribe. To sign. To agree.

SUSCRIPCIÓN. Subscription. Generally a written commitment that binds the subscriber to effect certain payments, in exchange for receiving certain benefits or services. (1) The act of writing one's name under a written instrument. (2) Obligation to make periodic payments in order to receive periodic benefits or services. Generally refers to periodical publications.

SUSODICHO. Above-mentioned, aforesaid, aforementioned. Already mentioned. Previously referred to.

SUSPENDIDO. Suspended. Postponed. Pending. In a temporary stop.

SUSPENSIÓN. Suspension. A temporary stop or interruption.

SUSPENSIÓN DE GARANTÍAS CONSTITUCIONALES. Consequence arising out of a state of emergency in which the government has declared a temporary suspension of all the rights protected under the constitution.

SUSPENSIVO. Suspensive. That which causes delay or temporary stop.

SUSPENSO, EN. In suspense, in abeyance. (1) A temporary stop in the proceedings. (2) To suspend a lawyer or judicial officer in the performance of his or her duties.

SUSTANTIVO. Substantive. An essential part. Relating to what is essential.

SUSTENTO. Maintenance; support.

T

TABLA DE IMPUESTOS. Tax table.

TABLILLA. Auto license plate.

TABLÓN DE ANUNCIOS. Bulletin board. Board where reports or notices are made public. Exposed to public view.

TACHA. Objection; scratch. (1) Line drawn over something written to discard it. (2) Defect, flaw. (3) Disqualification.

TACHABLE. Challengeable. That which can be erased or deleted from.

TACHA DE TESTIGOS. The impeachment or disqualification of a witness. To challenge a witness' testimony by questioning its validity because of lack of credibility.

TACHADURA. Something to cancel or strike out. In documents, refers to a correction or an amendment.

TACHAR. (1) To erase or to scratch. (2) To challenge a witness. (3) To cancel or eliminate an endorsement to a negotiable instrument without affecting the validity of the document itself. (4) To object to the personal qualification of a person for a particular function; or to the existence of a right claimed; or to the validity of an instrument.

TÁCITA RECONDUCCIÓN. Extension or renewal of an expired lease term by order of law.

TÁCITO. Tacit. Silent. What is expressed not with words, but by acts or behavior. Implied.

TALA. The systematic destruction of forests or areas by fire or demolition, or cutting them in large amounts.

TALENTO. Talent. The special ability inherent in some people to do something extraordinary.

TALIÓN. Punishment equal to the offense. For example, an eye for an eye. Requital. An expression of revenge. A punishment materially equal to the offense received. Ancient law which allows retaliation. Doing an evil for an evil.

TALÓN. Receipt, coupon or stub.

TALONARIO. Receipt, coupon or stub book; a voucher. A book used to keep track of certain transactions.

TALLA. Ransom, reward. Bounty offered for the capture of a fugitive, or the release of a captive.

TALLER. Workshop. Place where work is performed.

TANTEAR. Exercising the right to purchase a good or realty by payment of the bid price.

TANTEO. Approximate estimate; payment of the bid price; review, inspection.

TARA. Tare. (1) An allowance or abatement of a certain weight or quantity which the seller makes to the buyer, on account of the weight of such box, cask, etc. (2) Defect.

TARIFA. Tariff. Schedule of prices, rates, duties or taxes that must be paid for an item or the performance of a job.

TASA. Rate. (1) What determines value or price from a tax law point of view. (2) The amount of money paid in exchange for a specific public service received. (3) **Tasa de cambio.** Rate of exchange. (4) **Tasa de impuesto.** Tax rate. (5) **Tasa de interés.** Rate of interest.

TASACIÓN. Appraisal, assessment, valuation. The act of setting the amount of tax to be paid on an item. The determination of the value of one thing.

TASADOR. Appraiser. A person appointed to estimate the value of something.

TASAR. Assess, appraise. To set an estimated value on something.

TAXATIVAMENTE. Limited. That which has been expressly enumerated. The declaration referring exclusively to those things enunciated. Excluding what has been left of the list.

351

TAXATIVO. Restrictive, limited, conditioned. Specifically mentioned.

TECNOCRACIA. Technocracy. Political regime where the government is controlled by the technocrats that regulate all the activities of a nation.

TELA DE JUICIO, EN. A matter in dispute, under advisement, contested.

TEMARIO. Agenda, schedule of items, order of the day.

TEMERARIO. Rashly; baseless; malicious. A plaintiff who shows no ground or cause of action.

TEMOR. Fear. Apprehension of something.

TEMPORAL. Temporal. (1) Relating to time, as opposed to the eternal. That which passes with time. Seasonal or temporary. (2) Employee without stability, hired to perform a transitory activity.

TENDERO. Salesperson in the retail business. The person in charge of a store.

TENEDOR. Holder, keeper, beneficiary, payee.

TENEDOR DE ACCIONES. Stockholder, shareholder. Person who owns shares of stock in a corporation.

TENEDOR DE BONOS. Bondholder. Person who owns a bond.

TENEDOR DE BUENA FE. Bona fide holder for value; holder in due course.

TENEDOR DE PAGARE. Noteholder.

TENEDOR DE PÓLIZA. Policyholder. Person who owns a policy of insurance, whether he or she is the insured or not.

TENEDOR DE LIBROS. Bookkeeper. Person who keeps books in a systematic way, keeping records of all business transactions.

TENENCIA. Tenancy. (1) Occupancy and actual possession of a thing. (2) Term of office. The period during which an elected officer is entitled to hold office with all privileges and duties. (3) **Tenencia**

conjunta. Co-tenancy; tenancy in common. (4) **Tenencia común.** Tenancy in common. (5) **Tenencia vitalicia.** Tenancy for life.

TENENCIA DE LOS HIJOS. Child custody.

TENER. To have, hold, own.

TENTATIVA DEL DELITO. Attempt to commit a crime. Efforts made to commit a crime which were frustrated by unforeseen circumstances outside the control of the perpetrator.

TERCERÍA. (1) Intervention by a third party into a lawsuit to protect his or her rights. (2) The mediation or arbitration of a dispute by a third party.

TERCERÍA COADYUVANTE. Intervention by a third party into a lawsuit in support of one party.

TERCERÍA DE DOMINIO. Intervention by a third party into a lawsuit with the purpose of claiming ownership of goods which are the subject matter of the lawsuit.

TERCERÍA DE MEJOR DERECHO. Intervention by a third party into a lawsuit, alleging a preferred right.

TERCERÍA EXCLUYENTE. Intervention by a third party into a lawsuit, opposing both parties.

TERCERISTA. Intervenor, intervener.

TERCERO. Third party. Arbitrator, mediator, umpire. (1) One different from the defendant and plaintiff interested in a lawsuit. (2) One called to settle a conflict.

TERCERO EN EL PROCESO. Third party in interest. Party with the right to intervene in a pending suit at any stage of the proceedings, as any judgment imposed may affect their rights.

TERCIAR. To mediate or arbitrate.

TEOCRACIA. Theocracy. Government of a state by a god. Government of a state by priests who claim divine authority.

TÉRMINO. Term; limit, deadline. A fixed period. A set date.

TÉRMINO CIERTO. Fixed or specified period. A specific period. A certain point in time established to determine a moment. A precise date. Fixed term, term stated by day, month and year.

TÉRMINO CONVENCIONAL. Term fixed by a contract or agreement between parties. Agreed period. A point in time that has been accepted by the parties in a contract. It opposes the time that is determined by the judge.

TÉRMINO DE ENCARCELAMIENTO. Term of imprisonment.

TÉRMINO DE GRACIA. Grace period. (1) Portion of time during which the party in a contract is exempt from performing an obligation. (2) Time during which payment is not owed. The specific rights granted during this time should be specified in the contract. Sometimes payment is still owed but is deferred to a future moment when the grace period expires. (3) In insurance law it is the time beyond the due date of a premium during which the policy is still in force and payment can be made to maintain the insurance.

TÉRMINO DE PRUEBA. Time allowed to parties in a lawsuit to produce evidence.

TÉRMINO DEL CARGO. Term of office. Period of time during which an elected or appointed official has the right to hold the position and perform his duties.

TÉRMINO EXTRAORDINARIO. Period of time (longer than the usual term allowed by court rules) allowing parties to a lawsuit to produce evidence from a distant place (e.g., a foreign nation).

TÉRMINO FATAL. Deadline. Term which cannot be extended. A fixed and absolute compliance date that cannot be extended by which the obligation needs to be fulfilled.

TÉRMINO INCIERTO. Uncertain term. Term of time defined by an act or circumstance which cannot be ascertained; for example, the death of the insured in a life insurance contract.

TÉRMINO JUDICIAL. Time or deadline fixed by judge. Judicial term. Period of time established by the court according to the proceedings during which a procedural practice or act should be performed by the parties or the court.

TÉRMINO LEGAL. Time or deadline fixed by law.

TÉRMINO ORDINARIO. The specified period of time allowed by court rules to parties in a lawsuit to do something.

TÉRMINO PROBATORIO. Probatory term. Time allowed for the production of evidence. Period of time included in the judicial term during which the specific practice of producing evidence should be performed by the parties.

TÉRMINO PRORROGABLE. Extendable term. Period of time which can be extended. The term of a contract which can be prolonged.

TERRATENIENTE. Landholder, land owner.

TERRENO COLINDANTE. Abutting property.

TERRITORIAL. Territorial. Having to do with a particular area.

TERRITORIALIDAD. Territorial. Having to do with a particular area.

TERRITORIO. Territory. (1) A part of a country separated from the rest. (2) Geographical area under the jurisdiction of another country or sovereign land.

TERROR. Terror. Fright; dread. Overwhelming fear caused by the presence of danger.

TERRORISMO. Terrorism. Violent acts performed to inspire terror to impact a political process.

TERRORISTA. Terrorist. One who systematically uses terror as a means of coercion. The person whose ideas are fanatical and believes in attacking and causing harm, death and destruction to innocent people in order to obtain his or her goal.

TESIS. Thesis. Conclusion arrived at, following reasonable thoughts. Work presented in writing and orally explained to the faculty in order to obtain a university degree.

TESORO. Treasure. (1) Things hidden in the earth, discovered by chance, and which no one can prove his property. (2) Treasury. The government office which manages public revenues.

355

TESORO NACIONAL. National treasury. Treasury formed by the state to meet national expenses. Public revenues.

TESTADO. Testate. Person who dies having made a will.

TESTADOR. Testator, devisor. (1) Person who makes or has made a will. (2) Person who is legally capable of making a will.

TESTADORA. Testatrix.

TESTAFERRO. Person allowing another to use his or her name to hide the name of the real owner.

TESTAMENTO. Will. Instrument by which a person makes a disposition of his property, to take effect after his or her death, and which by its own nature is ambulatory and revocable during his or her lifetime.

TESTAMENTO ABIERTO. Oral or nuncupative will. Oral will declared or dictated by the testator in his or her last sickness before a sufficient number of witnesses, and afterwards reduced to writing.

TESTAMENTO CERRADO. Sealed or mystic will. Sealed will given by a testator to a notary in a closed or sealed letter, before witnesses, expressing that the letter contains the testator's will.

TESTAMENTO MUTUO. Mutual or reciprocal will.

TESTAMENTO OLÓGRAFO. Holographic will. One that is entirely handwritten, dated and signed by the testator himself or herself.

TESTAMENTOS ESPECIALES. Wills arising out of particular and specific conditions and hence lacking standard legal formalities.

TESTAR. To make a will.

TESTIFICAR. Testify. To be a witness in a lawsuit.

TESTIGO. Witness. One who sees or perceives a thing. Person who gives testimony of an event ocurring in his or her presence.

TESTIGO DE CARGO. Witness for the prosecution. The one who testifies against the defendant.

TESTIGO DE DESCARGO. Witness for the defense. The one who testifies in support of the defendant.

TESTIGO HÁBIL. Competent witness. One who is legally qualified to testify in a case.

TESTIGO INHÁBIL. Incompetent witness. One who is not legally qualified to testify in a case.

TESTIGO INSTRUMENTAL. Attesting witness. Subscribing witness. Regarding documents, the one who signs in order to attest a signing party.

TESTIGO OCULAR. Eyewitness. When the act happens in the presence of the witness and is seen and experienced by him or her.

TESTIGO PRESENCIAL. Eyewitness. The person who testifies to an act that occurred in his or her presence.

TESTIMONIAL. Testimonial. Pertaining to testimony. The kind of evidence obtained from the testimony of a witness.

TESTIMONIO. Testimony. Evidence given by a witness under oath. Oral affirmations, trial statements or deposition of a fact, known by the witness.

TEXTO. Text. The words contained in documents.

TIEMPO. Time. Term.

TIMBRE. Stamp, seal; stamps tax. Stamps, required by law on certain documents, indicating that the fees or charges imposed by law have been paid.

TIMO. Swindle, cheating. To defraud somebody by an intentionally false representation.

TINTERILLO. Shyster lawyer, pettifogger. A dishonest lawyer.

TIPICIDAD. Quality of typical. The condition consisting of acting in a wrongful manner which is already described in the law as a crime.

TÍPICO. Typical. Criminal conduct already described in a statute.

TIRANÍA. Tyranny. Arbitrary government. Regime whereby power is exercised arbitrarily without reason, right or justice.

TIRANO. Tyrant. A despot. A ruler who acts arbitrarily. The cruel and despotic ruler of a country, who acts arbitrarily disregarding the law and justice.

TÍTERE. Puppet. Person who allows him or herself to be used by others to serve their purpose, while pretending that his or her acts are the product of a free will.

TITULADO. Licensed. Having a title. (1) The person who has received a degree. (2) Something that is properly documented. Having a name.

TITULAR. Titleholder. Owner of record; security holder.

TÍTULO. Title. Means whereby the owner of real property has the just possession of his property. Also, the evidence of such property.

TÍTULO ABSOLUTO. Absolute title. Title which excludes all others not compatible with it.

TÍTULO A LA ORDEN. Order instrument. Document issued to the order of a named person, or anybody specified by that person.

TÍTULO AL PORTADOR. Bearer instrument. Any document issued to the bearer. Document that does not specify the name of the titleholder. Any person who holds it is therefore entitled to the rights derived from it.

TÍTULO EJECUTIVO. Plaintiff's right of execution. Document which enables a creditor to get paid from a debtor's property by merely requesting judicial enforcement, and without providing evidence of the creditor's rights.

TÍTULO GRATUITO. Lucrative title. Conveyance of a title without giving anything in exchange for it. Title acquired by gift.

TÍTULO INSCRIBIBLE. Recordable instrument. Any document which can be recorded in any public record.

TÍTULO LUCRATIVO. See "Título Gratuito".

TÍTULO NOMINATIVO. Credit instrument bearing a name. Document issued to a named person, who is the only one entitled to the rights derived from it.

TÍTULO ONEROSO. Onerous title. Conveyance of a title for valuable consideration.

TOGA. Gown. A long robe worn by judges and scholars.

TOXICOMANÍA. Drug addiction.

TOLERAR. Tolerate. To allow so as not to hinder; to permit though not wholly approved of.

TOMA DE POSESIÓN. Taking of possession. Entry. Taking office. Act of taking right; with regard to personal property, the physical delivery of the property to another. Taking of office. To be invested with the rights and duties inherent to a public charge or employment.

TOMADOR. Drawee, payee.

TONELAJE. Tonnage. Capacity of a ship to carry freight, calculated in tons.

TORMENTOS. Torments. Submitting the accused to torture in order to obtain his or her confession of committing a crime. The extraction of testimony through the use of torture or force.

TORTURAR. To torture. To inflict intense pain to the body or mind of another.

TRABAJADOR. Worker.

TRABAJADOR EVENTUAL. Temporary worker. Person employed for a fixed, temporary period of time.

TRABAJADOR OCACIONAL. Occasional worker. Person who works for a brief, undetermined period.

TRABAJO. Labor, work.

TRABAJO A DESTAJO. Piecework. Work paid according to the number of items produced, as opposed to by the hour.

TRABAJO A TIEMPO COMPLETO. Full-time job.

TRABAJO EVENTUAL. Job or work. The job for which a person has been hired in a non-permanent basis.

TRABAJO FORZADO. Hard labor. Obligation to do any kind of job imposed to a convicted person as part of punishment with the purpose of rehabilitation.

TRACTO SUCESIVO. Contract of successive execution. One of the parties to the contract must perform continually or repeatedly. The obligation is not due at once but rather periodically.

TRADICIÓN. Delivery, tradition, transfer. (1) Material delivery of property in order to transfer title or ownership. (2) Act of giving control of a thing to another.

TRAFICANTE. Trafficker. Merchant. Person who trades and deals in commerce.

TRÁFICO DE DROGAS. Drug traffic or trade.

TRAICIÓN. Treason. Crime of attempting to overthrow one's own country.

TRAIDOR. Traitor. Person who betrays the confidence given to him or her. A disloyal act against something that should have been protected.

TRAMITACIÓN. Action. Procedure or series of actions. Practices or handling necessary to carry out an administrative or judicial matter according to law or practice.

TRAMITAR. To carry out. The successive acts performed pursuant to judicial proceeding according to the procedure established by law.

TRÁMITE. Proceedings. Those steps necessary to accomplish an official act.

TRÁMITE JUDICIAL. Legal or judicial proceeding. To prosecute an action.

TRAMPA. Trap; catch. Deceitful device or act intended to misrepresent facts in order to defraud.

TRANSACCIÓN. Transaction; settlement; bilateral juridical act, whereby the parties make reciprocal concessions or settle obligations. Agreement reached by parties in a controversy in order to put an end to it or avoid a lawsuit.

TRANSAR. To transact; to compromise.

TRANSCRIPCIÓN. Transcription. Written record of a trial or hearing. A full and complete copy of an original document.

TRANSEÚNTE. Transient. A passer by, one without fixed residence or abode in the state.

TRANSFERENCIA. Transference. Act upon which a person transmits any right or property to another.

TRANSFERIR. Transfer, convey, make over. The act by which ownership is passed to another. The act performed with the intent to pass and transmit property or rights to another.

TRANSGREDIR. To transgress; to be guilty of a misdemeanor or crime.

TRANSGRESIÓN. Violation, breach. Violation of a prohibition or order. Breaking the law.

TRANSGRESOR. Infringer; offender. The person who commits a crime. The one who violates a law or right. The offendant.

TRANSIGENCIA. Settling. The act of settling a dispute. By giving up part of a right and assuming part of the obligation.

TRANSIGIR. To settle, to compromise. The act intended to compound by accommodating the differences.

TRANSITO. Traffic. The passing of persons or any kind of vehicle along streets or any other route of transportation.

TRANSITORIO. Transitory. That which has a limited and short term or duration.

TRANSMISIBLE. Transmissible, transferable. That which may go from one person or place to another.

TRANSMISIÓN. Transmission. The act of passing something to another place or persons.

TRANSPORTE. Transport. Any vehicle used for transportation. To carry an object or person from one place to another.

TRASLADAR. To transfer, move. (1) The act of moving something from one place to another. (2) To give notice of an act to one of the parties to a lawsuit.

TRASLADO. Transfer. (1) The moving of one thing or person to another place. (2) A written notice served on a party or a judicial officer seeking either defenses from the other party or a transfer of the matter to another forum. (3) Transfer of property or other rights from one person to another. (4) Copy of an original document.

TRASPASAR. To convey. To transfer. To trespass. The conduct intended with the purpose of entering a place. (1) A crime consisting of entering a place against or without the owner's authorization. (2) The act performed to convey property. The transmission of a title of property to the new owner.

TRASPASO. Assignment, conveyance. To transmit a right or property to another person. (1) The unlawful entry into another's property without or against the owner's authority. (2) The transmission of the title of property to another.

TRASTORNADO. Disturbed. (1) Something which is not in its ordinary state. (2) Person who is not of sound mind.

TRASTORNO. Disturbance. A disorder.

TRASTORNO MENTAL TRANSITORIO. Temporary insanity. Brief mental disturbance caused by a sudden or unexpected event, which clears without permanent damage.

TRATA DE BLANCAS. Women traded for purposes of prostitution.

TRATA DE ESCLAVOS. Slave trade.

TRATADISTA. Scholarly writer. Commentator. A person who masters a subject and writes about it.

TRATADO. Treaty. In international law, agreement between two or more nations.

TRATO. Deal. Treatment. Agreement. Unlawful contact. (1) The act of entering into an agreement. A pact. (2) The dealing in a commercial manner. (3) The way in which a person is treated. (4) Illicit or illegal touch between persons. Sexual intercourse.

TRAVESTÍ. Person who dresses in clothes of the opposite sex.

TREGUA. Truce. Agreement between belligerents to stop hostilities temporarily.

TRIBUNA. Rostrum, pulpit. A place where a speaker stands to address the public.

TRIBUNAL. Court, tribunal. Judge or judges who undertake any jurisdictional function.

TRIBUNAL A QUO. Court "a quo" (Lat.). The court from which a case has been removed.

TRIBUNAL AD QUEM. Court "ad quem" (Lat.). The court to which a case has been sent from an inferior one.

TRIBUTABLE. Taxable. Subject to taxation.

TRIBUTAR. To pay taxes. The act of paying taxes.

TRIBUTARIO. Tributary. Relative or having to do with taxes.

TRIBUTO. Taxes. Tax, tribute or any other fiscal obligation placed on individuals to support the government.

TRIUNVIRATO. Triumvirate. Authority and power shared among three persons.

TROCAR. Barter. To exchange one thing for another.

TRUEQUE. Barter. Exchange of goods without using money.

TUICIÓN. Protection, custody. The act and effect of defending or protecting someone.

TUITIVO. Protective. That which protects, guards or defends.

TURNO. Turn. Shift. (1) Order in which something corresponds or pertains to someone. (2) The moment in which a court or judge among various is responsible for receiving pleas and practicing the initial acts in a lawsuit. See "Juez de Turno" and "Juzgado de Turno".

TUTELA. Guardianship. Tutelage. Institution created by law to protect minors and those who are incompetent or unable to take care of themselves, and by which a capable person takes care of the rights and property of the incapable.

TUTOR. Guardian. Person who is in charge of a tutelage or guardianship. (1) **Tutor ad litem.** Guardian ad litem. Guardian appointed by the court to represent and protect the rights of a minor or incompetent.

TUTORÍA. Guardianship. The office duty, or authority of a guardian.

U

UCE. Your honor. Expression of respect used when addressing the judge.

UCENCIA. Your excellency.

UJIER. Usher. Court officer; bailiff. Sometimes in charge of practicing some proceedings.

ÚLTIMA INSTANCIA. Last resort.

ÚLTIMA VOLUNTAD. Last will. Last wishes that a person expresses before his or her death.

ULTIMAR. To end, conclude, finalize; to murder.

ULTIMATUM. (Lat.) The last. (1) The final request or proposition made in negotiating something. (2) A final and definitive resolution issued by one nation to another stating its last communication before engaging in war. (3) A threat.

ULTRA PETITA. (Lat.) Expression used when a judge has given to the plaintiff more than what he or she sued for.

ULTRA VIRES. (Lat.) Transcending authority. Acts performed beyond the limits of the scope of the faculties or powers.

ULTRA VIRES HEREDITATIS. (Lat.) "Beyond the forces of the hereditary succession." It refers to the obligation created upon the acceptance of the inheritance without the "Beneficio de Inventario" or benefit of inventory to pay all the debts of the deceased.

ULTRAJE. Outrage, contempt, insult, abuse, offense; rape. It may refer to acts that offend public morality or norms.

ULTRAJE AL PUDOR. Sexual abuse of a person without intercourse.

ULTRAJADA. The victim of a rape or an outrage or injurious abuse.

ULTRAJADOR. Rapist; offender.

ULTRAJAR. To rape, violate; to offend, insult.

UNÁNIME. Unanimous. Without dissent.

UNANIMIDAD. Unanimity. Agreement of all the persons concerned. Approved with the consent of each one consulted or at least without a negative vote.

ÚNICA INSTANCIA. Proceeding before one authority which permits no appeal.

UNICAMERAL. Unicameral. One chamber. Legislative body in which there is no division between chambers. There is only one body.

UNIDAD FAMILIAR. Household.

UNIDAD MONETARIA. Currency. Coin or paper used by a country as a medium of exchange.

UNIFICACIÓN. Unification. The act of different things becoming a unit.

UNILATERAL. Unilateral. One-sided.

UNIÓN. Union, marriage, alliance. (1) The joining together of persons, organizations, or things for a particular purpose. (2) An organization of workers, formed to negotiate with employers on wages, working conditions, etc.

UNIPERSONAL. Unipersonal. Pertaining to just one person. The act, right or obligation of one person only.

UNIR. To unite, merge, combine, consolidate.

UNIVERSAL. Universal. Pertaining to all without exception. Relative to the universe. Relative to the whole rights and obligations. In successions, the whole estate can be left either to one heir or in proportional parts to many. Refers to everything a person has or owes.

UNIVERSALIDAD. Universality, totality. The total of goods (property) or rights that are considered in a legal sense as a whole and to which a different set of rules applies other than those applicable to each of its components individually.

UNIVERSIDAD. University. Institution of higher learning, offering instruction in the arts and sciences, and conferring degrees.

UNIVERSITARIO. Relative to a university.

URBANIZAR. The act of planning and developing cities and towns. To create a town in an uninhabited place.

URGENCIA. Urgency. (1) That which must be done, or dealt with, quickly. (2) In need of expeditious medical care.

URNA. Ballot box. Used to deposit votes in a public or private election.

U.R.S.S. U.S.S.R. The former Union of Soviet and Socialist Republics.

USANZA. Usage, custom. (1) A custom in a locality concerning particular transactions. (2) Uniform practice or course of conduct followed in certain lines of business or professions. Something that is done because it is the general practice and considered a binding conduct to the people of that place or business.

USÍA. Your honor. Expression of respect used when addressing the judge.

USO. Use. Custom, practice; usance. (1) The right to benefit from another person's goods according to the necessities of the user. (2) Rule of conduct originated from the general practice. (3) The enjoyment of possession of property.

USO CONVENCIONAL. Conventional use. The normal use of a good.

USO COMERCIAL. Commercial use. The general and accepted commercial practice.

USO DE RAZÓN. Prudence. Refers to the mental condition of a normal and reasonable person.

USO LOCAL. To limit to local use. (1) According to the local practice. (2) That can be used only in a specific place limited to local use.

USOS. Uses. See "Uso".

USUAL. Usual, customary, common. Something done frequently. That conduct or act which is the general practice. Something done by virtue of custom. What is ordinary. The performance executed according to the use commonly established. Happening in a habitual or customary manner.

USUARIO. User, usufructuary. The one who enjoys the right to use a thing. Holder of a concession.

USUCAPIÓN. Usucapion. Adverse possession, prescription. To assert a right or title to a thing or land as a result of uninterrupted and long-continued enjoyment of it.

USUFRUCTO. Usufruct. The right to use and enjoy another's property, provided it be without altering its substance.

USUFRUCTUARIO. Usufructuary. One who has the usufruct or right of enjoying something in which he has no property.

USURA. Usury; interest; profit. Interest paid for borrowed money which exceeds that allowed by law or charged by the average lender.

USURARIO. Relative to usury; see "Usura".

USURERO. Usurer. One who lends at an interest rate higher than the rate allowed by law.

USURPACIÓN. Usurpation. The unlawful encroachment or assumption of the use of property, power or authority that belongs to another.

USURPACIÓN DE FUNCIONES PÚBLICAS. Public functions usurpation. Crime by a public officeholder consisting of acting beyond the scope of authority entrusted to the officeholder.

USURPADOR. Usurper. One who seizes and holds the property, rights, or office of another without a legal right.

UTILIDAD. Utility. profit.

UTILIDADES. Benefits. See "Utilidad".

UTILIDAD PÚBLICA. Public utility. Particular convenience for the general welfare.

UTERINO. Uterine. Pertaining to the womb. Born from the same mother.

UTOPIA. Something ideal. So perfect that it can only exist in the mind.

UT SUPRA. Above. Refers to something written in previous pages.

UXORICIDA. Uxoricide (male). Husband who murders his wife.

UXIORICIDIO. Wife murder.

V

VACACIÓN. Vacation. When a court suspends activities.

VACANTE. Vacant, empty. (1) Empty post, position or job. (2) Deprived of contents.

VAGABUNDO. Vagabond, vagrant. A homeless wanderer without means to make an honest livelihood.

VAGANCIA. Vagrancy. The act of going from place to place without visible means of support, without working though able to do so, and living on the charity of others.

VAGO. Vagabond, vagrant. Also see "Vagabundo".

VALE. Voucher, I.O.U., promissory note. (1) A receipt which serves as evidence of payment or discharge of a debt. (2) A document that serves to recognize a liability and authorize the disbursement of cash.

VALEDERO. Valid; binding, effective.

VALER. (1) Worth, value. See "Valor". (2) To produce, yield.

VALÍA. Worth; value; influence.

VALIDAR. To validate. To make valid; sanction; affirm.

VALIDEZ. Validity, force. Legal sufficiency. Capable of being enforced.

VÁLIDO. Valid. That which has legal effects and can be enforced.

VALOR. Value, significance; valor, courage; worth; price.

VALOR NOMINAL. Nominal or face value. In stocks, it refers to the par value. It does not correspond to the current price nor to the price at which they were first sold.

VALOR RECIBIDO. Value received. Expression used to show that proper consideration has been received in exchange for an obligation.

370

VALORAR. To appraise. The act of ascertaining the value of a thing.

VALORACIÓN. Valuation; appraisal. The act of establishing the value of something.

VALORACIÓN DE LAS PRUEBAS. Evaluation of the evidence. The weight given to the evidence by the fact finder in a case.

VALORADOR. Appraiser. The person who determines the value of something.

VALORES. Valuables; stocks; securities; bonds; assets.

VALORES NEGOCIABLES. Negotiable instruments.

VALORIZACIÓN. Valuation, appraisal. The estimated value of a thing.

VALORIZAR. To value, appraise. To establish the value of something.

VALUACIÓN. Valuation, appraisal. See "Valorización".

VALUAR. To appraise, rate, price.

VARADO. Beached. When a ship has run aground.

VARIACIÓN. Variance. (1) A discrepancy or disagreement between two instruments or two allegations, which by law ought to be consistent. (2) Departure from the literal requirements of a zoning ordinance.

VARÓN. Male.

VASALLO. Vassal. The subject of a lord. A feudal tenant.

VECINDAD. Vicinity, neighborhood. Legal residence (town).

VECINDARIO. Neighborhood. (1) The place where one's house is located. (2) Collective name for the people who inhabit a neighborhood.

VECINO. Neighbor. That which adjoins something.

VEDA. Prohibition, interdiction, veto. Normally refers to a time when hunting and/or fishing is prohibited.

VEDADO. Prohibited, suspended, forbidden.

VEHÍCULO. Vehicle. Means of transportation, generally by land.

VEJAR. To annoy; to criticize.

VEJEZ. Old age.

VENAL. Venal, corruptible; salable, marketable. Pertaining to something that is bought.

VENCEDOR. Prevailing party in a lawsuit. Winner.

VENCER. To defeat; to mature, fall due. To overcome; to win.

VENCIDO. Due. Defeated. (1) Being conquered or beaten by another. (2) An obligation that is payable because the period allowed to pay has expired. (3) Loser in a lawsuit.

VENCIMIENTO. Maturity; expiration date.

VENDEDOR. Seller, salesman, vendor.

VENDER. To sell. To exchange goods or properties for a price.

VENDETA. Vendetta. A private blood feud.

VENENO. Poison.

VENÉREA. Venereal. Relative to sex.

VENIA. Permission. Authorization to perform or do something.

VENIA DE LA SALA. With the court's permission.

VENGANZA. Revenge.

VENTA. Sale. Contract whereby one party, the seller, obliges him or herself to transfer the ownership of a property to another party, the buyer, who agrees to pay its price.

VENTA A PLAZO. Installment sale. The contract by which one person, the seller, transfers property to another, the buyer, who undertakes the obligation to pay the price in periodic amounts until the debt is satisfied.

VENTA AL CONTADO. Cash sale. Sales contract by which the seller gives property to the buyer who pays the full price at once.

VENTA AL CRÉDITO. Sale on credit. The sales contract by which property is transferred from seller and delivered to buyer at the time of the contract but payment is deferred to a future moment.

VENTA AL POR MAYOR. Wholesale. A sale in large quantities, usually to retailers.

VENTA CON RETRACTO. Sale with right of redemption. Sales agreement by which the seller reserves the right to take back the goods sold by returning the money he or she received.

VENTA HIPOTECARIA. Foreclosure sale. Also see "Venta Judicial".

VENTA JUDICIAL. Judicial or foreclosure sale. The sale of real property persuant to a court order.

VENTA PÚBLICA. Public sale. Sale by public auction.

VERBAL. Verbal, oral.

VERDAD. Truth.

VERDUGO. Executioner. Person who carries out the death penalty.

VEREDICTO. Verdict. The decision arrived at by a jury.

VER UNA CAUSA. To try or hear a case.

VETAR. To veto.

VETO. Veto. Refusal of assent by the executive officer whose assent is necessary for a law to pass.

VÍA. Path; procedure, method; street, road.

VÍA EJECUTIVA. Executive proceeding. (1) Short procedure to try a case. (2) Procedure before the executive branch.

VÍA JUDICIAL. Judicial proceeding, court action.

VIABILIDAD. Viability. Capable of being exercised or done.

VIABLE. Viable. Livable. Having the possibility to live. That which can be done. Possible.

VIÁTICO O DIETAS. Allowance; payment of daily expenses. Subsidy of government officials or diplomats being transferred to a new destination.

VICE GOBERNADOR. Lieutenant governor.

VICE MINISTRO. Vice Minister. The second in rank after the minister.

VICE PRESIDENTE. Vice President. The second in command after the president.

VICIAR. To invalidate, annul; to adulterate.

VICIO. Vice. (1) A fault, defect, or imperfection. (2) Immoral conduct with probable damage to the body or spirit.

VICIO OCULTO. Hidden defect. Defect that is unknown to the buyer at the time of purchase.

VICIOS PROCESALES. Procedural mistake or defect.

VÍCTIMA. Victim. The object of a crime.

VICTIMARIO. One who has committed a crime.

VIDUAL. Pertaining to widowhood.

VIGENCIA. Operation or term of a law. The life, term or duration of a contract, statute, or law.

VIGENTE. In force; outstanding. (1) A law or statute in effect. (2) Currently existing.

VIGILANCIA. Vigilance. Watchfulness; precaution.

VIGILANTE. Watchman. One who guards, patrols, and oversees property.

VIL. Vile, base, low, mean.

VINCULACIÓN. Entailing, linking, encumbering.

VÍNCULO. Tie, bond, encumbrance, entail. The limitation on how real property is to descend.

VINDICTA PÚBLICA. Public censure, punishment or revenge. The prosecutor's office.

VINDICATORIO. Vengeful, vindictive.

VIOLACIÓN. Violation. Infringement. (1) Breach of right, duty, or law. (2) A rape.

VIOLACIÓN DE DOMICILIO. Trespass on the domicile of another.

VIOLADOR. Infringer or violator. (1) Person who has violated the law. (2) Rapist.

VIOLAR. To violate, infringe; to rape.

VIOLENCIA. Violence. Unjust or unwarranted use of force.

VIOLENCIA FÍSICA IRRESISTIBLE. Actual physical force used against a person.

VIOLENCIA CARNAL. Sexual assault.

VIOLENTAR. To force, break into; to assault.

VIS. (Lat.) Any kind of force, violence, or disturbance relating to a person or his or her property.

VIS ABSOLUTE. (Lat.) Absolute violence. A superior and irresistible force.

VIS COMPULSIVE. (Lat.) Force exerted by menaces or terror to compel another to do an act against his or her will.

VISA. An official endorsement on a passport denoting that it has been examined and that the bearer is permitted to proceed.

VISA CONSULAR. Consular visa. Permission granted by a consular official to enter a foreign country.

VISAR. To officially examine and approve something. To certify.

VISITAR. To inspect, call on, or examine. To search with a warrant. To visit.

VISTA. (1) Trial, hearing; interview; judgment. (2) Sight, vision. (3) Document which contains the legal opinion of a decision-maker.

VISTO. Examined, approved. Whereas.

VISTOS. The legal opinions of the prosecutor.

VITALICIO. For life; annuity.

VIUDA. Widow.

VIUDEZ. Widowhood.

VIUDO. Widower.

VIVIENDA. House. The place where a person lives.

VOCACIÓN. Vocation. Calling to do something. One's occupation or profession.

VOCAL. Member of a board or commission authorized to speak and give opinions in the name of the group.

VOCERO. Spokesman; attorney. Person authorized to speak for another.

VOLITIVO. Regarding a person's will to do something.

VOLUNTAD. Will, consent, disposition.

VOLUNTAD EXPRESA. Express consent. When someone's consent is given in a positive, direct and unequivocal manner.

VOLUNTAD TÁCITA. Implied consent. When someone's consent is given as manifested by signs, actions, or facts which raise a presumption that the consent has been given.

VOLUNTARIO. Voluntary; noncontentious.

VOTACIÓN. Voting, balloting.

VOTADOR. Voter, elector.

VOTAR. To vote.

VOTO. Vote, ballot. The formal expression of one's will, preference or choice.

VOTO DIRECTO. Direct vote. Vote which is directly counted in an election, as opposed to a vote used to designate a representative who will do the ultimate voting.

VOTO INDIRECTO. Indirect vote. Vote used to designate a representative who will do the ultimate voting.

VOTO SECRETO. Secret vote or ballot.

VOZ. Voice.

VULNERAR. To injure, violate.

X

XENELAXIA. In international law, the power of a nation at war to deport the nationals of the enemy state.

XENO. Foreigner, foreign, strange.

XENODOQUIA. Hospitality; friendly reception of foreigners.

XENOFOBIA. Xenophobia. Hatred, fear or hostility towards all foreign persons or things.

Y

YACENTE. Vacant, lying. (1) Person who lies on the ground. (2) An inheritance that has not been claimed or divided.

YACIMIENTO. Bed, layer. (1) **Yacimiento mineral.** A mineral outcropping capable of exploitation. (2) Mineral layer or deposit.

YERNO. Son-in-law.

YERRO. Error or mistake.

YUGO. Yoke. Oppression, confinement, imprisonment.

YUSIÓN. A command or precept.

Z

ZACAPELA. A quarrel.

ZANJAR. To resolve a conflict; to settle amicably.

ZAR. Czar. Title of the former emperors of Russia.

ZONA. Zone, area. (1) **Zona Fiscal.** Name given to an administrative area. (2) Taxing district.

ZONA DE GUERRA. War zone.

ZONA FRANCA. Free zone. Area or territory where duty-free items can be purchased.

ZORRA. Prostitute; fox. Also see "Prostituta".

ZOZOBRAR. In maritime law. When a ship is in danger of capsizing.

*

Diccionario Legal
Español-Inglés/Inglés-Español

Traducciones de Términos, Frases y Definiciones
de Conceptos de Terminología Legal Moderna en
Inglé y Español

*

A

A.G. "Attorney General". (1) Procurador General o Fiscal General de un Estado. El funcionario de mayor rango encargado de hacer cumplir la ley. (2) U.S.A.G. Procurador General de la nación. El que está al mando del Departamento de Justicia y es además miembro del gabinete presidencial.

A.L.R. "American Law Report". Serie extensa de libros que publica ciertos precedentes legales importantes en forma comentada.

A CONTRARIO SENSU. (Lat.) En sentido contrario.

A POSTERIORI. (Lat.) Con posterioridad. Después del hecho. Razonamiento del efecto a la causa.

A PRIORI. (Lat.) Literalmente "Por lo que precede". Razonamiento que es independiente de la experiencia.

A QUO. (Lat.) De donde. Dícese generalmente del tribunal en donde se inició el caso o de donde viene.

ABANDONMENT. (1) Abandonar. Renunciar a todos los derechos de propiedad que pueda tener uno, con la intención de no intentar recuperarlos. (2) **Abandonment of Lawsuit.** Desistimiento. Acto de abandonar un recurso interpuesto o el mismo proceso. (3) **Abandonment of Husband or Wife.** Abandono del marido o de la mujer. Dejar, sin su consentimiento, al otro cónyuge con la intención de no regresar.
(4) **Abandonment of Patent Rights.** Abandono del derecho de patente. Cuando el inventor deja transcurrir el término señalado por ley para solicitar la patente o cuando a muchas personas se les permite ver el invento no patentado.

ABATEMENT. (1) Disminución o reducción. (2) **Nuisance Abatement.** Una molestia pública, un daño, un perjuicio. (3) **Tax Abatement.** Disminuir la carga fiscal. Reducción en los impuestos.

ABDICATION. Acto de Abdicar Renunciar. Dimisión. Renunciar a un puesto público o al trono si se trata de un rey.

ABDICATE. Abdicar. Renunciar a un cargo público. Ver "ABDICATION".

ABDUCTION. Delito de rapto o secuestro, delito cometido al llevarse a una persona que está bajo la custodia de otra.

ABET. Alentar, incitar, solicitar, inducir, ordenar o ayudar a una persona a cometer un delito.

ABETTOR. El incitador, alentador o asistente en la comisión de un crimen.

ABEYANCE. Posponer. Estado de suspensión o espera.

ABIDE. Obedecer. Observar, someterse, atenerse. Actuar de acuerdo a la ley o sentencia.

ABILITY TO PAY. Capacidad económica para satisfacer la deuda. Principio que un arbitrador puede utilizar al considerar cuanto debe pagar el demandado. Rara vez el jurado utiliza este principio.

ABJUDICATIO. Remover a alguien de la corte. Perder algo por decreto judicial.

ABJURATION. Adjuración. Renuncia mediante juramento a propiedades, derechos, convicciones, religión y opiniones.

ABODE. Domicilio o residencia de una persona natural o jurídica.

ABOLISH. Abolir, derogar, anular. Eliminar por completo y permanentemente alguna ley, reglamento o estatuto.

ABORTION. Aborto. Provocar de modo expreso la interrupción del embarazo, destruyendo el feto.

ABRIDGE. (1) Resumir. Condensar o abreviar un texto.
(2) **Abridge a Right.** Disminuir un derecho.

ABROGATION. Derogar. Terminar, anular o dejar sin efecto una ley anterior por otra posterior. Terminar el efecto de una ley.

ABSCOND. Desaparecer, evadir, fugarse para evitar un arresto, una demanda o persecusión de acreedores.

ABSENTEE. Ausente. Aquél que está ausente, por ejemplo de su domicilio o residencia.

ABSENTEE VOTING. Voto en ausencia. Voto por correspondencia. Voto efectuado por correo por aquél que no puede acudir al lugar de votación.

ABSENTIA. Ausencia. Que no está presente.

ABSOLUTE. Completo; perfecto, final. Sin condición o gravamen, incondicional.

ABSOLUTE LIABILITY. Responsabilidad civil sin necesidad de probar culpa o negligencia.

ABSOLUTE NUISANCE. Perjuicio o daño absoluto. Cuando un daño no incluye negligencia alguna.

ABSOLUTISM. Absolutismo. Forma de gobierno mediante la cual el grupo gobernante ejerce el poder sin restricción o limitación alguna.

ABSOLVE. Absolver, amnistía, perdón. Liberación de la obligación de pagar una deuda. El acto de absolver no sólo se aplica a deudas si no también a delitos.

ABSORPTION. Continuación de la existencia de una compañía o un derecho al ser incorporado(a) a otro(a) de mayor importancia o volumen.

ABSTAIN. Abstenerse de algún acto. Privarse.

ABSTENTION DOCTRINE. Doctrina jurídica que permite a una Corte Federal, según su discreción, abstenerse de tomar jurisdicción para evitar conflictos innecesarios con la administración de otro estado, sobre sus asuntos o leyes.

ABSTRACT. Resumen, sumario, extracto. Substraer. (1) **Abstract of Title.** De título. Resumen o sumario de la historia de un título de propiedad en el cual constan sus antiguos dueños y gravámenes. (2) **Abstract of Record.** Resumen de un caso o juicio para ser visto en la apelación.

ABSTRACTION. Substracción; hurto. Tomar algo, usualmente dinero, con la intención de cometer un fraude.

ABUSE. Abuso. (1) **Abuse of Discretion.** De discreción o de libre albedrío. Sobrepasar la suficiente discreción legal. Acción

385

arbitraria e injustificada. (2) **Abuse of a Child.** De un menor. Aprovecharse sexualmente de un menor.

ABUSE OF POWER. Abuso de autoridad. Abuso del poder cedido a una persona, usualmente en violación de la ley.

ABUSE OF PROCESS. Abuso malicioso del proceso legal por una parte con un fin ilegal.

ABUT. Colindar. Tener los linderos uno al lado del otro. Predios contiguos.

ABUTTER. Colindantes. Dueño colindante. Personas que poseen fincas vecinas o que colindan.

ACADEMIC QUESTION. Punto legal innecesario e inaplicable para resolver un caso. Punto hipotético.

ACCEDE. Acceder; acordar; conceder.

ACCELERATED DEPRECIATION. Varios métodos de depreciar activos, con deducciones mayores en los primeros años de vida del activo.

ACCELERATION. Acortar o reducir el período de tiempo para fijar un interés anticipado.

ACCELERATION CLAUSE. Cláusula de aceleración. Cláusula en un contrato de préstamo mediante la cual se establece que una deuda puede quedar vencida y pagada anticipadamente.

ACCEPT. Recibir o aceptar.

ACCEPTANCE. (1) En contrato, aceptación de una oferta. Acto mediante el cual se origina o surge un contrato. (2) **Banker's Acceptance.** Carta o documento mediante el cual el banco promete pagar una suma cierta de dinero en una fecha próxima. (3) En la venta de mercadería, el acto mediante el cual una parte acepta los bienes sujetos a un contrato de venta comercial. También hay aceptación (a) calificada, (b) expresa, (c) implícita, y (d) condicional.

ACCESS. Acceso. (1) Oportunidad de acceso a la calle a través de un lote. (2) Derecho de acceso a un documento público. (3) **Multiple Access.** Acceso múltiple. Defensa alegada en juicios de filiacion y paternidad, invocando actos sexuales multiples de parte de la maure con muchos hombres. (4) **Access to Counsel.** Acceso a un abogado.

ACCESSION. Acrecencia, accesión, adhesión. (1) Derecho a una cosa que viene a formar parte de otra que ya le pertenece. (2) **(International Law)** La aceptación, absoluta o condicional, por una o varias naciones, de un tratado ya concluído entre otros estados soberanos.

ACCESSORY. (1) Cómplice. Quien ayuda o contribuye a cometer un delito sin estar presente al momento del mismo. (2) **Accessory Before the Fact.** Quien ayuda a preparar la comisión del delito. (3) **Accessory After the Fact.** Quien ayuda a encubrir el delito o al criminal. (4) Accesorio. Algo conectado a otra cosa más importante.

ACCIDENT. Accidente. Acontecimiento inesperado, predecible o no, con o sin culpa.

ACCOMMODATE. Acomodar. Poner a otra persona en una posición o sitio conveniente. Usualmente consiste en actuar como co-deudor.

ACCOMMODATION PAPERS. Carta de acomodación. Carta, documento o pagaré firmado por una persona como favor para ayudar a otra a conseguir un préstamo.

ACCOMPLICE. Cómplice. Una persona que provoca o facilita, con conocimiento de causa, la realización de un hecho o delito.

ACCORD. Acuerdo o convenio mediante el cual una persona se compromete a dar o pagar algo distinto o diferente de aquello que le es en realidad debido, y la otra persona lo acepta.

ACCORD AND SATISFACTION. Transacción. Acuerdo para el pago en dinero de otra suma, distinta a la debida, y de menor valor, a cambio del extinguimiento de la obligación, y aceptada con el propósito de extinguir la obligación. (1) Método de resolver un reclamo o pleito mediante el cual una parte ofrece y acepta algo en liquidación de la disputa, a cambio del extinguimiento total de la antigua obligación o pleito. (2) Una defensa afirmativa que debe ser alegada en los escritos del demandado.

ACCOUNT. Cuenta. (1) Lista detallada de los créditos y deudas entre las partes. (2) **Account Payable.** Cuenta por pagar. Deuda aún no pagada, usualmente a los suplidores. (3) **Account**

Receivable. Cuenta por cobrar. Deuda aún no cobrada, usualmente a los clientes. (4) **Account Stated.** Cuenta convenida. Detalle preciso de lo debido hecho por el acreedor y aceptado por el deudor. (5) **Account Balance.** El saldo de una cuenta. (6) **Current Account.** Cuenta corriente. Lo opuesto de una cuenta convenida.

ACCOUNTANT. Contador. Aquél que se especializa en la preparación de estados financieros; el que lleva la contabilidad.

ACCOUNTING. Contabilidad. Método usado para llevar los estados financieros. Forma de registrar los ingresos y gastos.

ACCREDIT. Acreditar. Reconocer oficialmente el estado civil o legal de algo o alguien.

ACCRETION. (1) Acrecer; aumentar. (2) Aumento en la superficie de un terreno o predio por causas naturales. (3) Aumento en los bienes de un fideicomiso.

ACCROACH. Usurpación. Tomar o ejercitar un poder o autoridad sin derecho a ello.

ACCRUAL BASIS. Base devengada. Método de contabilidad que determina los gastos incurridos y el ingreso devengado, se haya o no realmente recibido el dinero en efectivo.

ACCRUE. (1) Devengado, acumulado. Que es debido y está por ser pagado. (2) **Accrue Dividend.** Dividendo devengado. Dividendo que ha sido declarado pero aún no ha sido pagado. (3) **Accrue Cause of Action.** Momento en el cual un pleito puede ser procesado.

ACCUMULATED DIVIDENDS. Dividendos pagaderos a los accionistas que aún no han sido pagados.

ACCUMULATED EARNINGS TAX. Impuesto federal sobre las ganancias acumuladas y no distribuídas como dividendos de una sociedad anónima.

ACCUMULATED PROFITS OR SURPLUS. Ganancias acumuladas en exceso del capital inicial y las obligaciones existentes.

ACCUMULATION. (1) Acumulación. Aumento debido a la continua o repetida adición. (2) **Accumulation Trust.** Fideicomiso acumulativo. Fideicomiso que retiene sus rentas en lugar de distribuirlas a sus beneficiarios.

ACCUMULATIVE SENTENCE. Sentencia por acumulación. Condena adicional a uno ya condenado.

ACCUSATION. Acusación. Cargo formalmente hecho ante la autoridad competente imputando un delito a alguien.

ACCUSATORY BODY. Gran jurado. Cuerpo jurídico que determina si una persona debe ser acusada de un delito.

ACCUSE. Acusar, denunciar, delatar. Cargo formalmente hecho ante la autoridad competente imputando un delito a alguien.

ACCUSED. Acusado. Aquél contra quien la acusación es imputada.

ACID TEST RATIO. Método de análisis financiero que compara la relación entre el efectivo y las cuentas por cobrar contra los pasivos.

ACKNOWLEDGED INSTRUMENT. Declaración formal ante un oficial o notario, realizada por una persona que firma un instrumento bajo juramento. Usualmente, lleva un certificado del oficial o notario.

ACKNOWLEDGMENT. Reconocimiento, confirmación. Declaración admitiendo que algo es genuino.

ACQUAINTED. Conocido. Persona o documento del cual se tiene conocimiento de su existencia.

ACQUEST. Adquirido. Algo comprado, no heredado.

ACQUIESCE. Consentir. Estar de acuerdo con algo en forma tácita.

ACQUIESCENCE. Aquiescencia, consentimiento, conformidad. Consentimiento mediante silencio.

ACQUIRE. Adquirir, obtener.

ACQUIRED RIGHT. Derecho adquirido.

ACQUISITION CHARGE. Cláusula que penaliza un pago anticipado o acelerado. Cargo adicional a lo debido por pagar o cancelar la totalidad de una deuda antes de su vencimiento.

ACQUIT. Absolver. Exonerar. Liberar de una culpa u obligación.

ACQUITTAL. Absolución, finiquitar. Que absuelve a una persona de una acusación u obligación.

ACQUITTANCE. Convenio escrito liberando una obligación de pagar dinero. Carta de pago liberando una obligación.

ACT. (1) Acto. (2) **Legislative Act.** Ley pasada por una o ambas cámaras de la legislatura. (3) **Criminal Act.** Un delito o acto criminal. (4) **Private Act.** Actos de personas privadas en relación a sus asuntos. (5) **Public Act.** Acto público.

ACT IN PAIS. Acto fuera de Autos. Acto realizado fuera de la corte y que no forma parte del procedimiento.

ACT OF GOD. Acto de la naturaleza. Fuerza mayor. Caso fortuito; evento que ha ocurrido enteramente causado por la naturaleza.

ACT OF STATE DOCTRINE. Doctrina del acto soberano de otro Estado, mediante la cual una Corte en los Estados Unidos no puede disputar la legalidad de procedimientos legales en otro país en ejercicio de su poder soberano.

ACTING. Actuando. Efectuando o desempeñando los poderes de otro.

ACTIO. (Lat.) Acción. Derecho y procedimiento judicial para hacer valer el derecho de alguien.

ACTION. Acción. (1) Conducta o comportamiento. (2) Demanda formal ante la Corte para hacer valer un derecho. (3) **Civil Action.** Acción jurídica, basada en estatutos, ley consuetudinaria o equidad. (4) **Wrongful Death Action.** Acción jurídica a consecuencia de una muerte. (5) **Action in Equity.** Una acción jurídica basada en principios de equidad y justicia. (6) **Action in Rem.** Una acción jurídica proseguida contra un bien o una casa. (7) **Common Law Action.** Una acción basada en derecho consuetudinario. (8) **In Personam Action.** Una acción personal para recobrar daños por un agravio.

ACTIONABLE. Accionable, procesable. (1) Capaz de motivar una acción. (2) **Actionable Fraud.** Un fraude justiciable. (3) **Actionable Negligence.** Negligencia procesable. (4) **Actionable Misrepresentation.** Una declaración falsa, la cual es procesable. (5) **Actionable Per Se.** Palabras que por sí solas son difamantes o calumniosas. (6) **Actionable Words.**

Véase "Actionable Per Se". (7) **Actionable Tort.** Un agravio el cual surge a consecuencia de violar una obligación o un deber legal.

ACTIVE. Activo. Que implica acción, movimiento o actuación.

ACTUAL. Real. Que existe en el presente; lo opuesto a teórico.

ACTUAL AUTHORITY. Autorización real. La autorización que tiene un agente porque le ha sido dada, o porque puede creer, con razón, que así le ha sido dada por el principal.

ACTUAL CASH VALUE. Valor real en efectivo. El valor que justamente tendría un objeto en el mercado.

ACTUARIAL METHOD. Método actuarial. Forma de llevar la contabilidad en un libro para tal fin.

ACTUARY. Actuario. La persona que se especializa en las ciencias actuariales basadas en estadísticas y probabilidades.

AD DAMNUM. (Lat.) Para los daños. Parte de la demanda que fija la cuantía por daños.

AD HOC. (Lat.) Para éste. Para este propósito en especial.

AD HOMINEM. (Lat.) A la persona. Usualmente son argumentos dirigidos personalmente contra el oponente.

AD IDEM. (Lat.) A lo mismo. Que tiende a probar el mismo punto.

AD INFINITUM. (Lat.) Sin límites. Para siempre.

AD INTERIM. (Lat.) Mientras tanto, por ahora.

AD LITEM. (Lat.) Para el litigio. Guardian Ad Litem. Una persona designada para representar a un menor de edad o a un incapacitado durante un litigo.

AD QUEM. (Lat.) Al cual. El tribunal **ad quem** es el tribunal superior al cual un caso es enviado en grado de apelación final.

AD SECTAM. (Lat.) Por la demanda de.

AD VALOREM. (Lat.) De acuerdo a su valor. (1) **Ad Valorem Tax.** Impuestos basados de acuerdo al valor de la propiedad.

AD VITAM. (Lat.) De por vida.

ADDICT. Adicto. Persona que depende del uso de algo hasta el extremo de no poder controlar su uso, generalmente drogas.

ADDITUR. (Lat.) (1) Facultad de una corte para incrementar la cantidad concedida al demandante por el jurado. (2) Facultad de una Corte en grado de apelación de negar al demandante la apelación si el demandado acuerda pagar al demandante cierta cantidad de dinero adicional.

ADDUCE. Aducir. Traer o presentar pruebas en un juicio.

ADEEM. Revocar.

ADEMPTION. (1) Revocación o anulación de una herencia. Cuando el causante dispone de los bienes dejados antes de morir con intención de que no le toquen a quien estaban destinados. (2) Entregar anticipadamente el legado al legatario antes de la muerte del causante.

ADEQUATE. Adecuado, suficiente. (1) **Adequate Notice.** Suficiente aviso a otra parte para proteger o defender sus derechos. (2) **Adequate Remedy at Law.** Una doctrina equitativa que impide el uso de un recurso equitativo si el demandante tiene un recurso adecuado bajo la ley.

ADHESION. Adhesión. (1) Adhesión de un país a los principios de un tratado ya existente. (2) **Adhesion Contract.** Usualmente contrato bajo el cual todo el poder de negociación está en manos de una de las partes.

ADJACENT. Adyacente. Cercano o próximo.

ADJECTIVE LAW. Ley adjetiva o derecho procesal. Normas legales que señalan el procedimiento o la forma en que funciona la corte o agencia administrativa.

ADJOINING OWNER. Propietario limítrofe o colindante. Propietario de una finca cuyos límites tocan los de otra.

ADJOURN. Levantar, posponer, o suspender una sesión o reunión.

ADJOURNMENT. Suspensión temporal o definitiva de una sesión judicial o legislativa.

ADJUDGE. Juzgar. Un fallo judicial por una corte de competencia jurisdiccional. Véase "Judgment".

ADJUDICATE. Fallar, adjudicar. Cuando una corte, en ejercicio de sus facultades, decide un caso.

ADJUDICATION. Adjudicación. Dictar o proferir sentencia formalmente. En un litigio, la resolución del pleito o la disputa entre las partes.

ADJUDICATION PROCESS. El proceso de adjudicar un caso o pleito entre las partes.

ADJUNCT. Adjunto. Unir una cosa con otra, pero en una forma secundaria.

ADJUNCTION. Adjunción. Unir permanentemente.

ADJURATION. Juramento.

ADJUST. Ajustar, arreglar, regular, transar. Llegar a un acuerdo, especialmente en asuntos monetarios.

ADJUSTED BASIS. Base ajustada. El costo u otra base usada para fijar el valor de una propiedad, reducido por la depreciación permitida, y aumentado por las mejoras de capital.

ADJUSTED COST BASIS. Costo base ajustado. Base usada para establecer el impuesto sobre la renta. Consiste del costo original de una propiedad, más adiciones de capital, menos depreciación.

ADJUSTED GROSS INCOME. Renta bruta ajustada. Es usada para calcular el impuesto federal sobre la renta de personas naturales. Se refiere al ingreso bruto, menos ciertas deducciones permitidas por la ley.

ADJUSTER. Ajustador. (1) Persona que transa o determina la cuantía de un reclamo. (2) **Claims Adjuster.** Persona que actúa en nombre de una compañía de seguros para decidir si un reclamo será pagado.

ADJUSTMENT SECURITIES. Acciones Ajustadas. Acciones emitidas durante el proceso de reorganización de una sociedad anónima. Usualmente tienen un valor inferior a las acciones originales.

ADMEASURE. Repartir. Repartir acciones.

ADMINISTER. Administrar. (1) Administrar un negocio. (2) Establecer y distribuir los bienes de un difunto. (3) Dar u otorgar juramento.

ADMINISTRATIVE AGENCY. Agencia administrativa. Subdivisión del gobierno, usualmente en la rama ejecutiva, encargada de regular e implementar ciertas leyes.

ADMINISTRATIVE BOARD. Junta administrativa. Término muy amplio que en ocasiones se refiere a agencias administrativas. Usualmente atienden asuntos de interés público.

ADMINISTRATIVE DISCRETION. Discresión administrativa. Derecho de un funcionario público de ejercer ciertas obligaciones dentro del marco de su juicio profesional y sentido común.

ADMINISTRATIVE LAW. Derecho Administrativo. (1) Normas que señalan el procedimiento y modo en que una agencia administrativa ha de funcionar. (2) Regulaciones establecidas por una agencia administrativa.

ADMINISTRATIVE LAW JUDGE. (Abreviado: A.L.J.). Juez de lo administrativo. Preside durante audiencias de una agencia administrativa.

ADMINISTRATIVE PROCEDURE ACT. (Abreviado: A.P.A.). Ley de Procedimiento Administrativo. Ley que señala los procedimientos y las pautas aplicables a una agencia administrativa al resolver conflictos o disputas con el público o con personas afectadas por decisiones administrativas.

ADMINISTRATIVE REMEDY. Remedio administrativo. Medio de hacer valer un derecho por la vía administrativa.

ADMINISTRATOR. Administrador. Persona señalada por la corte para supervisar y entregar el caudal hereditario. Si es señalado en el testamento se llama ejecutor. Véase "Executor".

ADMIRALTY. Almirantazgo. Relativo al Derecho del Mar. (1) **Admiralty Law.** Derecho Marítimo. (2) **Admiralty Court.** Corte de derecho marítimo.

ADMISSIBLE. Admisible, aceptable. Que puede ser usado como evidencia para decidir el mérito de una causa.

ADMISSION. Admisión. (1) Afirmación voluntaria de que algo es cierto. (2) **Admission to the Bar.** Admitido a ejercer ante una corte o al Colegio de Abogados. (3) **Admission to Bail.** Admisión de Fianza. Que se puede liberar si se consigna la fianza determinada. (4) **Admission of Evidence.** Admisión de evidencia que puede ser considerada en el juicio. (5) El proceso de admitir a una persona como emigrante. (6) Concepto evidencial usado en litigio para probar la existencia o la inexistencia de un hecho. Véase "Adoptive Admission".

ADMISSIONS. Admisiones. Confesiones o reconocimiento voluntario de algo.

ADMIT. Admitir. Véase "Admission".

ADMONISH. Amonestar, prevenir, regañar. Aconsejar sobre malas prácticas o advertir sobre los posibles daños de una ofensa.

ADMONITION. Amonestación. Un aviso o reprensión hecha por la corte al jurado o a uno de los abogados con respecto a sus obligaciones. Un regaño.

ADOPT. Adoptar. (1) Hacer de uno; tomar o aceptar propiedad o ideas. (2) Pasar una ley, darle vigencia y vigor. (3) Darle a un menor, hijo de otro, todos los derechos como si hubiese sido propio. En algunos Estados puede adoptarse a un mayor de edad.

ADOPTION. Adopción. Véase "Adopt".

ADOPTIVE ADMISSION. Admisión adoptiva. Aprobación de lo afirmado por otro mediante silencio u otro acto, al no negar lo afirmado.

ADS. Abreviatura de Ad Sectam. Véase esa palabra.

ADULT. Adulto. Persona mayor de la edad establecida en un estado para tener plenos derechos.

ADULTERATION. Adulteración. Cambiar algo puro o genuino usualmente mezclando o añadiendo algo de inferior calidad.

ADULTERY. Adulterio. Coito voluntario entre una persona casada y otra que no es su cónyuge.

ADVANCE. Avance. (1) Pagar dinero antes de deberlo. (2) Aumento en el precio. (3) Requerir un juicio inmediato. (4) **Advance**

395

Sheet. Panfleto que contiene una decisión judicial que aún no ha sido codificada.

ADVANCEMENT. Avance o anticipación de herencia. Dinero o propiedad dada por el futuro difunto a sus herederos como anticipo de la porción que les tocaría de la herencia.

ADVENTURE. Aventura. (1) Riesgo comercial. (2) Envío de bienes por barco. (3) Una empresa comercial.

ADVERSARY PROCEEDINGS. Proceso en el cual las partes son adversarias y están representadas.

ADVERSARY SYSTEM. Sistema Adversario. Opuesto al sistema inquisitorio. Sistema judicial basado en leyes, reglas y procedimientos mediante el cual la corte opera como árbitro imparcial e independiente entre dos partes en oposición. Cada parte actúa para obtener los mayores beneficios para sí misma dentro del marco jurídico.

ADVERSE. Adverso, opuesto. Tener un interés contrario a la otra parte.

ADVERSE INFERENCE RULE. Regla de presunción de adversidad. Cuando una agencia administrativa presume o infiere que la prueba retenida y no presentada por una parte es adversa a esa parte.

ADVERSE INTEREST. Interés contrario. Conflicto de interés que tiene un testigo contra una parte.

ADVERSE PARTY. Parte adversa. Aquella parte que está opuesta o que tiene un interés contrario a la otra parte.

ADVERSE POSSESSION. Prescripción adquisitiva. Posesión adversa; Poseer tierra abierta y continuamente sin ser su dueño por el tiempo que señala la ley para adquirir su título.

ADVERSE WITNESS. Un testigo con un interés adverso a la parte que lo está interrogando. Véase "Adverse Interest".

ADVICE. Notificación o aviso.

ADVISE. Consejo. Asesoría dada por un abogado a su cliente.

ADVISE & CONSENT. Consulta y consentimiento. Derecho constitucional del Senado para aconsejar al Presidente sobre tratados y nombramientos de funcionarios presidenciales de alto rango, así como de dar su consentimiento a tales tratados o nombramientos.

ADVISEMENT. Consideración. Deliberación que hace el juez sobre un caso antes de fallar, y luego de haber escuchado las pruebas y los argumentos de las partes.

ADVISORY JURY. Jurado de Consulta. Jurado que puede ser llamado por un juez federal para decidir sobre cuestiones de hecho que el juez podría por sí solo resolver.

ADVISORY OPINION. Opinión legal emitida por ciertos tribunales a instancias de la asamblea legislativa o de algún funcionario público, sin que hubiese un caso concreto ante el tribunal.

ADVOCACY. Abogacía. Presentar o defender un caso, derecho o posición.

ADVOCATE. Abogar. (1) Hablar por otro. (2) Hablar a favor de algo.

AEQUITAS. (Lat.) Equidad, justicia.

AFFAIR. Asunto, demanda. Acción o evento que puede originar una demanda.

AFFECT. Afectar; cambiar.

AFFECTED CLASS. Clase afectada. (1) Personas que sufren en la actualidad los efectos de discriminaciones pasadas. (2) Personas que forman parte en las acciones de un grupo, (Véase "Class Action") y que han sido perjudicadas.

AFFECTING COMMERCE. Que afecta al comercio. Usualmente se refiere a una actividad que puede obstruir el libre flujo de comercio.

AFFIANT. Deponente, declarante. Aquél que manifiesta algo por escrito bajo juramento.

AFFIDAVIT. Afidávit. Declaración jurada. Testimonio o declaración hecha bajo juramento ante un funcionario competente.

AFFILIATE. Afiliado, aliado, asociado. Persona o compañía que mantiene estrechos vínculos comerciales internos con otra compañía. Si una compañia tiene cierto porcentaje de acciones con derecho a votos de otra compañía, ambas podrían considerarse como afiliadas.

AFFILIATION. Afiliación, asociación. Acto de aliarse o afiliarse a otro.

AFFILIATION PROCEEDINGS. Juicio de filiación. Procedimiento judicial para determinar si una persona es el padre de un menor.

AFFINITY. Afinidad. Parentesco contraído por matrimonio.

AFFIRM. Afirmar. Hacer firme, repetir un acuerdo, confirmar. (1) Cuando una corte superior confirma una resolución apelada o un caso apelado. (2) Cuando declarar bajo juramento está en contra de los principios religiosos de una persona, afirmar equivale a jurar sobre la Biblia. (3) **Affirm Judgment.** Confirmar la decisión o el fallo de una corte inferior.

AFFIRMANCE. Afirmación. Véase "Affirm".

AFFIRMATION. Afirmación. Declaración formal en lugar de declaración bajo juramento, aplicable a casos en que jurar en nombre de Dios va contra los principios religiosos de una persona.

AFFIRMATIVE ACTION. Acción Afirmativa. (1) Cualquier medida tomada para remediar un mal en lugar de castigar al causante. (2) Medidas tomadas por empleadores para remediar discriminaciones laborales, raciales o basadas en el sexo. (3) Programas de empleo establecidos por estatutos y reglas federales, diseñados para remediar la práctica discriminatoria de ciertos patronos con relación al empleo de grupos minoritarios.

AFFIRMATIVE DEFENSE. Defensa. Defensa afirmativa. En una demanda por lesiones, el demandado puede afirmar, en su defensa, que el demandante fue negligente y que eso provocó la lesión. Son las defensas legales que interpone el demandado para demostrar que no tiene responsabilidad civil por los daños o perjuicios sufridos por el demandante. Las defensas afirmativas deben ser alegadas al principio del litigio o se consideran perdidas por el demandado.

AFFIRMATIVE ORDER. Orden afirmativa. Orden emitida por una autoridad competente, ordenando la cesación de una conducta y la toma de medidas positivas para reparar los daños.

AFFIRMATIVE RELIEF. Remedio afirmativo. Dictamen de la corte emitido a favor del demandado que no sólo niega lo pedido por el demandante, sino que le otorga algo al demandado.

AFFIX. Adherir. Adherir algo físicamente, usualmente en forma permanente.

AFORESAID. Antedicho. Se refiere a lo anteriormente mencionado.

AFORETHOUGHT. Premeditado. Pensado con anticipación.

AFTER–ACQUIRED PROPERTY. Propiedad posteriormente adquirida. Propiedad que se adquiere después de cierto evento. En los contratos de hipoteca, puede haber una cláusula de propiedad subsecuentemente adquirida mediante la cual se grava a cualquier propiedad añadida a la propiedad hipotecada igual que si hubiese sido gravada con la hipoteca original.

AFTER–ACQUIRED TITLE. Título de propiedad subsecuentemente adquirido. (1) Principio legal que señala que si una persona que no posee justo título sobre una propiedad la transfiere y luego adquiere el justo título sobre ella, el justo título pasa automática y directamente a quien la propiedad fue transferida. (2) Cláusula a veces encontrada en escrituras de hipoteca al efecto de que cualquier mejora o adición a la propiedad hipotecada se considerará hipotecada como si hubiera existido bajo la hipoteca original.

AFTER–BORN CHILD. Hijo póstumo. Hijo nacido con posterioridad al testamento. Principio legal que señala que el hijo póstumo heredará en igualdad con los otros, salvo una expresa exclusión testamentaria.

AGAINST INTEREST. Contra interés. Afirmación por el demandante que puede perjudicarlo.

AGAINST THE EVIDENCE. Contra la evidencia. Que va contra el peso o preponderancia de la evidencia.

AGE OF CONSENT. Edad para consentir. Edad a partir de la cual una persona se puede casar sin la aprobación de los padres. Edad a partir de la cual una mujer puede consentir legalmente a tener relaciones sexuales sin que se considere una violación por parte del hombre.

AGE OF MAJORITY. Mayoría de edad. Edad a partir de la cual una persona adquiere plenos derechos. Usualmente 18 años.

AGE OF REASON. Edad de la razón. Edad a partir de la cual un menor es capaz de razonar y actuar con responsabilidad. Usualmente 7 años.

AGENCY. Agencia. Mandato. Relación o contrato mediante el cual una persona actúa a nombre o representación de otra con la autorización de esta última.

AGENCY SHOP. Acuerdo entre patrón y sindicato o unión laboral mediante el cual todo empleado no sindicalizado tiene que pagar al sindicato una mensualidad, tal y como si estuviese sindicalizado, para mantener su calidad de empleado.

AGENT. Agente. Persona autorizada para actuar por cuenta de otra.

AGGRAVATED ASSAULT. Agresión mayor. Usualmente definida por cada ley estatal. Tipo de agresión más seria y peligrosa que la simple agresión, usualmente incluyendo el uso de un arma.

AGGRAVATING CIRCUMSTANCES. Circunstancias agravantes. Véase "Aggravation".

AGGRAVATION. Agravante. Actos o hechos que agravan, haciendo más serio un delito, sin ser parte de la definición legal del delito cometido.

AGGREGATION DOCTRINE. Doctrina de la agregación. Principio federal que prohíbe acumular o sumar la cuantía de diferentes demandas para alcanzar la cantidad mínima requerida (US $20,000) para entablar una demanda ante una corte federal.

AGGRESSIVE COLLECTION. Cobro coactivo. Distintos medios de cobrar una deuda, usualmente por vía ejecutiva, embargando o secuestrando.

AGGRESSOR. Agresor. El que primero usa fuerza o violencia en un altercado.

400

AGGRIEVED PARTY. Parte agraviada o perjudicada. Aquél cuyo derecho o propiedad ha sido afectado por la decisión de la corte, o violado por un particular.

AGIO. Agio. Dinero pagado al convertir la moneda de un país a la de otro, o la diferencia existente entre tasas de interés.

AGING SCHEDULE. Lista que detalla por cuanto tiempo han sido debidas las cuentas por cobrar y cuáles de ellas se encuentran en mora.

AGRARIAN REFORM. Reforma agraria. Leyes que dividen grandes extensiones de tierra para distribuirla en porciones equitativas entre los pequeños granjeros.

AGREED CASE. Caso acordado. Caso donde los hechos importantes son establecidos por las partes de modo que el juez no tenga que resolver cuestiones de hecho, sino decidir solamente sobre los puntos legales controversiales.

AGREEMENT. Acuerdo, arreglo. (1) Concierto de voluntad. (2) Un contrato. (3) Intención de dos o más personas de realizar un contrato.

AGRICULTURAL MARKETING AGREEMENT ACT. Ley Federal que regula el mercadeo de productos agrícolas y fija precios, protegiendo a los granjeros.

AID AND ABET. Ayuda e instiga. Ayudar, instigar, incitar, o encubrir un delito.

AID AND COMFORT. (1) Ayudar y confortar. (2) Ayudar y confortar al enemigo es un delito de traición bajo la Constitución de los Estados Unidos.

AIDER AND ABETTOR. Uno que ayuda a otro a cometer un crimen.

AIDER BY VERDICT. Presunción legal de que una vez que ha sido revelado el veredicto, los hechos que se necesitaron para llegar al veredicto han sido debidamente alegados y probados.

AIR RIGHTS. (1) Derecho a construir sobre la superficie de una finca. (2) El derecho a uso razonable de todo el espacio aéreo sobre una propiedad.

AIRBILL. Conocimiento de embarque aéreo. Documento que contiene en detalle los bienes o mercancías transportados por avión.

AJUDICATION. Decisión judicial mediante la cual se le quita algo a una persona.

ALCOMETER. Medidor de alcohol. Aparato usado para medir el nivel de alcohol de una persona detenida por manejar en estado de embriaguez.

ALDERMAN. Regidor. Persona elegida para un cargo en el consejo de una ciudad, u otra institución gubernamental local.

ALEATORY CONTRACT. Contrato Aleatorio. Contrato cuyos efectos dependen de un hecho o evento incierto o inseguro. Los juegos de azar, la lotería, y los contratos de seguros son ejemplos de este tipo de contrato.

ALIA. (Lat.) Otra cosa, otra persona.

ALIAS. Alias. Abreviatura de "Alias dictus" (Lat.). Llamado. (1) Sirve para indicar que un nombre se usa en lugar del verdadero. (2) Un auto mandamiento alias es aquél que emite la corte cuando otro que se dictó antes no fue efectivo.

ALIBI. Coartada. Excusa dada para indicar que al momento de la comisión de un delito, el sospechoso estaba en otro lugar.

ALIEN. Extranjero. Aquél que no es ciudadano de un país.

ALIEN REGISTRATION ACT. Ley Federal sobre el registro de extranjeros. Requiere que todo extranjero mayor de trece años sea registrado anualmente además de reportar sus huellas digitales.

ALIENABLE. Enajenable. Que puede ser removido, tomado, negado o transferido.

ALIENATE. Transferir o traspasar una propiedad a otra persona.

ALIENATION. Traspaso. Acto de traspasar o transferir un terreno.

ALIENATION CLAUSE. Cláusula de un contrato de seguro sobre traspaso de la propiedad. Establece que de ser vendida o transferida la propiedad asegurada, la póliza de seguro termina.

ALIENI JURIS. (Lat.) Que está bajo el control legal o custodia de otro.

ALIMONY. Pensión alimenticia que debe pagar un cónyuge divorciado a su ex-cónyuge para su manutención personal.

ALIQUOT. Alícuota. Una parte; parte proporcional o fraccional.

ALIUNDE. De otro lado, lugar o frente. Que proviene de afuera de un documento.

ALIVE. Vivo. No tiene un significado legal preciso. Para efectos de la herencia, puede ser desde el momento de la concepción.

ALL–EVENTS TEST. Principio en materia fiscal que establece que cuando los impuestos se calculan sobre la base devengada, la renta pertenece al contribuyente una vez que han ocurrido todos los eventos necesarios para tal ingreso y cuando el mismo puede ser calculado con certeza.

ALL FAULTS. Con todos los defectos. Cuando un bien es vendido en esta forma, significa que posiblemente adolece de un defecto y el comprador sabe que lo compra tal como lo ve y le es descrito.

ALL FOURS. Dos precedentes o casos que son similares y exactamente iguales en todos sus aspectos legales relevantes.

ALLEGATION. Alegación. Afirmación en una demanda o petición que establece hechos que el demandante espera probar.

ALLEGE. Alegar. Exponer o presentar hechos en una demanda o petición.

ALLEGIANCE. (1) Lealtad o fidelidad al estado de donde proviene. (2) **Local Allegiance.** Lealtad local. Fidelidad temporal al estado en donde se vive.

ALLIANCE. (1) Relación o unión entre personas o familias. (2) En derecho internacional, la unión o alianza entre dos o más países.

ALLOCATION. Distribución. Prorratear. (1) Poner algo en un lugar en vez de ponerlo en otro. (2) **Allocation of Income.** Distribuir el ingreso según diferentes fuentes.

ALLOCUTION. Alocución, discurso. La oportunidad dada a un acusado para que diga por qué no debe condenársele o si tiene algo que decir antes de que la sentencia se dicte.

ALLODIAL. Alodial. Libre de toda carga. Palabra usada antiguamente para indicar que una propiedad estaba libre de todo agravio.

ALLOGRAPH. Documento escrito por una persona a nombre de otra.

ALLONGE. Papel adherido a un documento negociable para agregar los endosos que no caben.

ALLOTMENT. Repartición. (1) **Allotment Certificate.** Certificado de repartición mediante el cual se le enseña a los posibles futuros compradores de acciones de una compañía cuántas pueden comprar y cada cuanto tiempo. (2) **Land Allotment.** Parcelación. División de un terreno en parcelas para venderlas.

ALLOWANCE. Pensión. Asignación. (1) Pago regular de dinero. (2) Deducción. (3) Tomar algo en consideración.

ALLUVION. Aluvión. Aumento en un terreno causado por la naturaleza. Véase "Accretion".

ALLUVIUM. Aluvión. Véase "Alluvion".

ALTER EGO. Otro ego. Principio legal que permite a una corte responsabilizar personalmente a quien usa una sociedad anónima para efectuar sus propios negocios.

ALTERATION. Alteración. (1) Hacer que una cosa sea diferente de lo que era sin destruir su identidad. (2) Escribir sobre o borrar un documento, cambiando su significado.

ALTERCATION. Un intercambio verbal con pasión o rabia.

ALTERNATE VALUATION DATE. Fecha de avalúo alternativa. Regla de Derecho Fiscal Federal que le permite al administrador de los bienes de un yacente calcular el valor de la propiedad usando la fecha de la muerte del difunto u otra fecha alternativa (por ejemplo: cuando se vende).

ALTERNATIVE CONTRACT. Contrato con alternativas de cumplimiento, dando a las partes varias opciones para cumplir con el contrato.

ALTERNATIVE PLEADING. Demanda con hechos alternativos. Alegar, en una demanda o petición, hechos que son inconsistentes y que no podrían, por lógica, existir al mismo tiempo.

ALTERNATIVE RELIEF. Remedio alternativo. Solicitar a la corte remedios que se contradicen, como el retorno de lo prestado y su valor.

ALTERNATIVE WRIT. Auto o mandamiento alternativo. Antigua orden que daba la corte a una parte para que compareciera y estableciera la razón por la que algo no debía hacerse o permitirse.

AM. JUR. American Jurisprudence. Jurisprudencia americana. Una enciclopedia de derecho.

AMALGAMATION. Amalgamar. Unión total de dos cosas en una.

AMBASSADOR. Embajador. Máximo representante de un estado en otro.

AMBIGUITY. Ambigüedad. La posibilidad de que algo sea interpretado de más de una manera.

AMBIT. Línea limítrofe. Límite. Frontera.

AMBULANCE CHASER. Dícese del abogado que solicita clientes impropiamente o que trata de que las personas se demanden.

AMBULATORY. Ambulatorio. Capaz de ser movido o revocado. Que se mueve.

AMEND. Enmendar. Corrección o cambio en un documento o ley.

AMENDMENT. Enmienda. (1) Cambio en una ley. (2) Cambios en la Constitución de los Estados Unidos incorporados luego de que se promulgara. (3) Corrección de una demanda después de haber sido ratificada en la corte.

AMERCEMENT. Multa que se impone a un funcionario por una falta.

AMERICAN ARBITRATION ASSOCIATION. Asociación Norteamericana de Arbitraje. Organismo que proporciona árbitros para
solucionar disputas.

AMERICAN BAR ASSOCIATION. Asociación Norteamericana de
Abogados. La más grande asociación voluntaria de abogados en
los Estados Unidos.

AMERICAN CLAUSE. Cláusula americana. Disposición en un
contrato de seguro marítimo que responsabiliza por el valor total
de un reclamo a la compañía que originalmente vendió la póliza
de seguro aun cuando otras compañías subsecuentemente
hubieran vendido pólizas protegiendo los mismos bienes.

AMERICAN DIGEST SYSTEM. Sistema del Compendio
Americano. Recopilación de sumarios de todos los casos
reportados en los Estados Unidos desde el siglo XVI.

AMERICAN LAW INSTITUTE. Instituto de Derecho Norte-
americano. Organismo educativo de investigación legal.

AMERICAN LAW REPORT. Reportes de Derecho Norte-
americano. Libros que publican las decisiones y comentarios sobre
casos importantes.

AMERICAN RULE. Regla americana. Establece que el triunfador
en una acción legal no puede cobrar honorarios de su abogado a
la parte perdedora.

AMICABLE ACTION. Acción amigable, iniciada con el acuerdo de
ambas partes.

AMICUS CURIAE. (Lat.) Amigo de la corte. Parte a quien se le
permite comparecer ante una demanda para exponer sus
argumentos aun cuando de otra forma no tendría derecho a ello.

AMNESTY. Amnistía. Perdón general dado por el gobierno a
alguien culpable de un delito.

AMORTIZATION. Amortización. (1) Pagar una deuda en forma
periódica y regular con pagos iguales. (2) Partir el valor y costo
de un bien intangible año por año sobre su tiempo estimado de
vida útil. (3) División de los beneficios y costos de intangibles
para efectos fiscales.

AMOTION. Remoción. Por ejemplo, sacar a un arrendatario de una propiedad; sacar a un funcionario de su cargo.

AMOUNT IN CONTROVERSY. La cantidad en daños que debe ser alegada para que una Corte Federal tenga jurisdicción.

ANALOGY. Analogía. Razonamiento en base a similitudes.

ANALYTICAL JURISPRUDENCE. Jurisprudencia analítica. Método para estudiar diversos sistemas legales basado en el análisis de sus principios en abstracto sin considerar sus aplicaciones prácticas.

ANARCHIST. Anarquista. (1) Aquél que aboga por la derogación violenta de todos los gobiernos. (2) Aquél que cree que no hay buen gobierno.

ANARCHY. Anarquía. Ausencia de gobierno, ley u orden social.

ANATHEMA. Excomunión. Castigo religioso mediante el cual los miembros de una iglesia no pueden dirigirse al miembro castigado.

ANCIENT. Viejo. Antiguo. De vieja data.

ANCIENT LIGHTS. Servidumbre de luz bajo la cual las ventanas que han recibido la luz del exterior por cierto tiempo no pueden ser obstruidas por los propietarios de los terrenos colindantes.

ANCIENT WRITINGS. Presunción de que los documentos antiguos que han sido mantenidos y custodiados adecuadamente son genuinos.

ANCILLARY. Ancilario, auxiliar subordinado. Procedimiento que ayuda a otro procedimiento considerado como el principal.

ANCILLARY ADMINISTRATION. Procedimiento característico del estado en que una persona muerta había tenido propiedad, pero que es diferente del procedimiento acostumbrado en el estado donde esa persona residía o tenía la mayoría de sus bienes.

ANCILLARY JURISDICTION. Jurisdicción subordinada. Facultad de una corte para decidir los asuntos subordinados al asunto principal, aun cuando de otra forma no hubiese podido decidir los asuntos subordinados.

AND/OR. Y/o. Término vago. Mejor reemplazado por la palabra exacta.

ANIMO. (Lat.) Con la intención.

ANIMUS. (Lat.) Animo; intención.

ANIMUS ET FACTUM. (Lat.) El ánimo de hacer algo y el hacerlo.

ANN. Abreviatura de anual o anotado.

ANNEX. Anexo. Algo menor adjunto a algo mayor.

ANNEXATION. Anexar. Unir algo menor a algo mayor.

ANNOTATED STATUTES. Leyes anotadas. Libros que recopilan leyes anotándolas con comentarios.

ANNOTATION. Anotación. Explicación de un precedente legal, usualmente del texto de la decisión misma.

ANNUAL EXCLUSION. Exclusión anual. Cantidad de dinero que se puede excluir al calcular el impuesto a las donaciones sin usar el crédito unificado al que cada persona tiene derecho.

ANNUAL PERCENTAGE RATE. Tarifa del porcentaje de interés anual. Expresa de una manera estandarizada el costo anual real de un préstamo.

ANNUAL REPORT OR STATEMENT. Reporte o informe anual que muchas sociedades anónimas deben presentar a sus accionistas y al gobierno.

ANNUITY. Anualidad, renta anual. Una suma de dinero usualmente pagada a una persona en plazos determinados por un período determinado o de por vida.

ANNUL. Anular. Declarar nulo. Dejar sin valor.

ANNULMENT. Anulación. Acto de anular. Eliminar por completo la validez de algo desde su inicio.

ANOMALOUS OR ANOMALY. Anómalo. Excepción a una regla. Que no es lo normal.

ANONYMOUS. Anónimo. De autor desconocido. Abreviado "anon.".

ANSWER. Contestación a la demanda. Primera alegación o defensa hecha por el demandando.

ANTE. (Lat.) Antes. Que precede.

ANTE LITEM MOTAM. (Lat.) Antes de que la demanda o el litigio comience.

ANTE NATUS. (Lat.) Nacido antes. Que nació antes que alguien o algo.

ANTECEDENT DEBT. Deuda antecedente. Una deuda que precede en tiempo a otra transacción. En materia de quiebra, es aquella deuda debida con suficiente anticipación al registro de la quiebra que es considerada como una deuda válida.

ANTEDATE. Prefechar. Darle a un documento fecha anterior a la de su real creación. Puede ser considerado un delito.

ANTENUPTIAL. Antes del matrimonio. (1) **Antenuptial Agreement.** Acuerdo prenupcial que establece la forma en que los bienes serán administrados durante el matrimonio, cómo serán divididos en caso de divorcio y cómo serán transferidos en caso de muerte.

ANTICIPATION. Anticipación. (1) Hacer algo antes de lo debido o simplemente antes de algo. (2) Derecho a pagar una hipoteca antes que se venza sin tener que pagar un exceso por ello. (3) Derecho en algunos contratos de restar dinero al pagar antes de tiempo. (4) En derecho de patente, una persona ha sido anticipada si otra persona ha patentado algo sustancialmente igual.

ANTICIPATORY BREACH. Incumplimiento anticipado. (1) Incumplir una obligación contractual luego de haberla contratado, pero antes de la fecha de su cumplimiento. (2) El derecho que posee una parte a un contrato comercial para iniciar una demanda cuando la otra parte al contrato lo repudia anticipadamente.

ANTIDUMPING ACT. Ley federal que prohibe la venta de mercaderías dentro de los Estados Unidos a un precio menor del que se vende en su país de origen.

ANTILAPSE STATUTE. Ley que les permite heredar a los herederos de una persona que tenía derecho a heredar pero que muere antes que el testador.

ANTIMONY. Antimonia. Inconsistencia en una ley o entre ideas.

ANTI-RACKETEERING ACT. Ley federal que prohibe la extorsión e interferencia con el comercio entre los diversos estados de los Estados Unidos.

ANTITRUST ACT. Ley federal contra el monopolio. Protege al comercio en contra del monopolio y del ajuste de precios que perjudican a los pequeños comerciantes.

APEX RULE. Regla del ápice. Permite que un minero explote una vena mineral en tierras públicas desde la superficie hasta cualquier punto en el subsuelo de esa tierra pública si la vena mineral sale de donde tiene su concesión.

APP. CT. Abreviatura de corte de apelación.

APPARENT. Aparente. (1) Fácilmente visto. Que parece cierto. (2) **Apparent Authority.** Autorización o autoridad aparente. Que parece tener un agente.

APPEAL. Apelar. Pedir a una corte superior que revise la decisión de una corte inferior.

APPEAL BOND. Fianza o bono consignado para pagar los costos de la otra parte en caso de que la apelación no se conduzca honestamente.

APPEALABLE ORDER. Acción suficientemente finalizatoria o terminante dada por un juez de manera tal que si es apelada no afecta la forma en que se está llevando el caso ante el juez.

APPEAL IN FORMA PAUPERIS. (Lat.) El privilegio que se da a una persona pobre para apelar su caso sin pagar costos o poner fianza.

APPEALS COUNCIL. Consejo de Apelaciones. El órgano ante el que se apela la decisión de un juez de lo administrativo, especialmente en materias del seguro social.

APPEARANCE. Comparecencia, aparecer. Presentarse ante la corte como parte en un juicio o como abogado de una parte.

APPELLANT. Apelante. Recurrente. El que apela.

APPELLATE. Corte de Apelación. Ante quien se apela.

APPELLATE RULES. Reglas que rigen los procedimientos ante las cortes de apelación.

APPELEE. Apelado. La parte generalmente beneficiada con la decisión que se apela.

APPEND. Agregar. Añadir algo a otra cosa.

APPENDIX. Apéndice. Documentos adjuntos a escritos en soporte de una posición tomada ante una corte de apelación.

APPERTAIN. Que pertenece a algo; que está relacionado o conectado con algo. Véase "Appurtenance".

APPLICANT. Aplicante. Uno que solicita algo.

APPLICATION. Aplicación. (1) Efecto y acción de aplicar ante una entidad. (2) La aplicación de un precepto legal a un caso específico.

APPLY. Aplicar, pedir, solicitar, anteponer una petición, usualmente por escrito.

APPOINT. Designar. Dar un trabajo a alguien.

APPOINTEE. Designado. A quien se le da un trabajo.

APPOINTER. Designador. El que designa o nombra a alguien para un trabajo.

APPOINTMENT. Cita, nombramiento, designación.

APPOINTOR. Designador, nombrador, apoderado.

APPORTION. Prorratear; dividir por partes.

APPORTIONMENT. Prorrateo. Cuota que le corresponde a alguien sobre aquello que se divide en partes.

APPOSE. Cuestionar. Examinar al custodio de ciertos registros sobre ellos.

APPRAISAL. Avalúo, tasación. (1) Estimación del valor de algo por un perito imparcial. (2) **Appraisal Remedy.** Remedio dado por la corte a los accionistas minoritarios de una sociedad para que se tasen sus acciones a un precio justo en base a su valor antes de que cierto evento extraordinario sea llevado a cabo por los accionistas mayoritarios.

APPRAISER. Evaluador. Tasador. Perito que fija el precio de una cosa.

APPRECIABLE. Apreciable. (1) Que puede ser estimado o percibido por los sentidos. (2) Que existe pero no es necesariamente de gran valor. (3) Capaz de aumentar de valor.

APPRECIATE. Apreciar. (1) Aumentar en valor. (2) Estimar el valor de algo. (3) Entender.

APPRECIATION. Apreciación. (1) Incremento en el valor de una propiedad, excluyendo los incrementos debidos a las mejoras realizadas. (2) Cualquier aumento de valor.

APPREHEND. Arrestar. Privar a una persona de su libertad.

APPREHENSION. Aprensión. (1) Arresto de una persona. (2) Miedo. (3) Conocimiento de algo.

APPRENTICESHIP. Aprendizaje. Relación entre el maestro y la persona que estudia una artesanía o profesión.

APPROACH, RIGHT OF. En derecho marítimo internacional, el derecho de un buque de guerra en acercarse a otro buque para determinar su nacionalidad.

APPROPRIATE. (1) Tomar dominio, incautar, tomar posesión de. (2) Apto o justo.

APPROPRIATION. Apropiación, asignación. (1) Disposición legislativa de un dinero para un propósito especial. (2) Apropiación por el gobierno de propiedad para uso público. (3) Tomar algo sin derecho a ello. (4) La asignación de un dinero para una inversión mayor a largo plazo.

APPROVAL. Aprobación. Venta hecha bajo aprobación es aquella en la cual el comprador puede devolver lo comprado si no está satisfecho, aun cuando los bienes hubiesen sido todo lo que el vendedor prometió.

APPROXIMATION. Aproximación. Doctrina de equidad que permite a un juez mantener un fideicomiso de beneficencia o caridad, variando sus términos, cuando de por sí no podría seguir funcionando.

APPURTENANCE. Perteneciente a, anexado o añadido a. Algo accesorio está necesariamente ligado al uso y goce de otra cosa principal. Usualmente se refiere a servidumbre perteneciente a una propiedad.

APPURTENANT. Perteneciente. Véase "Appurtenance".

ARBITER. (1) Compra simultánea de bienes en un mercado y su venta en otro mercado para lucrar con la diferencia de precios. (2) Arbitro.

ARBITRAGE. La compra y venta de bienes, acciones o moneda en diferentes mercados para captar la ganancia entre las diferencias en precio entre los mercados.

ARBITRAMENT. Fallo arbitral. Decisión de un juez de arbitraje o árbitro sobre la materia en disputa.

ARBITRARILY. Arbitrariamente. (1) Hecho contrario a la razón. (2) Que depende de la voluntad de una persona.

ARBITRARY. Arbitrario. Veáse "Arbitrarily". Usualmente está relacionado a la mala fe o a un capricho.

ARBITRATION. Arbitraje. Someter formalmente una disputa a una persona para que decida la controversia.

ARBITRATION ACTS. Leyes de arbitraje. Permiten que ciertos asuntos sean ventilados ante árbitros, a cuyas decisiones se les da validez.

ARBITRATION OF EXCHANGE. La compra y venta simultánea de letras de cambio en diversos mercados para lucrar con la diferencia de precio de las monedas en los mercados.

ARBITRATOR. Arbitrador. Arbitro. Persona que resuelve un arbitraje.

AREAWIDE AGREEMENT. Convención colectiva y contrato de trabajo geográfico. Convención colectiva negociada por un sindicato con las empresas de un área geográfica.

413

ARGUENDO. Como argumento; objeto de razonamiento o de argumento. Asumir que algo es cierto, lo sea o no, para discutir un punto.

ARGUMENT. Argumento. (1) Persuasión por medio de la presentación de hechos, leyes y el razonamiento que las relaciona. (2) La presentación oral ante una corte de los argumentos de una parte.

ARGUMENTATIVE. Argumentativo. Expresión de hechos y conclusiones.

ARISE. Surgir, levantarse. Provenir.

ARISTOCRACY. Aristocracia. Gobierno de la clase noble.

ARMED ROBBERY. Robo a mano armada. Quitarle la propiedad a alguien mientras se le amenaza con un arma.

ARMISTICE. Armisticio. Suspensión total de una guerra entre dos naciones con la esperanza de que la suspensión sea permanente.

ARM'S LENGTH. Trato, acuerdo o negocio entre partes con intereses diversos.

ARMS, RIGHT TO. Derecho a tener armas. Derecho constitucional a que la ciudadanía tenga armas, pero que no permite portarlas en violación de leyes estatales o federales.

ARRAIGN. Acusar, denunciar, emplazar. Traer a un acusado ante la corte para que escuche la acusación y la conteste.

ARRAIGNMENT. Acusación, denuncia. Véase "Arraign".

ARRANGEMENT WITH CREDITORS. Arreglo con los acreedores. Plan hecho de acuerdo a la ley federal de quiebra o bancarrota para que un deudor pague menos de lo que debe a sus acreedores a fin de levantar (o evitar) la quiebra o ganar tiempo para pagar y no quebrar por completo.

ARRAY. Grupo dentro del cual se ha de seleccionar el jurado. (1) **Challenge to the Array.** Una objeción contra el procedimiento seguido para escoger aquellas personas de las cuales se ha de seleccionar el jurado.

ARREARAGES. Mora o atrasos. Dinero debido con plazo vencido y aún no pagado.

ARREARS. Mora. Véase "Arrearages".

ARREST. Arresto. Detención oficial de una persona para que responda a cargos penales.

ARREST OF JUDGMENT. Suspensión temporal de los efectos de una sentencia.

ARREST RECORD. Reporte de arresto. Reporte hecho por la policía cuando realiza una detención o arresto.

ARREST WARRANT. Orden de arresto.

ARROGATION. Arrogación. (1) Adopción de un adulto. (2) Reclamar o tomar algo sin derecho a ello.

ARSON. Incendio premeditado. Delito de incendiar maliciosa e ilegalmente un edificio.

ART. Arte. (1) Conocimiento o habilidad especial. (2) Proceso o método. (3) Abreviatura de artículo.

ARTICLE. Artículo. Una parte separada y distinta de un documento.

ARTICLED CLERK. Aprendiz de abogado (en Inglaterra).

ARTICLES. Artículos. (1) Partes separadas dentro de un documento. (2) Ley con muchas partes. (3) Sistema de leyes o reglas. (4) Alguna clase de contratos como los de una sociedad civil o de beneficencia.

ARTICLES OF CONFEDERATION. Artículos de la Confederación. Documento que mantenía a las primeras trece colonias unidas antes de la existencia de la Constitución.

ARTICLES OF INCORPORATION. Pacto social. Documento de origen, o mediante el cual se constituye una sociedad mercantil.

ARTICULATED PLEADING. Demanda que numera los hechos. Cada hecho está numerado por separado en la demanda.

ARTICULO MORTIS. (Lat.) Agonía de muerte. Que está a punto de morir.

ARTIFICE. Un esquema de ingenios. Que conlleva trampa o fraude.

ARTIFICIAL PERSON. Persona artificial o ficticia. Entidad o cosa a la cual la ley le reconoce derechos y obligaciones como una persona o como una sociedad mercantil.

ARTISAN'S LIEN. El derecho por estatuto que tiene un artesano en retener un objeto hasta que se le pague por su labor.

AS IS. Tal como está. Algo vendido con un posible defecto y que el comprador recibe en la condición en que se ve y sin garantía alguna.

AS PER. De acuerdo con.

ASCENDANTS. Ascendientes. Padres, abuelos.

ASCENT. Ascender. Cuando el derecho hereditario es uno ascendente con respecto al difunto.

ASPORTATION. Extracción. Tomar o llevarse cosas ilegalmente.

ASSAILANT. Asaltante. Persona que asalta o roba.

ASSASSIN. Asesino. Persona que mata a otra.

ASSASSINATE. Asesinar. Acto de matar a una persona.

ASSASSINATION. Asesinato. Matar a alguien.

ASSAULT. Asalto. Acto de asaltar o robar.

ASSAY. Ensayar. Experimentar o probar. (1) Examinar algo para descubrir su tamaño, medidas, peso, calidad, etc. (2) Prueba para establecer la pureza de un metal.

ASSEMBLAGE. Asamblea. Agregado. Combinar cosas pequeñas para formar una grande; por ejemplo, parcelas en un terreno grande. Véase "Assembly".

ASSEMBLY. Asamblea. (1) Reunión multitudinaria. (2) Casa gubernamental de menor jerarquía en las legislaturas estatales. (3) Derecho constitucional del pueblo a reunirse políticamente para protestar.

ASSENT. Asentir. Dar consentimiento o aprobación para algo.

416

ASSERVATION. Afirmación o protesta bajo juramento.

ASSESS. Amillarar, tasar, avaluar, calcular, imponer. (1) Establecer el valor de algo. (2) Determinar el valor de una propiedad para efectos fiscales. (3) Imputar el valor de una mejora pública a cada una de las propiedades beneficiadas por la mejora.

ASSESSABLE. Imponible. (1) Que debe pagar extra. (2) Que debe pagar impuestos.

ASSESSED VALUATION. Avalúo catastral. Valor real dado a un bien inmueble para efectos fiscales. Usualmente menor al valor comercial en el mercado.

ASSESSMENT RATIO. Porcentaje del valor comercial de un bien al cual el gobierno avalúa para efectos fiscales.

ASSESSMENT WORK. Minar o efectuar en una concesión sobre tierras de uso público, a fin de no perder el derecho a la concesión o reclamo del derecho minero.

ASSESSOR. Asesor. Tasador, avaluador. (1) Funcionario encargado de avaluar propiedades para efectos fiscales. (2) Persona que aconseja al juez durante una demanda sobre asuntos de carácter científico o técnico.

ASSET DEPRECIATION RANGE. Determinar la extensión de una depreciación. Método para calcular el tiempo de vida útil de un activo.

ASSETS. Activos. Cualquier dinero, propiedad o derecho relacionado con dinero que se debe a una persona o que alguien posee. (1) **Capital Assets.** Bienes de capital sujetos a un régimen fiscal especial. (2) **Current Assets.** Activos corrientes, usualmente efectivo, pagarés, acciones. (3) **Fixed Assets.** Activos fijos, que son difíciles de convertir en dinero. (4) **Tangible Assets.** Activos con cualidades físicas, por ejemplo, edificios.

ASSIGN. Asignar, ceder, traspasar, aplicar. Transferir un instrumento, una propiedad, un derecho o un artículo a otro. Designar algo para un propósito o a alguien para cumplir con un deber.

ASSIGNABILITY. Cualidad legal que permite que algo se transfiera, asigne o ceda.

417

ASSIGNEE. Cesionario. El que recibe aquello que se asigna, cede o transfiere. El beneficiario de una cesión.

ASSIGNMENT. El acto de transferir, asignar o ceder.

ASSIGNOR. Cedente. El que da en asignación, transferencia o cesión. Aquél que cede un derecho a otro.

ASSISTANCE OF COUNSEL. Derecho a ser aconsejado por un abogado.

ASSISTANCE, WRIT OF. Auto o mandamiento de asistencia, el cual autoriza a la policía a ayudar a la persona a quien el juez le reconoce el derecho de posesión de un terreno para que tome efectivamente la propiedad.

ASSOCIATE COMPANY. Compañía asociada. Aquélla controlada por otra compañía matriz.

ASSOCIATE JUSTICE. Juez Asociado. Nombre o título de cada juez en una corte de apelación, excepto el del Juez Presidente del Tribunal.

ASSOCIATION. Asociación. (1) Palabra común que indica unión de un grupo de personas para un propósito particular. (2) Clase de entidad financiera o sociedad civil que para efectos fiscales se grava como una sociedad mercantil.

ASSUME. Asumir. (1) Tomar o ejercer las responsabilidades de alguien. (2) Pretender.

ASSUMPSIT. (1) Palabra antigua que significa promesa, contrato o pacto. (2) (Lat.) El prometió.

ASSUMPTION. Asunción, presunción. (1) Asumir una obligación o deuda. (2) Un supuesto.

ASSUMPTION OF RISK. Asunción de riesgo. Principio legal que impide al demandante recuperar lo perdido cuando él mismo se expuso a ciertos peligros.

ASSURANCE. Seguro, seguridad. Prenda o garantía.

ASSURED. Asegurado. Aquél que tiene un seguro.

ASYLUM. Asilo. Derecho que tiene un estado de proteger a personas de ser procesadas penalmente por otros estados.

AT BAR. Ante la corte. Cuando se ventila un caso en la corte.

AT ISSUE. Disputa; en controversia. Una demanda está en controversia cuando un lado expone los hechos claramente y el otro los niega.

AT LARGE. Ilimitado.

AT LAW. Por o según la ley.

AT RISK. En riesgo o peligro.

ATS. "At suit of". En demanda.

ATTACHE. Agregado.

ATTACHMENT. Embargo, secuestro. (1) Quitarle la propiedad a alguien para ponerla a disposición de la corte. (2) Documento agregado a otro.

ATTACHMENT BOND. Bono o fianza de embargo. Bono entregado a la corte para liberar la propiedad embargada o secuestrada.

ATTAINDER. Eliminación completa de los derechos civiles y de toda la propiedad privada de una persona condenada a muerte por haber cometido traición u otra felonía.

ATTEMPT. Tentativa. Atentado. (1) Hechos que sobrepasan los actos preparatorios para cometer un crimen pero que no son suficientes para constituir el crimen en sí. (2) Intentar un crimen.

ATTENDANCE. Comparecencia. Presencia ante la corte.

ATTEST. Atestar. Declarar. Afirmar algo.

ATTESTATION. Atestación, testimonio. Actuar como testigo de la firma de un documento y firmar cuando uno fue testigo de la firma de tal documento.

ATTORN. Palabra arcaica que entre otras cosas significa el reconocimiento de un nuevo arrendador por parte del arrendatario.

ATTORNEY. Abogado. **Attorney in Fact.** Apoderado o representante legal. Aquél que representa a otro. No tiene que ser abogado.

ATTORNEY GENERAL. Procurador General de la Nación. Procurador General de un estado en particular.

ATTORNEY OF RECORD. Abogado registrado en la corte como quien representa a una persona.

ATTORNEY–CLIENT PRIVILEGE. Secreto entre abogado y cliente. Derecho y deber de un abogado de retener o rehusarse a dar información sobre lo conversado con su cliente.

ATTORNEY'S LIEN. Embargo o retención de dinero de bienes del cliente hecho por el abogado para cobrar sus honorarios.

ATTRACTIVE NUISANCE. Peligro atractivo. Doctrina de la responsabilidad civil según la cual el dueño de cierta propiedad de índole peligrosa (por ejemplo: mina explosiva) es responsable absolutamente por los daños causados a niños, ya que la propiedad atrae la atención de niños a no ser que el dueño tome medidas extraordinarias.

ATTRIBUTION. Atribución. Decidir que algo que parece de alguien en realidad pertenece a otro.

ATT'Y. Abreviatura de "attorney". Véase esa palabra.

AUCTION. Subasta. Remate. Venta pública por apuestas al mejor postor.

AUCTIONEER. Subastador. El que realiza la subasta.

AUDIT. Auditoría. Revisión oficial de una cuenta o estado financiero de una sociedad.

AUDIT TRAIL. Contra referencia entre un registro contable y su fuente original para explicarla propiamente.

AUDITOR. Auditor. Persona que revisa cuentas y decide si están en orden.

AUGMENTED ESTATE. Caudal acrecentado. Propiedad dejada por un difunto luego de realizar sustracciones y aumentos.

AUTHENTIC. Auténtico. Legalizado.

AUTHENTICATION. Autenticación. Dar autoridad o validez legal a una persona.

AUTHOR. Autor. Aquél que produce algo nuevo.

AUTHORITIES. Autoridades. Los orígenes legales que apoyan una posición legal.

AUTHORITY. Autoridad, autorización. (1) **Apparent Authority.** Permiso tácito para hacer algo. (2) **Express Authority.** Poder expreso para actuar a nombre de alguien. (3) **General Authority.** Derecho legal de actuar.

AUTHORIZATION CARD. Tarjeta de autorización. Permiso dado por un trabajador al sindicato para que lo represente.

AUTHORIZE. Autorizar. (1) Dar autorización. (2) Legal u oficialmente permitido.

AUTOCRACY. Autocracia. Gobierno de una persona.

AUTOPSY. Autopsia. Examen médico o forense hecho a un difunto para establecer la causa de muerte.

AUTRE. (Fr.) Otro. (1) **Autre Vie.** Durante la vida de otro. (2) **Autre Droit.** Durante el tiempo de otra ley o derecho. (3) Antiguamente, antes.

AUTREFOIS ACQUIT. (Fr.) Absuelto con anterioridad por la misma causa.

AUTREFOIS CONVICTED. (Fr.) Ya condenado por la misma causa.

AUXILIARY. Auxiliar. Que ayuda, que es subsecuente o subsidiario.

AVAILS. Ganancias o productos.

AVER. Declarar, alegar. Establecer algo clara y formalmente.

AVERAGE. Promedio. (1) Término matemático que se refiere al término medio de algo. (2) Avería. En Derecho Marítimo, una pérdida en términos de seguros marítimos.

AVERMENT. Testimonio. Afirmación de una cosa haciéndola evidente.

AVIATION ACT. Ley Federal de Aviación que crea la Administración Federal de Aviación, encargada de todo lo relativo al transporte y navegación aéreos.

A VINCULO MATRIMONI. (Lat.) De los vínculos del matrimonio. Tipo de divorcio.

AVOID. Anular. Dejar sin efectos; sin ningún valor.

AVOIDABLE. Anulable. Capaz de ser anulado.

AVOIDANCE. (1) Escapar o evadir. (2) Al alegar, es la aceptación de los hechos presentados por la otra parte. Sin embargo, se alegan también las razones por las cuales no debe dársele valor legal a dichos hechos.

AVOW. Reconocer y justiciar un acto.

AVOWAL. Declaración que le permite a la corte conocer lo que el testigo hubiera contestado a la pregunta propuesta.

AVULSION. Avulsión. Repentina pérdida o ganancia de superficie de un terreno debido a causas naturales.

AWARD. Dar o entregar mediante un derecho formal. (1) La cantidad de dinero que un jurado concede a la parte triunfadora. (2) Dar o asignar mediante sentencia o fallo arbitral.

AXIOM. Axioma. Verdad básica de la cual se deducen otras.

A.W.W. "Average Weekly Wages". Salario promedio semanal usado para calcular compensaciones e indemnizaciones laborales.

B

B.C. (1) Siglas de "Before Christ". Antes de Cristo. (2) Abreviatura de "British Columbia" y "Bankruptcy Court".

B.F. Abreviatura de Bona Fide (Lat.). Buena fe. Abreviatura de Bonum Factum. Aprobado.

B.F.O.Q. "Bona Fide Occupational Qualification". Necesidad legítima y aprobada de un empleador para discriminar por raza, sexo, religión, edad, etc., al contratar empleados.

B.F.P. "Bona Fide Purchaser". Comprador de buena fe. Aquél que compra algo honestamente, paga un precio justo y desconoce el que otra persona, si existe, reclame la cosa comprada.

BABY ACT. Ley estatal que permite usar la minoría de edad como defensa en una demanda por razón de un contrato hecho por un menor.

BACK. Endosar. Firmar o asumir la responsabilidad financiera de algo. Aprobar dinero para una empresa.

BACKUP WITHHOLDING. Retención adicional de impuestos sobre ciertos intereses y dividendos.

BACKBOND. Una obligación de indemnización con respecto a un fiador de dinero.

BAD DEBT. Deuda incobrable. Cuenta mala.

BAD FAITH. Mala fe. Deshonestidad al negociar con otra persona. No implica fraude.

BADGE OF FRAUD. Fuerte indicio de fraude. Usualmente se utiliza para determinar si se transfiere propiedad en perjuicio de acreedores.

BAIL. Fianza. Caución o dinero que pone una persona a disposición de la corte para permitir la libertad provisional de una persona hasta el momento del juicio.

BAILEE. Depositario. Persona a quien se le presta o a quien se le da en depósito algo.

BAILIFF. Alguacil. Oficial de baja jerarquía encargado de mantener orden en la corte.

BAILMENT. Depósito. Entrega temporal de propiedad a una persona distinta del dueño. Por ejemplo: dejar un automóvil en un taller.

BAILOR. Depositante. Aquél que entrega o presta a otro. (1) El que paga una fianza.

BAIL–OUT. Evitar que una persona caiga en una pérdida financiera.

BAIT AND SWITCH. Enseñar un artículo como anzuelo o señuelo para que los clientes vengan a la tienda y luego convencerlos de que compren otro artículo. Puede ser ilegal si el primer artículo nunca estuvo en realidad para la venta.

BALANCE. Saldo. Cantidad que sobra. Diferencia entre lo debido y el pago hecho que da el saldo debido. (1) **In Balance or Balanced**; en balance o balanceado. Que no sobra o queda nada. Auditoría en la cual débitos y créditos se igualan.

BALANCE OF PAYMENT. Balanza de pagos. A veces se refiere a la balanza comercial de un país más otras transacciones financieras como los préstamos internacionales.

BALANCE OF TRADE. Usualmente denota la balanza comercial internacional de un país. La diferencia entre las exportaciones y las importaciones de un país.

BALANCE SHEET. Hoja de balance. Estado de contabilidad, balance de situación. Sumario completo y detallado del valor de una compañía desglosado por pasivos y activos. Balance general.

BALANCING TEST. Doctrina constitucional bajo la cual la corte balancea los derechos constitucionales de una persona contra los derechos de un estado de proteger a sus ciudadanos. La doctrina se usa comúnmente en casos de libertad de palabra e igual protección de la ley.

BALLOON PAYMENT OR LOAN. Pago o préstamo global o redondeado. Aquel préstamo a plazos en el cual el último pago es mucho mayor que los otros.

BALLOT. Balota. (1) Papel usado para votar en una elección. (2) Voto total en una elección. (3) Lista de candidatos en una elección.

BAN. Anuncio o publicación. Proclamación de una ley.

BANC. Pleno del tribunal cuando una corte considera un caso, estando todos los magistrados presentes.

BANISHMENT. Destierro. Expulsar a una persona de un país y enviarlo a otro.

BANK. Banco. (1) Entidad que puede ejercer el negocio de banca como tomar depósitos y dar préstamos. (2) **Bank Bill or Bank Note.** Letra Bancaria. Documento que promete pagar a solicitud del portador una cantidad fija de dinero. Este documento es tratado como si fuera dinero. (3) **Bank Credit.** Promesa escrita dada por el banco que le permite a una persona tomar prestado hasta cierta cantidad de dinero. (4) **Bank Draft.** Giro bancario. Cheque o documento similar hecho por un oficial del banco para retirar dinero del banco o depósitos a cuenta del banco. (5) **Bank Paper.** Documento bancario suficientemente bueno como para ser comprado o negociado por el banco.

BANK HOLDINGS COMPANY ACT. Ley federal que exige a los bancos reportar transferencias de grandes cantidades de dinero, y exige a las personas reportar si mantienen cuentas con grandes cantidades de dinero o si efectúan envíos de grandes sumas dentro o fuera del país.

BANKER'S LIEN. Gravamen bancario. Derecho que tiene el banco de retener propiedad del cliente bajo custodia si un cliente le debe con plazo vencido.

BANKRUPT. Quebrado. El sujeto en un procedimiento de quiebra.

BANKRUPTCY. Quiebra. (1) Procedimiento bajo la Ley Federal de Quiebra mediante la cual una persona se libra de todas sus deudas una vez que entrega a la corte todas sus propiedades y

425

bienes. (2) También el procedimiento mediante el cual una organización o sociedad en problemas económicos se reestructura o se liquida para pagar a los acreedores. (3) **Voluntary Bankruptcy.** Quiebra voluntaria solicitada por el deudor. (4) **Involuntary Bankruptcy.** Quiebra involuntaria solicitada por los acreedores.

BAR. Grupo de abogados. (1) Todos los abogados a quienes se les permite ejercer en una corte. (2) Parte de la corte en donde el prisionero se ubica. (3) Barrera o prohibición. (4) La misma corte o juez que preside un juicio.

BAR ACT. Ley estatal que establece lo que un abogado puede o no hacer.

BAR ASSOCIATION. Asociación voluntaria de abogados.

BAR EXAMINATION. Reválida. Examen que tiene que pasar un graduado en derecho para poder ejercer la profesion. La mayoría de los estados usan el examen multi-estatal.

BARE. Falto o escaso. Descubierto con muy limitados efectos legales.

BARGAIN. Negocio. Trato. Convenio. Entendimiento mutuo, contratar. Regatear.

BARGAINING AGENT. Sindicato que tiene la representación exclusiva de todos los empleados de cierta clase en una compañía.

BARGAINING UNIT. Aquellos empleados de una compañía que son representados en grupo por el sindicato.

BAROMETER. Barómetro. Indicador comercial que muestra la tendencia económica.

BARRATRY. (1) Demanda fraudulenta, pleito. Activar una demanda o promover una discusión o pleito para lucrar. (2) Baratería. Actos fraudulentos o ilegales hechos por el capitán o la tripulación en perjuicio del dueño del buque.

BARRISTER. Abogado que expone un caso ante las cortes de Inglaterra.

BARTER. Trueque. Cambio de cosa por cosa en lugar de dinero por cosas.

BARTER EXCHANGE. Trueque; intercambio de bienes sin que medie dinero.

BASE. Base. Inferior o subordinado. Básico. Aquello a lo que se le añade algo.

BASIC FORM OR POLICY. Póliza básica. Aquélla que cubre los riesgos comúnmente asegurados en una póliza.

BASIC PATENT. Patente básica. Patente pionera. Aquella completamente nueva que origina un nuevo campo para descubrimientos o inventos.

BASIS. Base asumida del costo de una propiedad para calcular las ganancias o pérdidas para efectos fiscales. Usualmente es el precio de compra.

BASIS OF BARGAIN. La razón o entendimiento principal en que se basa un acuerdo o contrato para vender bienes.

BASTARD. Bastardo. Hijo ilegítimo.

BASTARDY ACTION. Juicio de filiación. Acción legal para que el padre de un niño lo reconozca como su hijo.

BATTERED CHILD. Niño que sufre abuso físico o emocional.

BATTERY. Agresión. Aplicación ilegal de fuerza o violencia física en la persona de otro.

BEAR ARMS. Derecho a portar armas. Véase "Arms, Right to".

BEAR MARKET. Caída general en los precios de las acciones o valores.

BEAR RAIDING. Atentado ilegal por parte de inversionistas para producir la caída del precio de una acción mediante la rápida venta en serie.

BEARER. Portador. Poseedor de un documento negociable que se ha hecho pagadero al portador o endosado sin indicar que es pagadero a nombre u orden de una persona en particular, o hecho pagadero a "cash" (en efectivo).

BEHOOF. Uso o beneficio.

BELIEF. Creencia. Firmeza de la verdad o realidad de una idea que se apoya entre el conocimiento y la sospecha.

BELIEF–ACTION RULE. Principio de la creencia-acción. Establece que uno puede creer sin restricciones en todo lo que desee, pero que no se puede hacer todo lo que se desea.

BELLIGERENT. Beligerante. (1) Un país en guerra contra otro. (2) Rebeldes que han organizado un gobierno mientras pelean de modo que la lucha se considera legal según los parámetros internacionales.

BELOW. Inferior. Corte de menor jerarquía.

BENCH. Tribunal o banco. Los jueces que forman el tribunal. El lugar donde se sienta el juez.

BENCH CONFERENCE. Reunión del juez con los abogados de ambas partes frente a su banco y fuera del oído del jurado.

BENCH WARRANT. Orden de detención emitida directamente por el juez para que la policía arreste a una persona.

BENEFICIAL ASSOCIATION. Asociación benéfica que usa el dinero de sus miembros para prestarlo a otros que lo necesitan.

BENEFICAL INTEREST. Interés beneficioso. Derecho a las ganancias que resulten de un contrato, propiedades o bienes en lugar del derecho a la propiedad en sí.

BENEFICIARY. Beneficiario. (1) Persona en cuyo interés se constituye un fideicomiso. (2) Persona a quien se le paga el beneficio de una póliza de seguro. (3) El que hereda de un testamento. (4) El que se beneficia o es dueño de algo para efectos fiscales.

BENEFIT. Beneficio. Ventaja, ganancia, privilegio. Dinero pagado por una aseguradora, pensión de jubilación, empleador, etc.

BENEFIT OF BARGAIN RULE. Principio del beneficio de lo negociado. En una demanda por fraude en la venta de algo por un precio mayor a su valor real, el comprador tiene derecho a recuperar la diferencia entre lo que pagó y lo que realmente vale el bien. En algunos casos puede recuperarse el precio de lo que se le prometió o dijo que valía menos lo que realmente vale.

BENEFIT SOCIETY. Sociedad benéfica. Véase "Beneficial Association".

BENEFITS. Beneficios; prestaciones.

BENEVOLENT CORPORATION OR ASSOCIATION. Sociedad o asociación de beneficencia que no tiene fin de lucro sino que actúa por caridad.

BEQUEATH. Legado. Dar derechos personales o inmuebles mediante testamento. Dar cualquier cosa por testamento.

BEQUEST. Legado. Asignación testamentaria. Véase "Bequeath".

BEST EVIDENCE. Mejor prueba o evidencia. Principio que requiere que se presente la prueba más confiable y disponible. Si el original está disponible, una copia no es suficiente.

BESTIALITY. Bestialismo. Delito de un ser humano de mantener relaciones sexuales con un animal.

BEST USE. Mejor uso. El valor que una propiedad hubiera tenido de haberse usado en la forma más lucrativa.

BESTOW. Dar. Otorgar algo.

BET. Apuesta.

BETA. Medida que señala cuan paralelo va el valor de una acción y sus dividendos en comparación con el mercado de valores.

BETRAY. Traicionar. Revelar o entregar algo al enemigo.

429

BETRAYAL OF CONFIDENCE. Traición o falta a la confianza. Revelar un secreto.

BETTERMENT. Mejoras. (1) Modificaciones que mejoran una propiedad y constituyen algo más que simples reparaciones. (2) **Betterment Act.** Ley que le permite al arrendatario recuperar del arrendador el valor de las mejoras.

BEYOND A REASONABLE DOUBT. Más allá de una duda razonable. Nivel de prueba requerido para condenar a una persona. Para condenar se requiere que el jurado esté completamente convencido de la culpabilidad del reo.

BIANNUAL. Dos veces al año.

BIAS. Prejuicio. Parcialidad. Predisposición. (1) Opinión preconcebida de algo que imposibilita una resolución imparcial. (2) Opinión preconcebida de la parte, hecha por el juez.

BICAMERAL. Bicameral. Con dos cámaras o asambleas.

BID. Propuesta. Proposición. (1) Oferta de pagar un precio solicitado en una subasta. (2) Aplicación para un nuevo trabajo ante el mismo patrono. (3) Ofrecimiento de realizar un trabajo o suministrar bienes al precio de un bien en subasta sin la intención de comprar.

BIDDER. Postor. Licitador. Proponente. Aquél que hace una oferta o licitación.

BID SHOPPING. Revelar a una persona los precios de las proposiciones o propuestas más bajas para que pueda presentar una propuesta mejor en una licitación.

BIENNIAL. Bienal. Una vez cada dos años.

BIENNIUM. Bienio. Período de dos años.

BIFURCATED TRIAL. Juicio bifurcado. Audiencias para cuestiones legales separadas y distintas de un mismo caso.

BIG BOARD. Indicador del precio de valores de Nueva York.
Nombre popular para la lista de precios de los valores de la Bolsa
de Valores de Nueva York.

BIG EIGHT. Las ocho firmas más grandes de contadores en los
Estados Unidos.

BIGAMY. Bigamia. Delito de estar casado con más de una persona
a la vez.

BILATERAL CONTRACT. Contrato bilateral. Aquel contrato que
involucra una promesa por una parte a cambio de la promesa de
la otra part. Ejemplo: una persona dice, "te prometo que te vendo
mi carro", por un lado; por el otro, el comprador dice, "te prometo
pagar el precio."

BILL. Escrito, cuenta, documento negociable, pagaré o giro.
(1) Escrito formal enviado a una corte superior informando de
ciertos hechos o solicitando cierta acción. (2) Proyecto de ley en la
legislatura. (3) Ley emitida por el órgano legislativo en funciones
judiciales. (4) Declaración poco común de mucha importancia
como **Bill of Rights**: Carta o Declaración de Derechos. (5) **Bill
of Lading.** Conocimiento de embarque. Lista de mercancía
embarcada. (6) **Bill of Exchange.** Factura de Cambio.
Documento negociable mediante el cual una persona instruye a
otra para que pague cierta suma de dinero a un tercero. (7) **Bill
of Indictment.** Acusación ante un gran jurado. Escrito que
detalla en corte la acusación de un delito. (8) Palabra
antiguamente usada para indicar demanda, solicitud o petición en
una corte de equidad. (9) **Bill of Review.** Solicitud de revisión.
Petición hecha para que la corte deseche o anule una resolución
anterior para un nuevo juicio. No es una reapertura del juicio
anterior. (10) **Bill of Particulars.** Explicación minuciosa de los
hechos que fundan la demanda solicitada por el demandado.

BILL OF RIGHTS. Declaración de Derechos. Las primeras diez
enmiendas de la Constitución de los Estados Unidos de América.

BILLING CYCLE. Período de procesamiento de cuentas. Intervalo
de tiempo entre las fechas en que las cuentas son enviadas a los
clientes.

BIND. Atar, obligar legalmente, comprometer.

BINDER. Cobertura provisional de un seguro. (1) Abono inicial en la compra de una casa.

BINDING AUTHORITIES. Autoridad comprometedora. Fuente de precedentes legales que deben considerarse al decidir un caso.

BINDING INSTRUCTIONS. Instrucciones que debe seguir el jurado respecto a la decisión a tomar si encuentra probados ciertos hechos.

BINDING OVER. Libertad bajo fianza. (1) Transferir a un presunto reo de corte dentro del mismo sistema.

BIRTH. Nacimiento. (1) **Birth Certificate.** Certificado de nacimiento. (2) **Birth Record.** Registro o inscripción del nacimiento.

BLACK ACRE. Nombre inventado para representar un terreno o bien inmueble al explicar o enseñar derecho.

BLACK LETTER LAW. Principios legales que representan los principios básicos seguidos por muchos jueces en la mayoría de los estados. Nombre informal dado generalmente a los principios legales básicos de una jurisdicción en particular.

BLACK MARKET. Mercado negro. Vender bienes que son robados, prohibidos o controlados sin someterse al control legal.

BLACK LIST. Lista negra. Contiene nombres de personas con quien no se debe hacer negocios.

BLACK MAIL. Chantaje. Extorsión. Solicitar ilegalmente dinero mediante la amenaza de revelar la conducta ilegal de una persona o de destruir su reputación.

BLANK. En blanco. (1) Espacios dejados sin llenar en un documento escrito o impreso. (2) Documento modelo con espacios vacíos para llenarse.

BLANK ENDORSEMENT. Endoso en blanco. Hacer un documento negociable pagadero al portador mediante la firma del documento sin especificar a quien se le endosa o firma.

BLASPHEMY. Blasfemia. Ridiculizar a Dios o a la religión.

BLOCK POSITIONS. Colocación en masa. Acción de un corredor de valores al comprar una porción de un paquete grande de valores que su cliente quiere vender porque no las puede vender inmediatamente para luego venderlas por partes.

BLOCKED. (1) Bloqueado, congelado. Restringir la salida o conversión de moneda de un país a otro. (2) Congelar o suspender pagos o retiros de fondos en una cuenta bancaria.

BLOTTER. Registro o informe policíaco. Contiene información sobre el arresto de una persona, sus datos e información sobre lo que ocasionó el arresto.

BLUE BOOK. (1) Libro que muestra la forma correcta de abreviar las referencias de jurisprudencia. (2) Documentos diplomáticos. (3) Lista de nombres de funcionarios del gobierno o de una organización.

BLUE CHIP. Acciones selectas por ser de compañías estables y lucrativas.

BLUE–SKY LAWS. Leyes que regulan la venta de valores en los mercados estatales.

BOARD. Junta, directiva. (1) Personas nombradas o elegidas públicamente para ejercer una función pública. (2) Grupo de personas que dentro de una sociedad privada ejercen una función de administración.

BOARDER. Huésped, pensionista. Persona que paga por comer continuamente en una casa (en ocasiones también paga por una habitación).

BODY. Cuerpo. (1) Corporación. Una persona o sociedad. (2) Colección de leyes. (3) Parte más importante de un documento.

BODY EXECUTION. Orden de detención o arresto. Autoridad legal para quitarle la libertad a una persona y someterla a arresto.

BOGUS. Falso, postizo. Falso y con intenciones de engañar.

433

BOILER–ROOM SALES. Venta de valores hechas bajo gran presión, usualmente por teléfono y a través de fuentes poco comprobables.

BONA. Bienes. Bueno. (1) Propiedades, posesiones. (2) Honestamente; de buena fe.

BONA FIDE. De buena fe. Honestamente.

BONA FIDE PURCHASER. Comprador de buena fe. El que compra algo honestamente, paga un precio razonable y desconoce el que otra persona tenga un reclamo sobre lo comprado.

BONA INMOBILIA. Bienes inmuebles. Propiedad inmueble. Terrenos.

BOND. Bono, título, fianza. (1) Documento que refleja la deuda de una compañía o del gobierno. Se compromete a pagar un porcentaje de interés por cierto tiempo y al vencimiento del préstamo se cancela lo prestado. (2) **Adjustment Bond.** Bono emitido al reorganizar una sociedad o corporación. (3) **Convertible Bond.** Bono que puede convertirse en acciones. (4) **Coupon Bond.** Bono de cupones que se entregan periódicamente para reclamar los intereses. (5) **Debenture Bond.** Bono respaldado por la confianza en un gobierno o entidad más que en sus propiedades. (6) **Guaranteed Bond.** Bono garantizado por una compañía distinta a aquella que lo emite. (7) **Municipal Bond.** Emitido por gobiernos locales para financiar proyectos locales. (8) **Serial Bond.** Bonos emitidos a la vez con distintas fechas de pago cada uno. (9) **Series Bond.** Bonos exactamente iguales pero emitidos en intervalos de tiempo. (10) **Term Bond.** Bonos que se vencen todos a la vez. (11) **Appeal Bond.** Bono o fianza de apelación para cubrir los gastos de la parte que triunfa en la apelación si pierde el apelante. (12) **Attachment Bond.** Fianza de embargo. Puesta como garantía para liberar un bien embargado. (13) **Fidelity Bond.** Fianza de fidelidad para proteger a una empresa de hurtos por parte de sus empleados.

BONDED WAREHOUSE. Almacén de aduanas. Depósito fiscal. Bodega donde se guardan bienes hasta que paguen el impuesto que les corresponde.

BONDSMAN. Fiador. La persona que paga una fianza.

BONIFICATION. Bonificación. El no cobrar impuesto sobre bienes para la exportación. Tiene el mismo efecto que la devolución de impuestos.

BOOKKEEPER. Tenedor de libros. Contador.

BOOKKEEPING. Contabilidad. Llevar por escrito las transacciones financieras de una compañía de forma sistemática.

BOOT. Añadido a una negociación.

BOOTSTRAP SALE. Usar los activos de una compañía recién comprada para pagar parte del costo de comprar la compañía.

BOROUGH. Municipio, villa, ayuntamiento. División territorial y política de un estado.

BORROWER. Prestatario. Persona que pide dinero prestado.

BOTTOMRY. Préstamo a la gruesa. Préstamo para reparar o equipar un buque.

BOUGHT AND SOLD NOTES. Notificaciones de compra y venta hechas por un corredor de valores al comprador y al vendedor.

BOYCOTT. Boicot. Negación de comerciar con una empresa y el intento de que otros tampoco negocien con ella.

BRACKET. Categoría, grupo, clase. Usualmente se refiere a un nivel en una escala de impuestos.

BRAIN DEATH RULE. Principio de muerte del cerebro. De acuerdo a este principio una persona está muerta cuando el cerebro deja de funcionar total e irreversiblemente aunque otras partes del cuerpo aún funcionen.

BRANDEIS BRIEF. Resumen de un caso apelado que incluye estudios sociológicos y económicos además de argumentos legales.

BREACH. Violación, incumplimiento. Violar una ley o no cumplir una obligación.

BREACH OF CONTRACT. Violación de contrato. Dejar de hacer lo que se contrató sin excusa legal alguna. Incluye el impedir que la otra parte cumpla lo que contrató para hacer.

BREACH OF PEACE. Alteración de la paz u orden público. Término vago que es tratado de diferente forma por los diversos estados.

BREACH OF PROMISE. Incumplimiento o violación de los esponsales. Romper la promesa de contraer matrimonio.

BREACH OF TRUST. Abuso o violación de confianza. Falta de un fiduciario de hacer algo para lo cual se le requiere.

BREAKING. Violación de domicilio. Usar la fuerza o algún modo de destruir la propiedad, usualmente para entrar ilegalmente a un inmueble.

BREAKING A CASE. Resolución de un delito. (1) Discusión informal de un caso por los jueces de apelación.

BREAKING BULK OR BAIL. Delito de abrir un recipiente o envase encomendado a quien lo abrió y hurtar parte de su contenido.

BREATHALYZER. Examen diseñado para determinar el porcentaje de alcohol en la sangre de una persona detenida por manejar embriagada.

BREVE. Auto o mandamiento. Orden judicial.

BRIBERY. Soborno. Cohecho. Ofrecer, dar, recibir o pedir cualquier cosa de valor para influenciar la acción de un funcionario público.

BRIDGE LOAN. Préstamo o financiamiento a corto plazo.

BRIEF. Resumen, alegato. (1) Sumario escrito de las ideas o contenido de un documento. (2) Escrito preparado por una parte para explicar su caso al tribunal. (3) Resumen de una opinión pública en un caso. (4) Ropa interior de caballero.

BROAD FORM. Cobertura amplia. Tipo de seguro que cubre más que los riesgos básicos de una casa.

BROAD INTERPRETATION. Interpretación amplia de la ley basada en el espíritu e intención real en lugar de en su sentido literal.

BROCAGE. Corretaje. Intermediario en una actividad.

BROKER. Corredor. Agente contratado para negociar. (1) **Insurance Broker.** Corredor de Seguros. (2) **Real Estate Broker.** Corredor de Bienes Raíces. (3) **Securities Broker.** Corredor de Valores.

BROKERAGE. Corretaje. Intermediación en una actividad o negociación.

BROTHER. Colega. Abogado, hermano.

BROTUM FULMEN. (Lat.) Sentencia que no puede ejecutarse debido a una imperfección obvia.

BROWN DECISION. Jurisprudencia de la Corte Suprema Federal que declara inconstitucional la segregación racial en las escuelas públicas.

BUCKET SHOP. Negocio fraudulento de aceptar órdenes de vender o comprar valores sin negociarlos.

BUDGET. Presupuesto. (1) Dinero estimado para un propósito especial. (2) Dinero estimado que se usará en un período de tiempo.

BUGGERY. Sodomía, bestialidad. Sexo anal. Sexo de forma no natural. Delito contra la naturaleza del ser humano.

BUILDING CODE. Código de construcción. Contiene las leyes de construcción y uso de edificios.

BUILDING LINE. Línea de edificación. Distancia del límite de un terreno dentro de la cual no se puede edificar o construir.

BULK TRANSFER. Transferencia en masa o en volumen que no está en el curso ordinario de un negocio. Tiende a perjudicar a los acreedores.

BULL MARKET. Subida general del mercado de valores.

BULLETIN. Boletín. Publicaciones legales, como panfletos, que contienen una legislación.

BUMPING. (1) Acción de un empleado de menor jerarquía de ocupar un cargo de otro empleado de mayor rango. (2) Acción de una aerolínea de rehusar acomodar a un pasajero en el avión porque se vendieron más boletos aéreos que asientos disponibles.

BURDEN OF PROOF. Carga o peso de la prueba. En cieirtos casos la obligación de la parte que alega un hecho o un derecho de probar con evidencias la realidad de lo que se alega o reclama.

BUREAU. Oficina, agencia.

BUREAUCRACY. Burocracia. (1) Organización con menos personal en los niveles superiores que en los inferiores. (2) Delegación de autoridad de nivel a nivel en dirección descendiente. (3) Sistema rígido de papeleo y procedimientos.

BUFORD DOCTRINE. Doctrina que establece que las cortes federales pueden rehusarse a conocer casos que involucren leyes estatales complejas.

BURGLARY. Hurto. Violación de domicilio para cometer un delito. Algunos estados no requieren que la violación del domicilio sea con fuerza o destrucción.

BURSAR. Tesorero. Persona que administra dinero de una organización.

BUSINESS. Negocio, asunto.

BUSINESS AGENT. Agente comercial. Delegado sindical. (1) Persona que representa a una compañía en negociaciones. (2) Aquél que representa al sindicato en negociaciones laborales.

BUSINESS EXPENSE. Gasto necesario para producir la renta de un comercio o empresa.

BUSINESS JUDGMENT RULE. Principio de discreción comercial que establece que si la decisión se dio de forma razonada y prudente, aunque el efecto sea perjudicial, ninguna corte la investigará.

BUSINESS RECORD EXCEPTION. Excepción al principio procesal de que la promesa referencial o de oídas no se admite en corte, que establece que cierto tipo de documentos creados y mantenidos por negocios son aceptables como evidencia en procedimientos legales.

"BUT FOR" RULE. Principio que establece que la negligencia de por sí no hace a una persona responsable de los daños causados a menos que la negligencia causase los daños.

BUY. Compra.

BUY AMERICAN ACTS. Leyes que protegen a los productos hechos en los Estados Unidos. Usualmente dirigidas a las compras del gobierno.

BUY AND SELL AGREEMENT. Acuerdo de compra y venta mediante el cual los asociados en un negocio acuerdan comprarse sus porciones si uno muere o se retira del negocio.

BUYER 60 CONTRACT. Contrato de compra de acciones a un valor superior al valor en el momento de la compra, con el derecho a pagar 60 días después de la compra.

BY-BIDDING. Postor que eleva el precio de un bien subastado o en licitación sin la intención real de comprarlo.

BY-PRODUCT. Subproducto.

BUYER. Comprador. La persona que paga con dinero para adquirir un producto.

BY-LAWS. Estatutos. Reglas o reglamentos adoptados por una sociedad o corporación.

C

C. (1) Cent, cents. (2) Derechos de autor.

C.A. "Court of Appeals". Corte de Apelación.

C.A.B. "Civil Aeronautics Board". Junta de Aeronáutica Civil.

C.A.F. "Cost and Freight". Costo y Flete. Precio de una mercancía que incluye su costo y el costo de su flete. No incluye el seguro.

C.C.A. "Circuit Court of Appeals". Corte de Apelación de Circuito.

C.D. "Certificate of Deposit". Certificado de Depósito. Documento que demuestra la existencia de un depósito a plazo.

C.F.I. "Cost Freight and Insurance". Costo, flete y seguro. Precio de un producto que incluye su costo, el costo del flete y el costo del seguro.

C.I.A. "Central Inteligence Agency". Agencia Central de Inteligencia.

C.J. (1) "Chief Justice". Magistrado Presidente. (2) Corpus Juris. Enciclopedia legal. (3) "Circuit Judge". Juez de Circuito.

C.J.S. Corpus Juris Secundum. Edición actualizada de la Enciclopedia de Derecho Corpus Juris.

C.L. "Civil Law". Derecho Civil.

C.L.A. "Certified Legal Assistant". Asistente Legal Certificado por la Asociación Nacional de Asistentes Legales.

C.O.D. "Collect on Delivery". Cobrado al entregarse. Indica que el precio de los bienes o cargos de entrega serán pagados a la persona por el destinatario.

C.P.A. "Certified Public Accountant". Contador Público Autorizado.

C.P.I. "Consumer Price Index". Indice de precios del consumidor. Indice que refleja el precio promedio de ciertos bienes comprados por el consumidor. Es usado como un índice para medir la inflación económica.

CABINET. Gabinete. Junta asesora de máxima jerarquía en un gobierno.

CAFETERIA PLAN. Plan de beneficio para empleados que le permite al trabajador seleccionar uno de varios beneficios ofrecidos por el patrono. Estos planes están libres de impuestos.

CALENDAR. Calendario de juicios. Lista de casos listos para audiencia.

CALL. Llamada. Convocatoria, opción. (1) Anuncio público. (2) Cobro formal de una deuda de acuerdo al contrato.

CALL PREMIUM. En el mercado de valores, la cantidad de dinero que, sobre el valor nominal, debe pagar una compañía cuando desea volver a comprar los valores que ha emitido.

CALLABLE. (1) Redimibles o pagaderos a la vista. (2) **Callable Bonds.** Redimibles por la compañía que los paga antes de su fecha de vencimiento.

CALUMNY. Calumnia. Falsa acusación. Delito que consiste en decir una mentira sobre otra persona.

CANCEL. Cancelar. Eliminar la validez de un documento; destruir sus efectos.

CANCELLATION. Cancelación. Terminar un contrato o rehusarse a seguir con un contrato debido a que la otra parte no ha cumplido su obligación.

CANCELLATION CLAUSE. Cláusula que permite la cancelación de un contrato al ocurrir cierto evento.

CANCELLED CHECK. Cheque cancelado.

CANDIDATE. Candidato. Persona que aspira ser designado o elegido.

CANON. Canon. (1) Ley, regla, principio. (2) **Canons of Judicial Ethics.** Reglas y normas de ética seguida por los miembros de la magistratura. (3) **Canons of Professional Responsibility.** Normas y principios que describen el comportamiento profesional de un abogado ante la corte, el público y otros miembros de la profesión.

CANON LAW. Derecho Canónico. Ley de la religión cristiana.

CANONICAL DISABILITY. Impotencia física incurable o incapacidad de copular.

CANVASS. Escudriñar, examinar. (1) Escrutinio de votos en una elección para determinar la autenticidad de cada uno y la precisión del total. (2) Solicitar ventas u órdenes a domicilio. (3) Muestrario estadístico.

CAPACITY. (1) Capacidad. Habilidad de hacer algo. (2) Derecho legal de hacer algo.

CAPITAL. Capital. (1) De mayor jerarquía. Por ejemplo, el delito que conlleva pena capital o de muerte es un delito capital. (2) Activos o valores. (3) **Capital Assets.** Activos o propiedad que no está a la venta. (4) **Capital Budget.** Presupuesto para inversiones a largo plazo. (5) **Capital Cost.** Mejoras a la propiedad que pueden deducirse de los impuestos. (6) **Capital Gains Tax.** Impuesto a las ganancias de capital. (7) **Capital Goods.** Bienes usados en la producción de otros bienes. (8) **Capital Returns.** En impuestos, pagos recibidos y no gravados por ser el retorno de dinero ya pagado. (9) **Capital Stocks.** Acciones cambiadas por dinero invertido en una compañía. (10) **Capital Surplus.** Exceso sobre el valor nominal de una acción pagado por los accionistas a la compañía.

CAPITALISM. Capitalismo. Doctrina económica que permite que la empresa privada controle los medios de producción y comercio en un mercado más o menos sin restricciones.

CAPITALIZATION. El total de los valores emitidos por una compañía, por ejemplo, bonos o acciones.

CAPITALIZE. Capitalizar. (1) Emitir acciones o valores para cubrir una inversión. (2) Calcular el valor presente de una inversión.

CAPRICIOUS. Caprichoso. Que no está basado en la razón, la ley o los hechos.

CAPTION. Encabezamiento. Parte introductoria de un documento que contiene el nombre de las partes, el caso, la corte, etc.

CARE. Custodiar. Cuidar, cuidado, diligencia. Un concepto crítico en la ley de negligencia. (1) **Reasonable Care.** Cuidado razonable que se espera de una persona normal bajo ciertas circunstancias. (2) **Ordinary Care.** El cuidado y la diligencia que una persona normal debe usar en situaciones ordinarias. Véase "Diligence", "Due care", "Negligence".

CARNAL KNOWLEDGE. Contacto o relación sexual. Coito.

CARRIER. Transportador, portador. Persona u organización dedicada al transporte de personas o cosas.

CARRIER'S LIEN. Gravamen o garantía del transportador. Derecho del que transporta de retener los bienes transportados hasta que el porte del transporte sea pagado.

CARRY BACK OR CARRY OVER. Regla Fiscal que le permite al contribuyente usar sus pérdidas para reducir el impuesto a pagar en los años anteriores o posteriores al año en que se produjo la pérdida.

CARTE BLANCHE. (Fr.) Término que significa autoridad sin límite o con poder plenipotenciario.

CARTEL. Consorcio, monopolio. Empresas dedicadas a la misma actividad comercial agrupadas para limitar la competencia entre ellas y acabar con la competencia de otros.

CASE. Caso. Demanda. Juicio.

CASE IN CHIEF. Esa parte de un juicio en que un litigante expone y plantea su caso ante la corte.

CASE IN POINT. Precedente legal de una misma corte u otra superior que decide un caso similar.

CASE LAW. Derecho jurisprudencial o basado en precedentes judiciales. Leyes y principios legales los cuales están basados en casos decididos por las cortes. Precedentes legales. Derecho creado a través de las decisiones judiciales.

CASE METHOD OR CASE SYSTEM. Método de enseñanza por casos. Forma de enseñar el derecho en la mayoría de las universidades norteamericanas, bajo la cual se estudian casos que sirven como precedentes para obtener de ellos principios legales.

CASE WORKER. Trabajador social asignado a trabajar con clientes en comunidades de bajos recursos económicos.

CASEBOOK. Libro de casos. Texto que se usa en las Universidades y que contiene los precedentes legales.

CASH. Dinero en efectivo.

CASH BASIS. Base en efectivo. Método de contabilidad que muestra las ganancias y pérdidas de una compañía según se producen los ingresos y egresos.

CASH FLOW. (1) Efectivo que recibe una persona o compañía menos el que gasta en un período de tiempo. (2) Ganancias netas más depreciación.

CASH OUT. Vender. Convertir en dinero una cosa por medio de venta.

CASH PRICE. Precio de venta en efectivo. Valor de un bien si es pagado en efectivo.

CASH VALUE. Valor en efectivo o valor en el mercado. Valor que tendría un bien al venderse públicamente en el mercado.

CASHIER'S CHECK. Cheque de gerencia. Cheque que el banco certifica que será pagado, emitido a nombre del banco y firmado por un oficial del banco.

CASUAL. Casual, accidental.

CASUAL EMPLOYMENT. Un empleo ocasional por un período indeterminado y sin requisitos técnicos para el empleado.

CASUALTY. Pérdida, accidente. (1) Una persona herida o muerta. (2) Accidente imprevisto.

CASUALTY LOSS. Pérdida fortuita o accidental. Pérdida que puede ser deducible para efectos fiscales o cubierta bajo una póliza de seguro.

CASUS BELLI. (Lat.) Un evento que justifica o puede causar una guerra.

CASUS FORTUITO. (Lat.) Hecho inevitable o fortuito, (que causa un accidente.)

CAUCUS. Junta dentro de un grupo. (1) Reunión de electores para elegir delegados a una convención. (2) Subgrupo informal de un cuerpo mayor.

CAUSA. (Lat.) Causa, razón. Aquello que produce un efecto.

CAUSA MORTIS. (Lat.) Una acción tomada por causa de muerte.

CAUSATION. El hecho que hace que algo ocurra o suceda. Una doctrina importante en la ley de negligencia y en Derecho Criminal.

CAUSE. Causa. (1) Aquello que produce un efecto. (2) Motivo o razón para algo. (3) Demanda o acción legal. (4) Abreviación de "Just Cause" o causa justificada para reemplazar o destituir un funcionario o empleado de su cargo. (5) **Direct or Immediate Cause.** Acción que causa un evento. Véase "Proximate Cause". (6) **Superseding Cause.** Un evento que interviene entre la acción inicial y el resultado final y torna la acción inicial inofensiva.

CAUSE OF ACTION. Fundamento legal y material de una demanda. Causa de Acción. (1) Hechos que sostienen una demanda. (2) Derecho sobre el cual se basa una demanda o un pleito.

CAUTION. Cautela. Advertencia. Amonestación. Advertencia formalmente dada.

CAUTIONARY INSTRUCTION. Instrucciones de cautela. Instrucciones dictadas al jurado advirtiéndole que no considere evidencia extraña al juicio al momento de emitir su veredicto.

CAVEAT. (Lat.) Advertencia. A riesgo de. (1) **Caveat Emptor.** Compra efectuada a riesgo del comprador. (2) Dejadlo precaverse. Advertencia dada al juez o a un oficial notificándole que tiene que tener cuidado con sus actos.

CEASE AND DESIST ORDER. Orden de cesar y desistir. Orden dada por una agencia administrativa o una corte que prohibe a alguien seguir con una actividad o una conducta particular.

CEDE. Ceder. Transferir. Asignar. Contrato mediante el cual una persona transfiere sus derechos y obligaciones a otra.

CELEBRATION. Celebración. Ceremonia formal.

CENSOR. Çensor. El que censura algo. Uno que revisa una publicación o una película para ver que el contenido no ofenda la moral pública.

CENSORSHIP. Censura. (1) Negación de la libertad de expresión o de prensa. (2) Revisión de libros o publicaciones por razones de moralidad.

CENSURE. Censurar. Reprimenda formal. Reprobar una acción.

CENSUS BUREAU. Oficina de censos. Agencia federal que cuenta a la población cada 10 años y mantiene estadísticas oficiales.

CENTER OF GRAVITY DOCTRINE. Doctrina del centro de gravedad. Principio legal que establece que en caso de haber conflicto de leyes, una corte debe escoger la ley del estado que tiene los contactos o las relaciones más importantes con los hechos, personas o derechos de la demanda.

CEREMONIAL MARRIAGE. Matrimonio ejecutado por una persona competente con licencia válida y en cumplimiento de las leyes estatales respectivas.

CERTAIN. Seguro, preciso, libre de duda, definitivo, sin ambigüedad.

CERTAINTY. Certeza. Véase "Certain".

CERTIFICATE. Certificado. Afirmación escrita de que algo ha sido hecho o de que se satisfizo algún requisito formal. (1) **Certificate of Acknowledgment.** Certificado de reconocimiento dado por un notario. (2) **Certificate of Convenience and Necessity.** Licencia de operación para empresas de servicio público. (3) **Certificate of Deposit.** Certificado de depósito. Depósito a plazo en un banco que recibe un interés preferencial. (4) **Certificate of Occupancy.** Certificado de ocupación. Permite el uso de un edificio por haber cumplido con las regulaciones de zonificación y construcción. (5) **Certificate of Incorporation.** Instrumento legal mediante el cual una compañía es incorporada bajo los estatutos de un estado. (6) **Certificate of Good Conduct.** Un escrito oficial que verifica el buen carácter de una persona para ciertas actividades. (7) **Certificate of Redemption.** Documento que prueba que una persona ha redimido una propiedad después de su venta judicial. (8) **Certificate of Title.** Documento que verifica el título de la propiedad, usualmente mediante un seguro de título. Véase "Title Insurance", "Insurance".

CERTIFICATION. Certificación. (1) Proceso mediante el cual una corte federal remite una cuestión relacionada con la ley estatal a la máxima corte de dicho estado y se abstiene de resolver el caso hasta tanto esa cuestión legal sea decidida por la corte estatal. (2) **Certification Proceeding.** Mecanismo laboral mediante el cual los empleados seleccionan a un sindicato laboral para que los represente ante el patrón.

CERTIFIED. Certificado. Oficialmente aprobado o revisado.

CERTIFIED PUBLIC ACCOUNTANT. Contador Público Certificado.

CERTIORARI. (Lat.) Auto de avocación mediante el cual una corte superior solicita a una inferior que le remita una causa para determinar si han habido irregularidades en el procedimiento. Véase "Writ of Certiorari".

CESSION. Cesión, traspaso.

447

CESSIONARY BANKRUPT. Cesión de lo quebrado o fallido. Cesión que hace una persona de todos sus bienes para que sean divididos entre sus acreedores.

CESTUI QUE. (Lat.) Aquél que. (1) **"Cestui que" Trust.** Beneficiario de un fideicomiso, fideicomisario.

CHAIN. Cadena. (1) **Chain of Custody.** En la ley de evidencia, aquél que en un juicio presenta evidencia física de una cosa, debe demonstrar su posesión desde el momento del recibo hasta el juicio. (2) **Chain of Title.** Cadena, resumen o historia del título de propiedad. Lista que contiene en orden consecutivo los traspasos de un bien inmueble. (3) **Chain Picketing.** Cadena o línea de piqueteo. Piqueteo en varios establecimientos de una misma empresa.

CHALLENGE. Recusación, objeción, tacha.

CHAMBER OF COMMERCE. Cámara de Comercio. Asociación que promueve el comercio de su área.

CHAMBERS. Despacho del juez. (1) **In Chambers.** En el despacho del juez y fuera de la sala de corte.

CHAMPERTY. Comprar el derecho en un litigio a cambio de participación en la ganancias del proceso.

CHANCELLOR. Canciller. Juez. (1) **Cabeza del sistema universitario estatal.** (2) **Juez de equidad.**

CHANCERY. Cancillería. (1) **Jurisprudencia de una corte en función de corte de equidad.** (2) **Corte de Equidad.**

CHANGE OF VENUE. Cambiar el sitio donde se ha de desenvolver un procedimiento legal. Cambio de tribunal.

CHAPTER ELEVEN. Capítulo Once. Capítulos de las leyes federales de quiebra mediante los cuales se reorganiza un negocio bajo la supervisión de una corte federal para formar una nueva sociedad anónima donde los acreedores se convierten en accionistas.

CHAPTER SEVEN. Capítulo Siete. Ley de quiebra para las personas naturales. Véase "Bankruptcy".

CHAPTER THIRTEEN. Capítulo Trece o procedimiento de rehabilitación bajo la ley de quiebra, mediante el cual se le permite a un individuo o pequeña empresa pagar sólo parte de su deuda, u obtener mayores plazos en sus deudas, o ambos. Una vez que la corte aprueba el plan, los acreedores deben aceptarlo.

CHARACTER EVIDENCE. Prueba testimonial del carácter o solvencia moral de una persona. Testimonio acerca de los hábitos y la reputación de una persona.

CHARGE. Cargo, imputación, obligación, carga. (1) Instrucciones finales que da el juez al jurado. (2) Acusación formal de un delito. (3) Cuando se compra algo a plazo.

CHARGE D'AFFAIRE. (Fr.) Encargado de negocios en una misión diplomática cuando no hay embajador.

CHARGE OFF. Disminución del valor de algún activo en los registros de una compañía.

CHARITABLE. Caritativo o de beneficencia. (1) **Charitable Institution.** Institución de beneficencia. (2) **Charitable Contribution.** Contribución de Beneficencia hecha al gobierno o a una institución de caridad, religiosa, científica, educativa o similar; estas contribuciones son deducibles de impuestos. (3) **Charitable Deduction.** Deducción de beneficencia. Véase "Charitable Contribution". (4) **Charitable Trust.** Fideicomiso para el bien público.

CHARITY. Caridad o beneficencia. Que no tiene fines de lucro.

CHARTER. (1) Contrato de flete mediante el cual se alquila un buque, avión, etc. (2) Pacto social o escritura que contiene los artículos mediante los cuales se constituye una sociedad o una corporación.

CHARTERED ACCOUNTANT. Contador Público Autorizado en Inglaterra.

CHATTEL. Bien mueble. Propiedad personal; animales. (1) **Chattel Mortgage.** Hipoteca sobre bien mueble. (2) **Chattel Paper.** Documento que muestra que una deuda está garantizada por otros bienes.

CHEAT. Engañar, estafar.

CHECK. Cheque. Documento negociable mediante el cual una persona instruye a su banco para que le pague una suma cierta de dinero a otra persona.

CHECK–OFF. Sistema mediante el cual un sindicato cobra por descuento directo del salario, a través de la empresa, la mensualidad de sus miembros.

CHECKS AND BALANCES. La división del poder gubernamental entre varias ramas, cada una con igual peso, para evitar el poder absoluto de una rama.

CHICANERY. Trampa, fraude.

CHIEF. Jefe. El que tiene mayor jerarquía sobre otros. **Chief Justice.** Magistrado Presidente.

CHILD. Niño, menor de edad. (1) **Child Abuse.** Cualquier tipo de crueldad o abuso que afecta el bienestar de un niño. (2) **Child Support.** Obligación legal de los padres de pagar por el mantenimiento económico de sus hijos.

CHILLING. Congelado. (1) Una conspiración para no inflar el precio de un artículo y así adquirirlo barato. (2) **Chilling Effect.** Efecto desalentador que tiene una ley cuando procura que las personas no hagan uso de un derecho constitucional.

CHOATE. Completo. Cuando algo se ha perfeccionado o madurado. Véase "Inchoate".

CHOICE OF LAW. Seleccionar la Ley. El mecanismo o análisis mediante el cual una corte decide qué ley aplicar a un caso que puede ser regido por las leyes de diferentes estados.

CHOSE. Cosa. Objeto de propiedad personal.

CHOSE IN ACTION. Derecho de entablar una demanda para recuperar una deuda o dinero.

CHURNING. Acción de un corredor mediante la cual éste ejecuta transacciones sin la autorización de su cliente en detrimento de éste para ganar mayor comisión.

CIRCUIT. Circuito. (1) **Circuit Court.** Corte de circuito. Nombre dado a la corte de cierto nivel en un estado. No es igual en todos los estados. (2) **Circuit Court of Appeals.** Corte de Apelaciones.

CIRCULAR NOTE. Un instrumento similar a una carta de crédito, girado por un banco local contra un banco corresponsal en el exterior, pagadero a un viajero.

CIRCUMSTANCIAL EVIDENCE. Prueba o evidencia circunstancial, no basada en observaciones directas del hecho que se quiere probar. Que indirectamente prueba un hecho principal alegado.

CITATION. Emplazamiento, citación. (1) Orden para que comparezca alguien ante la corte. (2) Referencia a un precedente o autoridad legal indicando donde se encuentra. En derecho jurisprudencial, cada ley o caso debe citar su origen.

CITATOR. Citador. Libros que indican lo acontecido a un caso o afirmación luego de ser ventilado. Indica si se anuló o si se sigue como precedente. También cita a todos los otros casos que citan a un caso en particular como autoridad de un principio o una norma de derecho.

CITE. Cita. (1) Orden dada a una persona para que concurra a la corte. (2) Se refiere a precedentes legales, describiendo dónde se puede encontrar la autoridad citada.

CITIZEN. Ciudadano. (1) **U.S. Citizen.** Persona nacida o naturalizada en los Estados Unidos. (2) La persona con residencia en un estado de los Estados Unidos es ciudadano de ese estado.

CITIZEN'S ARREST. Arresto por un ciudadano. Arresto efectuado por una persona privada en lugar de un policía.

CIVIL. Civil. (1) Que no es criminal o penal. (2) Relacionado al gobierno.

CIVIL ACTION. Acción Civil. Toda demanda o pleito que no sea penal. Acción para recuperar algo o protejer o ejercer un derecho.

CIVIL COMMITMENT. Interdicción civil. Orden no penal que interna a una persona en un hospital mental por locura, alcoholismo o drogadicción.

CIVIL DEATH. Muerte civil. Pérdida de todos los derechos civiles. Usualmente se refiere al condenado a cadena perpetua.

CIVIL DISABILITIES. Incapacidad civil. Pérdida de algunos derechos. Usualmente luego de ser condenado. Por ejemplo: derecho al voto, a ocupar puestos públicos, etc.

CIVIL DISOBEDIENCE. Desobediencia Civil. Violación de una ley para demostrar su injusticia o para llamar la atención sobre un problema.

CIVIL JURY TRIAL. Un juicio civil donde un jurado resuelve toda disputa sobre los hechos en cuestión. La corte resuelve toda cuestión de índole legal.

CIVIL LAW. Derecho civil. (1) Derecho Romano. (2) Derecho basado en un código. (3) Gobierno de civiles en lugar de militares. (4) Gobierno organizado en lugar de un gobierno anárquico. Sistema jurídico basado en códigos de derecho en vez de opiniones jurídicas o precedentes legales.

CIVIL LIABILITY. La obligación de una persona de pagar por los daños después de un pleito.

CIVIL LIBERTIES. Derechos civiles. Derechos garantizados en la constitución a todas las personas en el país.

CIVIL PROCEDURE. Derecho procesal civil. Reglas o normas que regulan el procedimiento en casos no penales. Las reglas conocidas como "Rules of Civil Procedure" que regulan todas las fases de un pleito.

CIVIL RIGHTS. Derechos Civiles. Véase "Civil Liberties". (1) **Civil Rights Acts.** Leyes federales aprobadas después de la guerra civil, que prohiben la discriminación por razón de raza, color, edad, sexo, religión o nacionalidad.

CIVIL SERVICE. Servicio Civil. Término que generalmente se usa para identificar a empleados gubernamentales, sean federales o estatales; los empleados gubernamentales usualmente son regidos por leyes que protegen los derechos de los empleados.

CIVIL SUIT. Demanda civil. Véase "Civil Action".

CIVILIAN. Ciudadano privado. Que no es miembro de las fuerzas armadas.

CLAIM. Reclamo, demanda.

CLAIM ADJUSTER. Ajustador de reclamos. Persona que determina el valor de un reclamo en una compañía de seguros.

CLAIM AND DELIVERY. Acción antigua para recobrar una cosa más los daños causados.

CLAIM FOR RELIEF. Base de la demanda moderna. Lo que el demandante solicita si los hechos alegados son probados.

CLAIMANT. Demandante, reclamante. El que acude a una corte iniciando un juicio contra otro en reclamo de algo.

CLASS ACTION. Demanda conjunta, acción colectiva. Demanda interpuesta por todos los que están en igualdad de situación. Normalmente es iniciada por una persona quien solicita que la corte lo certifique como representante de una clase. La querella por los daños a repararse es aquélla de la clase (o del grupo) y no del demandante.

CLASS DIRECTORS. Directores de corporaciones cuyos períodos como directores son escalonados.

CLASS GIFT. Donaciones a personas de una misma clase, como los nietos. La cuota para cada miembro de la clase depende del número de miembros de la clase.

CLASSIFIED. Clasificado, secreto. Que no es accesible a todos.

CLAUSE. Cláusula, párrafo, oración.

CLEAN HANDS. De buena fe. Actuar honesta y justamente en la demanda que se tramita. Doctrina de equidad que ayuda a aquellos que actúan de buena fe.

CLEAR. Despejar. (1) Pago de un cheque por el Banco contra el cual se giró. (2) Libre de dudas y restricciones. (3) Libre de gravámenes o impuestos.

CLEAR AND CONVINCING PROOF. Prueba clara y convincente. Evidencia con mayor peso que la requerida en asuntos civiles, i.e., la evidencia de mayor peso. Evidencia que es clara y convincente pero no necesariamente libre de duda razonable.

CLEAR AND PRESENT DANGER. Doctrina de censura de la libertad de expresión, limitándola si tiende a causar violencia o peligro.

CLEAR TITLE. Título limpio. Que no tiene restricciones o dudas.

CLEARANCE CARD. (1) Documento de aduana dado a un buque para que zarpe. (2) Carta de buena conducta dada a un empleado cuando deja el trabajo.

CLEARING. Véase "Clear". (1) Acción de eliminar las causas que pesan sobre un título. (2) Zarpe de un buque luego de cumplir con las regulaciones aduaneras y de salud. (3) Liquidación de balances.

CLEARINGHOUSE. Asociación o lugar donde los bancos cambian cheques girados contra cada uno de los diversos bancos, y donde saldan sus cuentas cada día.

CLEMENCY. Clemencia. Trato indulgente a un criminal; reducción de la pena de un criminal.

CLERICAL ERROR. Error de oficina. Error cometido mientras se copiaba un documento o se escribía algo en contraposición al error de juicio o en la decisión.

CLERK. Secretario, oficinista. Secretario o empleado de un juzgado que mantiene registros, archivos, etc.

CLERKSHIP. Pasantía. Empleo de un estudiante de Derecho en un juzgado u oficina de abogados en una posición temporal para entrenarlo en la práctica del Derecho.

CLIENT. Cliente. Aquél que emplea los servicios de un abogado.

CLIENT SECURITY FUND. Fondo establecido por abogados en diferentes estados para compensar a clientes que han sido defraudados por un abogado deshonesto.

CLIENT PRIVILEGE. El derecho de un cliente a mantener secretas las comunicaciones con su abogado.

CLOSE. Cerrado. Terminado. Clausurado.

CLOSE CORPORATION. Sociedad anónima de unos cuantos dueños. El capital está en manos de pocos y la sociedad no vende acciones.

CLOSED MORTGAGE. Hipoteca cerrada. Que no puede ser prepagada sin el consentimiento del hipotecario.

CLOSED SHOP. Tienda cerrada. Empresa agremiada. Empresa que no puede contratar empleados para ciertos puestos si no pertenecen a un determinado sindicato.

CLOSED–END MORTGAGE. Hipoteca de fin cerrado. Que no permite préstamos adicionales bajo el mismo contrato.

CLOSELY HELD. Con pocos dueños. Compañía cuyos dueños son una familia u otra compañía.

CLOSING. Cierre. Consumación de la transacción que implica el traspaso de un bien inmueble. Incluye la determinación de la hipoteca, el pago, y la entrega del título.

CLOTURE. Procedimiento legislativo que permite terminar la discusión sobre una ley propuesta y llamar a votación sobre la misma.

CLOUD ON TITLE. Gravamen sobre un título o acción que se puede interponer sobre el inmueble, disminuyendo su valor.

CO. Prefijo de con, juntos, en unidad. Abreviatura de compañía o condado.

COACHING. Acto de entrenar. Acción de un abogado instruyendo a un testigo sobre cómo declarar.

CO–CONSPIRATORS RULE. Regla de la co-conspiración. La declaración de un miembro de una conspiración puede usarse contra cualquier otro miembro como evidencia.

CODE. Código. (1) Cuerpo de leyes que forma un sistema completo de legislación sobre alguna materia. (2) Recopilación de las leyes de un país.

CODE CIVIL. Código Civil. Leyes francesas de 1804 que han sido modificadas hasta la actualidad.

CODE OF FEDERAL REGULATIONS. Código de Regulaciones Federales. Compilación de regulaciones federales emitidas por las agencias federales y basadas en las leyes del Congreso. Las regulaciones tienen la misma autoridad que una ley.

CODE OF JUDICIAL CONDUCT. Código de conducta judicial. Reglas de conducta que un juez debe seguir.

CODE OF PROFESSIONAL RESPONSIBILITY. Código de responsabilidad profesional o código de ética. Regula la profesión legal. Contiene los principios éticos y prohibiciones generales para los que ejercen la profesión legal.

CODEX. Código. Libro.

CO–DEFENDANT. Co-demandado, co-acusado, co-encausado. Una de varias partes demandadas en el mismo pleito.

CODE OF MILITARY JUSTICE. Código de justicia militar. Reglas y procedimientos para implementar las leyes aplicables a los miembros de las fuerzas armadas.

CODICIL. Codicilo. Suplemento, modificación o adición que se le hace a un testamento.

CODIFICATION. Codificación. Acción de codificar o hacer un código.

CO–EMPTION. Comprar todo lo disponible de una misma mercancía.

COERCION. Coerción. Fuerza. Hacer que una persona actúe contra su voluntad mediante amenazas o el uso de la fuerza.

COGNATION. Cognación. Consanguinidad. Relación de sangre. Parentesco lineal en lugar del colateral.

COGNIZANCE. Conocimiento. Competencia. Jurisdicción. Poder judicial de conocer un asunto para resolverlo.

COGNOVIT JUDGMENT. Admitir o confesar la sentencia o el fallo de la corte.

COGNOVIT NOTE. Pagaré donde el deudor confiesa deber dinero y admite la sentencia, o permite que el acreedor mismo declare la sentencia a nombre del deudor.

CO–HABITATION. Cohabitación. (1) Vivir juntos. (2) Vivir como marido y mujer. (3) Vivir juntos y tener relaciones sexuales.

COIF. Cofia. Toca. (1) Pieza antiguamente usada por jueces para sujetarse la peluca. (2) Una fraternidad legal de honor compuesta por los mejores estudiantes de Derecho.

CO–INSURANCE. Seguro de riesgo compartido. División del riesgo entre la compañía de seguros y el cliente.

COLLAPSIBLE CORPORATION. Corporación establecida para convertir sus ingresos ordinarios en ganancias de capital.

COLLATERAL. Colateral. Al lado. Dinero o propiedad dada en garantía para respaldar un préstamo.

COLLATERAL ATTACK. Evitar los efectos de una decisión judicial mediante la acción ante otra corte.

COLLATERAL ESTOPPEL. Prohibición de tomar una acción o posición en una corte cuando dicha acción o posición ha sido rechazada en otra corte.

COLLATERAL FACT. Hechos y disputas que no son centrales a la acción ante a la corte.

COLLATERAL WARRANTY. Garantía colateral. (1) Garantía hecha por un ascendiente sobre bienes inmuebles. (2) Garantía sobre un título inmueble hecha por una persona distinta de la que vende. El pleito sólo puede ser iniciado por el comprador original.

COLLATION. Colación. Confrontación. (1) Comparar una copia con su original. (2) Agrupación en partes iguales.

COLLECT. Cobrar. Recaudar.

COLLECTIVE BARGAINING. Negociación colectiva. Negociación que realiza una empresa y un sindicato sobre las condiciones de trabajo.

COLLECTIVE BARGAINING AGREEMENT. Convención colectiva. Contrato que resulta de una negociación colectiva. Véase "Collective Bargaining".

COLLECTIVE BARGAINING UNIT. Unidad de negociación colectiva. Todos los empleados de un mismo departamento o clase de una empresa que forman una unidad para negociaciones.

COLLECTIVISM. Colectivismo, comunismo, socialismo.

COLLECTOR. Albacea, cobrador. Ejecutor o administrador temporal de una herencia.

COLLOQUIUM. Explicación o alegato que hace el demandante en su demanda por calumnia o difamación.

COLLOQUY. Coloquio. Conferencia en privado que tienen los abogados y el juez durante el juicio.

COLLUSION. Confabulación. (1) Acuerdo secreto de dos o más personas para cometer un fraude. (2) Acuerdo entre varias partes para usar medios ilegales para lograr un fin ilegal.

COLOR OF TITLE. Título aparente. Que probablemente no es un título válido pero que parece serlo.

COLORABLE. Falso, aparentemente cierto pero que no lo es.

CO-MARKER. Cogirador, fiador. Persona que además de otra, firma un documento negociable responsabilizándose por el pago.

COMBINATION. Combinación. (1) Grupo que trabaja para un propósito ilegal. (2) Unión de dos o más inventos para crear uno nuevo.

COMFORT LETTER. Carta dada por un contador indicando que luego de una revisión informal, los registros contables aparecen en orden aunque la aprobación oficial requeriría una auditoría.

COMITY. Cortesía y respeto. (1) Aceptar algo no como un deber legal sino como gesto de buena voluntad. (2) **Judicial Comity.** Cuando una corte reconoce las leyes o decisiones de otra corte foránea por cortesía y respeto.

COMMERCE. Comercio.

COMMERCE CLAUSE. Disposición constitucional que le permite al Congreso regular y controlar el comercio internacional y entre estados. También llamado poder del comercio o "commerce power."

COMMERCIAL CODE. Código uniforme de comercio aprobado por la mayoría de los Estados. Véase "U.C.C." o "Uniform Commercial Code".

COMMERCIAL INSURANCE. Seguro contra riesgo comercial. (1) Seguro que protege a una compañía si otra no cumple con su obligación contractual. (2) Seguro contra pérdidas comerciales fuera del control de la compañía aseguradora.

COMMERCIAL PAPER. Instrumento negociable. Usualmente se refiere a obligaciones de corto plazo.

COMMERCIAL UNIT. Artículos o grupo de bienes que, de ser separados, perderían su valor comercial.

COMMINGLING. Juntar o unir el dinero de dos personas en una cuenta bancaria.

COMMISSION. Comisión. (1) Encargo gubernamental. (2) Organización encargada de un asunto. (3) Pago basado en un porcentaje de la venta o de la ganancia.

COMMISSIONER. Comisionado. (1) Cabeza de una agencia gubernamental. (2) Encargado por una corte para bregar por un asunto especial como una venta de un bien, recibir un testimonio, etc.

COMMITMENT. Compromiso. Auto de prisión. Proceso formal de poner a una persona bajo custodia de otra.

COMMITMENT FEE. Pago hecho a un prestamista por hacer un préstamo o abrir una línea de crédito.

COMMITTEE. Comité. (1) Subgrupo de otro. (2) Especie de fideicomiso creado por un juez para administrar los bienes de un incompetente o una compañía en bancarrota.

COMMODITIES. Véase "Commodity".

COMMODITY. Mercancía, producto. (1) Cualquier cosa que se produce, compra o vende. (2) Materia prima o parcialmente producida. (3) Lo que se produce en una granja o finca, e.g., grano.

COMMON. Común, regular. (1) Algo utilizado o compartido por varias personas. (2) Usual, ordinario, que se aplica a muchos.

COMMON COUNCIL. Consejo local. Cuerpo legislativo de un pueblo o ciudad.

COMMON DISASTER. Desastre común. La cláusula en un testamento que señala el destino de una herencia si el heredero muere en un accidente conjuntamente con el testador.

COMMON ENEMY DOCTRINE. Doctrina del enemigo común. Le permite a un terrateniente cambiar el curso de un río aún sobre la tierra de otro, si el río pasa por su tierra.

COMMON FUND RULE. Regla del fondo común. Señala que si una persona demanda algo y otros se benefician con la decisión, el actor tiene derecho a retirar del fondo los gastos y honorarios del juicio antes que los otros obtengan beneficio del fondo.

COMMON LAW. Derecho Consuetudinario. Derecho Anglosajón. (1) Ley creada mediante precedentes judiciales en vez de por código, estatuto o legislación. (2) Ley originada en Inglaterra y variada por la costumbre, las prácticas y la tradición.

COMMON LAW ACTION. Acción de Derecho Consuetudinario. Demanda basada en el derecho consuetudinario, en vez de en una ley, equidad, o derecho civil.

COMMON LAW MARRIAGE. Matrimonio de hecho. Matrimonio creado sin una ceremonia formal, sino por acuerdo entre ambas partes, seguido por cohabitación.

COMMON MARKET. Mercado Común. Unión económica establecida en Europa entre varias naciones.

COMMON PLEAS COURT. Corte de Demandas Comunes. Nombre dado a varias cortes civiles de distintas clases.

COMMON SCHEME. (Plan or design). Maquinación común. (1) Cuando dos o más personas planean el mismo crimen. (2) Dos o más crímenes planeados conjuntamente. (3) División de terreno en parcelas con iguales restricciones de uso.

COMMON STOCK. Acciones comunes. Acciones de una corporación cuyo valor depende de la compañía. Usualmente los accionistas tienen derecho a voto.

COMMON TENANCY. Concepto de propiedad donde todas las partes tienen un interés en el bien o inmueble sin derecho a pasar ese interés por testamento o herencia.

COMMON TRUST FUND. Fondo común que recibe contribuciones de varias entidades y es administrado por un fideicomiso.

COMMONWEALTH. Comunidad política. (1) País o estado democrático o políticamente organizado.

COMMUNISM. Comunismo. Sistema político que aspira a la colectivización de los medios de producción, a la repartición, según las necesidades, de los bienes de consumo, y a la supresión de las clases sociales.

COMMUNITY. Comunidad. (1) Término vago que puede indicar un grupo de vecinos de mucha o poca gente. (2) Grupo con intereses comunes.

COMMUNITY OF INTEREST. Término usado para describir el interés común que tienen varias partes en un proyecto o comercio.

COMMUNITY PROPERTY. Comunidad de ganancias o de propiedad. Propiedad por partes iguales del marido y la mujer. Los estados que siguen este sistema consideran que la propiedad de los cónyuges les pertenece a ambos por igual, indistintamente de a nombre de quien se encuentre.

COMMUNITY TRUST. Organización creada para administrar un fondo de beneficencia o fideicomiso público.

COMMUTATION. Conmutación de la pena o sentencia. Cambiar una condena por otra menos grave.

COMMUTATIVE CONTRACT. Contrato conmutativo. Aquél por el cual ambas partes reciben y dan en equivalencia.

COMP. (1) Abreviatura de compilación. (2) Abreviatura de compensación.

COMPACT. Pacto, convenio. Acuerdo o contrato usualmente entre estados.

COMPACT CLAUSE. Cláusula constitucional de convenio que prohíbe a los estados realizar pactos entre sí o con otros países sin la aprobación del Congreso.

COMPANY. Compañía. Cualquier organización establecida para comerciar.

COMPARATIVE NEGLIGENCE. Regulación que determina la cantidad de culpa de cada parte en un accidente, usualmente en términos de porcentaje, y los daños son distribuidos entre los diferentes actores en relación directa al porcentaje de culpa. Si el demandante es culpable, sus daños son reducidos proporcionalmente.

COMPARATIVE RECTITUDE. Principio legal mediante el cual, después de un divorcio, la compensación se otorga a la parte que durante el matrimonio se comportó mejor.

COMPEL. Obligar. Cuando el actor es obligado a hacer algo a través de miedo, presión o coerción.

COMPELLING STATE INTEREST. Razón que tiene un estado para limitar mediante sus leyes los derechos constitucionales de una persona.

COMPENSATING BALANCE. Balance que un individuo debe mantener en un banco o en una cuenta corriente que no produce intereses para compensar al banco por préstamos u otros servicios.

COMPENSATORY DAMAGES. Indemnización; resarcimiento de daños y perjuicios. Pago hecho por el demandado por pérdidas reales sufridas por el demandante.

COMPETENCY PROCEEDING. Procedimiento para determinar la competencia o capacidad legal de una persona antes de decidir si tiene que comparecer en un juicio penal.

COMPETENT. Competente. Calificado propiamente; adecuado.

COMPETENT EVIDENCE. Prueba relevante para demostrar el punto en controversia y adecuada para tal fin.

COMPILED STATUTES. Leyes compiladas. Véase "Code".

COMPLAINANT. Demandante, querellante, acusador.

COMPLAINT. Demanda, querella. (1) Primer documento de un procedimiento judicial, el cual contiene la razón del pleito, los principios legales sobre los cuales se basa el pleito, los hechos, la afirmación del daño causado al demandante, la reclamación del remedio, etc. (2) Cualquier queja oficialmente presentada a una autoridad.

COMPLETE VOLUNTARY TRUST. Fideicomiso voluntario y completo. Aquél que se establece con todos sus detalles.

COMPLEX TRUST. Fideicomiso complejo. Que no es simple, y bajo el cual el fiduciario tiene discreción de pagar o acumular ingresos.

COMPLIANCE. Acatamiento. Actuar de acuerdo a la ley.

COMPLICITY. Complicidad; estar envuelto en la ejecución de un crimen.

COMPOSITION. Ajuste o arreglo entre un deudor y sus acreedores, normalmente extendiendo el término del vencimiento de la deuda o conviniendo en recibir menos que lo acordado originalmente.

COMPOUND. Capitalizar, transar. (1) Combinar varias cosas en una. (2) Compromiso. Transar de manera que los acreedores acepten menos de lo debido.

COMPOUND INTEREST. Interés compuesto. Interés sobre el interés.

COMPOUND LARCENY. Delito agravado. Delito que lleva una pena mayor por las circunstancias que lo rodean y por la forma en que se cometió.

COMPOUNDING A FELONY. Cuando una persona acepta un soborno monetario para no procesar un delito cometido contra esa persona.

COMPREHENSIVE ZONING PLAN. Plan comprensivo para el desarrollo urbano de una comunidad.

COMPRISES. Incluye, abarca.

COMPROMISE. Compromiso, arreglo.

COMPROMISE AND SETTLEMENT. Acuerdo entre las partes de una disputa pare transar y resolver la disputa según términos negociados entre las partes.

COMPROMISE VERDICT. Veredicto comprometido o por acomodo. Veredicto entre jurados que se alcanza cuando unos miembros abandonan sus fuertes opiniones a cambio de que otros abandonen también sus fuertes opiniones, en lugar de un veredicto alcanzado por un acuerdo total de todos los miembros.

COMPTROLLER. Contralor general. Contador supremo o máximo de un gobierno o compañía.

COMPULSION. Por fuerza; coerción.

COMPULSORY. Involuntario; por fuerza legal o legislativa.

COMPULSORY PROCESS. Jurisdicción o procedimiento coactivo. Obligar a una persona a presentarse ante una corte o legislatura, usualmente mediante citación o emplazamiento.

CON. Abreviación de "contra". (1) Por otro lado. (2) Con, junto. (3) Abreviación de "constitucional."

CONCENTRATION BANKING. Sistema de pagos locales que se canalizan y transfieren mediante el correo y los bancos locales.

CONCEPTION. Concepción. La idea completa de un inventor para una invención. El día de la concepción es aquél en el cual la idea completa se escribe.

CONCERT OF ACTION RULE. Principio de derecho criminal que señala que un acuerdo entre dos personas para cometer un crimen no será una conspiración si el delito intentado es tal que requiere por definición el concurso de dos personas.

CONCILIATION. Conciliación. Proceso de acercar a dos personas a una solución y compromiso voluntario con respecto a una disputa.

CONCLUSION OF LAW. Conclusión legal. Conclusiones hechas al aplicar las leyes apropiadas a los hechos de un caso.

CONCLUSIVE. Concluyente, decisivo. (1) Más allá de una disputa; que termina un debate. (2) **Conclusive Evidence.** Evidencia que es irrefutable y concluyente. (3) **Conclusive Presumption.** Un supuesto que debe ser aceptado como hecho.

CONCORDAT. Pacto, convenio entre dos países.

CONCUR. Concurrir; estar de acuerdo.

CONCURRENT. Concurrente; que tienen igual autoridad.
(1) **Concurrent Jurisdiction.** Competencia concurrente. Cuando dos cortes tienen el poder de resolver los mismos casos.
(2) **Concurrent Sentences.** Sentencias con condenas que corren al mismo tiempo.

CONCURRING OPINION. Opinión concurrente. Opinión dada por un juez con respecto a la decisión en un caso pero sin estar de acuerdo con el análisis o el contenido de la opinión jurídica dictada por la mayoría.

CONDEMN. Condenar. (1) Encontrar a alguien culpable de un delito. (2) Expropiar. Cuando el gobierno toma propiedad privada sin consentimiento del dueño. (3) Decisión de una corte autorizando la expropiación de un buque. (4) Decisión oficial de que un edificio no sirve para su propósito o uso dadas sus condiciones físicas.

CONDITION. Condición. (1) Evento futuro e incierto que crea o destruye derechos. (2) **Express Condition.** Condición expresa en un contrato. (3) **Implied Condition.** Condición implícita que se deduce del texto de un contrato. (4) **Condition Precedent.** Condición precedente. Cuando un evento debe suceder antes que se cree un derecho u obligación. (5) **Subsequent Condition.** Condición subsecuente. Si un evento futuro sucede, un derecho u obligación es extinguido o creado. (6) **Independent Condition.** Una obligación que debe ser cumplida sin referencia a otras condiciones colaterales.

CONDITIONAL. Condicional. Que depende de una condición; inseguro; dependiente de un evento futuro.

CONDOMINIUM. Condominio. Sistema bajo el cual varias personas son dueñas de una unidad en un edificio compuesto de unidades múltiples.

CONDONATION. Condonación. Perdón voluntario de parte de un cónyuge a la acción del otro, que es suficiente para quitarle a esa acción la razón de ser causa de divorcio.

CONDONE. Véase "Condonation".

CONFEDERACY. Confederación. (1) Personas reunidas para cometer un acto ilegal. (2) Unión flexible de gobiernos independientes.

CONFERENCE COMMITTEE. Reunión de ambas cámaras de una legislatura para trabajar juntas resolviendo diferencias entre las versiones de una ley pasada por ambas cámaras.

CONFESS. Confesar. Véase "Confesión".

CONFESSION. Confession. (1) Declaración voluntaria de culpabilidad. (2) Cualquier admisión de un mal criminal.

CONFESSION AND AVOIDANCE. Véase "Affirmative Defense". Cuando una parte admite los hechos pero alega eventos adicionales que neutralizan el efecto legal de la demanda.

CONFESSION OF JUDGMENT. Confesión o admisión de sentencia. (1) Cuando un prestatario firma de antemano una confesión para que el prestamista obtenga sentencia ejecutiva contra aquél si no paga cual lo acordado. Estas sentencias no son favorecidas por las cortes.

CONFIDENTIAL RELATION. Relación confidencial o fiduciaria mediante la cual una persona, basada en tal relación, tiene derecho a esperar un cuidado y atención mayor de parte de otra.

CONFIDENTIALITY. Confidencialidad. Estado de ser confidencial; algo privado.

CONFIRMATION. Confirmación. (1) Aprobación formal. (2) Noticia de que algo ha sido recibido. (3) Traspaso del título de propiedad de un inmueble a alguien que tiene la posesión del bien. (4) Contrato o acuerdo que reafirma algo que hubiese sido difícil de probar o ejecutar. (5) Aprobación legislativa de un nombramiento hecho por el ejecutivo.

CONFISCATION. Confiscación. Expropiación de propiedad privada realizada por el gobierno sin indemnización.

CONFLICT OF INTEREST. Conflicto de intereses. Posición en la que está una persona cuando sus aspiraciones y necesidades personales podrían llevarle a violar el deber fiduciario que pueda tener para con otra persona.

CONFLICT OF LAWS. Conflicto de leyes. Cuando las leyes de más de un estado o país pueden ser aplicadas a un caso y el juez debe escoger entre ellas.

CONFORMED COPY. Copia auténtica. Copia que concuerda o se conforma con su original.

CONFRONTATION. Careo. Confrontación. Derecho que tiene quien es acusado de un delito para ver y hacer preguntas a todos los testigos en su contra.

CONFUSION. Confusión. Fusión. Cuando se mezclan o juntan los bienes o las acciones de dos partes al punto en que no se sabe quién es el dueño de los bienes o activos.

CONGLOMERATE. Conglomerado. Compañía que es dueña de otras en diversas industrias.

CONGRESS. Congreso. (1) Organo legislativo de los Estados Unidos. (2) Reunión de funcionarios.

CONGRESSIONAL RECORD. Actas o Registros del Congreso. Registro diario de cómo se votó en cada ley y de lo que se dijo en el Congreso.

CONGRESSMAN. Miembro del Congreso. Término comúnmente usado para referirse a un miembro de la Cámara de Representantes.

CONJOINT. Conjunto. Asociado. Que tiene un interés junto a otros.

CONJUGAL. Conyugal. Relativo al matrimonio.

CONNIVANCE. Connivencia. (1) Permiso o asentimiento tácito o indirecto para la comisión de un crimen. (2) Consentimiento o ayuda que da un cónyuge al otro para realizar actos en los cuales basaron su divorcio.

CONSANGUINITY. Consanguinidad. Parentesco o relación de sangre.

CONSCIENTIOUS OBJECTOR. El que tiene una objeción de conciencia por motivos religiosos o morales para participar en una guerra.

CONSECUTIVE SENTENCE. Sentencia acumulativa. Término adicional de condena a quien está cumpliendo otra condena anterior. El término adicional comienza luego de haberse cumplido el primero.

CONSCRIPTION. Servicio militar obligatorio.

CONSENT. Consentimiento. Acuerdo voluntario y activo. (1) **Express Consent.** Una autorización expresa que no requiere mayor explicación. (2) **Implied Consent.** Acuerdo o autorización manifestada por los hechos, la inacción o el silencio de alguien, aunque no fue expresado.

CONSENT DECREE. Decreto o sentencia por consentimiento. (1) Divorcio otorgado en contra del demandado, quien no se opuso al divorcio. (2) Transar en una demanda en la cual se acuerda hacer algo sin admitir culpa sobre lo que causó la demanda.

CONSENT JUDGMENT. Un fallo jurídico con el consentimiento y en contra de la parte demandada.

CONSEQUENTIAL DAMAGES. Daños consecuentes. Pérdidas o daños, incluso corporales, causados por un acto injusto y que no se presentan inmediatamente sino como resultado o consecuencia de ese acto injusto.

CONSERVATOR. Curador. Administrador de la propiedad de alguien que no puede administrarla legalmente.

CONSIDERATION. Causa. (1) Motivo principal por el cual una persona realiza un contrato. Sin causa un contrato no es válido. (2) Algo de valor recibido o prometido que induce a una persona a realizar un contrato. (3) Uno de los elementos esenciales para la formación de un contrato.

CONSIGNMENT. Consignación. Entregar algo para un fin determinado. Entregar algo a alguien para transportarlo o venderlo.

CONSOLIDATE. Consolidar. Unir. Juntar mercancía suelta para transportarla en un solo embarque.

CONSOLIDATED STATEMENT. Informe financiero que refleja el estado financiero de varias compañías legalmente separadas pero combinadas como si se tratara de una sola.

CONSOLIDATION. Consolidación. (1) Proceso judicial que combina varias demandas como una sola demanda ya que son de la misma materia general y entre las mismas partes. (2) Unión de dos corporaciones para formar una nueva.

CONSORTIUM. Consorcio. Derecho de un cónyuge al amor y servicio del otro. (1) **Loss of Consortium.** Pérdida del consorcio; es base material para una demanda. Por ejemplo, el esposo de una mujer gravemente herida en un accidente puede demandar al causante del accidente por su pérdida del consorcio.

CONSPICUOUS. Obvio. Prominente. Notable.

CONSPIRACY. Conspiración. Dos o más personas unidas para cometer un acto ilegal.

CONSTABLE. Alguacil, policía, condestable. Funcionario de paz de poca jerarquía que realiza trabajos relacionados a los de la corte.

CONSTANT PAYMENT MORTGAGE. Hipoteca común de vivienda. Típica clase de hipoteca de vivienda con mensualidades iguales, en la cual una proporción del pago va a reducir la deuda capital y la otra porción sirve para pagar intereses hasta la cancelación del préstamo.

CONSTITUTION. Constitución El documento principal de un país que establece los derechos básicos y la estructura del gobierno.

CONSTITUTIONAL. Constitucional. Que tiene consistencia o que está en congruencia con la constitución.

CONSTITUTIONAL LAW. Derecho Constitucional. Rama del derecho relativa a la organización, estructura y funcionamiento de un estado o de la constitución.

CONSTITUTIONAL RIGHTS. Derechos Constitucionales. Aquéllos consagrados o protegidos por la constitución.

CONSTRUCTION. Interpretación. Normas de interpretación sobre el significado y efecto legal de las palabras de una ley ambigua o dudosa hecha en base no sólo al significado de las palabras sino incluyendo las circunstancias bajo las cuales la ley fue aprobada.

CONSTRUCTION DRAW. Clase de hipoteca o contrato de construcción que permite al constructor obtener dinero según el progreso de la construcción.

CONSTRUCTIVE. Deducido, implícito. Tal como si. Verdad legal aún cuando no lo sea materialmente.

CONSTRUCTIVE CONTRACT. Véase "Quasi-contract".

CONSTRUCTIVE DESERTION. Abandono Implícito. Forzar a un cónyuge a abandonar al otro. El cónyuge forzado a abandonar puede demandar al otro por abandono implícito ya que este último es el causante del abandono.

CONSTRUCTIVE EVICTION. Acciones que, tomadas por un arrendador, hacen la propiedad inhabitable, causando daños al inquilino.

CONSTRUCTIVE KNOWLEDGE. Conocimiento sobreentendido o implícito. Conocimiento que se supone tiene una persona en una situación particular. Igual que "Constructive Notice".

CONSTRUCTIVE NOTICE. Véase "Constructive Knowledge".

CONSTRUCTIVE RECEIPT OF INCOME. Ingreso de Renta Implícito. La persona que adquiere control de una renta es gravada sobre ese ingreso aún cuando no reciba materialmente el dinero en efectivo.

CONSTRUCTIVE TRUST. Fideicomiso implícito. Situación en la cual una persona tiene el título de propiedad de algo que justamente debe ser de otro. La corte considera entonces que el que tiene el título no tiene más que un fideicomiso implícito del verdadero dueño.

CONSTRUE. Determinar el efecto y significado de un documento.

CONSUETUDO. (Lat.) Consuetudinariamente. Costumbre. Aquello que se hace repetidamente en forma de hábito desde tiempo atrás.

CONSUL. Cónsul. Representante de un país en otro, que atiende los asuntos o negocios de su país y de sus ciudadanos pero no necesariamente los asuntos políticos.

CONSULTATION. Acto de consultar con un médico, abogado o profesional.

CONSUMER. Consumidor. Persona que compra algo para uso personal en lugar de para uso comercial.

CONSUMER CREDIT. Crédito para el consumidor. Usualmente dinero, propiedad o servicio ofrecido a una persona a crédito para su uso personal, familiar o del hogar.

CONSUMER CREDIT PROTECTION ACT. Ley federal que requiere que el prestamista divulgue en términos legibles los términos y las condiciones cuando otorga un préstamo o crédito al consumidor.

CONSUMER PRICE INDEX. Lista de precios para el consumidor. Estadística que muestra los precios promedio de bienes y servicios adquiridos por el consumidor.

CONSUMER PROTECTION LAWS. Leyes estatales dirigidas a proteger a los consumidores en ciertas transacciones.

CONSUMMATE. Consumar, completar, terminar.

CONSUMMATION. Consumación. (1) Completar una cosa. Llevar a cabo un acuerdo. (2) Completar un matrimonio al tener contacto sexual.

CONTEMNER. Aquél que está en desacato por desobedecer una orden de la corte.

CONTEMPLATION OF DEATH. Expectación o contemplación de muerte. Acto realizado e influenciado en expectativa inminente de muerte.

CONTEMPT. Desacato. (1) Acto realizado para obstruir o indignar a la corte o al trabajo que ella realiza. (2) Desobediencia intencional de una orden judicial, administrativa o de procedimiento legislativo.

CONTEST. Disputar, litigar, impugnar. (1) Oponerse y defenderse contra una demanda. (2) Oponerse a la validez de un testamento.

CONTEXT. Contexto. Orden de composición o tejido de un estatuto, contrato, u otro escrito con consecuencias legales.

CONTIGUOUS. Contiguo. Adyacente.

CONTINGENT. Contingente. Eventual. Fortuito. Posible pero no asegurado. Que depende de acciones futuras que pueden o no pasar.

CONTINGENT FEE. Pacto de cuotalitis. Honorarios que recibe el abogado de su cliente, establecidos en un porcentaje de la cuantía recuperada o de las etapas en que se ventile el juicio. Por ejemplo; 25% si se transa; 20% si se resuelve en primera instancia; 30% si se resuelve en segunda instancia.

CONTINUANCE. Aplazamiento. Posposición de un juicio o audiencia para otra fecha.

CONTINUING APPROPRIATION. Apropiación de dinero hecha por el gobierno que continúa automáticamente hasta que se revoca.

CONTINUING JURISDICTION. Competencia de una corte para seguir conociendo un caso si se necesita cambiar una orden o acto.

CONTINUING OFFENSE. Delito continuado. Un solo delito que puede contener muchos actos individuales durante un período de tiempo. Por ejemplo: Conspiración.

473

CONTRA. Contra. (1) **Contra Bonos Mores (Lat.).** Contra las buenas costumbres. (2) **Contra Accounts.** Cuentas hechas para mostrar sustracciones de otras cuentas.

CONTRABAND. Contrabando. Propiedad o bienes que no se pueden producir o poseer legalmente. Bienes exportados o importados en contra de las leyes.

CONTRACT. Contrato. Acuerdo entre dos o más personas que crea una obligación para hacer o no hacer algo determinado. (1) **Bilateral Contract.** Contrato bilateral. Aquél en el cual ambas partes se prometen algo. (2) **Unilateral Contract.** Contrato unilateral. Una parte promete algo a cambio de una acción de la otra parte. Para que exista un contrato debe haber una oferta aceptada con sus respectivas causas. (3) **Conditional Contract.** Un contrato que depende en su ejecución en una o varias condiciones. (4) **Divisible Contract.** Cuando un contrato es parcelable en varias partes. (5) **Indivisible Contract.** Contrato que debe ser cumplido en su totalidad antes que la otra parte tenga que cumplir con sus obligaciones contractuales.

CONTRACT CLAUSE. Cláusula constitucional que prohibe a los estados abolir el derecho a contratar o negarle sus efectos legales.

CONTRACT FOR DEED. Un acuerdo de entregar un título de propiedad al cumplirse ciertas condiciones. Por ejemplo: al completarse los pagos de compra de una propiedad.

CONTRACT FOR SALE OF GOODS. Tipo de contrato mercantil regulado por el "Uniform Commercial Code" sobre bienes muebles.

CONTRACTOR. Contratista. Persona que realiza un trabajo, usualmente relacionado con la construcción, y que conserva el control de su propio trabajo así como del método y detalles del mismo.

CONTRAVENTION. Contravención. Algo hecho en violación de la ley.

CONTRIBUTE. Contribuir.

CONTRIBUTION. Contribución. (1) Cuota en el pago de una deuda entre personas responsables por pagar la misma. (2) Derecho de quien ha pagado por completo una deuda de recuperar la cuota de otro a quien le correspondía hacer parte del pago.

CONTRIBUTORY. Contributorio. (1) Persona que debe pagar el valor de sus acciones en una compañía que cierra negocios y debe dinero. (2) Algún acto que contribuye a un evento.

CONTRIBUTORY NEGLIGENCE. Negligencia contribuyente. Actos realizados por el demandante sin el cuidado que una persona prudente y ordinaria tendría, y que sumados a la negligencia del demandado son la causa de los daños.

CONTROLLED SUBSTANCE ACT. Ley de las Sustancias Controladas. Controla la producción, venta y uso de drogas, medicinas o sustancias peligrosas.

CONTROLLER. Contralor. Aquél encargado de controlar y fiscalizar los gastos.

CONTROVERSY. Controversia. Cualquier demanda civil que involucra verdaderos derechos legales; más que una violación potencial o asumida de esos derechos.

CONTROVERT. Controvertir, disputar, negar, oponerse.

CONTUMACY. Contumacia. (1) Renuncia a comparecer ante la corte cuando así se requiere por ley. (2) Renuncia a obedecer una orden legal. Véase "Contempt".

CONTUMELY. Ofensa insolente.

CONVENIENCE AND NECESSITY. Conveniencia y necesidad. Las condiciones que tienen que existir antes que se le otorgue una licencia de operación a una empresa de transportación.

CONVENTION. Convención. (1) Reunión de representantes. (2) Acuerdo entre países sobre asuntos que no son ni políticos ni financieros.

CONVENTIONAL. Convencional. Usual, ordinario. Causado por un acuerdo entre las partes en lugar de ser originado por disposición de la ley.

CONVENTIONAL LOAN. Hipoteca sobre bienes inmuebles sin participación o garantías gubernamentales.

CONVERSION. Apropiación indebida. (1) Cualquier acto que priva a un propietario de su derecho sin su consentimiento ni causa justa. (2) Conversión o intercambio de propiedad. Por ejemplo: entregar un tipo de acciones de una compañía a cambio de acciones de otra clase.

CONVERTIBLE. Convertible. Bono o acción preferencial que puede ser intercambiada por acciones comunes.

CONVEYANCE. (1) Traspaso del título de un bien inmueble. (2) Cualquier traspaso de título de propiedad.

CONVICT. Convicto. (1) Condenado. Persona en prisión. (2) Condenar. Encontrar a una persona culpable de un delito.

CONVICTION. Condena. Decisión judicial la cual encuentra a una persona culpable de un delito.

CO-OWNER. Una de dos o más personas dueñas de una propiedad, sea mueble o inmueble.

COOLING OFF PERIOD. (1) Período de enfriamiento durante el cual ninguna parte en un litigio debe tomar acción alguna. (2) Tiempo durante el cual un comprador puede cancelar una compra. (3) Demora automática entre la demanda de divorcio y la audiencia.

COOPERATIVE. Cooperativa. Organización formada para ayudar a sus miembros. Puede ser agraria, de vivienda, o de crédito.

COORDINATE JURISDICTION. Competencia concurrente. Poder que tienen dos o más cortes para resolver una misma causa.

COP A PLEA. Declaración de culpabilidad. Acuerdo de un acusado de declararse culpable, si se cambia la acusación por un delito u ofensa de menor grado.

COPARCENARY. Copropietario. Herencia conjunta.

COPYRIGHT. Derecho de autor. Derecho de un autor, creado por leyes federales, de beneficiarse de las copias y distribución de lo que haya creado. El tiempo de duración de este derecho es el de la vida del autor más cincuenta años; cuando los derechos son propiedad de una compañía, este derecho dura setenta y cinco años.

CORAM. (Lat.) Ante. En presencia de.

CO-RESPONDENT. (1) Una de dos o más personas demandadas. (2) Dícese de la persona que es cómplice o tiene relaciones con el cónyuge demandado en una demanda de divorcio por adulterio.

CORNER. Acaparar. Monopolizar. Tener suficiente cantidad de acciones o productos como para poder controlar su precio.

COROLLARY. Corolario. Deducción o inferencia obtenida de un argumento lógico.

CORONER. Médico forense. Doctor u oficial gubernamental que determina la causa de una muerte violenta o sospechosa.

CORPORAL PUNISHMENT. Castigo corporal.

CORPORATE. Corporativo. Relativo a una sociedad anónima.

CORPORATE VEIL. Velo corporativo. Principio legal que asume que los actos de una sociedad anónima no son los actos de sus accionistas y que estos no pueden ser responsabilizados por los actos de la corporación.

CORPORATION. Corporación. Sociedad anónima organizada bajo las leyes estatales o federales que le dan existencia como una persona ficticia. La corporación se establece para realizar negocios o cualquier actividad lícita.

CORPORATION COUNSEL. Abogado que representa a un municipio, ciudad, o una corporación en asuntos civiles.

CORPOREAL. Corpóreo. Tangible. Que se ve y tiene substancia.

CORPUS. (Lat.) Cuerpo. Parte principal de una cosa.

477

CORPUS DELICTI. (Lat.) Cuerpo del delito. (1) Objeto material sobre el cual se cometió un delito. (2) Hechos que demuestran que un delito ha sido cometido.

CORPUS JURIS. (Lat.) Enciclopedia de Derecho. Su versión actualizada es el Corpus Juris Secundum.

CORPUS JURIS CIVILIS. (Lat.) Código de leyes civiles. Código Civil. Leyes principales escritas por los romanos.

CORRECTIONAL. Actividad que tiene por objetivo corregir algo. Usualmente se refiere a una cárcel, prisión o penitenciaría.

CORRELATIVE. Correlativo. Ideas que tienen relación mutua y dependen unas de otras para su significado.

CORRESPONDENT. Corresponsal. (1) Persona que cobra una hipoteca en representación del prestamista. (2) Banco o compañía financiera que presta servicios por otro.

CORROBORATE. Corroborar. (1) Añadir hechos o pruebas para fortalecer la evidencia ya presentada. (2) Ratificar o apoyar lo que otro dice.

CORRUPT. Corrupto. Corrompido; moralmente incorrecto.

CORRUPT PRACTICES ACT. Ley de probidad electoral; ley contra prácticas corruptas. (1) Ley que regula las campañas políticas. (2) Ley que regula las actividades financieras internacionales de las sociedades anónimas.

CONSIGNATORY. Relativo a consignación. Véase "Consigner".

COSIGNER. Cosignatario. Quien firma junto con otro un documento. En algunos estados tiene responsabilidad solidaria; en ótros es un mero fiador al que se recurre sólo si el deudor principal no cumple.

COST AND FREIGHT. Costo y flete. Precio de un artículo que refleja su costo más el flete, pero no incluye el seguro u otro gasto adicional.

COST OF LIVING ADJUSTMENT. Ajuste según el costo de vida. Ajuste salarial que aumenta automáticamente con la inflación.

COST OF LIVING ALLOWANCE. Asignación por el costo de vida. Paga adicional por vivir en un área cuyo costo de vida es alto.

COST PLUS CONTRACT. Contrato de construcción por administración. Contrato de construcción bajo el cual la paga del constructor se calcula según el costo de los materiales, más la mano de obra y un porcentaje fijo sobre tal valor.

COSTS. Costo, costas, gastos del juicio. Los gastos incurridos por una parte en una demanda.

COUNCIL. Consejo. Cuerpo legislativo local, de una ciudad o municipio.

COUNSEL. Consejero. (1) Abogado que representa a un cliente. (2) Consejo. (3) **Of Counsel.** Abogado asistente en un caso, no el principal.

COUNSEL, RIGHT TO. Derecho a tener un abogado. Garantía constitucional que tiene todo acusado a ser defendido por un abogado.

COUNSELLOR. Abogado.

COUNT. Cargo. Cada parte de una demanda que debe describir los hechos y las bases legales de lo alegado. Una demanda puede tener varios cargos.

COUNTER. Contra. En oposición.

COUNTERCLAIM. Contrademanda. Respuesta que da el demandado a una demanda mediante la cual demanda al demandante.

COUNTERFEIT. Falsificación. Moneda falsificada. Copiar o imitar algo para hacerlo pasar como el original.

COUNTERMAND. Revocar. Contramandar. Cambiar o retirar instrucciones.

479

COUNTER OFFER. Contra oferta. (1) Rechazo de una oferta mediante la proposición de una nueva oferta. (2) Según el U.C.C., en casos de venta de bienes, una contra oferta puede funcionar como una propuesta de términos nuevos para el contrato de venta.

COUNTERPART. Contraparte, duplicado. (1) Copia de un documento. (2) Copia sin firmar de un documento firmado. (3) Copia de un documento firmado por una parte, y dada a la otra parte que ha firmado el original.

COUNTERSIGN. Refrendar. Firmar un documento en adición a la firma ya puesta para ratificar su validez.

COUNTERVAILING. Contrarrestar. Sopesar. Compensar.

COUNTY. Condado. División política de un territorio estatal. Generalmente, cada condado tiene su sistema judicial y administrativo propio.

COUPON. Cupón. Certificado de interés o dividendo que debe ser redimido en cierta fecha. El cupón se separa del documento principal y se presenta para su cobro.

COURSE OF BUSINESS. Curso de los negocios. Lo que se hace normalmente en la actividad comercial de una empresa en particular.

COURSE OF DEALING. Transcurso de las negociaciones. Se refiere a la historia o forma en que dos personas han negociado entre sí.

COURSE OF EMPLOYMENT. Transcurso del empleo. Directamente relacionado al empleo; durante horas laborables o en el lugar del empleo.

COURT. Corte. (1) Lugar donde trabajan los jueces. (2) Los mismos jueces en un área determinada. (3) **Criminal Court.** Una corte que sólo trata con asuntos criminales. (4) **Civil Court.** Una corte que sólo trata con asuntos civiles. (5) **Equity or Chancery Court.** Corte que actúa con equidad. (6) **Trial Court.** Término general que describe la corte donde se enjuicia un caso. (7) **Law Court.** Corte que examina casos en base a principios o precedentes legales. (8) **Administrative Court.** Corte

Administrativa. Corte que determina asuntos administrativos.
(9) **Federal Court.** Cualquier corte establecida bajo leyes
federales. (10) **Supreme Court.** Corte Suprema.
(11) **Bankruptcy Court.** Corte federal que trata con asuntos de
bancarrota.

COURT MARTIAL. Corte marcial. Corte militar para el
juzgamiento de los miembros del servicio militar de acuerdo al
Código Militar. (1) **Summary Court Martial.** Corte marcial
sumarias o para faltas leves. (2) **Special Court Martial.** Corte
marcial especial, para asuntos intermedios, y cuyo poder incluye
imponer penas de cárcel. (3) **General Court Martial.** Corte
marcial general que trata con delitos mayores y puede imponer
pena de muerte.

COURT OF APPEALS. Corte de apelaciones. (1) Corte que
resuelve apelaciones. Generalmente, es una corte intermedia,
aunque en ciertos estados es la máxima corte estatal. (2) **U.S.
Court of Appeals.** Una de las doce cortes federales de apelación.

COURT OF CLAIMS. Corte de reclamaciones. Corte que trata con
juicios en los que se demanda en contra del gobierno de los
Estados Unidos.

COURT OF PROBATE. Tribunal de sucesiones. Corte que resuelve
asuntos de herencia, testamentos, y que en ocasiones toma a su
cargo asuntos de menores o personas legalmente incapacitadas.

COURT REPORTER. Persona que transcribe lo sucedido en un
proceso judicial.

COURT RULES. Reglas y normas adoptadas por las cortes que
regulan las prácticas y los procedimientos ante las cortes. Véase
"Federal Rules of Civil Procedure", "Federal Rules of Criminal
Procedure", "Federal Rules of Appelate Procedure" y "Federal
Rules of Evidence".

COURTESY. Derecho que tiene el marido viudo a una parte de la
propiedad de su difunta esposa.

COVENANT. Pacto. Convenio. Promesa escrita, acuerdo o
restricción, usualmente en un título de propiedad. Generalmente
tiene el efecto de crear un contrato. (1) **Covenant for Quiet**

Enjoyment. Garantía de posesión sin trastornos legales; garantía de posesión quieta y pacífica. (2) **Covenant Running with the Land.** Obligación unida al fundo o terreno.

COVER. Cubrir; proteger.

COVERAGE. Cobertura. Cuantía y clase de protección en una póliza de seguro.

COVERTURE. Casada. Estatus de una mujer casada. Derechos y deberes de una mujer casada.

CRAFT UNION. Sindicato gremialista. Sindicato en el cual sus miembros tienen el mismo oficio.

CREDENTIALS. Credenciales. Documento que demuestra la autoridad de una persona.

CREDIBILITY. Credibilidad. Veracidad de un testigo.

CREDIT. Crédito. (1) Derecho a posponer el pago de algo. (2) Dinero prestado. (3) Deducción de lo que se debe. (4) **Credit Card.** Tarjeta de crédito.

CREDIT LINE. Línea de crédito. Promesa que hace un banco o institución de conceder un préstamo hasta cierta suma para que un comerciante realice negocios.

CREDITOR. Acreedor. Persona a quien se le debe algo.

CREDITOR'S MEETING. Junta de acreedores; concurso de acreedores. Reunión de acreedores de una persona en quiebra.

CREDITS. Créditos. Registro en un libro de contabilidad del dinero que le deben a uno.

CRIME. Crimen. Violación a la ley penal o criminal. (1) **Capital Crime.** Crimen por el cual se puede dar la pena de muerte. (2) **Organized Crime.** Término usado para describir crímenes que son producto de actividades coordinadas por grupos de criminales (por ejemplo, narcóticos, juegos, etc.). (3) **Statutory Crime.** Crimen creado por ley.

CRIME AGAINST NATURE. Véase "Sodomy".

CRIMINAL. Criminal. (1) Relativo al crimen. (2) Ilegal. (3) El que comete un delito. (4) **Criminal Action.** Acción o acusación criminal. Procedimiento para enjuiciar a un delincuente. (5) **Criminal Behavior.** Comportamiento criminal. (6) **Criminal Capacity.** Cuando el actor tiene la capacidad para saber que comete un crimen. (7) **Criminal Charge.** La descripción del cargo criminal contra un acusado. (8) **Criminal Contempt.** Cargos criminales por obstruir un proceso o una investigación legal. (9) **Criminal Conversation.** Adulterio. Provocar un adulterio. (10) **Criminal Forfeiture.** Confiscación por el estado de un bien usado en un delito. (11) **Criminal Intent.** Actuar con un propósito criminal. (12) **Criminal Proceeding or Prosecution.** El procesamiento judicial de un criminal.

CRIMINOLOGY. Criminología. Estudio de las causas, prevención y castigo de los delitos.

CROSS–ACTION. (1) Contra demanda. (2) Demanda contra alguien que lo demanda a uno. (3) Sinónimo de "cross-claim," "cross-demand," y "cross-complaint."

CROSS–EXAMINATION. Contrainterrogación; repreguntar. Examinar a un testigo de la otra parte.

CROSS–PICKETING. Piqueteo de dos o más sindicatos que alegan que representan a los mismos trabajadores.

CRUEL AND UNUSUAL PUNISHMENT. Penas crueles e inusuales. Penas abolidas por ser excesivas y en contra de la moral.

CRUELTY. Crueldad. Acto que hace sufrir, ya sea física o moralmente.

CULPABLE. Culpable. El que debe responder de un acto. Responsable.

CULPRIT. Culpado, reo, delincuente. Aquél que ha cometido un delito.

CUMULATIVE EVIDENCE. Evidencia acumulativa. Prueba que demuestra algo ya probado.

CUMULATIVE SENTENCE. Sentencia acumulativa. Condena que se suma a una que ya está siendo cumplida.

CUMULATIVE VOTING. Voto acumulativo. Sistema de elección corporativa bajo el cual cada accionista tiene derecho a un total de votos igual al número de posiciones que existan para elegir, multiplicado por el número de acciones que posee el accionista.

CURATOR. Curador. Persona designada por la corte para representar o administrar los bienes de otro que no puede valerse por sí mismo.

CURFEW. Toque de queda. Período de tiempo durante el cual la movilización está prohibida por razones de guerra o seguridad nacional.

CURRENT. Corriente, actual. Que sucede en estos momentos. Que tiene vigencia.

CUSTODIAL INTERROGATION. Interrogación custodial. Interrogatorio conducido por la policía inmediatamente después de que una persona ha sido privada de su libertad.

CUSTODY. Custodia. Término de carácter general que abarca distintas formas de cuidado, atención y vigilancia.

CUSTOM. Costumbre. El comportamiento social de las personas de un área geográfica determinada. También se aplica en el caso de un negocio en particular, cuya forma de práctica eventualmente adquiere importancia y significado legal.

CUSTOM HOUSE. Aduana. Despacho por donde pasan los bienes que entran o salen de un país para ser revisados e inspeccionados, y donde se pagan los impuestos.

CUSTOMS. Impuestos o derechos aduaneros. (1) Impuesto sobre bienes que se importan o exportan. (2) Oficina que grava los bienes que se importan o exportan. (3) **Customs Court.** Corte que conoce de asuntos aduaneros.

CY-PRES. Tan cerca como sea posible. Doctrina que permite a un juez interpretar un testamento, que de otra forma no sería válido, de la manera más cercana posible a la intención del testador. Hoy día se utiliza para darle validez a fideicomisos de caridad o beneficencia.

D

D. Sigla de "Defendant." Demandado, acusado.

D.B.A. Sigla de "Doing Business As." Literalmente, "haciendo negocios como". Indica bajo qué nombre se realiza una transacción comercial.

D.C. (1) **District Court.** Corte de Distrito. Tribunal usualmente de primera instancia. (2) **District of Columbia.** Distrito de Columbia. Distrito especial en el cual se encuentra la Capital de los Estados Unidos.

D.E.A. Siglas del "Drug Enforcement Administration". Agencia para la Represión del Narcotráfico. Oficina del Departamento de Justicia de los Estados Unidos que lucha contra el narcotráfico.

D.J. Siglas de "District Judge." Juez de Distrito.

D.O.D. Siglas de "Department of Defense". Departamento de Defensa o Ministerio de Defensa de los Estados Unidos.

D.O.T. Siglas de "Department of Transportation". Ministerio de Transporte. Regula el transporte entre los estados mediante sus agencias, tales como la Administración Federal de Aviación, Administración Federal de Carreteras, etc.

D.W.I. (1) Véase "Driving While Intoxicated". Manejando en estado de embriaguez. (2) **Died Without Issue.** Morir sin decendencia.

DACTYLOGRAPHY. Dactilografía. Estudio de la identificación de huellas digitales.

DAMAGES. Daños y perjuicios. (1) Dinero que la corte ordena que sea pagado a quien sufre una pérdida o un daño a cuenta del causante. (2) **Actual and Compensatory Damages.** Daños actuales y compensatorios directamente relacionados a la cuantía de la pérdida. (3) **Punitive Damages.** Daños punitivos o ejemplares. Daños concedidos al demandante para castigar al demandado y así indicar a otros que un acto determinado es ofensivo a la corte. (4) **Nominal Damages.** Daños nominales. Se conceden cuando, la pérdida es insignificante o cuando probado el daño, no se puede determinar su valor.

DANGEROUS INSTRUMENTALITY. Instrumento peligroso. Cosas que son en sí peligrosas, como las armas de fuego.

DATE OF ISSUE. Fecha de vigencia. (1) Fecha en que un documento comienza a tener efecto. No es necesariamente la fecha en que se firma.

DAY-BOOK. Diario. Registro de los eventos diarios de un comerciante.

DAY CERTAIN. Fecha o plazo cierto. Fecha futura y específica. Normalmente es la fecha en que la corte comienza un juicio.

DAY IN COURT. Expresión que indica el derecho que tiene toda persona de ser notificada sobre el proceso en el cual se involucra su interés, así como de ser escuchada en audiencia.

DE BENE ESSE. (Lat.) Provisional, sujeto a futuro ataque o cambio. Declaración testimonial "De Bene Esse" es aquella hecha fuera de corte y usada cuando el testigo no puede aparecer en el proceso.

DE FACTO. (Lat.) De hecho. Situación que existe, sea o no legal.

DE JURE. (Lat.) De derecho; legítimo; legal. Que tiene su base en la ley.

DE NOVO. (Lat.) Nuevo. Completamente nuevo; desde el principio.

DEAD. Muerto. Sin valor, sin usar, obsoleto.

DEAD FREIGHT. Flete que se paga por aquella parte del buque que va vacía.

DEAD MAN'S STATUTE. Ley que prohibe cierto tipo de evidencia oral que atribuye al difunto declaraciones contrarias al testamento. Es excluída de la audiencia para invalidar un testamento.

DEADLINE. Plazo final para un acontecimiento. Ultima fecha en que un evento debe ocurrir.

DEADLY FORCE. Uso de fuerza letal.

DEADLY WEAPON. Instrumento mortal o letal.

DEALER. Negociante, traficante, comerciante. (1) Persona que compra y vende como comerciante. (2) Bajo las leyes de intercambio de bienes, bonos y valores, un "dealer" es aquél que compra para sí y revende en lugar del intermediario que compra para otros.

DEATH. Muerte. Fin de la vida.

DEATHBED DECLARATION. Declaración, que rinde quien está a punto de morir sobre quien le mató y cómo sucedió.

DEBARMENT. Exclusión, prohibición. Excluir a una persona de hacer algo. Véase "Disbarment".

DEBAUCHERY. Libertinaje sexual. Orgía. Relaciones sexuales ilegales.

DEBENTURE. Bono, pagaré, vale. Obligación de pagar un dinero que no está garantizado con propiedades.

DEBITS. Débitos. Registro en libros de contabilidad del dinero que una persona debe o que ha pagado. Lo opuesto a crédito.

DEBT. Deuda. Dinero debido.

DEBT FINANCING. Financiamiento por endeudamiento. Dinero que una compañía adquiere mediante la venta de bonos o pagarés, en lugar de la venta de acciones.

DEBT SERVICE. Servicio sobre la deuda. Los intereses y cargos debidos sobre una deuda, incluyendo los pagos sobre la deuda principal.

DEBTOR. Deudor. Aquél que debe dinero o tiene que pagar una deuda.

DECEDENT. Difunto, muerto, fallecido, finado.

DECEIT. Dolo, engaño, fraude, trampa. Afirmación falsa e intencional dirigida a engañar y sorprender a otra persona causándole un perjuicio. Véase "Misrepresentation", "artifice", "fraud".

DECISION. Decisión, fallo, resolución. Conclusión legal hecha por una corte después de considerar la ley y los hechos.

DECISION ON THE MERITS. Decisión final que resuelve completamente un pleito con el efecto de impedir otra demanda entre las mismas partes y el mismo objeto.

DECLARANT. Declarante. Persona que rinde una afirmación o declaración.

DECLARATION. Declaración. (1) Afirmación no jurada realizada fuera de la corte. (2) Afirmación formal de un hecho. (3) Proclamación pública. (4) Anuncio sobre la disposición de dineros.

DECLARATION OF TRUST. Declaración de Fideicomiso. Afirmación del que tiene control sobre una propiedad, estableciendo que la tiene para el beneficio de otra persona.

DECLARATORY JUDGMENT. Sentencia declaratoria. Decisión judicial que declara un derecho sin conceder un remedio o sin ordenar algo. Procedimiento judicial para definir y aclarar los derechos de las partes.

DECLARATORY STATUTE. Ley declaratoria. Ley dictada para aclarar otra o explicar su sentido.

DECREE. Decreto. (1) Sentencia que anuncia las consecuencias legales de los hechos probados y ordena que se ejecute la decisión judicial. (2) Proclamación u orden dada por aquél que tiene autoridad absoluta para dar órdenes.

DECRIMINALIZATION. (1) Legalización de un acto ilegal. (2) Acto oficial que convierte una conducta delictiva en una sin consecuencias criminales.

DEDICATION. Dedicación. Donación de un derecho o propiedad para el uso público.

DEDUCTIBLE. Deducible. Aquello que puede ser sustraído de otra cosa. (1) Cantidad de dinero que se sustrae de la renta para efectos fiscales. (2) Aquella parte de una pérdida que debe ser pagada por un asegurado antes de que la aseguradora pague el resto.

DEDUCTION. Deducción. (1) Conclusión lógica obtenida de principios y hechos probados. (2) Sustracción de dinero debido. (3) Sustracción de la renta para efectos fiscales. (4) **Itemized Deductions.** Deducciones detalladas. Aquellas deducciones de la renta bruta ajustada de gastos no comerciales. (5) **Standard Deduction.** El deducir un porcentaje fijo de la renta bruta en lugar de utilizar las deducciones detalladas.

DEED. Título de propiedad. Escritura de transferencia de propiedad; escritura. Documento firmado y entregado por una persona a otra transfiriendo una propiedad inmueble.

DEED OF TRUST. Escritura de creación de un fideicomiso. Un instrumento legal usado en ciertos estados en vez de una hipoteca donde la propiedad es otorgada a un fideicomiso hasta cumplir con los términos del contrato de compra.

DEEM. Juzgar, considerar.

DEEP POCKET. Bolsillo profundo. Expresión que indica que una persona, entre varios posibles demandados, tiene los recursos económicos para pagar la demanda. Esta es la persona a la que el demandante usualmente demanda.

DEFACE. Desfigurar. Hacer algo ilegible; estropear, mutilar. (1) Hacer ilegible un documento. (2) Destruir deliberadamente un monumento, bandera, edificio, etc.

DEFALCATION. Malversación, desfalco. (1) Malversación de dineros encomendados a uno para un propósito determinado. Usualmente se refiere a funcionarios públicos o de una corporación. (2) Resarcimiento o recuperación. Disminución de una deuda mediante la deducción de un crédito menor que tenía el deudor contra el acreedor.

DEFAMATION. Difamación. Perjuicio causado a la reputación de una persona mediante afirmaciones falsas y maliciosas. Incluye calumnia e injuria.

DEFAULT. Contumacia, rebeldía, incumplimiento, omisión, mora. (1) Incumplimiento de un deber legal. (2) Omisión de cumplir con un requisito en un procedimiento legal o en un juicio.

DEFAULT JUDGMENT. Cuando la sentencia es dictada contra una parte por no defender el caso o por omisión de las obligaciones impuestas por la corte.

DEFEASANCE. Resolutorio. Un instrumento que neutraliza o termina algún derecho o título.

DEFEASANCE CLAUSE. Cláusula resolutoria. Parte del contrato de hipoteca que establece la terminación del contrato una vez se han hecho todos los pagos.

DEFEASIBLE. Revocable, anulable. Sujeto a terminación por un acto o evento futuro.

DEFECT. Defecto. (1) Ausencia de algún requisito legal que hace a una cosa insuficiente. (2) Un defecto que resulta en una obligación civil.

DEFENDANT. Demandado, acusado. Persona contra quien se entabla una causa o proceso civil o penal.

DEFENDANT IN ERROR. Apelado. La parte en una apelación que no interpuso el recurso de apelación.

DEFENSE. Defensa. (1) Hechos, derechos y alegatos presentados por el demandado. (2) **Defense Attorney.** Abogado que representa al acusado o demandado, defendiendo a su cliente.

DEFICIENCY JUDGMENT. Sentencia por deficiencia. Una decisión judicial que requiere que una persona pague la diferecia o deficiencia que existe entre el dinero obtenido en la liquidación o remate de un activo que garantiza una deuda, y la deuda.

DEFICIT. Deficit. (1) Menos de lo que debe ser. (2) Cuando los egresos exceden los ingresos.

DEFINITIVE. Definitivo. Algo que concluye totalmente una demanda o resuelve un punto legal.

DEFINITE SENTENCE. Sentencia definitiva. Véase "Determinate sentence".

DEFRAUD. Defraudar, estafar, engañar. Actuar con malicia para aprovecharse de otro.

DEGREE. Grado. (1) División usada para indicar distancia o separación entre cosas o para indicar la gravedad de ellas. (2) **Degree of Proof.** Nivel inicial de prueba necesaria para resolver un caso (3) **Degree of Negligence.** El nivel o grado de negligencia de un actor. Véase "Negligence".

DEL CREDERE. Agente vendedor de bienes de otra persona que le garantiza al dueño que el comprador tiene dinero para comprar a crédito.

DELEGATION. Delegación. (1) Autorización dada por una persona a otra. (2) Acción de tomar la deuda de otra persona con su consentimiento. (3) **Delegation of Powers.** Transferencia de los poderes gubernamentales de una rama del gobierno a otra.

DELINQUENCY. Delincuencia. Omisión o violación de un deber.

DELINQUENT. Delincuente. (1) Vencido y debido. (2) Incumplimiento intencional de una obligación. (3) **Juvenile Delinquent.** Delincuente juvenil. Menor de edad que comete un acto ilegal o que se ha comportado mal.

DELIST. Remover acciones del mercado de valores.

DELIVERY. Entrega. Transferencia de propiedad mueble o inmueble.

DEMAND. Demanda. (1) Reclamo de un derecho ante una corte. (2) **On Demand.** A la vista. Refiérese al documento pagadero cuando se presenta. (3) **Demand Loan/Note.** Préstamo o pagaré pagaderos a la vista o cuando es presentados para pago. (4) **Demand Deposit.** Depósitos bancarios que se pueden retirar sin previo aviso.

DEMEANOR. Proceder, comportamiento; conducta de alguien.

DEMISE. (1) Fallecimiento, muerte. (2) Traspaso de bienes. (3) Arrendamiento.

DEMOCRACY. Democracia. Forma de gobernar basada en un sistema de representación en el cual participan todos los ciudadanos del estado.

DEMONSTRATIVE EVIDENCE. Evidencia demostrativa. Cualquier prueba, excepto la testimonial, percibida por los sentidos. Por ejemplo: exhibición de un arma de fuego.

DEMONSTRATIVE LEGACY. Legado demostrativo. Legado pagadero, de una parte en particular, del caudal hereditario.

DEMUR. Excepcionar, objeción.

DEMURRAGE. Detención, estadía. Demora. Dinero pagado al dueño de un buque o tren por la demora de su partida.

DEMURRER. Incidente o excepción. Interpuesta para desechar o desestimar una demanda. Normalmente indica que aunque sea cierto lo que alega el demandante, no existen bases legales contra el demandado.

DENATURALIZATION. Desnaturalización. Pérdida involuntaria de la ciudadanía previamente adquirida por naturalización.

DENIAL. Negación. (1) Parte de la contestación a la demanda en la cual se niegan los hechos alegados en la demanda.
(2) Denegación, rechazo.

DEP. (1) Abreviación de "Deputy" asistente. (2) Abreviación de "Department" departamento.

DEPENDENT. Dependiente. (1) Persona mantenida por otra.
(2) Condicional. Por ejemplo, un "Dependent Contract" es un contrato condicionado en el cual una parte no tiene que realizar ningún acto hasta que la otra haya hecho algo.

DEPENDENT RELATIVE REVOCATION. Doctrina que establece que si un testador revoca su testamento para realizar otro en el futuro, de no llegar a realizarlo se presume que hubiese deseado la validez del revocado en vez de no tener testamento alguno.

DEPLETION ALLOWANCE. Deducción fiscal concedida a los que explotan el subsuelo.

DEPONENT. Deponente. Persona que hace una declaración jurada ante un notario o autoridad competente. Véase "Deposition".

DEPORTATION. Deportación. Sacar a una persona de un país y enviarla a otro.

DEPOSE. Deponer. (1) Tomar una declaración jurada de una persona ante una autoridad competente. Véase "Deposition". (2) Sacar por la fuerza a una persona de su cargo público.

DEPOSIT. Depósito. (1) Dar una cosa a otra persona para que la cuide y guarde. (2) Dar dinero a alguien como abono o adelanto de una compra. (3) Dinero dado a un banco para que lo guarde y sobre el que se gana intereses. (4) **Time Deposit.** Depósito a Plazo. Debe ser mantenido en el banco por cierto período de tiempo. (5) **Demand Deposit.** Depósito a la vista. Pagadero en cualquier momento. (6) **Certified Deposit.** Depósito a plazo fijo.

DEPOSIT IN COURT. Entrega de un dinero al tribunal para que determine a quién le corresponde.

DEPOSITARY. Depositario. (1) Persona a quien se le entrega algo en depósito para que lo guarde. (2) Depositaría. Lugar donde se deposita algo.

DEPOSITION. Deposición. Declaración jurada de una persona fuera de los estrados del tribunal. Es uno de los métodos más comunes e importantes para obtener evidencia y establecer los hechos en cualquier litigio. Una parte obtiene una citación que se entrega a la persona (deponente) que debe atestiguar. Dicha persona debe responder a varias preguntas ante un funcionario de la corte, quien transcribe todas las preguntas y respuestas durante la sesión.

DEPOSITOR. Depositante. Quien da algo a otro en depósito para que se lo guarde.

DEPOSITORY. Depositorio. (1) Lugar donde se deposita algo. (2) Depositario. Persona ante quien se deposita algo.

DEPRECIATION. Depreciación. Pérdida o disminución del valor de una cosa.

DEPUTY. Asistente, suplente, diputado. Funcionario autorizado para actuar por otro. Usualmente el segundo al mando de una organización.

DERELICT. Abandonado. (1) Propiedad intencionalmente abandonada. (2) Buque abandonado sea o no intencionalmente.

DERELICTION. (1) Abandono de propiedad. (2) Negligencia en el desempeño de un cargo público.

DERIVATIVE ACTION. Demanda derivada. Acción legal entablada por el accionista de una sociedad a nombre de ella para hacer valer un derecho de ella contra un tercero.

DERIVATIVE EVIDENCE. Prueba derivada. Prueba recogida en base a otra obtenida ilegalmente. No tiene validez en la corte.

DERIVATIVE TORT. (1) Responsabilidad civil extracontractual derivada de un agravio. (2) Demanda por la responsabilidad civil extracontractual que tiene el patrón o principal por las actos de su agente o empleado.

DERIVATIVE WORK. Trabajo derivado. Significa que una obra continúa siendo propiedad del autor aunque se exprese en otra forma artística. Por ejemplo: radio, teatro.

DEROGATION. Derogación. Abolición parcial de una ley por medio de otra que la limita.

DEROGATORY CLAUSE. Cláusula derogatoria. Disposición secreta de un testador de que no será válido ningún testamento futuro que no incluya una frase secreta que sólo el testador conoce.

DESCENT. Descendiente. Herencia.

DESECRATE. Profanar. Destrucción o daño hecho a un edificio público.

DESERTION. Deserción. (1) Abandono de un puesto militar sin la intención de volver. (2) Abandono de un cónyuge o de un hijo sin la intención de reanudar los deberes que se tiene para con ellos. (3) Abandono de un cargo.

DESIRE. Deseo. En un testamento su definición varía desde una preferencia simple hasta una orden irrefutable.

DESPOIL. Robar, despojar. Quitar una cosa a alguien ilegalmente y mediante violencia.

DESTINATION CONTRACT. Negociación mediante la cual se contempla que el riesgo de pérdida o daño del embarque corren con el vendedor hasta que lleguen a su destino.

DESTITUTE. Indigente. Sin la habilidad o los medios para mantener su vida.

DESTITUTION. Indigencia. Pobreza.

DESTROY. Destruir. La eliminación de los efectos legales de un documento.

DETAINER. Detención. (1) Mantener o retener ilegalmente la propiedad de otra persona. (2) Retener a una persona contra su voluntad. (3) Auto u orden de detención para mantener a una persona bajo custodia.

DETENTION. Detención. (1) Retención de una persona contra su voluntad. (2) **Detention for Questioning.** Detención hecha por un policía u oficial para interrogar a una persona.

DETER. Acción diseñada para prevenir o desalentar otra acción indeseable.

DETERMINABLE. Determinable. Que puede ser decidido o determinado.

DETERMINATE SENTENCE. Sentencia fija. Pena establecida exactamente por ley, la cual no está sujeta a disminución.

DETERMINE. Determinar, decidir.

DETINUE. Acción reivindicatoria. Para recuperar un bien que está siendo retenido ilegalmente.

DETOURNEMENT. Apropiación indebida, desfalco, malversación. Tomar dinero encomendado a uno y usarlo para el beneficio propio. Normalmente por un sirviente.

DETRACTION. Quitar. Sacar bienes de un caudal hereditario y transferir el título de esos bienes a otro.

DETRIMENT. Detrimento. Cualquier pérdida o daño. Perjuicio.

496

DETRIMENTAL RELIANCE. Confianza perjudicial. La acción ejecutada por una persona basada en una promesa contractual la cual no es cumplida, causándole daños y perjuicios.

DEVALUATION. Devaluación. Reducción del valor de la moneda de un país, usualmente en relación o referencia a la moneda de otro país.

DEVEST. Quitar, salir de algo, privar. Despojar.

DEVIATION. Desviación. (1) Salir del curso normal. (2) Cambio en los términos contractuales originales. (3) Permitir que se ignoren términos de un testamento para alcanzar la intención del testador.

DEVISE. Legado. Disposición en un testamento dejando bienes, usualmente inmuebles, a una persona.

DEVISEE. Legatario. Recibidor de bienes legados.

DEVISOR. Testador. El que deja bienes inmuebles por testamento.

DEVOLUTION. Entrega, transferencia. (1) Traspaso legal de un derecho, obligación, título o propiedad. (2) En Inglaterra, la decentralización gubernamental.

DICTUM. (Lat.) Opinión emitida por un Juez al decidir un caso que no es parte central o medular de su conclusión. Si la opinión emitida no es necesaria para alcanzar el resultado final de la decisión, es dictum. El dictum no tiene fuerza de precedente pero puede ser alegado para reforzar otro caso.

DIES. (Lat.) Días.

DIET. Dieta. Cuerpo u órgano legislativo.

DIGEST. Digesto. Recopilación de normas y precedentes legales, usualmente con comentarios de expertos.

DILATORY. Dilatorio. Que intenta ganar tiempo o retrasar un evento.

DILIGENCE. Diligencia. (1) Cuidadoso y prudente. (2) **Due Diligence.** Normalmente se refiere a las investigaciones de todos los hechos relevantes antes de emitir acciones en la bolsa de valores. Dichos hechos deben ser publicados antes de venderse las acciones.

DIMINISHED RESPONSIBILITY. Disminución de responsabilidad. Estado mental en el que se encuentra un delincuente al cometer un delito, y que puede ser causa de atenuación de la pena. Por ejemplo, retraso mental.

DIMINUTION. Disminución. (1) **Diminution in Value.** Disminución del valor. Una forma de medir los daños causados a la propiedad o a un derecho, equivalente a la diferencia entre el valor del bien antes y después del daño. (2) **Diminution of Damages.** Disminución o mitigación de los daños. Véase "Mitigation of Damages".

DIPLOMACY. Diplomacia. Arte de negociar entre dos naciones para obtener relaciones políticas mutuamente satisfactorias.

DIPLOMATIC IMMUNITY. Inmunidad diplomática. Derecho de un representante diplomático a no ser procesado penalmente bajo las leyes del estado huésped.

DIRECT ACTION. Acción Directa. (1) Demanda contra la compañía de seguros de uno en lugar de contra la persona o la compañía de seguros de la persona que causa el daño. (2) Demanda de un accionista contra la compañía o dignatarios de la compañía en la cual es accionista, para hacer valer un derecho propio y no el de la compañía.

DIRECT ATTACK. Ataque directo. Procedimiento iniciado con el único propósito de ver una decisión judicial anulada, revocada, o impugnada.

DIRECT CAUSE. Causa directa. Véase "Proximate cause".

DIRECT EVIDENCE. Prueba directa. Evidencia testimonial de una persona que vio, tocó, u oyó lo sujeto a interrogación.

DIRECT EXAMINATION. Interrogación directa. Primeros interrogatorios hechos a un testigo por el abogado que lo llamó a declarar. Contrarios a los interrogatorios hechos a ese testigo por el abogado de la contraparte lo cual constituye "Cross-Examination".

DIRECT LINE. Ascendencia o descendencia por línea directa. Abuelos, padres, hijos, nietos.

DIRECT TAX. Impuesto directo. Impuesto sobre bienes inmuebles, basado en el valor de la propiedad.

DIRECTED VERDICT. Veredicto ordenado por el juez.

DIRECTOR. Director. Persona que dirije una organización, grupo o proyecto. En una corporación, el director es elegido por los accionistas para dirigir las actividades de la corporación.

DIRECTORY. Directorio. (1) Instrucción legal sin fuerza obligatoria. (2) **Mandatory Directory Trust.** Fideicomiso mandatorio con instrucciones expresas que no permiten discreción al fiduciario.

DISABILITY. Incapacidad. (1) **Legal Disability.** Incapacidad legal. Ausencia de capacidad legal para realizar un acto. (2) **Physical or Mental Disability.** Inhabilidad física o mental. La inhabilidad puede ser total o parcial, permanente o transitoria. Usualmente, la inhabilidad sufrida afecta la capacidad de una persona para trabajar. Véase "Worker's Compensation".

DISABLED. Incapacitado, lisiado, inválido.

DISAFFIRM. Negar, anular, repudiar. Retirar el consentimiento ya dado. Rehusar o negarse a cumplir promesas dadas o a mantener acciones pasadas.

DISBAR. Desaforar. Quitarle a un abogado el derecho de ejercer la abogacía. Excluirlo de la profesión.

DISCHARGE. Liberar, absolver, remover, pagar, terminar, cancelar. (1) **Discharge a Contract.** Terminar un contrato. (2) **Discharge a Prisoner.** Liberar a un prisionero. (3) **Discharge a Court Order.** Cancelar o revocar una orden judicial. (4) Cumplir con una obligación.

DISCIPLINARY RULES. Reglas de ética y responsabilidad profesional de los abogados.

DISCLAIM. Renuncia. Abandono.

DISCLAIMER. Renuncia, repudio. rechazo.

DISCLOSURE. Revelación. (1) La divulgación de un secreto.
(2) En derecho mercantil, y para la protección del consumidor, se
refiere a la información divulgada en el acuerdo de préstamo o en
una compra a crédito.

DISCONTINUANCE. Desestimación. Descontinuación de un
proceso por falta de causas que justifiquen la acción de la justicia.

DISCOUNT. Descuento. (1) Pago de intereses por adelantado.
(2) Cualquier reducción hecha a una suma de dinero.

DISCOUNT RATE. Tarifa de descuento. Cantidad, usualmente
expresada en términos de porcentajes, por medio de la cual se
reduce el valor futuro de un documento negociable.

DISCOVERED PERIL DOCTRINE. Doctrina del peligro
descubierto. Principio legal que le permite ganar el caso a un
demandante en una causa por negligencia, aun cuando también
exista negligencia por su parte. Es una excepción al principio de
negligencia contributoria. Los fundamentos de la doctrina son:
(a) Condición a la que se expone el demandante por su propia
negligencia, (b) descubrimiento por parte del demandado de la
condición peligrosa con suficiente tiempo para evitar el daño, y
(c) falta del demandado en utilizar los medios que evitarían el
daño.

DISCOVERY. Descubrimiento. (1) Determinación de lo que era
previamente desconocido. (2) Medios extra-judiciales para obtener
hechos e información relativa a un caso. Métodos para obtener e
intercambiar información entre las partes con el objeto de
establecer los hechos de un caso.

DISCREDIT. Desacreditar. Afectar la credibilidad de una persona
o documento.

DISCRETION. Discreción. Conducta legal que es prudente y guiada
por principios generales sin sujetarse a reglas específicas, y que
no es motivada por perjuicio, capricho o abuso.

DISCRETIONARY REVIEW. Revisión discrecional. Véase
"Certiorari".

DISCRETIONARY TRUST. Fideicomiso discrecional. Permite el uso de la discreción del fiduciario en su ejecución.

DISCRIMINATION. Discriminación. (1) No tratar a los iguales como iguales. (2) Tratar en forma diferente e ilegal a las personas por razones de raza, religión, sexo, o edad.

DISFRANCHISE. Quitar o privar a una persona de sus derechos como ciudadano.

DISHONOR. Incumplir. Rehusar el pago de un documento negociable cuando su pago es exigido.

DISMISS. Desechar una demanda o un caso. Orden judicial que declara sin lugar un proceso.

DISORDERLY HOUSE. Casa o establecimiento cuyos inquilinos practican actos contra la moral pública.

DISPARAGEMENT. Descrédito, menosprecio, rebaja. Desacreditar a alguien o algo.

DISPATCH. Despachar. Envío de mercancías, usualmente con cierta agilidad.

DISPENSATION. Exención. Permiso para hacer algo que está prohibido.

DISPOSE. Disponer, enajenar. Vender o transferir algo.

DISPOSITION. Disposición. Resultado final de una causa.

DISPOSSESSION. (1) Desposeer, despojar. (2) Juicio de desahucio entablado por el arrendador para sacar al arrendatario de la propiedad arrendada.

DISPROVE. Refutar. Probar lo contrario de lo alegado por la otra parte.

DISPUTE. Disputa. Contienda o desacuerdo entre dos partes acerca de sus obligaciones y derechos.

DISSEIZIN. Usurpación. Quitarle a una persona un bien inmueble sin tener derecho a hacerlo.

DISSENT. Disentir. Cuando un juez está en contra de la opinión de la mayoría en un caso.

DISSENTING OPINION. Opinión disidente. Escrito en el cual un juez expresa su desacuerdo con la opinión de la mayoría en un caso.

DISSOLUTION. Disolución, terminación. (1) **Dissolution of Contract.** Terminación de un Contrato. (2) **Dissolution of a Corporation.** Disolución de una sociedad anónima. (3) **Dissolution of Marriage.** Extinción del vínculo matrimonial basado en las diferencias irreconciliables de la pareja, sin que haya un cónyuge culpable.

DISTINGUISH. Distinguir o diferenciar. Establecer las diferencias básicas entre un caso alegado como precedente y el mismo caso en proceso. Demostrar que el caso invocado como precedente es irrelevante.

DISTRAIN. Embargar, secuestrar. Tomar la propiedad de otra persona por medios legales o ilegales.

DISTRESS. Angustia, secuestro, embargo. (1) Proceso de embargo. Véase "Distrain". (2) Tener una aflicción. (3) **Distress Sale.** Venta en la cual el precio de los bienes es más bajo de lo normal porque el vendedor ha sido forzado a liquidar dichos bienes.

DISTRIBUTEE. Heredero. Persona que recibe una herencia.

DISTRIBUTION. Distribución. Dividir por cuotas y partes.

DISTRIBUTIVE FINDING. Decisión de un jurado bajo la cual una parte del caso está a favor del demandado y otra a favor del demandante.

DISTRIBUTOR. Distribuidor de mercancías.

DISTRICT. Distrito. División política de un territorio.

DISTRICT ATTORNEY. Fiscal de Distrito. Máximo representante del Ministerio Público en un Distrito Federal o Estatal.

DISTRICT COURT. Corte de Distrito. (1) **Federal District Court.** Corte de procedimiento federal. Hay una en cada distrito federal que puede abarcar todo o parte de un Estado. (2) Corte de primera instancia en algunos estados y de apelación en otros estados.

DISTURBING THE PEACE. Alteración del orden público. Tiene diferente significado en diferentes estados.

DIVERSION. Desviación. Comerciar con mercancía en un área o mercado diferente del que estaba originalmente destinada, o en el cual se estaba autorizado. Destinar mercancía hacia un área o mercado donde no se ha autorizado la comercialización de ese producto.

DIVERSITY OF CITIZENSHIP JURISDICTION. Diversidad de ciudadanía. Principio que permite que una corte federal resuelva un caso en donde las partes son de distintos estados, o donde una parte es de un estado de los Estados Unidos, y la otra de otro país.

DIVERT. Desviar. Imcumplimiento contractual que surje si se comercia con productos en áreas no autorizadas.

DIVEST. Desposeer, despojar, enajenar.

DIVESTITURE ORDER. Orden de Desposeimiento. Orden judicial disponiendo que una compañía se deshaga de algo por razones de monopolio.

DIVIDEND. Dividendo. Ganancias distribuídas por una corporación. (1) **Asset Dividend.** Dividendo en propiedad o activo. Dividendo pagado con bienes de la corporación. (2) **Consent Dividend.** Dividendo declarado y no pagado. (3) **Constructive Dividend.** Dividendo implícito. Pago excesivo a una persona que se grava como dividendo recibido. (4) **Cumulative Dividend.** Dividendo acumulable. Si tales dividendos no se pagan regularmente, se acumulan y deben ser pagados antes de que se paguen los dividendos de acciones comunes. (5) **Deficiency Dividend.** Dividendo pagado para reponer uno anterior no pagado. (6) **Stock Dividend.** No es un dividendo real ya que se paga mediante la emisión de más acciones que se entregan en vez del dividendo.

DIVORCE. Divorcio. Terminación judicial de un matrimonio.

DOCK. El área especial adonde se mantiene a los acusados en una corte criminal.

DOCKET. (1) Lista de casos que esperan juicio o audiencia. (2) Libro del estado de los casos.

DOCTOR–PATIENT PRIVILEGE. Secreto profesional. El derecho de un paciente de mantener secretas sus comunicaciones con su médico. Generalmente, el médico no puede atestiguar sobre dichas comunicaciones sin la autorización del paciente.

DOCTRINE. Doctrina. Principio legal.

DOCUMENT. Documento. Escrito o documento que tiene efecto legal y que puede ser usado como prueba.

DOCUMENTARY EVIDENCE. Prueba documental. Evidencia presentada mediante escritos o documentos.

DOCUMENTARY STAMP. Estampilla, sello o timbre fiscal. Debe ponerse en algunos documentos antes de ser registrados en una oficina pública.

DOING BUSINESS. Realizar o efectuar negocios. Término que implica la actividad comercial necesaria para que se pueda demandar a la empresa o persona en el estado donde realiza sus negocios.

DOING BUSINESS AS. "Hacer negocios como..." Indica la calidad y el nombre en la cual se realiza una transacción comercial.

DOMAIN. Dominio. Propiedad y control absoluto de un bien, generalmente inmueble.

DOMESTIC INTERNATIONAL SALES CORPORATION D.I.S.C. Sociedad Anónima organizada bajo las leyes de algún estado de los Estados Unidos, y cuyos ingresos provienen de ventas realizadas en el extranjero.

DOMICILE. Domicilio. Lugar donde una persona vive permanentemente. En ocasiones las palabras "abode," "citizenship," "habitancy" y "residence" pueden ser tomadas como sinónimo de domicilio.

DOMINANT. Dominante. Que tiene derechos sobre otra persona o cosa. (1) **Dominant Estate.** Predio o finca dominante. Terreno que tiene derechos sobre otra finca.

DOMINION. Dominio. Control efectivo y real sobre una cosa.

DONATIO. (Lat.) Donación. Obsequio, regalo.

DONEE. Donatario. Persona a quien se le da un regalo o un poder.

DONOR. Donante. Persona que da un regalo u otorga un poder.

DORMANT. Durmiente. Que se encuentra inactivo.

DOUBLE INDEMNITY. Indemnización doble. Pago doble de un beneficio bajo una póliza de seguros al ocurrir condiciones específicas.

DOUBLE INSURANCE. Seguro doble. Seguro que se tiene sobre una cosa con más de una compañía de seguros.

DOUBLE TAXATION. Doble imposición fiscal. (1) Cuando el mismo bien o dinero es gravado dos veces por el gobierno en un período fijo. Por ejemplo, el impuesto sobre la renta de una sociedad además de los dividendos de esa misma sociedad.

DOUBLE WILL. Véase "Reciprocal Will".

DOUBT. Duda. Incertidumbre acerca de una prueba en un juicio.

DOW JONES AVERAGE. Precio promedio de las acciones de un grupo selecto de las industrias más grandes en los Estados Unidos.

DOWER. Derecho que tiene la viuda sobre parte de los bienes de su difunto esposo.

DOWN PAYMENT. Abono inicial. Dinero, usualmente en efectivo, entregado como pago inicial de una deuda contraída a plazo.

DRAFT. (1) Un documento negociable que es emitido por uno como pago a otro. Por ejemplo, un cheque. (2) Un borrador de un documento.

DRAW. (1) Emitir o preparar un documento legal. Por ejemplo, un giro, cheque, o contrato. (2) Retirar dinero de una cuenta bancaria. (3) **Draw a Jury.** Seleccionar a los miembros de un jurado.

DRAWBACK. (1) Devolución o reembolso de impuesto. Reembolso que hace el fisco al contribuyente que ha pagado impuesto de importación sobre bienes que son reexportados. (2) Desventaja, inconveniente.

DRAWEE. Girado, librado. Persona a la que se le ordena o instruye mediante cierto documento negociable que pague o haga efectivo dicho documento. Usualmente es el banco en el cual se tiene la cuenta corriente contra la cual se gira.

DRAWER. Girador, librador. Persona que emite un documento negociable ordenando a otra persona que lo pague. Usualmente el girador es quien gira o firma el cheque.

DUCES TECUM. (Lat.) "Traiga consigo". Frase usualmente usada con una citación de la corte que requiere que un testigo traiga a la corte ciertos documentos u objetos.

DUE. (1) Pagadero, vencido, debido, cumplido. (2) Apto, justo, propio. Por ejemplo, usar el cuidado necesario dentro de las circunstancias es "due care". (3) **Due Process.** Doctrina constitucional que protege a cada ciudadano contra acciones arbitrarias y que requiere un proceso legal antes de despojar a alguien de algun bien o derecho.

DUMP. Vender un artículo en otro país a menor precio del que se vende en el país de origen.

DUN. Demandar el pago de una deuda vencida.

DUPLICATE. Duplicar; duplicado. (1) Copia. (2) Documento nuevo hecho para reemplazar a su original.

DURESS. Coacción, compulsión. Presión ejercida ilegalmente sobre otra persona para que haga lo que de otra forma no hubiese hecho.

DUTY. Obligación, deber. (1) Deber de observar la ley. (2) Obligación legal hacia otra persona. (3) Cualquier obligación, bien sea legal, moral, o ética.

DWELLING DEFENSE. Véase "Castle Doctrine".

506

DYING DECLARATION. Declaración en el lecho de muerte. Testimonio extrajudicial acerca de las circuntancias de su muerte dado por quien está falleciendo.

E

E.B.I.T. Siglas de "Earnings Before Interest and Taxes." Ganancias obtenidas antes de sacar los intereses e impuestos.

E.G. Siglas de "Exampli Gratia" (Lat.). Literalmente "Por ejemplo".

E.P.S. Siglas de "Earnings per Share". Literalmente "Ganancias por acción".

E.R.I.S.A. Siglas de "Employee Retirement Income Security Act". Ley Federal que rige la administración de pensiones.

EARLIER MATURITY RULE. Regla de vencimiento anticipado bajo la cual los bonos que se vencen primero son pagados antes que otras deudas.

EARNED INCOME. Ingreso o renta ganada. Dinero o compensación recibida por trabajar. No incluye ganancias obtenidas por poseer propiedades. (1) **Earned Income Credit.** Crédito de renta ganada. Beneficio otorgado a trabajadores de pocos ingresos.

EARNEST MONEY. Fianza, arras. Depósito pagado por el comprador para asegurarle a un vendedor el cumplimiento de un contrato.

EARNINGS PER SHARE. Ganancia por acción. Ganancia de una sociedad disponible para ser pagada como dividendo, y dividida entre el número de acciones comunes en manos de los inversionistas.

EASEMENT. Servidumbre. Derecho que tiene el público, gobierno o persona para usar parte de un terreno de una forma en especial. La finca sobre la que pesa el gravamen o servidumbre es la sirviente ("servient"), y aquélla que es beneficiada se llama dominante ("dominant"). El concepto del "easement" es uno de los más importantes en el área de derecho inmobiliario.

ECONOMIC STRIKE. Huelga por conflicto económico.

EDICT. Edicto. Ley dictada por un rey o alto Jefe de Estado.

EDUCATIONAL EXPENSES. Gastos educacionales pagados para alcanzar un nivel de conocimiento o proficiencia, o una preparación académica.

EFFECTS. Efectos. Bienes personales de un testador o de un difunto. Propiedad personal.

EFFICIENT CAUSE. Véase "Proximate Cause".

EIGHTEENTH AMENDMENT. Decimoctava enmienda a la Constitución de los EE.UU., mediante la cual se prohibía la venta de bebidas alcohólicas. Esta enmienda ha sido derogada.

EJECTMENT. Lanzamiento. Demanda para recuperar una propiedad por quien ha sido privado del uso de la misma.

EJUSDEM GENERIS. (Lat.) Del mismo género. Regla bajo la cual las palabras generales son interpretadas en su sentido más limitado, cuando el texto anterior a las palabras generales consiste de una lista especifica o limitada de palabras o cosas.

ELECTION. Elección. (1) Acto de elegir. (2) Escoger entre derechos o remedios legales.

ELECTOR. Votante. El que emite su voto.

ELEEMOSYNARY. Caritativo; de caridad. Que no tiene fines de lucro.

ELEMENT. Elemento; ingrediente de algo; factor.

ELIGIBILITY. Elegibilidad. Que tiene capacidad para un cargo.

ELOIGN. Véase "Eloignment".

ELOIGNMENT. Ocultar bienes para mantenerlos fuerta del alcance de la corte.

ELOIN. Véase "Eloignment".

EMANCIPATION. Emancipación. Dejar en libertad. Por ejemplo, un hijo se emancipa cuando tiene edad suficiente para actuar sin estar bajo el control de sus padres.

509

EMBARGO. Embargo. Restricción impuesta por un país sobre la venta o compra de mercancias de otro país.

EMBEZZLEMENT. Apropiación indebida. Delito cometido por el que se apropia de bienes o dineros que le han sido dados para un propósito.

EMBLEMENTS. Derecho del arrendatario a cosechar y recoger los frutos de la tierra que arrienda.

EMBRACERY. Soborno. Cohecho. Delito cometido por quien intenta sobornar a un jurado.

EMERGENCY DOCTRINE. Doctrina de la emergencia. (1) Una persona no tiene que observar durante una emergencia el mismo cuidado que se le requeriría bajo diferentes circunstancias. (2) Si no está presente la persona apropiada para autorizar tratamiento médico de emergencia, el tratamiento necesario para salvar una vida puede ser suministrado.

EMINENT DOMAIN. Dominio Eminente o Supremo. Poder de una entidad gubernamental para expropiar forzosamente, con indemnización, una propiedad para el bien común.

EMIT. Emitir. Poner en circulación.

EMOLUMENT. Emolumento. Pago por trabajo.

EMPLOYER. Empleador, patrono, empresario. El que contrata los servicios de otro.

EMPLOYMENT. Empleo; ocupación. Actividad ejercida con retribución económica.

EN BANC. (Fr.) Pleno. Audiencia donde todos los jueces de la corte están presentes para decidir un caso.

ENACT. Promulgar. Sancionar, poner en vigencia una ley.

ENCROACHMENT. Intrusión, invasión, usurpación. Intrusión ilegal sobre la propiedad ajena.

ENCUMBER. Gravar, afectar. Véase "Encumbrance".

ENCUMBRANCE. Gravamen. Carga sobre una propiedad, por ejemplo, una hipoteca.

ENDORSE. Endoso. Véase "Indorse".

ENDORSEMENT. Endoso. Firmar un documento. Firmar un documento negociable para transferirlo a un tercero. Véase "Indorsement".

ENDOWMENT. Dotación, fundación. (1) Fondo para donación de caridad o beneficencia. (2) **Endowment Policy.** Póliza dotal que paga una cantidad fija en un tiempo establecido, o que paga una cantidad a un beneficiario cuando muere el asegurado.

ENFORCEABILITY. Ejecutabilidad. Que puede hacerse valer.

ENFORCEMENT. Observación. Cumplimiento. Ejecución. Ejecución de una ley; hacer valer un derecho.

ENFRANCHISEMENT. (1) Poner en libertad. (2) Otorgar el derecho a votar.

ENGAGE. Comprometer; participar en algo.

ENGAGEMENT. Compromiso.

ENHANCE. Aumentar, acrecentar.

ENJOIN. Prohibir, requerir, ordenar. Orden de una corte prohibiéndole a alguien hacer algo o indicándole qué hacer.

ENJOYMENT. Goce, uso, disfrute, usufructo.

ENROLL. Alistar; matricular; inscribir.

ENSUE. Resultar. Lo que sigue lógicamente a algo.

ENTAIL. Vincular. Propiedad que se transmite sólo a los hijos de los hijos, etc.

ENTER. Entrar. Registrar formalmente.

ENTER JUDGMENT. Registrar una sentencia o un fallo en los libros de la corte.

ENTERPRISE. Negocio, empresa, actividad.

ENTICE. Seducir, atraer, tentar. Persuadir a uno menor para que venga a un lugar solitario con la intención de aprovecharse de él/ella sexualmente.

ENTITLE. Autorizado. Facultado. Con derecho a algo.

ENTITLEMENT. Estar titulado para ejercer. Tener derecho a algo.

ENTITY. Entidad. Persona jurídica ficticia.

ENTRAPMENT. Acto por el cual un funcionario público induce a una persona a cometer un delito que de otra forma la persona no hubiera cometido.

ENTREPRENEUR. Hombre de negocios, empresario.

ENTRUST. Confiar. Entregar o depositar algo con alguien en quien uno confía para que lo cuide.

ENTRY. Entrada, anotación.

ENVIRONMENTAL IMPACT STATEMENT. Estudio y documentación del impacto que tendrá un proyecto sobre el medio ambiente.

ENVOY. Enviado diplomático.

EQUAL DEGREE. Del mismo grado. Que tienen el mismo grado en la línea de afinidad o consanguinidad.

EQUALIZE. Igualar. Poner en condición similar. Emparejar.

EQUITABLE. Equitativo, justo. (1) **Equitable Election.** Elección equitativa. Principio que impone la obligación de elegir entre dos cosas posibles cuando no es justo obtener ambas. (2) Cuando la corte considera que algo existe, por razones de equidad o justicia, aunque en estricta legalidad no existe.

EQUITABLE ACTION. Un pleito que requiere un remedio equitativo.

EQUITABLE ESTOPPEL. Cuando la conducta o los actos de alguien le impiden tomar una posición contraria a esos actos en el futuro, por razones de justicia.

EQUITABLE ABSTENTION DOCTRINE. Doctrina judicial que permite a una corte abstenerse de tomar jurisdicción sobre un caso cuando sería ofensivo a otro estado.

EQUITY. Equidad, justicia. (1) Justicia en un caso particular. (2) Poder de un magistrado para hacer justicia cuando las leyes no proveerían una solución justa. (3) El valor residual de la propiedad luego de que todas las obligaciones han sido canceladas. (4) Acciones de una corporación.

EQUITY FINANCING. Adquisición de dinero para financiar un proyecto mediante la venta de acciones en lugar de pedir un préstamo.

EQUIVALENTS DOCTRINE. Principio de la equivalencia o similitud, mediante el cual se considera como una misma máquina aquellas que aunque tengan patentes distintas, realizan la misma función de manera similar. En estos casos, la máquina con la primera patente está protegida por las leyes de patentes.

ERASURE OF RECORD. Procedimiento mediante el cual se limpia el historial penal y criminal de una persona o se hace inaccesible al público.

ERGO. (Lat.) Por tanto, luego, pues.

ERRATUM. (Lat.) Error.

ERROR. Error, sea inofensivo o significativo, en un proceso legal.

ESCALATOR CLAUSE. Cláusula de ajuste. Cláusula que permite que aumente o disminuya el salario de un obrero dependiendo de las fluctuaciones del costo de la vida.

ESCAPE CLAUSE. Cláusula de escape. Aquélla que en un contrato libera a una parte de completar cierta obligación si se dan ciertas circunstancias.

ESCHEAT. Revertir. Bienes que se revierten al estado si su dueño muere sin testar y no se encuentra un heredero.

513

ESCOBEDO RULE. Principio que impide usar su declaración contra un detenido, si este pidió un abogado y se le negó.

ESCROW. Plica. Depósito. Dinero, propiedad o documento entregado, a un tercero para que lo guarde hasta la realización de la obligación, y por medio de cuya entrega se le obliga a algo.

ESQ. Abreviación de esquire. Título dado en Inglaterra a algunos abogados. En los Estados Unidos se escribe generalmente a continuación del nombre del abogado.

ESSENCE. Esencia. Los términos esenciales de un contrato.

ESTATE. Masa hereditaria; bienes, propiedades, patrimonio. (1) El interés que tiene una persona en cierta propiedad. (2) La propiedad misma sobre la cual se tiene un interés. Uno de los conceptos básicos en el área de bienes raíces.

ESTIN DOCTRINE. Principio que señala que mientras un estado debe reconocer el divorcio otorgado en otro estado, no tiene por qué reconocer la sentencia de manutención si el estado que expidió la sentencia no tenía jurisdicción sobre el demandado.

ESTOPPEL. Impedimento. Principio legal que impide a alguien, basado en los actos propios, reclamar algo opuesto a lo dicho o actuado por la propia persona.

ESTOPPEL BY JUDGMENT. Impedimento para reclamar algo por haber sido resuelto previamente por medio de una sentencia si se refiere a la misma reclamación y a las mismas partes.

ESTOVER. Pensión alimenticia. Véase "Alimony". (1) Pensión dada para abastecer las necesidades básicas. (2) Derecho del arrendatario de cortar los árboles del predio arrendado para satisfacer ciertas necesidades básicas.

ET AL. (Lat.) Y otros.

ET SEQ. (Lat.) Y los que siguen.

ET UX. (Lat.) Y esposa.

ET UIR. (Lat.) Y esposo.

ETHICS. Ética. (1) Normas de comportamiento profesional para abogados y jueces. (2) Nivel de conducta justa en general.

EURODOLLAR. Moneda de curso legal en los Estados Unidos depositada en bancos fuera de los Estados Unidos.

EUTHANASIA. Eutanasia. Muerte por misericordia. Muerte causada a una persona que padece una enfermedad gravísima sin posibilidades de recuperación para abreviar su sufrimiento.

EVASION. Evasión. Acto ilegal de no pagar o de pagar en una cantidad inferior a los impuestos debidos.

EVASIVE. Evasivo. Calidad de una demanda que no señala cargos definidos ni concretos.

EVERGREEN CONTRACT. Contrato que continúa automáticamente llegado el plazo pactado si las partes no dan aviso previo de su intención de cancelarlo.

EVICTION. Evicción. Acción del arrendador contra el arrendatario para sacarlo del bien arrendado.

EVIDENCE. Evidencia, prueba. (1) Cualquier prueba o información presentada en un juicio. (2) Información que puede usarse en un caso futuro. (3) Demostración que sirve como prueba. (4) Testimonio, deposición o declaración ante una corte. Puede ser oral o escrita.

EXACTION. Extorsión. Exacción. Requerimiento ilegal que hace un funcionario público a otra persona para que pague por servicios que no tenían por qué cobrarse.

EXAMINATION. Investigación, examen, interrogatorio. (1) Cualquier investigación. (2) Interrogatorio hecho a un testigo. (3) **Direct Examination.** Interrogatorio hecho al testigo por quien lo llama a testificar. (4) **Cross Examination.** Interrogatorio hecho al testigo por la otra parte.

EXCEPTION. Excepción. (1) Objeción formal contra la decisión de un juez durante un juicio. (2) Excluir algo de un contrato.

EXCHANGE. Intercambio. Trueque. (1) Transacción de cambio de bienes en la cual no se incluye dinero ni se fija el valor monetario de lo cambiado. (2) Institución organizada para intercambiar valores tales como acciones. (3) Pago de deudas en diferentes lugares mediante la transferencia de créditos.

EXCISE TAXES. (1) Impuesto al consumo, manufactura o venta de bienes. (2) Impuesto gravado sobre un servicio o actividad.

EXCITED UTTERANCE. Declaración en estado de excitación. Excepción al principio de no admitir testimonio sobre rumores o declaraciones hechas por un tercero fuera de la corte.

EXCLUSIONARY CLAUSE. Cláusula excluyente o de exclusión. Pacto en un contrato que pretende limitar los remedios legales de los que puede disponer una parte en caso de violación del contrato.

EXCLUSIONARY RULE. Principio de exclusión. Regla que prohíbe utilizar pruebas en un juicio, aun cuando sean relevantes, si fueron obtenidas ilegalmente o en violación de un derecho.

EXCLUSIVE. Exclusivo. Uno solo.

EX CONTRACTU. (Lat.) Por contrato. Que surge de un contrato.

EXCULPATE. Exculpar. Demostrar que alguien no es culpable.

EXCULPATORY CLAUSE. Cláusula exculpatoria. Cláusula de un contrato que libera de responsabilidad a una de las partes.

EXCUSE. Excusa. Argumento que sirve en un juicio para justificar una acción o evento.

EX DELICTO. Por delito. Que surge de un delito.

EXECUTE. Ejecutar. Completar, firmar, cumplir, realizar. Llevar a cabo un contrato.

EXECUTION. Ejecución. (1) Llevar a cabo o completar. (2) Firmar un documento. (3) Ejecutar a una persona condenada a muerte. (4) Cumplir con una orden judicial.

EXECUTIVE. Ejecutivo. Organo ejecutivo del estado. (1) Funcionario de alto nivel.

EXECUTIVE AGREEMENT. Acuerdo del órgano ejecutivo de un gobierno el cual requiere el consentimiento del senado para su validez.

EXECUTIVE PRIVELEGE. Secreto ejecutivo. Derecho del Presidente y de ciertos funcionarios de retener información y no divulgarla al público.

EXECUTOR. Albacea testamentario. Ejecutor testamentario. Persona designada por el testador para administrar sus bienes luego de su muerte.

EXECUTORY. Ejecutable, incompleto; que depende en un acto o evento futuro.

EXECUTRIX. Femenino de "executor".

EXEMPLARS. Muestras, modelo. Identificaciones físicas tomadas de un demandado tales como huellas digitales, muestras de sangre, caligrafía, etc.

EXEMPLARY DAMAGES. Daños punitivos ejemplares. Son otorgados al demandante para castigar al demandado. Daños aumentados por sobre los daños sufridos para compensar al demandante.

EXEMPLIFICATION. Copia certificada.

EXEMPT. Exonerado de impuesto u obligación. Deudor que, bajo una ley, puede reclamar ciertos bienes en calidad de libres de todo gravamen.

EXEQUATUR. (Lat.) Dar validez en una corte local a una sentencia extranjera.

EXHAUSTION OF REMEDIES. Agotamiento de remedios. (1) Principio que requiere que antes de someter una controversia administrativa a una corte, deben agotarse todos los remedios ante la agencia donde se originó la controversia. (2) En el área penal, se refiere al agotamiento de recursos estatales antes de hacer uso de recursos federales.

EXHIBIT. (1) Exhibir. Presentar como prueba. (2) Documento de prueba.

EXONERATION. Exoneración. (1) Liberar de culpa. (2) Quitar una carga; liberar de una obligación. (3) Derecho de aquél que paga una deuda por otro de recuperar del deudor lo que pagó. (4) Acto de recibir el pago de un documento negociable.

EX PARTE. (Lat.) Con la concurrencia de una sola parte.

EXPATRIATION. Expatriación. Acto voluntario de abandonar la ciudadanía de un país y adoptar la de otro.

EXPECTANCY. Un derecho futuro; normalmente se refiere a una expectativa sobre un bien inmueble.

EXPEL. Expulsar. Echar a alguien de un terreno, normalmente mediante el uso de la fuerza.

EXPERT WITNESS. Testigo perito. La persona que testifica en un caso como el experto en una materia.

EXPIRATION. Expiración, vencimiento, cumplimiento.

EXPIRE. Expirar. Caducar. (1) Que venció. Que ya no tiene validez. (2) Morir.

EXPLICIT. Explícito, sin ambigüedad, claro.

EXPLOIT. Explotar. (1) Explotar un recurso natural. (2) Abusar de algo.

EXPORT. Exportar; enviar fuera del país.

EXPOSITORY STATUTE. Ley explicativa. Ley publicada para explicar otra anterior.

EXPRESS. Expreso. Claro, directo, manifestado explícitamente.

EXPRESSIO UNIUS ET EXCLUSIO ALTERIUS. (Lat.) Norma de interpretación legislativa bajo la cual la expresión de algo específico excluye lo no expresado.

EXPRESSION, FREEDOM OF. Libertad de expresión, uno de los derechos básicos de la constitución. Incluye la libertad de expresarse, la libertad de prensa, y la de tener reuniones públicas.

EXPROPRIATION. Expropiación. Tomar una propiedad privada para uso público.

EXPUNGE. Tachar, borrar completamente del registro o de los libros.

EXTEND. Extender. (1) Alargar un período de tiempo. (2) Posponer la fecha de vencimiento.

EXTENUATING CIRCUMSTANCES. Circunstancias atenuantes. Hechos que disminuyen la pena de un delito.

EXTERRITORIALITY. Privilegio de embajadores y funcionarios diplomáticos de no someterse a las leyes del país huésped.

EXTINGUISH. Abolir un derecho; extinguir una obligación o deuda.

EXTORT. Extorsionar; obtener algo ilegalmente.

EXTORTION. Extorsión. Obtención ilegal de dineros o bienes mediante amenazas, fuerza o poder público aparente.

EXTRADITION. Extradición. Entrega que un país hace a otro de una persona para que sea juzgada o penada en el país que solicita la entrega de la persona.

EXTRAJUDICIAL. Extrajudicial. (1) Que no tiene relación con lo actuado por la corte. (2) Más allá de los límites de la corte. (3) Que no tiene efecto legal a pesar de ser dicho por el juez.

EXTRAORDINARY REMEDIES. Remedios extraordinarios. Remedios concedidos por la corte sólo si los recursos comunes y legales no son suficientes para hacer justicia.

EXTRATERRITORIALITY. Extraterritorialidad. Aplicación de la ley de un país fuera de su territorio.

EXTRINSIC EVIDENCE. Prueba extrínseca. Prueba que se encuentra fuera del documento en cuestión.

EYEWITNESS. Testigo presencial u ocular. Persona que declara sobre hechos que acontecieron en su presencia.

F

F. Registro Federal Primera serie. (1) **F. 2d.** Segunda serie del Registro Federal. (2) **16 F.** Página 16 y siguiente.

F.A.A. Siglas de "Federal Aviation Administration". Agencia Federal de Aviación de los Estados Unidos.

F.A.S. Siglas de "Free Alongside Ship". Libre de Costo Junto al Buque. Término que indica que el precio de un bien incluye el transporte terrestre del mismo, y que la entrega de los bienes será al lado del barco.

F.B.I. Siglas de "Federal Bureau of Investigation". Agencia Federal de Investigaciones. Departamento del Ministerio de Gobierno que investiga los delitos federales no asignados a otras agencias.

F.D.A. Siglas de "Federal Drug Administration". Agencia Federal que regula y vela por la seguridad de los alimentos y medicinas.

F.D.I.C. Siglas de "Federal Deposit Insurance Corporation". Corporación Aseguradora de Depósitos Federales. Una entidad gubernamental que asegura depósitos bancarios individuales hasta una cierta cantidad.

F.M.V. Sigla de "Fair Market Value". Valor comercial o de mercado de un artículo.

F.O.B. Sigla de "Free on Board". Libre de gastos abordo. El precio FOB incluye el costo del transporte hasta el lugar designado en el contrato y el costo de cargar la mercancía en el barco.

F.Y. Sigla de "Fiscal Year". Año Fiscal.

FABRICATE. Fabricar o elaborar una fantasía o un objeto. Inventar algo falsamente, como por ejemplo la evidencia en un caso.

FACE. Apariencia, la cara de algo. Lenguaje de un documento que incluye todo lo que hay en él y excluye todo lo que no está en él.

FACE VALUE. Valor nominal. El valor monetario formalmente dado o escrito en un documento o instrumento financiero, normalmente al momento de su vencimiento.

FACILITATION. Facilitación. En derecho criminal, la ayuda intencional por uno para facilitarle a otro la comisión de un delito.

FACSIMILE. Facsímile. Copia exacta de un original.

FACT. Hecho. Evento. (1) Cualquier cosa que sucedió. (2) Algo real opuesto a lo que debería ser o que no es. (3) Algo real opuesto a la suposición.

FACTO. (Lat.) De hecho.

FACTOR. Factor, consignatario. Agente comercial usado para vender mercancía bajo consignación que recibe una comisión sobre la venta.

FACTORAGE. La comisión ganada por un consignatario.

FACTORING. La venta, con descuento que hace una firma, de sus cuentas por cobrar a un factor. El factor corre con el riesgo de cobrar las cuentas, y su ganancia es normalmente el descuento de la compra.

FACT QUESTION. Cuestión o punto decidido mediante el estudio de los hechos de un caso, en vez de las leyes o estatutos.

FACT SITUATION. Estado de los hechos. Resumen de los hechos de un caso sin comentarios legales.

FACTS IN ISSUE. Los hechos que serán decididos por el tribunal.

FAIL. Falta, falla, quebrar, declarar bancarrota. Véase "Failure".

FAILURE. Falta, culpa, falla, desliz, descuido, quiebra, bancarrota. Esta palabra se usa junto a muchos otros términos legales para describir con precisión alguna falla, falta o evento. Por ejemplo, "Failure of Title", cuando el título de la propiedad está en duda.

FAILURE OF CONSIDERATION. Término que indica que la consideración ofrecida como parte de un contrato, transferencia o pacto ya no es válida.

FAILURE TO STATE A CAUSE OF ACTION. Cuando el demandante no alega en su querella los hechos necesarios para establecer un caso válido.

FAINT PLEADER. Demandante tendencioso. Aquél que demanda algo falso.

FAINT PLEADING. Demanda o alegación falsificada o ficticia.

FAIR. Justo. Razonable. Imparcial, honrado. Palabra usada para modificar otros términos legales.

FAIR COMPETITION. Competencia justa y honrada entre comerciantes.

FAIR CONSIDERATION. Consideración justa. Algo equivalente. Cuando la consideración ofrecida en un contrato es razonable y está libre de duda bajo las circunstancias.

FAIR CREDIT BILLING ACT. Ley federal que facilita la resolución de conflictos entre las compañías de crédito y el consumidor.

FAIR CREDIT REPORTING ACTS. Estatutos y reglamentos que protegen el crédito de los ciudadanos y la forma en que la información crediticia es divulgada.

FAIR LABOR STANDARDS ACT. Ley federal diseñada para protejer a los trabajadores de compañías involucradas en comercio interestatal.

FAIR MARKET VALUE. Valor comercial justo o de mercado de un artículo.

FAIR RENTAL VALUE. Valor justo de arriendo.

FAIR TRIAL. Juicio justo. Juicio llevado ante un juez competente, imparcial y bajo una atmósfera judicial apropiada.

FAIT ACCOMPLI. (Lat.) Acción tomada y completada.

FALSE. Falso. Que no es cierto.

FALSE ARREST. Detención o arresto ilegal. Arresto indebido e intencionalmente hecho por un oficial.

FALSE PRETENSES. Pretensiones o apariencias falsas. Falsas demostraciones con la intención de aprovecharse de otro.

FALSE REPRESENTATION. Representación falsa hecha con intenciones de engañar. Similar a las pretensiones falsas pero que da lugar a una demanda civil.

FALSE SWEARING. Mentira dicha en una declaración bajo juramento.

FAMILY COURT. Tribunal que atiende asuntos de familia que involucran a menores.

FAMILY LAW. Derecho familiar. Derecho de familia.

FANNIE MAE. Véase "Federal National Mortgage Association".

FARE. Peaje, tarifa, pasaje.

FARM. Granja; finca.

FARM LABOR CONTRACTOR REGISTRATION ACT. Ley de Registro de los Contratistas de Mano de Obra Agrícola.

FARMER. Granjero; productor; agricultor.

FARMING. Actividades agropecuarias.

FAULT. Culpa. Negligencia por ausencia de cuidado.

FAUNTLEROY DOCTRINE. Doctrina que requiere que una sentencia dictada en un estado de los Estados Unidos sea reconocida por los otros estados.

FAVORED BENEFICIARY. Beneficiario o heredero favorecido. Persona involucrada en la preparación del testamento que resulta favorecido por sobre otros que tenían iguales derechos.

FEASANCE. Cumplimiento. Hacer algo. Cumplir un deber.

FED. Abreviación de "Federal". (1) Sistema federal de reserva. Banco central de los Estados Unidos.

FEDERAL. (1) Gobierno central que une a varios estados relegando ciertos poderes a los estados. (2) **U.S. Federal Government.** Gobierno Nacional opuesto al de cada estado.

FEDERAL COMMON LAW. Derecho Común Federal. Leyes basadas en la jurisprudencia desarrollada por los jueces que atienden casos federales.

FEDERAL COMMUNICATIONS COMMISSION (F.C.C.). Comisión Federal de Comunicaciones. Agencia federal que regula, a nivel nacional, los canales de televisión y radio, los teléfonos, el telégrafo, la televisión cablegráfica, y las comunicaciones vía satélite.

FEDERAL DEPOSIT INSURANCE CORPORATION (F.D.I.C.). Agencia federal independiente creada para asegurar el dinero depositado en ciertos bancos.

FEDERAL DISTRICT COURT. Corte de Distrito Federal. Tribunal Federal de Primera Instancia.

FEDERAL EXCISE TAXES. Impuestos federales sobre artículos de uso y consumo.

FEDERAL GOVERNMENT. Gobierno federal.

FEDERAL HOME LOAN MORTGAGE CORPORATION. Agencia federal que compra hipotecas de entidades financieras que forman parte del sistema bancario federal.

FEDERAL HOUSING ADMINISTRATION (F.H.A.). Administración Federal de Viviendas. Agencia federal creada para asegurar préstamos de hipoteca hechos por prestamistas aprobados por ella misma.

FEDERAL INSURANCE CONTRIBUTIONS ACT (F.I.C.A.). Ley de Contribución al Seguro Social.

FEDERAL JURIDICTION. Juridicción federal. Basada en el Artículo III de la constitución y en las leyes del Congreso.

FEDERAL NATIONAL MORTGAGE ASSOCIATION. Organización gubernamental creada para establecer un mercado secundario para ciertas hipotecas garantizadas en parte por agencias federales.

FEDERAL OFFENSE. Crimen definido y designado por el congreso federal.

FEDERAL QUESTION. Cuestión federal. Casos que tratan de cuestiones constitucionales y leyes o tratados federales, y cuya jurisdicción reside en las cortes federales.

FEDERAL REGISTER. Gaceta diaria del gobierno federal que publica todas las acciones reglamentarias del gobierno federal.

FEDERAL REPORTER. Registro Federal. Recoge los casos vistos por cortes federales, menos los de la Corte Suprema.

FEDERAL RULES. Reglas federales. (1) **Federal Rules of Appellate Procedure.** Reglas de procedimientos para los casos apelados en las cortes federales. (2) **Federal Rules of Civil Procedure.** Reglas de procedimiento para casos civiles en las cortes federales. (3) **Federal Rules of Criminal Procedure.** Reglas sobre el proceso criminal en las cortes federales. (4) **Federal Rules of Evidence.** Reglas sobre la admisión de evidencia en casos federales.

FEDERAL TAX LIEN. Gravamen por impuesto federal.

FEDERAL TORT CLAIMS ACT. Ley federal que permite demandar al gobierno federal por daños y perjuicios bajo ciertas condiciones.

FEDERAL UNEMPLOYMENT TAX. Ley Federal de Contribución para el Desempleo (FUTA).

FEE. (1) Honorario. (2) Herencia que no tiene limitaciones. (3) Caudal hereditario sin restricciones que va directo a los herederos.

FEE SIMPLE. Derecho de propiedad el cual puede ser absoluto o condicional. Si es absoluto, el dueño puede hacer lo que desee con la propiedad; si es condicional, el beneficiario de la propiedad debe observar ciertas condiciones para beneficiarse. En ciertos casos, la violación resulta en la pérdida de la propiedad (fee simple defeasible).

FELON. Convicto o ex-convicto. Persona que ha cometido un delito serio y que fue juzgada y sentenciada.

FELONIOUS. Criminal. Felón. Término de derecho criminal usado cuando algo es hecho con intenciones criminales.

FELONY. Crimen o delito grave. Puede ser un crimen federal o estatal que resulta en un castigo serio y en la pérdida de los derechos civiles.

FELLOWSHIP. Beca. Pensión (1) Dinero para realizar pesquisas o investigaciones. (2) Dinero que se obsequia a un estudiante para cubrir los gastos de sus estudios.

FETUS. Feto. Producto humano de la concepción desde que pasa el período embrionario hasta el momento del parto.

FEUDALISM. Feudalismo. Sistema basado en la relación entre el señor, dueño de la tierra y el vasallo, quien trabaja la tierra.

FIAT. Orden o decisión arbitraria.

FICTION OF LAW. Ficción legal. Una ficción legal es la presunción legal de que algo que es falso o que no existe es en realidad cierto.

FIDELITY BOND. Bono de fidelidad. Seguro contra la posible deshonestidad de alguien que está en una posición de confianza.

FIDUCIARY. Fiduciario. (1) Aquél que administra el dinero en nombre de otro. (2) Relación de confianza entre dos personas, uno con mayor conocimiento y poder que el otro. (3) Cualquier relación en la cual uno actúa en nombre de otro bajo un grado de confianza. (Por ejemplo, abogado-cliente).

FIELD WAREHOUSE RECEIPT. Documento que prueba que se han recibido ciertos bienes en depósito.

FIFO. Véase "First in, first out".

FIFTEENTH AMENDMENT. Enmienda decimoquinta a la Constitución. Garantiza el derecho constitucional al voto sin considerar la raza, el color o el origen de la persona.

FIFTH AMENDMENT. Quinta enmienda a la Constitución. Garantiza el debido proceso legal para quitarle a una persona su libertad, su vida o su propiedad.

FIGHTING WORDS. Palabras de altercado o pelea. Palabras dirigidas a una persona, quien al oírlas provoca actos de violencia.

FILE. Registro. (1) Incluir un documento en un caso al dárselo al oficial de la corte. (2) Expediente.

FILIATION PROCEEDING. Proceso civil para determinar si un hombre es el padre natural de un niño(a), y así imponer al padre la obligación de mantener a su hijo(a).

FILIBUSTER. Táctica legislativa para obstruir nueva legislación mediante el uso de discursos prolongados.

FILING OF RETURN. Presentación de la declaración. Acto de declarar los ingresos para el pago de impuestos.

FILING STATUS. Estado civil elegido o asignado al presentar la declaración de impuestos, para efectos fiscales.

FINAL ARGUMENT. Alegato de conclusión. Argumento final en un caso.

FINAL DECISION. Una decisión judicial final, la cual, de no ser apelada dentro de un tiempo fijo, torna irreversible la decisión.

FINAL JUDGMENT. Veredicto final.

FINANCE CHARGE. Costo por financiamiento, cargos financieros.

FINANCIAL INSTITUTIONS. Instituciones financieras. Organizaciones involucradas en negocios financieros y regidas por leyes estatales y federales. Por ejemplo, los bancos.

FINDING. Decisión, fallo, sentencia. (1) Generalmente se refiere a una decisión sobre un hecho o una conclusión legal basada en los hechos del caso.

FINE. Multa. Castigo que consiste en el pago de una suma de dinero a un tribunal.

FINGERPRINTS. Huellas digitales.

FIREARM. Arma de fuego. Arma que funciona a fuerza de pólvora. Por ejemplo un revólver.

FIRM OFFER. Oferta en firme. Oferta escrita hecha por un comerciante que se mantiene abierta por un período de tiempo. Es una clase de opción que no requiere una causa o consideración para ser válida.

FIRST AMENDMENT. Primera enmienda a la Constitución. Garantiza la libertad de expresión, religión, prensa y asociación.

FIRST COME BASIS. En atención al primero en presentarse. Criterio o base utilizada para atender a personas o asuntos en consideración al orden de llegada.

FIRST DEGREE MURDER. Asesinato u homicidio en primer grado. Asesinato cometido con alevosía y premeditación o un alto grado de crueldad y atrocidad.

FIRST IMPRESSION CASE. Un caso nuevo o único. Caso que no se asemeja a otros y que requiere un análisis legal que no puede basarse en los precedentes legales existentes.

FIRST-IN, FIRST-OUT. Primero en entrar, primero en salir. Término usado en contabilidad para el manejo de inventario.

FIRST LIEN. El primer gravamen sobre una propiedad o un artículo.

FIRST MORTGAGE. Primera hipoteca. Aquella hipoteca que es superior a todos los otros gravámenes sobre una propiedad. Que tiene preferencia en la prelación.

FISCAL. Fiscal. Que tiene que ver con cuestiones del fisco.

FISCAL YEAR. Año fiscal, ejercicio fiscal. Período de doce meses consecutivos considerados como un año para efectos fiscales.

FISHING TRIP OR EXPEDITION. Juicio temerario entablado para obtener información de un demandado a través de la corte.

FITNESS FOR A PARTICULAR PURPOSE. Apropiado para un determinado uso. Principio que establece la garantía implícita de que si un comerciante sabe o debiera saber que un artículo será usado para un propósito o fin determinado, el comerciante es responsable ante el comprador de que el artículo sea útil para cumplir su propósito o su fin.

FIXED CHARGES OR COST. Gastos fijos. Gastos de un negocio que son fijos aun cuando no existan ventas. Por ejemplo, la renta, luz, agua, etc.

FIXTURE. Cosas o muebles, adheridos o unidos a un inmueble.

FLAG OF CONVENIENCE. Bandera o abanderamiento de conveniencia. Registro de un buque en un país distinto de aquél en donde está su mayor negocio, porque tiene costos más bajos.

FLAGRANT. Flagrante. Que sucede en el momento en que se sorprende. Que es notorio.

FLAGRANT NECESSITY. Una emergencia que justifica legalmente una acción ilegal.

FLOAT. Cheques que han sido depositados en la cuenta del depositante, pero no han sido cobrados contra la cuenta del girador o dador.

FLOOR. (1) Lugar desde donde se habla en una asamblea. (2) También significa tener la palabra en una reunión.

FLOTSAM. Chatarra de un buque o sus accesorios encontrados a la deriva en el mar.

FOOD STAMPS. Cupones para alimentos.

FORBEARANCE. La demora de un acreedor en cobrar las obligaciones vencidas del deudor. Una forma de consideración legal.

529

FOR CAUSE. Por causa. Hecho con una sólida razón legal; por ejemplo, despedir a un empleado que ha robado.

FOR YOUR RECORDS. Para su archivo.

FORCE. Fuerza. (1) Violencia ilegal. (2) **In Force.** En vigor, que es válido.

FORCE MAJEURE. (Lat.) Fuerza mayor. Fuerza natural irresistible e inevitable.

FORCED HEIR. Heredero forzoso. Que no puede quedarse sin su cuota o parte de la herencia a menos que el testador tenga una causa legítima para ello.

FORECLOSE. El acto de ejecución para tomar la propiedad hipotecada.

FORECLOSURE. Juicio hipotecario. Dícese del juicio mediante el cual el acreedor hipotecario toma la propiedad hipotecada y la vende para pagar la deuda.

FOREIGN. Extranjero. Que pertenece o viene de otro país o estado.

FOREIGN ACCOUNT. Cuenta en el exterior.

FOREIGN CORPORATION. Una compañía creada en otra jurisdicción, sea otro estado o país.

FOREIGN EXCHANGE. Cambio de una moneda a otra moneda extranjera.

FOREIGN TAX CREDIT. Crédito por impuestos pagados en el extranjero.

FOREMAN. Presidente del jurado.

FORENSIC. Forense. Que tiene relación con el derecho y las cortes.

FORESEEABILITY. Previsibilidad, previsión. Aquello que cualquier persona razonable, prudente y cuidadosa esperaría o haría al momento de un determinado evento y bajo las mismas circunstancias.

FORFEIT. Perder un derecho por multa o confiscación. Pérdida de un derecho debido al incumplimiento de un deber, a la comisión de una ofensa, o al incumplimiento de un contrato.

FORGERY. Falsificación. (1) Emitir un documento falso o alterar uno legítimo para cometer un fraude. (2) El documento falsificado.

FORM. Forma, planilla, ejemplar. (1) Un modelo de documento. (2) Las palabras, arreglos, conducta, procesamiento y tecnicismos de un documento legal opuesto a la substancia del documento.

FORM LETTER. Carta modelo.

FORMS (TAX). Formularios de impuestos. (1) **940PR Employer's Annual Federal Unemployment Tax Return.** 940 Planilla para la declaración anual del patrono. La Contribución FUTA. (2) **941PR Employer's Quarterly Federal Tax Return 941PR.** Planilla para la declaración trimestral del patrono. La Contribución FICA. (3) **941c PR Statement to Correct Information Previously Reported Under the Federal Insurance Contribution Act.** 941c PR Planilla para la corrección de información facilitada anteriormente en cumplimiento de la ley FICA. (4) **942PR Employer's Quarterly Tax Return for Household Employees.** 942PR Planilla para la declaración trimestral del patrono de empleados domésticos. La Contribución FICA. (5) **943PR Employer's Annual Tax Return for Agricultural Employees.** 943PR Planilla para la declaración anual del patrono de empleados agrícolas. La contribución FICA. (6) 1040 **U.S. Individual Income Tax Return.** 1040 Declaración del impuesto sobre el ingreso personal en los Estados Unidos. Impuesto sobre la renta. (7) **1040A (same).** 1040A (idem). (8) **1040–ES Estimated Tax for Individuals.** 1040–ES Contribución Federal Estimada del Trabajo por Cuenta Propia (Puerto Rico). (9) **1040EZ Income Tax Return for Single Filers With No Dependents.** 1040EZ Declaración del impuesto sobre el ingreso para solteros sin dependientes. (10) **1040–PR.** 1040–PR Planilla para la declaración de la contribución federal sobre el trabajo por cuenta propia (Puerto Rico). (11) **Schedule A (1040).** Anexo A (1040). (12) **2848 Power of Attorney and Declaration of Representative.** 2848 Poder y declaración del representante. (13) **2848–D Tax Information Authorization and Declaration of Representatives.** 2848–D Declaración del representante y autorización para divulgar información tributaria. (14) **W–2 Wage and Tax Statement.** W–2 Comprobante de retribuciones e impuestos. (15) **W–3 Transmittal of Wage and Tax Statements.** W–3 Transmisión de comprobantes de salarios e impuestos. (16) **W–3PR Transmittal of Withholding Statements.** W–3PR Transmisión de comprobantes de retención (Puerto Rico). (17) **W–4 Employee's Withholding Allowance Certificate.** W–4 Certificado de descuentos del empleado para la retención. (18) **W–5 Earned Income Credit Advance Payment Certificate.** W–5 Certificado de derecho a pagos adelantados del crédito por ingreso del trabajo. (19) **499R–2/W–2PR Withholding Statement.** 499R–2/W–2PR Comprobante de retención (Puerto Rico).

FORMA PAUPERIS. Sin recursos económicos, indigente, pobre.

FORNICATION. Fornicación. Relaciones sexuales entre personas solteras.

FORSWEAR. Abjurar. Jurar algo sabiendo que es falso. Más amplio que perjurio pero no tan serio.

FORTHWITH. Inmediatamente.

FORTUITOUS. Fortuito. Que sucedió por accidente, sin previsión o anticipación.

FORUM. Foro. Corte. La jurisdicción en donde se conduce una acción legal.

FORUM NON CONVENIENS. (Lat.) Corte inconveniente. Principio que permite que un juez se niege a tomar jurisdicción sobre un caso si hay otra corte más apropiada, adecuada, o conveniente para conocer la causa.

FORUM SHOPPING. Escoger entre varias cortes la que uno cree que resolverá el caso a su favor.

FORWARD. Adelantar. (1) Fijar una tasa para transacciones futuras. (2) Enviar.

FOSTER CHILD. Hijo(a) de crianza. Menor bajo custodia y manutención de un adulto que no lo ha adoptado.

FOUNDATION.   Fundación. (1) Preguntas preliminares a un testigo para establecer la base necesaria para que su testimonio sea admitido como evidencia en el caso. (2) Fondo benéfico establecido para mantener y administrar contribuciones a instituciones no-lucrativas como hospitales, parroquias, etc.

FOUNDER OF A TRUST.   Fideicomitente.

FOURTEENTH AMENDMENT.   Decimocuarta enmienda a la Constitución. Prohíbe constitucionalmente a los estados aplicar leyes que restrinjan los privilegios e inmunidades de los ciudadanos de los Estados Unidos.

FOURTH AMENDMENT.   Cuarta enmienda a la Constitución. Derecho constitucional que prohíbe pesquisas y cateos excesivos y no razonables, requiriendo también que exista buena causa para cualquier orden de registro.

FRAME.   Complot. Expresión popular, que significa la incriminación de alguien con pruebas falsas.

FRANCHISE.   Franquicia. Derecho a usar el nombre de algún producto, marca o compañía para la venta de bienes o servicios. Normalmente se trata de un contrato que define cómo se ha de manejar una franquicia.

FRANKING PRIVILEGE.   Franquicia postal. Derecho a enviar cosas por correo sin costo.

FRATERNITY.   Fraternidad. Asociación de estudiantes de universidades.

FRAUD.   Fraude. Cualquier clase de estafa para aprovecharse de otro. La perversión intencional de la verdad con el objeto de que otro acepte lo dicho y actúe de conformidad con esto. Hay fraude civil y criminal.

FRAUDULENT.   Fraudulento. Que hace trampa o estafa.

FRAUDULENT CONCEALMENT.   Ocultamiento fraudulento. Esconder la verdad con el objeto de estafar a alguien.

FRAUDULENT INTENT.   Malicia. El estado mental del actor que demuestra malicia como parte de la estafa.

533

FREE ON BOARD. Véase "F.O.B.".

FREEDOM OF ASSOCIATION. Libertad o derecho de agrupación para cualquier propósito legal.

FREEDOM OF EXPRESSION. Libertad de expresión. Incluye el derecho a la libertad de religión y prensa, así como a la libertad de expresarse verbalmente.

FREEDOM OF INFORMATION ACT (F.O.I.A.). Ley federal que hace posible que la información recopilada por las agencias federales sea dada a conocer al público que la pide, a menos que dicha información solicitada del gobierno sea confidencial bajo la ley.

FREEDOM OF RELIGION. Libertad de religión. Libertad garantizada por la primera enmienda a la Constitución.

FREEHOLD. Dominio. Control absoluto sobre un bien inmueble.

FREE PORT. Puerto libre. Lugar donde los bienes se comercian sin entrar al país y sin pagar aranceles aduaneros.

FREEZE OUT. Acción tomada por la mayoria de los accionistas para forzar al accionista minoritario a que venda sus acciones.

FREIGHT. Carga.

FRESH OR HOT PURSUIT RULE. Derecho de un policía a perseguir a un sospechoso fuera de su jurisdicción.

FRINGE BENEFITS. Beneficios económicos o uso de infraestructura otorgados a una persona por su patrón, cuyos beneficios no son considerados como salario.

FRISK. Registro de una persona en particular, para determinar si la persona está armada.

FRIVOLOUS. Frívolo. Sin valor legal.

FRONTAGE ASSESSMENT. Impuesto de valorización de la propiedad. Es calculado en proporción al valor en que se incrementa un inmueble por una mejora realizada; por ejemplo, por mejoras a la calle frente a la que el dicho inmueble se halla situado.

FRUIT. Fruto. El producto de algo. Por ejemplo, la renta.

FRUIT OF POISONOUS TREE. Fruto del árbol envenenado. Doctrina que mantiene que toda evidencia obtenida mediante la violación de los derechos del acusado no será admitida en su juicio.

FRUSTRATION. Frustración. (1) **Frustration of Contract.** Frustación del Contrato. Sucede cuando resulta imposible ejecutar lo pactado debido a algún cambio no imputable a las partes. (2) **Frustration of Purpose.** Frustración del propósito. Sucede cuando es posible ejecutar lo pactado, más la razón primordial por la cual se mantiene el contrato ya no existe.

FUGITIVE. Fugitivo, prófugo. Aquel prófugo de la ley o la justicia.

FULL FAITH AND CREDIT. Doctrina del crédito absoluto. Principio constitucional que obliga a un juez a reconocer como válida la sentencia y las decisiones de las cortes de otro estado de los Estados Unidos.

FULL–TIME EMPLOYEE. Empleado a tiempo o jornada completa.

FULL–TIME JOB. Trabajo (empleo) a tiempo o jornada completa.

FULL–TIME STUDENT. Estudiante a tiempo completo. Estudiante que completa todas las materias asignadas en el transcurso de su carrera durante un período académico fijo.

FUNDAMENTAL RIGHTS. Derechos fundamentales otorgados por la constitución o la ley orgánica de un país.

FUNDS. Fondos. Dineros.

FUNGIBLE. Fungible. Cosas que son fácilmente reemplazables por otras de igual calidad y cantidad.

FUTURE DAMAGES. Daños y perjuicios futuros que pueden ser recuperados como parte de un caso.

FUTURES CONTRACT. Contrato para la compra de bienes en el futuro, aunque los bienes no existan o puedan ser identificados a un precio fijo y en cantidades definidas.

FUTURES TRADING. La compra y venta de contratos a un precio, y por cantidades fijas.

G

G.A.A.P. "General Accepted Accounting Principles". Principios de contabilidad generalmente aceptados para certificar el estado financiero de una entidad, empresa o corporación.

G.A.A.S. Normas de auditoría generalmente aceptadas para auditar una entidad, empresa o corporación.

G.A.T.T. "General Agreement on Tariffs and Trade". Acuerdo general sobre aranceles aduaneros y comercio. Convenio internacional que procura disminuir impuestos de importación y fomentar el comercio entre naciones.

G.N.P. Producto Nacional Bruto. Véase "Gross National Product".

GAG ORDER. Orden de desacato. (1) Mandato judicial instruyendo a un demandado para que guarde orden y respeto. (2) Orden judicial instruyendo a los abogados y testigos que no discutan o comenten el caso fuera de la corte.

GAIN. Ganancia. Provecho. Aquello que se obtiene como beneficio.

GAIN REALIZED. Ganancia realizada.

GAINFUL EMPLOYEE. Empleado retribuido, a quien se le paga por su labor.

GAINFUL EMPLOYMENT. Trabajo retribuido o lucrativo.

GAMBLER. Jugador. Apostador. Aventurero.

GAME LAW. Leyes que regulan la caza de animales.

GAOL. Prisión, carcel. (Término arcaico).

GARNISH. Embargar. Embargar un bien o dinero que se halla en manos de una tercera persona. Véase "Garnishment".

GARNISHEE. Embargado. Normalmente alguien que tiene bienes o dineros embargados pertenecientes a otro.

GARNISHMENT. Embargo. Procedimiento legal instaurado por el acreedor contra los bienes del deudor para rematar dichos bienes y cobrar el valor de lo debido.

GAULT. Caso de la corte suprema que reconoce a los delincuentes juveniles los mismos derechos que a los adultos.

GENERAL. General. Que se refiere a todo un grupo en contraposición a una parte.

GENERAL APPEARANCE. Comparecencia general. Aparecer ante la corte y someterse a su jurisdicción.

GENERAL ASSEMBLY. Asamblea General. El nombre dado a la asamblea legislativa de muchos estados.

GENERAL ASSIGNMENT FOR CREDITORS. Cesión general de los bienes del deudor a un fiduciario a favor de los acreedores para que éste los distribuya entre los acreedores.

GENERAL CREDITOR. Acreedor que no posee garantía alguna sobre un bien para asegurarse el cobro de lo que se le debe.

GENERAL EXECUTION. Orden judicial para que se tome cualquier propiedad personal del demandado para satisfacer la deuda por la que se le condenó.

GENERAL JURISDICTION. Competencia general. Poder de la corte para conocer cualquier caso que se presente dentro de su jurisdicción territorial.

GENERAL PARTNER. Socio general, quien es co-dueño de la propiedad colectiva de la sociedad y quien es personalmente responsable ante sus socios por las deudas del negocio.

GENERATION. Generación.

GENEVA CONVENTION. Acuerdo internacional escrito en 1864 que establece las normas y la conducta de naciones en guerra.

GENOCIDE. Genocidio. Plan sistemático para aniquilar a un grupo racial, político o cultural.

GENTLEMEN'S AGREEMENT. Pacto de caballeros. Que no tiene validez legal, pero sí moral.

GEODETIC SURVEY SYSTEM. Estudio topográfico en EE.UU. que deslinda e integra todo los terrenos del país mediante marcadores en puntos específicos.

GERMANE. Al punto, pertinente, afín, aplicable.

GERRYMANDER. División o demarcación injusta y arbitraria del territorio de un estado con fines políticos para favorecer a un candidato o a un partido.

GIFT. Regalo, obsequio, donación. Transferencia de un bien sin que se reciba un valor a cambio, o si el valor recibido a cambio está muy por debajo de lo entregado.

GIFT TAX. Impuesto a las donaciones.

GIST. Quid. (Lat.) La esencia o el fundamento del problema o de un litigio.

GIVEBACK. Devolver. Negociación colectiva en la que el sindicato acepta renunciar a ciertos beneficios, generalmente para conservar empleos.

GOING AND COMING RULE. Principio legal de la ida y vuelta al trabajo según el cual el trabajador que va o viene del trabajo no está protegido por las leyes de responsabilidad profesional.

GOING CONCERN. Una empresa que funciona y está establecida.

GOING PRIVATE. La reestructuración de una corporación de manera que sus acciones queden en posesión de pocas personas; tales acciones no están registradas en una bolsa de valores.

GOING PUBLIC. Venta de sus acciones que por vez primera hace una corporación al público en general.

GOOD. Bueno, válido.

GOOD BEHAVIOR. Buena conducta. Término que se refiere al comportamiento que debe obervar una persona en circunstancias determinadas.

GOOD CAUSE. Que no es arbitrario, una causa válida.

GOOD FAITH. Buena fe. (1) Honesto. (2) Para un comerciante esto significa mantener un comportamiento comercialmente razonable, de trato justo, y de buena fe en las negociaciones con otros.

GOOD FAITH PURCHASER. Comprador de buena fe. Aquél que compra sin tener conocimiento de circunstancias que hicieren que una persona prudente dudara del título ofrecido por el vendedor.

GOOD WILL. Buena fe. Buen crédito. Buen nombre, plusvalía, valor intrínsico. Valor superior al comercial que tiene un activo debido a ciertos factores como la buena reputación de la compañía, la honorabilidad de sus administradores, la preferencia del público, etc.

GOODS. Bienes. Término que puede significar cualquier propiedad o determinados artículos. (1) **Capital Goods.** Bienes de producción usados para producir bienes diferentes. Por ejemplo maquinaria y equipo. (2) **Consumer Goods.** Bienes de consumo usados para fines domésticos personales o familiares. (3) **Durable Goods.** Bienes duraderos, que tienen un largo período de vida. (4) **Fungible Goods.** Bienes fungibles. Bienes que tienen igual calidad y valor que otros del mismo género. Por ejemplo café, arroz, etc.

GOODS AND CHATTELS. Bienes muebles. Artículos de propiedad personal.

GOODTIME ALLOWANCE. Tiempo de gracia. Reducción, por buena conducta, del tiempo penal que debe cumplir un preso durante su reclusion en la cárcel.

GOODWILL. Véase "Good Will".

GOVERNMENT. Gobierno. Conjunto de personas que gobiernan un estado o pais.

GOVERNMENTAL IMMUNITY. Principio legal bajo el cual el gobierno federal, estatal o local no puede ser demandado, excepto en casos en que el mismo gobierno lo permita.

GOVERNOR. Gobernador. Usualmente el puesto político más alto en el gobierno estatal.

GRAB LAW. Leyes de embargo, secuestros, remates y ejecuciones forzosas.

GRACE PERIOD. Período de gracia. (1) En materia de seguros, se refiere a los días en que se mantiene válida la póliza después de que se venza la prima. (2) En contratos, se refiere a un período adicional al pactado para cumplir con el contrato.

GRAND JURY. Gran Jurado. Jurado que determina el mérito de la causa o de la acusación. No establece la inocencia o culpabilidad del acusado; esto corresponde al Jurado del juicio. Véase "Petit Jury".

GRAND LARCENY. Robo de mayor cuantía. Delito en el cual el valor de lo apropiado sobrepasa cierta suma establecida por ley.

GRANDFATHER CLAUSE. Cláusula dentro de una nueva ley que permite que aquéllos que ya están dedicados a la actividad regulada por la ley estén exentos de las nuevas reglas.

GRANT. Conceder. (1) Transferencia de bienes inmuebles usualmente mediante una escritura pública. (2) Regalo, obsequio, subsidio.

GRANTEE. Concesionario o donatario. Persona a quien se le concede algo.

GRANTOR. Concedente, cesionista, donante. Persona que concede o regala algo a otra persona. **Grantor of a Trust**. Cesionista para un fideicomiso.

GRAVAMEN. Parte medular o material de una demanda.

GREAT WRIT OF LIBERTY. Ver "Habeas corpus".

GRIEVANCE. Agravio. En derecho laboral, la queja presentada por los trabajadores respecto a las condiciones laborales para resolverlas mediante mecanismos provistos en la convención colectiva. Reclamo por algún acto opresivo, discriminatorio o injusto.

GROSS. Total, general, absoluto, bruto. (1) **Gross Estate**. Valor total del caudal hereditario. (2) **Gross Income**. Ingreso bruto. Cualquier ingreso independiente de su fuente. (3) **Gross Profit**. Utilidad bruta. (4) **Gross Receipts**. Entrada bruta. (5) **Gross Misdemeanor**. Delito que, sin ser insignificante o grave, es sin embargo serio bajo las leyes criminales. (6) **Gross Negligence**.

541

El incumplimiento de un deber, privado o público, por una falla seria del actor.

GROSS NATIONAL PRODUCT. Producto National Bruto. Valor de mercado, dentro de un país que, por el período de un año, tienen todos los bienes y servicios producidos en ese país, calculados de acuerdo al precio final en que éstos se venden, más el exceso de las exportaciones sobre las importaciones.

GROUNDS. Causa, motivo, base.

GROUP LIFE INSURANCE. Seguro de vida colectivo.

GUARANTEE. Garantía. (1) Persona a quien se le asegura mediante una garantía. (2) Contrato de garantía. (3) Obligación del garante.

GUARANTEE CLAUSE. Cláusula de garantía o fianza mediante la cual un tercero se convierte en garante o fiador de la persona obligada.

GUARANTOR. Garante. Aquél que da una garantía. Persona que asegura que una obligación se va a cumplir.

GUARANTY. Garantía. Promesa de cumplir una obligación.

GUARDIAN. Tutor. Curador. Encargado legalmente de otra persona o de sus bienes.

GUARDIAN AD LITEM. Curador durante el litigio. Encargado de los bienes o de la representación de una persona durante el juicio en el que está involucrada esta persona, normalmente un menor o un incapacitado.

GUEST. Huésped, invitado(a). (1) Una persona que ha pagado para hospedarse en un hotel, motel o posada. (2) Una persona que es un pasajero(a) en un automóvil. (3) Invitado a una casa o un club.

GUEST STATUTE. Ley de algunos estados que prohíbe al pasajero de un auto demandar al conductor en caso de accidente si viajaba en el auto como invitado, a menos que el accidente fuera causado por algo más que la negligencia ordinaria del conductor.

GUILTY. Culpable. (1) Responsable de un delito. (2) Condenado por un delito. (3) Responsable por un mal civil.

H

H.D.C. "Holder in Due Course". Tenedor legítimo o de buena fe de un instrumento negociable.

H.L. Siglas de House of Lords, Cámara de los Lores o de los Pares en Inglaterra.

H.R. Siglas de House of Representatives, Cámara de Representantes. Una de las partes del Congreso o Poder Legislativo.

HABEAS CORPUS. (Lat.) Habeas Corpus. Orden judicial para que una persona detenida se presente ante la corte para examinarla o liberarla del arresto indebido.

HABENDUM CLAUSE. Parte de una escritura pública que describe los derechos de propiedad transferidos.

HABIT. Hábito o costumbre; vicio; vestido. Acciones que resultan de hábito, costumbre o repetición.

HABITABILITY. Habitabilidad. Condición de una vivienda que permite a sus habitantes vivir en ella sin exponer a peligros su salud o su seguridad.

HABITUAL. Habitual. Acostumbrado. Acciones tomadas por costumbre.

HABITUAL INTEMPERANCE. Intemperancia o inmoderación habitual. Embriaguez o drogadicción regular suficientemente seria para interferir con las relaciones en el trabajo o en el hogar.

HAGUE TRIBUNAL. Corte de arbitraje internacional para resolver conflictos entre naciones.

HALFWAY HOUSE. Institución diseñada para rehabilitar a personas que han salido recientemente de un hospital o de una prisión.

HAMMER SALE. Venta forzosa. Remate judicial. Cualquier subasta.

HANDICAPPED. Lisiado, incapacitado, minusválido.

HARASSMENT. Acosamiento. Molestia. Acciones o palabras que tienden a molestar, alarmar o atormentar ilegalmente a otra persona.

HARBOR. Refugiar, encubrir. Ocultar a un criminal.

HARDSHIP CASE. Caso de daño irreparable.

HARMLESS ERROR. Un error trivial o meramente formal que no perjudica los derechos substanciales de una persona y que no afecta la decisión final de un caso.

HARTER ACT. Ley federal que prohíbe, en los conocimientos de embarque, cualquier cláusula que libere de responsabilidad civil a los propietarios del buque por daño en la carga.

HAZARD. Peligro, riesgo. Cualquier riesgo o peligro de pérdida o daño.

HEAD OF HOUSEHOLD. Cabeza de familia. La persona responsable por mantener el bienestar de una familia. Hay beneficios fiscales para estas personas.

HEADNOTE. Resumen. Sumario del dictamen de un caso publicado conjuntamente con la decisión de la corte.

HEALTH BENEFITS. Beneficios médico-hospitalarios.

HEALTH INSURANCE. Seguro de enfermedad, seguro médico.

HEARING. Audiencia. Procedimiento abierto al público ante una agencia administrativa, tribunal, comisionados o árbitro donde las partes presentan pruebas y luego se emite una decisión.

HEARING AID. Audífono.

HEARING DE NOVO. Una audiencia nueva o por segunda vez, sin tomar en cuenta los acontecimientos de la primera audiencia.

HEARSAY EVIDENCE. Testimonio de referencia o de oídas. Testimonio en el que se manifiesta la verdad de aquello que llegó a conocimiento del testigo a través de lo dicho por otro.

HEART BALM ACT. Leyes que prohíben el derecho a demandar por el incumplimiento de una promesa de matrimonio o seducción a una persona mayor de edad.

HEAT OF PASSION. Al calor de la pasión. Arrebato de cólera. En la ley criminal, se refiere a crímenes cometidos por pasión o rabia provocada por otro. Estado de violencia incontrolable en el cual se encuentra una persona, y que puede alegarse como motivo para reducir el grado del crimen pasando de asesinato a homicidio sin premeditación.

HEIR. Heredero. (1) El que recibe bienes en herencia. (2) El que tiene derecho a heredar. (3) El beneficiario de una herencia.

HELD. Decidido. La esencia de una decisión jurídica en el sistema legal anglo-americano.

HENCEFORTH. En lo sucesivo.

HEREAFTER. En lo sucesivo. De aquí en adelante.

HEREDITAMENT. Heredable. Bienes susceptibles de ser heredados.

HEREDITARY. Hereditario. Aquello que es susceptible de ser heredado.

HEREIN. Contenido aquí adentro.

HEREUNDER. (1) De acuerdo con el presente documento. (2) Más adelante en este documento.

HERMENEUTICS. Hermenéutica. Arte de redactar e interpretar los documentos legales así como los principios en ellos utilizados.

HIGH SCHOOL. Escuela secundaria; escuela superior.

HIGHEST AND BEST USE. El mayor y mejor uso. Para la valuación de bienes raíces, es el uso que resulta en el mayor y mejor provecho económico de un inmueble.

HIGHWAY. Calle o avenida pública. (1) Carretera que todos los ciudadanos tienen derecho a usar. (2) Autopista. Vía para el transito de autos a velocidad.

HIJACKING. Secuestror. (1) Asaltar. Asaltar bienes o el vehículo en el que éstos se transportan mientras están en tránsito. (2) También se refiere al acto de tomar control de un avión por fuerza y cambiar su destino.

HIT AND RUN ACCIDENT. Accidente vehicular con fuga. Accidente entre un vehículo y un peatón o entre dos vehículos, cuando el que maneja un vehículo escapa y desaparece del área del accidente sin dejar identificación.

HOBBY LOSS. Pérdida producida por un pasatiempo.

HOLD. Poseer, decidir. (1) Tener algo legalmente y con justo título. (2) Declarar conclusiones de ley en una sentencia. (3) La resolución legal sobre la cual se decide un caso.

HOLD–HARMLESS AGREEMENT. Contrato bajo el cual una parte asume la responsabilidad de un evento o situación, relevando a la otra parte de toda responsabilidad civil.

HOLDER. Tenedor. Aquél que tiene algo en su posesión.

HOLDER IN DUE COURSE. Tenedor de buena fe. Tenedor de un documento negociable que lo recibe por su justo valor, de buena fe y sin conocimiento de defensa o reclamo de ninguna otra persona.

HOLDING. La decisión de un caso. Parte de la opinión del juez en una sentencia que tiene la fuerza y el valor de precedente en casos subsiguientes. Véase "Held", "Hold".

HOLDING COMPANY. Compañía o sociedad tenedora de las acciones de otra(s) sociedad(es) o compañía(s).

HOLDING PERIOD. Período de tenencia.

HOLOGRAPH. Hológrafo. Aplícase al testamento o a la memoria testamentaria de puño y letra del testador.

HOME. Hogar familiar. Centro de la vida doméstica, social y cívica.

HOME LOAN. Préstamo garantizado por la residencia del deudor.

HOME OWNER'S WARRANTY. Garantía del propietario de una residencia o inmueble. Asegura que el bien está en buen estado y libre de defectos o gravámenes, ya sea por contrato o por ley, y que el garante es el propietario legal.

HOME RULE. El derecho de un gobierno estatal a la autonomía local.

HOMESTEAD. La casa y tierra donde vive una familia.

HOMESTEAD EXEMPTION. Exención que permite al dueño de una residencia que es su hogar tenerla a prueba de acreedores o de ciertos impuestos.

HOMICIDE. Homicidio. Matar a otra persona. No es necesariamente un crimen, por ejemplo, la defensa propia o la ejecución de un reo condenado a muerte, etc.

HOMOLOGATION. Homologación. Dar firmeza o aprobación judicial a ciertos actos de las partes.

HOMOSEXUAL. Homosexual.

HOMOSEXUALITY. Homosexualidad.

HONOR. Honrar. Aceptar un documento negociable para su pago.

HONORARIUM. Honorario. Obsequio. (1) Pago sin compromiso. (2) Pago a un abogado. (3) Pago voluntario por aquello que no podría cobrarse remuneración por vía legal o judicial.

HORNBOOK. Texto que contiene un sumario de los principios legales de una rama o área de derecho.

HOSPITAL INSURANCE BENEFITS TAX OR MEDICARE. Contribución para beneficios del seguro hospitalario.

HOSTAGE. Rehén. Persona capturada por alguien que amenaza con matarla a menos que las autoridades hagan lo que se les dice.

HOSTILE. Hostil. Alguien que actúa como enemigo.

HOT BLOOD. Apasionado. Véase "Heat of Passion".

HOT PURSUIT. Persecución inminente de un criminal o delincuente. Persecución iniciada inmediatamente después de la comisión de un delito o del descubrimiento de un delincuente. (1) Principio legal que permite a un policía cruzar su jurisdicción cuando está persiguiendo a un delincuente. (2) Principio que le permite a un ciudadano usar los medios razonables para recuperar sus bienes robados cuando lleva a cabo la persecución inmediata del delincuente.

HOTCHPOT. Colación de bienes. Reunir los bienes para dividirlos entre los herederos.

HOUSE. Una de las cámaras legislativas. Usualmente la cámara baja, la de los representantes.

HOUSE COUNSEL. Abogado de planta. Abogado que es empleado de una compañía y que trabaja en ella como asesor legal.

HOUSE OF REPRESENTATIVES. Cámara de los representantes. La cámara baja del órgano legislativo.

HOUSEBREAKING. Hurto que implica entrar ilegalmente en una residencia.

HOUSEHOLD. Unidad familiar.

HOUSEHOLD APPLIANCES. Enseres domésticos.

HOUSEWIFE. Ama de casa.

HUMANITARIAN DOCTRINE. Doctrina humanitaria. Véase "Last Clear Chance".

HUNG JURY. Jurado que, debido al desacuerdo entre sus miembros, se ve impedido de llegar a un veredicto.

HUSBAND–WIFE PRIVILEGE. Secreto matrimonial. En derecho procesal, las comunicaciones privadas entre los cónyuges gozan del privilegio de ser inadmisibles como evidencia en la corte, a opción de cualquiera de los dos cónyuges.

HYPOTHECATE. Hipotecar. Usar un bien como garantía hipotecaria sin darlo al prestamista.

HYPOTHETICAL QUESTION. Pregunta hipotética, basada en hechos asumidos y diseñada para extraer la opinion de la persona a quien se le hace la pregunta. Dicha persona es generalmente un experto o perito.

I

I.D.   Identificación. Prueba de identidad.

I.E.   (Lat.) Abreviatura del latín de "Id est", o eso es.

I.M.F.   Siglas de "International Monetary Fund". Fondo monetario internacional. Agencia de las Naciones Unidas que promueve el comercio mundial.

I.O.U.   Siglas que significan "I owe you". Yo te debo. Aceptación o reconocimiento escrito de una deuda, usualmente en forma de pagaré.

I.R.A.   Siglas de "Individual Retirement Account". Cuenta individual para la jubilación.

I.R.S.   "Internal Revenue Service". Agencia del gobierno federal de colección o cobro de impuestos.

IBID.   (Lat.) Ibidem. Igual. Lo mismo que.

ID.   (Lat.) Idem. Lo mismo que lo anterior.

IDENTITY.   Identidad. En derecho probatorio es aquello auténtico.

ILLEGAL.   Ilegal. Contrario a la ley penal. Violación de la ley.

ILLEGAL ENTRY.   Entrada ilegal al país.

ILLEGITIMATE.   Ilegítimo. (1) Que carece de autorización legal. (2) Contrario a la ley.

ILLICIT.   Ilícito. Prohibido.

ILLUSORY PROMISE.   Promesa ilusoria. Que parece prometer algo pero que en realidad no promete nada.

IMMATERIAL.   Inmaterial. Que no es relevante, pertinente o significativo.

IMMEDIATE CAUSE.   Causa inmediata. Evento final en una cadena de sucesos, el que produce el resultado en cuestión.

IMMEDIATE ISSUE. Hijos; niños.

IMMIGRANT. Inmigrante. Extranjero en un país.

IMMIGRATION. Inmigración. (1) Entrar en un pais con el propósito de obtener la residencia permanente en dicho país. (2) Oficina que se ocupa de los movimientos migratorios.

IMMINENT. Inminente. Que está a punto de suceder.

IMMORAL. Inmoral. Actos contra el bienestar público según las normas legales de una comunidad o la opinión mayoritaria de la comunidad.

IMMOVABLES. Inmuebles. En la ley civil, la tierra y las cosas naturales unidas permanentemente a la tierra, formando parte de ella.

IMMUNITY. Inmunidad. Privilegio que, para un acto o una función, exculpa a determinadas personas o instituciones de la responsabilidad que pudieran contraer en el ejercicio de sus funciones oficiales.

IMPARTIAL. Imparcial. Justo. Que no tiene favoritismos.

IMPEACH. Impugnar. (1) Demostrar que un testigo carece de credibilidad. (2) Procedimiento para remover a un funcionario público de su puesto oficial.

IMPEACHMENT. Acusación. Procedimiento criminal contra un oficial público, llevado ante una corte cuasi política. Dicho procedimiento comienza con una petición escrita, a veces llamada "actos de acusación".

IMPEDIMENT. Impedimento. Inhabilidad legal para contratar.

IMPERSONATION. Personificación. Hacerse pasar por un policía o funcionario que requiere una licencia especial.

IMPERTINENCE. Impertinencia. Que no viene al caso.

IMPLEAD. Demandar. Entablar un pleito contra un tercero para que participe en un caso existente.

IMPLIED. Implícito. Que se conoce indirectamente. (1) **Implied Authority.** Autorización implícita. (2) **Implied Terms.** Términos implícitos de un contrato. (Aunque no estén escritos son parte del contrato.)

IMPOSE. Imponer. Gravar mediante un impuesto o contribución.

IMPOSSIBILITY. Imposibilidad. Aquello que no puede ser hecho. (1) **Physically Impossible.** Físicamente imposible; por ejemplo, estar en dos lugares a la vez. (2) **Legally Impossible.** Legalmente imposible; por ejemplo, contratar a la edad de 4 años. (3) **Logically Impossible.** Lógicamente imposible; por ejemplo, vender algo muy por encima de su valor.

IMPOST. Impuesto. Gravamen o arancel aduanero. Véase "Duty".

IMPOUND. Depositar animales o bienes perdidos en un recinto cerrado.

IMPRACTICABILITY. Impracticabilidad. Difícil al extremo de resultar injusto e irrazonable requerir su ejecución.

IMPRISON. Encarcelar. Poner a una persona en una prisión.

IMPRISONMENT. Encarcelamiento. Encerrar en una cárcel.

IMPROVEMENT. Mejora. Adición o cambios a la tierra o a inmuebles que aumentan su valor.

IMPUTED. Imputado. Que se le atribuye a alguien. (1) **Imputed Income.** Dinero sujeto a impuesto sobre la renta aunque no se haya recibido. (2) **Imputed Knowledge.** Cuando la ley supone que alguien sabe ciertos hechos aunque no lo sepa en realidad. (3) **Imputed Negligence.** Cuando la ley atribuye la negligencia del actor a otra persona, como a los padres o al patrón.

IN BLANK. En blanco. Que no se ha llenado. Que no se han registrado letras, palabras o números.

IN COMMON. En común. Que pertenece a varios por igual o a la vez.

IN KIND. En especie.

IN LIEU OF. En lugar de.

IN PERSONAM. (Lat.) En persona.

551

INADMISSIBLE. Inadmisible. Hechos o pruebas que no pueden ser admitidos en un juicio.

INALIENABLE. Inalienable. Inajenable. Que no se puede vender o comprar o pasar de una persona a otra.

IN CAMERA. En la oficina del juez.

INC. Abreviatura de "incorporated". Incorporado. Organizado como sociedad anónima.

INCAPACITY. Incapacidad. Que carece de habilidad legal.

INCARCERATION. Encarcelación. Poner en prisión, privar de su libertad a alquien al encerrarlo en la cárcel.

INCEST. Incesto. Relaciones sexuales entre familiares cercanos.

INCHOATE. Imperfecto, parcial, sin terminar. Iniciado pero no terminado o madurado.

INCIDENTAL. Incidental. Que depende de algo primario o más importante.

INCITE. Incitar, provocar. Instigar a otra persona para que ejecute ciertos actos que de otro modo no hubiese realizado.

INCOME. Ingreso, renta.

INCOME TAX. Impuesto sobre la renta; contribución sobre ingresos.

INCOMPATIBILITY. Incompatibilidad. (1) Dos o más cosas que no pueden existir juntas. (2) Causal de divorcio por tener los cónyuges personalidades muy diferentes.

INCOMPETENCY. Incompetencia. Que carece de la habilidad legal o del derecho de hacer algo.

INCONSISTENT. Inconsistente. Que se contradice. Si una cosa es válida, y la otra no puede serlo, sería contradictorio pretender la validez de ambas.

INCORPORATE. Incorporar. Organizar en forma de sociedad anónima.

INCORPOREAL. Incorpóreo. Que no tiene cuerpo.

INCRIMINATE. Incriminar. Exponer o inculpar a alguien o a uno mismo por un delito.

INCRIMINATORY. Incriminatorio. Que tiende a incriminar. Que puede ser prueba de culpa.

INCROACHMENT. Véase "Encroachment".

INCULPATE. Inculpar. (1) Acusar de un delito. (2) Que implica culpa.

INCUR. Incurrir.

INDECENT. Indecente. Vulgar. Contrario a la decencia.

INDEFEASIBLE. Irrevocable. Que no puede ser abrogado o revocado.

INDEMNITY. Indemnizar. Reembolsar o compensar por los daños causados.

INDENTURE. Instrumento de contrato. (1) Escrito que contiene la venta de bonos cuya fecha de vencimiento e intereses están fijos. (2) Documento hipotecario donde consta un gravamen.

INDEPENDENT. Independiente. Algo que no está sujeto al control o a las leyes de otra entidad.

INDEPENDENT AGENCY. Agencia federal que no depende o forma parte de ningún ministerio.

INDETERMINATE. Indeterminado. Algo cuyo período de tiempo, duración o características no se han establecida.

INDICIA. Indicio. Circunstancias que hacen que un hecho sea probable pero no cierto.

INDICTMENT. Encausamiento. Procesamiento. Sumario. Acusación mediante gran jurado.

INDIGENT. Indigente. Pobre. Que carece de recursos económicos. Tiene derecho a un defensor gratuito.

INDIRECT EVIDENCE. Prueba indirecta. Evidencia o prueba que establece, a través de la consistencia de varios hechos relacionados, la veracidad de una hipótesis.

INDIRECT TAX. Impuesto indirecto. Que no se impone sobre una cosa o ingreso sino sobre un derecho, privilegio o evento.

INDISPENSABLE PARTY. Parte indispensable. Parte en un caso cuya presencia es necesaria para que el tribunal pueda tomar una decisión justa y completa con relación a las otras partes.

INDIVIDUAL INCOME. Ingreso personal. Rentas que obtiene una persona.

INDIVIDUAL RETIREMENT ACCOUNT (I.R.A.). Cuenta de jubilación individual. Cuenta bancaria similar a un fideicomiso en la cual un empleado que no está incluido en un programa de jubilación puede depositar cierta cantidad de dinero todos los años sin que ese dinero ni los intereses sean gravados con impuestos, hasta cuando se retiren en el futuro.

INDORSE. Endosar. Firmar un papel o documento. Firmar un documento para transferir su titularidad.

INDORSEMENT. Endoso. Firma en un documento. Generalmente en un documento o instrumento negociable para transferir el derecho contenido en él a otra persona.

INDUCEMENT. Persuación. Inducción. Aquella cosa, afirmación o promesa hecha por alguien para convencer a otro a entrar en un negocio.

INFAMY. Infamia. Pérdida de la reputación honrada debido a la condena criminal y a la pérdida de cierto derecho que acompaña la pérdida de la buena reputación.

INFANCY. Infancia. Minoría de edad.

INFERENCE. Inferencia. Deducción probable que resulta lógicamente de algún hecho probado.

INFERIOR COURT. Tribunal inferior. Cualquier tribunal excepto el de máxima jerarquía en un sistema legal.

IN FORMA PAUPERIS. (Lat.) Como si fuese pobre. Forma de entablar un juicio sin tener que pagar costos a la corte; normalmente sólo los indigentes o aquéllos sin recursos económicos pueden hacer uso de este derecho judicial.

INFORMATION. Acusación. (1) Denuncia jurada que constituye causa para abrir un sumario. (2) Conocimiento personal.

INFORMATION RETURN. Declaración informativa.

INFRA. (Lat.) Debajo. Dentro. Más adelante en un libro o escrito.

INFRACTION. Infracción. Violación de una ley de poco valor o importancia. Incumplimiento de un contrato u obligación.

INFRINGEMENT. Infracción. Violación. Término comúnmente usado con respecto a derechos de patente, propiedad literaria o marcas registradas.

INHABITANT. Habitante. Ciudadano. Alguien que reside o vive en un lugar de manera permanente y que lo considera como su domicilio.

INHERENT. Inherente. (1) Que se deriva y es inseparable de algo. (2) **Inherent Defect.** Defecto de fábrica que es difícil de descubrir. Defecto en un procedimiento o en una idea.

INHERIT. Heredar. Transmisión de bienes o derechos de un difunto con ocasión de su muerte.

INHERITANCE. Herencia. Bienes recibidos de un difunto, sea por testamento o por sucesión intestada.

INHERITANCE TAX. Impuesto sobre la herencia; impuesto sucesorio o de sucesiones.

INITIATIVE. Iniciativa. Proceso electoral para someter leyes o cambios constitucionales al voto directo.

INJUNCTION. Mandato. Orden judicial que prohíbe u ordena hacer algo.

INJURE. Lesionar. Dañar.

INJURY. Lesión. Daño.

INJUSTICE. Injusticia. Término comúnmente usado con respecto a decisiones de las cortes.

IN-LAW. Afín. Pariente por afinidad.

INNOCENT. Inocente. Que no tiene culpa. Absuelto.

INMATE. Prisionero. Persona que se encuentra encarcelada.

IN PERSONAM JURISDICTION. (Lat.) Poder que tiene la corte sobre un individuo, comparado con el poder que tiene, por ejemplo, sobre los inmuebles del mismo. Véase "In Rem Jurisdiction".

INQUEST. Indagación. Investigación llevada a cabo por el médico forense sobre la muerte violenta de alguien.

INQUISITIONAL SYSTEM. Sistema inquisitivo. Sistema mediante el cual el juez puede recabar pruebas, representar a la nación y decidir. Se opone al sistema adversario de los Estados Unidos.

IN REM JURISDICTION. (Lat.) Poder que tiene la corte sobre los inmuebles de un individuo, comparado con el poder que tiene, por ejemplo, sobre el individuo mismo. Véase "In Personam Jurisdiction".

INSANE. Loco. Demente. Persona que no tiene la capacidad mental para entender o razonar.

INSANITY. Locura. Demencia.

INSCRIPTION. Registrar. Registro de un documento en una oficina pública.

INSIDE TRADING. Comerciar conociendo información confidencial o restringida que sólo tienen ciertas personas en una organización.

INSIDER. Aquél que por su posición dentro de una organización tiene la ventaja de conocer cosas que no son del conocimiento público.

INSOLVENCY. Insolvencia. Inhabilidad para cumplir con los deberes económicos. Bancarrota. Véase "Insolvent".

INSOLVENT. Insolvente. En bancarrota. Aquél que no puede pagar sus deudas vencidas o cuyos activos son menores que su pasivo.

INSPECTION. Inspección. Derecho de revisar libros o a entrar en una propiedad para recoger evidencia durante la etapa de investigación prejudicial.

INSTALLMENT. Plazo. Pago por partes. Pagos parciales de una deuda efectuados regularmente.

INSTANCE. Instancia. Ocurrencia.

INSTANT. Inminente. Presente.

INSTANTER. Inmediatamente.

INSTIGATE. Instigar. Promover o procurar una acción.

INSTITUTION. Institución. Cualquier costumbre, sistema u organización firmemente establecida.

INSTRUCTION. Instrucción. Direcciones dadas por el juez al jurado sobre las leyes que deben considerar en sus deliberaciones, las cuales deben tomar en cuenta antes de llegar a un veredicto.

INSTRUMENT. Instrumento. Documento escrito. Abreviatura de documento negociable.

INSTRUMENTALITY. Agencia. Corporación totalmente controlada por otra.

INSURANCE. Seguro. Contrato mediante el cual una persona (asegurada) paga a otra (aseguradora) para que ésta le reembolse si sufre una pérdida determinada.

INSURED. Asegurado. Quien paga para que le reembolsen si sufre una pérdida.

INSURER. Asegurador. Quien reembolsa si el asegurado sufre una pérdida.

INSURRECTION. Insurrección. Rebelión violenta.

INTANGIBLES. Intangibles. Derechos en lugar de cosas.

INTEGRATED. Completo. (1) Que constituye un todo.
(2) **Integrated Agreement.** Cláusula en un contrato bajo la cual se expresa que el mismo contiene todos los términos del contrato y es la expresión completa y final de lo pactado.

INTELLIGIBILITY. Inteligibilidad. Claridad.

INTENDMENT. Intención. Sentido verdadero de una ley.

INTENT. Intención. Intento. Propósito.

INTER. Con. Entre.

INTER ALIA. (Lat.) Entre otras cosas.

INTER VIVOS. (Lat.) Entre vivos.

INTERDICTION. Interdicción. Prohibición.

INTEREST. Interés. (1) Cualquier derecho en o sobre una propiedad. (2) Dinero adicional pagado por usar el dinero de otro. (3) El costo de usar dinero ajeno. (4) Participación o beneficio.

INTERLOCUTORY. Temporal, interlocutario, provisional. Que no es permanente o final.

INTERMEDIARY. Intermediario. Arbitro. Persona imparcial que se contrata para decidir un problema entre dos o más partes.

INTERNAL REVENUE SERVICE (I.R.S.). Servicio de Impuestos Internos; servicio federal de rentas internas. Agencia encargada de la recolección y el cobro de impuestos.

INTERNATIONAL COURT OF JUSTICE. Tribunal Internacional de Justicia. Tribunal de las Naciones Unidas.

INTERNATIONAL LAW. Derecho internacional. (1) **Public International Law.** Derecho Internacional Público. Se aplica a las relaciones de los países entre sí. (2) **Private International Law.** Derecho Internacional Privado. Principios que regulan el derecho y la jurisdicción de un país para considerar un caso, y la ley que se debe aplicar en sus cortes. Usualmente llamado conflicto de leyes.

INTERNATIONAL SHOE DOCTRINE. Principio contenido en un caso llamado Internacional Shoe mediante el cual se dispuso que, para que un estado pueda tener jurisdicción sobre una persona, ésta debe tener ciertos contactos mínimos con el demandado y con el estado donde se inicia el pleito.

INTERPLEADER. Acción legal a través de la cual el poseedor de una propiedad obliga a dos o más reclamantes de la misma a litigar entre sí el derecho pretendido.

INTERPRETATION. Interpretación. El hecho de decidir qué significa un documento mediante el estudio de su texto.

INTERROGATION. Interrogación. Examen oral hecho por la policía a un sospechoso o acusado.

INTERROGATORIES. Interrogatorios. Preguntas escritas de una parte a la otra para obtener respuestas a preguntas sobre determinados hechos.

INTERSTATE. Interestatal. Entre dos o más estados.

INTERSTATE COMMERCE. Comercio interestatal. Relaciones comerciales entre dos o más estados.

INTERVENING CAUSE. Causa interpuesta o sobreviviente. Causa que rompe una cadena de hechos y absuelve de culpa a la persona negligente que originalmente no cumplió con su responsabilidad.

INTERVENER. Interventor. Interviniente. Aquél que voluntariamente interviene en una demanda entre otras partes haciendo reclamaciones separadas o sumándose a cualquiera de las partes.

INTESTATE. Intestado. Morir sin testamento válido o dejar una porción de bienes sin mencionarlos en el testamento.

INTESTATE SUCCESSION. Sucesión intestada. Herencia dada a los herederos según las leyes estatales cuando no hay testamento.

INTOXICATION. Embriaguez. Cuando un individuo, después de tomar bebidas embriagadoras, pierde el uso normal de sus facultades físicas y mentales, volviéndose incapaz de comportarse como una persona razonable en circunstancias similares.

INURE. Entrar en efecto, validez o vigencia.

INVALID. Inválido. (1) Que no tiene validez. (2) Carente de fuerza legal.

INVENTION. Invención. Producir algo nuevo, inexistente o previamente desconocido.

INVENTORY. Existencia, inventario.

INVESTMENT. Inversión. Usar dinero para obtener o ganar más dinero.

INVESTMENT SECURITIES. Acciones, bonos, etc.

INVITATION. Invitación. (1) Decirle a alguien que entre en la propiedad de uno. (2) Tener inmuebles en forma tal que induzcan a pensar que el público puede entrar.

INVITEE. Invitado. Aquél que está en la propiedad de otro porque ha sido llamado.

INVOICE. Factura. Lista que contiene una serie de artículos vendidos o enviados. Generalmente incluye el precio de cada artículo indicado.

INVOLUNTARY. Involuntario. Sin querer.

INVOLUNTARY CONVERSIONS. Canjes involuntarios, expropiaciones involuntarias.

IRRECONCILABLE DIFFERENCES. Diferencias irreconciliables. Causal de divorcio sin que se requiera que un cónyuge se encuentre culpable.

IRRECUSABLE. Término que se refiere a obligaciones de contrato impuestas por ley sin necesidad del consentimiento de la persona afectada.

IRRELEVANT. Irrelevante. Que no tiene relación con el asunto en discusión.

IRREPARABLE INJURY. Daño irreparable. Daño que no se puede remediar económicamente.

ISSUE. Expedir. Girar, promulgar. Punto medular. (1) Punto eje o central en una discusión o demanda. (2) Hijo, descendiente. (3) Acciones o bonos emitidos u ofrecidos en venta al mismo tiempo. (4) Primera transferencia de un documento negociable.

ISSUE PRECLUSION. Cosa juzgada. Principio legal que prohíbe volver a litigar algo ya decidido.

ITEM. Artículo. Partida. (1) Renglón, sección o espacio separado e individualizado dentro de un todo. (2) Dinero designado para un propósito particular.

ITEMIZE. Detallar. Separar un todo por partes o artículos.

ITEMIZED DEDUCTIONS. Deducciones detalladas; deducciones especiales. Ciertas deducciones reconocidas por la ley que pueden ser detalladas por el contribuyente al presentar su declaración de impuestos.

J

J.D. Siglas de "Juris Doctor". Véase "Juris Doctor".

J.N.O.V. Véase "Judgment Non Obstante Veredicto".

JACTITATION. Jactancia. Alarde de algo falso.

JAIL. Cárcel, prisión.

JASON CLAUSE. Disposición incluida en el conocimiento de embarque mediante la cual el dueño de la carga se responsabiliza por cualquier daño a la carga aun cuando haya existido negligencia de otros.

JAY WALKING. Cruce de una calle de forma que no es legal ni segura.

JEOFAILE STATUTE. Ley en Luisiana y Francia que permite que las demandas y peticiones se corrijan libremente.

JEOPARDY ASSESSMENT. Acción legal llevada a cabo para incautar bienes de un contribuyente moroso por existir temor fundado de que evadirá su deuda fiscal y se despojará de los bienes en perjuicio del fisco.

JETSAM. Bienes arrojados de un buque para aligerar su peso durante una emergencia.

JETTISON. Arrojar cosas al mar para aligerar el peso de un buque durante una emergencia.

JOBBER. Mediador. Persona que compra y vende para otro.

JOHN DOE. Nombre ficticio dado a una persona en juicio, porque no se permite usar su verdadero nombre, o porque se trata de un menor.

JOINDER. Unión. Acumulación. Mecanismo legal para unir varias personas a un mismo caso bajo las reglas de la corte.

JOINT. Conjunto, mancomunado, unido. Se puede referir a un sinnúmero de acciones o eventos legales que están unidos.

JOINT AND SEVERAL. Mancomunado y solidario. Se refiere a casos en que todos los implicados conjuntamente, y cada uno en particular, son responsables por el total de los daños causados. Si unos no pueden pagar, los otros deberán pagar lo faltante.

JOINT AND SEVERAL CONTRACT. Contrato donde cada parte individualmente, y todas conjuntamente, se obligan bajo el contrato.

JOINT BANK ACCOUNT. Cuenta conjunta. Cuenta bancaria de la cual dos o más personas son propietarias, y tienen igual derecho a retirar y depositar dinero.

JOINT ENTERPRISE. Empresa conjunta o colectiva. Cuando varias personas se reúnen para una actividad o negocio de forma que las acciones de uno de los participantes afectan y obligan al grupo.

JOINT LIABILITY. Responsabilidad mancomunada. Cuando cada parte es responsable por el total de la obligación, aunque las otras partes también sean responsables y no tengan capacidad para cumplir con la obligación.

JOINT LIVES. Derecho que perdura mientras vivan todos aquellos que lo comparten.

JOINT RETURN. Declaración de rentas hecha en conjunto por ambos esposos.

JOINT VENTURE o JOINT ADVENTURE. Empresa o riesgo colectivo. Negocio donde participan varias personas o naciones.

JOKER. Cláusula o artículo de un contrato o instrumento que parece inofensivo pero que permite anular o evadir el contrato o el instrumento.

JOURNAL. Periódico. Publicación realizada cada cierto tiempo.

JOURNAL ENTRY. Entrada de un crédito o débito en los libros de contabilidad de una entidad.

JOURNALIST'S PRIVILEGE. Véase "News Person's Privilege".

JOYRIDING. Hurto de un automóvil para usarlo por un tiempo pero sin la intención de quedarse con él.

JUDGE. Juez. Juzgar. (1) Persona que decide un caso en la corte. (2) Acción de resolver o decidir un juicio.

JUDGMENT. Decisión, sentencia. Acto judicial que resuelve un conflicto presentado ante la corte.

JUDICARE. (Lat.) Juzgar, sentenciar.

JUDICATURE. El órgano judicial.

JUDICIAL. Judicial. (1) Relativo a una corte. (2) Relativo a un juez. (3) Organo del estado que atiende los litigios en las cortes.

JUDICIAL DISCRETION. Poder de libre discreción que posee una corte.

JUDICIAL IMMUNITY. Inmunidad contra demanda judicial que tiene un juez u otro oficial de la corte cuando actúa en una capacidad oficial, aun cuando actúe de mala fe.

JUDICIAL NOTICE. Aviso judicial. La capacidad de una corte para aceptar ciertos hechos como probados sin necesitad de evidencia (por ejemplo, el sol se pone en el oeste). Se refiere a hechos de conocimiento general.

JUDICIAL QUESTION. Cuestión para los tribunales. Decisión que debe tomar una corte y no el órgano legislativo o ejecutivo.

JUDICIAL REVIEW. Revisión judicial. Apelar. (1) Poder de una corte para examinar una ley o acto y declararlo inconstitucional, o para interpretar su sentido y aplicación. (2) Apelar una decisión administrativa a una corte.

JUDICIAL SALE. Venta judicial o legal. Venta efectuada bajo la orden de una corte.

JURIS DOCTOR. Doctor en Leyes. Diploma académico otorgado a un estudiante de leyes al graduarse.

JURISDICTION. Jurisdicción, competencia. (1) Area geográfica dentro de la cual un juez tiene facultad legal para conocer sus asuntos judiciales. (2) Poder que tiene un juez para conocer y resolver causas de litigio.

564

JURISPRUDENCE. Jurisprudencia. (1) Estudio de la filosofía, los principios y las doctrinas legales. (2) En un sentido menos común, se refiere a las decisiones de los jueces como precedentes legales.

JURIST. Jurista. El que estudia la ley.

JUROR. Jurado. Miembro de un jurado.

JURY. Jurado. Grupo de personas llamadas a decidir tanto sobre los hechos de un caso cuanto sobre la responsabilidad del demandado.

JURY LIST. Lista del jurado. (1) Contiene los nombres de las personas escogidas para actuar como jurado de conciencia en un juicio. (2) Lista de todas las personas que pueden ser seleccionadas como miembros de un jurado.

JURY TRIAL. Juicio por jurado. Juicio en el cual la responsabilidad la decide un jurado.

JUS. (Lat.) Justicia, derecho, etc.

JUST. Justo.

JUSTICE. Justicia. Magistrado.

JUSTICE DEPARTMENT. Ministerio de Justicia que representa al gobierno federal.

JUSTICIABLE. Justiciable. Que puede ser resuelto por una corte.

JUVENILE. Juvenil. Menor de edad. (1) Que no se considera un adulto mayor de edad para asuntos criminales. (2) Que no ha cumplido la mayoría de edad. (3) **Juvenile Court.** Tribunal Tutelar de Menores. Corte que resuelve asuntos sobre menores de edad.

K

K. Abreviatura de contrato.

KANGAROO COURT. Término usado para describir a un tribunal o un proceso legal donde se ignoran totalmente los derechos legales de un individuo y el resultado jurídico está predeterminado.

KEEP RECORDS. Llevar registros.

KEFAUVER–CELLAR ACT. Ley federal que le prohíbe a una compañía adquirir otra que se dedica al mismo negocio si el efecto es el de disminuir la competencia en ese mercado.

KEOGH PLAN ("H.R. 10 PLAN"). Programa de ahorro para la jubilación que está libre de impuestos para personas que tienen ingresos de trabajo por cuenta propia; es similar a la cuenta de jubilación individual "individual retirement account".

KEY NUMBERS. Números claves. Sistema de referencia usado en textos y libros legales para encontrar información sobre temas legales discutidos en otros casos.

KICKBACK. Pago indebido. Pago secreto dado a alguien, un empleado o un oficial público, con el objeto de inducir una compra o influir respecto a compras en el futuro.

KIN. Linaje, vínculo, parentesco.

KIND, IN. En especie. Que no es dinero.

KITING. Girar cheques sin fondos.

KNOWLEDGE. Conocimiento de los hechos o de la verdad. Una persona adquiere conocimiento cuando ha percibido algo con sus sentidos. La ley atribuye como presunción legal el conocimiento de ciertas cosas a ciertas personas. Por ejemplo, los ciudadanos conocen todas las leyes; el patrono se supone que conoce las acciones de sus empleados en la ejecución de sus labores, aunque no las conozca en realidad.

KNOWINGLY. A sabiendas. Con conocimiento completo e intencional.

L

LL.M. or LL.D. "Master of Laws" o "Doctor of Laws". Maestría o Doctorado en Leyes. Títulos universitarios avanzados de Derecho.

LABEL. Rótulo, etiqueta. Cualquier cosa escrita y añadida a un documento.

LABOR CONTRACT. Convenio colectivo. Contrato o convenio de trabajo firmado entre el empleador y el sindicato.

LABOR UNION. Unión de trabajadores; sindicato. Organización formalmente reconocida por el patrono y compuesta de empleados con el fin de mejorar las condiciones de trabajo.

LACHES. Falta de diligencia; tardanza. Concepto equitativo bajo el cual el retraso en reclamar algún derecho o remedio actúa como obstáculo para dicha reclamación.

LACKING. Falto, ausente, carente.

LAND. Tierra, terreno. Bienes raíces. Incluye el subsuelo, el suelo y el espacio aéreo de una propiedad.

LAND SALES CONTRACT. Contrato para la venta de un bien inmueble que no se registra en la oficina de registro de contratos de compraventa de inmuebles, y bajo el cual el vendedor retiene el título de propiedad hasta que se cumpla el plazo y los términos acordados.

LANDLORD. Arrendador. Dueño de un inmueble arrendado a inquilinos.

LANDMARK CASE. Caso sobresaliente que marca un cambio importante en las decisiones de la corte.

LAPSE. Lapso. Caducidad. Extinción de un derecho al no ser ejercido durante cierto tiempo.

LARCENY. Hurto de cualquier naturaleza.

LASCIVIOUS. Lascivo. Lujurioso; obsceno. Relativo a lujuria.

LAST RESORT. De última instancia. Tribunal ante el cual no se puede interponer ninguna apelación.

LATENT. Latente, pasivo.

LATERAL SUPPORT. Derecho a que un terreno o propiedad sea sostenido por el terreno adjunto.

LAUDUM. (Lat.) Laudo. Fallo o decisión.

LAW. Ley. Derecho.

LAWFUL. Legal. Permitido o autorizado por la ley. Que no está prohibido.

LAWSUIT. Litigio. Juicio; demanda. Procedimiento judicial para hacer valer un derecho.

LAWYER. Abogado o apoderado legal autorizado para ejercer ante una corte.

LAYOFF. Despido. Suspención del trabajo.

LEADING QUESTION. Una pregunta que le sugiere al testigo cómo debe contestarla.

LEASE. Arrendamiento; locación; alquiler. (1) Contrato para el uso de un bien por cierto tiempo a cambio de dinero.

LEASEBACK. Venta de una propiedad estableciendo el alquiler de la propiedad vendida, bajo cuya modalidad el arrendador es el comprador y el vendedor es el arrendatario del bien vendido.

LEASEHOLD. Derecho de arrendamiento. Bien inmueble que es objeto de un arrendamiento.

LEAVE OF ABSENCE. Licencia o permiso para ausentarse del empleo.

LEAVE OF COURT. Permiso de la corte o del juez.

LEGACY. Legado. (1) Dinero, propiedad o bienes dejados por testamento. (2) Porción hereditaria.

LEGAL. Legal. (1) Permitido por la ley. (2) Relacionado a la ley. (3) Jurídico.

LEGAL AGE. Mayoría de edad. Edad suficiente para que una persona contrate y sea considerada responsable de sus actos.

LEGAL ETHICS. Etica legal. Costumbres y normas que mantienen los abogados, y que rigen su compartamiento moral y profesional hacia otros abogados, sus clientes y las cortes.

LEGAL FEES. Honorarios legales. Honorarios profesionales que cobra un abogado por atender un asunto legal.

LEGAL REPRESENTATIVE. Representante legal o judicial. Uno que maneja los asuntos legales de otro ante una corte.

LEGAL RESIDENCE. Residencia legal. Lugar donde una persona vive habitualmente con la intención de permanecer indefinidamente en esa localidad.

LEGAL TENDER. Moneda de curso legal. Moneda autorizada por un estado para circular libremente en él.

LEGATEE. Legatario. Persona que recibe un legado.

LEGATION. Embajada. Miembros que componen una embajada.

LEGATOR. Testador. Aquel que hace un testamento y deja un legado a alguien.

LEGISLATE. Legislar. Dictar leyes.

LEGISLATION. Legislación. (1) Proceso de dictar leyes. (2) La ley propiamente dicha.

LEGISLATIVE. Legislativo. (1) Organo gubernamental que hace y dicta las leyes. (2) Referente a lo legislativo.

LEGITIMATE. Legítimo. Legal. (1) Reconocido por ley. (2) Hacer legal una cosa.

LEND. Prestar. Dar algo en calidad de préstamo.

LENDER. Prestamista. Persona que presta algo.

LESSEE. Arrendatario, inquilino. Persona que paga un alquiler por el uso de una cosa.

LESSOR. Arrendador. Persona que arrienda o alquila una cosa, generalmente de su propiedad, a cambio de dinero.

LET. Arrendar. Alquilar.

LETTERHEAD. Membrete. Papel membretado.

LETTER OF ADVICE. Notificación que hace el girador al girado sobre la emisión de un documento negociable.

LETTER OF CREDIT. Carta de crédito. Afirmación que hace un banco diciendo que pagará una obligación contraída por un comerciante en una transacción en particular, si ciertas condiciones se satisfacen.

LETTER OF INTENT. Un documento que describe un acuerdo preliminar que formará la base de un contrato. No otorga todos los derechos de un contrato.

LETTER RULING. Una opinión escrita por el "Internal Revenue Service" sobre cómo interpretar las leyes de impuestos con respecto a unos hechos específicos.

LETTERS PATENT. Un documento que otorga una patente o el título de una propiedad a alguien.

LETTERS ROGATORY. Cartas rogatorias. Solicitud que hace un juez a otro de distinta jurisdicción para que interrogue a cierto testigo y envíe su testimonio a la corte que mandó la carta.

LEVERAGE. Préstamo. Usualmente la adquisición de un préstamo mayor después de una inversión mínima de capital.

LEVY. Imponer. Embargar. Rematar, ejecutar, secuestrar. (1) Crear o cobrar un impuesto. (2) Incautar/secuestrar un bien del deudor para garantizar el pago a los acreedores.

LEWD. Lujurioso.

LEX. (Lat.) Ley.

LEX FORI. (Lat.) Ley del foro. Ley del lugar donde se decide o juzga el asunto.

LEX LOCI. (Lat.) Ley del lugar. (1) **Lex Loci Actua.** Ley del lugar donde se ejecutó el acto. (2) **Lex Loci Delictus.** Ley del lugar donde se cometió el delito.

LEXIS. Nombre de un sistema computarizado de investigación legal.

LIABILITY. Deuda. Obligación, responsabilidad.

LIABLE. Culpable, responsable. Persona que debe responder por las consecuencias de un acto u omisión.

LIBELANT. Demandante; libelista. Aquél que acude a la corte a presentar un reclamo contra otro llamado demandado.

LIBELOUS. Difamatorio. Que calumnia, injurioso. Que tiende a perjudicar la reputación de alguien.

LIBERTY. Libertad.

LICENSE. Licencia. Permiso. Autorización patente. Concesión. (1) **License Plate.** Matrícula o placa de automóvil.

LICENSEE. Concesionario. Persona autorizada para hacer algo. Aquél que tiene derecho a hacer uso de una concesión.

LIE. (1) Mentira. (2) Acción que existe o que es soportable.

LIE DETECTOR. Detector de mentiras. Polígrafo. Instrumento utilizado para determinar si un testigo miente. En general, los resultados de un polígrafo no son admisibles en corte.

LIEN. Carga. Gravamen. Obligación. Embargo, secuestro. Derecho a retener un bien o a imponer sobre él un gravamen hasta que quede satisfecha una deuda (tax lien, mechanic's lien, judgment lien, etc.).

LIFE. Vida. De por vida o durante la vida de.

LIFE ESTATE. Derecho de propiedad que una persona posee hasta su muerte pero que no puede pasar a sus herederos.

LIKE–KIND EXCHANGE. Intercambio de una cosa por otra de similar clase o especie. Este tipo de transferencia no es gravable con impuestos.

LIMINE. (Lat.) Al comienzo de.

LIMITATION. Limitación, restricción. (1) **Statute of Limitation.** Leyes que establecen cierto tiempo para poder hacer valer un derecho. Leyes de prescripción que señalan el período de tiempo dentro del cual se puede actuar legalmente.

LINE OF CREDIT. Línea de crédito. Crédito que le extiende a alguien un banco o un comerciante.

LINEUP. Procedimiento mediante el cual se le pide a un testigo que identifique al delincuente entre las personas presentes.

LINK–IN–CHAIN. Principio constitucional que protege a una persona contra la autoincriminación.

LIQUID. Líquido. (1) Un bien que se convierte fácilmente en dinero en efectivo. (2) Que tiene suficiente dinero en efectivo.

LIQUIDATE. Liquidar. (1) Pagar una deuda. (2) Ajustar la cuantía de una deuda. (3) Distribuir el dinero dejado en herencia o por una compañía que cierra sus operaciones.

LIQUIDATION. Liquidación. Terminación y cierre de una empresa mediante la venta de todos sus bienes.

LISTED SECURITY. Acción, bono o valor que ha satisfecho los requisitos de la bolsa o mercado de valores y que se intercambia en la bolsa.

LISTING. Acuerdo mediante el cual un corredor de bienes raíces puede vender una propiedad a nombre del dueño por una comisión.

LITERAL CONSTRUCTION. Interpretación literal. Interpretar un documento en base a su texto solamente, sin considerar la intención de las partes.

LITERARY PROPERTY. Propiedad literaria. Derecho de un autor sobre el control total de su obra.

LITERARY WORK. Obra o producción literaria. Cualquier trabajo literario expresado en palabras escritas, números o símbolos, sin considerar su forma física.

LITIGANT. Litigante. Una de las partes en un juicio.

LITIGATE. Litigar. Reclamar un derecho mediante una controversia judicial.

LIVING TRUST. Un fideicomiso establecido mientras una persona aún vive, en vez de llevarse a efecto bajo un testamento.

LIVING WILL. Un documento que expresa las intenciones de cómo quiere morir una persona si pierde el conocimiento a causa de una enfermedad o herida incurable.

LLOYD'S OF LONDON. Asociación de reaseguro con base en Londres, la más grande del mundo.

LOAN. Préstamo. Contrato mediante el cual una persona cede el uso de algo a alguien a cambio de otra cosa; generalmente dinero.

LOAN COMMITMENT. Promesa de una entidad prestamista de prestar dinero al cumplirse ciertas condiciones.

LOBBYING. Cabildeo. Intento de persuadir a un legislador para que vote de cierta forma en un proyecto de ley.

LOCAL ACTION. Demanda que sólo puede tramitarse en un lugar específico.

LOCATION. Marcar los límites de un terreno en el cual se ha hecho un descubrimiento mineral para reclamar el derecho a la explotación minera.

LOCATIVE CALLS. La descripción de un terreno en una escritura u otro documento utilizando marcas del terreno u objetos mediante los cuales el terreno puede identificarse precisamente.

LOCUS. (Lat.) Lugar, sitio.

LONG ARM STATUTE. Leyes estatales que permiten a una corte tomar jurisdicción sobre acciones contra personas o propiedades fuera del estado, sin violar los derechos constitucionales del demandado.

LONG TERM. Largo plazo. Que tiene una vigencia o duración extensa.

LOOPHOLE. Uso de un tecnicismo legal para evadir una ley o el pago de un impuesto.

LOSS. Pérdida. Daño.

LOSS LEADER. Mercancía vendida por debajo de su costo, normalmente para atraer compradores.

LOSS PAYABLE CLAUSE. Cláusula en una póliza de seguros que establece el orden o prioridad de pago si el seguro no es suficiente para pagar a todos los involucrados.

LOST WILL. Testamento perdido. Un testamento que alguna vez existió pero no se puede encontrar después de la muerte del testador. En algunos estados se permite que se prueben las cláusulas del testamento con evidencia oral.

LUMP SUM. Suma global. Cantidad total o alzada que se fija para varios objetos de la misma o diferente clase.

M

M.O. Modus Operandi (Lat.). Método o modo de operar. Usualmente se refiere al comportamiento criminal.

MAGISTERIAL PRECINCT. Distrito Jurisdiccional Magisterial. La parte de un territorio en la cual un magistrado, un alguacil o un juez de paz tiene facultad para ejercer su autoridad.

MAGISTRACY. Magistratura. Magistrado. (1) Todos los funcionarios públicos. (2) Todos los jueces y funcionarios que administran justicia. (3) Todos los jueces. (4) Todos los jueces de bajo rango o jerarquía así como los jueces de paz. (5) La oficina del magistrado.

MAGISTRATE. Magistrado. (1) Juez de bajo rango o jerarquía, usualmente con poderes y funciones limitadas. (2) Juez administrativo. Por ejemplo, un juez de una corte de policía. Este tipo de juez puede llevar a cabo los procedimientos preliminares o presupuestos procesales de un juicio y tratar asuntos criminales menores o faltas leves.

MAGNA CARTA. Carta Magna. El documento firmado por el Rey inglés en 1215 que definía y concedía derechos básicos por primera vez en Inglaterra. Estos incluían tanto los derechos personales y de propiedad, como los límites a los impuestos y a la interferencia religiosa.

MAGNUSON–MOSS ACT. Ley Magnuson-Moss. Ley federal que fija los parámetros de las garantías que deben tener los productos de venta al consumidor. Esta ley requiere que las garantías estén escritas en un lenguaje sencillo y claro.

MAIL FRAUD. Defraudación por correo. Delito federal que se comete cuando una persona defrauda a otra utilizando los servicios del correo.

MAIL ORDER DIVORCE. Divorcio solicitado por correo. Divorcio concedido por un país en el cual ninguno de los cónyuges vive y al cual ninguno ha viajado para conseguir el divorcio. Este tipo de divorcio no es válido en los Estados Unidos.

MAILBOX RULE. Principio legal mediante el cual una oferta es aceptada cuando se envía la aceptación por correo.

MAIM. Mutilar, cortar, lisiar.

MAIN PURPOSE DOCTRINE. Doctrina del propósito principal. La ley de fraudes requiere que sea escrito para ser ejecutable un contrato bajo el cual una persona asume la responsabilidad por las deudas de otra. La excepción a este principio es la "doctrina del propósito principal". Esta excepción es aplicable cuando la persona que asume la responsabilidad por la deuda de otra se compromete oralmente a cumplir con el contrato con el proposito principal de beneficiarse de alguna manera.

MAINTAIN. Mantener, sostener, defender. Evitar que caduque o que fracase. Continuar, hacer algo repetidamente.

MAINTENANCE. Conservación, sostenimiento. (1) Mantener. (2) Entrometerse en una demanda que no le concierne. Véase "Champerty". (3) Dar pensión alimenticia. Véase "Separate Maintenance". (4) Manutencion.

MAJOR AND MINOR FAULT RULE. Principio de la falta mayor y menor. En la ley marítima, la nave que es obviamente culpable de un accidente lleva la responsabilidad de probar la culpa de otra(s) nave(s). Cuando la evidencia establece en forma clara e incuestionable la culpa o falta de una nave, el navío responsable no puede disminuir su culpa o falta al cuestionar las acciones de otra(s) nave(s).

MAJOR DISPUTE. Disputa mayor. Una disputa mayor con respecto al derecho laboral, concerniente a la creación de un contrato laboral, mientras que una disputa menor concierne la interpretación del contrato existente cuando se aplica éste a una situación determinada.

MAJORITY. Mayoría. (1) Mayoría de edad. (2) Más de la mitad. (3) **Absolute Majority.** Mayoría absoluta. Más de la mitad de los votantes sufragaron. (4) **Simple Majority.** Mayoría simple. Más de la mitad de los votos de las personas que tienen derecho a votar.

MAKE PAYABLE TO. Literalmente "hacer pagadero a la orden de".

MAKE WHOLE. Compensar. Indemnizar. Poner a una persona que ha sufrido un daño en la posición económica en que estaba antes de que occurriera el daño.

MAKER. Otorgante, girador, librador. (1) La persona que inicialmente firma un documento negociable. (2) Persona que firma, crea o realiza algo.

MALA FIDES. (Lat.) Mala fe.

MALA IN SE. (Lat.) Véase "Malum In Se".

MALA PRAXIS. (Lat.) Véase "Malpractice".

MALEFACTOR. Malhechor. Persona que es culpable de un delito.

MALFEASANCE. Fechoría. Malversación. Mal hecho; acto ilegal. (1) Hacer mal. (2) Cometer un acto ilegal. Se aplica especialmente a funcionarios públicos.

MALICE. Malicia, mala intención. (1) Guardar rencor. (2) Hacer daño intencionalmente a otra persona. (3) No tener justificación moral ni legal para haber hecho daño a otra persona.

MALICE AFORETHOUGHT. Actuar mal premeditadamente. Cometer un delito con intención premeditada.

MALICIOUS. Malicioso. Actuar intencionalmente, con malos motivos y sin excusas.

MALICIOUS MISCHIEF. Agravio con malicia. El delito de destruir intencionalmente la propiedad ajena.

MALLORY RULE. Véase "McNabb-Mallory Rule".

MALO ANIMO. (Lat.) Con mala intención.

MALO GRATO. (Lat.) Sin intención.

MALPRACTICE. Mala conducta; tratamiento erróneo. Mala conducta profesional o falta irrazonable de habilidad en un área profesional.

577

MALUM IN SE. (Lat.) Malo por su naturaleza propia. Moralmente malo. Véase "Common Law Crimes".

MANAGER. Gerente. Administrador. Persona que se escoge para administrar un negocio o parte de él.

MANDAMUS. (Lat.) Orden de la corte dirigida a un funcionario público o a un departamento gubernamental.

MANDATE. Mandato, encargo, comisión. (1) Orden judicial de actuar. Véase "Mandamus". (2) Autorización para actuar.

MANDATORY. Obligatorio. Requerido. Deber que tiene que cumplirse.

MANDATORY AUTHORITY. Véase "Binding Authority".

MANIFEST. Manifestar, declarar. (1) Que es claramente visible; que no necesita prueba. (2) Documento por escrito que detalla artículos que han sido enviados o almacenados, dando descripción, valor e información sobre ellos. (3) Lista de pasajeros o carga que lleva un buque o avión.

MANIFESTO. Manifiesto. (1) Escrito del Jefe de Estado con relación a una acción internacional de importancia. (2) Declaración pública sobre principios políticos.

MANIPULATION. Manipulación. Crear una impresión falsa para lograr que se realice lo que el manipulador se propone.

MANN ACT. Ley federal en contra de transportar mujeres de un estado a otro para propósitos inmorales.

MANSLAUGHTER. Homicidio sin premeditación.

MANUFACTURER'S LIABILITY. Véase "Strict Liability". Responsabilidad civil por manufacturar algo.

MANUMISSION. Manumisión. El acto de liberar a una persona del control de otra.

MAPP RULE. Principio constitucional de Estados Unidos que establece que la evidencia obtenida ilegalmente no puede usarse en un proceso penal estatal.

MARBURY v. MADISON. Caso de la Corte Suprema de los Estados Unidos que establece el derecho del poder judicial a decidir si un acto del Congreso es constitucional. Este principio se conoce también como "judicial review."

MARGIN. Margen, borde. Porcentaje del precio de una acción que debe ser pagado en efectivo por el comprador, el resto podiendo financiarse a crédito.

MARGINAL RATE. Véase "Tax Rate".

MARITAL. Marital. Que tiene que ver con el matrimonio.

MARITAL AGREEMENTS. Acuerdos maritales. (1) Todo contrato entre personas casadas. (2) Contratos entre personas que están por casarse o que están por divorciarse.

MARITAL COMMUNICATIONS PRIVILEGE. Inmunidad conyugal. Derecho que tienen esposo y esposa de no testificar en contra del otro en un proceso penal.

MARITIME (MARINE) BELT. Véase "Territorial Waters".

MARITIME LAW. Derecho Marítimo. Leyes que regulan a los buques, el comercio marítimo y a los marineros.

MARK. Marca. (1) Una seña, por ejemplo la X, utilizada por el que no puede firmar. (2) Una indicación. (3) Véase "Trademark", "Service Mark", "Collective Mark" o "Certification Mark".

MARK DOWN. Descuento. Precio inferior a uno anteriormente dado a un mismo artículo.

MARK UP. Sobreprecio. Ganancia. Precio más alto con relación a otro en el mismo artículo.

MARKET. Mercado. (1) La región geográfica en la cual un producto puede venderse. (2) Las características económicas y sociales de los compradores.

MARKETABLE. Vendible. (1) Que puede venderse fácilmente por dinero en efectivo. (2) Que es comercialmente válido.

MARKETABLE TITLE ACTS. Leyes estatales que hacen posible determinar si un título de propiedad sobre un inmueble es válido, al indagar en el registro público a ver si hay algún otro registro sobre la propiedad durante un período de tiempo (p.ej., veinte años).

MARKET PRICE. Precio del mercado o de la plaza. Véase "Market Value".

MARKET VALUE. Valor en el mercado. El precio por el cual un vendedor y un comprador coinciden en transar en el curso ordinario del comercio.

MARKETING CONTRACT. Contrato o acuerdo entre una cooperativa y sus miembros a través del cual se venden ciertos artículos por un precio determinado.

MARRIAGE. Matrimonio, casamiento. Unión legal como esposo y esposa.

MARRIAGE SETTLEMENT. Acuerdo matrimonial. Un acuerdo antes del matrimonio en el cual cada parte modifica o cede derechos sobre propiedad. Estos derechos surgen a consequencia del matrimonio.

MARSHAL. Oficial en los tribunales de justicia de los Estados Unidos que tiene la función de mantener la paz, notificar órdenes legales, etc.; sus funciones son similares a las del "state sheriff". Véase "Sheriff".

MARSHALING. Poner en orden. Establecer el orden de las deudas cuando se van a dividir los activos.

MARTIAL LAW. Ley Marcial. Se da cuando la autoridad militar toma el control del gobierno. Donde los militares controlan tanto a los civiles cuanto los asuntos civiles.

MARTINDALE–HUBBEL. Conjunto de tomos informativos que clasifican a la mayoría de los abogados de cada estato tanto por su tipo de práctica cuanto en consideración al lugar donde tienen sus oficinas. También describen los bufetes internacionales y las leyes por nación y estado.

MASSACHUSETTS TRUST. Asociación voluntaria. Véase "Business Trust".

MASTER. Patrono. (1) **Master and servant.** Patrono y empleado. Persona que emplea a otra para que le sirva en sus asuntos, con derecho a controlar las acciones del empleado. (2) **Special Master.** Persona designada por la corte para que la represente en determinado acto o transacción. (3) **Master Agreement.** Convenio patronal. Convenio entre la unión (sindicato) y los representantes de una industria. (4) **Master Plan.** Plan maestro. Lineamientos para un plan de asuntos gubernamentales o municipales de viviendas, comercio, etc. (5) **Master Policy.** Póliza de seguro que cubre a un grupo de personas. (6) **Master Contract.** Acuerdo básico para comprar o alquilar equipo cuando se requiera, cada vez bajo las mismas condiciones. (7) **Master of a Ship.** Capitán. En derecho marítimo, quien está al mando de la navegación y la tripulación, el cuidado de la nave y la carga de ésta, y quien es el representante del dueño y su confidente.

MATERIAL. Importante. Probablemente necesario; que va a influir o tener efecto. (1) **Material Allegation.** Alegato esencial. (2) **Material Alteration.** Alteración substancial que cambia la esencia del documento.

MATERIAL EVIDENCE. Véase "Relevant Evidence".

MATERIAL FACT. Hechos influyentes. (1) En contratos, razón básica para la celebración de un contrato. (2) En alegatos, hecho central en la decisión de un caso. (3) En materia de seguros, hecho que, de haberse comunicado al asegurador, éste no hubiera otorgado la póliza, o no la hubiera suscrito en los términos que lo hizo.

MATERIAL ISSUE. Punto substancial. Cuestión que está en disputa entre las partes en un juicio y que es importante para decidir sobre la demanda.

MATERIAL WITNESS. Testigo esencial. Persona que puede dar testimonio que nadie más puede dar.

581

MATERIALMAN. Suplidor de materiales. Persona que suple de materiales a una construcción o reparación. También se le conoce como "supplier".

MATERNAL. Maternal. Que se refiere a la madre.

MATERNITY. Maternidad.

MATRIMONIAL ACTIONS. Acción que afecta el estado matrimonial. Por ejemplo, la disolución, la anulación del vínculo, la separación, etc.

MATTER. Asunto. (1) Hecho central, importante o necesario. (2) Hechos substanciales en una demanda o en una defensa.

MATTER OF FACT. Cuestión de hecho. Que puede deducirse por razonamiento en base al testimonio de los testigos y a otra evidencia.

MATTER OF LAW. Cuestión de derecho. Que puede resolverse aplicando la ley a los hechos del caso que no están en disputa o controversia.

MATTER OF RECORD. Cuestión de archivo. Cualquier cosa que puede probarse con sólo revisar los archivos de la corte.

MATURED. Véase "Liquidated" y "Maturity".

MATURITY. Vencimiento. Fecha en la que una deuda u otra obligación puede ser presentada al cobro.

MAXIM. Máxima, regla, axioma. Regla o idea que sirve de dirección en un caso.

MAYHEM. Mutilación. El delito de mutilar o de causar, en forma violenta, una herida seria y permanente a otra persona.

MAYOR. Alcalde. (1) Figura gubernamental que generalmente es la figura administrativa principal de una ciudad, pueblo u otro gobierno local. (2) **Mayor's Court.** Corte establecida en algunas ciudades de los Estados Unidos en la que el alcalde sirve de juez policial y cuya jurisdicción se limita a delitos leves que suceden dentro de la ciudad.

McCARRAN ACT. Ley federal de los Estados Unidos que permite a los estados regular y cobrar impuestos a compañías de seguros fuera del estado con respecto a clientes del estado en cuestión. Véase "Internal Security Acts".

McNABB–MALLORY RULE. Principio basado en un caso que establece que si alguien ha sido detenido por demasiado tiempo sin haber sido llevado ante un juez, cualquier confesión obtenida de esta persona es inválida y no puede usarse contra ella.

MEAN HIGH TIDE. Promedio de la marea alta. Promedio de la línea que alcanza la marea alta en un determinado período de tiempo. Utilizado para establecer el límite territorial sujeto a propiedad.

MEAN LOW TIDE. Promedio de la marea baja durante un período de tiempo.

MEANS. Medios, métodos. Recursos, dineros, propiedades o ingresos disponibles para mantener a una familia.

MEASURE OF DAMAGES. Las normas que miden el dinero necesario para compensar a alguien por daños y perjuicios.

MECHANICAL EQUIVALENT. Equivalencia mecánica. Dos cosas que hacen el mismo trabajo en la misma forma básica y producen el mismo resultado.

MECHANIC'S LIEN. Derecho que tiene un trabajador o contratista de retener o gravar una propiedad hasta que se le pague por su trabajo.

MEDIATE. Mediar, intervenir. En medio, secundario, incidental. Véase "Mediation".

MEDIATION. Mediación. Ayuda de un tercero en el arreglo de una disputa.

MEDICAID. "Ayuda Médica." Pagos de asistencia médica hechos por los gobiernos estatales y federales a personas de bajos ingresos que califican para los mismos.

MEDICAL EXAMINER. Examinador médico. Funcionario público que investiga las muertes violentas o inexplicables, y quien realiza las autopsias. Es la versión moderna del médico forense.

MEDICAL JURISPRUDENCE. Medicina legal; jurisprudencia médica.

MEDICARE. Pagos federales para el tratamiento médico de ancianos.

MEETING. Reunión, asamblea. En el área de Derecho, una asamblea de varias personas con el propósito de discutir y decidir sobre asuntos de interés común.

MEETING OF CREDITORS. Reunión de acreedores. Bajo la ley de quiebras consiste en la primera reunión de acreedores; en dicha reunión el deudor es interrogado, los acreedores hacen sus reclamos, y el fideicomisario en bancarrota aprueba o desaprueba los reclamos. También pueden haber reuniones intermedias, y en la reunión final se completan todos los asuntos del deudor ante la audiencia en la corte de quiebra.

MEETING OF MINDS. Acuerdo o concierto de voluntades. Acuerdo entre personas que van a realizar un contrato en cuanto atañe a los términos esenciales del mismo. Si no hay un entendimiento entre las partes, no hay contrato.

MELIORATION. Mejoras. Mejorar la propiedad más que repararla.

MEMBER. Miembro. (1) Cualquiera de las personas de una familia, corporación, legislatura, sindicato, etc. (2) Cualquiera de las extremidades del cuerpo.

MEMORANDUM. Memorandum. Sumario o nota informal de una reunión. (1) Nota de un miembro de una organización a otro.

MEMORANDUM DECISION. Decisión de la corte que no contiene los razonamientos que la llevaron a dicha decisión.

MEMORIAL. Memorial. (1) Documento presentado al órgano legislativo o ejecutivo por uno o más individuos, y que contiene peticiones o relato de hechos. (2) Nota corta; nota en borrador que contiene las decisiones de la corte y de la cual se sacará el registro de archivos de la corte.

MENS REA. (Lat.) Intención criminal. Propósito doloso. El estado mental de cometer algo prohibido.

MENTAL ANGUISH. Trauma mental. Sufrimiento mental y de sentimientos experimentado por una persona a la que se le ha hecho un daño físico o emocional.

MENTAL CAPACITY. La habilidad de razonar y entender la naturaleza y el efecto de un acto, por ejemplo, un acto de negocios o un acto criminal.

MENTAL CRUELTY. Trato mental cruel. Crueldad mental. Comportamiento de un cónyuge hacia el otro que causa daños físicos y mentales y que puede ser causa de divorcio.

MENTAL INCAPACITY; MENTAL INCOMPETENCY. Incapacidad mental. Cuando una persona es incapaz de entender, razonar y actuar con discreción en los asuntos diarios.

MENTAL STATE. Estado mental de una persona. Véase "Mental Capacity".

MERCANTILE. Mercantil. Comercial, que tiene que ver con las compras y ventas, etc.

MERCHANT. Comerciante. Una persona que se dedica a la compra y venta de mercancías. Generalmente se refiere a una persona que compra mercancía al por mayor y la vende al detalle. Un detallista.

MERCHANTABLE. Comerciable. (1) Que puede venderse porque reúne las cualidades exigidas. (2) **Merchantable Title.** Véase "Marketable Title Acts".

MERCY KILLING. Homicidio piadoso. Causar la muerte de una persona que está cerca de morir y que se cree deseaba la muerte. También se conoce como eutanasia.

MERGER. Fusión. Unión de dos o más cosas tales como corporaciones, contratos, derechos, etc., para existir formando parte de otra o convirtiéndose en una entidad nueva.

MERITS. Méritos. Fondo de la causa; méritos de la causa.

MESNE. Intermedio. (1) El medio entre dos extremos. (2) **Mense Process.** Abarca los documentos legales y los autos interlocutorios entre el principio y el fin del proceso.

MESSUAGE. La casa más su terreno circundante y sus construcciones externas. Véase "Curtilage".

METER. Medidor.

METES AND BOUNDS. Medir o describir un terreno por sus líneas limitantes, con sus puntos y ángulos limítrofes.

METROPOLITAN DISTRICT. Distrito metropolitano. Area que incluye, además de la ciudad, sus sitios aledaños; por ejemplo la ciudad y sus suburbios.

MIDDLEMAN. Intermediario. (1) Persona que acerca a dos otras para que realicen un trato. (2) Persona que le compra a una persona para venderle a otra. (3) Un agente o corredor.

MIGRATORY DIVORCE. Divorcio migratorio. Divorcio obtenido por una persona que se muda a otro lugar para obtener el divorcio.

MILITARY LAW. Derecho militar. La ley que regula a las fuerzas armadas y sus a miembros.

MIND AND MEMORY. "Mente y memoria." Frase que describe la capacidad mental adecuada para hacer un testamento.

MINERAL. Mineral. Toda sustancia que se encuentra en la tierra o sobre ella y que no es animal ni vegetal.

MINERAL LEASE. Arrendamiento del subsuelo. Acuerdo que da derecho a explorar en busca de minerales, y que permite la explotación del mineral.

MINERAL RIGHT. Derecho sobre los minerales. Otorga el derecho de extraer los minerales o de recibir pagos por los minerales extraídos.

MINIMAL (o MINIMUM) CONTACTS DOCTRINE. Doctrina del contacto mínimo. Principio que establece que para que una persona pueda ser demandada en un estado, esta persona debe haber llevado a cabo cierta mínima cantidad de actividades en ese estado. Véase "International Shoe Doctrine".

MINIMUM WAGE. Salario mínimo, establecido por la ley federal.

MINING LEASE. Arrendamiento minero.

MINISTER. Ministro. (1) Persona que actúa siguiendo las órdenes de otra persona o en representación de ella. (2) Representante diplomático; un embajador; un enviado. (3) El jefe de un departamento u organización gubernamental.

MINISTERIAL. Ministerial. Actos regulares y normales. Actos hechos en conformidad con los mandatos de la ley en vez de por discreción propia.

MINOR. Menor. (1) Persona que por no tener suficiente edad no está totalmente capacitada para ejercitar todos sus derechos y contraer cierta clase de obligaciones. (2) Menos; bajo.

MINOR DISPUTE. Disputa menor. Controversia laboral sobre la interpretación del contrato de trabajo. Véase "Major Dispute".

MINORITY. Minoría. (1) Ser menor de edad. (2) Menos de la mitad. (3) Grupo que representa un pequeño porcentaje del total de la población.

MINORITY OPINION. Opinión disidente o de la minoría.

MINORITY STOCKHOLDER. Accionista minoritario. Persona que tiene tan pocas acciones que no puede controlar la administración de la sociedad o compañía.

MINOR'S ESTATE. Propiedad que pertenece a un menor. Propiedad que debe ser administrada por un tutor porque el propietario es un menor de edad.

MINT. Casa de moneda. El sitio donde por ley se acuña el dinero.

MINUTE BOOK. Libro de actas o minutas. Libro de requisito llevado por el secretario del tribunal en el que se contienen sumarios de las decisiones de la corte.

MINUTES. Minutas. Notas escritas de una reunión.

MIRANDA WARNING. Lectura de los derechos del detenido. El aviso de derechos que se le debe dar a cualquier persona que va a ser arrestada o detenida por algún policía o funcionario público.

MISADVENTURE. Accidente; daño intencional; generalmente no tiene consecuencia legal.

MISAPPROPRIATION. Apropiación indebida. Tomar algo indebidamente pero no necesariamente ilegalmente.

MISBRANDING. Información falsa puesta intencionalmente en un producto.

MISCARRIAGE OF JUSTICE. Mala administración de justicia. Acción judicial que hace daño injusto a una persona.

MISCHIEF. Daño, perjuicio. (1) Hacer daño intencionalmente o por negligencia. (2) El problema o peligro que un acto legislativo pretende corregir.

MISCONDUCT. Mala conducta. Hacer algo prohibido intencional o voluntariamente.

MISDEMEANANT. Persona que comete un delito menor.

MISDEMEANOR. Delito menor. Ofensa penal menor. Una falta o contravención que conlleva multa o prisión por menos de un año.

MISFEASANCE. Acto legal hecho de una manera ilegal.

MISFORTUNE. Infortunio, desgracia. Un hecho verdaderamente accidental, que no pudo perverse.

MISJOINDER. Véase "Joinder".

MISLAID. Olvidar dónde se puso. Objeto colocado en algún lugar por una persona que olvidó dónde lo puso.

MISPRISION. (1) Fracasar en llevar a cabo un deber público. (2) No reportar o prevenir un delito. (3) Encubrir un delito.

MISREPRESENTATION. Falsedad. Testimonio falso. (1) **Innocent Misrepresentation.** Hacer una declaración o representación que es falsa sin saber que es falsa. (2) **Negligent Misrepresentation.** Hacer una declaración o una representación que es falsa, sin malicia, pero negligentemente ya que el actor puede comprobar los hechos fácilmente. (3) **Fraudulent Misrepresentation.** Hacer declaraciones o dar representaciones falsas, con malicia, sabiendo que son falsas o con la intención de engañar.

MISTAKE. Error.

MISTRIAL. Juicio nulo. Juicio que el juez declara nulo porque adolece de un defecto.

MITIGATING CIRCUMSTANCES. Circunstancias atenuantes. Hechos que no justifican o excusan la acción pero que sí disminuyen la pena así como la responsabilidad civil.

MITIGATION OF DAMAGES. Mitigar los daños. (1) Hechos que muestran que la cantidad reclamada es injustificada. (2) Principio que establece que una persona debe haber hecho todo lo posible para disminuir los daños que reclama como demandante, ya que de no hacerlo, esto rebajará la cantidad que puede recobrar.

MITTIMUS. (1) Sentencia judicial que ordena que un reo sea enviado a prisión. (2) Transferir expedientes de una corte a otra.

MIXED QUESTIONS. Preguntas mixtas. Preguntas legales que contienen tanto problemas de hecho como de derecho o conflictos relativos a leyes locales y extranjeras.

MIXED TRUST. Fondo mixto. Fondo constituido tanto para caridad como para uso de personas privadas.

M'NAGHTEN RULE. Regla M'Naghten. En la mayoría de las jurisdicciones de los Estados Unidos, bajo esta regla un acusado no es responsable por sus actos criminales si al cometer el delito su mente estaba afectada de tal manera que no entendía lo que hacía; o si entendía lo que hacía, no sabía que era ilegal.

MOBILE HOME. Vivienda móvil.

MODEL ACTS. Proyectos de ley propuestos por la Conferencia Nacional de Comisionados para uniformar leyes estatales que luego serán adoptadas como legislación uniforme por los estados (EE.UU.).

MODIFICATION. Modificación. Cambio o alteración.

MODO. (Lat.) Método, medio, manera.

MOIETY. (1) Mitad. (2) **Moiety Acts.** Leyes penales que confieren la mitad de la multa pagada por el acusado a la persona informante que dio inicio al proceso penal. (3) Una parte.

MONARCHY. Monarquía. Gobernación por reyes, reinas u otro gobernante real. Pueden ser absolutas o constitucionales.

MONETARY AGGREGATES. Agregado monetario. Subcategoría de "money supply". Véase "Money Supply".

MONEY. Dinero. La combinación de monedas y papel usados por un país en el intercambio de bienes o mercancía. (1) **Money Market.** Instituciones financieras que negocian a base de documentos de vencimiento a corto plazo. Como letras de cambio, aceptaciones bancarias, etc. (2) **Money Order.** Giro bancario o postal o de otra institución. (3) **Money Supply.** La cantidad de dinero circulante estipulada por la Reserva Federal (EE.UU.).

MONITION. Aviso o emplazamiento dictado por un juez.

MONOPOLY. Monopolio. La habilidad de una o pocas compañías de controlar la elaboración, venta, distribución o precio de un producto o servicio. Generalmente es ilegal.

MONROE DOCTRINE. Doctrina Monroe. Doctrina que afirma que los Estados Unidos se opondrá a cualquier interferencia europea en los asuntos del hemisferio occidental.

MONTHLY PAYMENTS. Pagos mensuales.

MONUMENT. Monumento. Poste, pila de piedras, límite natural, árbol marcado, etc., usados para marcar los límites de una propiedad.

MOOT. (1) Que ya no es importante, sobre lo que ya no se necesita decidir porque el problema está resuelto. (2) Sólo para practicar y argumentar, por ejemplo, Moot Court. Corte en la que los estudiantes de Derecho practican y argumentan sobre un caso. (3) Abstracto. Argumentos ficticios sobre un caso real. (4) Un tema de argumento que no está decidido, sobre el que no se ha llegado a una decisión judicial.

MORAL. Moral. (1) Que tiene que ver con la conciencia y los principios de buena conducta. (2) Que tiene que ver sólo con la conciencia, ya que no es obligatorio o prohibido por la ley. (3) Que depende de razonamientos o creencias, más que de la prueba positiva. En este sentido un testimonio podría ser "moral evidence", evidencia moral o "moral certainty", certeza moral. Las dos frases quieren decir que es muy posible que algo sea correcto.

MORAL TURPITUDE. Conducta inmoral. Hecho criminal que implica más que una violación técnica de la ley y prueba el mal carácter del actor.

MORATORIUM. Moratoria. Posponer algún acto o evento. (1) Un retraso impuesto. Por ejemplo, una ciudad puede, deliberadamente, suspender o retrasar temporalmente los permisos de construcción si es necesario para proteger el ambiente. (2) Toda demora deliberada, ya sea impuesta, requerida o acordada.

MORE FAVORABLE TERMS CLAUSE. Cláusula sobre términos más favorables. Disposición que puede contener un contrato laboral donde la unión de sindicatos se obliga a no dar términos laborales más favorables (salario, horas laborables, beneficios, condiciones de trabajo, etc.) a competidores de la compañía.

MORE OR LESS. Más o menos. Término utilizado en contratos bajo los cuales una pequeña variación en la cantidad o calidad de lo entregado de todas formas cumple con el contrato.

MORGUE. Morgue. Lugar donde se llevan los cuerpos no identificados o no reclamados para ser identificados.

MORTALITY TABLES. Tasa de mortandad. Estudio actuarial (o fórmula matemática) que predice cuantas personas de un mismo grupo de edad, sexo y otras características morirán en cada año que pasa.

MORTGAGE. Hipoteca, gravamen. Poner en garantía tierras, edificios u otros bienes raíces para obtener un préstamo. (1) **Mortgaged Deed.** Título de propiedad que se entrega a un tercero para comprobar una hipoteca. (2) **Mortgage Interest.** Interés hipotecario.

MORTGAGEE. Acreedor hipotecario. El que ha dado un préstamo a otro que le garantiza el pago con una hipoteca.

MORTGAGOR. Deudor hipotecario. El que recibe un préstamo garantizando el pago con una hipoteca.

MORTIS CAUSA. (Lat.) Por causa de muerte. Véase "Causa Mortis".

MORTMAIN. (1) Término antiguo utilizado para denominar la cesión o venta de tierras a una corporación o a una organización religiosa. (2) La acepción más moderna del término establece límites a las entregas hechas a la caridad en lecho de muerte porque éstas pueden causar desheredamientos de último minuto.

MOST FAVORED NATION. "Nación más favorecida." Acuerdo entre dos naciones que establece que cada una tratará a la otra como a una nación favorecida. El objeto principal de estos acuerdos es el de bajar los impuestos de importación y lograr la igualdad de tratamiento para las naciones más favorecidas.

MOST SUITABLE USE. Uso más apropiado. El uso adecuado para el que debe ser destinado un objeto. Véase "Highest and Best Use".

MOTION. Moción. (1) Petición para que el juez decida algo, o tome alguna otra acción. (2) La manera formal de proponer algo en una asamblea.

MOTIVE. Motivo. La razón por la cual una persona hace algo.

MOTOR CARRIER ACT. Ley federal que da al "Interstate Commerce Commission" el poder para regular las rutas y tarifas para carros, autobuses, camiones, etc., que transportan pasajeros o bienes entre estados con propósitos comerciales.

MOVABLES. Muebles. Propiedad personal.

MOVANT. Peticionante. Persona que presenta una moción.

MOVING EXPENSES. Gastos de mudanza.

MOVING PAPERS. Documentos que apoyan una petición, una moción o una demanda.

MUGGING. Robo callejero. Particularmente aquél en que se usa violencia.

MUGSHOT. Fotografía de un acusado para un archivo oficial de policía, luego de una redada. Se colocan en "mugbooks" o libros para la identificación posterior de criminales.

MULCT. Multa. Sanción pecuniaria.

MULIER. Término arcaico usado para referirse a un hijo(a) legítimo(a).

MULTIDISTRICT LITIGATION. Demandas o procesos fundados en los mismos hechos que están siendo tramitadas en distintas cortes de los distritos federales (EE.UU.). Estas deben ser transferidas a una sola corte donde serán decididas por un tribunal especial de acuerdo a normas especiales.

MULTIFARIOUSNESS. Desemejanza de alegatos. Juntar varios reclamos distintos en una sola demanda o varias materias distintas en un solo cuerpo legislativo.

MULTILATERAL AGREEMENT. Acuerdo multilateral. Acuerdo entre varias personas, compañías, gobiernos o naciones.

MULTILEVEL DISTRIBUTORSHIP. Esquema de ventas en el que se le promete a un participante una parte de la ganancia de toda venta que logre generar a través de una red de distribución. Dicho esquema puede ser ilegal. Véase "Pyramid Sales Scheme".

MULTINATIONAL CORPORATION. Compañía multinacional.
(1) Compañía con centros mayores de operación o subsidiarias en
varias naciones. (2) Compañía que simplemente hace negocios en
varias naciones.

MULTIPLE ACCESS. Acceso múltiple. Defensa para rechazar un
reclamo de paternidad en base a que la mujer tenía varios
amantes.

MULTIPLE EVIDENCE. Evidencia múltiple. Hechos que pueden
ser admitidos durante un juicio para probar hechos pero que no
pueden ser usados o considerados como evidencias para probar
hechos diferentes.

MULTIPLE LISTING. Sistema de publicidad para bienes raíces
donde los vendedores usan un vehículo común para anunciar las
ventas. Véase "Listing".

MULTIPLE OFFENSE. Ofensa múltiple. Acto que viola más de
una ley sin que ninguna exima a la otra totalmente.

MULTIPLE PARTY ACCOUNT. Cuenta conjunta. Cuenta de
banco conjunta con varios depositantes autorizados; no incluye la
cuenta de una organización.

MULTIPLE SENTENCES. Sentencias múltiples. Véase
"Cumulative Sentences".

MULTIPLICITY OF ACTIONS. Multiplicidad de acciones.
Presentar más de una demanda incorrectamente sobre un mismo
sujeto cuando una sola es necesaria.

MUNICIPAL. Municipal. Que tiene que ver con el gobierno local de
una ciudad, estado o condado.

MUNICIPAL CORPORATION. Institución municipal. Una ciudad
u otro gobierno local que se ha creado de acuerdo a las normas
estatales.

MUNICIPALITY. Municipalidad. Véase "Municipal Corporation".

MUNIMENTS. Documentos que contienen evidencia de títulos.

MURDER. Asesinato. Matar a otro ser humano sin excusa legal y premeditadamente.

MUTATIS MUTANDIS. (Lat.) Variando algunos detalles.

MUTILATION. Mutilación. (1) Cortar, rasgar, borrar o alterar de cualquier manera un documento, cambiando o destruyendo su efecto legal. (2) Véase "Mayhem".

MUTINY. Motín. (1) Rebelión en las fuerzas armadas. (2) Rebelión de los marinos en una nave.

MUTUAL. Mutualidad, mutuo. Hecho en conjunto, recíprocamente.

MUTUAL COMPANY. Compañía mutual. Compañía en la cual los consumidores son los dueños y reciben las ganancias de la compañía.

MUTUAL FUND. Fondo mutuo. Compañía de inversiones que invierte los fondos en acciones de otras compañías. La compañía hace esto vendiendo sus propias acciones al público.

MUTUAL MISTAKE. Error mutuo. Cuando un error o malentendido resulta en que ambas partes en un contrato se equivoquen en el entendimiento de uno de los términos esenciales del contrato. El error está en que el contrato no refleja lo acordado entre los contratantes.

MUTUAL STRIKE AID. Ayuda mutua para huelga. Compañías o industrias que acuerdan dar ayuda financiera a aquéllas que sufren una huelga.

MUTUALITY OF CONTRACT (u OBLIGATION). Contrato u obligación mutua. Principio según el cual cada parte debe estar comprometida a hacer algo para que el contrato sea obligatorio y válido. Si sólo una de las partes está obligada, no hay contrato.

N

N.A.L.A. "National Association of Legal Assistants". Asociación Nacional de Asistentes Legales.

N.A.R. "National Association of Realtors". Asociación Nacional de Corredores de Bienes Raíces.

N.A.S.A. "National Aeronautics and Space Administration". Administración Nacional de Aeronáutica y del Espacio.

N.B. (Lat.) "Nota bene". Literalmente "notar con atención".

N.C.D. (Lat.) "Nemine contra dicente". Literalmente "nadie en desacuerdo".

N.I.F.O. ("Next in, first out") Frase que se utiliza cuando se evalúan las unidades existentes en un inventario en base al costo de las unidades nuevas.

N.L.R.A. "National Labor Relations Act". Ley Nacional de Relaciones Laborales. Véase esta frase.

N.O.V. Véase "Non Obstante Veredicto".

N.O.W. "Negotiable Order of Withdrawal". Tipo de cuenta corriente que paga intereses.

N.P. Notary Public. Notario público.

N.R. (1) **New Reports.** Nuevos reportes. (2) **Not Reported.** No reportados. (3) **Non Resident.** Que no es residente.

N.Y.S.E. New York Stock Exchange. Bolsa de Valores de Nueva York. Centro de intercambio de acciones.

NAKED. Incompleto, sin fuerza.

NAPOLEONIC CODE. Código Napoleónico. Véase "Civil Code".

NARCOTIC. Narcótico. (1) Sustancias que ofuscan los sentidos y causan adicción. (2) Las sustancias antes descritas que son prohibidas por la ley.

NARR. Abreviatura del Latín "narratio." La declaración de una demanda.

NARRATIVE EVIDENCE. Evidencia testimonial. El testimonio del testigo cuando se da sin interrupciones o sin el cuestionamiento del abogado.

NATIONAL BANK. Banco nacional. Banco constituido bajo las leyes de los Estados Unidos en vez de las leyes estatales.

NATIONAL CONSULTATION RIGHTS. Derecho nacional de consulta. El derecho que tienen ciertas grandes uniones de sindicatos a sugerir cambios en la política federal respecto a personal.

NATIONAL ENVIRONMENT POLICY ACT. Ley de la política nacional sobre el ambiente que contiene las metas y proyectos de la política ambiental de los Estados Unidos. Ley federal que exige que los grandes proyectos presenten estudios sobre su impacto ambiental. Véase "Environmental Impact Statements."

NATIONAL LABOR RELATIONS ACT. Ley que crea el "National Labor Relations Board", Consejo o Junta Nacional de Relaciones Laborales y que establece reglas para todo tipo de contacto entre patrón y empleado (reconocimiento de sindicatos, huelgas, etc.).

NATIONAL REPORTER SYSTEM. Sistema que compila todos los casos de las cortes superiores, tanto estatales como federales, en un conjunto de libros.

NATIONALITY. Nacionalidad. El país de donde una persona es ciudadana.

NATIONALIZATION. Nacionalización. La apropiación de una industria por parte del estado, pagando o sin pagar por ésta.

NATIVE. Nativo. Ciudadano por nacimiento. Véase "Natural Born Citizen".

NATURAL AFFECTION. Afecto natural. Amor o lazos familiares entre personas directamente emparentadas.

NATURAL BORN CITIZEN. Ciudadano por nacimiento, incluyendo los nacidos de padres ciudadanos.

NATURAL DEATH ACTS. Leyes estatales que permiten que una persona dé instrucciones por escrito a los doctores para que no prolonguen su vida por medios artificiales si está cercana a la muerte por causa de una enfermedad o condición fatal.

NATURAL HEIR. Heredero natural. Un hijo o pariente cercano. Cualquier persona que heredaría si no existiera testamento.

NATURAL LAW. Ley o Derecho Natural. (1) Reglas de conducta practicadas en cualquier lugar por ser normas básicas de la conducta humana. (2) Leyes básicas de moral.

NATURAL OBJECT. Objeto natural. En derecho testamentario, sería la persona que heredaría si no existiera testamento.

NATURAL RESOURCES. Recursos naturales. (1) Materia prima que tendría valor económico si fuese extraída. (2) Cualquier lugar o producto natural que es beneficioso para alguien.

NATURALIZATION. Naturalización. El hecho de convertirse en ciudadano de un país.

NATURALIZED CITIZEN. Uno que, siendo extranjero por nacimiento, se convierte en ciudadano de un país.

NAVIGABLE WATERS. Aguas navegables. Aguas en/o adyacentes a un país que constituyen un lugar de paso continuo para naves comerciales que vienen del mar.

NE EXEAT. (Lat.) Escrito de la corte que prohíbe a una persona dejar un área determinada.

NE VARIETUR. (Lat.) "Do not alter it". "Que no sea alterado". Palabras escritas por el notario después de autenticar un documento.

NEAR v. MINNESOTA. Caso de la Corte Suprema en 1931 que prohíbe muchas de las restricciones que hasta ese momento había tenido la prensa.

NEAR–MONEY. Literalmente "casi dinero". Véase "Quick Assets".

NECESSARILY INCLUDED OFFENSE. Véase "Lesser Included Offense".

NECESSARY. Necesario. (1) Física o lógicamente inevitable. (2) Requerido legalmente. (3) Apropiado o que ayudaría.

NECESSITY. Necesidad. Cualquier cosa que constituya fuerza irresistible o coacción, o una acción importante pero no requerida.

NEGATIVE AVERMENT. Aseveración negativa, en vez de negación de una declaración hecha por otra persona.

NEGATIVE COVENANT. Acuerdo de no hacer algo, normalmente por contrato.

NEGATIVE EASEMENT. Véase "Easement".

NEGATIVE PREGNANT. Negación que en realidad implica una afirmación.

NEGLECT. Negligencia, descuido. (1) El no hacer algo que debió hacerse. (2) Ausencia de cuidado al hacer algo. (3) Negligencia en cuidar apropiadamente a un niño. (4) La violación de un deber o una obligación hacia otra persona que resulta en daños y perjuicios a esa persona.

NEGLIGENCE. Negligencia. (1) No haber ejercido una cantidad razonable de cuidado en una situación que causó daño a algo o a alguien. (2) El dejar de cumplir con un deber, cuya omisión causa daño a alguien. (3) **Criminal Negligence.** Negligencia criminal, conducta negligente tipificada como delito. (4) Un sinnúmero de palabras con la palabra "negligence" se usan modificando su significado, por ejemplo: (5) **Contributory Negligence:** cuando dos personas son negligentes en un evento que causa daño a una de esas personas, la parte perjudicada no puede reclamar contra el otro actor, ya que él también fue negligente. (6) **Comparative Negligence:** cuando hay varios actores negligentes, los daños a una persona por dicha negligencia son recuperables en proporción directa al grado o porcentaje de negligencia de cada actor. (7) **Criminal Negligence:** un crimen que por ley se basa en un acto que no toma en consideración el riesgo y peligro para el público o para las personas. (8) **Gross Negligence:** la falta intencional en cumplir un deber obvio al actuar, sin tomar en consideración el efecto sobre personas o propiedad que tal acto pueda tener. (9) **Imputed Negligence:** se refiere a la doctrina que hace a una persona responsable por los actos de otra persona. (10) **Ordinary Negligence:** la omisión en el grado de cuidado que un hombre razonable usaría en sus actividades. (11) **Willful, Wanton or Reckless Negligence:** términos que se refieren a las acciones de quien ha actuado intencionalmente en una forma irrazonable, ignorando el daño que normalmente surge de tal acto. (12) **Negligence Per Se:** un acto que viola la conducta establecida por ley u ordenanza, y que muestra negligencia sin tener que probar que se ha violado un deber.

NEGLIGENT. Negligente. Descuidado. Véase "Negligence".

NEGOTIABLE. Negociable. Documento que puede cambiar de propietario por endoso con una firma, transfiriendo el título a otra persona.

NEGOCIABLE INSTRUMENT. Documento o instrumento negociable. Documento firmado que contiene la promesa incondicional de pagar determinada suma de dinero, ya sea cuando se demande o en un futuro determinado.

NEGOTIATE. Negociar. (1) Discutir, tratar, convenir. (2) Discutir una situación en la que se va a comprometer. (3) Transferir un documento negociable.

NEGOTIATION. Negociación. Véase "Negotiate".

NEM.CON. Abreviatura de "Nemine Contradicente". Véase esa frase.

NEMINE CONTRADICENTE. (Lat.) Literalmente "Nadie se opone"; una decisión o votación unánime.

NEMO. (Lat.) Nadie, ninguna persona.

NEPOTISM. Nepotismo. Dar empleo público a, o contratar obras públicas con, parientes.

NET. Neto. La cantidad que resulta después de restar otra cantidad.

NET ASSET VALUE. Valor activo neto. Véase "Net Book Value".

NET BOOK VALUE. Valor líquido neto en los libros o valor neto de los activos. La cantidad de la propiedad de una compañía que respalda cada acción o bono que ésta emite.

NET CONTRACT (o LISTING). Venta en la que la comisión del agente se determina en base a la cantidad en que el precio de venta sobrepasa una cantidad determinada.

NET LEASE. Arrendamiento neto. Arrendamiento en el cual el arrendatario, además de pagar la renta, corre con los gastos de la propiedad, como impuestos y mantenimiento.

NET PROFIT. Utilidad neta. Beneficio resultante luego de las sustracciones.

NET WORTH METHOD. Método de calcular los ingresos cuando una persona ha declarado sus ingresos gravables por el impuesto sobre la renta sin pruebas documentales. El método consiste en probar que una persona ha adquirido más activos de los que pudieran haber sido comprados con el ingreso declarado.

NEUTRAL. Una posición indiferente, neutral, imparcial, inactiva.

NEUTRALITY LAWS. Leyes de neutralidad. Leyes que prohíben a los Estados Unidos dar ayuda militar en contra de cualquier país con el cual los Estados Unidos está en paz.

NEUTRALIZE. Neutralizar. Disminuir el efecto de un testimonio perjudicial, mostrando que el testigo ha dado un testimonio contradictorio. Véase también "Impeach".

NEW AND USEFUL. Nuevo y útil. En materia de patentes de inventos, algo es nuevo y útil cuando resulta en algo práctico hecho de una nueva manera.

NEWLY DISCOVERED EVIDENCE. Evidencia crucial descubierta después de terminado el juicio.

NEWS PERSON'S PRIVILEGE. Secreto de periodistas. Derecho constitucional que tienen los reporteros y afines de mantener sus fuentes de información en secreto.

NEXT CAUSE. Véase "Proximate Cause".

NEXT FRIEND. Tutor informal. Persona que actúa formalmente por un menor ante una corte sin ser su tutor legal.

NEXT OF KIN. Parientes más cercanos. (1) Persona con el parentesco más cercana a un difunto. (2) Las personas con derecho a heredar en una sucesión intestada.

NIHIL. (Lat.) Nada.

NIL. (Lat.) Nada.

NINETEENTH AMENDMENT. Decimonovena enmienda a la Constitución de los Estados Unidos que dio el derecho de votar a la mujer.

NINTH AMENDMENT. Novena enmienda a la Constitución de los Estados Unidos, la cual establece que aunque ciertos derechos específicos están delineados en la Constitución, esto no quiere decir que otros derechos que no se listan están derrogados o prohibidos.

NISI. (Lat.) "A menos que". Orden, sentencia o edicto de un juez que tendrá efecto "a menos que" la persona contra la cual se dicta se presente a la corte a demostrar por qué no debe llevarse a cabo lo dictado.

NISI PRIUS. (Lat.) "A menos que antes." En EE.UU. el tribunal de primera instancia ante el cual se determinan hechos frente a un jurado.

NIXON v. UNITED STATES. Caso de 1974 ante la Corte Suprema que rehusó reconocer el derecho ejecutivo (executive privilege) que pretendía mantener como secretas las cintas magnetofónicas grabadas por el presidente. Dichas cintas eran solicitadas como evidencia en un juicio penal.

NO ACTION CLAUSE. Cláusula de no actuar. Cláusula que se incluye en muchos contratos de seguros de responsabilidad civil, en la cual se establece que la compañía de seguros no tiene que pagar hasta que, como resultado de una demanda, se establezca, ya sea por el tribunal o por arreglo, la suma que se debe pagar.

NO ACTION LETTER. Carta en contra de acción. Una carta escrita por un abogado de una agencia gubernamental donde indica si la agencia tomaría acción legal ante ciertos hechos.

NO BILL. No hay caso. Declaración hecha por un gran jurado en la que establece que no encuentran pruebas suficientes para procesar a la persona por el delito que se le acusa.

NO CONTEST. No contest clause. Cláusula de no desafiar, que de estar incluida en un testamento, significa que el que tiene derecho a heredar no puede desafiar lo dispuesto, bajo pena de perder lo que para él se había dispuesto. Véase "Nolo contendere".

NO EVIDENCE. Que no hay suficiente evidencia para justificar lo que se demanda.

NO EYEWITNESS RULE. Regla para cuando no hay testigos. Cuando una persona muere en un accidente sin que haya testigos, el jurado puede presumir que el difunto actuó con prudencia inmediatamente antes de su muerte.

NO FAULT. No hay falta. Sin culpa. (1) Tipo de póliza de automóviles en la que la compañía de cada auto paga los gastos hasta cierta cantidad, no importa quien tenga la culpa por el accidente. (2) Se dice de un divorcio causado simplemente porque el matrimonio no resultó.

NO LIMIT ORDER. Orden de hacer algo sin importar los límites. Orden que da un cliente a un agente de bolsa para comprar o vender ciertas acciones sin importar la cantidad de dinero.

NOLENS VOLEMS. (Lat.) Estando o no dispuesto.

NOLLE PROSEQUI. (Lat.) La terminación de una causa penal debido a que el fiscal decidió o acordó detener el proceso.

NOLO CONTENDERE. (Lat.) No lo desafiaré. Cuando un acusado no admite el cargo pero no lo niega. Es igual a declararse culpable.

NOMINAL. Nominal. (1) Por nombre solamente. Que tiene un nombre. (2) Que no es real o substancial.

NOMINEE. Nominado. (1) Persona escogida como candidato para un puesto público. (2) Persona escogida como representante de otra persona. (3) **Nominee Trust.** Fideicomiso en el que una persona acepta por escrito mantener propiedades a beneficio de otra persona indeterminada.

NON. (Lat.) Prefijo de "no" o "not", "do not", "should not", "did not", etc.

NON COMPOS MENTIS. (Lat.) No ésta en control de sus facultades mentales. Demente.

NON OBSTANTE VEREDICTO. (Lat.) No obstante el veredicto. Veredicto que no se mantiene. Decisión a pesar del veredicto.

NON PROFIT. (Lat.) Sin fines de lucro, de caridad.

NON PROS. (Lat.) Sin seguimiento. Véase "Non prosequitur".

NON PROSEQUITUR. (Lat.) No le dio seguimiento. Veredicto que favorece al demandado porque el demandante no prosiguió con su acción.

NON SUI JURIS. Sin su facultad o derecho. Un menor, un demente, etc.

NO VULT CONTENDERE. Véase "Nolo contendere".

NONACQUIESCENCE. Cuando el Servicios de Rentas Internas anuncia estar en desacuerdo con una decisión de la corte de impuestos.

NONAGE. Sin la edad. Que no tiene la edad legal, que sigue siendo menor.

NONCONFORMING GOODS. Artículos que no están en conformidad con lo contratado.

NONCONFORMING LOT. Parcela de terreno con un tamaño, forma o localización que no concuerda con las leyes de zonificación urbana.

NONCONFORMING USE. El uso de un terreno que es permitido a pesar de que ése tipo de uso no está de acuerdo con la zonificación del área urbana.

NON–CONTESTABLE CLAUSE. Disposición en una póliza de seguros que prohíbe a la compañía de seguros negar un reclamo aun cuando la compañía sospecha fraude o error.

NONFEASANCE. Incumplimiento. Dejar de cumplir una tarea, especialmente cuando se trata de un funcionario público.

NONINTERVENTION WILL. Testamento válido en varios estados que faculta al albacea para manejar los bienes sin supervisión de la corte y sin bono de garantía.

NONPROFIT CORPORATION. Sociedad sin fines de lucro. Sociedad que no tiene dueños y que no da nada de sus ingresos a sus miembros. Véase "Charitable".

NONRECOURSE LOAN. Préstamo sin recurso. Préstamo en el cual el prestamista sólo puede ejecutar a hipoteca de la propiedad que se puso de garantía para la deuda.

NONSUIT. Caducidad de la instancia, porque el demandado no pudo darle seguimiento.

NONSUPPORT. Falta de manutención al cónyuge. No dar comida, vestido, ni casa.

NONWORK DAY. Día no laborable. Día en que no se trabaja.

NORMAL LAW. Ley normal. La ley como se le aplica a una persona en pleno uso de su facultades, capaz de actuar por sí mismo.

NORRIS-LA GUARDIA ACT. Ley federal puesta en vigor en 1932 para prevenir varios tipos de mandamientos judiciales en contra de las huelgas y de los llamados "yellow dog contracts". Véase esta frase.

NOSCITUR A SOCIIS. (Lat.) "Que se conoce por sus asociados." (1) Regla según la cual el significado de una palabra se conoce buscando el significado de las otras en el contexto. (2) Se usa par indicar que el carácter de una persona quizás sea igual al de sus amistades.

NOT FOUND. Véase "No Bill".

NOTARY PUBLIC. Notario Público. Funcionario semi público que puede recibir juramentos, certificar la validez de documentos y dar fe de otras cuestiones que se necesitan para negocios y materias legales.

NOTATION VOTING. Voto por anotación. Votar sin reunión.

NOTE. Pagaré. Documento que dice que la persona que firma promete pagar determinada suma de dinero en cierto tiempo.

NOTES OF DECISIONS. Literalmente "notas de decisiones". Referencias a casos que discuten las leyes, compiladas en libros de leyes comentadas.

NOTICE. Noticia. (1) Conocimiento de ciertos hechos. (2) Recibo formal o conocimiento de ciertos hechos. (3) Notificación.

NOVATION. Novación. La sustitución, por acuerdo, de un contrato viejo por uno nuevo. También la sustitución de una persona por la persona que es responsable por el nuevo contrato.

NOVELTY. Innovación. Nueva. Original. Para adquirir una patente, el invento tiene que llevar acabo una nueva función o realizar una vieja función de una manera completamente nueva.

NUDE. Que le falta algo esencial para ser legalmente válido.

NUDUM PACTUM. (Lat.) "Nude pact", contrato sin causa. Promesa de dar o hacer sin compensación, sólo por buena voluntad o afecto.

605

NUGATORY. Ineficaz, fútil, sin valor. Inválido, que no tiene fuerza ni efecto.

NUISANCE. Perjuicio. Molestia, cualquier cosa que incomode o moleste irrazonablemente, y que perjudique el uso de su propiedad a una persona o su bienestar o la salud pública.

NULL. Nulo. Que ya no tiene efecto o validez legal.

NULLA BONA. (Lat.) "No hay bienes". La respuesta de un comisario a un juez cuando este ha mandado embargar unos bienes y tales bienes no existen.

NULLITY. Nulidad. Que no tiene fuerza o efecto legal.

NUNC PRO TUNC. (Lat.) "De ahora para entonces". Que tiene efecto retroactivo.

NUNCUPATIVE WILL. Testamento oral.

O

O.A.S. Siglas de "Organization of American States". Organización de los Estados Americanos.

O.P.I.C. Siglas de "Overseas Private Investment Corporation". Sociedad Extranjera de Inversión Privada. Agencia para el fomento de inversiones privadas en el extranjero.

O.R. Siglas de "Own Recognizance". Obligación propia.

O.S.H.A. Siglas de "Occupational Safety and Health Administration". Véase ese término.

O.T.C. Sigla de "Over the counter". Véase esa frase.

OATH. Juramento. Juramento formal por medio del cual una persona certifica que va a decir la verdad o que va a hacer algo. (1) **Oath of Witnesses.** Juramento que pronuncia un testigo de decir la verdad. (2) **Oath of Allegiance.** Juramento de fidelidad que hace un funcionario gubernamental.

OBITER DICTUM. (Lat.) Véase "Dictum".

OBJECT. Objeto. (1) Propósito. (2) Objetar. Reclamar por la impropiedad, injusticia, o ilegalidad de una acción de la contraparte en un juicio o en una audiencia, y pedir al juez que se manifieste sobre ello. (3) Decir que una acción del juez está errada.

OBJECTION. Objeción. (1) Acción de objetar. (2) Desaprobar. Durante un proceso jurídico, interponer una protesta a un acto illegal, incorrecto o inoportuno.

OBLIGATION. Obligación. Palabra de mucho uso que puede significar cualquier deber (legal o moral) como cualquier obligación impuesta por un contrato; una promesa formal y por escrito de pagar dinero; un deber para con el gobierno; etc.

OBLIGEE. Obligante. Parte activa en una obligación. A quien se le debe la obligación.

OBLIGOR. Obligado. Parte pasiva en una obligación. Quien debe la obligación.

OBLITERATION. Borrar o tachar palabras escritas. También se aplica cuando las palabras tachadas aún se ven.

OBLIVION. Amnistía, perdón. Acto de olvidar y perdonar.

OBSCENE. Obsceno. Indecente, lascivo. Acto que ofende las normas morales y de decencia en una comunidad. Acto que no tiene valor moral, artístico, literario, político o científico y cuyo objeto es la lujuria.

OBSCENITY. Obscenidad. Véase "Obscene".

OBSOLESCENCE. Obsolescencia. Que no se usa más. Lo que se encuentra en desuso.

OBSTRUCTING JUSTICE. Interferir con el debido curso de una investigación o un proceso judicial, ya sea con actos o con palabras.

OCCUPANCY. Ocupación. (1) Posesión física de alguna propiedad (tierra o edificio) con o sin título de propiedad. (2) Otra palabra para indicar "adverse possession" (véase esta palabra). (3) Otra palabra para indicar "federal pre-emption". Véase "Pre emption".

OCCUPATION. (1) Ocupación, oficio. (2) Posesión física.

OCCUPATIONAL. Ocupacional. Relativo a oficio o profesión.

OCCUPATIONAL DISEASE. Enfermedad relacionada a un oficio. Enfermedad que se propaga o se manifiesta entre los trabajadores de un mismo campo (por ejemplo, asbestosis).

OCCUPATIONAL SAFETY AND HEALTH ADMINISTRATION. Administración de Seguridad y Salubridad Ocupacional. (EE.UU.) Agencia federal que vigila la aplicación de los requisitos de seguridad y salubridad de los obreros en las industrias y en sus oficios.

OCCUPYING CLAIMANT ACTS. (EE.UU.) Leyes estatales que otorgan al poseedor de buena fe de una propiedad (terreno), que resulta no ser el propietario, el derecho de cobrarle al verdadero dueño de los terrenos por las mejoras realizadas.

OCCUPYING THE FIELD. (EE.UU.) Bajo la ley federal ninguna ley estatal puede controlar materias de importancia nacional. Por ejemplo, la realización de un tratado internacional.

ODD LOT. Número de acciones vendidas en cantidad menor a la que usualmente se venden. Este número es casi siempre menos de 100 acciones.

OF AGE. De edad. Que ya no es menor. Persona mayor de edad.

OF COUNSEL. (1) Persona empleada como abogado en un caso. (2) Abogado que ayuda al abogado principal en un caso. (3) Abogado que aconseja a una firma o que es temporalmente miembro de ésta.

OF COURSE. Cuestión de derecho. Acciones que una persona lleva a cabo en una demanda sin consultar al juez, o si lo consulta, sabe que cuenta con la aprobación automática de la ley.

OF GRACE. Véase "Grace".

OF RECORD. Registrado. Que ha sido registrado formalmente en un registro o archivo público. Que forma parte oficial de un expediente legal.

OFF. Pospuesto indefinidamente.

OFFENDER. Ofendedor, ofensor, injuriador. Persona que hace daño a otra o viola la ley.

OFFENSE. Ofensa. Delito, falta. Cualquier violación de la ley.

OFFER. Oferta. (1) Hacer una propuesta. Requisito indispensable para la existencia de un contrato. (2) Tratar de hacer que algo sea admitido como evidencia en un juicio. (3) Propuesta para hacer un trato.

OFFER IN COMPROMISE. Ofrecimiento de transacción. Oferta de transigir. Oferta de arreglar una disputa sin admitir responsabilidad.

ER OF PROOF. Ofrecimiento de la prueba (EE.UU.). Cuando la corte rechaza la admisión de cierta evidencia, sea ésta oral o física, el abogado puede indicarle al juez, sin que el jurado lo sepa, la evidencia que se proponía admitir. Es un procedimiento para preservar lo que fue ofrecido como evidencia en caso de que se apele la decisión de la corte.

OFFERING. Ofrecimiento. Venta de acciones. (1) **Primary Offering.** Venta por la compañía de una nueva emisión de acciones. (2) **Secondary Offering.** Reventa de acción ya emitida, por un inversionista que la posee. (3) **Private Offering.** Oferta hecha a un pequeño grupo de inversionistas que conocen algo de la empresa. (4) **Public Offering.** Oferta de acciones hecha al público en general.

OFFERING CIRCULAR. Documento que describe a una empresa y que debe acompañar toda venta de acciones públicas.

OFFICE. Cargo, despacho, oficina. (1) Poder de actuar, más el deber de actuar de cierta manera en un cargo público. (2) Abreviatura para "public office" (cargo público). (3) Un despacho, departamento u otra agencia gubernamental.

OFFICE AUDIT. Auditar. Hacer cuentas de un inventario, activo o pasivo.

OFFICEHOLDER. Empleado o funcionario público. Persona encargada de un despacho público.

OFFICER OF THE COURT. Cargo o funcionario de la corte. La frase incluye los cargos que ocupan los que trabajan en la corte y los abogados que litigan en ella.

OFFICERS. Dignatarios, funcionarios, ejecutivos. Las personas que dirigen una organización.

OFFICIAL. Oficial, ejecutivo, dignatario. Funcionario público dotado de cierta autoridad para actuar.

OFFICIAL GAZETTE. Gaceta Oficial. (EE.UU.) Publicación semanal que enumera las patentes, marcas de fabricación y avisos relacionados.

OFFICIAL IMMUNITY. Inmunidad de que goza un oficial público contra demandas civiles por actos oficiales.

OFFICIAL NOTICE. Aviso oficial. Es lo mismo que "judicial notice" (véase esa palabra), pero con respecto a una agencia administrativa y no a un juez.

OFFICIAL RECORDS. Registros oficiales. Reportes, declaraciones, registros o archivos de información, mantenidos por una agencia gubernamental.

OFFSET. Contra demanda. Cualquier reclamación o demanda hecha en contra de la reclamación original.

OLD AGE, SURVIVORS AND DISABILITY INSURANCE. Nombre formal para "Seguro Social". Programa basado en los sueldos de patrones y empleados que paga beneficios a trabajadores jubilados, incapacitados, dependientes y viudos.

OLIGARCHY. Oligarquía. Gobierno dirigido por un grupo pequeño de personas.

OLIGOPOLY. Oligopolio. Cuando unos pocos vendedores dominan el mercado de un producto en particular.

OLOGRAPH. Véase "Holograph".

OMBUDSMAN. (Sueco) Persona que actúa como "oficina de reinvindicación" del gobierno, con poder de investigar la mala conducta de los funcionarios públicos, ayudar a reparar daños causados por el gobierno y algunas veces procesar a los que han hecho mal o daño.

OMNIBUS. (Lat.) (1) Que contiene dos o más asuntos separados o independientes. (2) **Omnibus Bill.** Legislación que concierne a dos o más materias completamente diferentes.

OMNIBUS CLAUSE. Cláusula Omnibus. (1) Cláusula en un testamento o en un decreto que distribuye toda propiedad no mencionada específicamente. (2) Disposición en una póliza de seguro de automóvil que extiende el seguro a todas las personas que manejen el automóvil con permiso del dueño.

OMNIS o OMNE o OMNI o OMNIA. (Lat.) Todos, todas.

ON ACCOUNT. A crédito. Pago parcial de algo que se compró o que se debe.

ON ALL FOURS. Véase "All Fours".

ON DEMAND or ON CALL. A requerimiento. Cuando se requiera. Pagadero inmediatamente después de que se requiera o pida.

ON OR ABOUT. Aproximadamente. Frase usada cuando no es posible ser más exacto.

ON POINT. Una ley o un caso de jurisprudencia se encuentra "on point" si se aplica directamente a los hechos del caso actual.

ONEROUS. Oneroso. (1) Que conlleva una carga irrazonable o que favorece más a una parte. (2) **Onerous Contract.** Contrato a título oneroso. Que tiene cargas y beneficios para todas las partes. (3) **Onerous Title.** Título oneroso. El derecho sobre una propiedad por la que se ha pagado o se ha dado algo a cambio.

ONUS PROBANDI. (Lat.) La carga de la prueba. Véase "Burden of Proof".

OPEN. Abierto. (1) Comenzar un proceso jurídico. (2) Que es visible o que está disponible al público. (3) Quitar las restricciones; abrir o reabrir. (4) Visible o aparente. (5) Que no tiene límite de tiempo o de cantidad.

OPEN A JUDGMENT. Volver a considerar una sentencia o un fallo.

OPEN ACCOUNT (O OPEN CREDIT). Cuenta (o crédito) abierto. Cuenta que no ha sido cancelada o pagada. Una serie de transacciones que han dado lugar a ciertos créditos y débitos pero que se constituyen en un solo reclamo.

OPEN BID. Oferta abierta. Oferta para hacer un trabajo o proveer materiales, usualmente en el negocio de la construcción, bajo la cual se reserva el derecho de bajar el precio para competir con otras ofertas.

OPEN COURT. Corte abierta; audiencia pública. (1) Corte o tribunal que está formalmente en sesión para atender asuntos ese día. (2) Corte que permite la asistencia del público a sus audiencias.

OPEN LISTING. "Listado abierto". Contrato en materia de bienes raíces por donde cualquier agente que procure la venta consigue una comisión.

OPEN MORTGAGE. Hipoteca abierta. Hipoteca que puede ser pagada sin multa o recargo en cualquier período antes de su vencimiento.

OPEN ORDER. Orden abierta. Una orden de un comprador dada a su agente de bolsa para que compre acciones a un precio determinado o por debajo de éste. La orden se ha de ejecuta mientras esté vigente.

OPEN PRICE TERM. Precio no determinado en un contrato. Por ejemplo, cuando el precio depende de algún suceso o indicador del mercado.

OPEN SHOP. Negocio abierto. Empresa que emplea a trabajadores que no forman parte de un sindicato laboral, al igual que a trabajadores qie sí son miembros.

OPEN-END COMPANY. Compañía de capital variable. Fondo mutuo. Véase "Mutual Fund".

OPEN-END CONTRACT. Véase "Requirements Contract".

OPEN-END MORTGAGE. Acuerdo hipotecario que permite préstamos adicionales durante la vida de la hipoteca en base al mismo acuerdo. Véase "Open Account" "Open Mortgage" y "Close-end Mortgage".

OPEN-END SETTLEMENT. Compensación laboral. Pagos laborales que se le hacen al trabajador hasta que pueda volver a trabajar.

OPENING STATEMENT. Exposición inicial del caso. Exposición en la que los abogados de las partes expresan al jurado, al iniciar un juicio, su versión de los hechos, la manera cómo estos hechos serán probados y cómo se aplican las leyes al caso bajo consideración.

OPERATING. Operación. (1) Operar una empresa. (2) **Operating Expenses.** Gastos de operación (electricidad, renta y otros que son necesarios para mantener abierto el negocio). (3) **Operating Profits.** Ganancias de operaciones. Se calculan tomando las ventas menos el costo de los productos vendidos y los gastos de operación.

OPERATING COST. Costo de operación. Todos aquellos gastos incurridos para que funcione un negocio.

OPERATION OF LAW. Por efecto de la ley. La manera en la que ciertos derechos y obligaciones recaen automáticamente sobre una persona sin que ésta coopere para que suceda.

OPERATIVE WORDS (O PART). Palabras (o parte) esencial. La parte de un documento, por ejemplo, una escritura pública, en la cual los derechos son creados o traspasados.

OPINION. Opinión. (1) Declaración. La decisión que un juez ha tomado en un caso. (2) Dictamen que contiene las conclusiones del juez en ése caso. (3) **Majority Opinion.** Opinión mayoritaria. Cuando más de la mitad de los jueces en un caso concuerdan con el resultado del caso y las razones para llegar a éste. (4) **Plurality Opinion.** Cuando la mayoría de los jueces están de acuerdo con el resultado pero no con el razonamiento. (5) **Concurring Opinion.** Opinión que está de acuerdo con el resultado pero no con el razonamiento. (6) **Dissenting or Minority Opinion.** Opinión que no está de acuerdo con el resultado de un caso. (7) **Memorandum Opinion.** Opinión unánime y muy corta. (8) Documento preparado para un cliente por un abogado, mediante el cual éste da sus conclusiones sobre la ley y comó se aplica a los hechos que le interesan al cliente. (9) Opinión de un experto.

OPINION EVIDENCE. Prueba pericial. Evidencia en forma de opinion. Evidencia de lo que un testigo piensa, cree o concluye sobre los hechos, en vez de lo que el testigo oye, ve, etc. Esta clase de evidencia, por lo regular, sólo se acepta cuando proviene de peritos o expertos.

OPPORTUNITY COST. El porcentaje de intereses que alguien podría estar recibiendo, invirtiendo su dinero en vez de utilizarlo en un proyecto determinado.

OPPRESSION. Opresión. (1) Véase "Unconscionability". (2) Daño (usualmente físico) hecho por un servidor público en exceso de su autoridad.

OPPROBRIUM. Vergüenza o deshonra.

OPTION. Opción. Contrato bajo el cual se paga dinero por el derecho a comprar o vender algo a cierto precio durante un determinado período de tiempo.

OPTIONAL BOND. Callable bond (véase esa palabra). Bono que puede redimirse a la opción del emisor.

OPTIONAL WRIT. Véase "Show Cause Order".

ORAL ARGUMENT. Alegato o argumento oral. La argumentación oral que cada parte presenta en favor de sus hechos ante una corte de apelación.

ORAL CONTRACT. Contrato verbal. Contrato que no figura por escrito, ya sea en parte o en su totalidad pero que tiene todos los elementos que forman un contrato y que es válido.

ORAL EVIDENCE. Evidencia oral, presentada por un testigo.

ORDEAL. Prueba penosa. Forma antigua de juzgar donde se suponía que habría una decisión divina sobre un caso. Estas pruebas eran de agua o de fuego.

ORDER. Orden. (1) Mandamiento o dirección por escrito dado por un juez. (2) Mandamiento dado por un oficial público. (3) "A la orden de" es un mandamiento de pagar algo a alguien. (4) Instrucción de comprar o vender algo.

ORDINANCE. Estatuto, ordenanza. Regla, reglamento o ley local o de una ciudad.

ORDINARY. Ordinario, usual, lo acostumbrado. (1) Regular o usual. (2) Un oficial jurídico.

ORGANIC. Orgánico. Que es básico.

ORGANIZATION. Organización. Todas las formas de asociación (compañía, gobierno, municipio, fideicomiso) donde existen intereses comunes formales o legales.

ORGANIZED LABOR. Trabajadores sindicalizados. Trabajadores representados por un sindicato.

ORIGINAL. Original. Que no es una copia. Que no deriva autoridad de otra fuente.

ORIGINAL DOCUMENT RULE. Principio del documento original. Regla probatoria que estipula que la mejor evidencia de lo que un documento dice es el documento original. No se acepta una copia en la corte a menos que el original no esté disponible.

ORIGINAL JURISDICTION. Competencia de primera instancia. El poder de una corte de tomar un caso, verlo y decidirlo (a diferencia del "appellate jurisdiction" (competencia de segunda instancia) que es el poder de la corte para oír y decidir sobre casos apelados).

ORIGINAL PACKAGE DOCTRINE. Reglamento federal que estipula que un estado puede cobrar impuestos sobre un artículo importado sólo cuando se ha roto el empaque original ya que esto sustrae al artículo del comercio interestatal.

ORIGINATION FEE. Honorario por hallar o comenzar los trámites necesarios para un financiamiento, por ejemplo, la hipoteca de una casa.

ORPHAN. Huérfano. Que no tiene padre o madre o ninguno de los dos.

OSTENSIBLE. (1) Aparente o visible. (2) **Ostensible Authority.** Poder que una persona parece tener.

OUSTER. Lanzamiento, desahucio. Desposeimiento. Sacar a alguien de una propiedad.

OUTLAW. Un prófugo de la justicia, un fujitivo.

OUT OF COURT SETTLEMENT. Arreglo extrajudicial.
Compromiso o acuerdo privado que da por terminado un litigio. A
veces el arreglo es aprobado por orden del juez.

OUT OF POCKET. (1) Un pequeño pago en efectivo. (2) Pérdida
que se calcula por la diferencia entre el precio pagado por un
artículo y su verdadero valor. El "out of pocket rule" permite que
se use este indicador de las pérdidas para calcular los daños que
se le causaron a una persona que fue víctima de un fraude.

OUTCOME TEST. Cuando una corte federal considera un caso sólo
por motivo de que hay diversidad de ciudadanía, el resultado del
caso debe ser el mismo que se daría en la corte estatal. Si no
resulta así, la corte de apelación considerará que el juez no aplicó
bien la ley o que actuó incorrectamente.

OUTPUT CONTRACT. Convenio bajo el cual una industria se
compromete a vender toda su producción a un solo comprador y
éste acuerda en comprarla toda. Este contrato es válido aunque
las cantidades no estén definidas.

OUTS. Condiciones o promesas que, de no ser cumplidas por el
cliente, dan derecho a un banco a salirse de lo acordado.

OUTSIDE DIRECTOR. Véase "Director".

OUTSIDE SALESPERSON. Persona cuyo trabajo es hacer ventas
fuera del local del patrón, y quien puede deducir todos sus gastos
de trabajo de sus impuestos.

OUTSTANDING. (1) Por cobrar, por pagar. (2) Que todavía existe.
(3) Sobresaliente.

OUTSTROKE. Hacer túneles mineros o pozos en una propiedad
adjunta.

OVER. Sobre, al otro lado. (1) Que continúa. (2) Que se cambia o
que pasa de una persona, cosa o tiempo a otro.

OVER THE COUNTER. Valores que no se venden en la bolsa de
valores sino de agente a agente o directamente de agente a
cliente.

OVERDRAFT (o OVERDRAW). Sobregiro. Girar un cheque contra una cuenta de banco por una cantidad de dinero mayor de la que se tiene en esa cuenta.

OVERDUE. Vencido. Que el tiempo para cumplir una obligación ha pasado sin que ésta se cumpla.

OVERHEAD. Gastos generales. Gastos fijos y globales que no pueden ser designados una actividad o un producto.

OVERISSUE. Emisión excesiva. Cuando una compañía emite más acciones de las permitidas por el documento de incorporación (pacto social) o por la ley.

OVERLYING RIGHT. Derecho del propietario a tomar y usar el agua que existe debajo de su propiedad.

OVERPAYMENT. Pago en exceso.

OVERREACHING. Tomar injusta ventaja comercial por medio de fraude o ventas inconcebibles.

OVERRIDE. (1) Comisión pagada a un supervisor cuando un empleado realiza una venta. (2) Comisión pagada a un agente de bienes raíces cuando un propietario vende directamente al comprador que fue encontrado por el agente.

OVERRULE. Desestimar. Rechazar una objeción hecha durante un juicio. Denegar un resultado judicial a causa de un error en la aplicación de la ley o porque la ley ha cambiado.

OVERSUBSCRIPTION. Situación que se da cuando la demanda para adquirir acciones de una sociedad es mayor que el número de las acciones que existen.

OVERT. Abierto, claro. Cuando ya se ha dado el primer paso decisivo en la comisión de un delito. No se refiere a los actos preparatorios sino que ya se ha entrado en la ejecución misma de los actos delictivos.

OWING. Debido. Que no se ha pagado. Que está en deuda.

OWNER. Dueño. Término general que denomima a la persona que tiene el derecho o el título legal sobre una propiedad. El derecho de propiedad puede ser parcial, total, mancomunado, incondicional, condicional o de equidad.

OWNERSHIP. Propiedad, pertenencia, titularidad.

OYER AND TERMINER. (Francés) "Oír y decidir". Algunas cortes criminales superiores estatales llevan esta denominación.

OYEZ. "Oígase." Exclamación utilizada por el oficial del tribunal para llamar la atención a una proclamación o procedimiento de la corte o para dar comienzo a la sesión.

P

P. (1) Reporte del Pacífico. Véase "National Reporter System".
(2) **Plaintiff.** Demandante.

P.A. Véase "Professional Association".

P.C. "Professional Corporation". Asociación profesional.

P.J. Siglas de "Presiding Judge". Juez presidente. Magistrado
ponente.

P.L. Siglas de "Public Law". Derecho público. Una ley pública.

P.O.D. Siglas de "Payable on death". Cuenta bancaria o de otra
clase que paga a una persona al morir el depositante.

PACK. Término que indica que ha existido fraude en la selección
del jurado.

PACKAGER. (1) Corredor. (2) Una persona que hace arreglos o
paquetes como, por ejemplo, los de un grupo de viajeros.

PACKING. Tratar de obtener decisiones favorables de un jurado o
corte al colocar a una o más personas específicas en ese jurado o
corte.

PACT. Pacto, convenio. Acuerdo de voluntades. (1) **Nude Pact.**
Nudum Pactum (Lat.). Acuerdo sin efecto legal.

PACTUM. (Lat.) Pact. Pacto.

PAID IN. Pagado. Que ha sido proporcionado por los dueños, como
por ejemplo, el capital en una sociedad o compañía.

PAIN AND SUFFERING. Dolor y sufrimiento. Término que
describe el dolor físico y la agonía mental sufrida por una
víctima. Normalmente resulta en daños pecuniarios.

PAIRING. Dos personas que se oponen una a la otra en cuanto a
un proyecto de ley en la asamblea legislativa, y que convienen en
abstenerse de votar.

PAIS. (Fr.) (1) Fuera de la corte, informalmente. Extrajudicial.
(2) La campiña, el campo, el vecindario.

PALIMONY. Manutención. Pensión alimenticia entre personas que nunca estuvieron casadas.

PALM OFF. Engañar al público al vender artículos de un fabricante como si fueran de otro fabricante más famoso.

PALPABLE. Palpable. Claro, simple, que se ve con facilidad, que es notorio.

PALSGRAF DOCTRINE. Regla legal que establece que una persona sólo es responsable por aquellos daños anticipados a causa de acciones negligentes y no por daños inesperados que no se prevén al actuar negligentemente.

PANDER. Alcahuete. Promover o solicitar prostitución.

PANEL. Panel. (1) Lista de personas de la cual se escoge el jurado. (2) Grupo de jueces seleccionados para decidir un caso.

PAPER. Documento. "The papers" son todos los documentos relativos a una demanda o un caso.

PAR. Par. Valor nominal. Valor a la par. El valor pre-establecido de un documento, por ejemplo, una obligación o bono.

PARALEGAL. Persona que no es abogado, sino que está empleada, usualmente en una firma de abogados, para realizar una serie de trabajos relacionados con la práctica del Derecho.

PARAMOUNT TITLE. Título superior. Título que prevalece sobre otro que se le contrapone.

PARCENER. Coheredero. Cuando dos o más personas heredan igualmente la totalidad de una cosa.

PARDON. Perdón, indulto, amnistía. Facultad de un presidente o gobernador para liberar a una persona de su castigo por cometer un delito.

PARENS PATRIAE. El derecho que tiene un gobierno de hacerse cargo de un menor o de otra persona que legalmente no puede hacerse cargo de sí misma o que está incapacitada.

PARENT COMPANY. Compañía o casa matriz. Compañía que tiene poder sobre las decisiones de otra.

PARENT CORPORATION. Compañía controladora o casa matriz. Compañía que controla totalmente a otra compañía.

PARENTAL LIABILITY. Responsabilidad de los padres. Responsabilidad de los padres por el daño causado por sus hijos menores.

PARENTAL RIGHTS. Patria potestad. Derecho de los padres. Autoridad que los padres tienen sobre sus hijos no emancipados de acuerdo a las leyes.

PARI CAUSA. (Lat.) Con o por igual derecho.

PARI DELICTO. (Lat.) Igualmente culpable. "Doctrine of pari delicto" es la regla que dice que ninguna corte pondrá en efecto o dará vigor a un contrato inválido o ilegal.

PARI MATERIA. (Lat.) Sobre la misma materia. Asuntos interdependientes. Por ejemplo, actos que se deben leer juntos para ser entendidos.

PARI PASSU. (Lat.) Igual. Del mismo grado, sin preferencia.

PARITY. Igualdad, equivalente, intercambiable. Que están en una situación similar o de paridad.

PARLIAMENTARY LAW. Reglamento parlamentario. Reglas o costumbres que rigen un parlamento o algún tipo de reunión.

PARLIAMENTARY SYSTEM. Sistema parlamentario. Forma de gobierno que tiene un parlamento.

PAROL. Oral, que no está escrito.

PAROL CONTRACT. Contrato oral que tiene efecto legal.

PAROL EVIDENCE. Prueba oral. Declaración testimonial.

PAROL EVIDENCE RULE. Regla sobre pruebas verbales. Doctrina legal que dice que cuando las personas hacen sus acuerdos por escrito, el sentido y los términos de esos acuerdos no pueden contradecirse por medio de previos acuerdos verbales a no ser que haya habido un error o un fraude.

PAROLE. Libertad condicional o bajo palabra. Liberar a un reo antes de que se termine la sentencia; bajo tal situación la persona queda sujeta a observar buena conducta y a cumplir con las condiciones exigidas para su libertad.

PART PERFORMANCE. Cumplimiento parcial. Véase "Performance".

PART–TIME EMPLOYEE. Empleado a medio tiempo. Que no trabaja la jornada completa.

PART–TIME STUDENT. Estudiante de medio tiempo. Que no está matriculado en todos los cursos que corresponden a su carrera.

PARTIAL AVERAGE. Avería parcial o particular. Véase "Particular Average Loss".

PARTIAL INCAPACITY. Incapacidad parcial. Lesión que imposibilita a un trabajador para realizar parte de su trabajo o que disminuye el trabajo de esa persona.

PARTIAL LOSS. Pérdida parcial, que no es una pérdida total.

PARTIAL RELEASE. Liberar parcialmente una propiedad o una obligación o una causa legal.

PARTICEPS CRIMINIS. (Lat.) Cómplice. El que ayuda en un delito.

PARTICIPATION. Participación. (1) Una póliza de seguro en la que la persona asegurada paga cierto porcentaje de cualquier pérdida. (2) Convenio de préstamo en el que diferentes bancos se combinan para lograr un préstamo mayor. (3) Contrato de hipoteca en el cual el prestamista recibe parte de los dividendos de la empresa en adición a los intereses del préstamo.

PARTICULAR AVERAGE LOSS. Avería particular. Pérdida de propiedad durante su transporte o en alta mar donde la perdida la tiene que asumir el dueño de la propiedad.

PARTICULAR LIEN. Gravamen específico. Derecho a retener una propiedad específica debido a reclamos contra esa propiedad. Por ejemplo, un taller de mecánica tiene derecho a retener un automóvil reparado hasta que se pague la reparación hecha.

PARTICULARS. Datos, detalles. (1) Los detalles de un reclamo legal o de los diferentes artículos incluidos en una cuenta. Véase también "Bill of Particulars". (2) La descripción detallada de una propiedad que se va a vender en una subasta.

PARTIES. Partes. Véase "Party".

PARTITION. Segregación. División de un terreno de propiedad mancomunada en lotes más pequeños que pasan a ser propiedad de cada persona individualmente.

PARTNER. Socio, asociado. Miembro de una sociedad. (1) **General Partner.** Socio que participa en la administración del negocio y tiene una obligación legal ante la asociación. (2) **Limited Partner.** Socio cuyo interés se limita a su inversión.

PARTNERSHIP. Sociedad colectiva. (1) Contrato entre dos o más personas para llevar a cabo un negocio juntas y compartir los gastos, el trabajo, las ganancias y las pérdidas. (2) **Limited Partnership.** Sociedad de responsabilidad limitada. Persona jurídica en la cual, además de los socios llamados "General Partners", con responsabilidad ilimitada que administran la socieda, existen otros socios llamados "Limited Partners", que sólo contribuyen con capital y que sólo son responsables por la cantidad de capital que aportaron.

PARTNERSHIP INTEREST. Participación en una sociedad colectiva.

PARTY. Parte. (1) Persona que toma parte en algún asunto, caso o procedimiento. (2) **Real Party.** El demandante o el demandado en un pleito. (3) **Third Party.** Tercera persona. Persona que no está directamente involucrada pero que podría ser afectada. (4) Partido. Grupo de personas organizadas políticamente. (5) **Party Wall.** Pared entre dos propiedades colindantes.

PASS. Pasar, aprobar. (1) Decir o pronunciar sentencia. (2) Dictar legislación. (3) Examinar y determinar. (4) Transferir o ser transferido. (5) Que ha sido pasado fraudulentamente.

PASSBOOK. Libreta de ahorros. Libro donde se anotan los depósitos y retiros de una cuenta de ahorros.

PASSENGER. Pasajero. (1) Cualquier persona que viaja en un vehículo de motor y no es el conductor. (2) Persona que paga por viajar en un vehículo.

PASSIM. "Aquí y allá". Que se encuentra en varios lugares; en cualquier parte.

PASSION. Pasión. Furor, ira.

PASSIVE. Pasivo. (1) Inactivo. (2) Sumiso o permisivo, en vez de estar de acuerdo o participar en algo.

PASSIVE TRUST. Véase "Dry Trust".

PASSPORT. Pasaporte. (1) Documento de identificación o permiso que emite un país en favor de sus ciudadanos para que éstos puedan viajar. (2) Documento usado durante la guerra que sirve como salvo conducto para la persona que lo lleva.

PAST CONSIDERATION. Consideración o arras que se da o que tiene lugar antes de que se celebre un contrato. Véase "Consideration".

PAST RECOLLECTION. Véase "Recollection".

PAT.PEND. Abreviación de "Patent pending". Patente pendiente. Si se ha aplicado para obtener una patente y se concede la misma, ésta se considerará válida desde la fecha de la aplicación.

PATENT. Patente. (1) Visible, evidente, abiertamente. (2) Privilegio de invención. Derecho que se le concede al descubridor o inventor de algo para que él tenga control de la fabricación y venta de lo descubierto o inventado.

PATENT AND COPYRIGHT CLAUSE. Disposición constitucional que provee a los autores e inventores el control y uso exclusivo de su producto por un tiempo determinado bajo las leyes federales.

PATENT AND TRADEMARK OFFICE. Agencia Federal del Departamento de Comercio que decide y procesa las aplicaciones de patentes de invención y de marcas de fábrica.

PATENTABLE. Patentable. Posibilidad de que una invención o descubrimiento sea patentable. Para ser patentable, la invención debe incluir una idea nueva.

PATERNITY SUIT. Juicio de filiación. Acción judicial para probar que una persona es el padre de un hijo(a) ilegítimo(a) para obligarlo a pagar alimentos.

PATIENT–PHYSICIAN PRIVILEGE. Secreto médico. Derecho de un paciente a que se mantenga en privacidad toda comunicación con su médico, incluyendo los archivos del médico.

PATRIMONY. Patrimonio. (1) Todos los derechos y propiedades que han pasado o que pasarán al poder de una persona como legado de sus padres, abuelos, etc. (2) Todas las propiedades, derechos y responsabilidades a las que se les puede calcular un valor en dinero. (3) Los bienes de alguien.

PATRONAGE. Patrocinio. Auspicio. (1) Todos los clientes de una empresa, los que proporcionan negocios a una compañía. (2) El derecho que tienen algunos funcionarios públicos de nombrar individuos a ciertos cargos según su propia discreción.

PATTERN. Patrón. Conducta, intencionalmente regular, repetida.

PAUPER. Mendigo, indigente. Persona que no se puede mantener por sí misma y que requiere ayuda financiera del gobierno.

PAWN. (1) Empeño. Dar algún bien mueble a una persona como garantía de una deuda. (2) Prenda, el bien en sí.

PAYABLE. Pagadero. (1) Debido y pagadero. (2) Debido y exigible inmediatamente. (3) Pagadero al portador. Véase "Bearer". Pagadero a la orden. Véase "Order".

PAYEE. Beneficiario. Persona a la orden de quien se emite un documento negociable.

PAYMASTER. Pagador. Persona que paga.

PAYMENT. Pago. Complir con una obligación, total o parcialmente.

PAYMENT–GUARANTEE. Pago garantizado. Garantía del signatario de cumplir con la obligación si el instrumento firmado no es pagado por el deudor.

PAYMENT–VOUCHER. Comprobante de pago. Recibo que demuestra que un pago se ha hecho.

PAYOR. El pagador, el que debe complir con un pago.

PAYROLL. Nómina. Planilla. Lista que contiene el nombre y el salario de los empleados.

PEACE BOND. Bono para garantizar buena conducta por un tiempo determinado.

PEACE OFFICER. Oficial del orden público. Cualquier oficial con autoridad para hacer arrestos.

626

PEACEABLE POSSESSION. Ocupar un terreno o un edificio por cierto tiempo cuando no ha habido intentos legales o uso de la fuerza para desalojar a los ocupantes del mismo.

PECULATION. Peculado. Desfalco. Véase "Embezzlement".

PECUNIARY. Pecuniario. Monetario, que tiene que ver con dinero.

PECUNIARY INTEREST. Interés monetario.

PEDERASTY. Pederastia. Sodomía. Prácticas homosexuales entre hombres.

PEERS. Iguales. "Trial by jury of peers" quiere decir que los miembros del jurado son ciudadanos imparcialmente escogidos.

PEG. Ajustar el precio de algo, sea oficialmente o al manipular un mercado. Arbitrariamente o artificialmente. Arreglar o poner valor a algo.

PENAL. Penal. (1) Que tiene que ver con una multa o castigo. (2) **Penal Action.** Acción penal. Acción para determinar si una multa o castigo sería apropiado basándose en los alegatos radicados. (3) **Penal Bond.** Obligación penal; fianza para multa. (4) **Penal Damages.** Véase "Punitive Damages".

PENALTY. Multa, condena. (1) Castigo impuesto por la ley. (2) Suma de dinero que una persona promete pagar a otra si incumple algo contratado.

PENALTY CLAUSE. Cláusula penal. Disposición contractual que requiere el pago de una suma determinada si se hace algo que cambia las condiciones del contrato.

PENDENCY. Pendiente. (1) Que está pendiente. Véase "Pending". (2) **Notice of Pendency.** Aviso formal que se pone en los registros de propiedad para indicar que una demanda o reclamo se ha interpuesto en contra de la propiedad.

PENDENT JURISDICTION. Derecho que tienen las cortes federales de decidir un reclamo basado en cuestiones estatales bajo ciertas circunstancias. Doctrina procesal que permite a una corte federal considerar un reclamo basado en las leyes estatales con tal de que la corte tenga jurisdicción federal sobre las parte del pleito. Esto se determina si la evidencia establece tanto el reclamo federal como el estatal.

627

PENDENTE LITE. (Lat.) Pending the suit. Pleito pendiente. Que un pleito está en proceso. Litis pendiente.

PENDING. Pendiente. En trámite. Que no se ha decidido todavía; que está comenzado pero no terminado.

PENITENTIARY. Penitenciaría. Una prisión para personas condenadas por crímenes. Cárcel.

PENNOYER RULE. Doctrina jurisdiccional según la cual una corte no puede fallar contra una persona sobre la cual la corte no tiene jurisdicción.

PENNY STOCK. Acciones especulativas vendidas por menos de un dólar.

PENOLOGY. Penología. El estudio de la administración de prisiones y de la rehabilitación de criminales.

PENSION PLAN. Plan de jubilación. Plan establecido por el patrón para pagar la jubilación de empleados.

PEONAGE. Esclavitud o trabajo forzado para pagar una deuda.

PEOPLE. El pueblo. Una nación o estado. Todas las personas de una nación o estado como grupo. Personas. Gente.

PER. Por, a través, por medio de, durante.

PER CAPITA. Por cabeza. Dividido por el número de personas; a repartirse por partes iguales.

PER CURIAM. (Lat.) Por la corte. Una opinión respaldada por todos los jueces de una corte en particular y usualmente sin identificar el nombre del juez que dictó la decisión del caso.

PER DIEM. (Lat.) (1) Por día, día a día, cada día. (2) Una cantidad de dinero acordada como estipendio pagadero a una persona para gastos del trabajo tales como hospedaje y comida.

PER PAIS. (Lat.) Véase "País".

PER PROCURATION. En Derecho Inglés, significa actuar como agente solo con autoridad limitada. Se abrevia "per.proc." o "p.p."

PER QUOD. (Lat.) Por eso. Por cuyos actos. Palabra que antecede a una especificación de detalles necesarios.

PER SE. (Lat.) En y por sí mismo.

PER STIRPES. (Lat.) Por estirpe. Método de dividir el patrimonio dejado por una persona a sus herederos, en el cual se dividen los bienes por representación o por grupo familiar.

PERCENTAGE DEPLETION. Véase "Depletion Allowance".

PERCENTAGE LEASE. Alquiler en base a porcentaje. Alquiler o renta de una propiedad con el canon o la suma de arrendamiento calculado en base a un porcentaje del valor de las ventas.

PERCEPTION. Percepción. Palabra antigua que significaba tomar en posesión algo para descontar o pagar una deuda.

PEREMPTORY. Perentorio. (1) Absoluto; concluso; final o arbitrario. (2) Que no requiere ninguna explicación o motivo.

PEREMPTORY RULING. Fallo perentorio. Fallo de un juez que le quita al jurado la decisión final de un juicio. Véase "Directed Verdict" o "Judgement Non Obstante Veredicto".

PERFECT o PERFECTED. Perfecto. Completo. Sin defecto, que se puede hacer cumplir.

PERFECT TENDER RULE. Principio raramente aplicado que establece que un contrato comercial debe cumplirse al detalle para ser válido.

PERFECTION OF SECURITY INTEREST. Todos los pasos necesarios para que un acreedor tenga derecho de pignoración sobre un bien.

PERFORMANCE. Cumplimiento, ejecución, desempeño. (1) Ejecutar un contrato, promesa o alguna otra obligación de acuerdo con los términos de un contrato, dando lugar así a la desaparición de la obligación. (2) **Specific Performance.** Cumplir exactamente lo que se ha contratado. (3) **Part Performance.** Hacer algo confiando en que existe un contrato. Cumplir parcialmente lo pactado.

PERFORMANCE BOND. Bono o fianza que asegura que algo se cumplirá.

PERIL. Riesgo. (1) Riesgo o accidente contra el cual se asegura algo con una póliza de seguro. (2) Peligro causado naturalmente, que no es producido por el hombre.

PERIODIC. Periódico. (1) Que sucede regularmente o cada cierto tiempo. (2) **Periodic Alimony.** El pago de cierta suma que se paga cada cierto tiempo para manutención. (3) **Periodic Tenancy.** Arrendamiento que continúa de mes a mes, o año tras año, a menos que se dé por terminado.

PERIODIC PAYMENTS. Pagos periódicos, plazos.

PERJURY. Perjurio. Mentir estando bajo juramento.

PERKS. Véase "Perquisites".

PERMANENT. Permanente. Por tiempo indefinido.

PERMISSION. Licencia para hacer algo que sería ilegal sin previa autorización.

PERMISSIVE. Permisivo. (1) Permitido. Lo opuesto a aprobado expresamente. (2) Por derecho. (3) Indulgente o tolerante.

PERMIT. Permiso. (1) Un documento oficial que permite hacer algo. (2) **Permit Card.** Documento otorgado por un sindicato que permite a una persona que no es miembro del sindicato trabajar en un empleo al no haber suficientes miembros del sindicato para ejecutar una labor.

PERPETRATOR. Autor. La persona que comete un delito.

PERPETUAL. Perpetuo. (1) **Perpetual Succession.** Sucesión perpetua. (2) Duración perpetua. La existencia continua de una corporación o sociedad anónima como una entidad jurídica aunque sus dueños, directores o administradores cambien.

PERPETUATING TESTIMONY. Perpetuación de un testimonio. Procedimiento para tomar y preservar el testimonio de personas que tienen muy mala salud, que son muy ancianas o que están por abandonar un lugar.

PERPETUITY. Perpetuidad. (1) Para siempre. (2) **Rule Against Perpetuities.** Regla que prohíbe posponer la transferencia de una propiedad por un período mayor a la vida de una persona en existencia más 21 años.

PERQUISITES. Emolumentos. Beneficios de un empleo además del salario, por ejemplo, el uso personal de un carro de la compañía.

PERSON. Persona. (1) Un ser humano o persona natural. (2) Una corporación o persona jurídica. (3) Cualquier otro ser que pueda demandar y ser demandado con identidad legal.

PERSONA NON GRATA. (Lat.) (1) Persona que no es querida, que no es bien recibida. (2) Persona que es rechazada como embajador de una nación o de cualquier otro cargo representativo de una nación.

PERSONAL. Personal. Particular. Privado. (1) Que tiene que ver con seres humanos. (2) Que tiene que ver con bienes muebles o propiedad personal. (3) **Personal Effects.** Efectos personales. Puede ser desde cualquier propiedad mueble, hasta los bienes que normalmente lleva consigo una persona.

PERSONAL EXCEPTIONS. Exenciones personales. Deducciones del impuesto que se le permiten a las personas.

PERSONAL EXPENSES. Gastos personales. Gastos hechos por una persona que pueden ser descontados del impuesto.

PERSONAL INCOME. Ingresos personales sujetos a impuestos.

PERSONAL INJURY. Lesión corporal, lesión personal. (1) Cualquier daño hecho a los derechos de una persona, excepto a los derechos de propiedad. (2) Acción Legal que se puede tomar basada en la negligencia de alguien, como por ejemplo en un accidente de tránsito.

PERSONAL JURISDICTION. La jurisdicción de una corte sobre una persona.

PERSONAL PROPERTY TAX. Impuesto sobre bienes muebles.

PERSONAL PROPERTY. (1) Propiedad personal. Bienes que no son propios de una empresa sino de una persona. (2) Bienes muebles. (3) **Personal Property Tax.** Impuesto sobre un inmueble.

PERSONAL REPRESENTATIVE. Albacea. Término en general usado para denominar al ejecutor o administrador de los bienes de un difunto.

PERSONAL TRUST. Fideicomiso personal. Fideicomiso a favor de uno o varios individuos y sus familiares.

PERSONAL USE PROPERTY. Propiedad de uso personal.

PERSONALTY. Bienes muebles; propiedad personal.

PERSUASIVE AUTHORITY. Toda fuente de derecho que un juez utiliza para decidir un caso.

PERTINENT. Pertinente. (1) Que es relevante para un asunto. (2) Perteneciente a una cosa.

PERVERSE VERDICT. Veredicto del jurado que no siguió las instrucciones del juez en la aplicación de la ley.

PETIT JURY. Jurado de conciencia usado en un juicio para decidir la culpabilidad o inocencia del acusado.

PETITION. Petición. (1) Pedir algo por escrito a una corte que ha tomado una acción en particular. Por ejemplo, el cambio de una orden. (2) Pedir algo por escrito a un servidor público, un memorial.

PETITION IN BANKRUPTCY. Petición de quiebra. Solicitud presentada en juicio de quiebra.

PETITIONER. Peticionario, demandante. El que demanda.

PETITORY ACTION. Acción petitoria. Juicio petitorio para establecer el título de una propiedad o terreno. Lo opuesto a pedir la posesión física de una propiedad.

PETTY. Pequeño o sin importancia.

PHYSICAL. Físico. (1) Que tiene que ver con el cuerpo de una persona, en vez de su mente. (2) Real; lo opuesto a imaginario. Véase "Physical Fact".

PHYSICAL FACT. Hecho tangible. (1) Ley natural irrefutable o hecho científico. (2) Algo visible, audible o de otra forma perceptible por los sentidos. (3) **Physical Fact Rule.** Principio que establece que la evidencia contraria a las leyes naturales puede justificar que el juez decida el caso sin el jurado.

PHYSICAL INCAPACITY. Incapacidad física. (1) Impotencia. (2) Lesión que impide trabajar.

PHYSICIAN–PATIENT PRIVILEGE. Secreto médico. Véase "Patient-Physician Privilege".

PICKETING. Piqueteo (Mex.). Personas que se reúnen afuera de un recinto de trabajo para crear disturbios con sus actividades o para informar a terceros sobre las injusticias, opiniones, etc., del lugar que se piquetea.

PIECEWORK. Trabajo a destajo; trabajo por desajuste; trabajo que se paga por unidad completada.

PIERCING THE CORPORATE VEIL. Levantar o descubrir or penetrar el velo corporativo. Doctrina legal aplicable a sociedades anónimas que de utilizarse ignora a la corporación como entidad jurídica. Impone sobre sus directores y oficiales -en forma personal y no como representantes de la corporación- la responsabilidad civil por los actos de esa corporación.

PIONEER PATENT. Patente básica u original. Patente para un invento o aparato enteramente nuevo, no para un pequeño mejoramiento de una existente. Patente que abre una nueva era de experimentación o desarrollo.

PIRACY. Piratería. (1) Atacar y saquear o robar un buque o aeronave. (2) Reproducir en todo o en parte un libro, película, artículo, tecnología, etc., total o parcialmente, protegida por la ley o por el derecho de autor, sin tener permiso.

PLACE. Lugar, colocar. Termino impreciso. Arreglar una venta o transacción financiera.

PLACEMENT. Ubicación. Colocación. (1) Arreglar un préstamo o hipoteca combinando prestamista y prestatario. (2) Dar trabajo a una persona. (3) Coordinar la venta de valores.

PLACITORY. Que tiene que ver con alegatos. Véase "Pleading" o "Pleas".

PLACITUM. (Lat.) Término antiguo utilizado para denominar una variedad de cosas como acuerdos, leyes, decisiones judiciales, demandas, alegatos, etc.

PLAGIARISM. Plagio. Tomar todo o parte de un escrito de otra persona y hacerlo pasar como propio. Véase también "Infringement Copyright".

PLAIN ERROR RULE. Principio que establece que una corte de apelación puede cambiar una decisión por un error de procedimiento, aunque no se haya hecho una objeción con respecto al error.

PLAIN MEANING RULE. Principio que establece que si el texto de la ley está claro, debe tomarse en su sentido más simple y no interpretarlo.

PLAIN VIEW DOCTRINE. Regla que establece que si un policía encuentra alguna evidencia mientras está actuando dentro de sus funciones legales, se puede utilizar ese artículo como prueba en un juicio criminal, aunque no haya habido orden de allanamiento o registro.

PLAINTIFF. Demandante. Persona que demanda a otra persona. Quien comienza un pleito.

PLAINTIFF ERROR. Véase "Apellant".

PLAT O PLOT. Plano o mapa que muestra un área o terreno que va a ser subdividida y construida. Un "plat map" da la descripción legal de las parcelas de terreno por lotes, calles y número de cuadras.

PLEA. Alegato. La contestación formal de un demandado a un cargo criminal o una demanda civil. Defensa.

PLEA BARGAINING. Arreglo entre el fiscal y el acusado o su abogado en el cual se negocia una confesión de culpabilidad a cambio de que se le atenúen los cargos o se le reduzca la sentencia.

PLEAD. Alegar, defender.

PLEADING. Alegación, defensa, informe. (1) Declaraciones formales en orden lógico sobre los hechos en los que se basa un caso, y que contempla, por otra parte, las bases para la demanda o la defensa del pleito. (2) Alegatos de las partes que afirman o niegan algún hecho o declaración.

PLEBISCITE. Plebiscito. El voto popular a favor o en contra de una nueva ley o asunto de gran interés y repercusión.

PLEDGE. Prenda, pignoración. Entregar la posesión física de un bien mueble propio a un acreedor para que lo mantenga en su poder hasta que se le pague la deuda al acreedor.

PLENARY. Plenario. Pleno. Completo. (1) Todas las personas o todas las cosas. (2) **Plenary Jurisdiction.** Poder completo de una corte de tomar decisiones sobre todas las personas o cosas involucradas en un juicio. (3) **Plenary Session.** Reunión de todos los miembros de un órgano legislativo u otro grupo grande.

PLENIPOTENCIARY. Plenipotenciario. Persona que posee plenos poderes, normalmente representante de un Estado.

PLOTTAGE. El valor adicional que tienen dos terrenos por encontrarse juntos y poder ser vendidos como una unidad.

PLOW BACK. Reinvertir dividendos en el negocio en vez de repartirlos a los dueños.

PLURALITY. Pluralidad. El número mayor.

PLURIES. Muchos; muchas cosas interrelacionadas. Tercer proceso cuando los dos primeros han sido inefectivos.

POCKET PART. La adición hecha en forma de panfleto para actualizar los libros de derecho hasta que salga una nueva edición.

POINT. Punto, cuestión. Una proposición, argumento o pregunta legal que surge en un juicio.

POINT RESERVED. Véase "Reserve". "Reserving Decision".

POISONOUS TREE. Véase "Fruit of Poisonous Tree".

POLICE COURT. Corte local de baja jerarquía con diversidad de funciones, pero casi siempre con la potestad para manejar casos de delitos menores.

POLICE POWER. El derecho y potestad de todo gobierno de crear y hacer cumplir leyes que provean la seguridad, salud y bienestar social de un pueblo.

POLICY. Política. Práctica. Póliza. (1) Los lineamientos generales del procedimiento de una organización. (2) El propósito general de un estatuto o ley. (3) **Public Policy.** Política a seguir para el bienestar general de un estado y su pueblo. (4) **Insurance Policies.** Póliza de seguros. Véase "Insurance".

POLITICAL CRIME OR OFFENSE. Crimen u ofensa política. Delito en contra del gobierno, por ejemplo, traición o sedición. Usualmente estos delitos son de violencia en contra del orden establecido.

POLITICAL QUESTION. Cuestión política. Asunto sobre el que la corte no decidirá porque implica una resolución que debe ser tomada por el órgano ejecutivo. Por ejemplo, decidir si una nación extranjera se ha independizado o no.

POLITICAL RIGHTS. Derechos políticos. Derechos que conciernen a la participación de un ciudadano en el gobierno, como, por ejemplo, el derecho de votar.

POLLING THE JURY. Encuestar al jurado. Preguntar individualmente a cada miembro del jurado cuál es su decisión.

POLL. Lista de personas que pueden votar.

POLLS. "A challenge to the polls". Objeción a la selección de un miembro del jurado en particular, hecha antes de que el jurado se convoque. Usualmente cuando se trata de un gran jurado.

POLYGAMY. Poligamia. Tener más de un esposo o esposa. Es un delito.

POLYGRAPH. Polígrafo. Detector de mentiras.

POOL. Fondos en común. (1) Combinación de recursos de individuos o compañías en una empresa comercial común. (2) Acuerdo entre compañías para no competir entre ellas y compartir los dividendos. Este tipo de acuerdo que usualmente es ilegal porque viola las leyes antimonopolistas. (3) Dinero reunido para una apuesta.

POPULAR. Popular. Que pertenece al pueblo.

PORNOGRAPHIC. Pornográfico. Obsceno.

PORT AUTHORITY. Autoridad portuaria. Agencias federales, estatales o interestatales que regulan el tráfico marítimo y promueven negocios en los puertos.

PORT OF ENTRY. Puerto de entrada. Puerto por donde tanto inmigrantes como artículos importados pueden entrar en un país y donde están las oficinas de aduanas.

PORTFOLIO. Lista de valores. Todas las inversiones que posee una persona u organización.

PORTFOLIO INTEREST. Interés procedente de valores de inversión.

POSITIVE EVIDENCE. Evidencia positiva. Véase "Direct Evidence".

POSITIVE LAW. Derecho positivo. Ley que ha sido promulgada por el órgano legislativo.

POSSE COMITATUS. (Lat.) The power of the state. El poder de la ciudadanía. Grupo de individuos que puede ser llamado por las autoridades para hacer cumplir la ley, usualmente en una situación de emergencia. Se abrevia "posse."

POSSESSION. Posesión. (1) Propiedad y dominio de los bienes personales. (2) Dominio de terrenos y edificios. (3) Simplemente tener algo.

POSSESSORY ACTION. Acción posesoria. Acción legal para obtener el control físico de una propiedad. Opuesto a aquél que intenta conseguir el título legal. Como por ejemplo una evicción.

POSSIBILITY OF ISSUE. Véase "Fertile Octogenarian Rule".

POST. Fijar. (1) Anunciar algo al público poniendo un anuncio en un lugar prominente. (2) Poner algo en el correo. Véase "Posting".

POST-CONVICTION REMEDIES. Procedimiento para apelar penas o sentencias de personas condenadas.

POSTDATE. Posfechar. Poner una fecha en un documento que es posterior a la fecha en que el documento fue firmado.

POSTHUMOUS. Póstumo. Después de la muerte.

POSTING. Hacer un asiento en un libro de contabilidad.

POST-MORTEM. Después de muerto. Examinación o autopsia de un cuerpo para determinar la causa de muerte.

POST-OBIT. Acuerdo bajo el cual un prestatario promete pagar una suma mayor de dinero después de la muerte de alguien de quien el prestatario espera heredar.

POST-TRIAL MOTION. Procedimiento que solicita un nuevo juicio o que se modifique el resultado de un juicio.

POUND. Lugar o depósito donde se guardan artículos confiscados.

POUROVER WILL. Testamento que deja dinero o propiedades a un fideicomiso existente bajo cuyas condiciones se distribuirán el dinero o propiedades.

POVERTY AFFIDAVIT. Declaraciones de pobreza. Documento firmado bajo juramento que declara que una persona es lo suficientemente pobre como para ser acreedora a la asistencia pública. También le facilita tener defensor público, el no pagar tarifas de la corte, etc.

POWER. Poder. (1) Derecho de hacer algo. (2) La autoridad para hacer algo.

POWER OF APPOINTMENT. Poder de disponer. Parte de un testamento, escritura o documento separado que da a alguien el poder de decidir quién recibe qué o cómo debe usarse.

POWER OF ATTORNEY. Poder. Mandato. Documento autorizando a una persona a actuar como representante de la persona que otorga el documento.

POWER OF SALE. Poder de venta que se otorga en una hipoteca.

PRACTICABLE. Factible, ejecutable. Que se puede hacer.

PRACTICE. Práctica. (1) Costumbre, hábito o repetición regular de algo. (2) Procedimiento formal de la corte. (3) Practicar una profesión o hacer cosas que sólo se le permiten a quienes ejercen una profesión.

PRAECIPE. Solicitud formal pidiendo que un funcionario del juzgado, por ejemplo, el secretario del tribunal, tome una acción.

PRAEDIAL. Predial. Que se refiere a un predio.

PRAYER. Petición, solicitud. La parte de una petición legal que contiene una queja o solicita indemnización.

PREAMBLE. Preámbulo, introducción.

PREAPPOINTED EVIDENCE. Evidencia o prueba requerida por adelantado.

PRECEDENT. Precedente. La decisión de una corte sobre una cuestión de derecho que confiere autoridad o dirección sobre cómo decidir en una cuestión similar en otro caso futuro.

PRECEPT. Precepto. (1) Orden o decreto de una persona con autoridad. (2) Una regla de conducta.

PRECINCT. Precinto. Distrito policial o electoral dentro de una ciudad.

PRECIPE. Véase "Praecipe".

PRECLUSION ORDER. Orden judicial que le prohíbe a una parte oponerse a los argumentos hechos por su rival basados en evidencia no admitida o producida por una parte.

PRECOGNITION. La examinación de un testigo antes de un juicio.

PRECONTRACT. Contrato que prohíbe a una persona hacer un contrato similar con una tercera persona.

PREDIAL. Véase "Praedial".

PRE–EMPTION. Prioridad. Derecho de comprar algo primero. (1) Derecho de hacer algo primero. (2) Supremacía sobre algo.

PREFERENCE. Preferencia. El derecho de un acreedor a ser pagado antes que a otros acreedores, normalmente en un caso de bancarrota.

PREJUDICE. Prejuicio. (1) Una opinión preconcebida. (2) Daño substancial a los derechos de alguien. (3) Que favorece a una de las partes.

PRELIMINARY EVIDENCE. Evidencia preliminar. Aquellos hechos necesarios para comenzar una audiencia o juicio; no necesariamente aquéllos que al final deciden la sentencia.

PRELIMINARY HEARING. Audiencia o vista preliminar. La primera exposición de un delito criminal en una corte.

PRELIMINARY INJUNCTION. Orden preliminar. Véase "Injunction".

PREMATURE WITHDRAWAL. Retirada prematura de fondos. Retiro de fondos depositados a plazo antes de la fecha pactada.

PREMEDITATION. Premeditación. (1) Pensar reflexivamente en una cosa antes de ejecutarla. (2) Proponerse de antemano cometer un delito, tomando previamente las medidas necesarias.

PREMISES. (1) Establecimiento. Un edificio y sus alrededores. (2) Premisas. La parte de un documento que explica el quién, el cómo y el cuándo de una transacción antes de explicar ésta en sí. (3) Las bases para una deducción lógica. Los hechos o argumentos en que se basa una conclusión.

PREMIUM. Prima. Costo de una póliza de seguro. (1) Dinero adicional pagado al comprar algo. (2) Bono.

PRENUPTIAL AGREEMENT. Esponsales. Contrato prematrimonial. Véase "Antenuptial Agreement".

PREPAID EXPENSE. Gastos pagados de antemano. Cualquier gasto o deuda que se paga antes de incurrir.

PREPAID INCOME. Dinero recibido, pero aún no ganado. Pago recibido con anterioridad a la ejecución del trabajo.

PREPAYMENT PENALTY. Multa o sobrecargo por pago adelantado. Dinero pagado como multa al cancelar una obligación antes de su vencimiento.

PREPONDERANCE OF EVIDENCE. Preponderancia de la prueba. No en cantidad ni número de testigos o hechos, sino en calidad, de convencimiento e importancia de los hechos probados.

PREROGATIVE. Prerrogativa. (1) Privilegio especial. (2) Poder oficial especial.

PRESCRIPTION. Prescripción. (1) Método de obtener el título legal de un bien personal. Se logra al mantener su posesión abierta y consecutivamente, por reclamarlo como propio. (2) El derecho de acceso a una senda, camino pluvial, luz, espacio abierto, etc., que se adquiere debido al uso continuo por largo tiempo (servidumbre). (3) Una orden o dirección o remedio. (4) Receta médica.

PRESENCE. Presencia.

PRESENT SENSE IMPRESSION. Declaración hecha durante o inmediatamente después de un evento por un participante u observador del evento. Es una de las excepciones a la regla de evidencia por referencia, y puede usarse tal declaración en la corte.

PRESENT. Presente. (1) Inmediato. (2) Véase "Presentment".

PRESENTMENT OR PRESENTATION. Acusación, presentación. Imputación de cargos.

PRESUMED INTENT. Intención presumida. Tener la intención de causar un efecto natural o probable por medio de acciones voluntarias. Criterio que considera que se tiene la intención de cometer el delito y sus consecuencias.

PRESUMPTION. Presunción, suposición, conjetura. Conclusión o indicio. La certeza de un hecho conduce a la certeza de otro. Una conclusión legal basada en que si un hecho existe o es cierto, otro hecho también existe y es cierto a no ser que se pruebe lo contrario. (1) **Rebuttable Presumption.** Suposición que puede ser refutada al probar lo contrario. (2) **Irrebuttable Presumption.** Que una vez probado un hecho, un supuesto está establecido, por ejemplo, un niño de cinco años no puede cometer un crimen.

PRESUMPTIVE. Presunto. Que puede deducirse.

PRESUMPTIVE TRUST. Véase "Resulting Trust".

PRETERMITTED HEIR. Descendiente que intencionalmente se deja fuera de un testamento o que nació después de que el testamento fuera hecho.

PRE–TRIAL DISCOVERY. Mecanismos procesales para obtener información de las partes.

PRE–TRIAL ORDER. Ordenes de la corte que controlan cómo se desenvuelve el juicio.

PREVAILING PARTY. Parte victoriosa. La persona o parte que gana el juicio.

PREVENTIVE DETENTION. Detención preventiva. Detener a una o varias personas en contra de su voluntad porque se sospecha que cometieron un delito o que han perdido sus facultades.

PREVENTIVE LAW. Derecho preventivo. Asistencia legal e información creada para ayudar a las personas a evitar problemas legales.

PRICE–FIXING. Acción cooperativa para mantener los precios entre empresas.

PRIMA FACIE. A primera vista. Hecho que inicialmente podría considerarse como cierto a menos que se descubriera una evidencia contradictoria.

PRIMARY ELECTION. Elección primaria. Proceso electoral por el cual un partido político selecciona a sus candidatos para competir para un puesto en una elección popular.

PRIMARY EVIDENCE. Evidencia primaria. La mejor evidencia para probar un punto.

PRIMARY JURISDICTION DOCTRINE. Si el caso trata de materias sobre cuya decisión actúa una agencia administrativa, esta doctrina le permite a la corte mantenerse al margen del caso y abstenerse hasta que la agencia tenga la oportunidad de resolver el caso.

PRIME. Primario; original; más importante.

PRIMOGENITURE. Primogénito(a). El/la primer(a) hijo(a).

PRINCIPAL. Principal. (1) Jefe más importante. Primario. (2) Actor directamente involucrado en la comisión de un delito. (3) Mandante. El que solicita a otro que le represente.

PRINCIPAL PLACE OF BUSINESS. Lugar principal de negocios. Plaza más importante en la que una empresa realiza sus negocios.

PRINCIPLE. Principio. (1) Una verdad legal básica. (2) Doctrina. (3) Una generalización.

PRIOR INCONSISTENT STATEMENTS. Manifestaciones anteriores inconsistentes. Declaraciones hechas por un testigo fuera de la corte que contradicen a su testimonio en corte, y que pueden usarse solamente para desacreditar su testimonio.

PRIORITY. Prioridad. (1) Preferencia de una cosa sobre otra. (2) El derecho de tener preferencia sobre otro.

PRISON. Prisión. Lugar donde son recluidas las personas que se encuentran cumpliendo una pena por haber cometido un delito.

PRISONER. Prisionero. Cualquier persona privada de su libertad, ya sea porque se le acusa de haber cometido un delito o porque se le ha condenado por haberlo cometido.

PRIVACY. Privacidad. El derecho de tener una vida privada.

PRIVACY ACT. Leyes que regulan la privacidad. Leyes federales y estatales que restringen el acceso a la información personal y financiera de un individuo y que prohíben el uso de aparatos electrónicos y otros tipos de vigilancia.

PRIVATE. Privado. Que concierne a individuos y no al público en general o al gobierno.

PRIVATE ATTORNEY GENERAL. Individuo que va a las cortes para hacer cumplir los derechos públicos de todos los ciudadanos.

PRIVATE CITIZEN. Ciudadano particular. Que no tiene carácter público ni oficial.

PRIVATE INTERNATIONAL LAW. Derecho internacional privado. Leyes que rigen las relaciones entre particulares de diversas naciones o estados. Véase "Conflict of Laws".

PRIVATE LAW. Derecho privado. (1) Legislación que afecta a una persona o grupo, lo opuesto a derecho político. (2) La ley que regula las relaciones entre personas o grupos mercantiles, civiles, etc.

PRIVIES. Véase "Privity" o "Privy".

PRIVILEGE. Secreto. Privilegio. (1) Una ventaja; el derecho a trato preferencial. (2) Derecho básico. (3) El derecho o el deber de mantener en secreto cierta información debido a una relación especial. Por ejemplo, relación entre marido y mujer, periodista e informante, etc.

PRIVILEGED COMMUNICATION. Comunicaciones protegidas por el secreto profesional. Derecho a mantener secreto el contenido de una comunicación. Véase "Confidentiality" y "Privilege".

PRIVITY. Relación común o financiera. Copartícipes.

PRIVY. (1) Personas que tienen una relación común. (2) "Privado".

PRIZE. Premio, recompensa.

PRIZE LAW. Derecho sobre los barcos capturados en guerras.

PRO. A favor. Por.

PRO BONO PUBLICO. (Lat.) Para el bienestar público.

PRO FORMA. (Lat.) (1) Mera formalidad. (2) Proyectar. (3) Ante proyecto.

PRO RATA. (Lat.) Por partes. Proporcionalmente, de acuerdo a una relación, un porcentaje o una medida.

PRO SE. (Lat.) Para sí mismo. En su propio interés.

PRO TANTO. (Lat.) En una porción igual, por la misma cantidad.

PRO TEM o PRO TEMPORE. (Lat.) Temporalmente, provisionalmente.

PROBABLE CAUSE. Causa presunta; motivo fundado. Causa que justifica una acción legal.

PROBATE. El proceso de validar un testamento y distribuir la propiedad contenida en él.

PROBATION. (1) Libertad condicional. (2) Libertad dada a una persona condenada por un delito. Estar fuera de la cárcel bajo condiciones supervisadas. (3) Período de prueba.

PROBATIONER. Persona bajo libertad condicional.

PROBATIVE. Probatorio. Que tiende a probar o que prueba algo.

PROBATIVE FACTS. Véase "Evidentiary Facts".

PROCEDURAL LAW. Derecho o ley procesal. Las reglas del procedimiento para llevar a cabo una demanda.

PROCEDURE. Procedimiento. Las reglas y métodos para llevar a cabo una demanda hasta su conclusión.

PROCEEDINGS. Actuaciones; proceso. (1) Un caso en la corte. (2) El procedimiento de un caso en la corte. (3) El historial de un caso. (4) Cualquier acción tomada por un órgano gubernamental.

PROCEEDS. Producto, ganancia. Dinero o propiedad ganados en una transacción.

PROCESS. Proceso, auto, citación. (1) Orden de la corte que cita al demandado a que se presente ante ésta. (2) Cualquier decisión de la corte que pone formalmente bajo su disposición a una persona o propiedad. (3) Método legal de operar. (4) Reglas de tramitación.

PROCESS SERVER. Notificador. Entregador de la citación. Persona con autoridad legal para formalmente entregar documentos de la corte al demandado, tales como citaciones, notificaciones.

PROCLAMATION. Proclamación. Declaración formal de un gobierno hecha para el conocimiento general.

PROCTOR. Apoderado. Procurador. (1) Alguien nombrado para manejar los asuntos de otra persona. (2) Un abogado o representante, especialmente en la ley marítima.

PROCURE. Adquirir; causar. Hacer que algo suceda, hacer algo para alguien.

PROCURING CAUSE. Causa inmediata. Lo que directamente origina un hecho. Véase "Proximate Cause".

PRODUCE. (1) Producir. Enseñar, mostrar. (2) **Motion to Produce o Motion for Production.** Son peticiones para que el juez ordene a la otra parte mostrar al peticionario documentos específicos.

PRODUCING CAUSE. Véase "Proximate Cause" y "Procuring Cause".

PRODUCT LIABILITY. Responsabilidad derivada del producto. La responsabilidad de un fabricante o vendedor de un producto de pagar por daños causados al comprador o a terceras personas por defectos en el producto.

PROFESSIONAL ASSOCIATION. Asociación profesional. Cualquier grupo de profesionales que se organizan para propósitos sociales, educativos, de lucro, etc. Por ejemplo, un colegio de abogados.

PROFESSIONAL PREPARER. Profesional especializado en la preparación de declaraciones de impuestos.

PROFESSIONAL RESPONSIBILITY. Responsabilidad professional. Véase "Code of Professional Responsibility".

PROFFER o PROFER o PROFERT. Oferta o presentación.

PROFIT. Ganancia. Todos los beneficios, incluyendo dinero y valorización de propiedades. Que se obtienen en una transacción.

PROFIT AND LOSS STATEMENT. Balance de ganancias y pérdidas. Utilidad.

PROFIT SHARING. Participación en los beneficios. Plan establecido por los empleadores para distribuir parte de las ganancias de la compañía entre sus empleados.

PROFITEERING. Usura. Obtener ganancias irrazonables, tomando ventaja de circunstancias especiales.

PROGRESSIVE TAX. Impuesto progresivo. Sistema de impuestos que impone un mayor porcentaje a medida que se hacen mayores las sumas ganadas. Lo opuesto a "regressive tax".

PROHIBITED DEGREES. Relación consanguínea demasiado cercana que no permite el matrimonio legal.

PROHIBITION. Prohibición. Orden o advertencia que prohíbe realizar ciertas acciones.

PROLIXITY. Usar demasiadas palabras, hechos, teorías, etc., en documentos presentados en la corte.

PROMISE. Promesa. Declaración que, moral o legalmente, o de otra manera, obliga a quien declara a hacer algo. Afirmación de hacer algo en el futuro.

PROMISSORY ESTOPPEL. Impedimento promisorio. Principio bajo el cual si una persona hace una promesa a otra, y esta última persona actúa basándose en la promesa, la ley obligará al promitente a cumplirla.

PROMISSORY NOTE. Pagaré. Promesa escrita de pagar una suma de dinero en una fecha dada o cuando se requiera.

PROMOTER. Promotor. Persona que forma una sociedad o corporación. Quien promueve algo.

PROMULGATE. Promulgar. Publicar; anunciar oficialmente. Dar a conocer.

PRONOUNCE. Pronunciar. Dicho formal y oficialmente.

PROOF. Prueba. (1) Evidencia que da validez a un argumento. Los hechos sobre los cuales se puede basar una conclusión. (2) El resultado de evidencia convincente.

PROPER. Apropiado. Adecuado, justo.

PROPERTY. Propiedad. (1) Propiedad de una cosa. El derecho legal de propiedad sobre algo. (2) Cualquier cosa que sea o pueda ser apropiada. (3) **Real Property.** Una propiedad inmueble, bienes raíces. (4) **Personal Property.** Bienes muebles.

PROPERTY TAX. Impuesto patrimonial. Impuesto sobre la propiedad basado en el valor de la misma.

PROPONENT. Oferente. La persona que ofrece o propone algo. Persona que hace una proposición.

PROPOSAL. Propuesta. (1) Oferta que puede ser aceptada y que de serlo crearía un contrato. (2) Exposición preliminar o exploratoria de una idea para su discusión.

PROPRIETARY. Propietario. Que tiene que ver con la propiedad. Dueño.

PROPRIETORSHIP. Propiedad. Dueño.

PRO–RATE. Prorratear. Dividir en partes proporcionales o por acciones. Véase "Pro Rate".

PROROGATION. Prórroga. Demora, continuación. Extensión del término.

PROSECUTE. Procesar, encausar, enjuiciar. (1) Comenzar y darle seguimiento a una demanda civil. (2) Acusar a una persona de haber cometido un delito y llevarla a juicio.

PROSECUTION. El acto de procesar, encausar o enjuiciar un caso, sea en lo criminal o en lo civil.

PROSECUTOR. Acusador público, fiscal. (1) Funcionario público que presenta el caso a nombre del Estado contra una persona acusada de haber cometido un delito; tal funcionario solicita a la corte que condene al acusado.

PROSECUTORIAL DISCRETION. El poder que tiene un acusador público para decidir si proceder o no a acusar a una persona de un delito; facultad para ver qué tan seria debe ser la acusación, qué pena solicitar, etc.

PROSPECTIVE. Que se anticipa. Que tiene que ver con el futuro.

PROSPECTUS. (Lat.) Prospecto. (1) Documento que tiene como objeto describir una corporación para interesar a las personas en comprar acciones de esa compañía. (2) Cualquier oferta que tiene el propósito de interesar a las personas en comprar títulos o valores. (3) Documento que tiene el propósito de interesar a las personas en algún negocio.

PROSSER ON TORTS. Libro escrito por un tratadista llamado Prosser sobre cómo establecer daños y perjuicios bajo ciertas teorías y doctrinas legales. Véase "Torts".

PROSTITUTION. Prostitución. Persona que ofrece su cuerpo para propósitos sexuales a cambio de dinero.

PROTECTIVE CUSTODY. Custodia protectora. Poner a una persona en la cárcel, una institución mental, en un lugar secreto, etc., para su propia seguridad, quiéralo o no la persona. Esta situación se le puede presentar a un testigo en un caso que involucre a un acusado peligroso; a un ebrio; a un enfermo mental, etc.

PROTECTIVE ORDER o PROTECTION ORDER. (1) Orden de la corte que permite temporalmente a una parte no mostrar a la otra documentos que han sido solicitados. (2) Cualquier orden de la corte que protege a una persona acusada, molestada o con problemas similares. (3) Orden de la corte que pone a una persona bajo protección custodiada.

PROTECTORATE. Protectorado. País al cual otro le maneja sus relaciones internacionales.

PROTEST. Protesta. (1) Declaración escrita en la cual se hace saber que no se está de acuerdo con un pago legal, judicial o multa, pero que se paga, reservándose el derecho de recuperar el dinero. (2) Certificado formal de que se ha desatendido el pago de un documento negociable cuando éste fue presentado para su pago.

PROTHONOTARY. Protonotario. El oficial mayor de algunas cortes.

PROTOCOL. Protocolo. (1) Documento preliminar de un acuerdo o reunión entre naciones. (2) Formalidades. (3) Etiqueta de la diplomacia internacional. (4) Sumario corto de un documento. (5) Las minutas de una reunión.

PROVE. Probar, establecer con certeza.

PROVISIONAL. Provisional. Temporal o preliminar. Que no es permanente.

PROVISO. Condición. Limitación contenida en un documento.

PROVOCATION. Provocación. El acto de causar una reacción de ira en otra persona para que actúe de cierta manera.

PROXIMATE CAUSE. Causa inmediata. La causa real de un accidente o daño. Aquello que directamente produce un resultado.

PROXY. Poder, delegación. Apoderado. (1) Persona que actúa a nombre de otra. (2) Documento que da el derecho a una persona para actuar por otra.

PRURIENT INTEREST. Interés obsesivo o vergonzoso en cosas inmorales o sexuales.

PUBLIC. Público. (1) Que tiene que ver con el estado, la nación o la comunidad en general. (2) Los habitantes de un lugar. Las personas en general.

PUBLIC DEFENDER. Defensor de oficio. Defensor público. Abogado contratado por el gobierno para representar a personas pobres acusadas de un delito.

PUBLIC DOMAIN. Dominio público. Propiedades que pertenecen a la nación. (2) Para el uso público. Que ya no está protegido por una patente o derecho de autor.

PUBLIC INTEREST. Interés público. (1) Término general para referirse a cualquier cosa que afecte al público, la economía, la salud y los derechos de la comunidad.

PUBLIC LAW. Derecho público. El estudio de la ley que tiene que ver con el manejo del gobierno o las relaciones entre las personas y el gobierno.

PUBLIC OFFICE. Puesto público. Término utilizado para referirse a cualquier cargo en el gobierno con funciones independientes.

PUBLIC POLICY. Política pública. Política gubernamental para el bienestar público.

PUBLIC UTILITY. Empresa de servicios públicos, tales como la electricidad, obras públicas, el alcantarillado, etc.

PUBLICATION. Publicación. Hacer público.

PUFFING. Declaraciones hechas por un vendedor con respecto a su producto haciendo alarde del producto en forma general. No son promesas o declaraciones específicas sobre el producto.

PUNISHMENT. Castigo. Multa o pena contra una persona impuesta por la corte.

PUNITIVE DAMAGES. Daños punitivos o ejemplares. Cantidad de dinero superior al valor del perjuicio que es otorgada por la corte a una persona cuando ha sufrido un daño que le ha sido causado de forma maliciosa o mal intencionada por otra persona.

PURCHASE AGREEMENT u ORDER. Orden de compra. Documento que autoriza a una persona a entregar mercancías o propiedad o a realizar un servicio para otra persona que promete pagar.

PURE PLEA. Defensa afirmativa. Defensa que exime de culpabilidad. Alegato que no necesita nada más para ser decidido por el juez. Aceptación de una acusación presentando una justificación aceptable.

PURGE. Purgar. (1) Disculpar. Exonerar de los cargos o de la culpa de algo o de un contrato. (2) En materia testamentaria, significa omitir a una persona mencionada en el testamento para que esta persona no herede nada sin alterar el resto del testamento.

PURPORT. (1) Pretender, dar la impresión, aparentar. (2) El significado, la intención, el propósito o la substancia de algo.

PURSUANT. Conforme a; de acuerdo con; de conformidad con.

PUTATIVE. Putativo, alegado, supuesto. Que es de conocimiento general. Que aparenta ser.

PYROMANIA. Piromanía. Atracción por el fuego.

Q

Q.B. Siglas de Queen's Bench. Audiencia Real.

QUA. (Lat.) Como. Considerado como. Como a sí mismo. En su carácter de.

QUAE. (Lat.) Cosas. Ciertas cosas. Cosas ya mencionadas.

QUAE EST EADEM. (Lat.) Lo que es lo mismo.

QUAERE. Una pregunta, una duda.

QUALIFICATION. Calificación. (1) Que posee las cualidades personales o aptitudes necesarias para ocupar un puesto público. (2) Limitación o restricción.

QUALIFIED. Condicional, limitado, calificado. Que reúne los requisitos.

QUALIFIED ACCEPTANCE. Aceptación condicionada. Aceptación que puede ser condicional o parcial y que altera la suma, forma o lugar de pago. En asuntos contractuales esta forma de aceptación varía los términos de la oferta por lo que se convierte en una contra oferta.

QUALIFIED EARNED INCOME. Ingreso producto del trabajo considerado para los fines del cálculo de ingresos al trabajar ambos cónyuges.

QUALIFIED INDORSEMENT. Endoso limitado o condicional. Firmar un instrumento negociable limitando la responsabilidad de pago. Limita o califica la responsabilidad del endosante.

QUALIFIED PRIVILEGE. Privilegio condicionado. (1) El derecho de publicar o decir algo que perjudica a una persona si ésto se hace sin malicia. (2) El derecho, bajo determinadas circunstancias, de retener información y no dársela a la otra parte en un juicio.

QUALIFIED. Véase "Qualification".

QUALIFY. Véase "Qualification".

QUANTUM MERUIT. (Lat.) Tanto como se merece. Doctrina equitativa que reconoce la responsabilidad civil a consecuencia del beneficio recibido por un contrato implícito.

QUANTUM VALEBAT. (Lat.) Tanto como vale.

QUARANTINE. Cuarentena. El derecho legal que tiene un gobierno de mantener aislados, por un período de tiempo, una nave, una persona, animales, etc., así como de prohibir el transporte de mercancías, con el propósito de prevenir la propagación de una enfermedad, peste, etc.

QUASH. Anular, invalidar.

QUASI. (Lat.) Casi. Parecido a; como si...; una clase de....

QUASI o CONSTRUCTIVE CONTRACT. Cuasi contrato. Una obligación casi contractual creada, no por un acuerdo, sino por la ley.

QUASI CORPORATION. Véase "Joint Stock Company".

QUASI IN REM. (Lat.) Véase "In Rem". Jurisdicción de la corte sobre un bien que también otorga jurisdicción sobre una persona.

QUASI–JUDICIAL. Cuando una agencia administrativa actúa como una corte.

QUASI–LEGISLATIVE. Cuando una agencia administrativa actúa como un cuerpo legislativo y crea reglamentos.

QUERY. Pregunta.

QUESTION. Pregunta, cuestionamiento, problema. (1) Materia que se va a investigar, debatir, etc. (2) Un punto en disputa en un pleito; materia que será decidída por un juez o jurado.

QUESTIONER. Interrogador. Persona que hace preguntas.

QUESTIONNAIRE. Cuestionario. Documento que contiene preguntas.

QUICK ASSETS. Los activos de una compañía que pueden ser fácil y rápidamente convertidos en activos líquidos para uso inmediato en caso de emergencia.

QUID PRO QUO. Una cosa por otra. Dar alguna cosa de valor por otra. Consideración o intercambio que hace un contrato válido.

QUIET. Tranquilo, quieto. Libre de interferencias o interrupciones.

QUIET ENJOYMENT. Posesión y goce pacífico de una propiedad.

QUIETUS. (Lat.) Descargo final de una obligación o deuda.

QUIT. Dejar, cesar. Renunciar. (1) Irse y abandonar la posesión de un lugar. (2) Estar libre o absuelto de una deuda o de un cargo criminal.

QUITCLAIM DEED. Finiquito. Escritura que traspasa al comprador todos los derechos de un título que el vendedor posee. Renuncia de derechos.

QUO ANIMO. (Lat.) "Con qué intención o motivo".

QUORUM. El mínimo número de personas que deben estar presentes para que una votación o cualquier otra acción de un grupo sea válida.

QUOTA. Cuota. (1) Meta o cantidad asignada. (2) Límite. (3) Parte proporcional de una responsabilidad.

QUOTATION. Cita. Reproducción textual de una ley o caso para fundar un argumento.

QUOTE. Citar; cotizar un precio.

QUO WARRANTO. (Lat.) "Con qué autoridad".

R

RACKET. Extorsión sistematizada. Actividades para ganar dinero mediante actos ilegales. Indica una conducta ilegal contínua.

RACKETEERING. Extorsión por crimen organizado o en gran escala. Conducta organizada de juegos ilegales, tráfico de narcóticos, prostitución, etc.

RAISE. Levantar, cuestionar, presentar. (1) **Raise an Issue.** Presentar un punto legal en una demanda o en un juicio. (2) **Raise a Presumption.** Levantar una presunción.

RAKE OFF. Ganancia o tajada ilegal. Estratagema para que las ganancias de un negocio no se reporten en los libros del negocio.

RANGE. Parámetro o extensión. En el área de bienes raíces, se refiere a una o varias parcelas de terreno que han sido identificadas en un estudio topográfico del gobierno.

RANSOM. Dinero o propiedad pagada a cambio de poner en libertad a una persona secuestrada, o para liberar a personas o propiedades capturadas durante la guerra. En la ley inglesa antigua, dinero pagado para obtener el perdón por un gran crimen.

RAPE. Violar. (1) Coito ilícito con una mujer u hombre sin su consentimiento o mediante el uso de fuerza o amenaza de fuerza. En ciertos casos, este crimen se define en términos de actos sexuales que no son naturales. (2) **Statutory Rape.** Crimen cometido al tener relaciones sexuales con un menor de edad, con o sin el consentimiento del menor.

RATE. Tarifa, tasa, tipo de interés, impuesto. Cantidad fijada por fórmulas matemáticas o ajustadas de acuerdo con ciertas normas.

RATIFY. Ratificar, aprobar, hacer válido, sancionar.

RATIFICATION. Confirmación de un acto previo. Por ejemplo, cuando el presidente firma un tratado, éste debe ser ratificado por el Senado.

RATIO DECIDENDI. (Lat.) El punto en el caso que determina la decisión del juez.

RATIO LEGIS. (Lat.) Razón o propósito legislativo para pasar la ley; el problema o la situación que justifica la necesidad de la ley. Teoría sobre la cual se basa la ley.

RATIONAL BASIS (o PURPOSE) TEST. Principio bajo el cual la corte no debe cuestionar la sabiduría de la ley (o de una decisión administrativa) si la ley (o decisión) tiene una base razonable.

RAVISHMENT. Violación. Véase "Rape".

RE. (Lat.) Con respecto a.

READJUSTMENT. Reorganización de una compañía con problemas financieros llevada a cabo voluntariamente por sus accionistas.

REAFFIRMATION. Reafirmación. Acuerdo para pagar una deuda irrecuperable. Bajo la ley de contratos y bancarrota, si una deuda se reafirma (con la aprobación de la corte, en caso de bancarrota), el deudor es nuevamente responsable por ésta.

REAL. (1) Relacionado a terrenos o bienes inmuebles y a las cosas permanentemente conectadas a estos bienes, como los edificios. (2) **Real Defense.** Defensa real. Una defensa basada en la validez de un documento, además de las circunstancias que la rodean. Defensas reales incluyen: falsificación del documento, el hecho de que la persona que firma sea un menor o la alteración del documento.

REAL ESTATE. Bienes raíces o predios. Un bien inmueble. Se refiere a edificios, terrenos o propiedad integrada al predio.

REAL EVIDENCE. Evidencia física vista por el jurado. Por ejemplo, heridas, huellas digitales, armas usadas en el crimen, etc. Es un tipo de evidencia demostrativa.

REAL PARTY IN INTEREST. Alguien que tiene el derecho legal de presentar una demanda, aun cuando esta persona no será beneficiada por un fallo en su favor.

REALTOR. Corredor o vendedor de bienes raíces.

655

REALTY. Véase "Real Estate."

REAPPORTIONMENT. (1) Cambio de las fronteras de distritos legislativos para reflejar cambios en la población y así asegurar que el voto de cada persona tenga igual peso. (2) Cambiar los distritos electorales para que reflejen los cambios en la población según la constitución.

REASONABLE. Razonable, apropiado, racional, justo, equitativo, prudente, moderado. Término legal que normalmente se usa junto a otra palabra para indicar que la acción, expectación o actitud es justificada y prudente bajo tales circunstancias.

REASSESS. El revalúo de una propiedad o un bien.

REBELLION. Rebelión. Resistencia armada y organizada contra las leyes y operaciones del gobierno.

REBUS SIC STANTIBUS. (Lat.) Bajo las circunstancias corrientes. Doctrina dentro de la ley internacional que estipula que si las condiciones cambian después de establecerse un tratado, el tratado no tendrá efecto.

REBUT. Refutar. Contestar un cargo, refutar un supuesto, contradecir lo expuesto.

REBUTTABLE. Refutable, disputable. Que se puede contradecir.

REBUTTABLE PRESUMPTION. Presunción disputable. Presunción que puede refutarse con evidencia contraria.

RECAPITALIZATION. Recapitalización. Reajuste del tipo, cantidad, valor y prioridad de las acciones de una corporación.

RECEIVER. Recaudador, administrador judicial, síndico. Persona imparcial asignada por la corte que tiene la custodia de un bien, de un activo o de una propiedad durante una demanda.

RECEIVERSHIP. Procedimiento legal mediante el cual un administrador judicial es nombrado por la corte para proteger los bienes y activos de una persona o entidad.

RECEIVING STOLEN GOODS. Ofensa criminal que consiste en poseer propiedad sabiendo que ha sido robada.

RECENT THEFT RULE. Principio bajo el cual al encontrarse una cosa recientemente robada en poder de una persona, se infiere que él o ella es el ladrón.

RECESS. Receso. La suspensión temporal de una sesión de la corte. Receso corto tomado por la corte.

RECIDIVIST. Un criminal habitual, considerado como incorregible; criminal reincidente.

RECIPROCAL. Mutuo, recíproco. Intercambio; dar o recibir mutuamente.

RECIPROCAL TRADE AGREEMENT. Acuerdo entre dos países para reducir los impuestos de importación en la mercancía que se trafica entre ambos países.

RESCISION. Rescisión. Cancelar un contrato cuando la otra parte ha incumplido. Véase "Rescission" y "Rescind".

RECITAL. Narración. Declaración formal en un documento que explica las razones por las cuales se ha suscrito el documento o se ha hecho la transacción que atañe al documento. Cualquier lista de hechos específicos en un documento.

RECKLESS. Acto que es imprudente, descuidado, negligente o inconsecuente. Una acción que demuestra indiferencia a las consecuencias probables del acto.

RECLAIM. Reclamar o pedir algo. Pedir la restitución de un derecho o un objeto.

RECOGNITION. Ratificar, confirmar. Reconocer y admitir que una acción llevada a cabo por otra persona en nombre ajeno en realidad fue autorizada por uno.

RECOGNIZANCE. Reconocimiento. Obligación establecida frente a la corte para hacer algo.

RECOLLECTION. Acto de recordar.

RECORD. Registro. (1) Recuento formal de un caso, que contiene la historia completa de todas las acciones tomadas, opiniones escritas, papeles archivados, etc. El "record" puede incluir evidencia actual (testimonio, objetos físicos, etc.) como también la evidencia que fue rehusada por el juez. (2) Documentos que demuestran lo ocurrido ante una corte en un procedimiento legal y sobre los cuales la corte ha basado su veredicto. (3) Archivo, registro, acta, constancia, autos. En un procedimiento judicial, el "record" es utilizado para las apelaciones y para proteger a las partes.

RECORD, PUBLIC. Documento archivado o preparado por una agencia del gobierno, el cual puede ser inspeccionado por el público.

RECOUPMENT. Recuperar algo (especialmente dinero perdido). Contrademanda.

RECOURSE. Recurso o remedio. (1) Recurso legal que una persona tiene contra otra. En el área de instrumentos comerciales, se refiere a la capacidad para reclamar contra una de las partes que anteriormente poseía el instrumento. (2) El derecho de una persona que tiene un instrumento negociable de recibir pago por éste de cualquiera que lo endose, si la persona que lo giró en primera instancia se rehúsa a pagar.

RECOVER. Recobrar, recuperar, obtener un fallo judicial contra otro. Generalmente, recobrar los daños sufridos por medio de una acción legal.

RECOVERY. Recobro, recuperación. Lo que se recibe cuando la corte decide a favor de uno. La cantidad de dinero otorgada por un jurado al ganar una demanda.

RECTUM. (Lat.) Derecho; juicio o acusación.

RECUSATION. Recusación. Proceso por el cual un juez es descalificado (o se descalifica él o ella misma) para escuchar una demanda porque tiene interés o perjuicio sobre el caso.

REDDENDUM. (Lat.) Cláusula en una escritura o título de propiedad en que se reserva el derecho de reversión o sucesión.

REDEEM. Redimir, rescatar; cumplir con una obligación. Implica el cancelar un gravamen sobre una propiedad mediante el pago de la obligación o la deuda. Reclamo de una propiedad que ha sido hipotecada o empeñada.

REDEMPTION. Redención; rescate. La cancelación de un gravamen que restituye el terreno al dueño. El derecho que tiene un dueño a cancelar, dentro de un tiempo fijo, su obligación con una autoridad fiscal para que cualquier terreno que haya sido vendido para pagar impuestos morosos sea restituido al dueño.

REDEMPTION PERIOD. (1) Período de tiempo durante el cual se puede redimir una propiedad que ha sido vendida por subasta o venta pública después de un juicio hipotecario. (2) También se refiere al período para cancelar una deuda y así recobrar una propiedad que se ha vendido por orden judicial.

REDEMPTION PRICE. El precio que debe pagar un deudor para recobrar una propiedad vendida por orden judicial.

RED HERRING. En el área de finanzas, se refiere a la copia preliminar de un prospecto sometido para la aprobación de una agencia que regula la emisión de valores.

REDLINING. Negativa de un banco para hacer préstamos en un vecindario particular porque el vecindario se está deteriorando. Esta práctica viola las leyes federales y es prohibida por leyes de discriminación racial.

REDRESS. Reparación. Cumplimiento o pago por un mal acto para rectificarlo.

RED TAPE. Término que indica los requisitos interminables de una burocracia.

REDUCTIO AD ABSURDUM. (Lat.) Reducción a lo absurdo. Refutar un argumento al demostrar que éste puede llegar a una conclusión ridícula.

REDUNDANCY. Redundancia. Asunto repetitivo o irrelevante.

REENACTMENT RULE. Principio bajo el cual si una legislación reestablece una ley (ya sea para prevenir que ésta se expire o para hacer pequeños cambios), se adopta nuevamente la interpretación sobre la ley vieja hecha por las cortes o por el gobierno.

REFER. Referir, someter. Acción de un juez de pasar un caso o parte de un caso a una persona que ha sido asignada para tomar declaraciones, hacer recomendaciones, examinar documentos y tomar decisiones.

REFEREE. Arbitro, componedor, ponente. En el caso de bancarrota, se refiere a una persona asignada por la corte para intervenir en la venta o administración de los bienes.

REFERENCE. (1) Acuerdo en un contrato para someter o referir a arbitraje cualquier problema que surja con respecto al contrato. (2) Acto de mandar un caso a un funcionario auxiliar del tribunal. (3) Persona que provee información sobre el carácter, crédito, etc., de una persona.

REFERENDUM. Proceso bajo el cual el electorado tiene la oportunidad de aprobar un cambio de ley o una nueva constitución.

REFINANCE. Refinanciar. El acto de cancelar una deuda con fondos provenientes de un préstamo nuevo.

REFORM. Reforma, reformar, cambiar. Cuando se modifica un documento por las partes.

REFORMATION. Reposición. Procedimiento bajo el cual la corte modifica, corrige o reforma un acuerdo para que concuerde con la intención original de las personas que están haciendo el trato. La corte hace esto únicamente si existe un fraude o un error mutuo al haberse escrito el documento original.

REFORMATORY. Reformatorio. Prisión para jóvenes delincuentes.

REGISTER. Registro, archivo; inscribir. (1) Libro de hechos públicos en el cual se registran los nacimientos, las muertes y los matrimonios. (2) Oficial público que trabaja en estos libros. (3) Inscribir información dentro de estos libros.

REGISTER OF DEEDS. (1) Registrador de títulos de propiedad. (2) **Register a Trademark.** Registrar una marca. (3) **Register a Title.** Registrar un título. Inscribir un documento de propiedad.

REGISTERED. Registrado o registrada. Que ha sido inscrito y se tiene registro de su existencia y titular.

REGISTERED MAIL. Correo certificado o registrado.

REGULATE. Regular, reglamentar.

REGULATION. Reglamento. Una regla que tiene igual efecto que una ley, y que es impuesta por una agencia administrativa para regular ciertas actividades controladas por las leyes.

REGULATORY OFFENSE. Crímenes establecidos por violar un reglamento. Ofensa definida por una regla más que por una ley.

REHABILITATION. Rehabilitación. Restablecer la credibilidad, el poder, la autoridad, la dignidad o el derecho de algo. (1) En el área corporativa, cuando se trata de continuar las actividades de una compañía mediante su recapitulación o reestructuración financiera. (2) Cuando un testigo es examinado por una de las partes con el objeto de restablecer la credibilidad del testigo o aclarar parte de su testimonio.

REHEARING. Examinar los méritos de un caso por segunda vez.

REIMBURSE. Reembolsar, indemnizar. Pagar un gasto incurrido o daño causado.

REINSTATEMENT. Restablecer, reponer. En seguros, la restauración de los derechos de un asegurado después de que su póliza ha caducado.

REINSURANCE. Reaseguro. (1) Contrato a través del cual todo o parte del riesgo que tomó una compañía está reasegurado con otra compañía. (2) Mecanismo contractual para redistribuir riesgos en el área de seguros.

RELATED. Relacionado. Emparentado. Que tiene relación con otro.

RELATION. (1) Relación; pariente. Una persona relacionada a otra por familia. (2) Una ficción legal que relaciona un acto a otro evento.

RELATIVE. Pariente. Familiar.

RELATIVE FACT. Prueba circunstancial; hecho relativo o secundario.

RELATOR. Relator. Persona a nombre de quien el estado o un gobierno demanda a alguien.

661

RELEASE. Abandonar, liberar o descargar una demanda o derecho. Acción mediante la cual una persona libera a otra de una demanda u obligación legal.

RELEVANT. Relevante. Algo que tiene impacto sobre una cuestión o hecho. La evidencia es relevante si ésta tiende a probar o desaprobar una teoría o posición, la cual influirá en los resultados de la demanda. La evidencia debe ser relevante para ser aceptada o admitida por la corte.

RELIANCE. Acto de creer en un hecho o una representación (aunque ésta no sea cierta) y actuar de acuerdo con esa creencia.

RELIEF. Socorro, asistencia. Satisfacción o reparación brindada por la corte a la persona que demanda. Esta ayuda puede ser el retorno de una propiedad adquirida por otra persona, la ejecución de un contrato, etc.

REMAND. Devolver; reencarcelar; mandar de vuelta. Acto de una corte superior que manda un caso de vuelta a una corte inferior para que ésta tome las acciones ordenadas por la corte superior.

REMEDIAL. Reparador; reparar un daño o un mal. Ofrecer algún remedio legal. Véase "Remedy".

REMEDIAL LAW o STATUTE. Ley pasada para corregir algún defecto en la ley anterior. Ley reparadora.

REMEDY. Recurso; remedio. Manera por la cual un derecho se hace valer. Satisfacción recibida por un daño ocasionado. Medio por el cual la violación de derechos puede ser evitada, reparada o compensada.

REMIT. Enviar, remitir, transferir. En lo penal, se refiere a la reducción del período de condena.

REMISE. Liberar, renunciar o perdonar.

REMISSION. Renunciar o perdonar una deuda. Perdonar una ofensa o un daño causado.

REMITTITUR. Remisión, devolución. (1) El poder que tiene un juez para disminuir la cantidad de dinero determinado por el jurado a favor del demandante. (2) El poder que tiene una corte de apelación para negarle un nuevo juicio al demandado si el demandante acepta tomar una cantidad de dinero menor del que se le ofrece en el juicio.

REMOTE. Algo distante, remoto o inconsecuente.

REMOVAL. Remoción. Remover una cosa o persona. También se usa al remover un caso a las cortes federales o al descalificar a un juez.

REMUNERATION. Remuneración. Retribución generalmente económica por un ejercicio prestado.

RENDER. Pronunciar o declarar. Cuando un juez pronuncia una sentencia al hacer saber su decisión sobre un caso en la corte.

RENDITION. Cuando un estado entrega a otro estado un fugitivo de la justicia.

RENEW. Renovar, prorrogar. Mantener un acuerdo vivo; extender el período de una deuda.

RENT. Alquiler.

RENT STRIKE. Negativa de un inquilino a pagar la renta para forzar al propietario a que haga algo.

RENUNCIATION. Renuncia, renunciación; abandonar. Abandono de un derecho sin transferirlo a otra persona.

RENVOI. Doctrina bajo la cual una corte utiliza las leyes de un país extranjero para escoger las leyes que deben aplicarse al caso.

REORGANIZATION. Reorganización. El acto o proceso de reorganizar algo. En el área corporativa, se refiere a la restructuración de los pasivos y el capital de una compañía al cancelar obligaciones y valores existentes mediante la emisión de nuevas acciones, valores y bonos.

REPARATION. Reparación, corrección, enmienda, restauración. Pagar con el objeto de restaurar al ofendido lo equivalente a lo dañado o tomado. El acto de compensar con dinero por un daño causado.

REPEAL. Revocar, abrogar, derogar por un estatuto o una ley.

REPLEVIN. Acción legal para recobrar la propiedad personal que injustamente se encuentra en las manos de otra persona.

REPLY. Contestación, respuesta, réplica. En un proceso legal, la réplica es la respuesta del acusado o demandado a los alegatos del demandante. La réplica niega, admite o desconoce los hechos en la demanda.

REPORT. Reportar. Declaración oficial o formal de hechos o procedimientos.

REPORTER. (1) Volúmenes publicados donde figuran decisiones tomadas por la corte o por un grupo de cortes. (2) Persona que recopila reportes. (3) **Court Reporter.** La persona que registra los sucesos que se llevan a cabo en la corte.

REPRESENT. Representar. Decir o declarar ciertos hechos. Actuar como abogado de alguien representándolo.

REPRESENTATION. Representación. Cualquier declaración presentada para convencer a la otra persona de que ciertos hechos son ciertos.

REPRESENTATIVE ACTION. Demanda hecha por algunos accionistas de una corporación para reclamar derechos o para reparar daños causados a todos los accionistas en la compañía.

REPRIEVE. Suspensión temporal. Posponer la ejecución de una sentencia criminal por un período de tiempo.

REPUBLICATION. Renovar la validez de un testamento que ha sido revocado.

REPUDIATION. Repudiación, rechazo, renuncia. Por ejemplo, negativa a llevar a cabo el contrato.

REPUGNANCY. Inconsistencia. Cuando una de las cláusulas de un documento contradice a otra cláusula del mismo documento.

REQUEST FOR ADMISSION. Procedimiento usado en la fase inicial de un caso. La parte demandante puede dar una lista de los hechos a la contraparte y además solicitar que éstos sean admitidos o negados. Los hechos que son admitidos no necesitan ser probados en el juicio.

REQUEST FOR INSTRUCTIONS. En los casos en que hay un jurado, cualquiera de las partes de la demanda puede solicitar al juez que instruya al jurado, leyéndole ciertas instrucciones acerca de la ley tocante a los hechos del caso.

REQUIREMENTS CONTRACT. Contrato bajo el cual la cantidad exacta de mercancía por comprar será determinada por lo que el comprador necesita durante la vida del contrato.

REQUISITION. Requerimiento; solicitud. Demandar o solicitar algo formalmente. Por ejemplo, la toma de propiedad privada por el estado, o una demanda formal de un estado a otro.

REQUISITORY LETTERS. Veáse "Rogatory letters".

RES. (Lat.) Objeto, cosa; Cualquier objeto que conlleva derechos. Por ejemplo, una propiedad (la "res") le da al propietario el derecho a su uso y explotación. Esta palabra tiene un sinnúmero de aplicaciones, generalmente con referencia a derechos, sean o no relacionados con objetos tangibles.

RES CONTROVERSA. (Lat.) "Algo en controversia". Lo opuesto a res judicata.

RES DERELICTA. (Lat.) Propiedad abandonada.

RES GESTAE. (Lat.) "Cosas hechas". Todo lo dicho y hecho que forma parte del incidente o transacción. El principio de "res gestae" establece que cuando algo se dice espontánea y concurrentemente en una trifulca, un accidente, etc., lo dicho conlleva un grado de veracidad inherente, el cual torna lo dicho admisible como evidencia.

RES INTEGRA. (Lat.) Punto de ley no decidido. Pregunta legal sin precedente y generalmente sin haberse discutido.

RES IPSA LOQUITUR. (Lat.) "La cosa habla por sí misma". Presunción controvertible con prueba en contrario. Que establece que el demandado fue negligente, si aquello que ocasionó el daño estaba bajo el control absoluto del demandado, y que el suceso o accidente era uno que de ordinario no ocurre a menos que haya habido negligencia.

RES JUDICATA. (Lat.) "Algo decidido." "Asunto decidido por un juicio." Doctrina legal que previene que una de las partes de una demanda ponga en pleito por segunda vez algún hecho que fue decidido con anterioridad por otra corte.

RESCIND. Rescindir, abrogar. Deshacer o anular. Cancelar un contrato y anularlo desde su comienzo como si no hubiera existido.

RESCISSION OF CONTRACT. Deshacer, abrogar, rescindir o anular un contrato en su totalidad.

RESCISSIONARY DAMAGES. Daños y perjuicios sufridos por una persona que están relacionados con la rescisión o abrogación de una transacción.

RESCRIPT. Orden de un juez al secretario de la corte instruyendo cómo disponer de un caso. Decisión escrita, corta y usualmente no firmada, sobre un caso que es enviado por una corte de apelaciones a una corte inferior.

RESCUE DOCTRINE. Doctrina que dice que cuando una persona negligente pone a otra en peligro, y una tercera persona resulta herida mientras trata de ayudar, la tercera persona puede reclamar por sus daños contra la persona negligente.

RESERVE. Reserva. Reservarse un derecho. (1) Fondos designados para pagar gastos o pérdidas futuras. (2) Cuando un juez se reserva la decisión sobre una cuestión legal para el final del juicio.

RESETTLEMENT. Decreto que es reabierto por el juez para incluir algo que accidentalmente se dejó fuera del decreto.

RESIDENCE. Residencia. Lugar donde una parte reside para efectos legales. La residencia se basa en las intenciones de la parte de vivir permanentemente en un área, ciudad o estado.

RESIDENT AGENT. Agente asignado por una compañía que reside en otro estado para que actúe como representante legal de la compañía en un estado.

RESIDENT ALIEN. Una persona que tiene las intenciones de ser residente de un país pero que no es ciudadano de ese país. Dicha persona es documentada para efectos de inmigración.

RESIDUE. Residuo. Lo que queda del caudal hereditario después de cancelar todas las deudas y obligaciones del testador.

RESISTING AN OFFICER. Acto criminal realizado al resistir o estorbar a un oficial de la policía en el cumplimiento de sus deberes. Esto es un crimen aun cuando no se utilice la fuerza.

RESOLUTION. Resolución de una entidad adoptada por votación y que refleja la decisión de la entidad.

RESOLVE. Acordar, resolver. Tomar una decisión para hacer algo. Resolución de llevar a cabo una meta.

RESORT. Recurso. "A court of last resort" es una corte cuya decisión no puede ser apelada dentro del mismo sistema de la corte.

RESPONDEAT SUPERIOR. (Lat.) Doctrina que responsabiliza al patrón por las acciones negligentes de sus empleados, las cuales han sido realizadas por trabajadores en el desempeño de sus labores.

RESPONDENT. Demandado; apelado. Persona en contra de quien se hace una apelación. Esta persona puede muy bien ser el demandante o el acusado en una corte inferior.

RESPONSIVE. Respondente. Una alegación o documento que responde directamente a los puntos propuestos por el otro lado en un litigio. Argumento o declaración que contesta a una interrogante.

REST THE CASE. Terminar la presentación de pruebas. Cuando una parte termina la presentación de sus pruebas.

RESTITUTION. Restitución. Devolución, reintegración, restablecer. Acto que restituye algo al dueño legal. Término que designa el derecho de una persona a recobrar lo que ha perdido o el daño que ha sufrido. En la ley de contratos, restitución es usualmente la cantidad que pone al demandante en la situación financiera en que éste se encontraba antes del contrato.

RESTRAIN. Prohibir, vedar. Impedir que se haga algo.

RESTRAINT OF TRADE. Restricción o represión del comercio. Acuerdo ilegal o combinación que elimina la competencia y crea un monopolio, o que aumenta o manipula los precios artificialmente.

RESTRICTION. Limitación, restricción. Provisión que limita el uso de una propiedad, ya sea por el dueño o el arrendatario.

RESTRICTIVE COVENANT. Pacto restrictivo. Términos de un título de propiedad que limita el uso de la propiedad o que prohíbe el uso de la propiedad en cierta forma.

RESTRICTIVE ENDORSEMENT. Endoso restrictivo. Firmar un documento negociable limitando el uso del documento. Normalmente, dicha firma termina la negociabilidad del instrumento.

RETAIL PRICE. Precio al detalle. Precio de un objeto al venderse al por menor o en cantidades pequeñas.

RETAILER. Detallista. Comerciante que vende al mismo cliente materiales al por menor o artículos por pieza y no en grandes volúmenes.

RETAIN. Retener, usar, mantener o poseer algo.

RETAINER. (1) Acción de un cliente de emplear un abogado. (2) Acuerdo al que llega un cliente con su abogado. (3) Primer pago que le hace un cliente a su abogado, ya sea por un caso específico o por casos que puedan venir en el futuro.

RETALIATORY EVICTION. Acción vengativa tomada por un arrendador contra un inquilino que protesta por las condiciones de la propiedad; o arrendador que defiende sus derechos desalojando al inquilino de su propiedad.

RETALIATORY LAW. Restricciones impuestas por un estado a compañías incorporadas en otro estado con el objeto de igualar las condiciones bajo las cuales las compañías del primer estado operan en otros estados. Por ejemplo, si Maryland le cobra a las compañías de seguro de Virginia impuestos más altos de los que cobra Virginia, Virginia puede subir el precio de los impuestos a la compañías de seguro de Maryland.

RETIREMENT. Jubilación. Terminación de la relación laboral al llegar el trabajador a determinada edad.

RETRACTION. Retractación. Acción de retirar lo que se dijo.

RETRIAL. Nuevo proceso; nueva audiencia. Enjuiciar un caso por segunda vez.

RETRIBUTION. Retribución. Algo entregado o demandado en pago de algo. En derecho criminal, es el castigo impuesto a un criminal, basado en el hecho de que el pago por cometer el crimen debe ser un castigo.

RETURN. Devolución, declaración, restitución. (1) Regresar documentos a la corte con prueba de entrega. (2) Declaración con fines tributarios. (3) Renta sobre el capital.

RETURN DAY. Día de contestación o comparecencia. Día en el cual el acusado debe presentarse en la corte después de haber recibido una citación.

REVALUATION. Revaluación, revalorización. Cuando una moneda devaluada aumenta en su poder adquisitivo.

REVENUE. Ingreso, renta. Cualquier entrada de dinero o activos que puede ser gravable por el gobierno.

REVERSE. Reponer o anular una sentencia. Por ejemplo, cuando una corte superior revoca la sentencia, el veredicto o una orden de una corte inferior, ésta anula la sentencia de la corte inferior y la sustituye con su propia decisión o manda el caso de regreso a una corte inferior con instrucciones de lo que se debe hacer con el caso.

REVERSE DESCRIMINATION. Discriminación dirigida a un grupo o una clase de ciudadanos con el objeto de remediar un patrón discriminatorio sufrido por otro grupo o clase.

REVERSION. Reversión; derecho de sucesión. Interés u otro derecho futuro sobre una propiedad que es actualmente poseída por otro.

REVERT. Revertir. Regresar o devolver algún objeto o derecho a otro.

REVIEW. Revisión. Re-examinar una acción jurídica o administrativa. Revisión de un caso por un tribunal superior.

REVISE. Revisar, corregir.

REVISED STATUTES. Libro que contiene los estatutos de un estado o del gobierno federal, y que han sido revisados.

REVIVE. Revivir. Restaurar el efecto legal de algo. Por ejemplo, si un contrato ha expirado, éste puede ser revivido con una nueva promesa para llevarlo a cabo.

REVOCATION. Derogación, revocación. Eliminar algún poder o autoridad. Por ejemplo, retractar una oferta antes de que ésta haya sido aceptada, eliminando el poder que tiene la otra persona de aceptarla.

REVOKE. Derogar, revocar. Terminar el efecto legal de algo al cancelarlo o anularlo.

REVOLVING CREDIT. Tipo de contrato de crédito en el cual el deudor puede usar el crédito en cualquier forma con tal de que no se exceda una línea de crédito predeterminada.

RICO. Leyes estatales y federales diseñadas para combatir el crimen organizado.

RIDER. Anexo, adición, endoso. Documento adicional que está adherido a un documento superior.

RIGHT. (1) Derecho, título, autoridad. (2) Moral, ética o legalmente justo. (3) Habilidad legal que tiene una persona para hacer algo o controlar ciertas acciones de otra persona.

RIGHT OF ACTION. Derecho de acción. Reclamo que puede ser impuesto en una corte.

RIGHT OF FIRST REFUSAL. Derecho a tener la primera opción de comprar una propiedad cuando ésta esté en venta, o la opción de igualar cualquier otra oferta.

RIGHT OF WAY. Servidumbre de paso o derecho de paso. Derecho de atravesar sobre la propiedad de otra persona. Terreno en el cual se construye un camino.

RIGHT–TO–WORK LAWS. Leyes estatales que prohíben acuerdos laborales que requieran membresía en sindicatos, empleos preferenciales o prohibiciones similares antes que un trabajador pueda ser empleado.

RIOT. Tumulto, pelotera. Tres o más personas que cometen o amenazan con cometer un acto de violencia, un crimen, el uso de armas, e impiden toda acción oficial en protección del orden público.

RIPARIAN. Materia legal relacionada al uso de ríos, lagos o áreas adyacentes a estos cuerpos de agua.

RIPARIAN RIGHTS. Derechos ribereños. Derechos de uso que tiene un dueño de una propiedad que está a la orilla de un río o un lago.

RIPE. Maduro. Cuando un caso está listo para una decisión judicial ya que los hechos legales involucrados están lo suficientemente claros, evolucionados y presentados para tomar una decisión sobre el caso. Cualquier corte o agencia que tenga el poder de rehusar ciertos casos debe utilizar este método de análisis ("Ripenes Doctrine") para decidir si toma el caso o no. Este método también incluye la idea de que el caso debe presentar una controversia real.

ROBBERY. Robo, hurto. Acto ilegal de tomar una propiedad que le pertenece a otra persona usando la fuerza.

ROBINSON–PATMAN ACT. Ley federal que prohíbe la discriminación contra compradores mediante el cambio de precios de mercancía.

ROGATORY LETTERS. Solicitud que le hace un juez a otro pidiéndole a éste segundo que supervise el interrogatorio de un testigo y su testimonio.

ROE vs. WADE. Caso de la Corte Suprema de 1973 que protege el derecho de una mujer para tener un aborto en la fase inicial del embarazo.

ROLL. Lista. Registro de actos oficiales; lista de bienes gravables; censo de contribuyentes; registro tributario.

ROMAN LAW. Derecho civil o romano, derivado de las leyes y códigos originalmente usados por los romanos.

ROYALTY. Regalía. Derechos de patente. Compensación que se paga al propietario de una patente o de una tecnología por el uso de ésta.

RULE. Auto, fallo, reglamento, regla, principio. (1) (verbo) Determinar un punto legal o decidir una objeción presentada por uno de los lados en una disputa legal. La decisión es tomada por la persona encargada (juez, oficiales de audiencia, ponente, etc.). (2) Principio, criterio, norma o guía establecida. Un reglamento. (3) "Ley pequeña" hecha por un grupo o alguna agencia administrativa, generalmente para gobernar su trabajo interno. (4) Regla que rige los procedimientos jurídicos de la corte.

RULE AGAINST ACCUMULATIONS. Ley estatal que prohíbe el que un sindicato ahorre dinero por un período largo de tiempo.

RULE AGAINST PERPETUITIES. Principio que limita la transferencia de bienes por testamento. Véase "Perpetuities".

RULES OF EVIDENCE. Reglas que controlan el tipo de evidencia que puede ser admitida ante una corte.

RULE OF FOUR. Regla que dice que si cuatro miembros de la Corte Suprema quieren examinar un caso que ha llegado a la corte por auto de avocación, la corte lo tomará.

RULE OF LAW. Principio de derecho máximo, precepto de ley. Sistema gubernamental bajo el cual la autoridad máxima es la ley, no una persona o grupo de personas.

RULE OF LENIENCY. Regla bajo la cual cuando no está claro si la ley que se debe aplicar debería ser más o menos severa, se escoge la interpretación menos severa.

RULES COMMITTEE. Comité de la asamblea legislativa que regula todas las operaciones y los procedimientos parlamentarios.

RULES. (Federal) Reglas Federales. El congreso le ha dado a la Corte Suprema el poder de imponer reglas para las cortes federales inferiores. Las reglas son: civiles, federales, criminales, de procedimiento de apelación, y de evidencia. Los estados han adaptado reglas similares.

RULES DECISION ACT. Leyes federales que hacen que las leyes sustantivas de un estado se apliquen a las demandas en la corte federal.

RULING. Decisión, fallo. Decisión que toma un juez cuando una pregunta legal es presentada durante un juicio.

S

S.B.A. Siglas del "Small Business Administration." Agencia gubernamental para el fomento de pequeñas empresas.

S.B.I.C. Siglas del "Small Business Investment Company". Compañía con recursos para invertir en pequeñas empresas.

S.E.C. Siglas de "Securities and Exchange Commission". Comisión gubernamental en los Estados Unidos responsable por regular, supervisar y controlar las bolsas mercantiles y el mercado de valores.

SABOTAGE. Sabotaje. (1) Destrucción o daño intencional, o la producción deficiente, de materiales o bienes de defensa nacional. (2) Acción del obrero para perjudicar al patrono ejecutando mal un trabajo o provocando desperfectos en los talleres y máquinas.

SABOTEUR. Saboteador.

SAFE. Seguro, salvo, sin riesgo. (1) **Safe Deposit Box.** Caja de custodia; caja de seguridad. (2) **Safe Company.** Empresa de depósitos de seguridad.

SAFEKEEPING. Custodia, buena guarda.

SAFETY PAPER. Documento de seguridad o garantía.

SALARY. Salario, sueldo. Cantidad de dinero que se da a alguno para pagar un servicio o trabajo.

SALE. Venta. Acción y efecto de vender. Un contrato bajo el cual una propiedad es intercambiada por dinero. (1) **Absolute Sale.** Venta donde la transacción es completada y el comprador tiene derechos absolutos sobre la propiedad. (2) **As Is Sale.** Se vende como está a venta de una propiedad sin garantías. Término usado en ventas muebles que indica al comprador que la propiedad o el bien se vende en la condición en la cual se encuentra, con o sin defectos. (3) **Bulk Sale.** Venta en volumen o de todo los bienes de una empresa. (4) **Cash Sale.** Venta al contado. Venta en la que el precio se cancela inmediatamente. (5) **Conditional Sale.** Venta condicional. (6) **Credit Sale.** Venta donde el pago es parcial o totalmente diferido por un período de tiempo. (7) **Exclusive Sale.** Venta de propiedad en la cual el propietario tiene un agente o corredor exclusivo que vende la propiedad. (8) **Executory Sale.** Venta donde existe un contrato de venta, pero uno de los términos del contrato aún no se ha cumplido. Una venta incompleta. (9) **Forced Sale.** Venta forzada. Venta sin la autorización del dueño pero bajo un decreto, ley o un proceso legal. (10) **Fraudulent Sale.** Venta fraudulenta. Una venta con el objetivo de defraudar a los acreedores del dueño de la propiedad antes que éste declare bancarrota. (11) **Installment Sale.** Venta donde el comprador hace pagos periódicos y el vendedor retiene título sobre la propiedad vendida hasta el pago final. (12) **Judicial Sale.** Venta judicial o legal. (13) **Public Sale.** Venta judicial mediante anuncios al público en general. (14) **Tax Sale.** Venta judicial de terrenos o propiedad para pagar una deuda fiscal.

SALE AND LEASEBACK. Una transacción donde se vende una propiedad y luego ésta es arrendada por el comprador al vendedor por un período fijo.

SALE or EXCHANGE. Venta o permuta.

SALES AGREEMENT. Acuerdos o contratos referentes a la venta de una propiedad.

SALES CONTRACT. Contrato oral o escrito para la venta de una propiedad. En la venta de inmuebles, los contratos orales pueden ser inefectivos.

SALES TAX. Impuesto sobre ventas. Impuesto sobre ventas locales o estatales, donde el comprador paga el impuesto al comerciante, y luego el impuesto es enviado al estado.

SALVAGE. Salvamento, recuperación. (1) Propiedad recobrada después de un accidente. (2) En derecho marítimo, dinero que se le paga a un individuo que ha rescatado una propiedad de su destrucción.

SALVAGE VALUE. Valor residual.

SAME EVIDENCE TEST. Doctrina que establece que si la misma evidencia prueba culpable a una persona en dos causas separadas, una de las cuales ya ha sido adjudicadas, la segunda causa será prohibida por inconstitucional. Véase "Double Jeopardy".

SAME OFFENCE. Véase "Double Jeopardy".

SANCTION. Sanción. (1) Estar de acuerdo o confirmar las acciones de otra persona. (2) Una pena o castigo sujeto a una ley para asegurar que será obedecida. (3) Acción punitiva tomada por una nación contra otra.

SANITY. Cordura. Lo opuesto a demencia. (1) **Sanity hearing.** Audiencia donde se determina si una persona está mentalmente capacitada para ser enjuiciada, si debe ser internada en un hospital para enfermos mentales, u otros asuntos relacionados.

SATISFACTION. Satisfacción. Cancelar una deuda u obligación pagándola. (1) **Satisfaction Contract.** Contrato por medio del cual una persona promete hacer algún trabajo o proporcionar bienes que satisfagan a otra persona. (2) **Satisfaction of Judgment.** Documento escrito, firmado por el acreedor, el cual declara que la obligación judicial ya ha sido pagada.

SATISFIED. Satisfecho. **Satisfied Lien.** Gravamen liquidado o cancelado.

SATISFY. Liquidar, cancelar, pagar, satisfacer.

SAVE. Preservar, salvar. La protección y preservación de derechos cuando se cambia una ley o un contrato.

SAVE HARMLESS CLAUSE. Condición en un documento donde una de las partes accede a indemnizar a la otra contra ciertos daños y perjuicios.

SAVING CLAUSE. Cláusula de reserva o de salvedad o de excepción. Cláusula en un estatuto que crea una excepción.

SAVINGS. Ahorros.

SAVINGS ACCOUNT. Cuenta de ahorros.

SAVINGS BANK. Banco o caja de ahorros.

SAVINGS AND LOAN ASSOCIATION. Sociedad de ahorro y préstamo; asociación de préstamos para edificación. Uno de varios tipos de instituciones que hacen préstamos a compradores de casas o bienes raíces.

SAVINGS BOND. Bonos para ahorros; títulos de ahorro. Bonos diseñados para ahorrar dinero, emitidos por una entidad bancaria o por el gobierno.

SCANDAL. Rumor o reporte escandaloso. Comentario difamatorio.

SCHEDULE. Itinerario, planilla, lista. Una lista que va junto a un documento y explica detalladamente los puntos mencionados en el documento.

SCHEME. Un plan o esquema para lograr un objetivo.

SCHOLARSHIP. Beca. Dinero otorgado a un estudiante para que sufrage sus estudios sin la obligación de reembolsarlos.

SCHOOL BONDS. Bonos escolares.

SCIENTER. (Lat.) A sabiendas. Con intento de engaño. Cuando el acusado tiene conocimiento previo del acto que causó el daño. Este término es usado comúnmente en casos de fraude.

SCILICET. (Lat.) Palabra innecesaria y frecuentemente usada después de una declaración general para introducir una lista de ejemplos específicos.

SCINTILLA. Una chispa. Término evidencial que indica que la prueba es insignificante o insuficiente.

SCOPE OF EMPLOYMENT. Ambito laboral. Bajo la doctrina de "respondeat superior" (véase esa palabra), el patrono es responsable por los daños y perjuicios causados por el empleado mientras éste actúe dentro del ámbito o la esfera de su empleo.

SCRIP. Vale; certificado de acción fraccionaria; certificado provisional. Documento que da derecho a su posesor a obtener algo de valor.

SCRIPT. Escritura; un manuscrito. Documento escrito.

SCRIVENOR. Notario. Persona encargada de redactar contratos.

SCRUTINY. Escrutinio. (1) Recuento de votos. (2) Análisis detallado o minucioso.

SEA. Mar, océano; marino, marítimo. (1) **Sea Carrier.** Empresa de transporte marítimo. (2) **Sea Letter.** Pasaporte de buque, certificado de navegación, carta de mar. Normalmente usadas durante tiempos de guerra. (3) **Sea Peril.** Accidente, fortuna o riesgos de mar.

676

SEAL. Sello, timbre. Marca de identificación impresa en cera. CORPORATE SEAL. El sello de una corporación usado para autenticar documentos de la compañía.

SEALED. Sellado. SEALED BIDDING. Propuestas selladas. Método de someter propuestas en forma confidencial para realizar una obra, venta o un servicio.

SEARCH. Registro, allanamiento. Cuando la policía u otra persona oficial examina la propiedad, carro, casa, etc. de un individuo buscando evidencia de un crimen. Si se hace un allanamiento o un registro sin ninguna causa o sin una orden de registro, la búsqueda es prohibida por la Constitución y cualquier evidencia obtenida puede ser excluída en un juicio criminal. **Title Search.** Examen de los expedientes de un terreno o propiedad para confirmar a quién pertenece legalmente, y si existen hipotecas, derecho de retención, etc., sobre ésta.

SEARCH WARRANT. Orden de registro o de allanamiento. Permiso escrito dado por un juez o magistrado a un oficial del gobierno, el cual permite examinar cierto lugar para obtener evidencia de algún crimen, contrabando, o fruto de un crimen. El oficial tiene que tener una base razonable para que la corte le otorgue el permiso.

SEASONABLE. Oportunamente. Acción tomada dentro del tiempo permitido.

SEASONAL UNEMPLOYMENT. Desempleo estacional.

SEAT OF GOVERNMENT. Sede de gobierno.

SEAWORTHY. Apto para la navegación. Un buque que está apropiadamente construido, mantenido, abastecido, y cuya tripulación está preparada, para hacerse a la mar.

SECEDE. Secesión. Separarse. Retirar su afiliación de un grupo.

SECOND. Desecho, segunda; secundar, apoyar. (1) **Second Mortgage.** Segunda hipoteca, hipoteca de segundo grado. (2) **Second the Motion.** Apoyar la moción. (3) **Second Offender.** Reincidente. El que vuelve a incurrir en una culpa o delito.

SECOND AMENDMENT. (EE.UU.) Segunda emnienda a la Constitución de los Estados Unidos que establece el derecho a tener y a portar armas. Este derecho ha sido definido estrictamente por leyes estatales y federales.

SECONDARY. Secundario, subordinado. Véase "Second".

SECONDARY AUTHORITY. Autoridad secundaria; autoridad persuasiva. Un comentario sobre alguna ley, tal como una anotación, un artículo en un periódico, o una enciclopedia, el cual no tiene la importancia de una autoridad primaria tal como la ley o un estatuto.

SECONDARY BOYCOTT. Boicot secundario. Comúnmente, un boicot laboral dirigido a una empresa que hace negocio con otra empresa con la cual un sindicato tiene disputas. Presión indirecta. Véase "Boycott".

SECONDARY EVIDENCE. Véase "Hearsay".

SECRET. Secreto. (1) **Secret Partner.** Socio secreto. (2) **Secret Partnership.** Asociación secreta. (3) **Secret Police.** Policía secreta. (4) **Secret Trust.** Fideicomiso secreto.

SECRETARY OF STATE. Secretario de Estado. En el gobierno de los Estados Unidos, éste es el miembro del gabinete que está al mando del Departamento de Estado y está a cargo de las relaciones internacionales. En la mayoría de los gobiernos estatales, éste es el oficial que está a cargo de supervisar ciertos asuntos administrativos del gobierno estatal, como proporcionar licencias a corporaciones.

SECRETE. Esconder u ocultar una propiedad para que los acreedores no puedan recobrarla o embargarla.

SECTA. (Lat.) Juicio.

SECUNDUM. (Lat.) Procedente de; tal como; de acuerdo con; según.

SECURE. Seguro. Garantizado. Dar seguridad o garantía. Garantizar el pago de una deuda. Asegurar el cumplimiento de una promesa dándole a la persona una hipoteca, derecho de retención, empeño, etc.

SECURED. Garantizado, asegurado. Protegido por una hipoteca, derecho de retención, empeño, u otra garantía. La persona protegida se llama "SECURED CREDITOR" Acreedor asegurado o "SECURED PARTY" Parte asegurada. La deuda protegida se llama "SECURED LOAN" Préstamo asegurado.

678

SECURITIES. Valores, títulos. Acciones, bonos, pagarés, u otros docomentos que representen una o varias acciones en la compañía o una deuda que la compañía tiene. Véase "Security".

SECURITIES ACTS. Ley reguladora de las bolsas de valores. Leyes federales y estatales que regulan la venta de valores.

SECURITIES AND EXCHANGE COMMISSION. Comisión de Valores y Bolsas. Agencia federal que controla y regula la compra y venta de valores y las actividades bursátiles.

SECURITY. Garantía, indemnización, seguridad. (1) Propiedad que ha sido empeñada, hipotecada etc., como garantía de un préstamo u otras obligaciones. (2) **Security Interest.** Cualquier interés en una propiedad adquirido por medio de un contrato, con el propósito de garantizar el cumplimiento de una obligación. (3) Cualquier pagaré, acción, bono, instrumento, o valor que indica una obligación de una empresa privada o gubernamental. (4) Cualquier obligación, título o valor que otorga derechos legales al poseedor sobre alguna empresa o entidad gubernamental.

SECURITY DEPOSIT. Depósito de garantía. Dinero que un arrendatario paga por adelantado para pagar por posibles daños a una propiedad o para asegurar el fiel cumplimiento de los términos y condiciones de arrendamiento.

SECURITY FOR COSTS. Caución para costos. Darle dinero, propiedad o bonos a una corte para el pago de costos en caso que la persona pierda. Esto se hace, por ejemplo, cuando el acusado es de otro estado.

SEDICIOUS. Sedicioso. Promotor o actor en un tumulto, una rebelión, u otro levantamiento contra la autoridad.

SEDITION. Sedición. Comunicaciones cuyo motivo es el de inducir a las personas a formar una resistencia contra el gobierno.

SEDUCE. Seducir. Inducir a una persona a perder la castidad o realizar actos sexuales.

SEDUCTION. Seducción. Acción de seducir.

SEGREGATION. Segregación. La práctica inconstitucional de separar personas en viviendas, escuelas, etc., basándose en su raza, nacionalidad, etc.

SEISIN. Posesión.

SEIZE. Confiscar, embargar, secuestrar. Quitarle a uno alguna cosa en virtud de una ley o reglamento.

SEIZURE. Secuestro, embargo. (1) Acción de un oficial público de quitarle a una persona su propiedad por alguna violación a la ley, por un mandamiento o decisión en un juicio, o porque la propiedad va a ser usada como evidencia en un caso criminal. (2) Acción de detener a un individuo bajo custodia, ordenada por un funcionario, interrumpiendo su libertad de movimiento.

SELF–EMPLOYMENT TAX. Contribución de seguro social impuesto a las ganancias o entradas de una persona que trabaja para cuenta propia.

SELF–EXECUTING. De efecto inmediato, autoejecutable.

SELF–INFLICTED INJURY. Auto-lesión. Daño causado a uno mismo.

SELF–SERVING. Para ventaja propia.

SELECTIVE SERVICE LAW. Leyes que regulan la conscripción o el alistamiento en el servicio militar.

SELF–DEFENSE. Defensa propia. Derecho bajo el cual una persona puede defenderse contra otra que la está amenazando o usando fuerza física en su contra. La defensa propia se considera un derecho si la familia, la propiedad o el cuerpo de la persona está en peligro. El uso de fuerza para la defensa propia debe ser proporcional al riesgo percibido.

SELF–INCRIMINATION. Auto-incriminación. Todo lo que sea dicho o hecho por una persona que la incrimina en un delito.

SELF–INSURANCE. Seguro propio. Establecer un fondo monetario de seguro para pagar pérdidas en el futuro, en vez de comprar una póliza de seguro que cubra esas posibles pérdidas.

SELL. Vender. Disponer de propiedad mediante una venta.

SELLER. Vendedor. El que vende una propiedad o un bien a un comprador.

SEMBLE. (Fr.) "Parece que". Expresión usada en reportes legales al introducir una declaración que no ha sido claramente explicada por la corte.

SENATE. Senado. Cámara Superior de la legislatura, sea en un estado o en el congreso de los Estados Unidos. Los miembros del Senado son los senadores. En el Senado de los Estados Unidos, los senadores son elegidos por seis años, y cada estado tiene derecho a ser representado por dos senadores.

SENATOR. Senador. Miembro del senado.

SENIOR. Principal, mayor, más antiguo.

SENTENCE. Sentencia, fallo, decisión. El castigo dado a una persona que ha sido encontrada culpable de haber cometido un crimen. La sentencia es comúnmente dictada por el juez de la corte, pero a veces es dictada por el jurado. Véase "Concurrent and Cumulative Sentences".

SEPARABILITY CLAUSE. Cláusula en un contrato que declara que si una parte del contrato es nula, lo restante del contrato mantiene su validez.

SEPARABLE CONTROVERSY RULE. Ley federal que otorga jurisdicción a las cortes federales. El propósito de ésta ley es permitir que una corte decida todas las disputas entre las partes. El juez de la corte federal decide si aceptará el caso entero o sólo la parte de la demanda que trata con la cuestión federal.

SEPARATE ESTATE. Propiedad particular o aparte. Propiedad perteneciente sólo a una de dos personas casadas o asociadas en un negocio.

SEPARATE MAINTENANCE. Manutención aparte. Dinero que le paga una persona casada a la otra para mantenerla si la pareja no está viviendo junta como marido y mujer.

SEPARATE PROPERTY. Propiedad individual de un cónyuge fuera de la propiedad matrimonial.

SEPARATE TRIAL. Juicio o proceso individual. Juicios separados e individuales a los acusados de un crimen.

SEPARATION. Separación. (1) Marido y mujer viviendo separados por medio de un acuerdo ya sea antes del divorcio o en vez de un divorcio completo. (2) **Separation of Powers.** La división del gobierno federal en tres ramas: legislativa, judicial y ejecutiva. Cada rama actúa para prevenir que la otra acumule demasiado poder. (3) **Separation of Witness.** Cuando los testigos en un

681

caso se mantienen fuera de la sala donde se lleva a cabo el juicio hasta que cada uno sea llamado para atestiguar.

SEQUESTER. Secuestrar. Aislar o mantener aparte. Secuestrar al jurado es prohibirle el contacto con el mundo exterior mientras el juicio se lleva a cabo.

SERGEANT AT ARMS. Sargento de armas. Una persona asignada para mantener orden en una legislatura, corte o en reuniones grandes.

SERIAL BONDS. Bonos de vencimiento escalonado o en serie; obligaciones seriadas. Grupos de bonos emitidos al mismo tiempo, pero con diferente fecha de vencimiento y tasa de interés para cada bono.

SERIAL NOTE. Un pagaré que es pagado a plazos.

SERIATIM. (Lat.) Uno a la vez; por separado; individualmente.

SERIES. Serie. (1) Un grupo de libros de leyes arreglado por orden numérico. (2) **Series Bond.** Grupos de bonos por ejemplo, serie A, serie B, emitidos en diferentes fechas pero bajo la autoridad de la misma escritura.

SERVANT. Criado, sirviente; empleado.

SERVE. Servir; notificar. (1) **Serve A Sentence.** Cumplir o extinguir una sentencia o condena. (2) **Serve A Subpoena.** Cumplir la orden de citación. (3) **Serve A Summons.** Notificar o diligenciar una citación o un emplazamiento.

SERVICE. Servicio. (1) Labor o trabajo realizado por un individuo para otro. (2) Tiempo que un ciudadano sirve de soldado. (3) **Service of Process.** La entrega formal de una citación legal. (4) **Service Charge.** Cobro por servicio. Cobro de una comisión por una entidad bancaria o comercial para cubrir algún servicio al cliente.

SERVICES RENDERED. Servicios prestados.

SERVIENT. Sirviente, subordinado.

SERVITUDE. Servidumbre. Derecho que tiene una casa o propiedad sobre otra. (1) **Servitude of Drainage.** Servidumbre de desagüe. (2) **Servitude of Light and View.** Servidumbre de luces y vistas.

SESSION. Sesión. Tiempo durante el cual permanece reunido un cuerpo deliberante.

SET ASIDE. Posponer. (1) Cancelar, anular, revocar una sentencia de la corte. (2) Programa para mantener tierras fértiles sin producción para conservar el suelo y estabilizar el precio de las cosechas. (3) Cualquier programa de ahorro de bienes para darle uso en el futuro. (4) Programa federal que designa parte de los contratos federales para minorías o grupos que se encuentran en condiciones de desventaja.

SET-DOWN. Fijar la fecha de la causa en el calendario.

SET FOR TRIAL. Fijar fecha para juicio.

SET OF EXCHANGE. En derecho comercial, una letra original con todas las copias.

SET-OFF. Contraponer, reservar. Contrareclamación contra la demanda del demandante que tiene por objeto reducir o superar la cantidad de la demanda. Aplicar la prenda contra la deuda.

SETTLE. Transigir, componer, arreglar, determinar. (1) Concordar. Un acuerdo de como pagar una deuda, o de como disponer de un juicio o caso. (2) Finalizar, completar algo. (3) **Settle Out of Court.** Transar o arreglar extrajudicialmente. (4) **Settle a Strike.** Solucionar una huelga. (5) **Settle Up.** Pagar.

SETTLEMENT. Convenio, arreglo, acuerdo. Véase "Settle".

SETTLEMENT DATE. Fecha del acuerdo o arreglo.

SETTLOR. Fideicomitente. Fundador de un fideicomiso, el cual proporciona el dinero necesario para fundarlo.

SEVENTEENTH AMENDMENT. (EE.UU.) Decimoséptima enmienda constitucional que instruye la manera de elegir a los senadores por medio de votación popular.

SEVENTH AMENDMENT. (EE.UU.) Séptima enmienda constitucional que garantiza un juicio por jurado en casi todos los casos civiles federales.

SEVER. Separar o dividir.

SEVERABLE. Divisible, separable, excluíble. Capaz de dividirse y de mantener su identidad y existencia. Un contrato es separable si una parte es ilegal pero el resto del contrato es válido.

SEVERAL. Varios, diversos. Más de uno.

SEVERALLY. Solidariamente. Separadamente, cada cual por su parte. (1) **Severally Liable.** Responsable solidariamente; que cada persona solidariamente responsable puede ser demandada individualmente.

SEVERALTY OWNERSHIP. Posesión o propiedad exclusiva. Propiedad de una sola persona.

SEVERANCE. Cesantía; separación; división. Cuando una causa se separa de otras para ser llevada a juicio.

SEVERANCE PAY. Sueldo de despido. Dinero extra que se paga a un trabajador cuando se le deja cesante.

SEVERANCE TAX. Impuesto sobre extracción forestal o mineral.

SHAM. Ficticio. Transacción ficticia que puede ignorarse por ser falsa, fraudulenta o inconsecuente. **Sham Defense or Plea.** Defensa ficticia.

SHARE. Participación, cuota, parte. (1) Una porción. (2) Una acción en una corporación. (3) **Share Certificate.** Certificado de participación. Documento que otorga a una persona el derecho a cierto número de acciones.

SHARE ACCOUNTS. Cuenta de depósito. Una cuenta en una cooperativa de crédito.

SHARECROPPER. Agricultor que cultiva tierra ajena y paga el alquiler por la tierra con parte de su cosecha.

SHARE–FARMING. Aparcería. Contrato por el cual el dueño de una finca rústica la cede en explotación con reparto proporcional de los frutos o beneficios.

SHAREHOLDER. Accionista. Propietario de acciones de una sociedad comercial o industrial.

SHARES OF STOCK. Acciones, partes. Certificados que acreditan una participación en el capital de una corporación o sociedad por acciones.

SHERIFF. Alguacil. Funcionario jefe de un condado, quien está a cargo de atender notificaciones de demandas, llamar jurados, mantener el orden en el tribunal, y dirigir la cárcel del condado.

SHERIFF'S DEED. Documento de propiedad que es evidencia de una venta judicial.

SHERIFF'S SALE. Venta judicial. Venta por orden judicial autorizando la venta de la propiedad, por subasta pública, al mejor postor.

SHERMAN ANTITRUST ACT. Ley federal que prohibe cualquier conspiración o contrato que interfiera con el funcionamiento del mercado libre entre los estados.

SHIELDS LAW. Leyes de protección. Ley que protege la fuente de información de periodistas y escritores.

SHIPOWNER'S LIABILITY. Responsabilidades del naviero.

SHIPPING. Embarque; despacho, envío. (1) Transportar bienes por comisión. (2) Con relación a naves o movimiento de bienes por mar. (3) **Shipping Articles.** Contrato de empleo de los marineros.

SHIP'S. Relativo a un buque. (1) **Ship's Articles.** Contrato de empleo de los marineros. (2) **Ship's Papers.** Documentación de a bordo. (3) **Ship's Passport.** Pasaporte del buque, carta de mar.

SHOPLIFTER. Ladrón de tienda. Ladrón que hurta artículos que se venden en una tienda sustrayéndolos sin pagar.

SHOP STEWARD. Mayordomo de tienda o de taller. Oficial de un sindicato laboral responsable por representar a los miembros del sindicato.

SHOPLIFTING. Hurto de mercancías que se vende en tiendas.

SHORE. Costa, orilla. Tierra adjunta al mar.

SHORT. Breve, corto; escaso. (1) **Short Notice.** Aviso a corto plazo. (2) **Short Position or Sale.** Término usado en el mercado de valores para indicar que una persona tiene un riesgo financiero por tener menos acciones en mano de lo que necesita para cumplir con sus obligaciones contractuales. Normalmente, la persona vende acciones bajo un contrato a un precio fijo, con la idea de que en el futuro podrá comprar las mismas acciones a un precio reducido y así cumplir con el contrato. (3) **Short Term**

Paper. Letras, giros, o pagarés de vencimiento a corto plazo (a menos de un año).

SHORT-TERM. Corto plazo (a un año o menos).

SHOW CAUSE ORDER. Orden de presentar motivos justificativos o de mostrar causa. Orden judicial dirigida a una persona o entidad indicando que si no existe una excusa o razón válida para algo, la corte tomará ciertas medidas.

SICK BENEFIT. Subsidio o beneficio por invalidez; indemnización por causa de enfermedad; auxilio de invalidez.

SICK LEAVE. Licencia para ausentarse del empleo por enfermedad.

SICK PAY. Compensación por enfermedad.

SIGHT DRAFT. Una letra, giro o documento negociable pagadero a la vista.

SIGN. Firmar.

SIGNATURE. Firma.

SIGNER. Firmante, signatario.

SILENT. Silencioso. (1) **Silent Partner.** Socio comanditario o capitalista. (2) **Silent Partnership.** Comandita.

SIMPLE. Simple, sencillo. (1) **Simple Assault.** Asalto simple, acometimiento. (2) **Simple Battery.** Agresión simple. (3) **Simple Bond.** Obligación incondicional, pagaré. (4) **Simple Confession.** Declaración de culpabilidad. (5) **Simple Interest.** Interés simple. (6) **Simple Larceny.** Hurto sencillo. (7) **Simple Promise.** Promesa pura o simple. (8) **Simple Trust.** Fideicomiso puro o simple.

SINE QUA NON. (Lat.) "Sin la cual no". Condición imprescindible.

SINECURE. Sinecura. Empleo bien retribuido y que ocasiona poco trabajo.

SINGLE. Singular, solo; una persona soltera.

SINGLE PUBLICATION RULE. Regla que establece que cada difamación constituye una única causa para demandar, sin considerar el número de copias del material difamatorio que se hayan distribuido.

SINKING FUND. Fondo caja de amortización. Dinero u otros activos apartados para algún propósito especial como pagar bonos u otras deudas a largo plazo, o para reponer maquinaria.

SISTER CORPORATION. Dos compañías con el mismo dueño.

SIT. Celebrar una sesión legislativa, judicial, etc. (1) Estar formalmente organizado y llevar a cabo asuntos oficiales. (2) Ser miembro del tribunal.

SIT-DOWN STRIKE. Huelga de brazos cruzados o de brazos caídos.

SITTING. Junta, sesión, reunión. La parte del año durante el cual la corte está en sesión. **Sitting in Banc.** Sesión de todo el tribunal.

SITUS. (Lat.) Lugar, localidad. Usualmente el lugar donde un asunto tiene lazos legales.

SIXTEENTH AMENDMENT. Decimosexta enmienda a la Constitución de los Estados Unidos que permite gravar los ingresos personales de cada persona, ya sea natural o jurídica.

SIXTH AMENDMENT. Sexta enmienda a la Constitución de los Estados Unidos que garantiza a todo acusado el derecho a tener un juicio ante un jurado, y a enfrentarse a sus acusadores, así como contar con un defensor legal durante un proceso legal imparcial.

SIXTY-DAY NOTICE. Requisito federal bajo el cual cualquier parte de un contrato laboral, sea patrono o sindicato, debe dar aviso previo antes de renegociar o terminar el contrato. Durante este tiempo están prohibidas las huelgas y los cierres totales de las empresas.

SKELETON BILL OF EXCEPTIONS. Nota de excepciones con omisión de varios documentos.

SLANDER. Calumnia, difamación oral. Decir o proferir palabras falsas y maliciosas que perjudiquen la reputación de algún individuo, negocio o derechos propietarios.

SLANDERER. Calumniador, difamador. El que dice una calumnia u ofensa.

SLANDEROUS. Calumnioso, injurioso.

SLANDER PER SE. Difamación oral por lo dicho. Palabras que son consideradas difamatorias sin necesidad de probar que la persona difamada sufrió daños. Normalmente estas palabras se pueden incluir en una de las siguientes áreas: (1) La persona difamada cometió un crimen; (2) La persona difamada tiene alguna enfermedad ofensiva o repugnante; (3) La castidad de una mujer difamada fue deshonrada; o (4) La persona difamada ha sido acusada de actos que perjudican su profesión, comercio, ocupación o posición.

SLATE. Lista de candidatos para una elección o posición.

SLEEPING PARTNER. Socio secreto. Socio cuyo nombre no es conocido por el público.

SLIP LAW. Decreto legislativo publicado en un panfleto o una hoja suelta inmediatamente después de haber sido aprobado por la legislatura.

SLIP OPINION. Decisión de una corte publicada individualmente inmediatamente después de su dictamen.

SLUSH FUND. Dinero para cabildeo o para soborno.

SMALL BUSINESS ADMINISTRATION. Agencia gubernamental en los Estados Unidos que asiste a la pequeña empresa con préstamos, garantías y asistencia técnica.

SMALL BUSINESS CORPORATION. Sociedad anónima dedicada a la pequeña empresa.

SMALL BUSINESSMAN. Dueño de un negocio pequeño.

SMALL CLAIMS COURT. Corte con jurisdicción sobre casos pequeños. Estas cortes tienen un procedimiento simple y menos formal que las cortes de jurisdicción general.

SMALL TAX CASE PROCEDURE. Procedimiento tributario de menor cuantía.

SMUGGLE. Contrabandear. Introducir artículos prohibidos a un país o sin pagar los impuestos de introducción.

SMUGGLER. Contrabandista.

SMUGGLING. Contrabando. Delito cometido al introducir o sacar de un país objetos o cosas que estén prohibidas o sobre las cuales se debe pagar impuesto.

SOCIAL CONTRACT. Contrato social. Teoría que establece que la única base de existencia de un gobierno es aquella que cuenta con el consentimiento de los gobernados.

SOCIAL GUEST. Invitado social. Persona admitida a una propiedad con un fin social.

SOCIAL SECURITY BENEFITS. Beneficios del seguro social.

SODOMY. Sodomía. Actos sexuales inmorales. Sexo oral o anal o con animales.

SOLD. Vendido; convencido.

SOLE. Unico, solo, separado.

SOLE ACTOR DOCTRINE. Doctrina legal bajo la cual el patrono se responsabiliza por lo que haga o sepa su empleado o agente.

SOLE HEIR. Heredero único.

SOLE PROPIETOR. Empresario único. Persona que es el único dueño de un negocio.

SOLE PROPIETORSHIP. Propiedad de una sola persona. Tipo de empresa donde una persona es la dueña de la totalidad de la empresa, sin socios o accionistas.

SOLE REPRESENTATIVE. Representante o agente exclusivo.

SOLICIT. Solicitar, peticionar. Vender.

SOLICITATION. Solicitación. Acto de solicitar o pedir. Exigir fuertemente.

SOLICITOR. Abogado, procurador; solicitador. (1) Abogado inglés que maneja todos los asuntos legales con excepción de juicios. Véase "Barrister". (2) Título que se le da al jefe de abogados del gobierno.

SOLICITOR GENERAL. Abogado que representa al gobierno ante la Corte Suprema.

SOLIDARITY. Solidaridad. En derecho civil, cuando varias personas acceden a pagar a otra parte la misma suma de dinero, al mismo tiempo, bajo un mismo contrato. Bajo tal acuerdo, cualquiera de los obligados puede ser forzado a pagar la deuda completa, y el pago por uno exonera al resto de la obligación.

SOLITARY CONFINEMENT. Prisión incomunicada.

SOLVENCY. Solvencia. (1) Habilidad de poder pagar las deudas antes de que se venzan. (2) Poseer más activos que pasivos.

SOUND. Solvente, confiable; productivo; sano. (1) **Sound in Health.** Bien de salud. (2) **Sound Mind.** Juicio cabal; mente sana. (3) **Sound Value.** Valor justo; valor en estado sano.

SOVEREIGN IMMUNITY. Inmunidad soberana. Doctrina legal que impide una demanda contra el gobierno o una entidad gubernamental a no ser que el gobierno o la entidad gubernamental acceda y permita tal demanda.

SOVEREIGNTY. Soberanía. El poder supremo, absoluto e independiente bajo el cual un estado tiene el derecho a gobernarse. El poder de un estado de actuar en forma independiente y con autoridad.

SPEAKER OF THE HOUSE. Presidente de la Cámara de Representantes del Congreso.

SPECIAL. Especial, extraordinario. Que designa algo en particular, individual.

SPECIAL APPEARANCE. Comparecencia en corte limitada o especial.

SPECIAL ASSESSMENT. Tasación para mejoras. Impuesto sobre mejoras de bienes y raíces.

SPECIAL DAMAGES. Daños indirectos.

SPECIAL INTERROGATORIES. Interrogatorios especiales. Preguntas escritas por un juez para un jurado. Si las respuestas del jurado están en conflicto con el veredicto, el juez puede anular el veredicto.

SPECIAL TRUST. Fideicomiso especial.

SPECIAL USE PERMIT. Documento que permite variar el tipo de uso previamente planificado para una zona urbana. Véase "Zoning".

SPECIAL VERDICT. Veredicto sobre los hechos solamente, sin decisión final.

SPECIAL WARRANTY DEED. Título de propiedad que solo otorga los derechos que la persona que ejecuta el título posee sobre la propiedad.

SPECIFIC BEQUEST. Legado de una propiedad específica en un testamento. Por ejemplo: Mi reloj de plata.

SPECIFIC INTENT. Intención específica. Elemento de ciertos crímenes que requiere que para probar un crimen, por ejemplo hurto, debe establecerse que el estado mental del acusado era tal que el acusado tenía la intención de cometer el crimen.

SPECIFIC PERFORMANCE. Cumplimiento específico, cumplimiento material. Cumple con lo específicamente pactado. Realizar la obligación del contrato.

SPECTOGRAPH. Máquina que se usa para identificar la voz de otra persona.

SPECULATION. Especulación. La compra o venta de un bien con la esperanza de realizar una ganancia por medio del aumento o la baja de su precio.

SPECULATIVE DAMAGES. Daños eventuales o anticipados.

SPEECH or DEBATE CLAUSE. Artículo de la Constitución de los Estados Unidos que provee inmunidad a los miembros del Congreso durante debates o discursos en la legislatura.

SPEEDY TRIAL. Proceso imparcial sin demora al cual todo acusado de un crimen tiene derecho.

SPENDTHRIFT. Despilfarrador, derrochador. Persona que malgasta el dinero abiertamente y por consecuencia sus bienes pueden ser sujetos a la custodia y supervisión de la corte, resultando en un fideicomiso a favor de la persona bajo tutela.

SPLIT ACTION. Un juicio para decidir solamente parte de una demanda.

SPLIT SENTENCE. Sentencia de multa con suspensión de la encarcelación.

SPOKESMAN. Vocero, portavoz. Persona con la autoridad para hablar a nombre de otros.

SPONTANEOUS DECLARATION. Declaración espontánea. Declaración sobre un acontecimiento formulada a raíz de la impresión hecha por el acontecimiento, de tal modo que tal declaración no hubiese podido ser inventad o fabricada.

SPOT. En la bolsa de dinero o de granos, se refiere a una compra para entrega inmediata de dinero o de granos.

SPREAD. Márgen. La diferencia entre la oferta y la demanda de acciones, granos u otros bienes en un mercado financiero.

SPURIOUS. Espurio. Falso, sin mérito, contrahecho, imitado.

SQUATTER. Colono usurpador. El que se establece en tierras baldías para ganar título de propietario.

SQUATTER'S RIGHTS. Derechos de usurpador. Derecho que tiene un usurpador de quedarse en un terreno porque lo ha ocupado por largo tiempo.

SQUEEZE OUT. Medidas de consolidación implementadas por los accionistas mayoritarios de una corporación para comprar o neutralizar los derechos de los accionistas minoritarios.

STAKEHOLDER. Depositario. Persona sin intereses en una disputa que toma posesión de algo en disputa hasta que se determine quien tiene derecho a ello.

STAMP TAX. Impuesto cobrado por estampillas o timbres. Impuesto sobre ciertos documentos legales, tales como escrituras, que requieren estampillas para que éstos sean válidos.

STAND. Estrado. Lugar donde un testigo se sienta o se para al atestiguar.

STANDARD. Pautas o normas usadas en un oficio o profesión. (1) **Standard of Care.** Forma de comportamiento normalmente requerida de una persona ante una situación específica. Si el comportamiento de la persona se desvía de la norma, puede haber negligencia. (2) **Standard of Proof.** Nivel de prueba que se requiere en un caso para probar un hecho.

STANDING. Derecho de una persona a presentar una demanda en caso de encontrarse directamente afectada por los hechos ocurridos.

STANDING MUTE. Cuando el acusado criminal se niega a contestar una acusación. Generalmente en estos casos el juez considerara que el acusado se estima a sí mismo como no culpable.

STAR–CHAMBER. Corte en la antigua Inglaterra que tenía el poder de castigar a aquellas personas que desobedecieran al Rey. La frase STAR CHAMBER LAW aún se utiliza cuando un juez abusa de su poder al castigar severamente a un individuo.

STARE DECISIS. (Lat.) Acatar las decisiones, observar los precedentes. Norma legal, basada en decisiones previas, que debe aplicar la corte cuando ésta toma una decisión sobre un caso con hechos y principios legales similares. Este es el principio de Jurisprudencia que se atiene a casos anteriores sobre temas similares.

STATE. (1) Condición, situación, estado. (2) Mayor subdivisión política de los Estados Unidos. (3) **State Law.** Ley de un estado. (4) **State of War.** Estado de guerra. (5) **State Tax.** Impuesto estatal. (6) **State Unemployment Compensation.** Compensación estatal por desempleo o por cesantía.

STATE DEPARTMENT. Departmento de Estado, Secretaría de Relaciones Exteriores.

STATEHOOD. Estadidad. Que existe como estado.

STATE OF THE CASE. El estado en que se encuentra un caso dentro del proceso de litigio.

STATE'S EVIDENCE. Prueba de cargo. Testimonio contra el acusado.

STATEMENT. Declaración. (1) Cualquier declaración, escrita, oral o por comportamiento. (2) Documento que contiene las declaraciones de un testigo. (3) Estado de cuenta.

STATION HOUSE. Estación de Policía.

STATUS. Estado legal o civil. Condición básica. Relación entre el individuo y el resto de la comunidad. (1) **Status Crime.** Crimen que depende solamente del estado de una persona en vez de

693

regirse por lo que esa persona haya hecho. Por ejemplo, un vago puede ser condenado por vagancia. (2) **Status Quo.** En el mismo estado.

STATUTE. Ley. Estatuto. Ley pasada por la legislatura.

STATUTE OF FRAUDS. Ley de fraudes o contra fraudes. Varias leyes estatales que requieren que ciertos tipos de contratos estén escritos y firmados para poder ser válidos.

STATUTE OF LIMITATIONS. Ley de prescripción; estatuto de limitaciones. Ley que establece los períodos de tiempo que deben transcurrir para que un derecho se pierda por prescripción.

STATUTE OF WILLS. Ley que requiere que un testamento sea escrito, firmado y atestiguado para ser válido.

STATUTORY. Estatutario. Algo que tiene que ver con un estatuto; creado, definido o requerido por un estatuto.

STATUTORY CRIME. Crimen establecido por la ley.

STATUTORY LIEN. Gravamen legal.

STAY. Suspender, posponer. (1) **Stay of Execution.** Cuando un juez suspende la ejecución de una sentencia. (2) **Stay Law.** Estatutos que suspenden acciones legales, generalmente para proteger a los deudores en tiempos de crisis financiera a nivel nacional.

STEAL. Robar. Tomar algo en violación de un derecho legal o una ley criminal.

STENOGRAPHIC RECORD. Acta taquigráfica, transcripción estenográfica.

STEPCHILD. Hijastro(a). El hijo de un cónyuge con relación al otro cónyuge.

STEWARD. Administrador, mayordomo. Miembro de un sindicato laboral que representa a los obreros ante el patrón.

STICK UP. Saltear, atracar.

STIFLING A PROSECUTION. Aceptar dinero a cambio de no enjuiciar a un individuo en una caso criminal.

STIPULATE. Estipular. Pactar, convenir, acordar.

694

STIPULATION. Convenio, contrato, pacto. Acuerdo entre abogados de partes opuestas durante un juicio. Generalmente se hace por escrito y se relaciona con los procedimientos ante la corte o hechos que no necesitan prueba.

STIRPES. Estirpe. Aquella persona de donde una familia desciende. Raíz o tronco de una familia o linaje.

STOCK. Acciones. (1) **Blue Chip Stock.** Acciones de alto valor y buen récord financiero. (2) **Common Stock.** Acciones comunes. Acciones que solo reflejan un interés proporcional en el capital de una corporación. (3) **Control Stock.** Un bloque de acciones que controlan las acciones de la corporación. (4) **Convertible Stock.** Acciones que se pueden convertir en acciones comunes. (5) **Preferred Stock.** Acciones preferidas. Acciones que tienen ciertos derechos prioritarios. (6) **Registered Stock.** Acciones registradas bajo las leyes federales que rigen la compra/venta de valores. (7) **Stock Broker.** Agente que compra y vende acciones en nombre de otros. (8) **Stock Certificate.** Certificado de acciones. (9) **Stock Market or Exchange.** Bolsa de valores donde se compran y venden acciones. (10) **Voting Stock.** Acción con derecho de voto. El poseedor de estas acciones que tienen derecho de votación para la elección de la junta directiva de la corporación.

STOCK DIVIDENDS. Dividendos en acciones. Ganancia de una corporación que se reparte entre los accionistas en forma de acciones.

STOCK OPTION PLAN. Sistema o plan que ofrece varias opciones para comprar acciones.

STOCKHOLDER. Accionista; el que es dueño de acciones.

STOCKHOLDER'S LIABILITY. Responsabilidad de los accionistas ante los depositantes.

STOCKHOLDER'S MEETING. Asamblea, junta o reunión de accionistas.

STOP & FRISK. Detener y registrar a una persona sospechosa que puede estar armada.

STOP PAYMENT ORDER. Orden de no pago. Orden dirigida al pagador de un giro, cheque o instrumento negociable prohibiendo el pago del mismo.

STOPPAGE IN TRANSIT. Embargo por el vendedor de mercancías en tránsito. Derecho de un vendedor para suspender el tránsito de mercancías aun después que éstas hayan sido entregadas al transportador. Por ejemplo, si el vendedor descubre que el comprador está al borde de la bancarrota y no podrá pagar por la mercancía, el vendedor puede cancelar el envío.

STRAIGHT LINE DEPRECIATION. Depreciación uniforme.

STRANGER. Tercera persona que de ninguna forma toma parte en un trato.

STREAM OF COMMERCE. Literalmente, corriente o flujo del comercio. Término usado cuando la mercancía está en tránsito entre estados para indicar el libre movimiento comercial.

STRICKEN. Eliminado, tachado.

STRICT. Exacto, preciso. Gobernado por normas exactas.

STRICT CONSTRUCTION (OF A LAW). Interpretar una ley o estatuto de manera estricta y rigurosa.

STRICT LIABILITY. Responsabilidad objetiva. (1) Responsabilidad legal que cabe a alquien por perjuicios o daños causados, aunque esa persona no sea culpable. Por ejemplo, un vendedor puede ser responsable por daños y perjuicios causados por un producto defectuoso que él vendió, aunque él no haya fabricado tal producto. (2) Culpabilidad de una ofensa criminal aunque el acusado no haya cometido el crimen intencionalmente.

STRIKE. Huelga laboral. (1) **Strike a Bargain.** Llegar a un convenio, cerrar un trato. (2) **Strike Call.** Emplazamiento de huelga.

STRIKING A JURY. Selección del Jurado. Escoger a varios individuos para que sirvan de jurado en un caso.

STRING CITATION. Literalmente, lista de citaciones. Lista de casos y citaciones que siguen a una afirmación o conclusión legal para apoyarla.

STRUCTURED SETTLEMENT. Acuerdo que fija las condiciones de una disputa mediante el pago periódico de ciertas cantidades.

STYLE. Título de una persona.

SUA SPONTE. (Lat.) De su propia voluntad; voluntariamente.

SUB. (Lat.) Debajo de.

SUB JUDICE. (Lat.) Pendiente de una resolución judicial. Todavía no decidido porque el juez lo está considerando.

SUB NOMINE. Bajo el nombre de; a nombre de.

SUBCHAPTER "S" CORPORATION. Corporación pequeña establecida bajo las leyes fiscales de los Estados Unidos, donde las ganancias de la corporación son atribuídas a los accionistas para ser gravadas como sus ingresos personales.

SUBDELEGATION. Véase "Delegation".

SUBJECT MATTER JURISDICTION. Poder jurisdiccional de una corte para acoger y determinar un caso. Competencia para resolver la materia sujeta a su consideración.

SUBJECT OF A COUNTRY. Súbdito.

SUBJECT TO. Subordinado a; gobernado por; afectado por; limitado por. (1) **Subject to Duty.** Gravable, sujeto a derechos. (2) **Subject to Tax.** Tributable, sujeto a impuesto. (3) **Subject to Withholding.** Sujeto a retención.

SUBLEASE. Subalquiler. Subarriendo. Cuando el arrendatario alquila o arrienda parte de lo que ha arrendado, convirtiéndose en un subarrendador.

SUBLET. Subarrendar, subalquilar; subcontratar.

SUBMIT. Someter. (1) Poner una decisión en otras manos. (2) Conceder, ceder a. (3) Dar evidencia. (4) Ofrecer algo para su aprobación.

SUBORDINATION. Subordinación. Sujeción, dependencia.

SUBORN. Sobornar, cohechar.

SUBORNATION OF PERJURY. Instigación por soborno para que se cometa perjurio. Crimen cometido al pedir o forzar a una persona para que mienta bajo juramento.

SUBPOENA. Citación. Documento mediante el cual la corte ordena a una persona que comparezca ante ella a una hora fija o ante un oficial de la corte para atestiguar en un caso.

SUBPOENA AD TESTIFICANDUM. Citación de un testigo.

SUBPOENA DUCES TECUM. (Lat.) Citación para comparecer y producir documentos.

SUBROGATE. Abrogar, substituir.

SUBROGATION. Subrogación. Sustitución de una persona por otra en una demanda, de modo que la segunda persona puede llevar adelante la demanda de la persona sustituida.

SUBSCRIBE. Subscribir. Firmar al pie de un escrito. Obligarse uno a contribuir con otros al pago de una cantidad.

SUBSCRIBED AND SWORN TO. Suscrito y declarado bajo juramento.

SUBSEQUENT. Subsecuente, subsiguiente. (1) **Subsequent Condition.** Condición subsecuente. (2) **Subsequent Negligence.** Negligencia subsecuente.

SUBSIDIARY. Subsidiaria. Corporación donde la mayoría de las acciones son controladas por otra corporación.

SUBSIDIZE. Subvencionar. Concesión de dinero dada por el gobierno, ayuntamiento, etc., a una entidad o individuo para fomentar una obra o un sevicio de interés público.

SUBSTITUTED SERVICE. Notificación por edicto o por correo, citación que no se entrega directamente a la persona citada.

SUBSIDY. Subsidio. La donación de servicios o dinero por una entidad gubernamental a una empresa o actividad económica con el objeto de ayudar a su desarrollo.

SUBSTANCE. Substancia, esencia, fondo. Aquello que es esencial o material.

SUBSTANTIAL COMPLIANCE RULE. Norma que indica que se ha cumplido con los requisitos básicos de un contrato o un estatuto.

SUBSTANTIAL PERFORMANCE. Cumplimiento sustancial. Cuando una parte de un contrato ha cumplido con los términos esenciales del mismo y ha variado solamente el cumplimiento de términos insignificantes del contrato.

SUBSTANTIATE. Comprobar, verificar.

SUBSTANTIVE EVIDENCE. Prueba sustantiva. Evidencia que prueba hechos que están en disputa.

SUBSTANTIVE LAW. Derecho sustantivo. Ley básica que enuncia o contiene derechos y responsabilidades.

SUBTRACTION. Sustracción. Ofensa de negarle a una persona lo que tiene derecho bajo la ley.

SUBVERSION. Subversión. El acto o el proceso de derrocar, destruir o corromper algo, especialmente las actividades gubernamentales.

SUCCESSION. Sucesión. Heredar los bienes de alguien. Transferir derechos o bienes mediante herencia a causa de muerte.

SUCCESSOR. Sucesor, causa habiente. El que toma el lugar de otro.

SUCCESOR IN INTEREST. Sucesor de los intereses o propiedad de otro.

SUDDEN EMERGENCY DOCTRINE. Doctrina de la emergencia repentina. Cuando una persona se enfrenta a una emergencia inesperada la cual no fue resultado de sus acciones, las acciones tomadas en ese momento que son razonables y prudentes, no se consideran negligentes aunque después se descubran otras alternativas que hubiesen sido más seguras.

SUE. Demandar, empezar un pleito civil. Entablar un juicio.

SUFFER LOSS. Sufrir una pérdida.

SUFFICIENT CAUSE. Causa suficiente. Causa legal para destituir a un oficial público de su puesto. La causa de la destitución debe afectar la habilidad de la persona en servir el interés público y ejecutar su cargo.

SUFFRAGE. Sufragio, voto. Expresar la voluntad mediante votación.

SUI GENERIS. (Lat.) De su propio género; único; particular y específico en su clase.

SUI JURIS. (Lat.) Por derecho propio; de plena capacidad legal.

SUIT. Acción judicial, pleito, litigio. Demanda.

SUIT MONEY. Alimentos provisionales pagados durante un juicio matrimonial. El pago de honorarios por orden de la corte.

699

SUITOR. Demandante, actor. El que inicia un pleito.

SUMMARY. Recopilación, resumen; sumario.

SUMMARY JUDGMENT. Sentencia sumaria. Cuando una de las partes gana el caso antes de que haya un juicio, ya que la ley, al aplicarse a los hechos indisputibles del caso, es suficientes para justificar que el juez decida a favor de esa parte.

SUMMARY OF INCOME AND DEDUCTIONS. Resumen de ingresos y deducciones.

SUMMARY PROCESS. Proceso sumario. Audiencia en juicio abreviado.

SUMMATION. Resumen, conclusiones.

SUMMING UP. Sumario, resumir, alegación de bien probado.

SUMMON. Convocar, llamar; citar, emplazar.

SUMMONS. Convocatoria. Una citación o notificación entregada por un alguacil u otra persona autorizada informando a la persona demandada de la querella en su contra, y requiriendo que la persona comparezca ante la corte en cierta fecha para responder a la demanda, o se arriesga a perder el caso. **Summons and Complaint.** Emplazamiento y demanda.

SUMPTUARY LAWS. Leyes suntuarias. Leyes que controlan la venta o el uso de productos de lujo.

SUNSET LAW. Ley que requiere que una agencia gubernamental pruebe periódicamente a la legislatura la necesidad de su existencia.

SUNSHINE LAW. Ley que requiere que las reuniones de agencias gubernamentales sean abiertas al público. Véase "Freedom of Information Act".

SUO NOMINE. (Lat.) En su nombre.

SUPERIOR. Superior. (1) **Superior Court.** Tribunal superior o de máxima jerarquía. (2) Que tiene un grado más elevado.

SUPERSEDE. Reemplazar, desalojar. (1) Poner a un lado; eliminar; hacer innecesario. (2) Reemplazar una ley o documento por otro.

SUPERSEDEAS. (Lat.) Auto de suspensión del juicio. Orden de un tribunal superior a un juez inferior para que suspenda el juicio hasta nueva orden.

SUPERSEDING CAUSE. Causa reemplazable. Acción realizada por una tercera persona u otra fuerza, cuya intervención sirve para absolver de negligencia o responsabilidad a la persona que originalmente actuó de forma tal que causó daños a otra persona. Véase "Intervening Cause".

SUPERVENING. Nuevo, efectivo.

SUPERVENING CAUSE. Causa Sobreviniente. Causa subsecuente que por sí sola e independientemente de otra anterior, origina un daño.

SUPERVENING NEGLIGENCE. Negligencia sobreviniente. Establece responsabilidad cuando hay negligencia por el actor, aunque la víctima hubiese estado de antemano en una situación de peligro si aquel tuvo oportunidad de evitar el daño y la víctima no pudo evitar tal situación.

SUPERVISOR. Supervisor. (1) En algunos estados, el oficial principal de un condado o pueblo. (2) Cualquier persona con autoridad sobre otras.

SUPPLEMENTAL. Suplemental, suplementario.

SUPPLEMENTAL PLEADING. Alegato suplemental. Un alegato que presenta eventos ocurridos después que se entabló la demanda.

SUPPLEMENTARY PROCEEDINGS. Trámites para examinar al deudor y determinar si posee bienes embargables.

SUPPORT. Manutención. Sostener; apoyar; mantener. Obligación de un individuo de mantener económicamente a su familia.

SUPPORTING DOCUMENTS. Documentos justificativos o comprobantes.

SUPPOSITION. Suposición, supuesto. Hipótesis.

SUP-PRO. Véase "Supplementary Proceedings".

SUPRA. (Lat.) Sobre, antes, anterior, en la parte previa.

SUPREMACY CLAUSE. Cláusula de la Constitución de los Estados Unidos que declara que las leyes federales tienen primacía sobre las leyes estatales que son contrarias a las federales.

SUPREME COURT. Corte Suprema. Corte Superior en los Estados Unidos.

SUPPRESS. Suprimir. **Suppress Evidence.** Omitir evidencia en un juicio criminal al comprobar que fue obtenida ilegalmente.

SURCHARGE. Recargo, sobretasa. (1) Imponer una deuda u obligación personal a un fiduciario por contravenir sus deberes y mal administrar los bienes de un fideicomiso. (2) Cobro adicional por algún servicio.

SURETY. Fiador, garante. Persona o compañía que garantiza o asegura que una deuda u obligación contraida por otra persona será pagada por él/ella si hay algún incumplimiento.

SURETY BOND. Bono de garantía; figura de caución.

SURETY COMPANY. Institución de fianzas.

SURFACE RIGHTS. Derechos a la superficie. Cuando una persona que posee derechos de explotación minera también posee derechos al uso de la propiedad sobre la cual existe el derecho de minar.

SURNAME. Apellido.

SURPLUS. Excedente, sobrante, exceso, superávit.

SURPLUSAGE. Sobrante, excedente, impertinente. Algo irrelevante a un caso o un documento legal.

SURPRISE. Sorpresa. Cuando una de las partes en un juicio, sin culpa alguna, se encuentra con evidencia (oral o de otro tipo) totalmente inesperada que perjudica la presentación de su caso. Bajo ciertas circunstancias, el juez puede anular una sentencia, fallo, orden o procedimiento a causa de una sorpresa.

SURREBUTTER. Contestación a la refutación del demandado.

SURRENDER. Cesión, renuncia, entrega. En la ley de contratos, significa abandono de la propiedad o de algún derecho.

SURREPTITIOUS. Subrepticio. Algo hecho a escondidas.

SURROGATE. Subrogar. (1) Juez del tribunal testamentario. (2) Persona que toma el lugar de, o representa a otro.

SURTAX. Impuesto adicional, sobretasa, recargo tributario.

SURVEY. Investigación, examinación, interrogatorio, encuesta.

SURVIVAL STATUTES. Estatutos de supervivencia. Leyes estatales que permiten que en ciertos casos un juicio sea llevado a cabo por un familiar después de la muerte de otro familiar.

SURVIVING. Superviviente o sobreviviente. El que vive luego de la muerte de otro.

SURVIVING SPOUSE. Cónyuge sobreviviente.

SURVIVORSHIP. Supervivencia. Cuando una persona co-dueña de una propiedad se hace dueña única de la propiedad al morir la otra co-dueña.

SUSPECT. Sospechoso. Persona de quien se presume cometió un delito.

SUSPECT CLASSIFICATION. Clasificación sospechosa. Con respecto a la fórmula usada para determinar si una clasificación bajo la ley constituye la negación del derecho a un igual trato bajo la ley; clasificaciones sospechosas son aquellas basadas en raza, ciudadanía, nacionalidad o sexo.

SUSPEND. Interrumpir, descontinuar, cesar.

SUSPENDED SENTENCE. Sentencia suspendida, condena provisional.

SUSPENSION. Suspensión. Que sus efectos no están realizándose.

SUSPICION. Sospecha. Imaginar una cosa fundada en apariencias.

SUSTAIN. Sostener, sustentar, mantener. (1) Conceder. Cuando un juez está de acuerdo con una objeción y la pone en efecto. (2) Mantener una posición. (3) Apoyar o justificar. Si la evidencia justifica el veredicto, se dice que sostiene el veredicto.

SWEAR. Jurar; declarar bajo juramento.

SWEATING. Interrogar agresivamente y con amenazas a un sospechoso criminal. Este tipo de interrogatorio es inconstitucional.

SWEETHEART CONTRACT. Contrato de trabajo que incluye términos favorables para una de las partes, y cuyo propósito es mantener fuera a otra unión o sindicato laboral competidor.

SWIFT WITNESS. Testigo que se muestra muy ansioso para dar testimonio favorable a la parte que lo llamó a testificar.

SWINDLE. Estafa, timo; estafar, embaucar.

SWINDLER. Estafador, timador, embaucador.

SWORN STATEMENT OR DECLARATION. Declaración jurada. Manifestación expresada bajo la gravedad del juramento.

SYLLABUS. Resumen de una decisión de la corte la cual no forma parte de la opinión oficial. Resumen. Compendio del dictamen.

SYMPATHETIC STRIKE. Huelga solidaria o por solidaridad; huelga de apoyo a otros huelguistas.

SYNDICALISM. Sindicalismo. (1) **Criminal Syndicalism.** Sindicalismo criminal, provocar un crimen, sabotaje, etc., para tomarse una industria o afectar el sistema político.

SYNDICATE. Sindicato, consorcio. Asociación de individuos formada con el objeto de ejecutar algún proyecto financiero de interés común. (1) **Crime Syndicate.** Grupo de criminales organizados, un sindicato criminal.

SYNOPSIS. Sinopsis, suma, resumen.

T

T. Una vieja abreviatura del latín "testamentum". Testamento.

T.C. Abreviación para el Tribunal Tributario. Véase "Tax Court".

TABLE. (Verb) Suspender la deliberación sobre una ley propuesta por la legislatura.

TACIT. Tácito. Entendido sin que se diga expresamente; hecho en silencio, implícito.

TACKING. Acción de anexar un gravamen posterior al gravamen original sobre un inmueble, para adquirir prioridad sobre cualquier gravamen intermedio.

TAFT HARTLEY ACT. Una ley federal, pasada en 1947, que agregó varios derechos de patrono a los derechos de los sindicatos que aparecen en el "Wagner Act."

TAIL. Limitación de propiedad. Limitado solamente a niños, nietos etc.

TAINT. Convicción. (1) Condena por un delito mayor. (2) El convicto por un delito grave.

TAKE. Tomar. Sacar. Esta palabra tiene una variedad de significados, el más común es privar a una persona, sin su consentimiento, de un bien.

TAKE THE STAND. Dirigirse al banquillo. Testificar en la corte.

TAKE DOWN. El momento en que se lleva a cabo un acuerdo, como la fecha en que ciertos productos han sido entregados y pagados.

TAKE–OUT LOAN. Una hipoteca permanente que paga por un préstamo de construcción.

TAKE–OVER. Asumir la administración. Tomar control del manejo de algo; por ejemplo, asumir la administración de una compañía o negocio, sin que necesariamente medie una transferencia de título de propiedad.

TAKING THE FIFTH. Cuando un testigo o un sospechoso rehusa contestar una pregunta, amparándose en la quinta enmienda a la Constitución de los Estados Unidos, la cual le da el derecho a rehusarse a dar información que lo pueda incriminar.

TALESMAN. Jurado Suplente. Una persona tomada entre los presentes en la corte para que sirva de jurado.

TAMPER. Alterar. Hacer cambios ilegales o fraudulentos.

TANGIBLE. Tangible. Que se puede tocar; real.

TARE. Peso total de la mercancía menos el peso de la caja o recipiente.

TARGET. Blanco, objetivo. Algo a lo que se aspira. El propósito de una investigación.

TARIFF. Tarifa. (1) Impuesto de importación. (2) Lista o catálogo de precios o impuestos que se debe por artículos importados.

TAX. Impuesto. Contribución fiscal. Tributo fiscal impuesto sobre contribuyentes, quienes pueden ser personas naturales o jurídicas. (1) **Capital Gains Tax.** Impuestos sobre las ganancias de capital. Provisión en las leyes de impuestos bajo las cuales los impuestos sobre la venta o intercambio de bienes de capital son más bajos que los impuestos sobre entradas ordinarias. (2) **Estate Tax.** Impuesto hereditario. Impuesto sobre el derecho a transferir propiedad antes de morir. (3) **Gift Tax.** Impuesto sobre donaciones. Impuesto sobre propiedad transferida como regalo. (4) **Head Tax.** Impuesto por cabeza. (5) **Personal Property Tax.** Impuesto sobre la propiedad personal como automóviles, muebles, etc. (6) **Property Tax.** Impuesto sobre propiedad, como bienes inmuebles basado en el valor de la propiedad. (7) **Sales Tax.** Impuesto sobre la venta de bienes, basado en el valor del artículo vendido. (8) **Stock Transfer Tax.** Impuesto sobre la venta o transferencia de acciones; (9) **Surtax.** Impuesto adicional sobre cierto tipo de entradas, tales como intereses sobre dinero invertido, créditos recibidos, etc.

TAX ACCOUNT INFORMATION. Información relacionada con una cuenta de impuestos.

TAX ASSESSMENT. Avalúo fiscal. Valor dado a una propiedad para efectos de impuestos.

TAX AUDITOR. Auditor de impuestos; inspector de impuestos.

TAX AVOIDANCE. Reducir legalmente la cantidad de impuestos pagados, mediante el uso de las leyes fiscales disponibles.

TAX BASE. Base imponible. El valor total dado a todos los bienes inmuebles en un área, el cual determina la tarifa de impuestos sobre cada propiedad individual.

TAX BENEFIT RULE. Si la cantidad deducida de impuestos en un año es recuperada en otro año, la cantidad recuperada será considerada como ganancia para efectos fiscales y gravada como tal.

TAX BILL. Factura de impuestos; factura de contribución.

TAX BRACKET. Tramo de la escala del impuesto; tramo de la escala contributiva. Nivel impositivo.

TAX COMPUTATION. Cálculo de impuesto; cómputo de la contribución.

TAX COURT. Corte Fiscal. Corte Federal que considera apelaciones presentadas por contribuyentes cuando el Servicio de Rentas Internas les ha acusado de tener una deficiencia en el pago de sus impuestos.

TAX CREDIT. Crédito fiscal. Deducción sobre impuestos permitida a un contribuyente por haber pagado otros impuestos.

TAX DEDUCTION. Deducción sobre impuestos. Deducción sobre entradas y ganancias para calcular las entradas a las que se les, impondrán impuestos.

TAX DEED. Escritura traslativa de dominio por impuestos no pagados. Prueba de propiedad de tierra otorgada a un comprador por el gobierno, después de que el gobierno le ha quitado la propiedad a otra persona por no haber pagado sus impuestos. Véase "Tax Title".

TAX DISPUTE. Conflicto fiscal; controversia tributaria.

TAX EVASION. Evasión de impuestos. Pagar ilegalmente menos impuestos de lo que la ley exige. Véase "Tax Fraud".

TAX EXEMPT. (1) Propiedades tales como aquellas que pertenecen a escuelas, iglesias, etc. que no están sujeta a impuestos sobre inmuebles. (2) Inversiones, tales como bonos municipales que producen renta no gravable. (3) Entradas no gravables, tales como aquellas recibidas por organizaciones benéficas.

TAX FERRET. Persona que busca propiedades que no han sido gravadas o que denuncian a los que han evadido el impuesto, a cambio de una recompensa, usualmente un porcentaje de los impuestos recuperados.

TAX FORM. Formulario de impuestos, planilla de contribución.

TAX FRAUD. Fraude fiscal. Acto deliberado de un contribuyente al no pagar impuestos, o al pagar menos impuestos de los que son legalmente debidos.

TAX FREE. Libre de impuesto. Sin carga tributaria. No sujeto al pago de impuestos.

TAX HAVEN COUNTRY. País de refugio tributario o paraíso tributario.

TAX HOME. Domicilio tributario.

TAX LIABILITY. Impuesto por pagar.

TAX LIEN. Gravamen de impuestos. Gravamen creado por una ley, que existe a favor de un estado o municipio, sobre los bienes inmuebles de una persona que debe impuestos sobre propiedad.

TAX LIST. Lista de bienes o de contribuyentes para efectos tributarios.

TAX PACKAGE AND INSTRUCTIONS. Juego de formularios e instrucciones para el impuesto; juego de planillas e instrucciones para la contribución.

TAX PENALTY. Multa sobre impuestos; multa contributiva. Multa por pagar los impuestos con retraso.

TAX PREFERENCE ITEMS. Beneficios tributarios sujetos a impuestos mínimos.

TAX PREPARER. Preparador de declaraciones de impuestos; preparador de planillas de contribución o impuestos.

TAX RATE. Tasa o cuota de impuesto. El porcentaje de renta gravable pagada en impuestos. Véase "Tax Table".

TAX RETURN. Declaración de impuestos. Formulario usado para declarar y reportar los ingresos, deducciones, etc.

TAX SALE. Venta de bienes para recobrar los impuestos no pagados por la propiedad vendida.

TAX SHELTER. Abrigo tributario. Mecanismos fiscales usados para reducir o diferir el pago de impuestos

TAX STATEMENT (BILL). Estado de cuenta contributiva.

TAX STATUS. Posición ante el impuesto. Situación fiscal.

TAX TABLE. Tabla de impuestos; tabla de contribución en base a la renta gravable.

TAX TITLE. Título de propiedad obtenido por una venta tributaria para pagar impuestos atrasados. Véase "Tax Deed".

TAX YEAR. Ejercicio fiscal, año tributario; año contributivo.

TAXABLE. Tributable. Sujeto a impuestos.

TAXABLE INCOME. Ingreso gravable. Bajo las leyes fiscales federales, el ingreso bruto de los negocios o el ingreso ajustado de los individuos, menos deducciones y exoneraciones.

TAXING COSTS. Imponer gastos. Ordenar que una de las partes en una demanda pague a la otra parte sus gastos legales incurridos en perseguir el pleito.

TAXPAYER. Contribuyente. El que paga o tiene la obligación de pagar impuestos.

TAXPAYER IDENTIFICATION NUMBER (TIN). Número de identificación del contribuyente.

TAXPAYER SERVICE REPRESENTATIVE (TSR). Representante de servicios al contribuyente.

TAXPAYER SUIT. Demanda del contribuyente. Demanda presentada contra el gobierno por un contribuyente reclamándole por los usos que el gobierno le ha dado al dinero público.

TECHNICAL. Técnico. Que pertenece a una ciencia o arte. Los términos técnicos son conocidos como "palabras de arte".

TECHNICAL ANALYSIS. Análisis técnico. Tomar una decisión sobre vender o comprar acciones u otros valores, basándose en un estudio del historial de las mismas (precios, volumen de rentas, etc.).

TECHNICAL ERROR. Error cometido durante el curso de un juicio, el cual no tiene efecto alguno sobre el proceso o el resultado final.

TELLER. Cajero. Una persona que cuenta algo; por ejemplo un cajero de banco que recibe y paga dinero, o un contador de votos en una asamblea legislativa.

TEMPORARY. Temporáneo, temporario o temporal. Lo contrario de permanente en duración.

TEMPORARY DETENTION. El hecho de arrestar a alguien mientras se decide el curso de una acción criminal contra el detenido.

TEMPORARY DISABILITY. Período de recuperación en el que una persona no puede trabajar a causa de una herida. Dicho período continúa hasta que la persona se pueda reintegrar completamente a su trabajo.

TEMPORARY RESTRAINING ORDER. Juicio de amparo temporal. Orden judicial que prohibe a una persona tomar ciertas acciones antes de que se efectúe un juicio o audiencia.

TENANCY. Inquilinato. (1) La condición de ser un inquilino. (2) La duración de un contrato de alquiler.

TENANCY AT WILL. Tipo de posesión bajo la cual alguien usa o habita una propiedad con el permiso del dueño de la misma, puede ser sin tener un término fijo o con un período fijo que se puede cancelar inmediatamente.

TENANCY IN COMMON. Tenencia en común. Tipo de posesión conjunta bajo la cual cada dueño tiene un interés completo en la propiedad, y cuyo interés no termina con su muerte (el interés pasa a los herederos del dueño).

TENANCY FROM MONTH TO MONTH. Alquiler de mes en mes. Véase "Tenancy at Will".

TENANCY BY THE ENTIRETY. Tipo de posesión entre marido y mujer bajo la cual ambos son dueños de la propiedad y al morir uno el otro toma posesión total sobre la misma.

TENANT. Inquilino. Una persona que ocupa un terreno o edificio pagando un alquiler por su uso.

TENANT FOR LIFE. Inquilino de por vida. Inquilino que ocupa cierta propiedad mientras él u otra persona determinada esté viva.

TENANT FOR YEARS. Inquilino por años. Inquilino que tiene derecho al uso de cierta propiedad, con el permiso del dueño.

TENDER. Oferta, oferta de dinero, propuesta. Una oferta, combinada con la intención de hacer lo que se ofrece.

TENEMENT. Vivienda. Cualquier casa, apartamento, o edificio habitado por gente. En el sentido legal, significa cualquier derecho a una propiedad inmueble que es permanente.

TENOR. Tenor, contenido. Constitución, sentido general o contenido de un escrito o cosa.

TENTATIVE CREDIT. Crédito provisional.

TENTH AMENDMENT. Décima Enmienda. Enmienda a la constitución de los Estados Unidos bajo la cual todos los poderes no dados específicamente al gobierno federal son mantenidos por los estados y por la cuidadanía.

TENURE. Tenencia, posesión, pertenencia. (1) Tenencia de un cargo o una posición gubernamental. (2) La duración de un cargo o puesto.

TERM. Término. (1) Un período fijo. (2) Porción de tiempo dentro del cual algo debe suceder. (3) **Term of Art.** Terminología usada por los profesionales, peritos o técnicos en una disciplina.

TERMINATION. Terminación. Acabar, concluir o finalizar algo antes de lo anticipado.

711

TERRITORIAL. Territorial. Que tiene que ver con un área en particular. Por ejemplo, las aguas territoriales son aquellas que rodean a un país.

TERRITORIAL COURTS. Cortes territoriales. Las cortes en los territorios de los Estados Unidos (por ejemplo, las Islas Vírgenes).

TERRITORIAL WATERS. Aguas territoriales. Extensión marítima desde las costas de un estado sobre las cuales éste ejerce su soberanía. Se consideran parte de su jurisdicción.

TEST CASE. Causa instrumental, caso de prueba. Una querella entablada para establecer un principio o derecho legal importante.

TESTACY. Testado. Dejar un testamento válido. Sucesión testada es aquella que autoriza a dar y recibir una propiedad por medio de un testamento.

TESTAMENT. Testamento. Documento a través del cual una persona dispone la manera como su propiedad debe ser distribuida después de su muerte.

TESTAMENTARY. Testamentario. Que tiene que ver con un testamento.

TESTAMENTARY CAPACITY. Capacidad testamentaria. La habilidad del testador de saber y entender el efecto que tendrá el hacer un testamento, las transacciones que esto conlleva, la capacidad de entender cuáles son los bienes dejados bajo el testamento, y generalmente la naturaleza y medida de la propiedad dejada.

TESTATE. Testado. Alguien que ha hecho un testamento; alguien que muere dejando un testamento.

TESTATE SUCCESSION. Sucesión testamentaria. La adquisición de derechos o propiedad bajo un testamento.

TESTATOR. Testador. Persona que hace un testamento.

TESTATRIX. Testadora. Mujer que hace un testamento.

TESTIFY. Testificar. Dar evidencia bajo juramento.

TESTIMONIUM CLAUSE. Cláusula testimonial. La parte de una escritura u otro documento que contiene el nombre de quien firmó el documento, así como cuando y donde fue firmado.

TESTIMONY. Testimonio. Evidencia dada por un testigo bajo juramento.

TESTIS. (Lat.) Testigo. Persona que afirma algo para demostrar una cosa.

THEFT. Robo, hurto.

THEOCRACY. Teocracia. Gobierno cuya autoridad procede de Dios y es ejercida por sus ministros.

THEORY OF PLEADING DOCTRINE. Principio de derecho consuetudinario bajo el cual una persona tiene que probar su caso exactamente como lo alegó en su querella. De no hacerlo, perderá el caso aunque los hechos prueben otra teoría no alegada. Este principio no es válido hoy día en la mayoría de los tribunales.

THEORY OF THE CASE. Bases de la acción. (1) Hechos bajo los cuales se alega que existe el derecho a demandar. (2) Una interpretación de los hechos y las leyes de un caso que favorece a la parte que expuso la interpretación.

THIRD DEGREE. Interrogatorio severo. Métodos ilegales de interrogación para forzar a una persona a confesar un crimen.

THIRD PARTY or PERSON. Tercero. Una persona que no es parte de un trato, pleito o incidente, pero que puede tener derechos en ellos.

THIRTEENTH AMENDMENT. Décimo tercera enmienda. La enmienda constitucional de los Estados Unidos que abolió la esclavitud.

THREAT. Amenaza. Intención expresa de causar daño a una persona con objeto de modificar sus acciones o de causar daño a una propiedad.

THREE–JUDGE COURT. Corte de tres jueces. Tribunal de primera instancia federal creado específicamente para ver y decidir ciertos casos federales. Las decisiones en estos casos van directamente a la Corte Suprema para ser revisadas.

713

THREE–MILE LIMIT. Límite de tres millas. La distancia de la orilla (una legua marina o tres millas) usualmente reconocida como el límite de jurisdicción territorial de un país.

THROUGH BILL. Conocimiento corrido o directo. Conocimiento de embarque de mercancía que será transportada por más de un embarcador en secuencia.

THROWBACK RULE. Regla de retroceso. Si el beneficiario de un fideicomiso recibe distribuciones durante un año en exceso de los ingresos del fideicomiso en ese año, y el fideicomiso no ha pagado en años anteriores todos sus ingresos, el impuesto con que se gravará el exceso será pagado por el beneficiario ese año menos un crédito por el impuesto pagado previamente por el fideicomiso.

TICKET. Billete, boleta, papeleta, taquilla. (1) Lista de candidatos de un partido político. (2) Notificación de una violación a las leyes de tránsito. (3) Certificado que da derecho a entrar a usar algo (teatro, tren, etc.).

TIME IMMEMORIAL. Tiempo inmemorial. (1) Antes de lo que recuerda cualquier persona viva. (2) Antes de que existiera cualquier registro oral o escrito.

TIME IS OF THE ESSENCE OF CONTRACT. El plazo del contrato es de esencia. Cuando esta frase se encuentra en un contrato, lo acordado debe hacerse dentro de cierto tiempo o el contrato no se podrá cumplir.

TIME–PRICE DOCTRINE. Normas comerciales las cuales permiten que se cobre un precio más alto por cosas compradas a crédito que por las mismas cosas pagadas al contado.

TIME SAVING ACCOUNT. Cuenta de ahorro a término.

TIMELY. Oportuno. Hecho a tiempo. Por ejemplo, un pleito oportuno es aquel que se lleva a cabo antes de que se venza el período de prescripción.

TIPPEE. Persona a quien se le revela información confidencial sobre una compañía con el objeto de manipular un mercado de valores o la compra-venta de acciones.

TIPS DEEMED TO BE WAGES. Propinas consideradas como salarios.

TITHE. La décima parte del ingreso.

TITLE. Título. (1) Nombre que se da a una parte de una Ley. (2) Marca, estilo o designación distintiva. (3) Título que designa un derecho. Normalmente se usa con otra palabra para designar el tipo de título o derecho que es aplicable. "Marketable title", "torrens title", etc.

TITLE DOCUMENTS. Documentos que prueban la existencia de algún derecho legal, normalmente sobre algún bien, sea inmueble o mueble.

TITLE INSURANCE. Organización comercial que se especializa en investigar los títulos de propiedades inmuebles para poder garantizar a un comprador el buen título a una propiedad.

TITLE SEARCH. Investigar el registro de propiedad para determinar si el registro de una propiedad tiene algún defecto o limitación; por ejemplo, un gravamen.

TITLE STANDARD. Normas utilizadas para determinar si el título de una propiedad tiene algún defecto o es válido.

TO FILE A TAX RETURN. Presentar una declaración de impuestos.

TO ITEMIZE. Detallar. Desglosar un detalle.

TO QUALIFY. Calificar. Reunir los requisitos.

TOLL. (1) (Verbo) Vencer, prevenir. (2) (Sustantivo) Tasa o peaje. El dinero pagado por el derecho a usar algo, por ejemplo una carretera, puente, u otra propiedad pública.

TONNAGE TAX. Impuesto de tonelaje. Un impuesto para naves basado en su capacidad.

TORRENS TITLE SYSTEM. Sistema de registro de títulos de propiedad inmueble bajo el cual el título es inscrito y formalmente aprobado por la corte como "Certificado de Título", en vez de únicamente registrar la evidencia del título, como una escritura.

TORT. Responsabilidad Civil extracontractual. Agravio, daño legal, perjuicio. Un daño civil que no está basado en una obligación bajo un contrato. Para probar que un daño civil se ha cometido, se

715

debe probar (1) la existencia de una obligación legal de una persona a otra, (2) que la obligación fue violada, y (3) que la violación fue la causa directa del daño.

TORT–FEASOR o TORTFEASOR. El que comete un agravio.

TOTAL. Total. Completo para propósitos legales.

TOTALITARIANISM. Totalitarismo. Régimen bajo el cual el gobierno o el estado controla la mayoría de los detalles de la vida de cada persona.

TOTTEN TRUST. Fideicomiso creado cuando una persona deposita su propio dinero para el beneficio de otra, nombrándose a sí mismo fiduciario. De morir el fiduciario sin primero haber retirado su dinero del fideicomiso, el dinero se convertirá en propiedad del beneficiario.

TOUCH AND STAY. El derecho de un navío, bajo su póliza de seguro, de atracar y quedarse en ciertos puertos, pero sin poder hacer negocio allí.

TOWN. Municipio, pueblo. Una división civil y política de un estado, que varía en tamaño e importancia, pero que generalmente forma parte de un condado.

TOWNSHIP. Una división de terreno estatal que mide seis millas por cada lado y que varía en importancia como unidad de gobierno, dependiendo del estado.

TRACT INDEX. Indice de terreno. Registro público que contiene todas las escrituras, hipotecas, etc., de una región, parcela por parcela y numeradas con referencia a mapas de esa región.

TRADE. Comercio. (1) Comprar y vender. (2) Profesión u oficio. (3) Trueque, cambio.

TRADE AGREEMENT. Tratado o convenio comercial, acuerdo de intercambio. Convenio comercial. Un tratado entre naciones que permite la venta de ciertos artículos, y establece los impuestos de importación.

TRADEMARK. Marca registrada o comercial. Una marca definida, el lema o símbolo que una compañía puede reservar por ley para su uso exclusivo en la identificación de sus productos.

TRADE NAME. Nombre comercial. El nombre de un negocio. Normalmente está protegido legalmente en el área donde opera la compañía con respecto a los productos o servicios que vende.

TRADE or BUSINESS. Ocupación o negocio.

TRADE SECRET. Datos reservados sobre procesos industriales. Una fórmula, patrón, artículo o información usada en el mundo comercial que tiene valor especial por no ser comúnmente conocido. Mientras se mantenga el secreto, el poseedor puede explotarlo exclusivamente.

TRADE UNION. Gremio; sindicato gremial. Conjunto de trabajadores con el mismo o similar oficio, formado con el propósito de adquirir, mediante negociaciones con el patrono, las mejores condiciones laborales.

TRADITIONARY EVIDENCE. Evidencia tradicional. Evidencia derivada de tradición o reputación, o de declaraciones anteriormente hechas por personas ya muertas, con respecto a cuestiones de linaje, genealogía, líneas limítrofes, etc., cuando no hay testigos vivos que puedan testificar sobre estos asuntos.

TRAFFIC. Tráfico, circulación; comerciar, mercadear.

TRAITOR. Traidor. Uno que traiciona un deber.

TRANSACT. Tramitar; negociar; gestionar.

TRANSACTION. Transacción, gestión. (1) Trato comercial. (2) Un incidente; algo que ha ocurrido. (3) Serie de eventos que forman la base para una demanda civil o criminal.

TRANSCRIPT. Transcripción, copia. Registro literal de juicio.

TRANSFER. Transferencia, traspaso. Cambiar o trasladar de una persona a otra; como vender, otorgar o firmar algo a favor de otra persona; transferir de un lugar a otro lugar, por ejemplo, de una corte a otra, etc.

TRANSFER AGENT. Agente o agencia de transferencias; registrador. Una persona o institución que mantiene el registro de los que poseen acciones y bonos de una compañía. El agente de transferencias algunas veces también maneja el pago de dividendos e intereses.

TRANSFER PAYMENTS. Pagos de transferencia. Pagos hechos por el gobierno como bienestar social o seguro social, por los cuales el gobierno no recibe nada directamente.

TRANSFER TAX. Impuesto de transferencia. Renta sobre propiedad gravada cuando esta es transferida de una persona a otra. Usualmente afecta la transferencias de bienes inmuebles y también los bienes intangibles, por ejemplo, acciones.

TRANSFEROR. Cesionista, el que transfiere algo.

TRANSFERRED INTENT RULE. Si una persona trata de golpear a otra, pero golpea a un tercero en su lugar, la regla establece que él o ella legalmente intentó pegar a la tercera persona. Esta ficción legal le permite a la tercera persona demandar por agravio personal a quien la golpeó, y permite al gobierno acusar al actor de un crimen intencional.

TRANSITORY ACTION. Acción transitoria. Una demanda que puede presentarse en cualquiera de muchos lugares.

TRAUMA. Trauma. (1) Daño causado al cuerpo por un golpe externo. (2) Daño psicológico repentino. (3) Daño psicológico severo causado por un hecho específico del pasado.

TRAVEL ACT. La ley que establece como crimen federal el viajar entre estados o usar medios de transportación, comunicación o comercio entre estados para cometer un crimen.

TRAVELER'S CHECK. Cheque de viajero. Cheque de gerencia comprado en un banco para salvaguardar el dinero con que se viaja. Puede ser hecho efectivo únicamente cuando el comprador firma el cheque por segunda vez.

TRAVERSE. Contradicción, negación, contra demanda. Forma antigua de alegato bajo la cual los hechos presentados por la otra parte eran negados.

TREASON. Traición. Delito bajo el cual una persona intenta derrocar al gobierno de su propio país, o revela secretos de su país a otro país.

TREASURER. Tesorero. Persona encargada de administrar los dineros de una organización pero que no necesariamente se encargan de las decisiones financieras.

TREASURE–TROVE. Literalmente significa tesoro hallado. Dinero u otros artículos de valor hallados escondidos en la tierra u otro lugar privado, y cuyo dueño es desconocido. Dependiendo de la ley estatal, los tesoros hallados pertenecen al que los encontró, al dueño de la propiedad donde se hallaron, al estado, o una porción del tesoro a cada uno de estos.

TREASURY. Tesoro, tesorería. (1) Lugar donde se depositan las rentas públicas y otros ingresos gubernamentales, y de donde se pagan los gastos del gobierno. (2) Departamento gubernamental encargado del recaudo, administración, y desembolso de fondos públicos. Departamento de Hacienda.

TREASURY BILL. Bono de caja. Obligación del gobierno federal a corto plazo. Los bonos de caja se vencen a los tres, seis, o doce meses de su compra.

TREASURY BOND. Bono del estado. Bono a largo plazo emitido por el gobierno federal.

TREASURY CERTIFICATE. Certificado del estado. Certificado emitido por el gobierno federal que se vence en un año, y el cual paga intereses mediante cupones.

TREASURY NOTE. Nota del estado. Nota emitida por el gobierno federal que se vence dentro de uno a cinco años, la cual paga intereses mediante cupones.

TREASURY STOCK. Acciones de caja o tesorería. Acciones que han sido redimidas por la empresa que las emitió.

TREATISE. Tratado. Obra o libro extenso que trata de un tema legal.

TREATY. Tratado, pacto. Un acuerdo formal entre naciones sobre asuntos políticos, económicos, y sociales de importancia. La cláusula del tratado de la Constitución de los Estados Unidos requiere que por lo menos dos terceras partes de los miembros del Senado aprueben cualquier tratado firmado por el presidente.

TREBLE DAMAGES. Daños triplicados. Cuando la cantidad de daños sufridos por una persona es multiplicada por tres conforme a un estatuto, para disuadir la ejecución de ciertos actos injustos o contrarios a la ley.

TRESPASS. Traspasar, transgredir, violar. Interferencia ilegal con la persona, propiedad, o derechos de otro.

TRIAL. Juicio. Una audiencia judicial de un pleito civil o criminal que, regida de acuerdo a las leyes vigentes, tiene poder para decidir todas las cuestiones presentadas por las partes. Para tener un juicio, la corte debe tener la jurisdicción apropiada.

TRIAL BALANCE. En contabilidad balance de prueba. Cuando los créditos y los débitos de una cuenta son sumados independientemente para compararlos. Si no son iguales, hay un error en la contabilidad.

TRIAL COURT. Tribunal de primera instancia.

TRIBAL LANDS. Territorio indígena. Tierras ocupadas por una nación indígena. Una reserva indígena.

TRIBE. Tribu. Nación indígena.

TRIBUNAL. Tribunal. Corte. Lugar donde un juez administra justicia.

TRIER OF FACT. El que tiene la obligación exclusiva de decidir cuales son los hechos de un caso. Usualmente el jurado decide los hechos, pero si no hay jurado el juez asume la obligación.

TROVER. Reivindicación. Acción de recuperación de propiedad mueble. Acción bajo derecho consuetudinario donde una demanda es presentada por una persona que perdió posesión sobre un artículo mueble y quiere recobrarlo, en contra de la persona que encontró el artículo y no quiere devolverlo.

TRUE BILL. Acusación, formulada y aprobada por el gran jurado.

TRUE LEASE. Arrendamiento verdadero. Arrendamiento permitido por las leyes del Servicio de Rentas Internas bajo el cual el arrendador puede reclamar beneficios de propiedad, mientras que el arrendatario puede deducir los pagos de su renta.

TRUE PERSON DOCTRINE. La doctrina bajo la cual una persona totalmente sin culpa no necesita tratar de escapar antes de matar a otra que repentinamente la ataca con fuerza mortal.

TRUE VALUE RULE. Regla del valor del mercado. Cuando las acciones vendidas de una compañía no han sido pagadas en su totalidad, los accionistas de la compañía pueden ser consideradas responsables ante los acreedores de la misma por el déficit creado.

TRUST. Consorcio. Fideicomiso. (1) Un grupo de compañías que tienen un monopolio. (2) El derecho a cierta propiedad, mueble o inmueble, mantenida y administrada por una persona para el beneficio de otra. Los elementos de un fideicomiso son los siguientes: el nombramiento de un fiduciario para administrar el fideicomiso, un beneficiario, fondos o propiedad lo suficientemente identificable para poder ser transferidos al fiduciario con la intención de hacerlo dueño de la misma.

TRUST ALLOTMENT. Terrenos asignados por cierto tiempo a los indios americanos por el gobierno de los Estados Unidos pero mantenido por el gobierno en fideicomiso para beneficio de los indios.

TRUST CERTIFICATE. Certificado de participación en una sociedad inversionista. Documento que muestra que un bien se encuentra en fideicomiso como garantía de una deuda contraída por la compra de ese bien.

TRUST COMPANY. Compañía o institución fiduciaria. Un banco u otra organización que administra fideicomisos, actúa como ejecutor testamentario, y realiza otras funciones financieras.

TRUST DEPOSIT. Depósito especial. Dineros o bienes depositados en un banco para ser guardados aparte, muchas veces por razones legales o éticas, o usados para un propósito especial.

TRUST ESTATE. Bienes de fideicomiso. El derecho legal del fiduciario, el derecho legal del beneficiario, o el bien mismo.

TRUST EX–DELICTO or EX MALEFICIO or INVITUM. (Lat.) Fideicomiso "de crimen o delito". Fideicomiso instaurado por ley para evitar un mal intencionalmente causado por una persona.

TRUST FUND. Fondos fiduciarios. Dineros o bienes puestos en fideicomiso o apartados para un propósito especial.

TRUST INDENTURE. Escritura de fideicomiso. Documento que contiene los términos y condiciones que gobiernan las obligaciones del fiduciario y los derechos del beneficiario.

TRUST INSTRUMENT. Contrato de fideicomiso que incluye los poderes del fiduciario y los derechos de los beneficiarios. El

721

documento formal que crea el fideicomiso y contiene los poderes del fiduciario y los derechos del beneficiario.

TRUST OFFICER. Funcionario de la sección de fideicomisos. Persona que administra los fideicomisos en una compañía fiduciaria.

TRUST RECEIPT. Recibo fiduciario. Documento bajo el cual un comprador al por mayor accede a tomar posesión de los bienes comprados para el beneficio del prestamista. El comprador eventualmente adquiere título de los bienes cuando el préstamo es pagado.

TRUST STATE or TRUST THEORY JURISDICTION. Estado donde las leyes hipotecarias requieren que el título de propiedad de un bien hipotecado sea transferido a un fiduciario hasta que la hipoteca sea pagada.

TRUST TERRITORY. Territorio en fideicomiso. Un territorio puesto bajo la administración de una nación por las Naciones Unidas.

TRUSTEE. Fiduciario, síndico, patrono, consignatario. (1) Persona que mantiene dineros o bienes para el beneficio de otra persona. (2) Persona que mantiene una relación fiduciaria con otra; por ejemplo, un abogado, un agente, etc. (3) **Trustee In Bankruptcy**: persona nombrada por una corte de quiebra para administrar y distribuir la propiedad y los bienes de la persona en quiebra. (4) Prisionero cuya buena conducta le ha ganado un puesto de confianza.

TRUTH–IN–LENDING ACT. Acto federal que asegura que a todo consumidor con necesidad de obtener un préstamo personal se le dará la información necesaria sobre el costo del préstamo. También por este medio se otorga al deudor un período de gracia para rechazar o cancelar el préstamo.

TRY. Enjuiciar. Examinar e investigar una controversia, usando el método legal conocido como juicio, con el propósito de resolver todas las disputas en la controversia.

TUITION. Cuota escolar, costo de matrícula.

TURNCOAT WITNESS. Testigo renegado. Testigo del cual se esperaba un testimonio favorable, pero que, por el contrario, ofrece testimonio que favorece a la parte opuesta.

TURN–KEY CONTRACT. (1) Contrato de construcción bajo el cual un constructor acuerda completar un edificio hasta el punto en que esté listo para ser ocupado. (2) Contrato bajo el cual un perforador de pozos de petróleo acuerda completar un pozo hasta el punto en que esté listo para producir, y bajo el cual, por un precio acordado, el perforador también asume los riesgos de la construcción, excepto el riesgo de un pozo seco.

TURNOVER or TURNOVER RATE. Ciclo de compra y venta. El período de tiempo durante el cual el inventario o los activos financieros son comercializados.

TURNOVER ORDER. Orden judicial que requiere la transferencia de un bien a otra persona por ejemplo un artículo o un bien que se encuentra en disputa, etc.

TURPITUDE. Torpeza, infamia. Una actividad injusta, deshonesta o inmoral.

TUTELAGE. Tutelaje. Estar bajo la tutela y autoridad de otro.

TWELFTH AMENDMENT. Décimosegunda enmienda. La enmienda a la Constitución de los Estados Unidos que requiere que los electores voten separadamente para Presidente y Vice-Presidente.

TWENTIETH AMENDMENT. Duodécima enmienda. La enmienda de la Constitución de los Estados Unidos que adelantó la toma de posesión del Presidente y el comienzo de la sesión del congreso de marzo a enero.

TWENTY–FIFTH AMENDMENT. Vigésimo quinta enmienda. La enmienda a la constitución de los Estados Unidos que establece los procedimientos para nombrar un Presidente y un Vicepresidente en caso de muerte, destitución o renuncia.

TWENTY–FIRST AMENDMENT. Vigésimo primera enmienda. La enmienda a la Constitución de los Estados Unidos que terminó con la prohibición nacional contra la destilación y venta de bebidas alcohólicas.

TWENTY–FOURTH AMENDMENT. Vigésimo cuarta enmienda. La enmienda a la Constitución de los Estados Unidos que prohibe negarle a un ciudadano el derecho de votar por no haber pagado sus impuestos.

TWENTY–SECOND AMENDMENT. Vigésimo segunda enmienda. La enmienda a la Constitución de los Estados Unidos que prohibe a un presidente servir por 3 períodos consecutivos, y que limita a una persona a ejercer la presidencia por no más de 10 años consecutivos.

TWENTY–SIXTH AMENDMENT. Vigésimo sexta enmienda. La enmienda a la Constitución de los Estados Unidos que estableció los 18 años como la edad para poder votar.

TWENTY–THIRD AMENDMENT. Vigésimo tercera enmienda. La enmienda a la constitución de los Estados Unidos que le dio el derecho de votar a los residentes de Washington, D.C., en las elecciones presidenciales.

TWISTING. Mentir sobre los términos de una póliza de seguro para convencer a una persona de que cambie de compañía de seguros.

TWO ISSUE RULE. Si un juez comete un error en instruir al jurado sobre una disputa, pero hay más de un asunto en debate en el juicio, y no puede probarse que el jurado basó su veredicto en la instrucción errónea, el veredicto se considera correcto. Esta regla no se sigue en todos los estados.

TWO WITNESS RULE. Esta regla requiere que el elemento de falsedad en una convicción por perjurio sea apoyado por el testimonio directo de un testigo más alguna evidencia que corrobore este testimonio.

TWO TIER METHOD. Doble imposición fiscal. Doble imposición de impuestos sobre los ingresos de una corporación, primeramente cuando los ingresos son recibidos por la empresa, y después cuando son recibidos por los dueños de la misma.

TYING IN. Cuando un vendedor rehusa vender un producto salvo que el comprador también compre un segundo producto. Si el vendedor tiene un monopolio sobre un producto, "tying in" quiere decir, casarlo con otro producto. Puede ser una violación de las leyes antimonopolistas, especialmente si el derecho de comprar un producto patentado está conectado con la venta de un producto no patentado.

TYRANNY. Tiranía. Gobierno arbitrario y despótico. El uso severo y autocrático de un poder soberano, sea éste adquirido por métodos constitucionales o usurpados.

U

ULTIMATE FACTS. Hechos decisivos. Hechos esenciales para probar el caso de una de las partes.

ULTIMATE ISSUE. Cuestión decisiva. Punto medular en un caso.

ULTRA VIRES. (Lat.) Fuera de la facultad (de una sociedad anónima). Actos de una corporación que no están autorizados por ley o estatuto, o por los artículos que rigen a una corporación.

UMPIRE. Arbitro. Persona elegida por las partes de una disputa para decidir el conflicto.

UNALIENABLE. Inalienable. Que no se puede enajenar.

UNAMBIGUOUS. No ambiguo, inequívoco. Que está claro.

UNAMORTIZED. No amortizado. Bien que no ha sido desvalorizado periódicamente por su uso.

UNANIMOUS. Unánime. Con el acuerdo de la voluntad de todos.

UNANIMOUSLY. Unánimamente, por unanimidad. Con el acuerdo de todos.

UNAPPEALABLE. Inapelable, no sujeto a recurso.

UNASSIGNABLE. Intransferible. Que no puede cederse a otro.

UNATTACHED. No embargado. Que no ha sido afectado por embargo.

UNAUTORIZED. No autorizado.

UNAUTHORIZED PRACTICE. Práctica no autorizada o ilegal. Cuando individuos que no son abogados ejercen las funciones que solo se les permite a los abogados.

UNAVAILABLE. No disponible. En derecho de evidencia, cuando un testigo no está disponible para testificar por causa de muerte o falta de capacidad mental.

UNAVOIDABLE. Inevitable, que no se puede evitar.

UNAVOIDABLE ACCIDENT. Accidente inevitable. Accidente que ocurrió a pesar de que todos los actores involucrados tomaron precauciones razonables.

UNBALANCED BUDGET. Presupuesto desnivelado. Presupuesto que no ha sido balanceado.

UNBIASED. Imparcial, indiferente. Que no tiene prejuicios.

UNCLEAN HANDS. Literalmente "manos sucias". Véase "Clean Hands". Cuando el demandante o actor actuó de forma incorrecta y no merece el amparo de la corte.

UNCOLLECTIBLE. Incobrable, irrecuperable.

UNCONDITIONAL. Incondicional, absoluto. **Unconditional Pardon**. Amnistía incondicional.

UNCONSCIONABLE. Un contrato que es excesivamente opresivo para una de las partes y por éso queda sujeto a modificación por las cortes. Término que ha sido integrado a la ley de ventas, y que indica cuando hay opresión o desventaja indebida en el área comercial.

UNCONSTITUTIONAL. Inconstitucional. Contrario a la constitución.

UNCONTESTED. No disputado, no contencioso. Que no está en controversia.

UNCONTRADICTED. No impugnado o atacado.

UNCOVERED. Descubierto. Que no está oculto.

UNDECLARED. No declarado.

UNDER BOND. Bajo fianza.

UNDER CONTRACT. Bajo contrato, contratado.

UNDER OATH. Bajo juramento.

UNDER OBLIGATION. Obligado.

UNDER PENALTY OF. So pena de, bajo pena de. Término que denota la pena por violar la ley.

UNDER PROTEST. Bajo protesta. Véase "Protest".

UNDER SEAL. Bajo sello. Sellado. Que se ha puesto el sello.

UNDERCAPITALIZED. Con capital insuficiente.

UNDERSECRETARY. Subsecretario. Vice ministro.

UNDERSTANDING. Acuerdo, arreglo; entendimiento.

UNDERTAKING. Empresa; compromiso.

UNDERWRITE. Subscribir, asegurar.

UNDERWRITER. Subscriptor. (1) El que celebra un documento. (2) Asegurador. (3) Compañía aseguradora.

UNDERWRITING CONTRACT. Contrato de subscripción de valores.

UNDISPUTED. Indiscutible, que no se disputa, incontestable.

UNDUE. No vencido, más de lo debido, indebido. (1) Ilegal o incorrecto. (2) Que no está vencido. Que aún no se puede cobrar.

UNDUE INFLUENCE. Cuando la voluntad o el libre albedrío de una persona se frustra mediante el uso indebido de presión o intimidación.

UNEARNED. No ganado; no devengado. **Unearned Income.** Renta de inversiones.

UNEMPLOYMENT. Desempleo, paro forzoso.

UNEMPLOYMENT BENEFITS. Beneficios de desempleo. Cuando el estado paga a aquellas personas que han trabajado por un período mínimo de tiempo y han perdido el trabajo.

UNEMPLOYMENT COMPENSATION. Compensación por encontrarse desempleado.

UNENCUMBERED. Libre de gravamen, desahogado. Que no pesa ningún gravamen sobre el bien.

UNENFORCEABLE. Que no se puede hacer cumplir. Que no es ejecutable.

UNETHICAL CONDUCT. Comportamiento no ético. Acciones que violan las normas profesionales aplicables a los abogados u otros profesionales. Conducta por un abogado, bufete, o un juez que viola el código profesional.

UNFAIR. Injusto. Inicuo. Que no es justo.

UNFAIR COMPETITION. Compentencia injusta. El uso de fraude o deshonestidad en el mundo comercial. Normalmente se refiere a un artificio diseñado para adquirir una ventaja ilegal en una actividad comercial.

UNFIT. Incapaz, incompetente. Inadecuado para un fin.

UNFOUNDED. Sin lugar, improcedente. Carente de fundamento o bases.

UNFULFILLED. Incumplido.

UNFUNDED TRUST. Fideicomiso sin depósito de fondos.

UNIFORM. Uniforme. Regular. Cuando algo se aplica en general, igual e imparcialmente a todos.

UNIFORM ACTS (UNIFORM LAWS). Leyes que son uniformes entre los diferentes estados. Dichas leyes son propuestas por una comisión designada para escribir leyes en áreas donde se considera deseable tener uniformidad entre los diferentes estados (por ejemplo, la venta de bienes muebles, depósitos bancarios, cartas de crédito, crédito al consumidor, papel comercial). Dichas leyes muchas veces son adoptadas, entera o parcialmente, por muchos estados.

UNILATERAL. Unilateral. Que es hecho sólo por una de las partes. **Unilateral Mistake.** Error unilateral. Error cometido por una de las partes al interpretar los términos de un contrato. Generalmente no invalida el contrato, a menos que la otra parte haya tenido conocimiento del error.

UNIMPEACHEABLE. Intachable, irrecusable. Que no puede ser culpado por algo.

UNINCORPORATED. No incorporado. Que no ha sido organizado en forma de corporación.

UNINSURED. No asegurado, sin seguro. Que no tiene protección contra un riesgo.

UNION. Unión, sindicato, gremio laboral. Cualquier reunión de personas u organizaciones para un propósito en particular.

UNION CERTIFICATION. Certificación de un sindicato o gremio laboral. Proceso para certificar un sindicato laboral para que represente a los trabajadores ante el patrón. Véase "Certification Proceedings".

UNION SECURITY CLAUSE. Cláusula en un contrato entre el sindicato y el patrón que estipula las condiciones de empleo. A veces la cláusula requiere que todos las empleados pertenezcan al sindicato para poder trabajar con el patrón.

UNION SHOP. Empresa sindicalista. Compañía donde todos los trabajadores deben hacerse miembros del sindicato laboral vigente una vez que son empleados.

UNISSUED STOCK. Acciones no libradas o por emitir.

UNITED NATIONS. Naciones Unidas. Organización mundial con sede en Nueva York, EE.UU., que agrupa a las naciones del mundo para armonizar y mejorar las relaciones entre los países.

UNIT OWNERSHIP ACTS. Leyes estatales que regulan los condominios.

UNITED STATES ATTORNEY. Abogado de los EE.UU. Abogado nombrado por el Presidente para que trate con asuntos legales, ya sean civiles o criminales, en un distrito judicial de los EE.UU.

UNITED STATES COMMISSIONER. Comisionado de los EE.UU. Véase "Magistrate".

UNITED STATES COURT OF APPEALS. Corte de apelación de los EE.UU. Cortes federales que tienen jurisdicción sobre varios estados en un circuito y que consideran las apelaciones de las cortes de distrito de los EE.UU. en su circuito.

UNITED STATES COURTS. Cortes de los EE.UU. Incluyen la Cortes de Apelación, de Distrito, de Reclamo, de Aduana, etc.

UNITED STATES REPORTS. Volúmenes donde se publican las decisiones de la Corte Suprema de los EE.UU.

UNITY. Unidad. (1) **Unity of Interest.** Unidad de interés. En derecho de propiedad, significa que los co-dueños o coarrendatarios tienen que tener igual interés en su propiedad. (2) **Unity of Possession.** Posesión conjunta. Con respecto a una copropiedad, significa que todos los coarrendatarios tienen derecho a poseer y usar la propiedad en su totalidad. (3) **Unity**

of Time. Con respecto a una copropiedad, significa que los coarrendatarios tienen que adquirir su derecho a la propiedad al mismo tiempo. (4) **Unity of Title.** Con respecto a una copropiedad, significa que los coarrendatarios tienen que adquirir su derecho a la propiedad de un mismo título.

UNIVERSAL. Universal. Todo el mundo. Aquello que es general y total opuesto a lo particular y limitado.

UNIVERSAL SUFFRAGE. Sufragio o voto universal.

UNJUST. Injusto, inicuo. Que no ha sido hecho con justicia.

UNJUST ENRICHMENT. Enriquecimiento injusto. Principio legal que dicta que cuando una persona obtiene dinero o propiedad injustamente debe devolver lo obtenido al dueño legítimo.

UNJUSTIFIABLE. Injustificable, que no se puede justificar.

UNLAWFUL. Ilegal. Contrario a la ley.

UNLAWFUL DETAINER. Juicio de desahucio. Juicio para desalojar a una persona de una propiedad.

UNLIMITED LIABILITY. Responsabilidad sin límite. Responsabilidad que abarca la cuantía de los daños.

UNLIQUIDATED DAMAGES. Daños no liquidados o no determinados. Perjuicio que todavía no se ha calculado.

UNLIQUIDATED DEBT. Deuda sin liquidar. Que lo debido no se puede determinar mediante un simple cálculo.

UNMARKETABLE. Invendible, incomerciable. **Unmarketable Title.** Título incierto. Derecho de propiedad suceptible a litigio por un tercero.

UNPLEADED. No alegado.

UNPREJUDICED. Sin predisposición. Imparcial.

UNPREMEDITATED. No premeditado. Que el acto realizado no se medió con antelación.

UNPROFESSIONAL CONDUCT. Conducta antiprofesional.

UNPROVED. No probado, no demostrado. Hecho que no se ha comprobado.

731

UNREASONABLE. Irracional, exorbitante. **Unreasonable Search and Seizure.** Registro y embargo arbitrario, registros o secuestros arbitrarios, contrarios a la ley.

UNRECORDED. No registrado, no inscrito.

UNREFUNDABLE. No restituíble. Que no será devuelto o reembolsado.

UNRELATED OFFENSES. Ofensas o crímenes no relacionados.

UNSATISFIED. Insatisfecho, no liquidado. **Unsatisfied Judgment.** Decisión, fallo o sentencia que no se ha cumplido o que no ha sido liquidada o ejecutada.

UNSECURED. No garantizado; sin colateral. (1) **Unsecured Creditor.** Acreedor común o no garantizado. (2) **Unsecured Debt.** Deuda sin garantía. (3) **Unsecured Loan.** Préstamo sin caución o a descubierto.

UNSETTLED. Sin pagar, pendiente, insatisfecho.

UNSOUND. No firme, no sólido. (1) **Unsound of Mind.** Incapaz de razonar, demente. (2) **Unsound Securities.** Valores especulativos.

UNTENABLE. Insostenible.

UNWARRANTED. Sin justificación; no garantizado.

UNWRITTEN LAW. Ley no escrita. Cosas que la gente hace porque son consideradas justas, buenas y usuales.

U.S. Siglas de "United States". Estados Unidos.

U.S.A. Siglas de "United States of America". Estados Unidos de (Norte) América.

USE IMMUNITY. Véase "Immunity".

USER. Usuario, consumidor.

USE TAX. Impuesto sobre la utilización de bienes.

USUAL PLACE OF ABODE. Domicilio actual.

USUFRUCT. Usufructo. Derecho de usar algo pero sin cambiarlo o gastarlo. En derecho civil se refiere a usar algo o derivar beneficio de algún bien o propiedad, pero sin cambiar o destruir el bien o la propiedad.

USURER. Agiotista. Usurero. Persona que presta dinero con intereses excesivos.

USURP. Usurpar. Apoderarse de algo sin derecho.

USURY. Usura. Cobrar ilegalmente intereses altos.

U.S. DISTRICT COURT. Corte de Distrito Federal. Tribunal federal de primera instancia.

UTILITIES. Utilidades. Servicios públicos tales como electricidad, agua, alcantarillado, etc.

V

V. (1) Abreviación para "versus" o "contra," usada en el nombre de un caso. Por ejemplo, Smith **v.** Jones significa que Smith está demandado a Jones. (2) Abrevición de "volumen".

VACANCY. Lugar o empleo vacante. Que está disponible.

VACANT. Vacante, desocupado.

VACATE. Rescindir o anular una decisión; desocupar un lugar.

VADIUM. (Lat.) Empeño, fianza.

VAGRANCY. Vagancia. **Vagrancy Laws**. Leyes que prohíben la vagancia en lugares públicos.

VAGUE. Vago. Indefinido, incierto.

VAGUENESS DOCTRINE. Doctrina constitucional que requiere que toda ley criminal declare claramente lo que es requerido o prohibido.

VALID. Válido. Legal, suficiente, que contiene todas las formalidades necesarias bajo la ley.

VALIDITY. Validez; fuerza legal.

VALUABLE. Valioso, apreciable.

VALUABLE CONSIDERATION. Arras. En la ley de contratos, todo aquello de valor sobre lo cual se funda un contrato o una promesa legal.

VALUABLES. Artículos de valor, valores.

VALUATION. Avalúo, valuación, valorización.

VALUE. Valor, precio, valuación, justiprecio, aprecio. El valor de algo se puede definir como: (1) El costo de algo; (2) lo que costaría reemplazarlo; o (3) su precio al venderse en el mercado abierto. Véase "Market Value".

VALUER. Avaluador, tasador.

VANDALISM. Vandalismo. Destrucción intencional de propiedad ajena.

VARIANCE. Variación, cambio, desacuerdo. (1) Diferencia entre lo que es declarado en un informe y lo que se prueba en un juicio. (2) Permiso oficial para usar tierras o edificios. Una excepción a las regulaciones que rigen el tipo de desarollo urbano para el vecindario donde se encuentra la propiedad.

VENDEE. Comprador.

VENDOR. Vendedor.

VENDOR'S LIEN. Gravamen del vendedor. Principio equitativo que permite a un vendedor mantener un gravamen sobre lo vendido hasta que reciba el pago total de la venta.

VENIRE. (Lat.) Venir; comparecer en corte. Véase "Venire Facias".

VENIRE FACIAS. (Lat.) Auto de convocación del jurado. Mandato al alguacil para que escoja y reúna a un jurado.

VENIREMAN. Miembro del jurado.

VENTURE CAPITAL. Capital aventurado. Capital o dinero usado para financiar una nueva empresa o un nuevo producto.

VENUE. Sitio, jurisdicción, competencia. Lugar donde un caso puede llevarse a juicio. Varias cortes pueden tener jurisdicción para considerar un caso, pero la corte más apropiada será aquella que es más conveniente para las partes y para los testigos.

VERBAL. Verbal, de palabra, oral.

VERBATIM. (Lat.) Al pie de la letra.

VER NON. (Lat.) O no.

VERDICT. Veredicto, fallo, opinión. La decisión del jurado.
(1) **Verdict Contrary to Law.** Veredicto en oposición a la ley.
(2) **Verdict of Guilty.** Veredicto de culpabilidad o de condenación. (3) **Verdict of Not Guilty.** Veredicto absolutorio o de no culpabilidad, sentencia de no responsable.

VERIFY. Verificar, comprobar. (1) Jurar por escrito a la verdad o exactitud de un documento. (2) Confirmar; probar la verdad.

VERSUS. (Lat.) Contra.

VERTICAL TRUST. En la ley antimonopolista, el control de medios de producción desde la materia prima hasta el producto final.

VERTICAL UNION. Gremio o sindicato industrial que participa en todas las etapas de producción, desde la elaboración de la materia prima hasta la producción final.

VEST. Dar posesión. El acto de recibir un derecho en forma absoluta.

VESTED. Fijado, absoluto, efectivo. (1) **Vested Estate.** Propiedad de dominio pleno. (2) **Vested in Interest.** Con derecho de goce futuro. (3) **Vested in Possession.** Con derecho de goce actual. (4) **Vested Interests.** Intereses establecidos o creados. (5) **Vested Rights.** Derechos intrínsicos o adquiridos.

VETERANS ADMINISTRATION. Administración de Veteranos.

VETERANS PREFERENCE. Leyes federales y estatales que dan preferencia a veteranos de guerra en cuestiones de trabajo.

VETO. Vetar, prohibir. Cuando el Presidente o un gobernador se niega a firmar un proyecto de ley que ha sido aprobado por la legislatura, negando así su efecto legal. En el caso del Veto Presidencial, el proyecto de ley se convierte en ley si dos tercios del Congreso vota a su favor dentro de un período de tiempo después del veto.

VEXATIOUS LITIGATION. Acción civil no basada en fundamentos legales y cuyo objeto es enfadar e incomodar a la parte demandada. Véase "Malicious Prosecution".

VI ET ARMIS. (Lat.) Con fuerzas y armas. Véase "Trespass".

VICARIOUS LIABILITY. Responsabilidad vicaria. Responsabilidad legal de una persona por los actos de otra a consecuencia de la relación entre ambas.

VICE. Vicio. Defecto. Actividad criminal de carácter inmoral.

VIGILANCE. Vigilancia.

VIOLATE. Violar, infringir.

VIOLATION. Violación, infracción, atropello.

VIRTUE. Virtud. Algo que vale o es bueno.

VIS MAJOR. (Lat.) Fuerza mayor. Fuerza irresistible, desastre natural.

VISA. Endoso oficial de un pasaporte, certificando que ha sido examinado y aprobado. Permiso otorgado por un país para viajar a él.

VISITATION. Inspección, supervisión. Derecho de ver a los niños después de un divorcio o separación.

VITAL STATISTICS. Estadísticas públicas (por ejemplo, muertes, nacimientos, matrimonios, etc.) de un organismo gubernamental.

VITIATE. Viciar. Invalidar o debilitar algún acto o hecho.

VIZ. A saber.

VOID. Nulo, inválido. Sin efecto legal. (1) **Void Contract.** Contrato inválido. (2) **Void Judgement.** Sentencia nula. (3) **Void Marriage.** Matrimonio nulo. (4) **Void Process.** Procedimiento ilegal o nulo. (5) **Void Tax.** Impuesto ilegal.

VOIDABLE. Anulable, cancelable. Algo que puede ser anulado legalmente, pero que no es automáticamente nulo.

VOIR DIRE. (Fr.) Decir la verdad. Examen oral hecho a una persona para ver si existe alguna razón por la cual esa persona no debería ser miembro de un jurado.

VOLENTI NON FIT INJURIA. (Lat.) Cuando una persona se expone voluntariamente a una situación peligrosa, entendiendo sus riesgos, y tiene un accidente, se considera que asumió el riesgo y no puede recobrar por ningún daño sufrido. Véase "Assumption of Risk".

VOLSTEAD ACT. Ley federal ya anulada que prohibe la manufactura, venta o transportación de licor.

VOLUNTARY. Voluntario, sin interferencia o fuerza. (1) **Voluntary Arbitration.** Abritraje voluntario. (2) **Voluntary Assignment.** Cesión voluntaria. (3) **Voluntary Bankruptcy.** Bancarrota voluntaria. (4) **Voluntary Compliance.** Cumplimiento voluntario. (5) **Voluntary Confession.** Confesión espontánea. (6) **Voluntary Jurisdiction.** Jurisdicción voluntaria. (7) **Voluntary Petition.** Petición voluntaria.

VOLUNTEER INCOME TAX ASSISTANCE (VITA). Asistencia Voluntaria al Contribuyente sobre el impuesto a la renta.

VOTE OF CONFIDENCE. Voto de confianza.

VOTER. Votador, votante. Persona que tiene las cualidades necesarias para votar; persona que se ha registrado para votar; persona que ha votado.

VOTING RIGHTS ACT. Ley federal que prohíbe que un votante tenga que pasar ciertos parámetros de carácter y de habilidad para leer y escribir antes de poder votar.

VOTING STOCK. Acciones votantes o con derecho a votar. El poseedor de estas acciones o valores tiene derecho a votar en elecciones de directores y en elecciones sobre otras materias de importancia para una corporación.

VOTING STOCK RIGHT. Derecho que tiene un accionista de participar, mediante su voto, en las actividades de una corporación.

VOUCH. Atestiguar, certificar, verificar.

VOUCHER. Comprobante; vale; justificante; documento crediticio o probatorio.

VOYEURISM. Aberración sexual bajo la cual se deriva satisfacción sexual al observar los órganos o actos sexuales de otros, normalmente desde un escondite.

VS. Abreviación de "versus", usada en los títulos de casos. Véase "V".

W

W-2 FORM. Formulario en blanco usado por un empleado para declarar los ingresos y los impuestos pagados durante un año.

WAGE AND HOUR LAWS. Leyes que establecen el mínimo de los salarios y el máximo de las horas de trabajo.

WAGE ASSIGNMENT. Descuento salarial directo. Arreglo donde una persona permite que parte de su salario sea pagado directamente a un acreedor.

WAGE DISPUTE. Controversia o disputa sobre salarios.

WAGE EARNER'S PLAN. Plan que permite a una persona en bancarrota arreglar una forma de pago basada en el salario de la persona. Véase "Chapter Thirteen".

WAGER. Apostar; apuesta.

WAGES. Salario jornal, sueldo. Pago por el trabajo realizado.

WAGNER ACT. (EE.UU.) Ley federal que establece muchos de los derechos básicos de los sindicatos laborales.

WAITING PERIOD. Período de espera antes de que un contrato surta efecto.

WAIVE. Renunciar, desistir. Renunciar a un privilegio, derecho o beneficio con pleno conocimiento de lo que se está haciendo.

WAIVER. Renuncia, abandono. (1) **Express Waiver.** Renunciar explícitamente a un derecho o beneficio. (2) **Implied Waiver.** Cuando el comportamiento de una persona permite creer que hay abandono de un derecho o beneficio. (3) **Waiver of Immunity.** Renuncia de inmunidad. (4) **Waiver of Jury.** Renuncia del derecho de juicio ante jurado. (5) **Waiver of Notice.** Renuncia de citación o de aviso. (6) **Waiver of Performance.** Renuncia de cumplimiento específico. (7) **Waiver of Rights.** Renuncia de derechos. (8) **Waiver of Tort.** Renuncia a daños por agravio.

WANT. Desear; cuando algo falta. (1) **Want of Consideration.** Falta de causa contractual o arras. (2) **Want of Jurisdiction.** Falta de jurisdicción.

WANTON. (1) Descuidado, imprudente, malicioso. (2) Acción injustificable, desenfrenada y desconsiderada que pone en peligro el bienestar y los derechos de otros.

WAR CRIMES. Crímenes de guerra. Delitos cometidos por países o individuos que violan las leyes internacionales sobre la conducta durante guerras.

WARD. Custodia, guarda. (1) Persona puesta por la corte bajo el cuidado de un guardián. (2) División política de una ciudad.

WAREHOUSE. Almacén, depósito, bodega.

WAREHOUSEMAN. Almacenero, almacenador.

WARNING. Aviso, advertencia; caución.

WAREHOUSE RECEIPT. Certificado o conocimiento de almacén. Recibo que prueba que alguien es el propietario de un bien depositado en un almacén. Este recibo puede ser un documento negociable.

WARRANT. Orden, decreto, autorización, certificado o mandamiento. (1) Garantizar algo en un contrato o escritura. (2) Permiso dado por un juez a un oficial de policía para arrestar a una persona, realizar un allanamiento, etc. (3) Garantizar que determinados hechos son ciertos.

WARRANT OF ARREST. Auto de detención, mandamiento u orden de arresto.

WARRANTED. Garantizado. Que será tal como se ha manifestado.

WARRANTY. Garantía. (1) Cualquier promesa o aseveración de que determinados hechos son ciertos. (2) Obligación que tienen los vendedores para con los compradores de garantizar su producto. (3) Garantía que existe en ventas comerciales que protegen al comprador. Dichas garantías pueden ser expresas o tácitas, limitadas o completas, dependiendo de los términos del contrato de venta.

WARRANTY DEED. Escritura o título de propiedad con garantía de título. Título de propiedad garantizado por el vendedor por medio del cual se transfieren todos los derechos de propiedad al comprador.

WARRANTY OF TITLE. Garantía de título. Título de propiedad cuya legitimidad ha sido garantizada.

WASTE. Malgastar o derrochar un bien, aunque sea por el dueño, en perjuicio de otros ya sean sus herederos, vecinos, etc.

WATER MARK. Punto que designa el nivel más alto o más bajo del agua.

WATER RIGHTS. Derechos legales sobre el uso de recursos ribereños.

WATERED STOCK. Acciones diluídas, capital inflado. Acciones emitidas por una corporación en calidad de acciones, cuando en realidad no lo han sido, diluyendo así el valor de las otras acciones de la corporación.

WAYS AND MEANS. Medios y arbitrios.

WEDLOCK. Matrimonio.

WEIGHT OF EVIDENCE. Preponderancia de la prueba. La más convincente prueba en un pleito.

WELFARE. Previsión. (1) Beneficencia social. (2) Asistencia económica pública para cierta categoría de personas pobres. (3) Salud, bienestar, bienestar general.

WELFARE CLAUSE. Cláusula constitucional que permite al gobierno federal implementar leyes para el bienestar de la ciudadanía.

WELFARE RECIPIENT. Beneficiario de asistencia social.

WHEREAS. Por cuanto, visto que, en vista de.

WHEREAS CLAUSE. Considerandos, por cuantos.

WHEREBY. Por razón de.

WHEREFORE. Por lo cual.

WHITE ACRE. Véase "Black Acre".

WHITE COLLAR CRIMES. (1) Delitos cometidos por corporaciones o individuos como desfalco, alteración de precio, u otras violaciones fiscales cometidas en el trabajo. (2) Delitos no violentos.

WHOLESALE. Venta al por mayor. Venta de artículos en grandes cantidades.

WIDOWER. Viudo. El hombre a quien se le ha muerto su esposa.

WILL. Testamento. Documento en el cual una persona deja establecido como debe ser distribuida su propiedad después de su muerte.

WILL CONTEST. Litigio sobre un testamento.

WILLFUL. (1) Premeditado, intencional. (2) **Willful Misconduct.** Mala conducta intencional. (3) **Willful Neglect.** Descuido porfiado. (4) **Willful Tort.** Agravio intencional.

WITH ALL FAULTS. Tal cual, a riesgo del comprador. En contratos de ventas, indica que los bienes se venden tal como están y sin garantía alguna.

WITHDRAW. Retirar. (1) **Withdraw a Bid.** Rescindir una propuesta. (2) **Withdraw Charges.** Retirar acusaciones. (3) **Withdraw Funds.** Retirar o sacar fondos. (4) **Withdraw a Motion.** Rescindir la moción. (5) **Withdraw a Suit.** Desistir del pleito.

WITHHOLDING OF EVIDENCE. Esconder, destruir, o remover evidencia.

WITHHOLDING OF TAX. Retención de impuestos. Retención de impuesto que hace aquél que le paga al contribuyente para remitirlos directamente al gobierno.

WITHOUT JUSTIFICATION. Sin justa causa.

WITHOUT NOTICE. Sin aviso. En documentos comerciales, significa que el poseedor adquirió el documento de buena fe.

WITHOUT PREJUDICE. Sin perjuicio. Palabras que indican que las partes involucradas no han renunciado a ningún derecho o privilegio, excepto a aquellos derechos expresamente mencionados.

WITHOUT RECOURSE. Sin recurso. Palabras usadas cuando se endosa un documento negociable, indicando que si se rehúsa el pago el endosante no se hace responsable.

WITNESS. Testigo. (1) Persona que se encuentra presente cuando ocurre algún hecho. (2) Persona que declara bajo juramento. (3) **Witness against Himself.** Testigo contra sí mismo. (4) **Witness Fee.** Dieta de testigo. (5) **Witness for the Defense.** Testigo de la defensa. (6) **Witness for the Plaintiff.** Testigo de la parte demandante. (7) **Witness for the Prosecution.** Testigo de cargo. (8) **Witness Stand.** Silla de los testigos.

WORDS OF ART. Términos técnicos que son usados de una manera especial en una profesión determinada.

WORDS ACTIONABLE BY THEMSELVES. Palabras que por sí solas son difamatorias.

WORDS OF LIMITATION. Palabras en una escritura o en un testamento que limitan los derechos que se otorgan o traspasan a otra persona.

WORDS OF PURCHASE. La parte de una escritura o testamento que indica quien recibe las tierras.

WORK-PRODUCT RULE. Regla evidencial bajo la cual un abogado no tiene que mostrarle a la otra parte en un caso los frutos de su trabajo o de sus investigaciones sobre ese caso.

WORKERS' or WORKMEN'S COMPENSATION ACT. Estatutos que determinan los derechos de un trabajador que tuvo un accidente en su lugar de empleo. Estas leyes controlan el derecho de un obrero o trabajador a reclamar contra el patrón. También definen los beneficios que recibe el trabajador por accidentes o enfermedades relacionadas al empleo.

WORKING DAY. Día laborable. Día en que se trabaja normalmente.

WORKING TIME. Horas laborables. Horario en que se labora normalmente.

743

WORKER'S COMPENSATION. Compensación legal por accidentes de trabajo. Riesgos profesionales.

WORKSHEET. Hoja de computaciones, borrador. Hoja de trabajo. Hoja electrónica de trabajo.

WORLD COURT. Corte internacional de justicia. Véase "International Court of Justice".

WORTH. Valor; precio.

WORTHLESS. Sin valor.

WRIT. Mandato, orden, mandamiento. (1) Orden judicial requiriendo a una corte inferior, a un oficial gubernamental, o a una persona a que haga algo. (2) **Writ of Attachment.** Mandamiento de embargo, providencia de secuestro. (3) **Writ of Certiorari.** Auto de avocación; auto de certiorari. (4) **Writ of Ejectment.** Mandamiento de desalojo. (5) **Writ of Entry.** Acción para recobrar posesión de un inmueble. (6) **Writ of Error.** Auto de casación. (7) **Writ of Execution.** Auto ejecutivo. (8) **Writ of Habeas Corpus.** Auto de habeas corpus. (9) **Writ of Mandamus.** Mandamiento. (10) **Writ of Possession.** Auto de posesión, interdicto de despojo. (11) **Writ of Process.** Citación. (12) **Writ of Quo Warranto.** Auto de quo warranto. (13) **Writ of Replevin.** Auto de reivindicación. (14) **Writ of Summons.** Emplazamiento. (15) **Writ of Supersedeas.** Auto de suspensión o de sobreseimiento; mandamiento ordenando la paralización de los procedimientos.

WRITE–OFF. Anular. (1) Un crédito incobrable. (2) Remover de los libros una inversión o negocio que resultó en pérdida.

WRITING. Escrito.

WRITTEN AGREEMENT. Acuerdo por escrito.

WRITTEN CONTRACT. Contrato escrito.

WRITTEN LAW. Derecho o ley escrita. Véase "Statute, Law, Ordinance, Regulation".

WRONG. Daño, agravio; incorrecto.

WRONGFUL ACT. Un acto que viola los derechos de otro y que resulta en daños. Generalmente es un acto producido por la negligencia de alguien.

WRONGFUL DEATH ACTION. Demanda interpuesta por los beneficiarios de una persona muerta, contra quien le causó la muerte por negligencia o intencionalmente.

WRONGFUL DEATH STATUTE. Leyes que permiten a los beneficiarios de un difunto entablar un pleito para recobrar daños a causa de su muerte.

WRONGFUL LIFE ACTION. Demanda o pleito entablado por los padres de un niño(a), quien nació a causa de la negligencia de otra persona. Por ejemplo, en el caso de una esterilización médica mal efectuada, los padres pueden demandar al médico por negligencia.

Y

YEAR–AND–A–DAY RULE. Principio bajo el cual una muerte no puede ser atribuída a la mala conducta de una persona a menos que tal muerte haya ocurrido dentro de un año más un día después de la conducta.

YEAR–END. Fin de año. Período de cierre fiscal para la contabilidad.

YEA–AND–NAY VOTE. Votación por lista. Votación oral afirmativa (yea) o negativa (nay).

YELLOW DOG CONTRACT. Contrato que prohibe afiliación con un gremio.

YIELD. Ceder, rendir, dejar; rendimiento o beneficio recibido por una actividad comercial.

YOUTHFUL OFFENDER. Delincuente juvenil.

Z

ZEALOUS WITNESS. Testigo indebidamente afanoso.

ZONING. La división y organización de una ciudad o área urbana por distritos, los cuales son regulados por una legislación que controla el tipo de arquitectura y de estructuras o empresas que pueden operar en esos distritos. Las zonas o distritos normalmente están organizadas de acuerdo a un plan de desarrollo urbano. El objetivo de dicha legislación zonal es prevenir el desarrollo descontrolado de áreas urbanas y la contaminación y destrucción del ambiente.

ZONING RULES. Reglamentación urbanística.